Yamaha FJR1300
Service and Repair Manual

by Matthew Coombs

Models covered
FJR1300 2001 to 2005
FJR1300A 2003 to 2013
FJR1300AS 2006 to 2012

(5607-328)

© Haynes Publishing 2013

ABCDE
FGHIJ
KLMNO
PQRST

A book in the Haynes Service and Repair Manual Series

All rights reserved. No part of this book may be reproduced or transmitted in any form or by any means, electronic or mechanical, including photocopying, recording or by any information storage or retrieval system, without permission in writing from the copyright holder.

ISBN: **978 0 85733 607 1**

British Library Cataloguing in Publication Data
A catalogue record for this book is available from the British Library.

Library of Congress Catalog Card Number 2013933075

Printed in the USA

Haynes Publishing
Sparkford, Yeovil, Somerset BA22 7JJ, England

Haynes North America, Inc
861 Lawrence Drive, Newbury Park, California 91320, USA

Haynes Publishing Nordiska AB
Box 1504, 751 45 Uppsala, Sweden

Contents

LIVING WITH YOUR YAMAHA

Introduction
Yamaha – Musical instruments to motorcycles	Page	0•4
Acknowledgements	Page	0•8
About this manual	Page	0•8
Identification numbers	Page	0•9
Buying spare parts	Page	0•9
Safety first!	Page	0•10

Pre-ride checks
Engine oil level	Page	0•11
Suspension, steering and final drive	Page	0•11
Legal and safety	Page	0•11
Coolant level	Page	0•12
Brake fluid levels	Page	0•12
Clutch fluid level	Page	0•14
Tyres	Page	0•15
Model development	Page	0•16
Bike spec	Page	0•17

MAINTENANCE

Routine maintenance and servicing
Specifications	Page	1•1
Lubricants and fluids	Page	1•2
Maintenance schedule	Page	1•3
Component locations	Page	1•5
Maintenance procedures	Page	1•8

Contents

REPAIRS AND OVERHAUL

Engine, transmission and associated systems
Engine, clutch and transmission	Page	**2•1**
Cooling system	Page	**3•1**
Engine management system	Page	**4•1**

Chassis components
Frame and suspension	Page	**5•1**
Brakes, wheels and final drive	Page	**6•1**
Bodywork	Page	**7•1**

Electrical system
Page **8•1**

Wiring diagrams
Page **8•30**

REFERENCE

Tools and Workshop Tips	Page	**REF•2**
Security	Page	**REF•20**
Lubricants and fluids	Page	**REF•23**
Conversion factors	Page	**REF•26**
MOT Test Checks	Page	**REF•27**
Storage	Page	**REF•32**
Fault Finding	Page	**REF•35**
Technical Terms Explained	Page	**REF•44**

Index
Page **REF•48**

0•4 Introduction

Yamaha
Musical instruments to motorcycles

**The FS1E -
first bike of many sixteen year olds in the UK**

The Yamaha Motor Company

The Yamaha name can be traced back to 1889, when Torakusu Yamaha founded the Yamaha Organ Manufacturing Company. Such was the success of the company, that in 1897 it became Nippon Gakki Limited and manufactured a wide range of reed organs and pianos.

During World War II, Nippon Gakki's manufacturing base was utilised by the Japanese authorities to produce propellers and fuel tanks for their aviation industry. The end of the war brought about a huge public demand for low cost transport and many firms decided to utilise their obsolete aircraft tooling for the production of motorcycles. Nippon Gakki's first motorcycle went on sale in February 1955 and was named the 125 YA-1 Red Dragonfly. This machine was a copy of the German DKW RT125 motorcycle, featuring a single cylinder two-stroke engine with a four-speed gearbox. Due to the outstanding success of this model the motorcycle operation was separated from Nippon Gakki in July 1955 and the Yamaha Motor Company was formed.

The YA-1 also received acclaim by winning two of Japan's biggest road races, the Mount Fuji Climbing race and the Asama Volcano race. The high level of public demand for the YA-1 led to the development of a whole series of two-stroke singles and twins.

Having made a large impact on their home market, Yamahas were exported to the USA in 1958 and to the UK in 1962. In the UK the signing of an Anglo-Japanese trade

Introduction

agreement during 1962 enabled the sale of Japanese lightweight motorcycles and scooters in Britain. At that time, competition between the many motorcycle producers in Japan had reduced numbers significantly and by the end of the sixties, only the big-four which are familiar with today remained.

Yamaha Europe was founded in 1968 and based in Holland. Although originally set up to market marine products, the Dutch base is now the official European Headquarters and distribution centre. Yamaha motorcycles are built at factories in Holland, Denmark, Norway, Italy, France, Spain and Portugal. Yamahas are imported into the UK by Yamaha Motor UK Ltd, formerly Mitsui Machinery Sales (UK) Ltd. Mitsui and Co. were originally a trading house, handling the shipping, distribution and marketing of Japanese products into western countries. Ultimately Mitsui Machinery Sales was formed to handle Yamaha motorcycles and outboard motors.

Based on the technology derived from its motorcycle operation, Yamaha have produced many other products, such as automobile and lightweight aircraft engines, marine engines and boats, generators, pumps, ATVs, snowmobiles, golf cars, industrial robots, lawnmowers, swimming pools and archery equipment.

Two-strokes first

Part of Yamaha's success was a whole string of innovations in the two-stroke world. Autolube engine lubrication, torque induction, multi-ported engines, reed valves and power valves kept their two-strokes at the forefront of technology. Many advances were achieved with the use of racing as a development laboratory. They went to the USA in the late 1950s with an air-cooled 250cc twin but didn't hit the GPs until the early 1960s when Fumio Ito scored a hat-trick of sixth places in the Isle of Man TT, the Dutch TT and the Belgian GP. This experiment gave rise to the idea of the over-the-counter racer, an idea that became reality in the TD1, the first in an unmatched series of two-stroke racers that were the standard issue for privateers at national and international level for years and helped Yamaha develop their road engines. While privateers raced the twins, Yamaha built the outrageously complicated vee-four 250 for Phil Read and followed it with a vee-four 125 that Bill Ivy lapped the Isle of Man on at over 100mph! When the FIM regulations were changed to limit the smaller GP classes to two cylinders, these exotic bikes died but set the scene for an unparalleled dynasty of mass-produced racers based on the same technology as the road bikes.

In the 1960s and 70s the two-stroke engined YAS3 125, YDS1 to YDS7 250 and YR5 350 formed the core of Yamaha's range. By the mid-70s they had been superseded by the RD (Race-Developed) 125, 250, and 350 range of two-stroke twins, featuring improved 7-port engines with reed valve induction. Braking was improved by the use of an hydraulic brake on the front wheel of DX models, instead of the drum arrangement used previously, and cast alloy wheels were available as an option on later RD models. The RD350 was replaced by the RD400 in 1976.

Running parallel with the RD twins was a range of single-cylinder two-strokes. Used in a variety of chassis types, the engine was used in the popular 50 cc FS1-E moped, the V50 to 90 step-thrus, RS100 and 125, YB100 and the DT trail range.

The TD racers got water-cooling in 1973 to become the TZs, the most successful and numerous over-the-counter racers ever built. That same year, Jarno Saarinen became the first rider to win a 500cc GP on a four-cylinder two-stroke on the new in-line four which was effectively a pair of TZs side-by-side. TZs won everywhere – including the Daytona 200 and 500 races when overbored to 351cc. A 700cc TZ also appeared, one year later taken out to 750cc. Steve Baker won the first Formula 750 world title – one of the precursors of Superbike – on one in 1977. The following year Kenny Roberts won Yamaha's first world 500 title and would be succeeded by Wayne Rainey and Eddie Lawson before Mick Doohan and the NSR500 took over.

The air-cooled single and twin cylinder RD road bikes were eventually replaced by the LC series in 1980, featuring liquid-cooled engines, radical new styling, spiral pattern cast wheels and cantilever rear suspension (Yamaha's Monoshock). Of all the LC models, the RD350LC, or RD350R as it was later known, has made the most impact in the market. Later models had YPVS (Yamaha Power Valve System) engines, another first for Yamaha – this was essentially a valve located in the exhaust ports which was electronically operated to alter port timing to achieve maximum power output. The RD500LC was the largest two-stroke made by Yamaha and differed from the other LCs by the use of its vee-four cylinder engine.

With the exception of the RD350R, now manufactured in Brazil, the LC range has been discontinued. Two-stroke engined models have given way to environmental pressure, and thus with a few exceptions, such as the TZR125 and TZR250, are used only in scooters and small capacity bikes.

The Four-strokes

Yamaha concentrated solely on two-stroke models until 1970 when the XS1 was produced, their first four-stroke motorcycle. It was perhaps Yamaha's success with two-strokes that postponed an earlier

The distinctive paintwork and trim of the RD models

Introduction

move into the four-stroke motorcycle market, although their work with Toyota during the 1960s had given them a sound base in four-stroke technology.

The XS1 had a 650 cc twin-cylinder SOHC engine and was later to become known as the XS650, appearing also in the popular SE custom form. Yamaha introduced a three cylinder 750 cc engine in 1976, fitted in a sport-tourer frame and called the XS750, TX750 in the USA. The XS750 established itself well in the sport tourer class and remained in production with very few changes until uprated to 850 cc in 1980.

Other four-strokes followed in 1976, with the introduction of the XS250/360/400 series twins. The XS range was strengthened in 1978 by the four-cylinder XS1100.

The 1980s saw a new family of four-strokes, the XJ550, 650, 750 and 900 Fours. Improvements over the XS range amounted to a slimmer DOHC engine unit due to the relocation of the alternator behind the cylinders, electronic ignition and uprated braking and suspension systems. Models were available mainly in standard trim, although custom-styled Maxims were produced especially for the US market. The XJ650T was the first model from Yamaha to have a turbo-charged engine. Although these early XJ models have now been discontinued, their roots live on in the XJ600S and XJ900S Diversion (Seca II) models.

The FZR prefix encompasses the pure sports Yamaha models. With the exception of the 16-valve FZR400 and FZR600 models, the FZ/FZR750 and FZR1000 used 20-valve engines, two exhaust valves and three inlet valves per cylinder. This concept was called Genesis and gave improved gas flow to the combustion chambers. Other features of the new engine were the use of down-draught carburetors and the engine's inclined angle in the frame, plus the change to liquid-cooling.

The XS650 led the way for Yamaha's four-stroke range

Yamaha's XS750 was produced from 1976 to 1982 and then uprated to 850 cc

Introduction 0•7

Lightweight Deltabox design aluminium frames and uprated suspension improved the bikes's handling. The Genesis engine lives on in the YZF750 and 1000 models.

The Genesis concept was the basis of Yamaha's foray into four-stroke racing, first with a bike known simply as 'The Genesis', an FZ750 motor in a TT Formula 1 bike with which the factory attempted to steal the Honda RVF750's thunder at important events like the Suzuka 8 Hours and the Bol d'Or although they never fielded it for a whole World Championship season. That had to wait for the advent of the World Superbike Championship, although there was no full works team until 1995, instead it was left to individual importers to support teams. It was the Australian Dealer Team Yamaha which scored the factory's first World Superbike win in the series debut year of 1988. The rider? Mick Doohan. Slightly, embarrassingly, it was the steel framed FZ750 rather than the FZR homologation special that won races. The OW01 was a race winner, mainly in the hands of Fabrizio Pirovano, the factory's most successful Superbike racer with ten victories, but national success in the UK, Japan, and in the Daytona 200 has not been translated into World Championships for any of Yamaha's 750s.

The vee-twin engine has been the mainstay of the XV Virago range. Since 1981 XVs have been produced in 535, 700, 750, 920, 1000 and 1100 engine sizes, all using the same basic air-cooled sohc vee-twin engine. Other uses of vee engines have been in the XZ550 of the early 1980s, the XVZ12 Venture and the mighty VMX-12 V-Max.

Yamaha has always been a sporting-orientated company whose motto could be 'Racing Improves the Breed', so it's no surprise that the latest generation of lightweight sportsters are at the cutting edge of performance on and off the track. The R6 won more races than any other machine in the inaugural year of the World Supersports Championship, the R7 won a race in its debut year in World Superbike in the hands of the mercurial Noriyuki Haga, and the mighty 1000cc R1 ended Honda's domination of the Isle of Man F1 TT when David Jefferies won three races in a week in 1999.

A new family of four-strokes was released in 1980 with the introduction of the XJ range

FJR1300 – Smooth Operator

If you ever need proof that that the DNA of a design lives on through changes in engine capacity, name, and sundry other alterations that time, the markets and fashion dictate, Yamaha's FJ/FJR range would make a good case study. If you go back to the mid-1980s to the very first FJ, the 1100, you would find a motorcycle that looked initially like a serious competitor for Kawasaki's GPZ900 Ninja, a bike capable of winning the Production TT. However, the Yamaha was a much more rounded, simpler motorcycle. It was one of the last air-cooled multis from Japan, and crucially it was a just a little bit bigger in every direction to make it a more comfortable proposition as a long-distance machine especially if a passenger and luggage were involved. It was a true sports tourer.

The last of the air-cooled FJs was made in 1996, a long model life, and the model prefix wasn't reintroduced until 2001, albeit with an R added. The new FJ looked much more of a tourer than its ancestors but the dynamics of the two were not too different. Indeed, the FJR, tall screen and all, got top marks in many publications' sports tourer comparison tests. It was one of a class of tourers that followed the same sort of design ethos as an executive-level saloon car from a maker like BMW or Audi; lots of luxury, lots of toys to play with, and lots of presence. In its first incarnation, the FJR was at the cutting edge of the class and was an early adopter of ABS brakes as an optional fitment.

When the FJR1300 received the first of its two major upgrades in 2006 ABS became a standard fitting.

There was also the first attempts at air management with adjustable vents to help the

The very first FJR as launched in 2001

Introduction

The 2006 FJR with redesigned bodywork and panniers

The 2013 gets a fresh new look and a host of technical improvements

rider stay comfortable in hot or cold conditions and an adjustable screen. This was part of a set of quite significant changes to deal with overheating in what were now called Gen-1 FJRs. However, there was a new option for the Gen-2 FJR which most definitely fitted the parallel to luxury cars – a semi-automatic gearbox. And just like an automatic car has no clutch pedal, the AS version of the FJR1300 has no clutch lever. You change gear either with a pair of buttons on the left handlebar or with the conventional pedal – although it's a 'five up' box with neutral at the bottom rather than the conventional one-down/four-up.

Yamaha's Chip-Controlled Shift (YCC-S) has been achieved using the same transmission shafts, layout and clutch as the conventional gearbox housed in the same cases as the A model. The clutch is under electronic control of the engine management system's ECU which achieves changes in 0.2 seconds, smoothed by changes to the ignition timing, and operates automatically when the bike comes to a halt.

When the Gen-3 arrived in 2013 the machine had a facelift with new bodywork, headlight and instruments. LED lighting replaced a number of bulbs on the previous model. In a further echo of luxury four-wheeled motoring the on-board electronics now got three customisable information display pages, fly-by-wire throttle with switchable sport and touring modes, traction control, and cruise control – formerly a popular after-market addition – as standard.

The one thing that has never changed on the FJR is the basic motor architecture. Back in 2001 it was at the cutting edge of class performance but the opposition, notably from BMW, has out-powered the FJR. However, engine power is not all in this sector of the market and one of its features is strong brand and model loyalty. One look at FJR websites and forums soon reveals owners on the their second, third and even fourth bike. The original FJ's design objectives still make sense.

Acknowledgements

Our thanks are due to Fowlers of Bristol, Bransons of Yeovil and Nigel Potter of Wellington who supplied the machines featured in the illustrations throughout this manual. We would also like to thank NGK Spark Plugs (UK) Ltd for supplying the colour spark plug condition photographs, the Avon Rubber Company for supplying information on tyre fitting and Draper Tools Ltd for some of the workshop tools shown.

Thanks are also due to Julian Ryder who wrote the introduction 'Yamaha – musical instruments to motorcycles', and to Yamaha (UK) Ltd. who supplied model photographs.

About this Manual

The aim of this manual is to help you get the best value from your motorcycle. It can do so in several ways. It can help you decide what work must be done, even if you choose to have it done by a dealer; it provides information and procedures for routine maintenance and servicing; and it offers diagnostic and repair procedures to follow when trouble occurs.

We hope you use the manual to tackle the work yourself. For many simpler jobs, doing it yourself may be quicker than arranging an appointment to get the motorcycle into a dealer and making the trips to leave it and pick it up. More importantly, a lot of money can be saved by avoiding the expense the shop must pass on to you to cover its labour and overhead costs. An added benefit is the sense of satisfaction and accomplishment that you feel after doing the job yourself.

References to the left or right side of the motorcycle assume you are sitting on the seat, facing forward.

We take great pride in the accuracy of information given in this manual, but motorcycle manufacturers make alterations and design changes during the production run of a particular motorcycle of which they do not inform us. No liability can be accepted by the authors or publishers for loss, damage or injury caused by any errors in, or omissions from, the information given.

Illegal copying

It is the policy of Haynes Publishing to actively protect its Copyrights and Trade Marks. Legal action will be taken against anyone who unlawfully copies the cover or contents of this Manual. This includes all forms of unauthorised copying including digital, mechanical, and electronic in any form. Authorisation from Haynes Publishing will only be provided expressly and in writing. Illegal copying will also be reported to the appropriate statutory authorities.

Identification numbers 0•9

Frame and engine numbers

The frame number is stamped into the right-hand side of the steering head. The engine number is stamped into the back of the crankcase on the right-hand side. Both of these numbers should be recorded and kept in a safe place so they can be given to law enforcement officials in the event of a theft. The VIN plate is on the right-hand side of the frame. There is a model, colour and country code label under the seat.

The frame number, engine number, model and colour codes should also be kept in a handy place (such as with your driver's licence) so they are always available when purchasing or ordering parts for your machine.

The procedures in this manual identify differences between models either by stating the model year, or by the letter that denotes their year of production (see table below), whether they have ABS (letter A), and whether they have the YCC-S (Yamaha Chip-Controlled Shift system) (letter S in Europe and E in the US).

Buying spare parts

Once you have found all the identification numbers, record them for reference when buying parts. Since the manufacturers change specifications, parts and vendors (companies that manufacture various components on the machine), providing the ID numbers is the only way to be reasonably sure that you are buying the correct parts for your model.

Whenever possible, take the worn part to the dealer so direct comparison with the new component can be made. Along the trail from the manufacturer to the parts shelf, there are numerous places that the part can end up with the wrong number or be listed incorrectly.

The two places to purchase new parts for your motorcycle – the franchised or main dealer and the parts/accessories store – differ in the type of parts they carry. While dealers can obtain every single genuine part for your motorcycle, the accessory store is usually limited to normal high wear items such as brake pads, spark plugs and lubes. Rarely will an accessory outlet have major suspension components, camshafts, transmission gears, or engine cases.

Used parts can be obtained from breakers for roughly half the price of new ones, but you can't always be sure of what you're getting. Once again, take your worn part to the breaker for direct comparison, or when ordering by mail order make sure that you can return it if you are not happy.

Whether buying new, used or rebuilt parts, the best course is to deal directly with someone who specialises in your particular make.

Model/prod yr letter*	Production year	Model code (UK models)
FJR1300N	2001	5JW1
FJR1300P	2002	5JW4
FJR1300R	2003	5JWA
FJR1300AR	2003	5VS1
FJR1300S	2004	5JWG
FJR1300AS	2004	5VS7
FJR1300T	2005	5JWN
FJR1300AT	2005	5VSC/D/G
FJR1300AV	2006	3P61
FJR1300ASV (AEV)	2006	2D21
FJR1300AW	2007	3P67
FJR1300ASW (AEW)	2007	2D27
FJR1300AX	2008	3P6D
FJR1300ASX (AEX)	2008	2D2D
FJR1300AY	2009	3P6K
FJR1300ASY (AEY)	2009	2D2K
FJR1300AZ	2010	1CY5/7
FJR1300ASZ (AEZ)	2010	1DA5/7
FJR1300AA	2011	1CY9
FJR1300ASA (AEA)	2011	1DA9
FJR1300AB	2012	1CY9
FJR1300ASB (AEB)	2012	1DA9
FJR1300AD	2013	1MC1

__Note:__ California models have C added to the end

The model/colour/country code label (arrowed) is on the rear sub-frame

The engine number is stamped into the back of the crankcase on the right-hand side

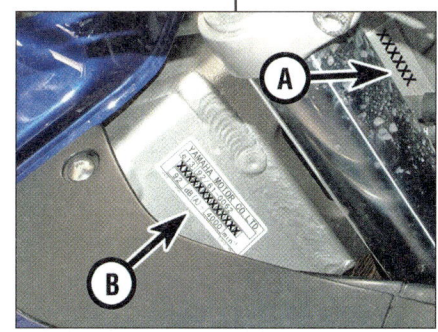

Frame number (A) and VIN label (B) are on the right-hand side of the steering head

Safety First!

Professional mechanics are trained in safe working procedures. However enthusiastic you may be about getting on with the job at hand, take the time to ensure that your safety is not put at risk. A moment's lack of attention can result in an accident, as can failure to observe simple precautions.

There will always be new ways of having accidents, and the following is not a comprehensive list of all dangers; it is intended rather to make you aware of the risks and to encourage a safe approach to all work you carry out on your bike.

Asbestos

● Certain friction, insulating, sealing and other products - such as brake pads, clutch linings, gaskets, etc. - contain asbestos. Extreme care must be taken to avoid inhalation of dust from such products since it is hazardous to health. If in doubt, assume that they do contain asbestos.

Fire

● Remember at all times that petrol is highly flammable. Never smoke or have any kind of naked flame around, when working on the vehicle. But the risk does not end there - a spark caused by an electrical short-circuit, by two metal surfaces contacting each other, by careless use of tools, or even by static electricity built up in your body under certain conditions, can ignite petrol vapour, which in a confined space is highly explosive. Never use petrol as a cleaning solvent. Use an approved safety solvent.

● Always disconnect the battery earth terminal before working on any part of the fuel or electrical system, and never risk spilling fuel on to a hot engine or exhaust.
● It is recommended that a fire extinguisher of a type suitable for fuel and electrical fires is kept handy in the garage or workplace at all times. Never try to extinguish a fuel or electrical fire with water.

Fumes

● Certain fumes are highly toxic and can quickly cause unconsciousness and even death if inhaled to any extent. Petrol vapour comes into this category, as do the vapours from certain solvents such as trichloro-ethylene. Any draining or pouring of such volatile fluids should be done in a well ventilated area.
● When using cleaning fluids and solvents, read the instructions carefully. Never use materials from unmarked containers - they may give off poisonous vapours.
● Never run the engine of a motor vehicle in an enclosed space such as a garage. Exhaust fumes contain carbon monoxide which is extremely poisonous; if you need to run the engine, always do so in the open air or at least have the rear of the vehicle outside the workplace.

The battery

● Never cause a spark, or allow a naked light near the vehicle's battery. It will normally be giving off a certain amount of hydrogen gas, which is highly explosive.

● Always disconnect the battery ground (earth) terminal before working on the fuel or electrical systems (except where noted).
● If possible, loosen the filler plugs or cover when charging the battery from an external source. Do not charge at an excessive rate or the battery may burst.
● Take care when topping up, cleaning or carrying the battery. The acid electrolyte, evenwhen diluted, is very corrosive and should not be allowed to contact the eyes or skin. Always wear rubber gloves and goggles or a face shield. If you ever need to prepare electrolyte yourself, always add the acid slowly to the water; never add the water to the acid.

Electricity

● When using an electric power tool, inspection light etc., always ensure that the appliance is correctly connected to its plug and that, where necessary, it is properly grounded (earthed). Do not use such appliances in damp conditions and, again, beware of creating a spark or applying excessive heat in the vicinity of fuel or fuel vapour. Also ensure that the appliances meet national safety standards.
● A severe electric shock can result from touching certain parts of the electrical system, such as the spark plug wires (HT leads), when the engine is running or being cranked, particularly if components are damp or the insulation is defective. Where an electronic ignition system is used, the secondary (HT) voltage is much higher and could prove fatal.

Remember...

✗ **Don't** start the engine without first ascertaining that the transmission is in neutral.
✗ **Don't** suddenly remove the pressure cap from a hot cooling system - cover it with a cloth and release the pressure gradually first, or you may get scalded by escaping coolant.
✗ **Don't** attempt to drain oil until you are sure it has cooled sufficiently to avoid scalding you.
✗ **Don't** grasp any part of the engine or exhaust system without first ascertaining that it is cool enough not to burn you.
✗ **Don't** allow brake fluid or antifreeze to contact the machine's paintwork or plastic components.
✗ **Don't** siphon toxic liquids such as fuel, hydraulic fluid or antifreeze by mouth, or allow them to remain on your skin.
✗ **Don't** inhale dust - it may be injurious to health (see Asbestos heading).
✗ **Don't** allow any spilled oil or grease to remain on the floor - wipe it up right away, before someone slips on it.
✗ **Don't** use ill-fitting spanners or other tools which may slip and cause injury.
✗ **Don't** lift a heavy component which may be beyond your capability - get assistance.

✗ **Don't** rush to finish a job or take unverified short cuts.
✗ **Don't** allow children or animals in or around an unattended vehicle.
✗ **Don't** inflate a tyre above the recommended pressure. Apart from overstressing the carcass, in extreme cases the tyre may blow off forcibly.
✓ **Do** ensure that the machine is supported securely at all times. This is especially important when the machine is blocked up to aid wheel or fork removal.
✓ **Do** take care when attempting to loosen a stubborn nut or bolt. It is generally better to pull on a spanner, rather than push, so that if you slip, you fall away from the machine rather than onto it.
✓ **Do** wear eye protection when using power tools such as drill, sander, bench grinder etc.
✓ **Do** use a barrier cream on your hands prior to undertaking dirty jobs - it will protect your skin from infection as well as making the dirt easier to remove afterwards; but make sure your hands aren't left slippery. Note that long-term contact with used engine oil can be a health hazard.
✓ **Do** keep loose clothing (cuffs, ties etc. and long hair) well out of the way of moving mechanical parts.

✓ **Do** remove rings, wristwatch etc., before working on the vehicle - especially the electrical system.
✓ **Do** keep your work area tidy - it is only too easy to fall over articles left lying around.
✓ **Do** exercise caution when compressing springs for removal or installation. Ensure that the tension is applied and released in a controlled manner, using suitable tools which preclude the possibility of the spring escaping violently.
✓ **Do** ensure that any lifting tackle used has a safe working load rating adequate for the job.
✓ **Do** get someone to check periodically that all is well, when working alone on the vehicle.
✓ **Do** carry out work in a logical sequence and check that everything is correctly assembled and tightened afterwards.
✓ **Do** remember that your vehicle's safety affects that of yourself and others. If in doubt on any point, get professional advice.
● If in spite of following these precautions, you are unfortunate enough to injure yourself, seek medical attention as soon as possible.

Pre-ride checks

Note: *The Pre-ride checks outlined in the owner's manual covers those items that should be inspected on a daily basis.*

Engine oil level

Before you start:
✔ Support the motorcycle on the centrestand, making sure it is on level ground.
✔ The oil level inspection window is located on the left-hand side of the engine. If necessary wipe the window so that it is clean.
✔ Start the engine and let it idle for 3 to 5 minutes.
Caution: Do not run the engine in an enclosed space such as a garage or workshop.
✔ Stop the engine and allow the oil level to stabilise for 2 to 3 minutes.

The correct oil:
● Modern, high-revving engines place great demands on their oil. It is very important that the correct oil for your bike is used.

● Always top up with a good quality oil of the specified type and viscosity and do not overfill the engine.

Oil type	API grade: SG or higher JASO T 903 grade: MA
Oil viscosity	SAE 10W40, 10W50, 15W40, 20W40, 20W50 according to climate

Caution: Do not use chemical additives or oils labelled "ENERGY CONSERVING". Such additives or oils could cause clutch slip.

Bike care:
● If you have to add oil frequently, check whether you have any oil leaks from the engine joints, oil seals and gaskets. If not, the engine could be burning oil, in which case there will be white smoke coming out of the exhaust (see *Fault Finding*).

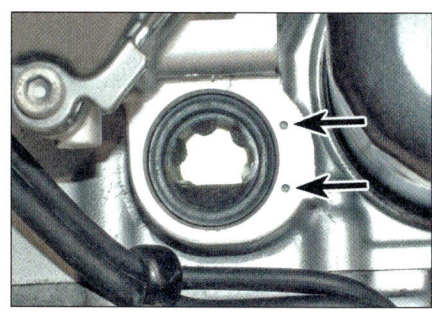

1 With the motorcycle vertical, the oil level should lie between the upper and lower level marks (arrowed).

2 If the level is on or below the lower line unscrew the oil filler cap.

3 Top up the engine with the recommended grade and type of oil to bring the level almost up to the upper line on the inspection window. Do not overfill.

4 Make sure the filler cap O-ring (arrowed) is in good condition and correctly seated before fitting the cap.

Suspension, steering and final drive

Suspension and Steering:
● Check that the front and rear suspension operates smoothly without binding (see Chapter 1).
● Check that the suspension is adjusted as required (see Chapter 5).
● Check that the steering moves smoothly from lock-to-lock.

Final drive:
● Check for signs of oil leakage around the final drive housing. If any is evident, check the final drive oil level (Chapter 1).

Legal and safety

Lighting and signalling:
● Take a minute to check that the headlights, tail and brake lights, licence plate light, instrument lights and turn signals all work correctly.
● Check that the horn sounds when the button is pressed.
● A working speedometer, graduated in mph, is a statutory requirement in the UK.

Safety:
● Check that the throttle grip rotates smoothly when opened and snaps shut when released, in all steering positions. Also check for the correct amount of cable freeplay (see Chapter 1).
● Check that the brake lever and pedal, clutch lever and gearchange lever operate smoothly. Lubricate them at the specified intervals or when necessary (see Chapter 1).
● Check that the engine shuts off when the kill switch is operated. Check the starter safety circuit (see Chapter 1).
● Check that the stand return springs hold the stands up securely when retracted.

Fuel:
● This may seem obvious, but check that you have enough fuel to complete your journey. If you smell petrol (gasoline) or notice signs of fuel leakage, rectify the cause immediately.
● Ensure you use the correct grade fuel – see Chapter 4 Specifications.

0•12 Pre-ride checks

Coolant level

Before you start:
✔ Support the motorcycle on the centrestand, making sure it is on level ground.
✔ Check the coolant level when the engine is cold as the level varies with temperature.
✔ On 2001 to 2005 models the coolant reservoir is located behind the right-hand fairing side panel. On 2006-on models the coolant reservoir is located behind the left-hand fairing side panel.
Caution: Do not run the engine in an enclosed space such as a garage or workshop.

Bike care:
● Use only the specified coolant mixture of 50% distilled water and 50% corrosion inhibited ethylene glycol anti-freeze – ready-mixed coolant is available in one litre containers. It is important that the correct proportion of anti-freeze is used in the system all year round, and not just in the winter. Do not top the system up using only water unless absolutely necessary, as the system will become too diluted. If water is used check and correct the mixture as soon as possible. If distilled water is not available, and you are in an area that has hard water, the system should be drained and refilled using the correct coolant mixture as soon as possible.
● Do not overfill the reservoir tank. If the coolant is significantly above the UPPER level line at any time, the surplus should be siphoned or drained off to prevent the possibility of it being expelled out of the overflow hose.
● If the coolant level falls steadily check the system for leaks (see Chapter 1). If no leaks are found and the level continues to fall, it is recommended that the machine is taken to a Yamaha dealer for a pressure test.

> ⚠ **Warning: DO NOT remove the pressure cap from the filler neck to add coolant. Topping up is done via the coolant reservoir tank filler. DO NOT leave open containers of coolant about, as it is poisonous.**

2001 TO 2005 MODELS

1 The coolant level should lie between the FULL and LOW level lines (arrowed) that are marked on the reservoir. If the coolant level is on or below the LOW line, remove the right fairing side panel (see Chapter 7).

2 Unscrew the upper mounting bolt (arrowed) and remove the cover, then remove the reservoir filler cap. Top up the reservoir with the recommended coolant mixture to the FULL level line.

2006-ON MODELS

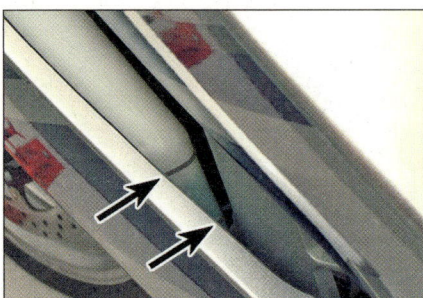 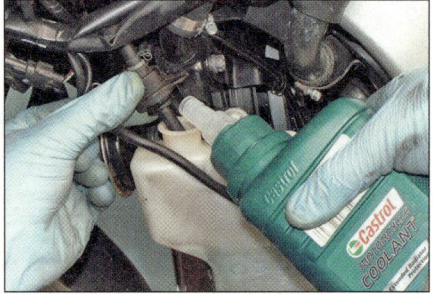

1 The coolant level should lie between the FULL and LOW level lines (arrowed) that are marked on the reservoir. If the coolant level is on or below the LOW line, remove the left fairing side panel (see Chapter 7).

2 Release the reservoir filler cap and move it to one side, and top up the reservoir with the recommended coolant mixture to the FULL level line using a suitable funnel if required.

Brake fluid levels

> ⚠ **Warning: Brake hydraulic fluid can harm your eyes and damage painted surfaces, so use extreme caution when handling and pouring it and cover surrounding surfaces with rag. Do not use fluid that has been standing open for some time, as it is hygroscopic (absorbs moisture from the air) which can cause a dangerous loss of braking effectiveness.**

Before you start:
✔ The front brake fluid reservoir is on the right-hand handlebar. The rear brake fluid reservoir is located behind the right-hand side cover.
✔ Make sure you have the correct hydraulic fluid – DOT 4.
✔ Wrap a rag around the reservoir being worked on to ensure that any spillage does not come into contact with painted surfaces.
✔ To check the fluid in the front reservoir turn the handlebars so the reservoir is level.
✔ To check the fluid in the rear reservoir support the motorcycle on the centrestand on level ground.

Bike care:
● The fluid in the front and rear brake master cylinder reservoirs will drop as the brake pads wear down. If the fluid level is low check the brake pads for wear (see Chapter 1), and replace them with new ones if necessary (see Chapter 6). Do not top the reservoir(s) up until the new pads have been fitted, and then check to see if topping up is still necessary – when the caliper pistons are pushed back to accommodate the extra thickness of the pads some fluid will be displaced back into the reservoir.
● If either fluid reservoir requires repeated topping-up there is a leak somewhere in the system. Check for signs of fluid leakage from the hydraulic hoses and/or brake system components – if found, rectify immediately (see Chapter 6).
● Check the operation of both brakes before taking the machine on the road; if there is evidence of air in the system (spongy feel to lever or pedal), it must be bled (see Chapter 6).

Pre-ride checks 0•13

FRONT BRAKE

1 The front brake fluid level is visible through the window in the reservoir body – it must be above the LOWER level line (arrowed).

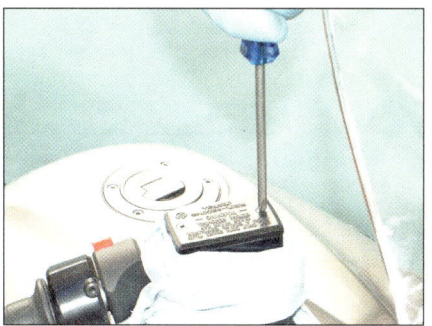

2 If the level is on or below the LOWER line, undo the reservoir cover screws and remove the cover, diaphragm plate and diaphragm.

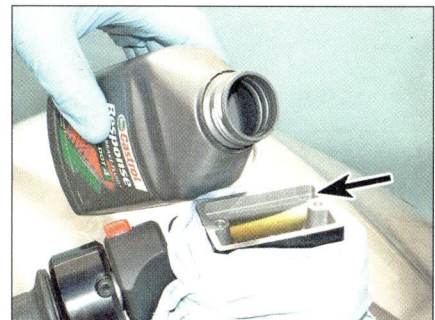

3 Top up with new clean DOT 4 hydraulic fluid, until the level is up to the upper level line cast inside the reservoir (arrowed). Do not overfill and take care to avoid spills (see **Warning** on page 0•12).

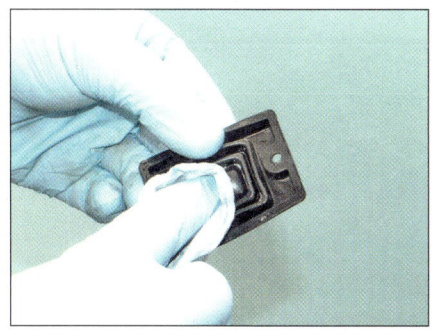

4 Wipe any moisture off the diaphragm with a tissue.

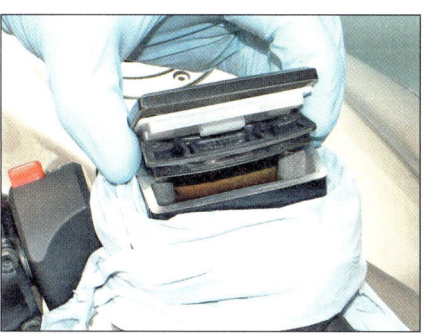

5 Make sure that the diaphragm is correctly seated before fitting the plate and cover. Secure the cover with its screws.

REAR BRAKE

6 Remove the right-hand side cover (see Chapter 7). The rear brake fluid level is visible through the reservoir body – it must be between the UPPER and LOWER level lines (arrowed).

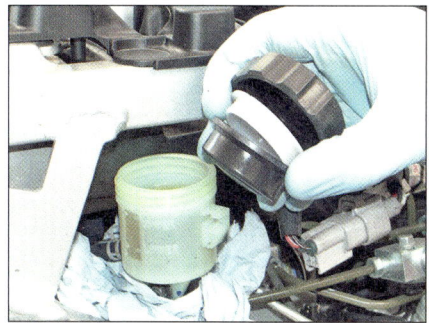

7 If the level is on or below the LOWER line, unscrew the reservoir cap, then remove the diaphragm plate and diaphragm.

8 Top up with new clean DOT 4 hydraulic fluid, until the level is up to the UPPER line. Do not overfill and take care to avoid spills (see **Warning** on page 0•12).

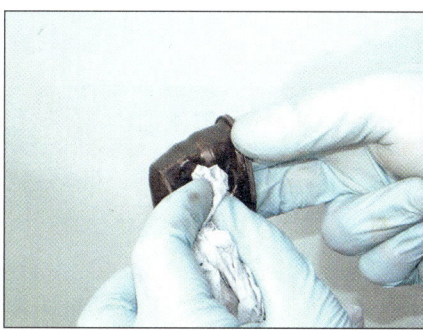

9 Wipe any moisture off the diaphragm with a tissue. Make sure that the diaphragm is correctly seated before fitting the plate and cap.

Pre-ride checks

Clutch fluid level

> **Warning:** Clutch hydraulic fluid can harm your eyes and damage painted surfaces, so use extreme caution when handling and pouring it and cover surrounding surfaces with rag. Do not use fluid from an opened container as it is hygroscopic (absorbs moisture from the air) which can cause a loss of clutch effectiveness.

Before you start:
✔ The clutch fluid reservoir is on the left-hand handlebar on models with a standard gearchange, and behind the left-hand side cover on models with YCC-S.
✔ Make sure you have the correct hydraulic fluid. DOT 4 is recommended.
✔ Wrap a rag around the reservoir on to ensure that any spillage does not come into contact with painted surfaces.
✔ Support the bike on the centrestand on level ground. Turn the handlebars so the reservoir is level.

Bike care:
● If the fluid reservoir requires repeated topping-up there is a leak somewhere in the system, which must be investigated immediately.
● Check for signs of fluid leakage from the hydraulic hose and release system components – if found, rectify immediately (see Chapter 2).
● Check the operation of the clutch before taking the machine on the road; if there is evidence of air in the system (spongy feel to lever, difficulty selecting gears and clutch drag), it must be bled (see Chapter 2).

STANDARD MODELS

1 The clutch fluid level is visible through the window in the reservoir body – it must be above the LOWER level line (arrowed).

2 If the level is on or below the LOWER line, undo the reservoir cover screws and remove the cover, diaphragm plate and diaphragm.

3 Top up with new clean DOT 4 hydraulic fluid, until the level is up to the upper level line cast inside the reservoir (arrowed). Do not overfill and take care to avoid spills (see **Warning** above).

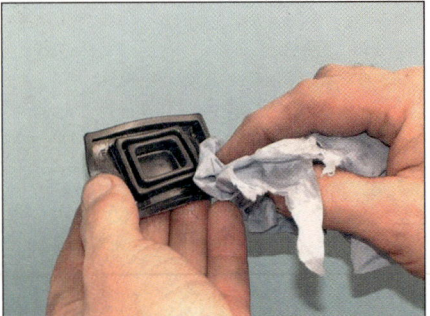

4 Wipe any moisture off the diaphragm with a tissue.

5 Make sure that the diaphragm is correctly seated before fitting the plate and cover. Secure the cover with its screws.

YCC-S MODELS

1 Remove the left-hand side cover (see Chapter 7). The clutch fluid level is visible through the reservoir body – it must be between the UPPER and LOWER level lines (arrowed).

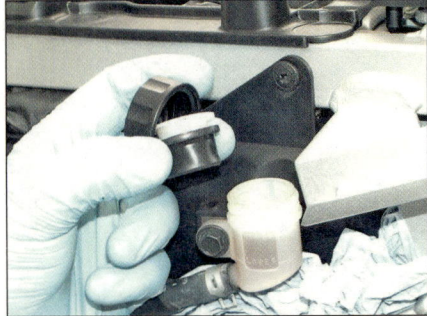

2 If the level is on or below the LOWER line, unscrew the reservoir cap, then remove the diaphragm plate and diaphragm.

3 Top up with new clean DOT 4 hydraulic fluid, until the level is up to the UPPER line. Do not overfill and take care to avoid spills (see **Warning** above).

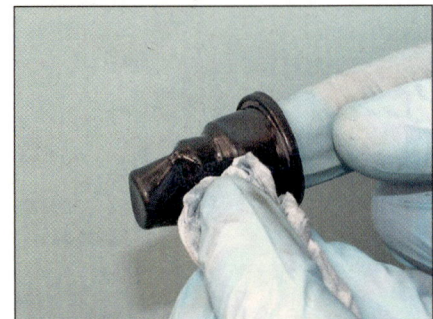

4 Wipe any moisture off the diaphragm with a tissue. Make sure that the diaphragm is correctly seated before fitting the plate and cap.

Pre-ride checks

Tyres

Tyre tread depth:
- At the time of writing UK law requires that tread depth must be at least 1 mm over 3/4 of the tread breadth all the way around the tyre, with no bald patches. Many riders, however, consider 2 mm tread depth minimum to be a safer limit. Yamaha recommends a minimum of 1.6 mm for each tyre. German law requires a minimum of 1.6 mm for each tyre.
- Most tyres incorporate wear indicators in the tread. Identify the location marking on the tyre sidewall to locate the indicator bar and replace the tyre if the tread has worn down to the bar.

The correct pressures:
- The tyres must be checked when **cold**, not immediately after riding. The pressure inside the tyre will increase when the tyre is hot. Note that tyre pressure will also change from one day to the next as air temperature changes.
- Correct tyre pressure will increase tyre life and provide maximum stability and ride comfort. Incorrect pressure will cause abnormal tread wear and unsafe handling. Low tyre pressures may cause the tyre to slip on the rim or come off.
- Use an accurate pressure gauge. Many forecourt gauges are wildly inaccurate. If you buy your own, spend as much as you can justify on a quality gauge.

Tyre care:
- Check the tyres carefully for cuts, tears, embedded nails or other sharp objects and excessive wear. Operation of the motorcycle with excessively worn tyres is extremely hazardous, as traction and handling are directly affected.
- Pick out any stones or nails that may have become embedded in the tyre tread. If left, they will eventually penetrate through the casing and cause a puncture.
- Make sure a dust cap is fitted. If tyre deflation occurs and it is not due to a slow puncture the valve core may be loose or it could be leaking past the seal. If a core tightening tool is incorporated in the dust cap check the valve is tight. Otherwise refer to Section 11 in Chapter 1.
- If tyre damage is apparent, or unexplained loss of pressure is experienced, seek the advice of a tyre fitting specialist without delay.

	Front	Rear
2001 and 2002 models		
Rider only (0 to 90 kg)	36 psi (2.5 Bar)	36 psi (2.5 Bar)
Rider and pillion (over 90 kg)	36 psi (2.5 Bar)	42 psi (2.9 Bar)
High speed riding	36 psi (2.5 Bar)	42 psi (2.9 Bar)
2003 to 2005 models		
Rider only (0 to 90 kg)	36 psi (2.5 Bar)	36 psi (2.5 Bar)
Rider and pillion (over 90 kg)	36 psi (2.5 Bar)	42 psi (2.9 Bar)
High speed riding	36 psi (2.5 Bar)	36 psi (2.5 Bar)
2006 to 2012 models		
All loads	39 psi (2.7 Bar)	42 psi (2.9 Bar)
2013-on models		
All loads	36 psi (2.5 Bar)	42 psi (2.9 Bar)

1 Remove the dust cap from the valve. Do not forget to fit the cap after checking the pressure.

2 Check pressures when the tyres are **cold**.

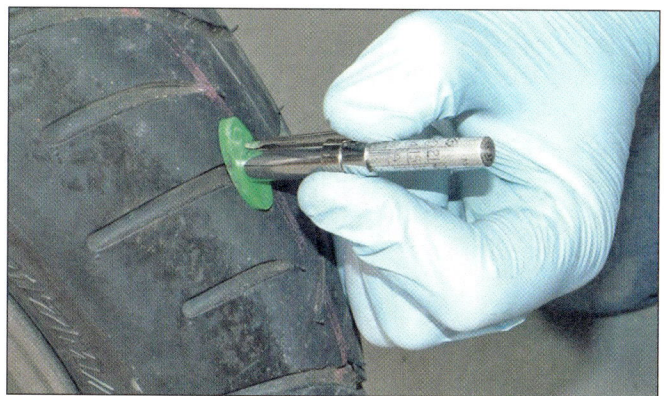

3 Measure tread depth at the centre of the tyre using a depth gauge.

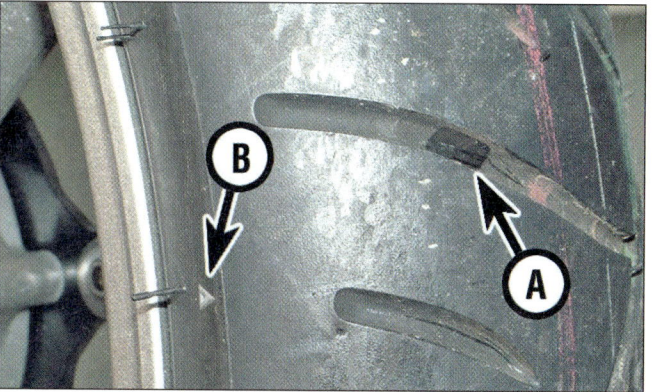

4 Tyre tread wear indicators (A) and its location marking (B) on the edge or sidewall (according to manufacturer).

Model development

The FJR1300 was launched in 2001 in the UK and Europe and in 2003 in the US.

The four cylinder engine is an in-line liquid-cooled unit with four valves per cylinder. Drive to the double overhead camshafts is by chain driven off the right-hand end of the crankshaft. The clutch is a conventional wet multi-plate unit actuated hydraulically, and the gearbox is 5-speed. Drive to the rear wheel is by shaft.

The fuel injection system supplies fuel and air to the engine via Mikuni throttle bodies and two intake valves per cylinder, with exhaust gases exiting via another two valves per cylinder into a four-into-two exhaust system with a closed-loop catalytic converter. An electronic engine management system controls both the injection system and the ignition system.

The engine sits in an aluminium frame using the engine as a stressed member.

Front suspension is by oil-damped cartridge forks with adjustable spring pre-load, rebound damping and compression damping. Rear suspension is by swingarm acting on a single shock absorber with adjustable spring pre-load and rebound damping, via a rising rate linkage. The swingarm houses the driveshaft in its left-hand arm.

The hydraulic braking system has two twin-opposed piston calipers acting on 298 mm discs at the front, and a single piston sliding caliper acting on a 282 mm disc at the rear.

In 2003 the front brake disc design changed and its diameter increased to 320 mm, the front turn signal design changed, and a lockable fairing pocket was added, an ABS system became available as an option (AR models), and an immobiliser system was introduced for certain markets.

In 2004 the idle speed control system on the throttle bodies changed, and the fuel pressure regulator was taken off the fuel rail and incorporated in the fuel pump assembly.

There were no changes in 2005.

In 2006 the FJR underwent a major revision in what was to become known as the Gen II model: there was a new fairing and bodywork with panniers fitted as standard, new instruments, new headlight and tail light, a new radiator with twin cooling fans, and an adjustable seat and handlebar height. ABS became standard across the range along with a new linked braking system – when the front brake lever is applied the system actuates both pairs of pistons in the left-hand front caliper but only one pair in the right-hand front caliper. When the rear brake pedal is applied the system actuates the rear caliper and the other pair of pistons in the right-hand caliper via a proportional control valve and a metering valve. YCC-S (Yamaha Chip Controlled Shift system) was introduced as an option (AS models) – this is a semi-automatic gearchange system that eliminates the use of a manual clutch lever. Instead gearchange is initiated either via a switch on the left handlebar or via a lever operated by the left foot (as normal), with the switch and lever connected to an electronic unit controlling the hydraulic actuator that releases and engages the clutch.

There were no changes in 2007.

In 2008 heated handlebar grips were added, and a new 3-mode ABS unit fitted along with upgraded wheel speed sensors. On AS models the YCC-S gear selection switch on the handlebar was modified.

In 2009 there was a new fault code for the engine management system, and on AS models the control unit for the YCC-S was modified.

There were no changes from 2010 to 2012.

For 2013 Yamaha introduced a third generation FJR, the Gen III model, with two significant technical features – YCC-T (Yamaha Chip Controlled Throttle system), and TCS (Traction Control System). YCC-T is a fly-by-wire throttle system that replaces the mechanical link between the throttle cables and the throttle valves with an electronic one. An electronic cruise-control system is a feature of YCC-T. TCS controls rear wheel spin under acceleration on slippery surfaces. There was also a new fairing and bodywork, new instruments and headlight, new throttle bodies, and 'stick' type ignition coils (the coil is incorporated in the spark plug cap) replace the conventional type, along with some minor detail changes around the bike.

Bike spec 0•17

Dimensions and weights
Note: *For California models add 1kg to weight*

2001 and 2002 UK/Europe models and 2003 US models
Overall length	2195 mm
Overall width	760 mm
Overall height	1420 mm
Seat height	805 mm
Wheelbase	1515 mm
Ground clearance	135 mm
Kerb weight	
Dry	237 kg
Wet	268 kg
Maximum weight capacity	208 kg

2003 (except US) to 2005 models
Overall length	2195 mm
Overall width	760 mm
Overall height	1435 mm
Seat height	805 mm
Wheelbase	1515 mm
Ground clearance	135 mm
Kerb weight	
Dry	
Standard models	244 kg
A models	251 kg
Wet	
Standard models	275 kg
A models	282 kg
Maximum weight capacity	
Standard models	201 kg
A models	194 kg

2006 to 2012 models
Overall length	2230 mm
Overall width	750 mm
Overall height	1450 mm
Seat height	
2006 and 2007 models	800 mm
2008 to 2012 models	805 mm
Wheelbase	1545 mm
Ground clearance	130 mm
Kerb weight (wet)	
A models	291 kg
AS models	295 kg
Maximum weight capacity	
A models	212 kg
AS models	208 kg

2013-on models
Overall length	2230 mm
Overall width	750 mm
Overall height	1325/1455 mm
Seat height	805/825 mm
Wheelbase	1545 mm
Ground clearance	130 mm
Kerb weight (wet)	
A models	289 kg
AS models	293 kg
Maximum weight capacity	
A models	215 kg
AS models	211 kg

0•18 Bike spec

Engine
Type	Four-stroke in-line four
Capacity	1298 cc
Bore	79.0 mm
Stroke	66.2 mm
Compression ratio	10.8 to 1
Cooling system	Liquid cooled
Clutch	Wet multi-plate, hydraulic
Transmission	Five-speed constant mesh
Final drive	Shaft
Camshafts	DOHC, chain-driven
Fuel system	Fuel injection
Ignition system	Computer-controlled digital transistorised with electronic advance

Chassis
Frame type	Aluminium, twin-spar diamond
Rake and trail	26°, 109 mm
Fuel tank	
Capacity (including reserve)	25 litres
Reserve volume	
2001 to 2005 models	5.0 litres
2006-on models	5.5 litres
Front suspension	
Type	Oil-damped 48 mm telescopic forks
Travel	135 mm
Adjustment	Spring pre-load, rebound damping, compression damping
Rear suspension	
Type	Single shock absorber, rising rate linkage, aluminium swingarm
Travel (at axle)	125 mm
Adjustment	Spring pre-load, rebound damping
Wheels	17 inch 3-spoke alloy
Tyres	
Front	120/70-ZR17M/C (58W)
Rear	180/55-ZR17M/C (73W)
Front brake	
2001 and 2002 models	Twin 298 mm floating discs with twin-opposed piston calipers
All other models	Twin 320 mm floating discs with twin-opposed piston calipers
Rear brake	Single 282 mm disc with single piston sliding caliper

Chapter 1
Routine maintenance and servicing

Contents

	Section number		Section number
Air filter	3	Idle speed	6
Battery	17	Nuts and bolts	16
Brake fluid level check	see *Pre-ride checks*	Pivot points and throttle cable lubrication	15
Brake system	1	Sidestand, centrestand and starter safety circuit	14
Clutch	2	Spark plugs	4
Clutch fluid level check	see *Pre-ride checks*	Steering head bearings	13
Coolant level check	see *Pre-ride checks*	Suspension	12
Cooling system	10	Throttle body synchronisation	6
Engine oil and filter	8	Throttle cables	7
Engine oil level check	see *Pre-ride checks*	Tyre pressure check	see *Pre-ride checks*
Engine wear assessment	see Chapter 2	Valve clearances	18
Final drive gear oil	9	Wheels, wheel bearings and tyres	11
Fuel and emission control systems	5		

Degrees of difficulty

Easy, suitable for novice with little experience	Fairly easy, suitable for beginner with some experience	Fairly difficult, suitable for competent DIY mechanic	Difficult, suitable for experienced DIY mechanic	Very difficult, suitable for expert DIY or professional

Specifications

Engine

Cylinder numbering .... 1 to 4 from left to right
Spark plugs
   2001 to 2012 models
      Type .... NGK CR8E or DENSO U24ESR-N
      Electrode gap .... 0.7 to 0.8 mm
   2013-on models
      Type .... NGK CPR8EA-9
      Electrode gap .... 0.7 to 0.8 mm
Throttle body synchronisation – intake vacuum at idle .... 220 to 280 mmHg
Throttle body synchronisation – max. difference between bodies ..... 10 mmHg
Engine idle speed .... 1000 to 1100 rpm
Valve clearances (COLD engine)
   Intake valves .... 0.15 to 0.22 mm
   Exhaust valves .... 0.18 to 0.25 mm

Specifications

Cycle parts

Throttle cable freeplay	3 to 5 mm
Tyre pressures (cold)	see Pre-ride checks

Lubricants and fluids

Engine oil
- Viscosity: SAE 10W40, 10W50, 15W40, 20W40, 20W50 according to climate
- Type: API grade SG or higher, JASO T 903 grade: MA, motorcycle oil

Engine oil capacity
- Oil change: 3.8 litres
- Oil and filter change: 4.0 litres
- Following engine overhaul – dry engine, new filter: 4.9 litres

Final drive oil type: Yamaha shaft drive gear oil (part No. 9079E-SH0001-00 for 2001 to 2012 models, 9079E-SH0002-00 for 2013-on models).

Final drive oil capacity: 0.2 litre

Coolant type: 50% distilled water, 50% silicate-free corrosion inhibited ethylene glycol anti-freeze

Coolant capacity
- 2001 to 2005 models
  - Radiator and engine: 3.3 litres
  - Reservoir: 0.25 litre
- 2006-on models
  - Radiator and engine: 2.6 litres
  - Reservoir: 0.25 litre

Brake fluid	DOT 4
Clutch fluid	DOT 4
Steering head bearings	Lithium based multi-purpose grease
Stand pivots, footrest pivots, gearchange lever pivot and brake pedal pivot	Lithium based multi-purpose grease
Wheel bearing seal lips	Lithium based multi-purpose grease
Throttle twistgrip	Lithium based multi-purpose grease
Throttle cables	Aerosol cable lubricant
Throttle cable ends	Lithium based multi-purpose grease
Front brake lever pivot and master cylinder pushrod end	Silicone grease
Clutch lever pivot and master cylinder pushrod end	Silicone grease
Rear brake caliper slider pins and boots	Silicone grease
Swingarm pivot bearings and seals	Lithium based multi-purpose grease
Shock absorber pivot bearing and seals	Lithium based multi-purpose grease
Suspension linkage pivot bearings and seals	Lithium based multi-purpose grease
Final drive shaft/UJ/housing splines	Molybdenum disulphide grease

Torque settings

Cooling system drain bolt	10 Nm
Engine oil check bolt	15 Nm
Engine oil drain bolt	43 Nm
Engine oil filter	17 Nm
Final drive oil drain bolt	23 Nm
Final drive oil filler bolt	23 Nm
Footrest bracket bolts (right-hand side)	28 Nm

Fork clamp bolts (top yoke)
- 2001 to 2005 models: 34 Nm
- 2006-on models: 26 Nm

Spark plugs: 13 Nm

Steering head bearing adjuster nut
- Initial setting: 52 Nm
- Final setting: 18 Nm

Steering stem nut: 115 Nm

Maintenance schedule – UK and Europe models

Note: *The Pre-ride checks outlined in the owner's manual cover those items that should be inspected before every ride. Also perform the pre-ride inspection at every maintenance interval (in addition to the procedures listed). The intervals listed below are the intervals recommended by the manufacturer for the models covered in this manual.*

Pre-ride
- [ ] See 'Pre-ride checks' at the beginning of this manual

After the initial 600 miles (1000 km)
Note: *This check is performed by a Yamaha dealer after the first 600 miles (1000 km) from new. Thereafter, maintenance is carried out according to the following intervals of the schedule.*

Every 6000 miles (10,000 km) or 12 months
- [ ] Check the brake pads for wear (Section 1)
- [ ] Check the brake system and brake light switch operation (Section 1)
- [ ] Check the clutch (Section 2)
- [ ] Clean the air filter element (Section 3)
- [ ] Check the spark plugs (Section 4)
- [ ] Check the fuel system, AIS (air induction system) and crankcase breather (Section 5)
- [ ] Check throttle body synchronisation and idle speed (Section 6)
- [ ] Check the throttle cables and adjust if necessary (Section 7, except 2013-on models)
- [ ] Change the engine oil (Section 8)
- [ ] Check the final drive and change the oil (Section 9)
- [ ] Check the cooling system (Section 10)
- [ ] Check the condition of the wheels, wheel bearings and tyres (Section 11)
- [ ] Check the front and rear suspension (Section 12)
- [ ] Check the steering head bearings and adjust if necessary (Section 13)
- [ ] Check the stands and starter safety circuit (Section 14)
- [ ] Lubricate the clutch, gearchange and brake levers, brake pedal, stand pivots, and the throttle cables (Section 15)
- [ ] Check the tightness of all nuts, bolts and fasteners (Section 16)
- [ ] Check the battery (Section 17)

Every 12,000 miles (19,500 km)
- [ ] Fit a new air filter element (Section 3)
- [ ] Fit new spark plugs (Section 4)
- [ ] Change the engine oil and fit a new filter (Section 8)
- [ ] Re-grease the shock absorber and suspension linkage bearings (Section 12)
- [ ] Re-grease the steering head bearings (Section 13)

Every 24,000 miles (39,000 km)
- [ ] Check the valve clearances and adjust if necessary (Section 18)

Every 30,000 miles (49,000 km)
- [ ] Re-grease the swingarm bearings (Section 12)

Every two years
- [ ] Change the brake fluid (Section 1)
- [ ] Change the clutch fluid (Section 2)

Every three years
- [ ] Change the coolant (Section 10)

Every four years
- [ ] Fit new brake hoses (Section 1)

Maintenance schedule – US models

Note: *The Pre-ride checks outlined in the owner's manual cover those items that should be inspected before every ride. Also perform the pre-ride inspection at every maintenance interval (in addition to the procedures listed). The intervals listed below are the intervals recommended by the manufacturer for the models covered in this manual.*

Pre-ride
- [ ] See 'Pre-ride checks' at the beginning of this manual

After the initial 600 miles (1000 km)
Note: *This check is performed by a Yamaha dealer after the first 600 miles (1000 km) from new. Thereafter, maintenance is carried out according to the following intervals of the schedule.*

Every 4000 miles (6500 km) or 6 months
- [ ] Check the brake pads for wear (Section 1)
- [ ] Check the brake system and brake light switch operation (Section 1)
- [ ] Check the clutch (Section 2)
- [ ] Clean the air filter element (Section 3)
- [ ] Check the spark plugs (Section 4)
- [ ] Check the fuel system, AIS (air induction system), crankcase breather and EVAP system (Section 5)
- [ ] Check and adjust throttle body synchronisation and idle speed (Section 6)
- [ ] Check the throttle cables and adjust if necessary (Section 7, except 2013-on models)
- [ ] Change the engine oil (Section 8)
- [ ] Check the final drive and change the oil (Section 9)
- [ ] Check the cooling system (Section 10)
- [ ] Check the condition of the wheels, wheel bearings and tyres (Section 11)
- [ ] Check the front and rear suspension (Section 12)
- [ ] Check the steering head bearings and adjust if necessary (Section 13)
- [ ] Check the stands and starter safety circuit (Section 14)
- [ ] Lubricate the clutch, gearchange and brake levers, brake pedal, stand pivots, and the throttle cables (Section 15)
- [ ] Check the tightness of all nuts, bolts and fasteners (Section 16)
- [ ] Check the battery (Section 17)

Every 8000 miles (13,000 km) or 12 months
- [ ] Fit new spark plugs (Section 4)
- [ ] Change the engine oil and fit a new filter (Section 8)

Every 12,000 miles (19,500 km) or 18 months
- [ ] Fit a new air filter element (Section 3)
- [ ] Re-grease the shock absorber and suspension linkage bearings (Section 12)
- [ ] Re-grease the steering head bearings (Section 13)

Every 16,000 miles (26,000 km) or two years
- [ ] Re-grease the swingarm bearings (Section 12)

Every 26,000 miles (42,000 km)
- [ ] Check the valve clearances and adjust if necessary (Section 18)

Every two years
- [ ] Change the brake fluid (Section 1)
- [ ] Change the clutch fluid (Section 2)
- [ ] Change the coolant (Section 10)

Every four years
- [ ] Fit new brake hoses (Section 1)

Component locations 1•5

Component locations on the right side (2001 to 2005 models)

1. Rear brake fluid reservoir
2. Idle speed adjuster
3. Steering head bearing adjuster
4. Front brake fluid reservoir
5. Throttle cable adjuster
6. Frame number
7. Battery
8. Coolant reservoir
9. Coolant drain bolt
10. Engine number
11. Rear brake light switch
12. Rear brake pedal height adjuster

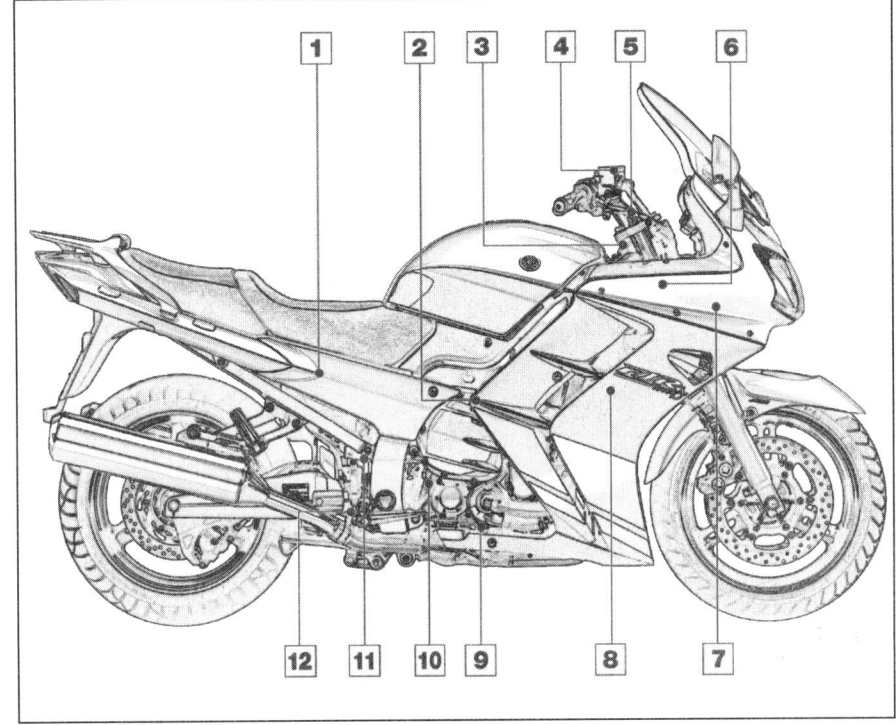

Component locations on the left side (2001 to 2005 models)

1. Clutch fluid reservoir
2. Cooling system pressure cap
3. Air filter
4. Final drive oil filler bolt
5. Final drive oil drain bolt
6. Oil filler cap
7. Oil filter
8. Oil level inspection window
9. Oil drain bolt

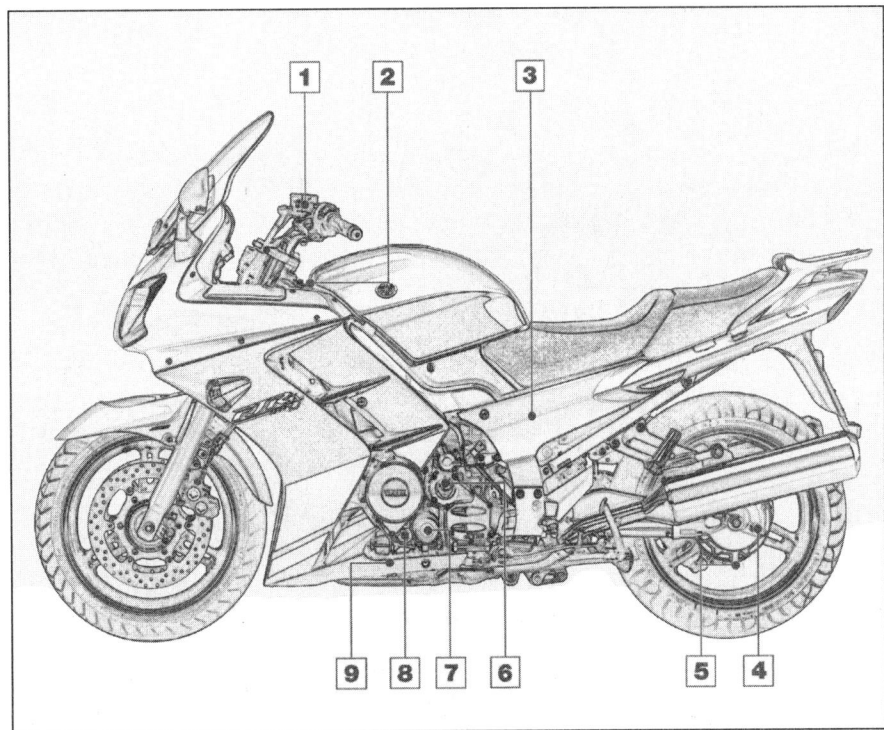

1•6 Component locations

Component locations on the right side (2006 to 2012 models)

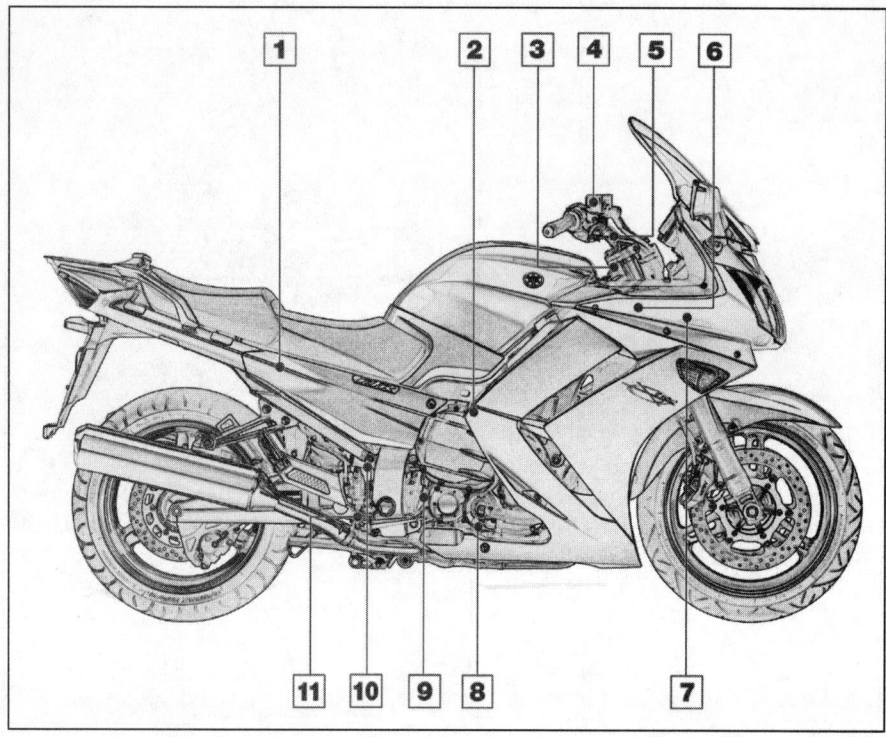

1. Rear brake fluid reservoir
2. Idle speed adjuster
3. Steering head bearing adjuster
4. Front brake fluid reservoir
5. Throttle cable adjuster
6. Frame number
7. Battery
8. Coolant drain bolt
9. Engine number
10. Rear brake light switch
11. Rear brake pedal height adjuster

Component locations on the left side (2006 to 2012 models)

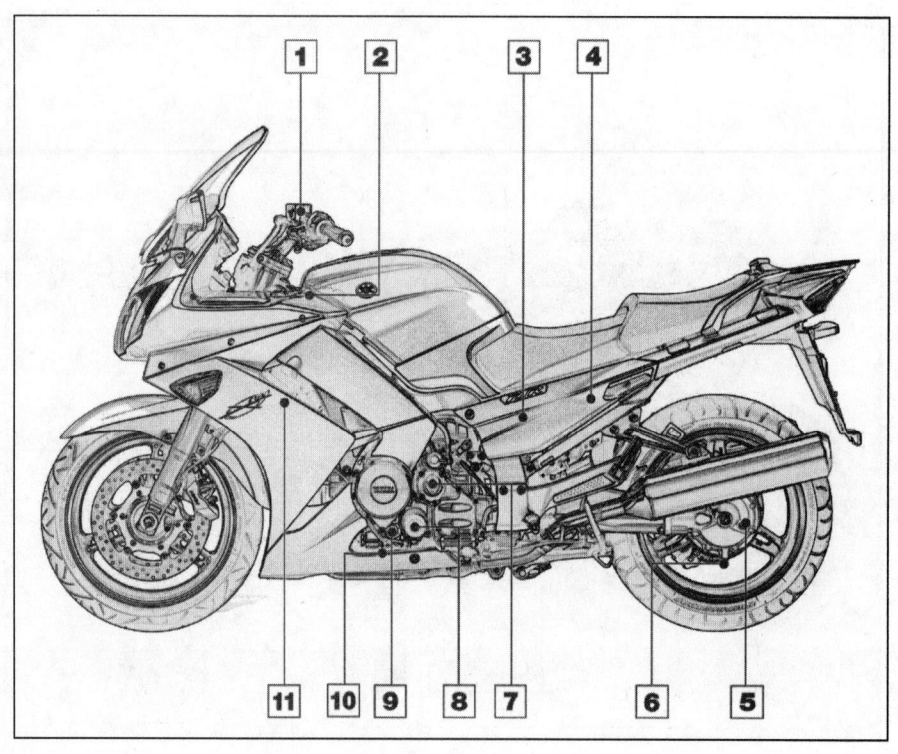

1. Clutch fluid reservoir (except YCC-S)
2. Cooling system pressure cap
3. Air filter
4. Clutch fluid reservoir (YCC-S)
5. Final drive oil filler bolt
6. Final drive oil drain bolt
7. Oil filler cap
8. Oil filter
9. Oil level inspection window
10. Oil drain bolt
11. Coolant reservoir

Component locations 1•7

Component locations on the right side (2013-on models)

1. Rear brake fluid reservoir
2. Steering head bearing adjuster
3. Front brake fluid reservoir
4. Throttle cable adjuster
5. Frame number
6. Battery
7. Coolant drain bolt
8. Engine number
9. Rear brake light switch
10. Rear brake pedal height adjuster

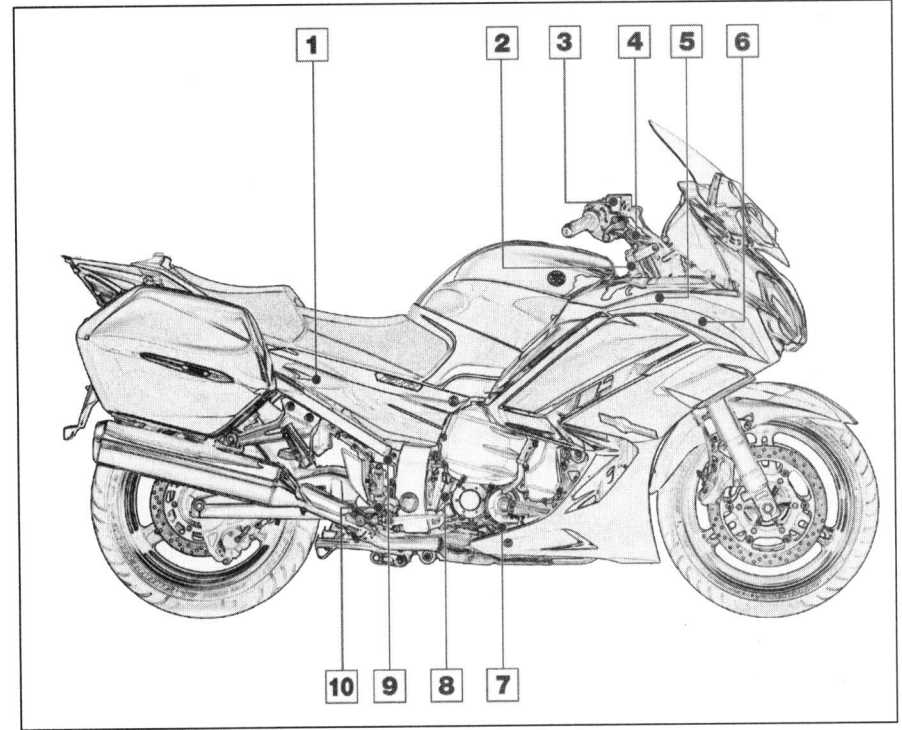

Component locations on the left side (2013-on models)

1. Clutch fluid reservoir (except YCC-S)
2. Cooling system pressure cap
3. Air filter
4. Clutch fluid reservoir (YCC-S)
5. Final drive oil filler bolt
6. Final drive oil drain bolt
7. Oil filler cap
8. Oil filter
9. Oil level inspection window
10. Oil drain bolt
11. Coolant reservoir

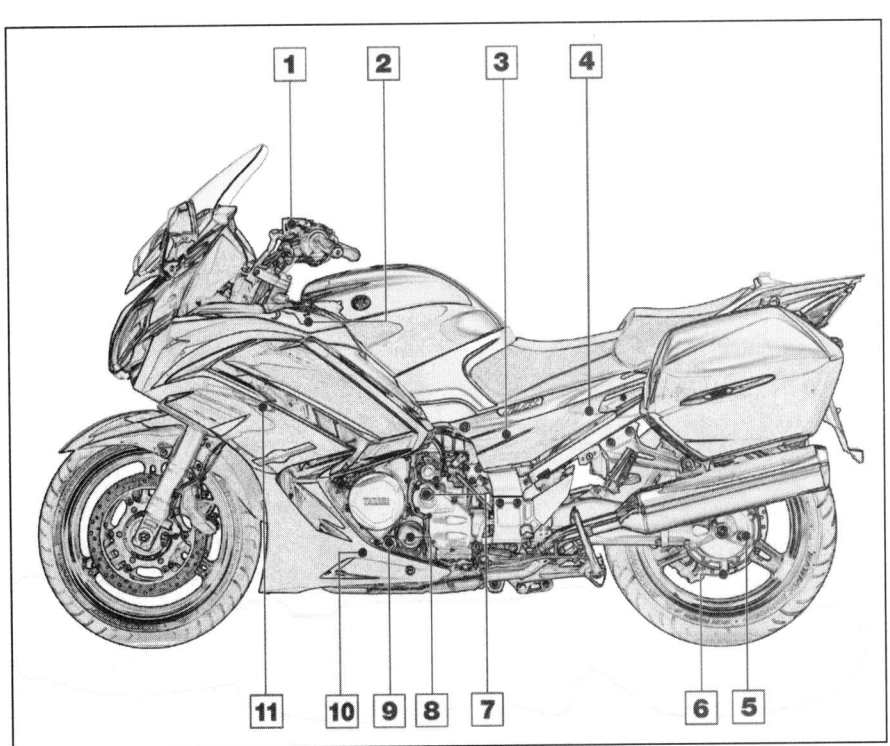

1•8 Routine maintenance and servicing

1 This Chapter is designed to help the home mechanic maintain his/her motorcycle for safety, economy, long life and peak performance.

2 Deciding where to start or plug into the routine maintenance schedule depends on several factors. If your motorcycle has been maintained according to the warranty standards and has just come out of warranty, start routine maintenance as it coincides with the next mileage or calendar interval. If you have owned the machine for some time but have never performed any maintenance on it, start at the nearest interval and include some additional procedures to ensure that nothing important is overlooked. If you have just had a major engine overhaul, then start the maintenance routine from the beginning. If you have a used machine and have no knowledge of its history or maintenance record, combine all the checks into one large service initially and then settle into the specified maintenance schedule.

3 Before beginning any maintenance or repair, clean the machine thoroughly, especially around the oil filter, oil drain plug, body panels, suspension, wheels, etc. Cleaning will help ensure that dirt does not contaminate the engine and will allow you to detect wear and damage that could otherwise easily go unnoticed. If you use a pressure washer make sure you do not direct the jet at wheel bearing and suspension seals and at the steering head, or at any electrical/ignition components and connectors.

4 Certain maintenance information is sometimes printed on labels attached to the motorcycle. If the information on the labels differs from that included here, use the information on the label.

1 Brake system

Brake pad wear check

1 Each front brake pad has a wear indicator in the form of a groove in the friction material **(see illustration)** – if the pads are worn to the bottom of the groove, they must be replaced with new ones (see Chapter 6).

2 Each rear brake pad has wear indicators in the form of raised sections on the pad base **(see illustration)** – the pad is worn when these almost contact the disc (if they do, you will hear a horrible noise, but you must replace them before this happens to avoid marking the disc). The raised sections may be difficult to see, but the amount of friction material remaining is easily visible, and the pads need replacing when the material is down to about 1 mm **(see illustration)**.

3 Yamaha specify a minimum thickness of 0.5 mm for front brake pads and 0.8 for the rear, but many would consider 1 mm to be a safer option for all pads. **Note:** *Some after-market pads may use different indicators to those on the original equipment.*

4 On 2001 to 2005 models check for different amounts of wear in the pads in each front caliper, and uneven wear across each pad – either situation is indicative of a sticking or seized piston or pistons. If uneven wear is found, the caliper(s) must be overhauled (see Chapter 6).

5 On 2006-on models check for different amounts of wear in each pad in the front left caliper, and in each opposed pad in the front right caliper, which is indicative of a sticking or seized piston or pistons (you can expect different amounts of wear between each pair of pads in the right caliper as one pair is actuated by the front brake lever while the other is actuated by the rear brake pedal). If uneven wear is found, the caliper(s) must be overhauled (see Chapter 6).

6 If the pads are dirty or if you are in doubt as to the amount of friction material remaining, remove them for inspection (see Chapter 6). If the pads are excessively worn, also check the brake discs (see Chapter 6).

Brake system check

7 A routine general check of the brake system will ensure that any problems are discovered and remedied before the rider's safety is jeopardised.

8 Check the brake pads for wear (see above) and make sure the fluid level in each reservoir is correct (see *Pre-ride checks*).

9 Check the brake lever and pedal pivots for sloppy or rough action, excessive play, bends, and other damage. Replace any damaged parts with new ones (see Chapter 5). Clean and lubricate the lever and pedal pivots if their action is stiff or rough (see Section 15). If the lever or pedal is spongy, bleed the brakes (see Chapter 6).

10 Look for leaks at the hose and pipe connections and check for cracks in the hoses, pipes and unions **(see illustration)**. If leakage or cracked or damaged hoses are found, fit new hoses as described in Chapter 6. Make sure all brake hose and pipe fasteners are tight. Similarly check for any signs of fluid leakage from the caliper and master cylinder – overhaul and seal replacement will be necessary if found (see Chapter 6).

11 Make sure the brake light operates when the front brake lever is pulled in. The front brake light switch, mounted on the underside of the master cylinder, is not adjustable. If it fails to operate properly, check it (see Chapter 8).

12 Make sure the brake light is activated just before the rear brake takes effect. The rear brake light switch is mounted behind the right-hand footrest bracket **(see illustration)** – for best access unscrew the footrest bracket bolts and displace the bracket **(see illustration)**. If adjustment is necessary, hold the switch body and turn the adjuster nut until the brake light is activated when required **(see illustration)** – do not turn the switch itself. If the brake light comes on too late or not at all, turn the ring clockwise so the switch is drawn up out of its bracket. If the brake light comes on too soon or is permanently on, turn the ring

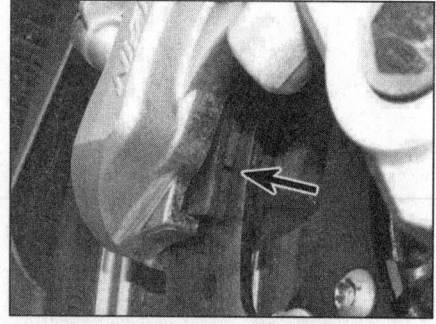

1.1 Front brake pad wear indicator cut-out (arrowed)

1.2a Rear brake pad wear indicators (arrowed)

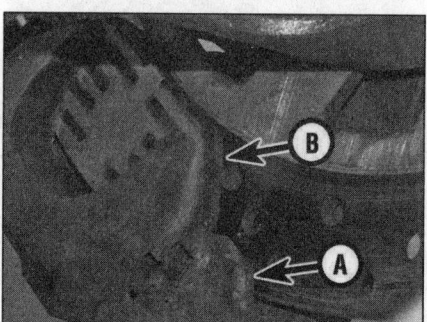

1.2b Rear brake pad wear indicator location (A) and friction material (B)

1.10 Check all hoses, pipes and unions for cracks and leaks

Routine maintenance and servicing 1•9

1.12a Rear brake light switch (arrowed) viewed from the back

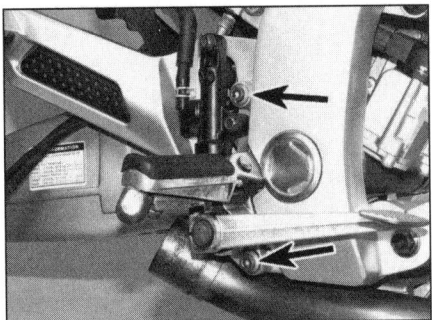

1.12b Unscrew the bolts (arrowed) and displace the bracket...

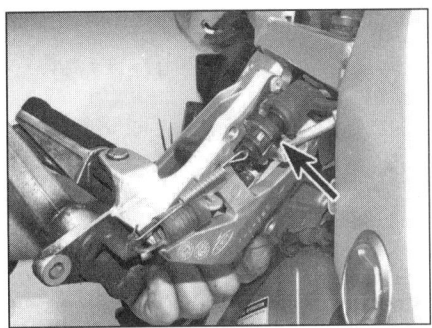

1.12c ...for best access to the switch adjuster nut (arrowed)

anti-clockwise so the switch is drawn down into the bracket. If the switch doesn't operate the brake light, check it (see Chapter 8). Note that if the switch is incorrectly adjusted on models with ABS fault code 23 may be shown, and on 2013-on models cruise control function may be affected. If removed tighten the footrest bracket bolts to the torque setting specified at the beginning of the Chapter.

13 On 2006-on models raise the front wheel off the ground by placing the bike on its centrestand and having an assistant press down on the rear. Press the rear brake pedal down and check that the front wheel is locked by the brake. If the wheel can be turned, there is a fault in the linked braking system (see Chapter 6).

14 The front brake lever has a span adjuster that alters the distance of the lever from the handlebar. Each setting is identified by a number in the adjuster ring aligning with the triangle on the lever – push the lever away from the handlebar and turn the adjuster ring to alter the span, making sure that the number specific to the desired setting is aligned with the triangle **(see illustrations)**. Position 1 gives maximum span, position 5 minimum span. Do not set the adjuster between the defined settings.

15 The end of the rear brake pedal should

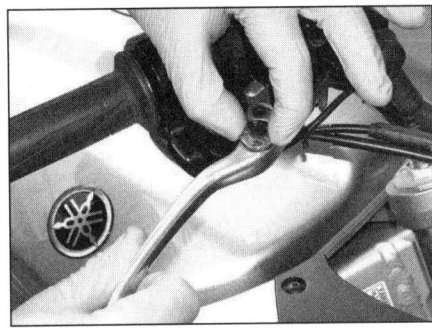

1.14a Push the lever away and turn the adjuster as required...

be 42 mm below the top of the footrest when measured as shown **(see illustration)**. It can be adjusted if necessary or if a different position is required to suit the rider's preference – slacken the locknut securing the clevis on the master cylinder pushrod, then turn the pushrod using a spanner on the rod's hex section until the pedal is at the desired height **(see illustration)**. If a non-standard position is used make sure the bottom of the pushrod is still visible through the hole in the clevis to ensure enough threads are engaged for security. On completion tighten the locknut. Adjust the rear brake light switch after adjusting the pedal height (see Step 12).

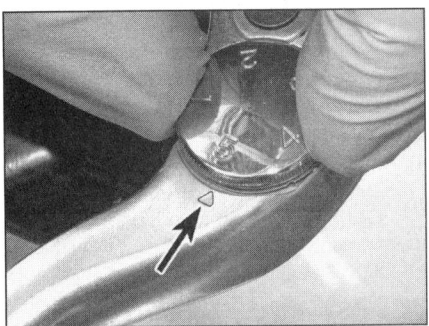

1.14b ...aligning the number with the triangle mark (arrowed)

Brake fluid change

16 The brake fluid should be changed every two years. Refer to Chapter 6 for details. Ensure that all the old fluid is pumped from the hydraulic system and that the level in the fluid reservoir is checked and the brakes tested before riding the motorcycle.

Brake hose change

17 The hoses will deteriorate with age and should be replaced with new ones every four years regardless of their apparent condition (see Chapter 6).

18 Always replace the banjo union sealing

1.15a Check the position of the pedal relative to the footrest...

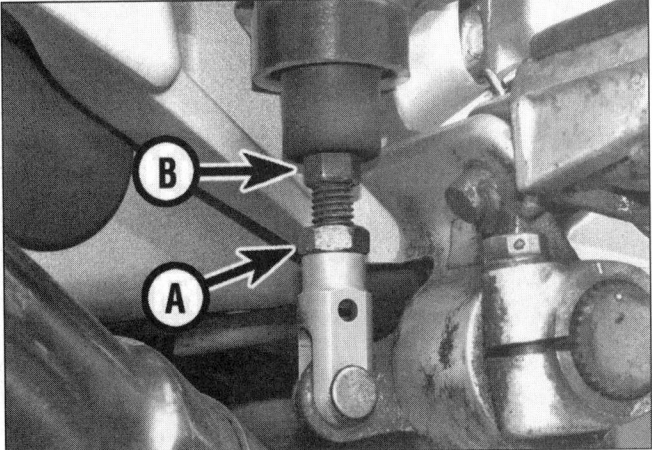

1.15b ...slacken the locknut (A) and turn the pushrod hex (B) to adjust

1•10 Routine maintenance and servicing

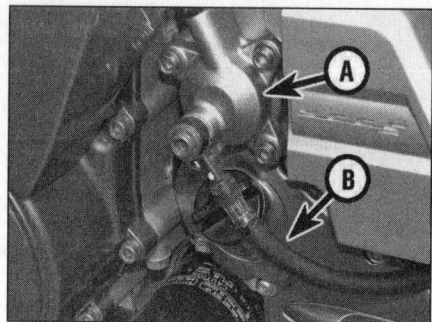

2.2 Clutch release cylinder (A) and hose (B)

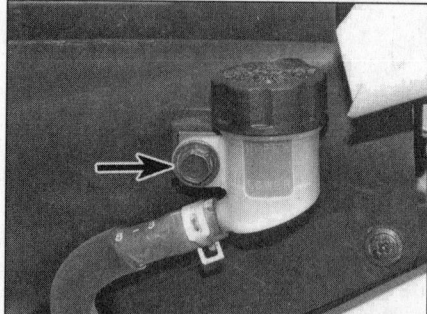

3.2a Unscrew the reservoir bolt (arrowed)

3.2b Release the trim clips, undo the screw and remove the shroud

washers with new ones when fitting the new hoses. Refill the system with new fluid and bleed the system as described in Chapter 6.

Brake master cylinder and caliper seals

19 Master cylinder and caliper seals will deteriorate over a period of time and lose their effectiveness, leading to sticky operation of the master cylinder or piston(s), or fluid loss. Although seal replacement is not subject to a specific time or mileage interval, it is advised after a high mileage has been covered and particularly if fluid leakage or poor brake action is apparent.

20 A rebuild kit for each master cylinder and caliper is available (see Chapter 6).

2 Clutch

All models

1 Make sure the fluid level in the reservoir is correct (see *Pre-ride checks*).
2 Look for leaks at the hose connections and check for cracks in the hose **(see illustration)**. If leaks or cracks are apparent, or the hose has deteriorated through age, renew the hose (see Chapter 2).
3 The clutch lever has a span adjuster that alters the distance of the lever from the handlebar in exactly the same way as the front brake lever – refer to Section 1, Step 14 for details.

Standard models

4 Check the clutch lever pivot and pushrod for sloppy or rough action, excessive play, bends, and other damage. Replace any damaged parts with new ones (see Chapter 5). Clean and lubricate the lever pivot and pushrod components if its action is stiff or rough (see Section 15).
5 Check the operation of the clutch. If there is evidence of air in the system (spongy feel to the lever, difficulty in engaging gear, drag when in gear), bleed the clutch (see Chapter 2). If the lever feels stiff or sticky, overhaul the release mechanism (see Chapter 2).
6 The clutch fluid should be changed every two years or whenever a master cylinder or release cylinder overhaul is carried out. Refer to Chapter 2 for details. Ensure that all the old fluid is pumped from the system and that the level in the fluid reservoir is checked and the clutch tested before riding the motorcycle.
7 Clutch release mechanism seals will deteriorate over a period of time and lose their effectiveness, leading to sticky operation of the master cylinder or the piston in the release cylinder, or fluid loss. Although seal replacement is not subject to a specific time or mileage interval, it is advised after a high mileage has been covered and particularly if fluid leakage or poor clutch action is apparent. A rebuild kit for the master cylinder is available; the release cylinder comes as a complete unit (see Chapter 2).

YCC-S models

8 The YCC-S system performs its own self-diagnosis on start up and during riding. In the event of a fault on start-up the YCC-S indicator and warning light will not go out, and in the event of a fault while riding the YCC-S indicator and warning light will come on. In either case refer to Chapter 2.
9 If there is evidence of difficulty in engaging gear or drag when in gear, the clutch release mechanism needs bleeding. Bleeding of the system is however a complex and precise procedure requiring the use of specialised equipment.
10 The system requires the same maintenance as standard models, i.e. fluid and hose replacement, and at the same intervals.

3 Air filter

Caution: If the machine is continually ridden in wet or dusty conditions, the filter should be replaced more frequently.

1 Remove the left-hand side cover (see Chapter 7).
2 On YCC-S models displace the clutch fluid reservoir, and on all models release the air intake shroud trim clips and undo the screw then remove the shroud **(see illustrations)**.
3 On YCC-S models displace the shift actuator (see Chapter 2, Section 19, Steps 2, 3 and 7).
4 Undo the air filter cover screws and remove the cover **(see illustrations)**.
5 Remove the filter element from the housing **(see illustration)**.

3.4a Move the wiring where necessary to access the screws (arrowed)...

3.4b ...then remove the cover...

3.5 ...and withdraw the filter

Routine maintenance and servicing

6 Either clean the element as described in Step 7 or replace it with a new one, according to service interval.
7 To clean the filter tap it on a hard surface to dislodge any dirt, then use compressed air to blow through it, directing the air in the opposite way to normal flow, i.e. from the outside **(see illustration)**. Do not use any solvents or cleaning agents on the element. If the element is excessively dirty or is damaged replace it with a new one.
8 Make sure the cover seal is in good condition and correctly seated **(see illustration)**. Fit the filter, making sure it seats correctly **(see illustration 3.5)**. Fit the cover **(see illustration 3.4b)** – where relevant make sure the wiring routes correctly **(see illustration)**.
9 On YCC-S models install the shift actuator (see Chapter 2, Section 19).
10 Fit the shroud **(see illustration 3.2b)**. On YCC-S models fit the clutch fluid reservoir **(see illustration 3.2a)**.
11 Install the left-hand side cover (see Chapter 7).

4 Spark plugs

Check

Special tools: *A spark plug socket is supplied in the motorcycle's tool kit (stored under the seat). A feeler gauge set or wire gauge is necessary for measuring the spark plug gap* **(see illustration 4.12a and b)**.

1 Raise or remove the fuel tank (see Chapter 4).
2 On 2001 to 2005 models unscrew the AIS control valve holder bolt **(see illustration)**.
3 Remove the T-bar **(see illustration)**. On 2006-on models remove the heat shield **(see illustrations)**.
4 On 2001 to 2012 models pull the cap off each plug **(see illustration)**.

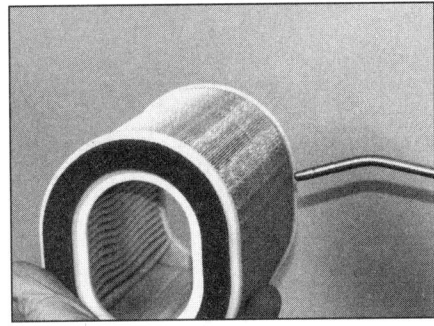
3.7 Direct compressed air from the outside

3.8a Check the seal (arrowed)

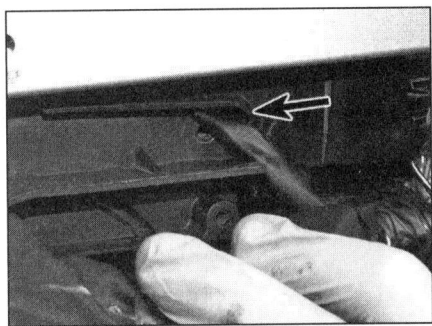
3.8b Make sure the wiring routes correctly, according to model (2010 shown)

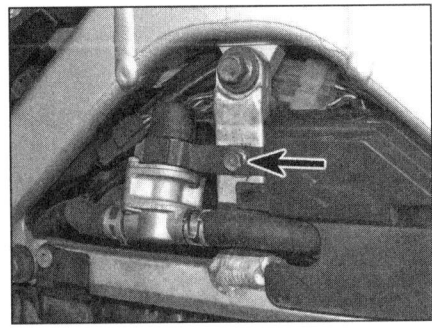
4.2 Unscrew the bolt (arrowed)

4.3a Unscrew the bolts (arrowed) and remove the T-bar

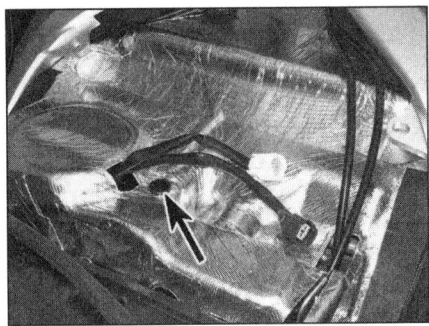
4.3b Release the trim clip (arrowed), thread the wiring through the hole and on 2013-on models slip the cables out of the slot...

4.3c ...and remove the shield

4.4 Pull the cap off the plug

1•12 Routine maintenance and servicing

4.5a On 2013-on models disconnect the wire connector from the coil...

4.5b ...and pull the coil out

4.7a Unscrew the plug...

4.7b ...and lift it out with the tool - the rubber insert should grip around the plug top

5 On 2013-on models disconnect the coil wiring connectors and pull the coils off the spark plugs **(see illustrations)**.
6 Clean around the base of each plug to prevent any dirt falling into the combustion chamber.
7 Using either the plug removing tool supplied in the bike's toolkit or a spark plug socket, unscrew and remove the plugs **(see illustrations)** – lay the plugs out in order so you know which cylinder each comes from.
8 Before cleaning the plug refer to the colour spark plug chart at the end of this manual and compare the firing end of each plug to those shown, identifying any abnormal condition and assessing its cause if necessary.
9 Clean the electrodes using a soft wire brush – if any deposits do not come off replace the plugs with new ones. Cleaning spark plugs by sandblasting is fine as long as you blow them with compressed air and clean them with a high flash-point solvent afterwards. Also clean any deposits off the white ceramic body of the plug.
10 Check the condition of the cleaned electrodes. Both the centre and side electrodes should have square edges and the side electrodes should be of uniform thickness. Check for evidence of a cracked or chipped insulator around the centre electrode. Check the plug threads, the washer and the ceramic insulator body for cracks and other damage.
11 If in doubt concerning the condition of the plugs, replace them with new ones, as the expense is minimal.
12 If the plugs can be re-used check the gap between the electrodes with a feeler gauge or wire type gauge **(see illustrations)**. The gap should be as given in the Specifications at the beginning of this chapter. If the electrodes have worn and the gap is wider than it should

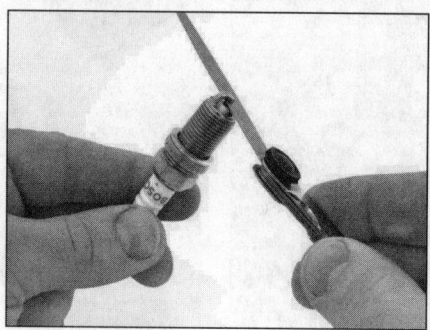

4.12a Using a feeler blade to measure the spark plug electrode gap

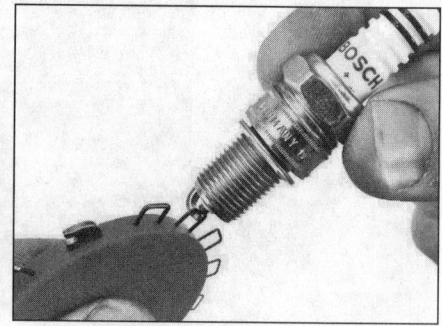

4.12b Using a wire gauge to measure the spark plug electrode gap

Routine maintenance and servicing 1•13

4.12c Adjusting the gap using the adjuster on a wire gauge

be, or for some reason the gap is narrower than it should be (if the plug has been dropped for instance) carefully bend the outer electrode as required to restore the correct gap – wire gauges have a special adjuster incorporated **(see illustration)**.

13 Fit the plug into the end of the tool, then use the tool to insert the plug **(see illustration 4.7b)**. Alternatively there are dedicated plug insertion tools, or you can use some hose (see **Haynes Hint**). Thread the plugs as far as possible into the head turning the tool or hose by hand, making sure they do not cross-thread. Once the plugs are finger-tight, tighten them using a spanner on the tool supplied or a socket drive **(see illustration 4.7a)**. If a torque wrench can be applied, tighten the spark plugs to the torque setting specified at the beginning of the Chapter. Otherwise, if new plugs are being used tighten them by 1/2 a turn after the washer has seated, and if the old plugs are being reused tighten them by 1/8 to 1/4 turn after they have seated, according to feel. Do not over-tighten them.

14 On 2001 to 2012 models fit the cap onto the plug and push it down so it is fully seated **(see illustration 4.4)**.

15 On 2013-on models fit the coil onto the plug and push it down so it is fully seated. Connect the wiring.

HAYNES HiNT As the plugs are quite recessed, slip a short length of hose over the end of the plug to use as a tool to thread it into place. The hose will grip the plug well enough to turn it, but will start to slip if the plug begins to cross-thread in the hole – this will prevent damaged threads.

16 On 2006-on models fit the heat shield **(see illustrations 4.3c and b)**.
17 Fit the T-bar and tighten the bolts to the torque setting specified in Chapter 4 **(see illustration 4.3a)**.
18 On 2001 to 2005 models fit the AIS control valve holder bolt **(see illustration 4.2)**.
19 Install the fuel tank (see Chapter 4).

HAYNES HiNT Stripped plug threads in the cylinder head can be repaired with a thread insert – see 'Tools and Workshop Tips' in the Reference section.

Renewal

20 At the prescribed interval, whatever the condition of the existing spark plugs, remove the plugs as described above and install new ones.

5 Fuel and emission control systems

⚠️ **Warning:** Petrol (gasoline) is extremely flammable, so take extra precautions when you work on any part of the fuel system. Don't smoke or allow open flames or bare light bulbs near the work area, and don't work in a garage where a natural gas-type appliance is present. If you spill any fuel on your skin, rinse it off immediately with soap and water. When you perform any kind of work on the fuel system, wear safety glasses and have a fire extinguisher suitable for a Class B type fire (flammable liquids) on hand.

1 Raise the fuel tank (see Chapter 4).

Fuel system

2 Check the fuel tank, the fuel supply hose, the return hose (2001 to 2005 models), the tank drain and breather hoses and the throttle body vacuum hoses for signs of leaks, cracks, deterioration or damage **(see illustrations)**. In particular check that there are no leaks from the fuel hose(s) or hose unions. Replace hoses with new ones as required, referring to the relevant section in Chapter 4. Note the

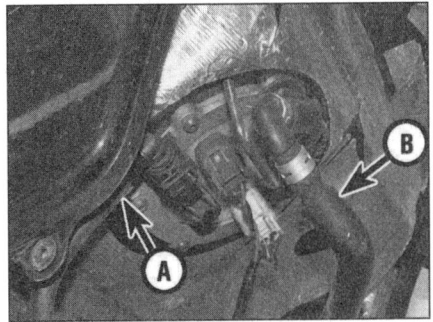

5.2a Fuel supply hose (A), fuel return hose (B – 2001 to 2005 models only)...

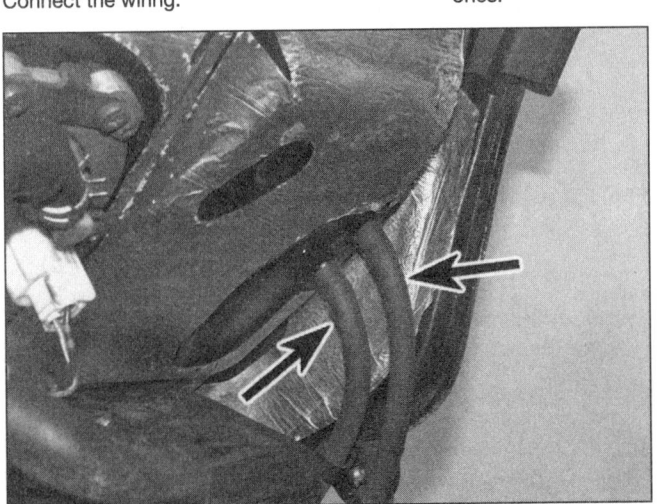

5.2b ...fuel tank drain and breather hoses (arrowed)...

5.2c ...throttle body vacuum hoses (arrowed – 2010 model shown)

1•14 Routine maintenance and servicing

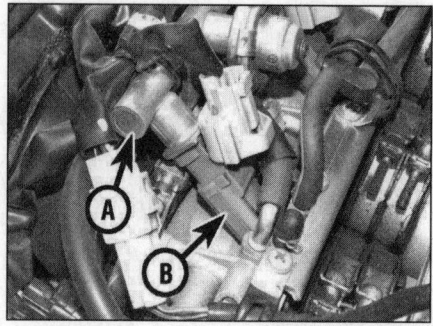

5.4 Fuel rail (A) and injector (B)

routing of each hose and how it is secured – it is advisable to make a sketch of the hoses before removing them to ensure they are correctly installed.

3 Check the joint between the fuel pump assembly mounting plate and the tank (see illustration 5.2a). If there is evidence of fuel leakage, check the bolts are tight (see Chapter 4 Specifications for the pump plate bolt torque setting). If the leak persists, remove the pump and fit a new seal (see Chapter 4).

4 Inspect the joints between the fuel rail, the injectors and the throttle bodies (see illustration). If there are any leaks, remove the injectors and fit new seals and O-rings (see Chapter 4).

5 Fuel filter renewal is not a service item. The filter is incorporated in the fuel pump assembly, and is not available as a spare part. If fuel starvation is experienced, and all other possibilities have been checked, a blocked filter could be the cause; in this event remove the pump and replace it with a new one (see Chapter 4).

6 Make sure the air filter housing ducts are in good condition and the clamps are secure on the throttle bodies (see illustration). Make sure the intake adapters between the throttle bodies and the cylinder head are in good condition and that the clamps securing them to the throttle bodies and the cylinder head are secure (see illustration).

Air induction system (AIS)

7 To reduce the amount of unburned hydrocarbons released in the exhaust gases, an air induction system (AIS) is fitted. The system consists of the control valve (mounted above the valve cover), the reed valves (fitted in the valve cover) and the hoses linking them (see illustrations). The control valve is actuated electronically by the ECU.

8 Under certain operating conditions, the valve allows filtered air to be drawn through the reed valves and cylinder head passages and into the exhaust ports. The air mixes with the exhaust gases, causing any unburned particles of the fuel in the mixture to be burnt in the exhaust port/pipes. This process changes a considerable amount of hydrocarbons and carbon monoxide into relatively harmless

5.6a Check each air duct and its clamp...

5.6b ...and the intake adapters and clamps

5.7a AIS control valve (arrowed) – 2001 to 2005 models

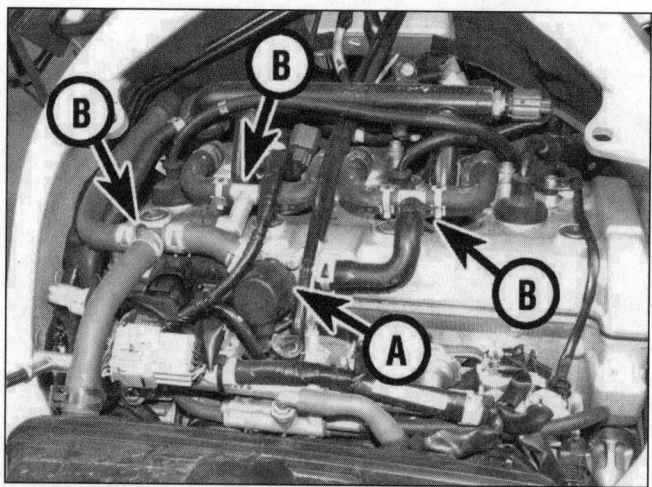

5.7b AIS control valve (A) and hoses (B) – 2006-on models

Routine maintenance and servicing 1•15

5.11 Crankcase breather hose (arrowed) shown with throttle bodies and air filter housing removed

carbon dioxide and water. The reed valves in the valve cover are fitted to prevent the flow of exhaust gases back up the cylinder head passages and into the air filter housing.

9 The system is not adjustable and requires little maintenance. Check that the hoses are not kinked or pinched, are in good condition and are securely connected at each end. Replace any hoses that are cracked, split or generally deteriorated with new ones. Make sure the control valve wiring connector is securely connected and no wires or terminals are loose or corroded.

10 Refer to Chapter 4 for further information on the system and for checks if it is believed to be faulty.

Crankcase breather

11 As far as you can see it with the throttle bodies in place check the condition of the crankcase breather hose that runs between the crankcase and the air filter housing **(see illustration)**. Check for cracks and splits and replace it with a new one if any are evident – remove the air filter housing to do this (see Chapter 4). Make sure the hose is not kinked or trapped, and is securely connected at each end.

EVAP system (California models)

12 Visually inspect all the system hoses between the fuel tank, the roll-over valve and the canister for kinks and splits and any other damage or deterioration. Make sure that the hoses are securely connected with a clamp on each end. Replace any hoses that are damaged or deteriorated.

13 Check the EVAP canister and the valve for cracks or other damage.

14 Refer to your dealer for further information and tests on the system. Note that there is an emission control system hose routing diagram on a label under the passenger seat.

6 Throttle body synchronisation and idle speed

⚠ **Warning:** *Petrol (gasoline) is extremely flammable, so take extra precautions when you work on any part of the fuel system. Don't smoke or allow open flames or bare light bulbs near the work area, and don't work in a garage where a natural gas-type appliance is present. If you spill any fuel on your skin, rinse it off immediately with soap and water. When you perform any kind of work on the fuel system, wear safety glasses and have a fire extinguisher suitable for a Class B type fire (flammable liquids) on hand.*

⚠ **Warning:** *Do not allow exhaust gases to build up in the work area; either perform the check outside or use an exhaust gas extraction system.*

1 Throttle body synchronisation ensures each throttle body passes the same amount of fuel/air mixture to each cylinder. This is done by measuring the vacuum produced in each throttle body. Throttle bodies that are out of synchronisation will result in increased fuel consumption, higher engine temperature, less than ideal throttle response and higher vibration levels. Before synchronising the throttle bodies, make sure that the air filter is clean or a new one has been fitted (according to service interval), idle speed is properly adjusted on 2001 to 2012 models (see below) and that the valve clearances were checked at the previous prescribed interval, or if they are due to be done check them before synchronisation (Section 18).

Throttle body synchronisation

Special tool: *A set of vacuum gauges or a manometer is necessary for this job.*

2 To synchronize the throttle bodies, you will need a manometer, such as the Morgan Carbtune Pro4, or a set of four vacuum gauges, with the necessary hoses and adapters (if required) to fit the take-off points **(see illustration)**. When using such equipment always read the instructions supplied. The hoses usually have some form of restrictor in them for damping the movement of the manometer rod or gauge needle – make sure these are fitted correctly if not already in place otherwise it will be difficult to get an accurate reading, and that in the case of the Carbtune the hoses are connected with the restrictors closest to the take-off points on the throttle bodies.

3 Support the machine on the centrestand on level ground. Start the engine and let it run until it reaches normal operating temperature, then shut it off. Raise the fuel tank (see Chapter 4).

4 Remove the blanking caps from the vacuum take-off stubs **(see illustration)**. Connect the gauge hoses to the stubs – make sure the No. 1 gauge is attached to the No. 1 (left-hand) throttle body, and so on.

5 Start the engine and let it idle, making sure the speed is still correct. If the gauges are fitted with damping adjustment, set this so that the needle flutter is just eliminated but so that they can still respond to small changes in pressure.

6 The vacuum readings should be between

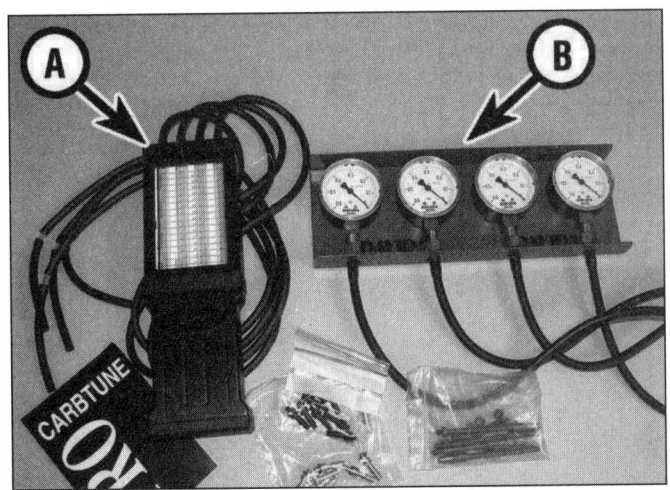

6.2 Carbtune Pro4 manometer (A) and a set of vacuum gauges (B)

6.4 Remove the caps (arrowed) and connect the gauge hoses

1•16 Routine maintenance and servicing

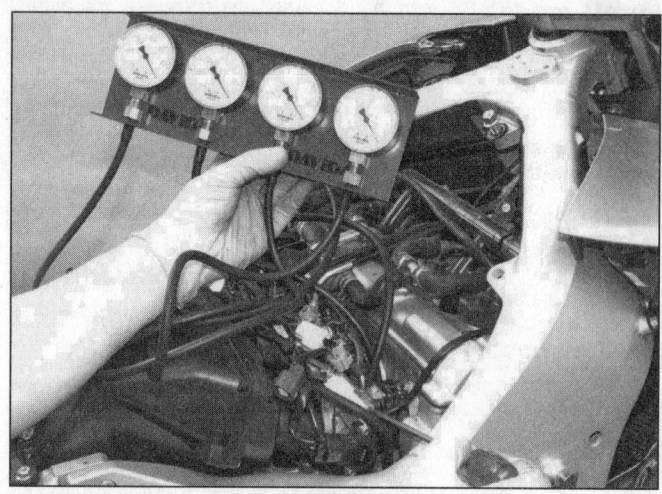

6.6 The gauges readings should read as described

6.7 Throttle body air screw (arrowed)

220 and 280 mmHg, and all readings within 10 mmHg of each other **(see illustration)**.

7 On 2001 to 2012 models the No. 3 throttle body is the base to which all the others are matched, and cannot itself be adjusted. If the vacuum readings on the others vary by more than 10 mmHg from No. 3, locate the air screws in the Nos. 1, 2 and 4 throttle bodies and adjust the throttle bodies as required by turning the appropriate air screw until the readings are the same as No. 3 **(see illustration)**. If an air screw is inadvertently removed, screw it in until it seats lightly, then back it out ¾ of a turn, and make any fine adjustment to its setting according to the gauge readings. **Note:** *Do not disturb the throttle valve adjustment screws situated in the linkage between the throttle bodies.*

8 On 2013-on models locate the air screws in the throttle bodies and identify the white painted one – this one is the base to which all the others are matched, and cannot itself be adjusted. If the vacuum readings on the others vary by more than 10 mmHg from the white one, adjust the throttle bodies as required by turning the appropriate air screw until the readings are the same as the base. If an air screw is inadvertently removed, screw it in until it seats lightly, then back it out ¾ of a turn, and make any fine adjustment to its setting according to the gauge readings. **Note:** *Do not disturb the throttle valve adjustment screws situated in the linkage between the throttle bodies.*

9 After each adjustment, open and close the throttle quickly two or three times to settle the linkage, and recheck the gauge readings, readjusting if necessary. When the adjustment is complete on 2001 to 2012 models check and adjust the idle speed (see below).

10 Remove the gauges and fit the blanking caps **(see illustration 6.4)**. Check throttle cable freeplay (Section 7). Install the fuel tank (see Chapter 4).

Idle speed

2001 to 2012 models

11 Check and adjust the idle speed before and after the throttle bodies are synchronised (balanced), after checking the valve clearances, and when it is obviously too high or too low. Before adjusting the idle speed, make sure the valve clearances were checked at the previous prescribed interval, and the spark plug gaps are correct and the air filter is clean. Also, turn the handlebars back-and-forth and see if the idle speed changes as this is done. If it does, the throttle cables may not be adjusted or routed correctly, or may be worn out. This is a dangerous condition that can cause loss of control of the bike. Be sure to correct this problem before proceeding.

12 The engine should be at normal operating temperature, which is usually reached after 10 to 15 minutes of stop-and-go riding. Make sure the transmission is in neutral.

13 The idle speed adjuster is located on the right-hand side of the bike, in a bracket on the top of the clutch cover **(see illustration)**. With the engine idling, turn the adjuster until the speed listed in this Chapter's Specifications is obtained.

14 Snap the throttle open and shut a few times, then recheck the idle speed. If necessary, repeat the adjustment procedure.

15 If a smooth, steady idle cannot be achieved, the throttle bodies may need synchronising (see above). Also check the intake manifold rubbers for cracks that will cause an air leak, resulting in a weak mixture.

2013 models

16 Idle speed is controlled automatically by the YCC-T system. If idle speed is not as specified at the beginning of the Chapter, take the bike to a Yamaha dealer.

7 Throttle cables

1 Make sure the throttle grip rotates smoothly and freely from fully closed to fully open with the front wheel turned at various angles. The grip should return automatically from fully open to fully closed when released. If the throttle sticks, check and lubricate the cable and twistgrip as described below.

Cable freeplay check and adjustment

2 Check for a small amount of freeplay in the cables, measured in terms of the amount of twistgrip rotation before the throttle opens, and compare the amount to that listed in this Chapter's Specifications for your model **(see illustration)**. If it's incorrect, adjust the cables to correct it as follows.

6.13 Idle speed adjuster (arrowed)

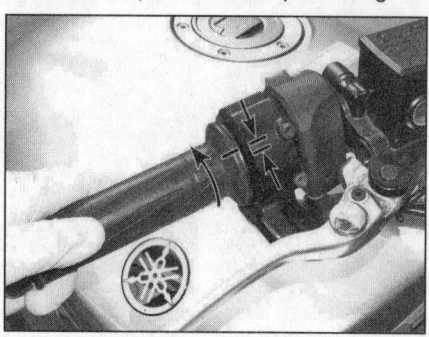

7.2 Throttle cable freeplay is measured in terms of twistgrip rotation

Routine maintenance and servicing

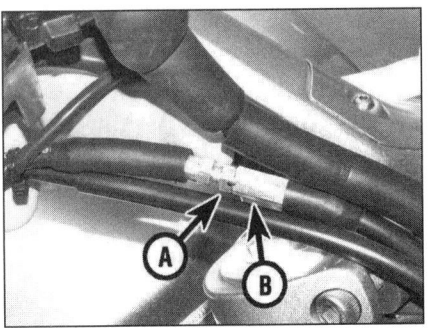

7.3 Slacken the adjuster locknut (A) and turn the adjuster (B) as required

7.5 Throttle cable adjuster locknut (A) and adjuster nut (B)

8.3 Unscrew the oil filler cap to act as a vent

3 Adjust freeplay using the adjuster in the throttle opening cable where it leaves the throttle pulley housing on the handlebar. Slide the rubber sleeve off the adjuster. Loosen the locknut and turn the adjuster in or out as required until the specified amount of freeplay is obtained (see this Chapter's Specifications), then retighten the locknut (see illustration).

4 On 2001 to 2012 models, if the adjuster has reached its limit of adjustment, reset it to its start point by turning it fully in, so that freeplay is at a maximum. Raise the fuel tank (see Chapter 4).

5 The adjuster at the throttle body end is on the rear cable in the bracket (see illustration). Fully slacken the top nut, then push the cable down until the bottom nut is free of the bracket, then thread the bottom nut up to increase freeplay or down to reduce it as required, then draw the cable up so the nut is captive in the bracket and tighten the locknut. Subsequent adjustments can be made at the throttle twistgrip end when required. If the cable cannot be adjusted as specified, replace it with a new one (see Chapter 4). Check that the throttle twistgrip operates smoothly and snaps shut quickly when released.

Warning: Turn the handlebars all the way through their travel with the engine idling. Idle speed should not change. If it does, the cables may be routed incorrectly. Correct this condition before riding the bike.

Cable and twistgrip lubrication

6 If the throttle sticks, this is probably due to a cable fault. Detach the cables from the throttle pulley (see Chapter 4) and lubricate them (see Section 15). Check that the inner cables slide freely and easily in the outer cables. If not, replace the cables with new ones.

7 With the cables removed, make sure the throttle twistgrip rotates freely on the handlebar – dirt combined with a lack of lubrication can cause the action to be stiff. If necessary refer to the relevant Steps in Section 5 of Chapter 5 and remove the twistgrip from the handlebar. Clean any old grease from the bar and the inside of the tube. Smear some lithium-based multi-purpose grease onto the bar, then refit the twistgrip.

8 Install the cables, making sure they are correctly routed (see Chapter 4). If this fails to improve the operation of the throttle, the cables must be replaced with new ones. Note that in very rare cases the fault could lie in the throttle bodies. Remove the fuel tank and check the action of the throttle pulley and linkage (see Chapter 4).

8 Engine oil and filter

Special tool: *A filter removing tool is necessary to remove the filter. You can purchase one as a Yamaha spare part or alternatively there are several after-market options (see Step 5).*

Warning: Be careful when draining the oil, as the exhaust, the engine, and the oil itself can cause severe burns.

1 Consistent routine oil and filter changes are the single most important maintenance procedure you can perform. The oil not only lubricates the internal parts of the engine, transmission and clutch, but it also acts as a coolant, a cleaner, a sealant, and a protector. Because of these demands, the oil takes a terrific amount of abuse and should be replaced often with new oil of the recommended grade and type. The oil filter must be changed with every second oil change, but as the cost of a filter is minimal consider doing it with every oil change.

HAYNES HiNT *Saving a little money on the difference in cost between a good oil and a cheap oil won't pay off if the engine is damaged.*

2 Before changing the oil, warm up the engine so the oil will drain easily. The oil drain bolt is on the underside of the engine, and the filter is on the left-hand side. When changing the filter remove the left and right-hand fairing side panels (see Chapter 7).

3 Place the bike on its centrestand. Position a large clean drain tray below the engine so it is under both the drain bolt and the filter, or use two small ones if a large enough one is not available. Unscrew the oil filler cap to vent the crankcase and to act as a reminder that there is no oil in the engine (see illustration).

4 Unscrew the oil drain bolt and allow the oil to flow into the tray (see illustrations). Remove the sealing washer from the bolt (see illustration 8.6b) – you may have to cut it off (see illustration). A new washer must be used.

8.4a Unscrew the oil drain bolt (arrowed)...

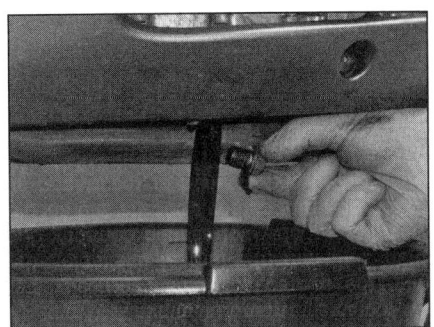

8.4b ...and allow the oil to completely drain

8.4c Because the washer compresses it can be tricky to remove

Routine maintenance and servicing

8.5a Unscrew the filter using a filter removing socket or strap...

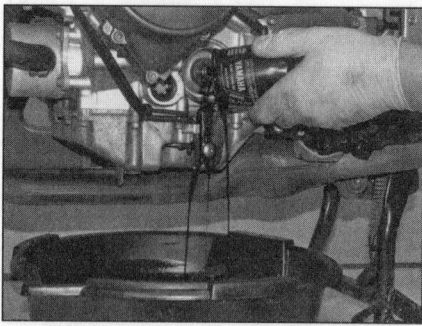

8.5b ...and allow the oil to drain

8.6a Fit a new sealing washer...

5 If changing the filter unscrew it using a filter socket (one can be obtained from Yamaha dealers under part No. 90890-01426, or otherwise there are commercially available equivalents available), filter pliers, or a filter removing strap or a chain-wrench, and tip any residual oil into the drain tray (see illustrations). The filter socket is preferable because it provides a means of tightening the new filter to the correct torque.

6 When the oil has completely drained, fit the new sealing washer onto the bolt, then fit the bolt into the sump and tighten it to the torque setting specified at the beginning of the Chapter (see illustrations). Do not overtighten it as the threads in the sump are easily damaged.

7 If the filter was changed, remove any cellophane from the end of the new filter. Check whether the seal is already greased (genuine Yamaha filters come pre-greased). If not, smear clean engine oil onto rubber seal. Thread the filter onto the engine (see illustration). Tighten it to the specified torque setting using the filter socket if available, or tighten the filter as tight as possible by hand, or by the number of turns specified on the filter itself or its packaging. Note: *Do not use a strap or chain-type filter removing tool to tighten the filter as you will damage it.*

8 Refill the engine using the recommended type and amount of oil (see Specifications) until the level is almost up to the upper mark on the inspection window with the motorcycle vertical (see illustrations). Do not overfill. Check the condition of the O-ring on the cap and replace it with a new one if it is damaged or worn (see illustration). Fit the cap.

9 Start the engine and let it run for two or three minutes (make sure that the oil level light extinguishes after a few seconds). Shut it off, wait a few minutes, then check the oil level again. If necessary, add more oil to bring the level close to the upper line, but do not go above it.

10 Check around the drain bolt and the filter for leaks. If leaks are evident, and the bolt and filter are correctly tightened using a new washer and a lubricated seal, there is another cause (such as dirt or corrosion) that must be investigated before riding the bike.

11 It is advisable to check that oil is flowing as it should – to do this slacken the oil check bolt on the upper right-hand front face of the cylinder head (see illustration). Start the engine and let it idle – oil should start to weep from the bleed hole fairly quickly. If no oil appears after one minute stop the engine immediately, then check the filter, oil passages and oil pump (see Chapter 2). If oil appears

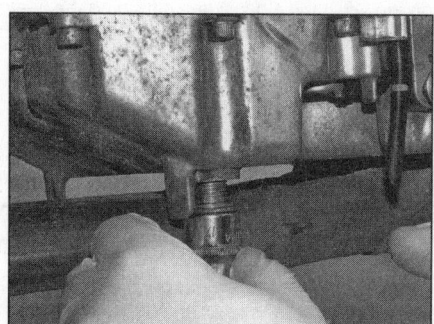

8.6b ...and tighten the bolt to the specified torque

8.7 Fit the filter and tighten it as described

8.8a Add the specified type and amount of oil...

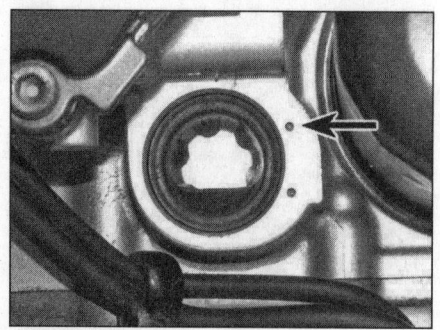

8.8b ...so the level is almost to the upper mark (arrowed) on the window

8.8c Make sure the O-ring (arrowed) is in good condition and correctly seated

8.11 Oil check bolt (arrowed) is located above the No. 4 exhaust port

Routine maintenance and servicing 1•19

as it should, tighten the check bolt to the specified torque setting, then stop the engine.
12 Install the fairing side panels (see Chapter 7).
13 The old oil drained from the engine cannot be re-used and should be disposed of properly. Check with your local refuse disposal company, disposal facility or environmental agency to see whether they will accept the used oil for recycling. Don't pour used oil into drains or onto the ground.

> **HAYNES HiNT** *Check the old oil carefully – if it is very metallic coloured, then the engine is experiencing wear from break-in (new engine) or from insufficient lubrication. If there are flakes or chips of metal in the oil, then something is drastically wrong internally and the engine will have to be disassembled for inspection and repair. If there are pieces of fibre-like material in the oil, the clutch is experiencing excessive wear and should be checked.*

Note: It is illegal and anti-social to dump oil down the drain. To find the location of your local oil recycling bank in the UK, call 08708 506 506 or visit www.oilbankline.org.uk

9.2a Unscrew the filler bolt (arrowed)

9 Final drive gear oil

Level check

1 Place the motorcycle on its centrestand on level ground. The check should be made after the machine has been standing for a few hours.
2 Unscrew the oil filler bolt and check that the oil is up to the edge of the filler hole, i.e. it is on the point of spilling out **(see illustrations)**. If the level is below this, look for signs of leakage, such as oil staining on the underside of the casing. If leakage is evident, the problem must be rectified to avoid the possibility of damage to the final drive and oil contaminating the rear tyre (see Chapter 6). Remove the sealing washer from the bolt **(see**

9.2b The oil should be at the edge of the hole (arrowed)

illustration 9.6b) – you may have to cut it off (see illustration 8.4c).
3 Top up the oil if necessary to the correct level using the type and grade specified at the beginning of the Chapter **(see illustration)**. Fit the filler bolt using a new sealing washer, and tighten it to the torque setting specified at the beginning of the Chapter **(see illustration)**.

Oil change

4 Place the motorcycle on its centrestand on level ground.
5 Place a drain tray under the drain bolt in the final drive housing. Unscrew the filler bolt **(see illustration 9.2a)**. Unscrew the drain bolt and allow the oil to drain into the pan **(see illustrations)**.
6 Clean any debris off the magnetic tip of the drain bolt **(see illustration)**. Remove the sealing washer from the bolt **(see illustration)**

9.3a Add some oil if necessary

9.3b Fit the bolt using a new sealing washer

9.5a Unscrew the drain bolt...

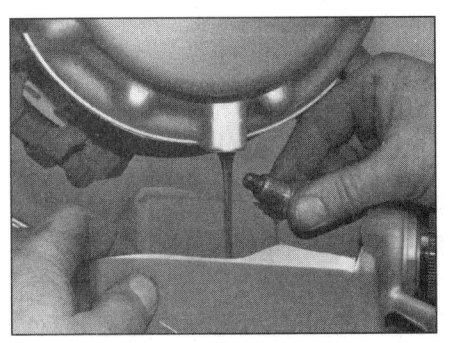

9.5b ...and drain the oil

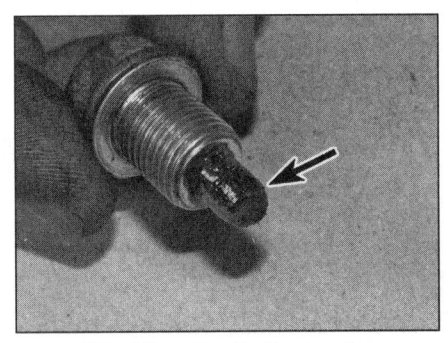

9.6a Clean the tip (arrowed)...

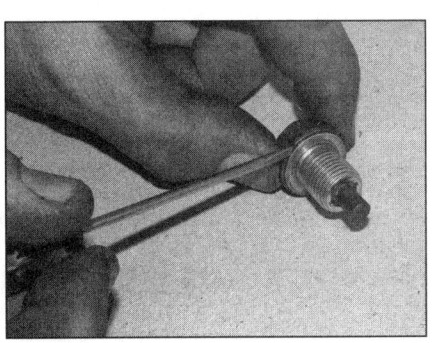

9.6b ...then remove the sealing washer

1•20 Routine maintenance and servicing

9.7a Fit a new sealing washer...

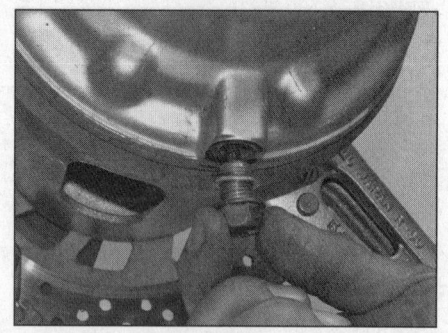

9.7b ...and tighten the bolt to the specified torque

10.3 Check all the coolant hoses as described

– you may have to cut it off **(see illustration 8.4c)**. A new washer must be used.

7 Fit a new sealing washer onto the bolt and tighten it to the torque setting specified at the beginning of the Chapter **(see illustrations)**.

8 Pour the gear oil specified at the beginning of the Chapter into the filler hole until it is up to the edge of the filler hole, i.e. it is on the point of spilling out **(see illustrations 9.3a and 9.2b)**.

9 Fit the filler bolt using a new sealing washer, and tighten it to the specified torque **(see illustration 9.3b)**.

10 Cooling system

Check

> **Warning:** *The engine must be cool before beginning this procedure.*

1 Check the coolant level in the reservoir (see *Pre-ride checks*).

2 Remove the fairing side panels (see Chapter 7), and the fuel tank (see Chapter 4).

3 Examine each rubber coolant hose along its entire length. Look for cracks, abrasions and other damage. Squeeze each hose at various points to see whether they are dried out or hard **(see illustration)**. They should feel firm, yet pliable, and return to their original shape when released. If necessary, replace them with new ones (see Chapter 3).

4 Check for evidence of leaks at each cooling system hose connection, around the pump on the right-hand side of the engine, at the inlet union on the front of the engine, the outlet unions on the top, and from the thermostat housing. Tighten the hose clips carefully to prevent future leaks. If the pump is leaking around the cover, check that the bolts are tight. If they are, remove the cover and replace the O-ring with a new one (see Chapter 3).

5 To prevent leakage of coolant from the cooling system to the lubrication system and vice versa, two seals are fitted on the pump shaft. The coolant seal on the water pump side is of the mechanical type and bears on the rear face of the impeller. The oil seal, which is mounted behind the mechanical seal, is of the normal feathered lip type. On the underside of the pump housing there is a drain hole **(see illustration)**. If either seal fails, the drain allows the coolant or oil (or both) to escape. If on inspection the drain shows signs of leakage, particularly with the engine running, remove the pump and replace and fit new seals (see Chapter 3).

6 Check the radiator for leaks and other damage. Leaks leave tell-tale scale deposits or coolant stains on the outside of the core below the leak. If leaks are noted, remove the radiator (see Chapter 3) and have it repaired or replace it with a new one – do not use a liquid leak-stop compound to try to repair leaks.

7 Check the radiator fins for mud, dirt and insects, which may impede the flow of air through. If the fins are dirty, remove the radiator (see Chapter 3) and clean it using water or low pressure compressed air directed through the fins from the inner side. If the fins are bent or distorted, straighten them carefully with a screwdriver **(see illustration)**. If the airflow is restricted by bent or damaged fins over more than 20% of the radiator's surface area, replace the radiator with a new one.

> **Warning:** *Do not remove the pressure cap when the engine is hot. It is good practice to cover the cap with a heavy cloth and turn the cap slowly anti-clockwise. If you hear a hissing sound (indicating that there is still pressure in the system), wait until it stops, then continue turning the cap until it can be removed.*

10.5 Check the pump drain hole (arrowed) for signs of leakage

10.7 Check the fins for obstruction and carefully straighten bent ones

Routine maintenance and servicing 1•21

10.8 Remove the pressure cap as described

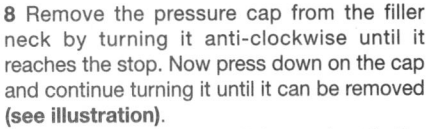

10.15a Unscrew the drain bolt...

10.15b ...and allow the coolant to drain

8 Remove the pressure cap from the filler neck by turning it anti-clockwise until it reaches the stop. Now press down on the cap and continue turning it until it can be removed **(see illustration)**.

9 Check the condition of the coolant in the system. If it is rust-coloured or if accumulations of scale are visible, drain, flush and refill the system with new coolant (see below). Check the antifreeze content of the coolant with an antifreeze hydrometer – a 50% content should give a reading of 1.084 at 5°C to 1.074 at 25°C, varying accordingly in between. The system must have the correct coolant mixture (see Specifications) – if the coolant is weak (too little anti-freeze) there will not be adequate protection against freezing and corrosion, and if it is too strong the ability to cool the engine is reduced. If the hydrometer indicates an incorrect mixture, drain, flush and refill the system (see below).

10 The function of the pressure cap is crucial to the correct running of the cooling system. Check the cap seal for cracks and other damage. If the coolant level consistently drops and/or the bike overheats, and no evidence of leaks can be found, have the cap pressure checked by a Yamaha dealer. If a new cap does not cure the problem have the entire system pressure checked by a dealer.

11 Fit the cap by turning it clockwise until it reaches the first stop then push down on it and continue turning until it can turn no further. Start the engine and let it reach normal operating temperature, then check for leaks again. As the coolant temperature increases, the electric fan(s) (mounted on the back of the radiator) should come on automatically and the temperature should begin to drop. If not, refer to Chapter 3 and check the fan(s) and fan circuit.

12 Check the oil cooler on the front of the engine for any signs of oil leakage between it and the engine. If there is leakage check the cooler bolts are tight. If the leakage persists you will have to fit a new O-ring between the cooler and the engine (see Chapter 2). Also check that the coolant hoses are secure on the cooler unions, and that there is no evidence of leakage from the body of the cooler. If there is, the cooler is damaged and must be replaced with a new one.

Coolant change

⚠️ *Warning: Allow the engine to cool completely before performing this maintenance operation. Also, don't allow anti-freeze to come into contact with your skin or the painted surfaces of the motorcycle. Rinse off spills immediately with plenty of water. Anti-freeze is highly toxic if ingested. Never leave anti-freeze lying around in an open container or in puddles on the floor; children and pets are attracted by its sweet smell and may drink it. Check with local authorities (councils) about disposing anti-freeze – many have collection centres that dispose it safely. Anti-freeze is also combustible, so don't store it near open flames.*

Draining

13 Support the bike upright on the centrestand on level ground. Remove the fairing side panels (see Chapter 7).

14 Remove the pressure cap from the filler neck by turning it anti-clockwise until it reaches a stop **(see illustration 10.8)**. If you hear a hissing sound (indicating there is still pressure in the system), wait until it stops. Now press down on the cap and continue turning the cap until it can be removed. Also remove the coolant reservoir cap.

15 Position a suitable container beneath the water pump on the right-hand side of the engine. Unscrew the drain bolt and allow the coolant to completely drain **(see illustrations)**. A new sealing washer is needed, but keep the old one for use during flushing if required.

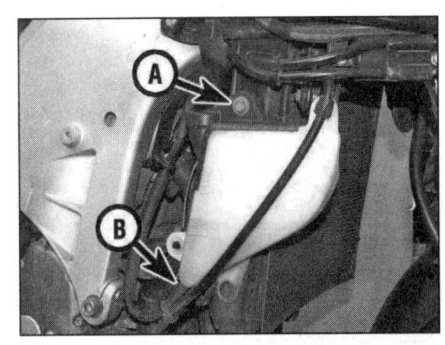

10.16 Unscrew the bolt (A) and remove the cover and cap, then detach the hose (B)

16 On 2001 to 2005 models unscrew the reservoir upper mounting bolt and remove the cover, then remove the filler cap **(see illustration)**. Hold a suitable container under the reservoir, then disconnect the hose from the bottom of the reservoir and allow it to drain into the container. Mop up any spilt coolant.

17 On 2006-on models release the cap from the top of the reservoir. Unscrew the bolts and displace the reservoir, freeing the breather hose from its groove, and lowering it so the cap hose is clear, then tip the coolant into the container **(see illustration)**. Flush the reservoir out, then refit it but leave the cap loose.

Flushing

18 Flush the system with clean tap water by inserting a hose in the filler neck. Allow the water to run through the system until it is clear and flows out cleanly. If the radiator is extremely corroded, remove it (see Chapter 3) and have it cleaned by a specialist. On 2001 to 2005 models also flush the reservoir, then reconnect the hose.

19 Clean the drain hole then fit the drain bolt using the old sealing washer.

20 Fill the cooling system via the filler neck with clean water mixed with a flushing compound **(see illustration 10.26)**. Make sure the flushing compound is compatible with aluminium components, and follow the manufacturer's instructions carefully. Fit the pressure cap.

21 Start the engine and allow it to reach normal operating temperature. Let it run for about ten minutes.

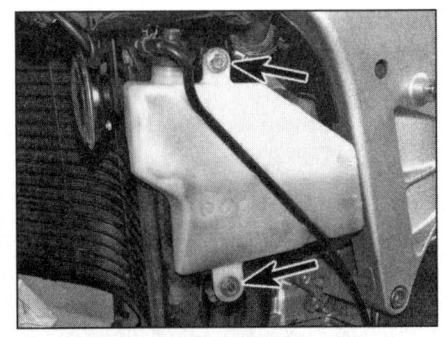

10.17 Unscrew the bolts (arrowed), then displace and drain the reservoir

1•22 Routine maintenance and servicing

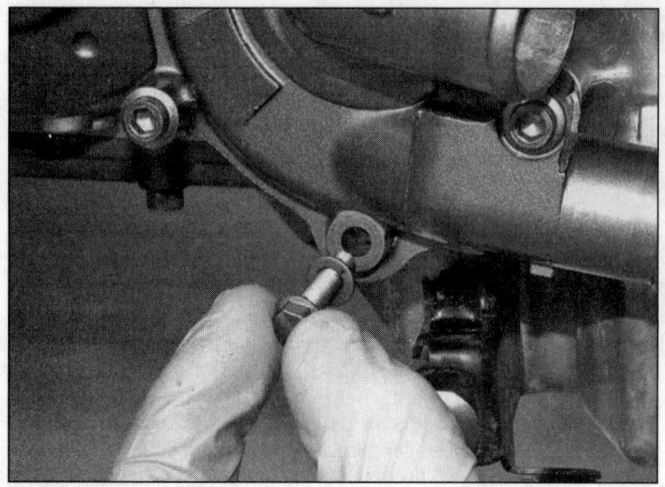

10.25 Fit a new sealing washer onto the drain bolt

10.26 Fill the system as described

22 Stop the engine. Let it cool for a while, then cover the pressure cap with a heavy rag and turn it anti-clockwise to the first stop, releasing any pressure that may be present in the system. Once the hissing stops, push down on the cap and remove it completely.
23 Drain the system once again.
24 Repeat Steps 20 to 23 using just clean water clean water.

Refilling
25 Fit the drain bolt using a new sealing washer and tighten it to the torque setting specified at the beginning of the Chapter **(see illustration)**. On 2001 to 2005 models reconnect the reservoir hose **(see illustration 10.16)**.
26 Fill the system to the base of the filler neck with the proper coolant mixture (see this Chapter's Specifications) **(see illustration)**. **Note:** *Pour the coolant in slowly to minimise the amount of air entering the system, and when full carefully wiggle the bike from side to side to dislodge any trapped air.* Fill the reservoir to the FULL level line (see *Pre-ride checks*).
27 Start the engine and allow it to idle for 2 to 3 minutes. Flick the throttle twistgrip part open 3 or 4 times, so that the engine speed rises to approximately 4000 rpm, then stop the engine. Any air trapped in the system should bleed back to the radiator filler neck.
28 If necessary top up the coolant level to the base of the filler neck and top up the reservoir to the FULL level line, then fit the pressure cap and reservoir cap.
29 Start the engine and allow it to reach normal operating temperature, then shut it off. Let the engine cool then remove the pressure cap as described in Step 22. Check that the coolant level is still up to the base of the filler neck. If it's low, add the specified mixture until it reaches the base of the filler neck. Refit the cap.
30 Check the coolant level in the reservoir and top up if necessary. Check the system for leaks.
31 Install the fairing side panels.

32 Do not dispose of the old coolant by pouring it down the drain. Instead pour it into a heavy plastic container, cap it tightly and take it into an authorised disposal site or service station – see *Warning* at the beginning of this Section.

11 Wheels, tyres and wheel bearings

Wheels
1 Cast wheels are virtually maintenance free, but they should be kept clean and checked periodically for cracks and other damage. Never attempt to repair cast wheels – if damaged they must be replaced with new ones. Also check wheel run-out and alignment (see Chapter 6). Check that the wheel balance weights are fixed firmly to the wheel rim. If you suspect that a weight has fallen off, have the wheel rebalanced by a motorcycle tyre specialist.

Tyres
2 Check the tyre condition and tread depth thoroughly – see *Pre-ride checks*.
3 Make sure the valve cap is in place and tight. Check the valve for signs of damage. If

11.6 Checking for play in the wheel bearings

tyre deflation occurs and it is not due to a slow puncture the valve core may be loose or it could be leaking past the seal – remove the cap and make sure the core is tight; if it is tight then it could be leaking – unscrew the core from the valve housing using a core removal tool (sometimes incorporated in the valve cap) and thread a new one in its place. A tool can be made quite easily by cutting a slot into the threaded end of a bolt using a hacksaw – the bolt must fit inside the valve housing and the slot must be the correct thickness to fit over the top of the core.

Wheel bearings
4 Wheel bearings will wear over a considerable mileage and should be checked periodically to avoid handling problems.
5 Place the motorcycle on its centrestand. To check the front wheel, have an assistant push down on the rear of the bike to raise the wheel off the ground.
6 Check for any play in the bearings by pushing and pulling the wheel against the hub **(see illustration)**. When checking the front wheel turn the handlebars to full lock on one side and hold the wheel against the lock. Also rotate the wheel and check that it turns smoothly and without any grating noises (bearing in mind that the brakes and final drive make some noise – do not confuse them).
7 If any play is detected in the hub, or if the wheel does not rotate smoothly (and this is not due to brake or transmission drag), remove the wheel and check the bearings for wear or damage (see Chapter 6).

12 Suspension

1 The suspension components must be maintained in top operating condition to ensure rider safety. Loose, worn or damaged suspension parts decrease the motorcycle's stability and control.

Routine maintenance and servicing 1•23

12.2 Check the action of the forks as described

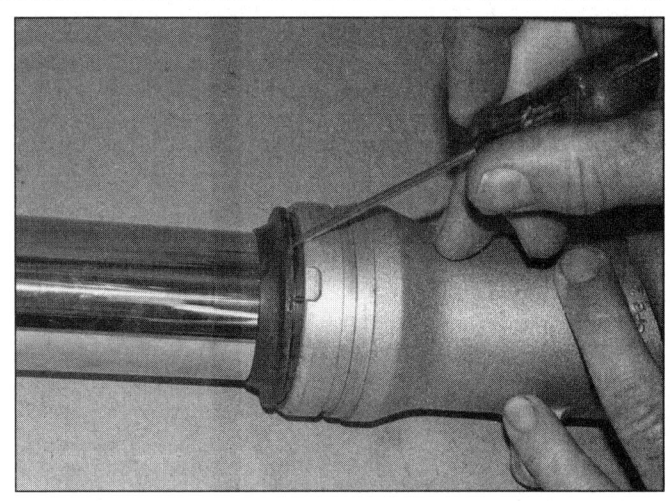

12.4 Carefully prise the seal out and check for corrosion

Front suspension check

2 While standing alongside the motorcycle (and with it off the stand), apply the front brake and push on the handlebars to compress the forks several times **(see illustration)**. See if they move up-and-down smoothly without binding. If binding is felt, the forks should be disassembled and inspected (see Chapter 5).

3 Inspect each fork inner tube for scratches, corrosion and pitting in the area of travel through the seals, which will cause seal failure, and for oil leakage, which means the seal has failed. If corrosion damage is excessive, new inner tubes should be fitted (see Chapter 5), or the fitted ones must be re-chromed using hard chrome. If leakage is evident, the seals must be replaced with new ones (see Chapter 5).

4 Carefully lever the dust seal out using a flat-bladed screwdriver and inspect the area around the oil seal **(see illustration)**. If there is evidence of corrosion on the oil seal and/or its retaining ring, spray the area with a penetrative lubricant. If the seal is corroding (from water getting under the rubber) it must be replaced with a new one (see Chapter 5). Press the dust seal back into the outer tube on completion.

Rear suspension check

5 Inspect the rear shock absorber for fluid leakage. If leakage is found, the shock must be replaced with a new one (see Chapter 5).

6 With the aid of an assistant to support the bike, compress the rear suspension several times **(see illustration)**. It should move up-and-down freely without binding. If any binding is felt, the worn or faulty component must be identified and checked. The problem could be due to either the shock absorber or its bush, or the suspension linkage or swingarm bearings.

7 Place the motorcycle on its centrestand so that the rear wheel is off the ground. Grab the swingarm and rock it from side-to-side **(see illustration)** – there should be no discernible movement at the rear.

8 Next, grasp the top of the rear wheel and pull it upwards **(see illustration)** – there should be no discernible freeplay before the shock absorber begins to compress.

9 If there's a little movement or a slight clicking can be heard, check the tightness of the swingarm pivot, referring to the procedure in Chapter 5, and re-check for movement. Also check the shock absorber mounting bolts/nuts and the suspension linkage mounting bolts/nuts. If there is still some noise or freeplay after everything has been correctly tightened then there is either a worn bush or bearing in the shock absorber mountings, or worn swingarm bearings, or worn linkage bearings. The worn components must be identified and replaced with new ones (see Chapter 5).

10 You can make a more accurate assessment by isolating the swingarm from the linkage – remove the rear wheel (see Chapter 6) and the bolt securing the linkage to the swingarm (see Chapter 5).

11 Grasp the rear of the swingarm with one hand and place your other hand at the junction of the swingarm and the frame. Try to move the rear of the swingarm from side-to-side. Any wear (play) in the bearings should be felt as movement between the swingarm and the frame at the front. If there is any play, the swingarm will be felt to move forward and backward at the front (not from side-to-side). Next, move the swingarm up and down through its full travel. It should move freely, without any binding or rough spots. If there is any play in the swingarm or if it does not move freely, remove the bearings for inspection (see Chapter 5).

12 With the linkage detached check the bearings for corrosion and wear and failure of the seals, referring to Chapter 5 for details, and

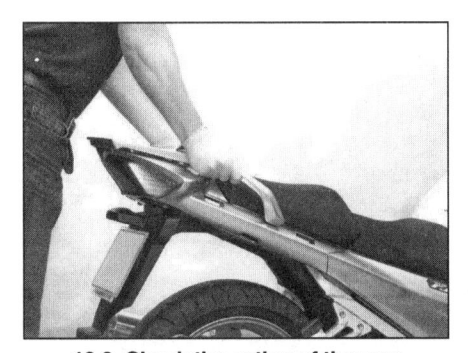

12.6 Check the action of the rear suspension as described

12.7 Checking for play in the swingarm bearings

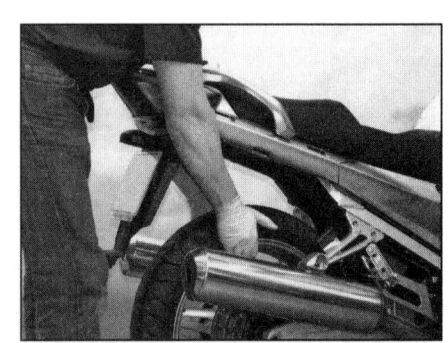

12.8 Checking for play in the rear shock mountings and the linkage bearings

1•24 Routine maintenance and servicing

clean and re-grease or replace components as required.

Front fork oil change

13 Although there is no set interval for changing the fork oil, the oil will degrade over a period of time and lose its damping qualities. Refer to Chapter 5 for details of front fork removal, oil draining and refilling. The forks do not need to be completely disassembled to change the oil.

Rear suspension bearing lubrication

14 Over a considerable mileage, and if the bike is often ridden in wet conditions (or through incorrect use of jet washers) the seals may fail and allow dirt and water to get in, in which case the grease in the bearings will be washed out or will harden.

15 At the specified service interval remove the shock absorber, linkage and swingarm and clean and re-grease the bearings (see Chapter 5).

13 Steering head bearings

Freeplay check and adjustment

1 Steering head bearings can become dented, rough or loose during normal use of the machine. In extreme cases, worn or loose steering head bearings can cause steering wobble – a condition that is potentially dangerous.

13.4 Feeling for play in the steering head bearings

Check

2 Place the motorcycle on its centrestand on level ground, and have an assistant push down on the rear of the bike to raise the front wheel off the ground. Always make sure that the bike is properly supported and secure.

3 Point the front wheel straight-ahead and slowly move the handlebars from lock to lock. Any dents, tightness or roughness in the bearing races will be felt – if the bearings are too tight the bars will not move smoothly and freely. Again point the wheel straight-ahead, and tap the front of the wheel to one side. The wheel should 'fall' under its own weight to the limit of its lock, indicating that the bearings are not too tight (take into account the restriction that cables, hoses and wiring may have). Check for similar movement to the other side.

4 Next, grasp the bottom of the forks and gently pull and push them forward and backward and side-to-side **(see illustration)**.

13.6a Unscrew the steering stem nut and remove the washer

13.6b Slacken the fork clamp bolt (arrowed) on each side

13.7a Displace the handlebar/yoke assembly...

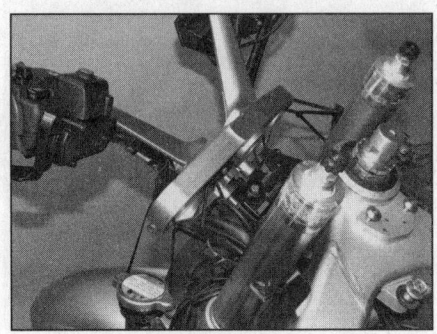

13.7b ...and support it as shown

> **HAYNES HINT** 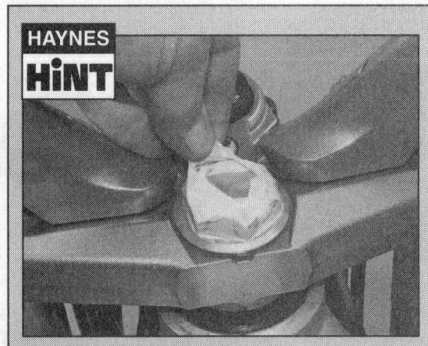
> Protect the finish of the steering stem nut by wrapping a layer of masking tape around it.

Any looseness or freeplay in the steering head bearings will be felt as front-to-rear or side-to-side movement of the forks. If play is felt, adjust the bearings as described below.

> **HAYNES HINT**
> Make sure you are not mistaking any movement between the bike and stand, or between the stand and the ground, for freeplay in the bearings. Do not pull and push the forks too hard – a gentle movement is all that is needed. Freeplay between the fork tubes due to worn bushes can also be misinterpreted as steering head bearing play – do not confuse the two.

Adjustment

Special tool: *Either the Yamaha special tool (part No. 90890-01403), equivalent peg spanner, or a suitably sized C-spanner is necessary for this procedure.*

5 As a precaution against accidental damage, remove the fairing side panels, fairing, and fuel tank (see Chapters 7 and 4).

6 Unscrew the steering stem nut and remove the washer **(see illustration)**. Slacken the fork clamp bolts in the top yoke **(see illustration)**.

7 Gently ease the top yoke/handlebar assembly up off the forks and displace it forwards, using cable-ties to secure it **(see illustrations)**.

8 Remove the tabbed lockwasher, noting how it fits **(see illustration)**. Unscrew the

13.8a Remove the lockwasher...

Routine maintenance and servicing 1•25

13.8b ...then unscrew the locknut and remove the rubber washer

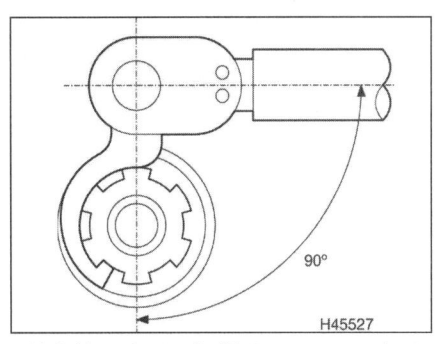

13.9 Yamaha tool with torque wrench at correct angle to tool

13.10 Adjust the bearings as described using a C-spanner

locknut and remove the rubber washer **(see illustration)** – the nut should only be finger-tight, but if necessary use a C-spanner.

9 To adjust the bearings as specified by Yamaha, a special service tool (part No. 90890-01403) and a torque wrench are required. If the tool is available, first slacken the adjuster nut slightly to take pressure off the bearing, then tighten the nut to the initial torque setting specified at the beginning of this Chapter. Make sure the torque wrench handle is at right-angles (90°) to the centre line between the adjuster nut and the service tool wrench socket **(see illustration)**. Now slacken the nut one turn, then tighten it to the final torque setting specified.

10 If the Yamaha tool is not available, use a C-spanner located in one of the notches to slacken the adjuster nut slightly to take pressure off the bearing, then tighten the nut until all freeplay is removed **(see illustration)**. Now tighten the nut a little more to pre-load the bearings. Now slacken the nut and retighten it, setting it so that all freeplay is just removed from the bearings, yet the steering is able to move freely from side to side. Tighten the nut only a little at a time, and after each adjustment repeat the checks outlined in Steps 2 to 4.

Caution: Take great care not to apply excessive pressure because this will cause premature failure of the bearings.

11 Turn the steering from lock to lock five times to settle the bearings, then recheck the adjustment or the torque setting depending on your method used. The object is to set the adjuster nut so that the bearings are under a very light loading, just enough to remove any freeplay.

12 With the bearings correctly adjusted, fit the rubber washer and the locknut **(see illustration 13.8b)**. Tighten the locknut finger-tight, then tighten it further until its notches align with those in the adjuster nut, making sure it does not turn as well. Fit the lockwasher so that the tabs fit into the notches in both the locknut and adjuster nut **(see illustration 13.8a)**.

13 Fit the top yoke/handlebar assembly onto the steering stem and forks **(see illustration 13.7a)**. Fit the washer and the steering stem nut and tighten the nut to the torque setting specified at the beginning of the Chapter **(see illustration)**. Tighten the fork clamp bolts to the specified torque **(see illustration 13.6b)**.

14 Check the bearing adjustment as described above and re-adjust if necessary.

15 Install the fuel tank (Chapter 4), fairing and fairing panels (Chapter 7) if removed.

Lubrication

16 Over a considerable time the grease in the bearings will be dispersed or will harden allowing the ingress of dirt and water.

17 At the specified service interval remove the steering stem and clean and re-grease the bearings (see Chapter 5).

14 Sidestand, centrestand and starter safety circuit

Stands

1 Check the stand springs for damage and distortion **(see illustration)**. The springs must be capable of retracting the stand fully and holding it retracted when the motorcycle is in use. If a spring is sagged or broken it must be replaced with a new one.

2 Lubricate the stand pivots regularly (see Section 15).

3 Check the stands and mounts for bends and cracks. Stands can often be repaired by welding.

13.13 Fit the washer and tighten the nut to the specified torque

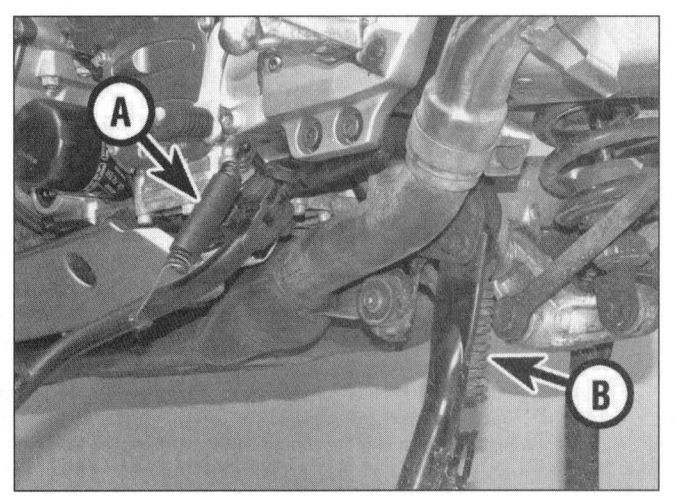

14.1 Check the sidestand springs (A) and the centrestand springs (B)

1•26 Routine maintenance and servicing

Starter safety circuit

Standard gearchange models

4 Check the operation of the starter safety circuit as follows:
- Make sure the transmission is in neutral, then retract the stand and start the engine. Pull in the clutch lever and select a gear. Keeping the clutch lever pulled in, extend the sidestand. The engine should stop as the sidestand is extended.
- Make sure the engine is in neutral and the sidestand is down, then start the engine. Pull the clutch lever in and select a gear. The engine should cut out.
- Check that when the sidestand is down the engine can only be started if the transmission is in neutral, and when the sidestand is up and the transmission is in gear the engine can only be started if the clutch lever is pulled in.

5 If the circuit does not operate as described, check the sidestand switch, neutral switch, clutch switch, starter circuit cut-off relay and diodes, and the wiring and connectors between them (see Chapter 8).

YCC-S models

6 Check the operation of the starter safety circuit as follows:
- Check that the engine cannot be started with the sidestand up unless either the brake lever or pedal is applied.
- Check that the engine cannot be started with the brake lever or pedal applied if the sidestand is down.
- Check that the engine stops if the sidestand is put down.

7 If the circuit does not operate as described, check the sidestand switch, neutral switch and brake light switches, and the wiring and connectors between them (see Chapter 8). If they are all good the YCC-S system could be faulty, in which case the warning light should come on and a fault code can be accessed (see Chapter 2).

15 Pivot points and throttle cable lubrication

Pivot points

1 As the clutch and brake lever pivots, footrest pivots, brake pedal, gearchange lever pivots and linkage, and stand pivots are exposed to the elements, they should be checked and lubricated at the specified service interval to ensure safe and trouble-free operation.

2 In order for the lubricant to be applied where it will do the most good, the component should be disassembled and cleaned (see Chapter 5). The lubricant recommended by Yamaha for each application is listed at the beginning of the Chapter. If an aerosol lubricant is being used, it can be applied to the pivot joint gaps and will usually work its way into the areas where friction occurs, so less disassembly of

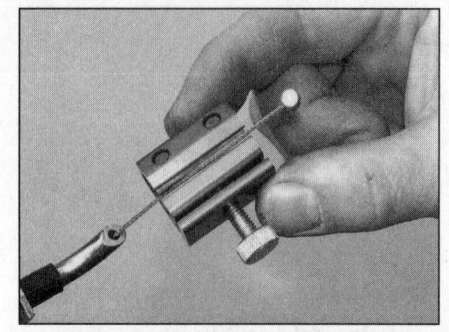

15.3a Fit the cable into the adapter...

the component is needed (however it is always better to do so and clean off all corrosion, dirt and old lubricant first). Apply grease sparingly as it may attract dirt (which could cause the controls to bind or wear at an accelerated rate).

Throttle cables

Special tool: *A cable lubricating adapter is necessary for this procedure.*

3 Disconnect the throttle cables from the twistgrip (see Chapter 4). Lubricate them with a pressure adapter and aerosol cable lubricant as shown **(see illustrations)**.

16 Nuts and bolts

1 Since vibration of the machine tends to loosen fasteners, all nuts, bolts, screws, etc. should be periodically checked for proper tightness.
2 Pay particular attention to the following, referring to the relevant Chapter:
Spark plugs
Engine oil drain bolt
Final drive housing oil drain bolt and filler bolt
Lever pivot bolts/nuts
Footrest and stand bolts/nuts
Engine mounting bolts/nuts
Shock absorber, suspension linkage and swingarm pivot bolts/nuts
Handlebar bolts/nuts (according to model)
Front fork clamp bolts (top and bottom yoke) and fork top bolts
Steering stem nut
Front wheel axle (2001 to 2005 models), front wheel axle bolt (2006-on models), axle clamp bolts
Rear wheel axle nut
Final drive housing nuts
Brake caliper and master cylinder mounting bolts
Brake hose banjo bolts and caliper bleed valves
Brake disc bolts
Exhaust system bolts/nuts

3 If a torque wrench is available, use it along with the torque settings given at the beginning of this and other Chapters.

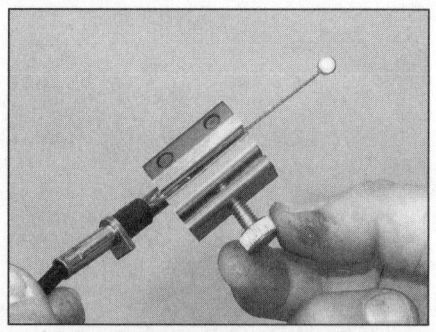

15.3b ...and tighten the screw to seal it in...

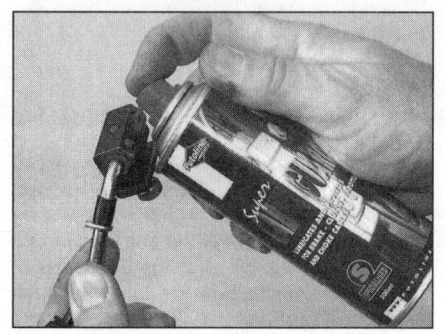

15.3c ...then apply the lubricant using the nozzle provided inserted in the hole in the adapter

17 Battery

1 All models covered in this manual are fitted with a sealed MF (maintenance free) battery. **Note:** *Do not attempt to remove the battery caps to check the electrolyte level or battery specific gravity. Removal will damage the caps, resulting in electrolyte leakage and battery damage.* All that should be done is to check that the terminals are clean and tight and that the casing is not damaged or leaking. See Chapter 8 for further details.

2 If the machine is not in regular use, disconnect the battery and give it a refresher charge every month to six weeks (see Chapter 8).

18 Valve clearances

Special tool: *A set of feeler gauges is necessary for this job* **(see illustration 18.5).**

1 The engine must be completely cool for this maintenance procedure, so let the bike stand overnight before beginning.
2 Remove the spark plugs (see Section 4). Remove the valve cover (see Chapter 2). On 2001 to 2012 models remove the cap from

Routine maintenance and servicing 1•27

the timing rotor cover **(see illustration)**. On 2013-on models remove the fairing right-hand side panel (see Chapter 2), then remove the timing rotor cover **(see illustration)**.

3 Each cylinder is referred to by a number. They are numbered 1 to 4 from left to right, viewed as seated normally on the bike. The intake valves are on the back of the head and the exhaust valves are on the front.

4 Using a spanner or socket on the timing rotor bolt and rotating in a clockwise direction only, turn the engine until the punch mark on each camshaft faces up in line with the arrow on the adjacent camshaft holder, so the camshaft lobes for the No. 1 (left-hand) cylinder face away from each other **(see illustrations)**. The No. 1 cylinder is now at TDC (top dead centre) on the compression stroke.

5 Check the clearances on the No. 1 cylinder intake and exhaust valves. Insert a feeler gauge of the same thickness as the correct valve clearance (see Specifications) between the camshaft lobe and follower of each valve and check that it is a firm sliding fit **(see illustration)** – you should feel a slight drag when the you pull the gauge out. If not, use the feeler gauges to measure the exact clearance. Record the measured clearance on your chart.

6 Now turn the engine clockwise 180° (half a turn) so that the camshaft lobes for the No. 2 cylinder are facing away from each other. The No. 2 cylinder is now at TDC on the compression stroke. Measure the clearances of the No. 2 cylinder valves using the method described in Step 5.

7 Now turn the engine clockwise 180° (half a turn) so that the camshaft lobes for the No. 4 cylinder are facing away from each other. The No. 4 cylinder is now at TDC on the compression stroke. Measure the clearances of the No. 4 cylinder valves using the method described in Step 5.

8 Now turn the engine clockwise 180° (half a turn) so that the camshaft lobes for the No. 3 cylinder are facing away from each other. The No. 3 cylinder is now at TDC on the compression stroke. Measure the clearances of the No. 3 cylinder valves using the method described in Step 5.

9 When all clearances have been measured and recorded, identify whether the clearance on any valve falls outside that specified. If it

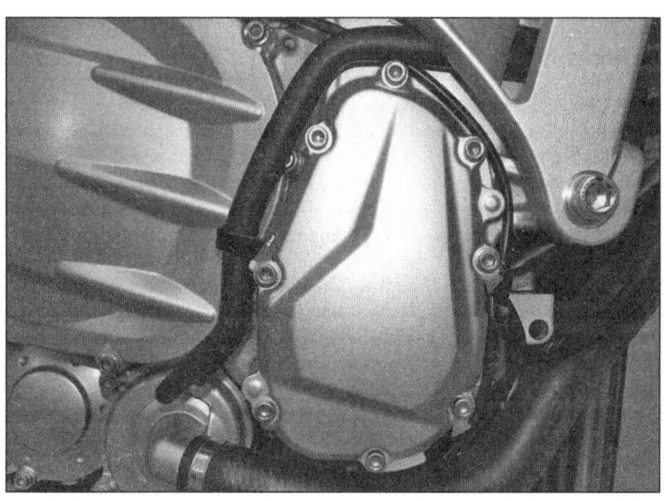

18.2a Unscrew the crankshaft end cap

18.2b Timing rotor cover is retained by 8 bolts – 2013-on models

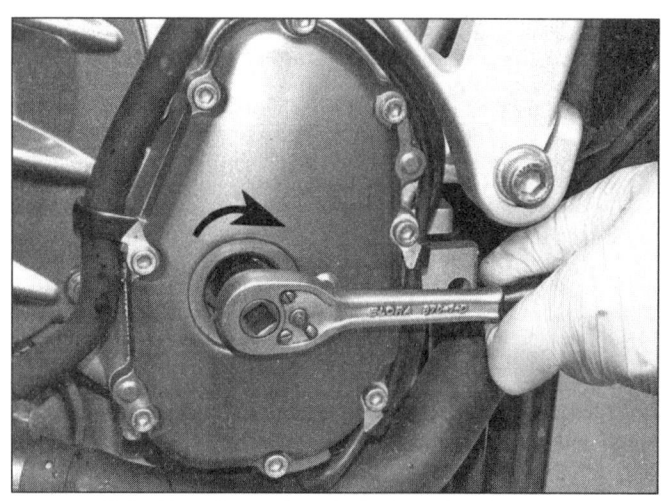

18.4a Turn the engine clockwise using the bolt...

18.4b ...until the punch marks (arrowed) are at the top

18.5 Insert the feeler gauge between the lobe and the shim as shown

1•28 Routine maintenance and servicing

18.11a Carefully lift out the follower...

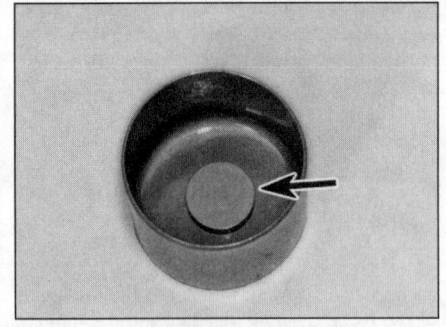

18.11b ...and retrieve the shim (arrowed) from inside it...

18.11c ...or from the top of the valve

does, the shim between the cam follower and the valve must be replaced with one of a thickness that will restore the correct clearance.

10 To replace a shim remove the camshafts (see Chapter 2). Place rags over the spark plug holes and the cam chain tunnel to prevent a shim from dropping into the engine on removal.

11 Remove the cam follower of the valve in question and retrieve the shim from inside the follower **(see illustrations)**. If it is not in the follower, pick it out of the top of the valve using either a magnet, a small screwdriver with a dab of grease on it (the shim will stick to the grease), or a screwdriver and a pair of pliers **(see illustration)**. Do not allow the shim to fall into the engine.

12 Measure the thickness of the shim using a micrometer **(see illustration)**. If a micrometer is not available a size should be marked on the upper face of the shim **(see illustration 18.11c)** – a shim marked 175 is 1.75 mm thick. If the mark is not visible, the shim thickness will have to be measured. It is recommended that the shim is measured anyway, to check that it has not worn.

13 Calculate the required replacement shim by using the formula $a = (b - c) + d$, where a is the required replacement shim size, b is the measured valve clearance, c is the specified valve clearance, and d is the existing shim thickness. For example:

The measured clearance of an exhaust valve is 0.30 mm, so b = 0.30

The specified clearance range for an exhaust valve is 0.18 to 0.25 mm, the mid-point being 0.22 mm, so c = 0.22

The thickness of the existing shim is 1.80 mm, so d = 1.8

Therefore, the required replacement shim a = 0.30 – 0.22 + 1.8 (a = 1.88 mm). Round this to the nearest available size, which is 1.90 mm. Shims are available in 0.05 mm increments from 1.20 mm to 2.40 mm.

14 If the required replacement shim is greater than 2.40 mm (the largest available), the valve is probably not seating correctly due to a build-up of carbon deposits and should be checked and cleaned or resurfaced as required (see Chapter 2).

15 Obtain the replacement shim, then lubricate it with molybdenum disulphide oil (a 50/50 mixture of molybdenum disulphide grease and engine oil) and fit it into its recess in the top of the valve, with the size marking facing up **(see illustration 18.11c)**. Check that the shim is correctly seated, then lubricate the follower with molybdenum disulphide oil and fit it onto the valve **(see illustration 18.11a)**.

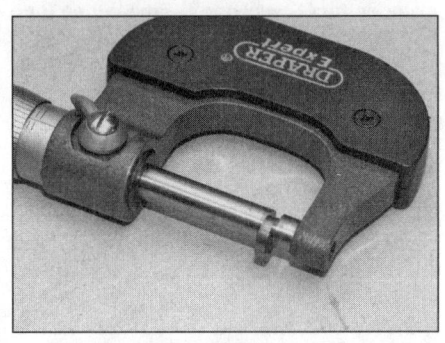

18.12 Check the thickness of the shim using a micrometer

Repeat the process for any other valves until the clearances are correct, then install the camshafts (see Chapter 2).

16 Rotate the crankshaft clockwise several turns to seat the new shim(s), then check the clearances again.

17 Install the valve cover (see Chapter 2). On 2001 to 2012 models fit the timing rotor cover cap **(see illustration 18.2)**. On 2013-on models install the timing rotor cover (see Chapter 2, Section 14).

18 Install the spark plugs (see Section 4). Check and adjust the idle speed (see Section 6).

Chapter 2
Engine, clutch and transmission

Contents

	Section number
Alternator rotor	13
Alternator stator	see Chapter 8
Balancer shafts	32
Cam chain, tensioner blade and guides	10
Cam chain tensioner	8
Camshafts and followers	9
Camshaft position sensor	see Chapter 4
Clutch check	see Chapter 1
Clutch	15
Clutch release mechanism – standard models	16
Clutch release mechanism – YCC-S models	17
Component access	2
Connecting rod and main bearing information	26
Connecting rod (big-end) bearings	29
Crankcases and cylinder bores	25
Crankcase separation and reassembly	24
Crankshaft and connecting rod removal and installation	27
Crankshaft position sensor	see Chapter 4
Cylinder head – removal and installation	11
Cylinder head and valves – overhaul	12
Engine wear assessment	3
Engine removal and installation	4
Engine overhaul – general information	5
Gearchange mechanism – standard models	18
Gearchange mechanism – YCC-S models	19

	Section number
General information	1
Idle speed	see Chapter 1
Main bearings	28
Middle gear shafts	23
Neutral switch	see Chapter 8
Oil and filter change	see Chapter 1
Oil cooler	6
Oil level check	see *Pre-ride checks*
Oil level sensor	see Chapter 8
Oil pump	22
Oil sump, strainer and pressure relief valve	21
Pistons	30
Piston rings	31
Running-in procedure	36
Selector drum and forks	35
Spark plugs	see Chapter 1
Starter clutch	13
Starter motor	see Chapter 8
Timing rotor	14
Transmission shaft overhaul	34
Transmission assembly removal and installation	33
Valve clearance check and adjustment	see Chapter 1
Valve cover	7
Water pump	see Chapter 3
YCC-S (Yamaha Chip Controlled Shift) system	20

Degrees of difficulty

Easy, suitable for novice with little experience	Fairly easy, suitable for beginner with some experience	Fairly difficult, suitable for competent DIY mechanic	Difficult, suitable for experienced DIY mechanic	Very difficult, suitable for expert DIY or professional

Specifications

General

Type	Four-stroke in-line four
Capacity	1298 cc
Bore	79.0 mm
Stroke	66.2 mm
Compression ratio	10.8 to 1
Cylinder numbering	1 to 4 from left to right
Cooling system	Liquid cooled
Lubrication	Wet sump, trochoid pump
Clutch	Wet multi-plate
Transmission	Five-speed constant mesh
Final drive	Shaft

Camshafts
Cam lobe height
  Standard .... 33.05 to 33.15 mm
  Service limit (min)
    Intake .... 32.05 mm
    Exhaust .... 32.95 mm
Journal diameter .... 24.459 to 24.472 mm
Holder diameter .... 24.500 to 24.521 mm
Journal oil clearance .... 0.028 to 0.062 mm
Runout (max) .... 0.03 mm
Cam chain type .... RH2015 – 136 links

Cylinder head
Warpage (max) .... 0.10 mm

Valves, guides and springs
Valve clearances .... see Chapter 1

Intake valves
Stem diameter
  Standard .... 4.975 to 4.990 mm
  Service limit (min) .... 4.945 mm
Guide bore diameter
  Standard .... 5.000 to 5.012 mm
  Service limit (max) .... 5.050 mm
Stem-to-guide clearance
  Standard .... 0.010 to 0.037 mm
  Service limit (max) .... 0.08 mm
Stem runout .... 0.01 mm
Head diameter .... 29.9 to 30.1 mm
Face width .... 1.2 to 2.0 mm
Seat width (on valve and in head) .... 0.9 to 1.1 mm
Margin thickness .... 0.8 to 1.2 mm

Exhaust valves
Stem diameter
  Standard .... 4.960 to 4.980 mm
  Service limit (min) .... 4.930 mm
Guide bore diameter
  Standard .... 5.000 to 5.012 mm
  Service limit (max) .... 5.050 mm
Stem-to-guide clearance
  Standard .... 0.020 to 0.052 mm
  Service limit (max) .... 0.105 mm
Stem runout .... 0.01 mm
Head diameter .... 25.9 to 26.1 mm
Face width .... 1.2 to 2.0 mm
Seat width
  Standard .... 0.9 to 1.1 mm
  Service limit (max) .... 1.6 mm
Margin thickness .... 0.5 to 0.9 mm

Valve springs
Free length
  Standard .... 39.7 mm
  Service limit (min) .... 37.7 mm
Spring bend (max) .... 1.7 mm

Clutch
Friction plates 9
Plain plates 8
Friction plate thickness
  Standard .... 2.9 to 3.1 mm
  Service limit (min) .... 2.8 mm
Plain plate thickness .... 1.9 to 2.1 mm
Plain plate warpage (max) .... 0.1 mm
Spring height
  Standard .... 6.78 mm
  Service limit (min) .... 6.44 mm

Lubrication system

Engine oil pressure (at 80 to 90°C)........................... 4.4 psi (0.3 Bar), engine idling
By-pass valve opening pressure .... 11.4 to 17.1 psi (0.78 to 1.18 Bar)
Relief valve opening pressure .... 70 to 81 psi (4.8 to 5.6 Bars)
Oil pump
  Inner rotor tip-to-outer rotor clearance
    Standard... less than 0.12 mm
    Service limit (max)..................................... 0.20 mm
  Outer rotor-to-body clearance
    Standard... 0.09 to 0.15 mm
    Service limit (max)..................................... 0.22 mm
  Rotor end-float
    Standard... 0.03 to 0.08 mm
    Service limit (max)..................................... 0.15 mm

Pistons

Piston diameter (measured 5 mm up from skirt, at 90° to piston pin axis)
  Standard... 78.965 to 78.980 mm
Piston-to-bore clearance
  Standard... 0.020 to 0.045 mm
  Service limit (max) .... 0.15 mm
Piston pin diameter
  Standard... 18.991 to 19.000 mm
  Service limit (min) .... 18.971 mm
Piston pin bore diameter in piston
  Standard... 19.004 to 19.015 mm
  Service limit (max) .... 19.045 mm
Piston pin-to-piston pin bore clearance
  Standard... 0.004 to 0.024 mm
  Service limit (max) .... 0.074 mm

Piston rings

Top compression ring
  Type .... Barrel
  Ring width... 2.8 mm
  Ring thickness .... 1.0 mm
  Ring end gap (installed)
    2001 to 2012 models
      Standard.. 0.35 to 0.45 mm
      Service limit (max).................................. 0.70 mm
    2013-on models
      Standard.. 0.20 to 0.30 mm
      Service limit (max).................................. 0.55 mm
  Piston ring-to-groove clearance
    Standard... 0.03 to 0.07 mm
    Service limit (max)..................................... 0.12 mm
2nd compression ring
  Type .... Taper
  Ring width... 2.9 mm
  Ring thickness .... 1.0 mm
  Ring end gap (installed)
    2001 to 2012 models
      Standard.. 0.75 to 0.85 mm
      Service limit (max).................................. 1.2 mm
    2013-on models
      Standard.. 0.35 to 0.45 mm
      Service limit (max).................................. 0.80 mm
  Piston ring-to-groove clearance
    Standard... 0.02 to 0.06 mm
    Service limit (max)..................................... 0.12 mm
Oil ring
  Ring width... 2.5 mm
  Ring thickness .... 2.0 mm
  Ring end gap (installed)
    2001 to 2012 models .... 0.20 to 0.60 mm
    2013-on models .... 0.20 to 0.70 mm
  Piston ring-to-groove clearance........................... 0.06 to 0.15 mm

Cylinder bores
Bore
   Standard.. 79.000 to 79.010 mm
   Service limit (max) .... 81.100 mm
Ovality (out-of-round) (max) .... 0.05 mm
Taper (max).. 0.05 mm
Cylinder compression
   Standard.. 228 psi (16.0 Bars) @ 400 rpm
   Maximum .... 255 psi (17.9 Bars)
   Minimum.. 198 psi (13.9 Bars)
   Max. difference between cylinders................ 14.5 psi (1.0 Bar)

Crankshaft and bearings
Main bearing oil clearance .... 0.027 to 0.045 mm
Runout (max) .... 0.03 mm

Connecting rods
Big-end side clearance...................................... 0.160 to 0.262 mm
Big-end oil clearance .... 0.031 to 0.048 mm
Small-end internal diameter................................ 19.005 to 19.018 mm

Gearchange mechanism
Selector fork shaft runout (max)......................... 0.10 mm

Transmission
Gear ratios (no. of teeth)
   Primary reduction .... 1.563 to 1 (75/48)
   1st gear... 2.529 to 1 (43/17)
   2nd gear.. 1.773 to 1 (39/22)
   3rd gear .... 1.348 to 1 (31/23)
   4th gear .... 1.077 to 1 (28/26)
   5th gear .... 0.929 to 1 (26/28)
   Middle gear
      2001 to 2005 models .... 0.972 to 1 (35/36)
      2006-on models .... 0.946 to 1 (35/37)
   Secondary reduction .... 0.777 to 1 (21/27)
   Final reduction .... 3.666 to 1 (33/9)

Torque settings
Alternator cover bolts....................................... 12 Nm
Alternator rotor bolt .... 130 Nm
Balancer shaft holder mounting bolt .... 14 Nm
Cam chain tensioner mounting bolts.................. 10 Nm
Camshaft holder bolts...................................... 10 Nm
Camshaft sprocket bolts................................... 24 Nm
Clutch cover bolts .... 12 Nm
Clutch hose banjo bolts .... 30 Nm
Clutch master cylinder clamp bolts .... 10 Nm
Clutch nut... 90 Nm
Clutch release cylinder bolts .... 10 Nm
Clutch spring retainer bolts .... 8 Nm
Connecting rod nuts
   Stage 1 torque .... 20 Nm
   Stage 2 angle .... 120° (1/3 turn)
Crankcase bolts
   9 mm bolts (numbers 1 to 10)
      Stage 1 and 3 torque .... 25 Nm
      Stage 4 angle .... 120° (1/3 turn)
   8 mm bolts (numbers 11 and 12) .... 24 Nm
   6 mm bolts (numbers 13 and 14) .... 12 Nm
   6 mm bolts (numbers 15 to 31) .... 10 Nm
Crankcase damper plate bolts........................... 12 Nm
Cylinder head 10 mm bolts
   Stage 1 and 3 torque .... 25 Nm
   Stage 4 angle .... 180° (1/2 turn)
Cylinder head 6 mm bolts .... 12 Nm
Engine mountings... *see Section 4*

Torque settings (continued)

Footrest bracket bolts (left-hand side)
    Lower (sidestand) bolts . . . . 65 Nm
    Upper (M8) bolts. . . . . 28 Nm
    Front (M10) bolt . . . . 49 Nm
Foot shift lever pivot bolt (YCC-S models). . . . . 16 Nm
Gearchange shaft centralising spring locating pin. . . . . 22 Nm
Gearchange shift actuator bolts (YCC-S models) . . . . 20 Nm
Gearchange shift actuator linkage rod bolts (YCC-S models). . . . . . . 10 Nm
Main oil gallery plug
    2001 to 2012 models . . . . 12 Nm
    2013-on models . . . . 8 Nm
Middle drive shaft bearing housing bolts . . . . 12 Nm
Middle driven shaft bearing housing/cover bolts. . . . . 25 Nm
Middle drive shaft nut
    2001 to 2012 models . . . . 110 Nm
    2013-on models . . . . 160 Nm
Middle shaft cover bolts. . . . . 12 Nm
Oil baffle plate bolts (clutch housing). . . . . 10 Nm
Oil baffle plate bolts (gearchange mechanism) . . . . 10 Nm
Oil baffle plate bolts (internal). . . . . 10 Nm
Oil cooler bolts . . . . 12 Nm
Oil delivery and return pipe bolts . . . . 10 Nm
Oil pump assembly bolts . . . . 12 Nm
Oil pump drive chain guide bolts
    2001 to 2005 models . . . . 10 Nm
    2006-on models . . . . 12 Nm
Oil pump mounting bolts
    2001 to 2005 models . . . . 10 Nm
    2006-on models . . . . 12 Nm
Oil strainer bolts . . . . 12 Nm
Oil sump bolts . . . . 12 Nm
Rear balancer shaft cover bolts . . . . 12 Nm
Selector drum bearing and shaft retainer plate bolts. . . . . 10 Nm
Starter clutch bolts. . . . . 32 Nm
Timing rotor bolt
    2001 to 2012 models . . . . 45 Nm
    2013-on models . . . . 65 Nm
Timing rotor cover bolts . . . . 12 Nm
Transmission input shaft bearing housing screws . . . . 12 Nm
Valve cover bolts . . . . 10 Nm

1 General information

The engine/transmission unit is a liquid-cooled in-line four cylinder. The engine has four valves per cylinder, operated by double overhead camshafts that are chain driven off the right-hand end of the crankshaft.

The engine/transmission unit is constructed in aluminium alloy and the crankcase divides horizontally. The one-piece forged crankshaft runs in five shell-type main bearings. The crankcase incorporates a wet sump, pressure fed lubrication system, and houses a chain driven oil pump. The system has an oil strainer in the pump pick-up, a pressure relief valve and by-pass valve, an oil filter, oil cooler, and an oil level sensor.

The right-hand end of the crankshaft carries the primary drive gear and the ignition timing rotor, and the left-hand end carries the alternator rotor and starter clutch, and the balancer shaft drive gear running two balancer shafts. The starter motor sits on the top of the crankcase behind the cylinders.

The water pump is on the right-hand side of the engine, and its drive shaft is keyed to the oil pump drive shaft.

The hydraulically-operated wet multi-plate clutch is gear driven off the crankshaft. The five-speed transmission is constant mesh. Final drive to the rear wheel is by shaft.

2 Component access

Operations possible with the engine in the frame

The components and assemblies listed below can be removed without having to remove the engine/transmission assembly from the frame. If however, a number of areas require attention at the same time, removal of the engine is recommended.

Valve cover
Cam chain tensioner
Camshafts, cam chain and blades
Throttle bodies

2•6 Engine, clutch and transmission

Cylinder head
Clutch
Rear balancer shaft
Gearchange mechanism
Timing rotor
Alternator
Starter motor
Starter clutch
Oil pump, oil strainer and oil pressure relief valve
Oil cooler
Water pump

Operations requiring engine removal

It is necessary to remove the engine/transmission assembly from the frame to gain access to the following components.
Crankshaft and bearings
Front balancer shaft
Connecting rods and bearings
Pistons and piston rings
Middle gear shafts
Transmission shafts
Selector drum and forks

3 Engine wear assessment

Cylinder compression check

Special tool: *A compression gauge is needed. You are best off using the type with a threaded hose and adaptor to fit the spark plug holes – there are cheaper ones that have a coned rubber tip that is pressed onto the spark plug hole, but they are not as good, especially when access is restricted. Depending on the outcome of the initial test, a squirt-type oil can may also be needed.*

1 Poor engine performance can be caused by leaking valves, incorrect valve clearances, a leaking head gasket, or worn pistons, piston rings or cylinder walls. A cylinder compression check will highlight these conditions and can also indicate the presence of excessive carbon deposits in the cylinder head, and a leakdown test (for which special equipment is needed – consult a Yamaha dealer) will pinpoint the actual cause(s) of the problem.
2 Start by making sure the valve clearances are correctly set (see Chapter 1). Also make sure the battery is well charged.
3 Run the engine until it is at normal operating temperature.
4 Remove the spark plug from the cylinder being tested, and pull the caps off or remove the coils from the other plugs according to model (see Chapter 1).
5 Make sure the gauge hose/adapter threads are the same as the spark plug (10 mm diameter x 1.0 mm pitch). Fit the gauge into the vacant spark plug hole **(see illustration)**.
6 With the ignition switch ON, the kill switch set to RUN, and the throttle held fully open, turn the engine over on the starter motor until the gauge reading has built up and stabilised.
7 Compare the reading on the gauge to the cylinder compression figures specified at the beginning of the Chapter.
8 Remove the gauge and refit the spark plug, leaving the cap off, then remove the other plug and fit the gauge into its hole. Repeat the test.
9 If a reading is low, it could be due to a worn cylinder bore, piston or rings, failure of the head gasket, or worn valve seats. To determine which is the cause, pour a small quantity of engine oil into the spark plug hole to seal the rings, then repeat the compression test. If the figures are noticeably higher the cause is worn cylinder, piston or rings. If there is no change the cause is a leaking head gasket or worn valve seats.
10 Although unlikely, if the reading is high there could be a build-up of carbon deposits in the combustion chamber. Remove the cylinder head and scrape all deposits off the piston and the cylinder head (Section 11).

Leak-down (cylinder leakage) test

11 A leak down or 'cylinder leakage' test is similar to a compression test in that it tells you how well a cylinder is sealing, but it does so by testing how much pressure is lost through leakage, as opposed to how much pressure is created through compression. Many professionals prefer a leak test to a compression test as it more accurately pin-points the cause of the problem before any disassembly is done and is therefore easy to tell where the leakage is occurring. Generally however the required equipment is more expensive than for a compression test and a source of compressed air is essential. If you think a test is needed take the bike to a suitably equipped dealer or workshop. If you decide to purchase your own equipment follow the manufacturer's instructions.
12 A leakage test can also be used in conjunction with a compression test to diagnose other kinds of problems, such as a faulty valve train component, incorrect valve timing, faulty ignition or fuel delivery problems.

Engine oil pressure check

Special tool: *An oil pressure gauge is required to perform this test.*

13 An oil pressure check can provide useful information about the condition of the engine's lubrication system, and can also be used as an indicator of excessive wear in the engine if no specific faults with the lubrication or pressure warning system are found.
14 This engine is fitted with an oil level sensor and warning light – there is no oil pressure switch and warning light. The oil level warning light should come on when the ignition is turned on, and then go out – if it doesn't, check the circuit (see Chapter 8). If the light stays on, or comes on whilst the engine is running, low oil level is indicated – stop the engine immediately and carry out an oil level check *(see Pre-ride checks)*. If the oil level is correct, drain the oil and remove the filter (see Chapter 1), and check the drained oil and the filter for sludge that reduces its ability to flow. Next remove the sump to check the pick-up strainer for blockage. Note that it is possible that the cause of the light staying on or coming on while the engine is running is an electrical fault, so make sure the oil level sensor, warning light and circuit are all functioning correctly (see Chapter 8). If all appears good an oil pressure check must be carried out. **Note:** *The warning light may flicker during sudden acceleration or deceleration or when riding up or down hill. Note that this is a characteristic of the system and provided the oil level is correct, does not indicate a fault.*
15 To check the oil pressure, a suitable gauge and adapter (which screws into the main oil gallery) will be needed. Yamaha produce a gauge (part Nos. 90890-03153 (2001 to 2006 models) or 90890-03120 (all other models)) and adapter (part No. 90890-03124 (all models)), for this purpose, or one can be obtained commercially. You will also need some rags to catch and mop up any residual oil that gets lost in between removing the gallery plug and fitting the gauge – support the bike on the sidestand to prevent excess oil loss.
16 Run the engine until it is at normal operating temperature. Remove the right-hand fairing side panel (see Chapter 7).
17 Unscrew the main oil gallery plug **(see illustration)** – note that a new O-ring will be needed. Screw the gauge adapter in its place, flexing the large-bore coolant pipe down to gain access. Connect the oil pressure gauge to the adapter.
18 Check the oil level (see *Pre-ride checks*).

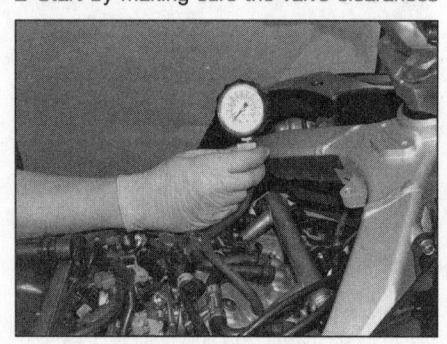

3.5 Compression tester in situ

3.17 Engine main oil galley plug (arrowed)

Engine, clutch and transmission 2•7

4.7a Unscrew the bolt (arrowed)

4.7b Unscrew the bolts (arrowed) and remove the T-bar

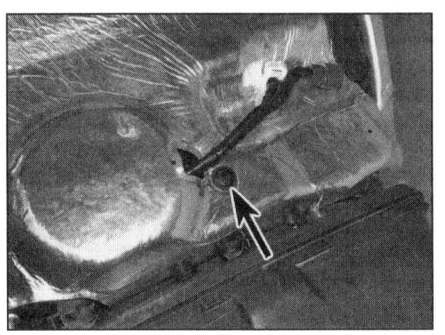

4.7c Release the trim clip (arrowed)...

4.7d ...and remove the shield

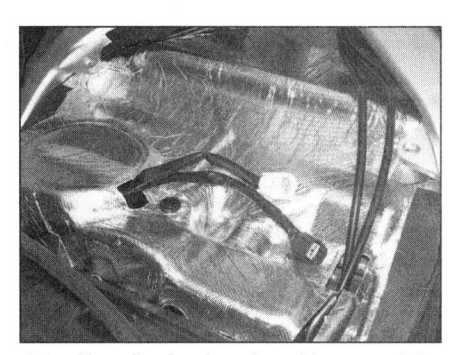

4.7e Also slip the throttle cables out of the slot – 2013-on models

19 Start the engine and allow it to idle whilst watching the gauge reading. The oil pressure should be similar to that given in the Specifications at the start of this Chapter – note that if the engine is not at normal temperature the reading will be high.

20 If the pressure is significantly lower than the standard, either the pick-up strainer is blocked, the pressure relief valve is stuck open, the oil pump or its drive mechanism is faulty, or there is other engine damage. Also make sure the correct grade oil is being used. Begin diagnosis by checking the oil strainer and relief valve, then check the oil pump (Section 22). If those items check out okay, and all passages are clear, chances are the bearing oil clearances are excessive and the engine needs to be overhauled.

21 If the pressure is too high, either an oil passage or the oil filter is clogged, the relief valve is stuck closed or the wrong grade of oil is being used.

22 If the pressure is as it should be, and if not already done, then check the oil level sensor, warning light and circuit (see Chapter 8).

23 Stop the engine and let it cool, then remove the gauge and adapter and fit the main oil gallery plug using a new O-ring smeared with grease, tightening it to the torque setting specified at the beginning of the Chapter.

⚠ *Warning: Be careful when removing the pressure gauge adapter as the exhaust pipes, the engine and the oil itself can cause severe burns.*

24 Check the oil level (see *Pre-ride checks*).

4 Engine removal and installation

Caution: The engine is very heavy. Engine removal and installation should be carried out with the aid of at least one assistant; personal injury or damage could occur if the engine falls or is dropped.

Note: As each mounting bolt is removed store it along with any related washer, nut and spacer to avoid parts getting mixed up, making installation easier. If you are removing the engine for an overhaul it is best to remove the alternator, timing rotor and clutch covers and slacken the alternator rotor bolt, timing rotor bolt and clutch nut with the engine still in the frame – refer to the relevant Sections in this Chapter.

Removal

1 Support the bike on the centrestand. Make sure the bike is on level ground, and tie the front brake on. Work can be made easier by raising the machine to a suitable working height on an hydraulic ramp or a suitable platform. Make sure the motorcycle is secure and will not topple over (also see *Tools and Workshop Tips* in the Reference section).

2 Remove the seat, the side covers and the fairing side panels (see Chapter 7).

3 Disconnect the negative (–ve) lead from the battery (see Chapter 8).

4 If the engine is dirty, particularly around its mountings, wash it thoroughly. This makes work much easier and rule out the possibility of caked on lumps of dirt falling into some vital component.

5 Drain the engine oil and the cooling system (see Chapter 1). If required remove the oil filter (see Chapter 1).

6 Remove the fuel tank (see Chapter 4).

7 On 2001 to 2005 models unscrew the AIS control valve holder bolt **(see illustration)**. On all models remove the T-bar **(see illustration)**. On 2006-on models remove the heat shield **(see illustrations)**.

8 Detach the AIS hoses from the valve cover and remove the control valve along with the hoses (see Chapter 4).

9 On 2001 to 2012 models pull the cap off

2•8 Engine, clutch and transmission

4.9 Pull the cap off the plug

4.11a Unscrew the bolt (arrowed)

4.11b Release the top of the guide on each side...

4.11c ...and remove it

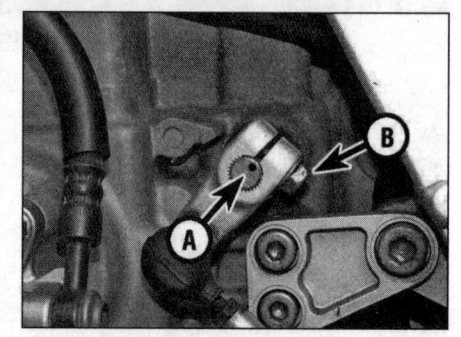

4.13 Alignment punch mark (A), gearchange arm pinch bolt (B)

each plug **(see illustration)**. On 2013-on models disconnect the coil wiring connectors and pull the coils off the spark plugs.

10 Remove the coolant reservoir and the radiator along with their hoses, noting the routing (see Chapter 3). Remove the thermostat housing and outlet pipe assembly along with all associated hoses (see Chapter 3). Detach and remove any remaining coolant hoses as required according to what work is to be carried out, noting their positions and routing.

11 Remove the exhaust system (see Chapter 4). On 2006-on models unscrew the air guide bolt **(see illustration)**. Remove the air guide from the front of the engine, noting how it locates **(see illustrations)**.

12 Remove the air filter housing and throttle body assembly (see Chapter 4). Plug the engine intake manifolds with clean rag.

13 On models with a standard gearchange, disconnect the sidestand switch wiring connector **(see illustration 4.14b)**. Feed the wiring down to the switch, releasing it from the guides and noting its routing. Note the alignment of the slit in the gearchange linkage arm with the punch mark on the shaft, then unscrew the pinch bolt and slide the arm off **(see illustration)**. Unscrew the footrest bracket bolts and remove the footrest bracket/gearchange lever assembly and sidestand assembly **(see illustrations 4.14c and d)**.

14 On models with YCC-S, remove the gear position sensor (see Chapter 8). Note the alignment of the punch marks on the gearchange linkage arm and shaft, then unscrew the pinch bolt and slide the arm off **(see illustration)**. Disconnect the sidestand switch wiring connector **(see illustration)**.

4.14a Alignment punch marks (A), gearchange arm pinch bolt (B) – YCC-S models

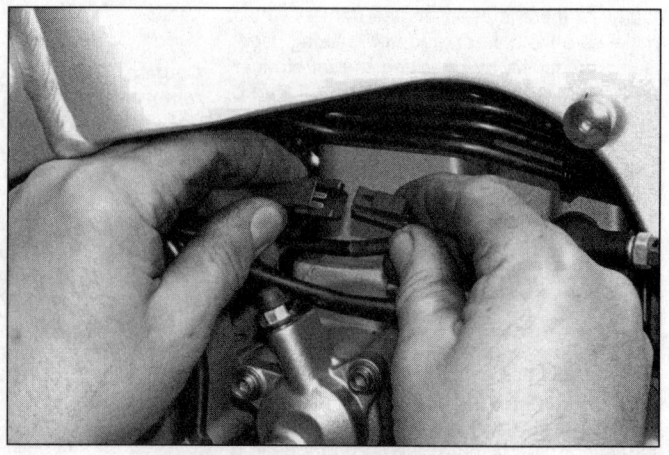

4.14b Disconnect the sidestand wiring

Engine, clutch and transmission 2•9

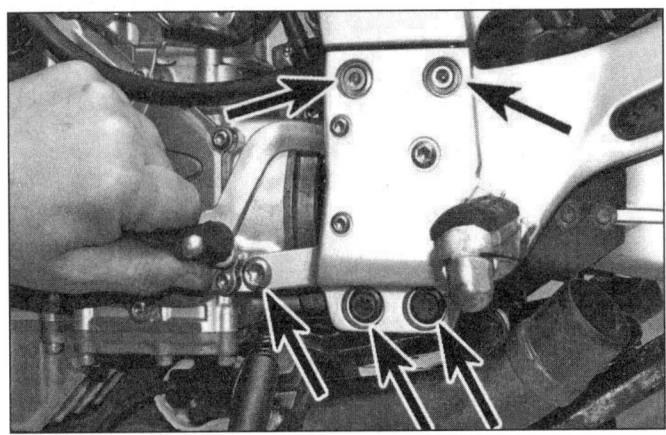

4.14c Unscrew the bolts (arrowed)...

4.14d ...and remove the assembly

Feed the wiring down to the switch, releasing it from the guides and noting its routing. Unscrew the footrest bracket bolts and displace the footrest bracket/gearchange lever assembly and remove the sidestand assembly **(see illustrations)** – support the footrest bracket/gearchange lever assembly so the foot shift switch wiring is not strained.

15 Displace the clutch release cylinder (Section 16) – there is no need to disconnect the hose.

16 Disconnect the alternator wiring connector **(see illustrations)**. Disconnect the starter motor lead **(see illustration)**. Disconnect the neutral switch (2001 to 2005 models and 2006-on AS models) or gear position switch (2006-on A models), speed sensor (2001 to 2005 models and 2006-on AS models), oil level sensor and crankshaft position sensor wiring connectors **(see illustration)**. Detach the engine earth lead **(see illustration)**. Release all engine related wiring from any ties on the frame and secure it to the engine, noting its routing.

17 If required remove the rear brake pedal (see Chapter 5) – this is not essential, but does get it out of the way.

18 Position an hydraulic or mechanical jack under the engine with a block of wood between the jack head and sump **(see illustration 4.27b)**. Make sure the jack is centrally positioned so the engine will not topple in any direction when the last mounting

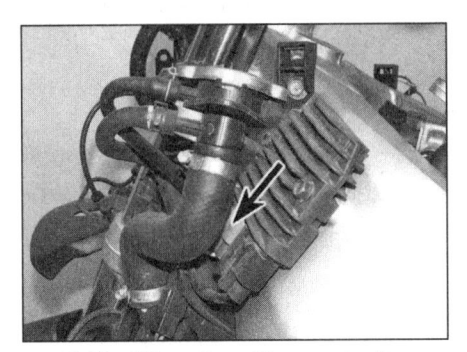

4.16a Alternator wiring connector (arrowed) – 2001 to 2005 models

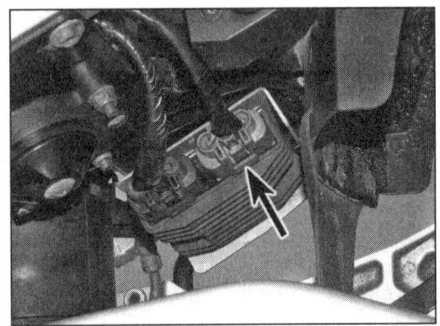

4.16b Alternator wiring connector (arrowed) – 2006-on models

4.16c Pull the boot back, unscrew the nut (arrowed) and detach the lead

4.16d Disconnect the various wiring connectors (arrowed – 2010 AS model shown)

4.16e Engine earth lead bolt (arrowed)

2•10 Engine, clutch and transmission

4.19 Unscrew the bolts (arrowed) and remove the bracket

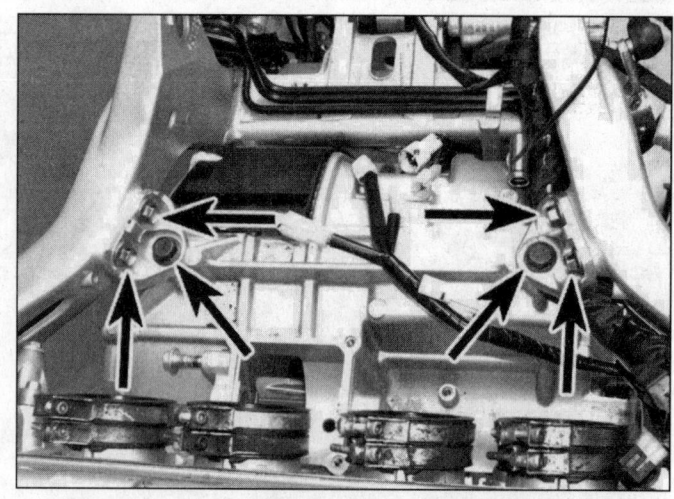

4.20 Unscrew the bolts (arrowed) and remove the brackets

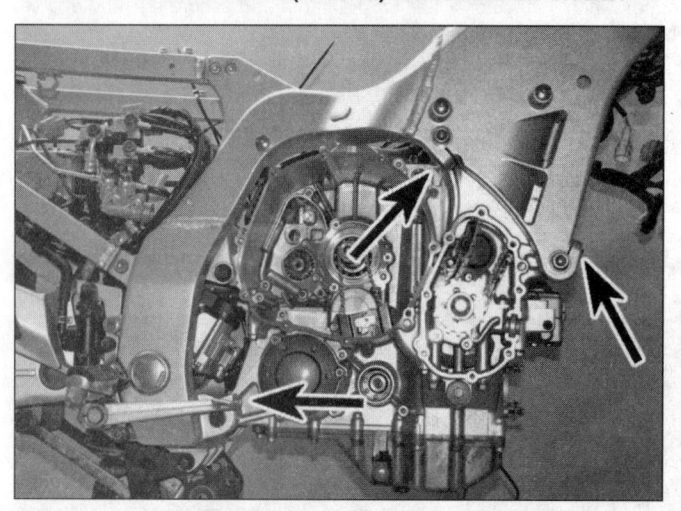

4.21 Slacken the pinch bolts (arrowed)

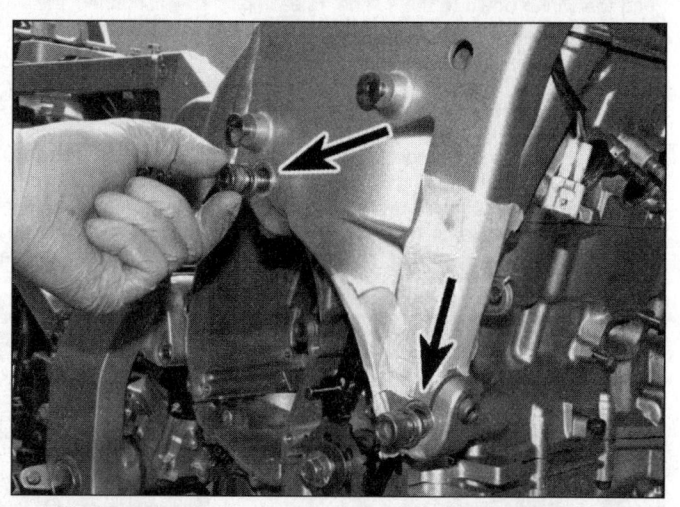

4.22a Remove the front and middle bolts and spacers on the right...

bolt is removed. Raise the jack to take the weight of the engine, but make sure it is not lifting the bike and taking the weight of that as well. The idea is to support the engine so that there is no pressure on any of the mounting bolts once they have been slackened, so they can be easily withdrawn.

19 Remove the engine bracket from the left-hand side (see illustration).

20 Remove the engine brackets from the top of the crankcase (see illustration).

21 Slacken the pinch bolts holding the front, middle and lower rear mounting bolt spacers (see illustration).

22 Unscrew the front and middle bolts on the right-hand side, noting the washers, and remove the spacers (see illustration). Unscrew the front and middle mounting bolts on the left-hand side, noting the washers (see illustration).

23 Unscrew the nut on the right-hand end of the upper rear mounting bolt (see illustration). Unscrew the adjuster bolt until its flange just contacts the frame so it is clear of the engine – to turn the adjuster you need to make a tool out of a piece of steel about 2 mm thick and 14 mm wide at one end so it fits into the cut-outs (see illustration). The width at the

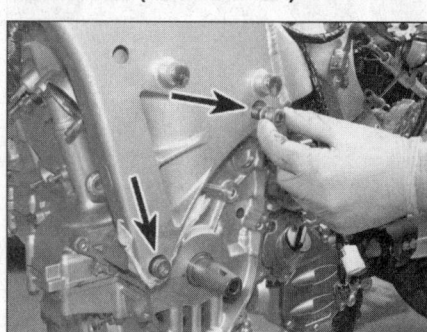

4.22b ...and the front and middle bolts on the left

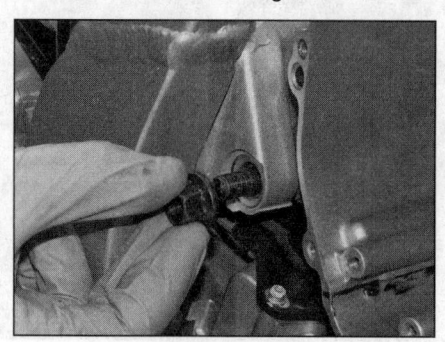

4.23a Unscrew the nut

4.23b Make a tool as described...

Engine, clutch and transmission 2•11

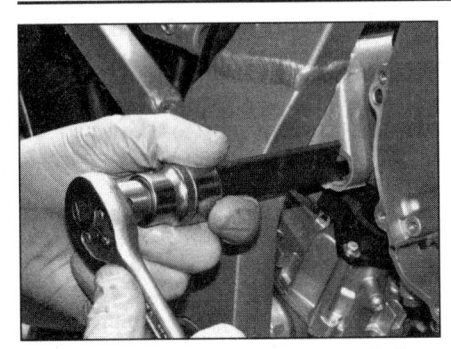

4.23c ...to unscrew the adjuster bolt

4.24 Remove the lower rear bolt

4.25 Remove the upper rear bolt

other end is not crucial as long as you can fit a socket onto it so a torque can be applied on installation **(see illustration)** – the piece shown is 25 mm wide and accepted a 23 mm socket.

24 Check that the engine is properly supported by the jack. Unscrew and withdraw the lower rear mounting bolt and remove the spacer **(see illustration)**.

25 Hold the engine and withdraw the upper rear mounting bolt **(see illustration)**.

26 The engine can now be removed from the frame (see *Caution* above). Check that all wiring, cables and hoses are free and clear, then carefully draw the engine forwards until the output shaft is clear of the universal joint **(see illustration 4.27c)**, then lower the jack a bit and manoeuvre the engine as required to clear the frame **(see illustration 4.27b)**. Fully lower the jack, then with the aid of an assistant remove the jack from under the engine and remove the engine from the right-hand side. Remove the universal joint if required **(see illustration 4.27a)**.

Installation

Note: *To prevent corrosion which could lead to bolts being seized, smear copper grease onto the bolt shafts, not the threads. This will prevent them seizing in the spacers or the engine or frame.*

27 Make sure the adjuster bolt for the upper rear mount is threaded fully into the frame. Smear molybdenum disulphide grease onto the splines on the output shaft and driveshaft and in the universal joint, then slide the UJ onto the driveshaft **(see illustration)**. Manoeuvre the engine into position under the frame and lift it onto the jack **(see illustration)**. Raise the engine to align all the mounting bolt holes, making sure that all cables and wiring are correctly routed and do not get trapped, and that the output shaft locates in the universal joint **(see illustration)**. Note that it may be necessary to adjust the jack as some of the bolts are installed and tightened to realign the other bolt holes.

28 Slide the upper rear mounting bolt in from the left-hand side **(see illustration 4.25)**.

29 Lubricate the threads of the lower rear mounting bolt with oil. Position the spacer between the engine and frame on the right-hand side and slide the bolt in, tightening it finger-tight only **(see illustration 4.24)**.

30 Fit the spacers for the front and middle mounting bolts on the right-hand side. Fit the bolts with their washers and tighten them finger-tight **(see illustration 4.22a)**.

31 Fit the front and middle mounting bolts with their washers on the left-hand side and tighten them finger-tight **(see illustration 4.22b)**.

32 On 2001 to 2005 models fit the three engine brackets and loosely fit the bolts **(see illustrations 4.19 and 20)**.

33 On 2006-on models fit the two top engine brackets and loosely fit the bolts **(see illustration 4.20)** – do not yet fit the bracket to the left-hand side.

34 On 2001 to 2005 models, using a torque wrench now tighten the bolts/nut in the following order to the specified torque setting:
1 Tighten the front and middle mounting bolts on the left-hand side to 55 Nm.
2 Tighten the lower rear mounting bolt to 45 Nm.
3 Tighten the adjuster bolt on the upper

4.27a Slide the UJ onto the driveshaft

4.27b Manoeuvre the engine into position...

4.27c ...and guide the output shaft into the UJ

2•12 Engine, clutch and transmission

rear mount to 18 Nm *(see illustration 4.23c)* – make sure the flange sits flat against the engine.
4 Fit the upper rear mounting bolt nut and tighten to 45 Nm *(see illustration 4.23a)*.
5 Tighten the front and middle mounting bolts on the left-hand side to 55 Nm (they may have loosened off a bit when tightening the other bolts).
6 Tighten the front and middle mounting bolts on the right-hand side to 55 Nm.
7 Tighten the spacer pinch bolts to 24 Nm *(see illustration 4.21)*.
8 Tighten the bolts on each top engine bracket until the heads contact the bracket and check the brackets and bolt heads all seat flat. Tighten the bolts into the engine to 36 Nm. Tighten the bolts into the frame to 16 Nm.
9 Tighten the bolts on the left-side engine bracket until the heads contact the bracket and check the brackets and bolt heads all seat flat. Tighten the bolt into the frame to 32 Nm. Tighten the bolts into the engine to 16 Nm.

35 On 2006-on models, using a torque wrench now tighten the bolts/nut in the following order to the specified torque setting:
1 Tighten the middle mounting bolt on the left-hand side to 49 Nm.
2 Tighten the lower rear mounting bolt to 45 Nm.
3 Tighten the adjuster bolt on the upper rear mount to 18 Nm *(see illustration 4.23c)* – make sure the flange sits flat against the engine.
4 Fit the upper rear mounting bolt nut and tighten to 45 Nm *(see illustration 4.23a)*.
5 Tighten the front mounting bolt on the left-hand side to 49 Nm.
6 Tighten the middle mounting bolt on the right-hand side to 49 Nm.
7 Tighten the front mounting bolt on the right-hand side to 49 Nm.
8 Tighten the spacer pinch bolts to 24 Nm *(see illustration 4.21)*.
9 Tighten the bolts on each top engine bracket until the heads contact the bracket and check the brackets and bolt heads all seat flat. Tighten the bolts into the engine to 37 Nm. Tighten the bolts into the frame to 16 Nm.

4.36 Route the hose through the air guide

10 Fit the left-side engine bracket and tighten the bolts until the heads contact the bracket then check the brackets and bolt heads all seat flat *(see illustration 4.19)*. Tighten the bolt into the frame to 32 Nm. Tighten the bolts into the engine to 16 Nm.
36 The remainder of the installation procedure is the reverse of removal, noting the following points:
● On 2001 to 2012 models route the coolant hose to the throttle bodies through the hole in the air guide **(see illustration)**.
● Use new gaskets on the exhaust pipe connections.
● Make sure all wires, cables and hoses are correctly routed and connected, and secured by any clips or ties.
● Fit and tighten the footrest/sidestand bracket bolts as follows – first clean the bolt threads, then apply some fresh non-permanent threadlock. Fit all the bolts finger-tight at first, then tighten the lower (sidestand) bolts first, then the upper (M8) bolts, then the front (M10) bolt, applying the correct torque setting to each bolt as specified at the beginning of the Chapter.
● Tighten the T-bar bolts to the torque setting specified at the beginning of Chapter 4.
● Refill the engine with the correct type and quantity of oil and coolant (see Chapter 1).
● On 2001 to 2012 models check throttle cable freeplay (see Chapter 1).
● Start the engine and check that there are no oil or coolant leaks.

5 Engine overhaul – general information

1 Before beginning the engine overhaul, read through the related procedures to familiarise yourself with the scope and requirements of the job. Overhauling an engine is not all that difficult, but it is time consuming. Check on the availability of parts and make sure that any necessary special tools are obtained in advance.
2 Most work can be done with a decent set of typical workshop hand tools, although a number of precision measuring tools are required for inspecting parts to determine if they are worn.
3 To ensure maximum life and minimum trouble from a rebuilt engine, everything must be assembled with care in a spotlessly clean environment.

Disassembly

4 Before disassembling the engine, thoroughly clean and degrease its external surfaces. This will prevent contamination of the engine internals, and will also make the job a lot easier and cleaner. A high flash-point solvent, such as paraffin (kerosene) can be used, or better still, a proprietary engine degreaser such as Gunk. Use old paintbrushes and toothbrushes to work the solvent into the various recesses of the casings. Take care to exclude solvent or water from the electrical components and intake and exhaust ports.

⚠ **Warning: The use of petrol (gasoline) as a cleaning agent should be avoided because of the risk of fire.**

5 When clean and dry, position the engine on the workbench, leaving suitable clear area for working. Gather a selection of small containers, plastic bags and some labels so that parts can be grouped together in an easily identifiable manner. Also get some paper and a pen so that notes can be taken. You will also need a supply of clean rag, which should be as absorbent as possible.
6 Before commencing work, read through the appropriate section so that some idea of the necessary procedure can be gained. When removing components note that great force is seldom required, unless specified (checking the specified torque setting of the particular bolt being removed will indicate how tight it is, and therefore how much force should be needed). In many cases, a component's reluctance to be removed is indicative of an incorrect approach or removal method – if in any doubt, re-check with the text.
7 When disassembling the engine, keep 'mated' parts that have been in contact with each other during engine operation together (i.e. each piston with its piston rings and connecting rod, valves with their associated components etc). These 'mated' parts must be reinstalled together and in their original location.
8 A complete engine/transmission disassembly should be done in the following general order with reference to the appropriate Sections.
Remove the valve cover
Remove the cam chain tensioner
Remove the camshafts
Remove the cylinder head
Remove the starter motor (see Chapter 8)
Remove the front balancer shaft
Remove the clutch
Remove the gearchange mechanism
Remove the alternator rotor
Remove timing rotor
Remove the cam chain guide blades
Remove the cam chain
Remove the sump and oil pump
Remove the middle gear shaft
Separate the crankcase halves
Remove the crankshaft
Remove the connecting rods and pistons
Remove the transmission shafts and the selector drum and forks

Reassembly

9 Reassembly is accomplished by reversing the general disassembly sequence.

Engine, clutch and transmission 2•13

6.6 Fit a new O-ring into the groove

7.8a Either release the wire clamp and disconnect the connector (arrowed)...

7.8b ...or unscrew the bolt (arrowed) and place the sensor aside

6 Oil cooler

Removal

1 The cooler is on the front of the engine. Remove the fairing side panels (see Chapter 7).
2 Drain the engine oil (see Chapter 1). Drain the coolant (see Chapter 1).
3 Slacken the cooler hose clamps and detach the hoses.
4 Unscrew the bolts and remove the cooler. Remove the O-ring – a new one must be used **(see illustration 6.6)**.
5 Check the cooler body for cracks and dents and any evidence of coolant leakage and replace it with a new one if necessary. Also check the hoses for splits, cracks, hardening and deterioration and fit new ones if required.

Installation

6 Installation is the reverse of removal, noting the following:
- Check the condition of the hoses and replace them with new ones if required.
- Ensure the mating surfaces of the crankcase and the cooler are clean and dry.
- Use a new O-ring on the cooler body and smear it with clean engine oil. Make sure it seats in its groove **(see illustration)**.
- Clean the threads of the bolts and apply a non-permanent thread locking compound, and tighten them to the torque setting specified at the beginning of the Chapter.
- Make sure the coolant hoses are pressed fully onto their unions and are secured by the clamps.
- Fill the engine with the correct type and quantity of oil (see Chapter 1).
- Refill the cooling system (see Chapter 1).

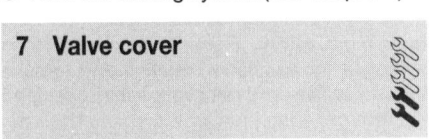

7 Valve cover

Removal

1 Remove the fuel tank (see Chapter 4).
2 On 2001 to 2005 unscrew the AIS control valve holder bolt **(see illustration 4.7a)**. On all models remove the T-bar **(see illustration 4.7b)**. On 2006-on models remove the heat shield **(see illustrations 4.7c and d)**.
3 Detach the throttle cables from the twistgrip, then draw them out through the frame and place them clear of the valve cover (see Chapter 4).
4 Detach the AIS hoses from the valve cover and remove the control valve along with the hoses (see Chapter 4).
5 On 2001 to 2012 models pull the cap off each plug **(see illustration 4.9)**.
6 On 2013-on models disconnect the coil wiring connectors and free the wiring from the cover, and pull the coils off the spark plugs.
7 Drain the cooling system (see Chapter 1). Remove the coolant outlet pipe assembly (see Chapter 3).
8 Either disconnect the CMP sensor wiring connector and remove the sensor with the valve cover, or if required for best access to the adjacent valve cover bolt displace the sensor from the cover and move it aside **(see illustrations)**.
9 Unscrew the valve cover bolts, noting the seals **(see illustration)**. Remove the seals if they are loose – if they are in poor condition replace them with new ones. Lift the cover off the cylinder head **(see illustration)**. If it is stuck, do not try to lever it off with a screwdriver. Tap it gently around the sides with a rubber hammer or block of wood to dislodge it. Take care not to damage the radiator fins.
10 Note the dowels that link the AIS air passages between the valve cover and cylinder head and remove them for safekeeping if loose **(see illustration)**.
11 The rubber gasket is reusable as long as it is not damaged, deformed or deteriorated – remove it if required **(see illustration 7.12)**.

Installation

12 Clean all old sealant of the cut-outs in the cylinder head, and if you are using the same gasket clean the sealant off the half-circle sections. If you have removed the gasket clean all old glue out of the groove in the cover. Cut the linking strips between the centre sections and perimeter of the new gasket in accordance with the old gasket. Smear grease into the

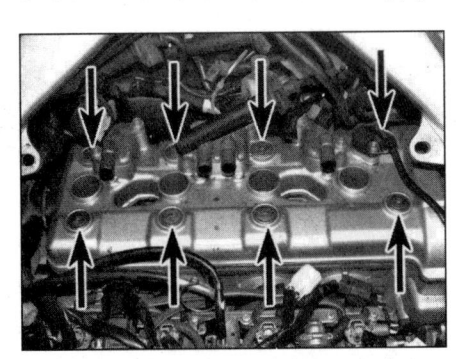

7.9a Valve cover bolts (arrowed)

7.9b Carefully remove the cover

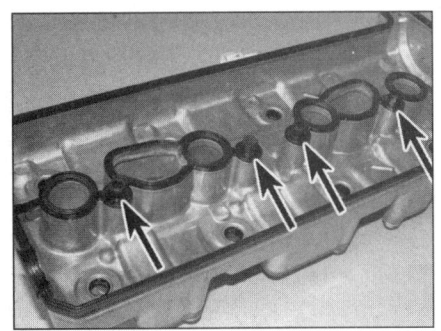

7.10 Air passage dowels (arrowed)

2•14 Engine, clutch and transmission

gasket groove in the cover to stick the gasket in place and make sure it is correctly seated all round **(see illustration)**. Apply a suitable sealant (Yamaha Bond 1215) to the cut-outs in the cylinder head.

13 If removed, fit the PAIR system dowels **(see illustration 7.10)**.

14 Position the valve cover on the cylinder head, making sure the gasket sections stay in place **(see illustration 7.9b)**. If removed, fit the seals into the cover, using new ones if required **(see illustration)**. Fit the bolts and tighten them to the torque setting specified at the beginning of the Chapter.

15 Install the remaining components in the reverse order of removal, referring to Chapter 4 where necessary.

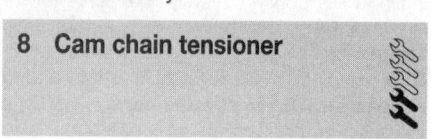

8 Cam chain tensioner

Removal

1 Remove the right-hand fairing side panel (see Chapter 7). Remove the fuel tank (see Chapter 4). Remove the clutch cover (Section 15) – this is to get clearance for a spanner to undo the tensioner lower bolt. Remove the rubber blanking cap from the frame **(see illustration)**. Remove the valve cover (see Section 7), then remove the timing rotor cover (see Section 14). Refer to Section 9, Step 4 and set the engine to TDC with cylinder No. 1 on its compression stroke.

2 Unscrew the tensioner cap bolt and remove

7.12 Make sure the gasket locates in the groove

the sealing washer **(see illustration)**. Note the arrow denoting the upper side of the tensioner.

3 Slacken the tensioner mounting bolts slightly **(see illustration 8.2)**. Insert a small flat-bladed screwdriver through the hole in the frame and into the end of the tensioner so that it engages the slot in the rod **(see illustration)**. Turn the screwdriver clockwise until it stops and hold it in this position while unscrewing the tensioner mounting bolts **(see illustration)**. Remove the bolts, then withdraw the tensioner, release and remove the screwdriver and remove the tensioner **(see illustration)** – the plunger will spring back out once the screwdriver is removed, but can be easily reset on installation.

4 Discard the gasket and sealing washer as new ones must be used on installation. Do not attempt to dismantle the tensioner.

7.14 Fit the seal (arrowed) with each bolt

Caution: Do not rotate the engine with the cam chain tensioner removed.

Check

5 Lightly push the end of the plunger with your finger while turning the screwdriver as in Step 3 and check that the plunger moves smoothly into the tensioner. Hold the plunger in the retracted position and remove the screwdriver, then gradually release finger pressure and check the plunger moves out smoothly and freely **(see illustration)**. If plunger movement is not as described replace the tensioner with a new one.

Installation

6 Ensure the tensioner and cylinder block surfaces are clean and dry.

7 Fit a new gasket onto the tensioner

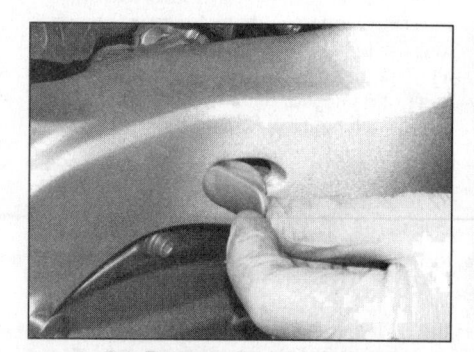

8.1 Remove the rubber cap

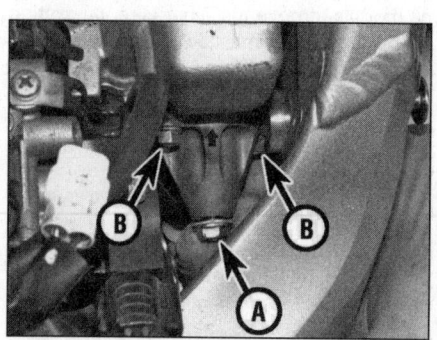

8.2 Tensioner cap bolt (A) and mounting bolts (B)

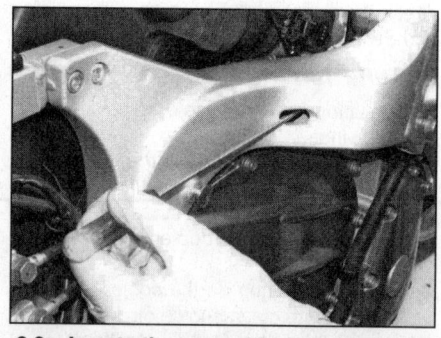

8.3a Locate the screwdriver and turn it to retract the plunger

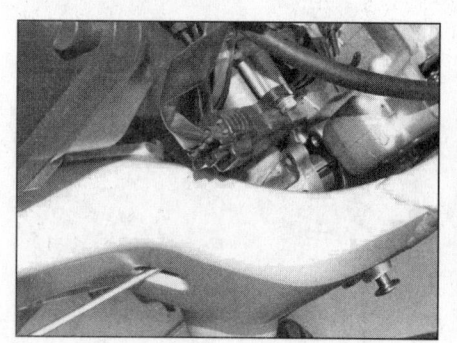

8.3b Draw the tensioner out...

8.3c ...then release the screwdriver and remove the tensioner

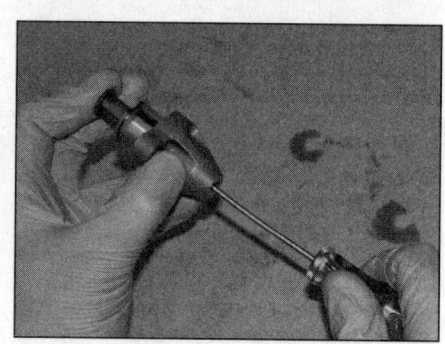

8.5 Check the tensioner as described

Engine, clutch and transmission 2•15

8.7 Fit the tensioner using a new gasket

body, then insert the mounting bolts **(see illustration)**.
8 Position the tensioner behind its bore with the arrow at the top, then fit the screwdriver through the frame and retract the plunger as in Step 3 **(see illustrations 8.3c and b)**. Fit the tensioner and tighten the bolts. Release and remove the screwdriver – you should hear the plunger spring out and take up the slack in the chain.

9 Fit the tensioner cap bolt with a new sealing washer and tighten it **(see illustration 8.2)**.
10 Check the valve timing position is correct, as described in Section 9, Step 4, and that the cam chain hasn't jumped a tooth on the sprockets whilst the tensioner was removed. Rotate the engine through two full turns and check the valve timing again.
11 Fit the rubber blanking cap **(see illustration 8.1)**. Install all remaining components.

9 Camshafts and followers

Removal

1 Remove the spark plugs (see Chapter 1).
2 Remove the valve cover (Section 7).
3 Remove the timing rotor cover (Section 14).
4 Using a spanner or socket on the timing rotor bolt and rotating in a clockwise direction only, turn the engine until the 'T' mark on the rotor faces to the rear and aligns with the crankcase mating surfaces, and the punch mark on each camshaft faces up in line with the arrow on the adjacent camshaft holder **(see illustrations)**. If the 'T' mark on the rotor is positioned correctly but the punch marks aren't, rotate the engine clockwise 360° (one full turn) so that the 'T' mark again faces back and aligns with the crankcase mating surfaces – the marks will now be aligned as described and the No. 1 cylinder will be at TDC (top dead centre) on the compression stroke.
5 If the engine is in the frame remove the rubber blanking cap from it **(see illustration 8.1)**. Remove the right-hand side cover (see Chapter 7). Unscrew the cam chain tensioner cap bolt and remove the sealing washer **(see illustration 8.2)**. Insert a small flat-bladed screwdriver through the hole in the frame and into the end of the tensioner so that it engages the slot in the rod **(see illustration 8.3a)**. Turn the screwdriver clockwise until it stops and secure it in this position as shown while removing and installing the camshafts **(see illustration)**. If the engine is out of the frame remove the cam chain tensioner (Section 8).

9.4a Turn the engine clockwise using the bolt...

9.4b ...until the T mark faces back in line with the crankcase surfaces (arrowed)...

9.4c ...and the punch marks (arrowed) are at the top

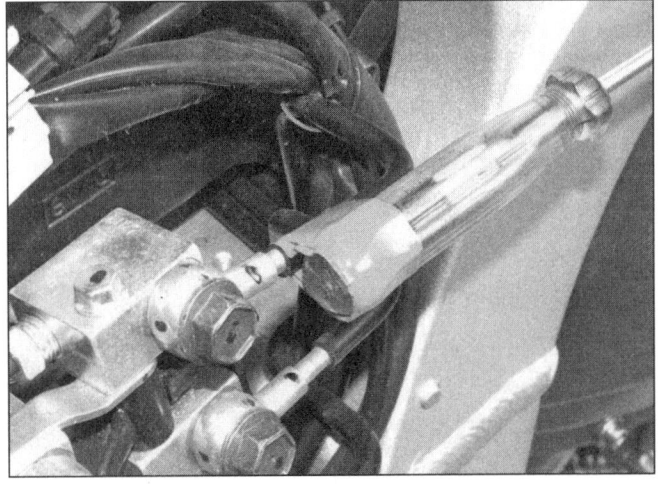

9.5 Secure the screwdriver handle using some tape so it cannot turn

2•16 Engine, clutch and transmission

9.6 Note the ID letter/number and directional arrow on each holder

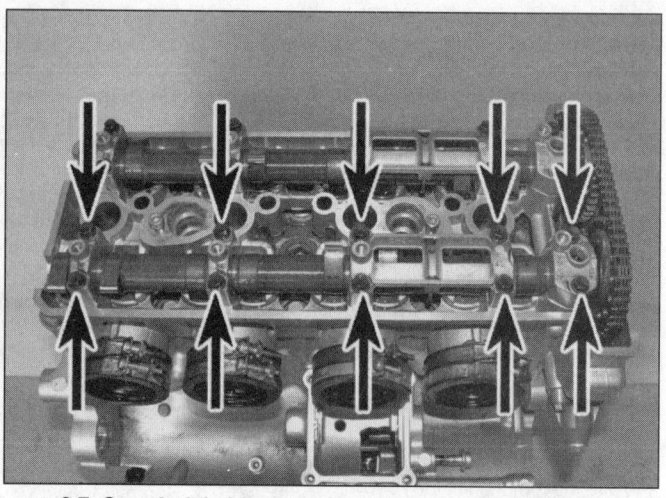

9.7 Camshaft holder bolts (arrowed) – intake camshaft

6 Before disturbing the camshafts and their holders, identify and note the timing and location marks. The intake camshaft holders are marked I1, I2, I3 and I from left to right and with the arrow on each pointing to the right-hand side of the engine. The exhaust camshaft holders are marked E1, E2, E3 and E from left to right and with the arrow on each pointing to the right-hand side of the engine **(see illustration)**. At TDC for No. 1 cylinder the punch mark on the lobe at the right-hand end faces up and aligns with the arrow on the I3 and E3 holders. The intake and exhaust camshafts and sprockets on all except 2013 models are identical; on 2013-on models the camshafts are different but the sprockets are identical. It is essential that each is refitted in its original place to ensure mated parts stay together, so mark each with an I or E according to its location. If you are in any doubt as to the alignment or position of any of the components, or if the described marks are not visible, make your own alignment marks between all components (including alignment marks between each shaft and its sprocket if the sprockets are being detached), and also between a tooth on each sprocket (including the timing sprocket on the crankshaft) and its corresponding link on the chain, before disturbing them. These markings ensure that the valve timing can be correctly set up on assembly. As it is easy to be a tooth out on installation, marking between a tooth on each sprocket and its link in the chain is especially useful.

7 Working on one camshaft at a time and starting with the intake shaft if removing both, unscrew the camshaft holder bolts evenly and a little at a time in a criss-cross pattern, starting from the outside and working towards the centre **(see illustration)**. Slacken the bolts above any cam lobes that are pressing onto a valve last in the sequence so that the pressure from the open valves cannot cause the camshaft to bend.

Caution: If the bolts are loosened carelessly and the holders do not come away from the head squarely, a holder is likely to break. If this happens the complete cylinder head assembly must be replaced with a new one as the holders are matched to the head and cannot be obtained separately. Also, the camshaft could be damaged if the holder bolts are not slackened evenly and the pressure from a depressed valve causes a shaft to bend.

8 Lift off the camshaft holders **(see illustration)**. Retrieve the dowels from either the holder or the cylinder head if they are loose.

9 Disengage the chain from the intake camshaft sprocket and lift the camshaft out of the head, then repeat for the exhaust camshaft **(see illustrations 9.30a and 9.29a)**. With both camshafts removed secure the cam chain to prevent it dropping into the crankcase, and avoid rotating the crankshaft in case the chain jams between the timing sprocket and the case.

10 If required remove the cam chain front guide blade, tensioner blade and cam chain (see Section 10).

11 If the followers and shims are being removed from the cylinder head, obtain a container which is divided into sixteen compartments, and label each compartment with the location of a valve, i.e. intake or exhaust camshaft, left or right valve. If a container is not available, use labelled plastic bags (egg cartons also do very well!). Remove the cam follower of the valve in question using a magnet or the suction created by a valve lapping tool, or long nosed pliers can be used with care **(see illustration 9.25b)**. Retrieve the shim either from the inside of the follower **(see illustration)**, or pick it out of the top of the valve spring retainer using either a magnet, a screwdriver with a dab of grease on it (the shim will stick to the grease), or a very small screwdriver and a pair of pliers **(see illustration 9.25a)**. Do not allow the shim to fall into the engine.

12 If required unscrew the sprocket bolts and take the sprockets off the camshafts **(see illustration)**. Both sprockets are identical

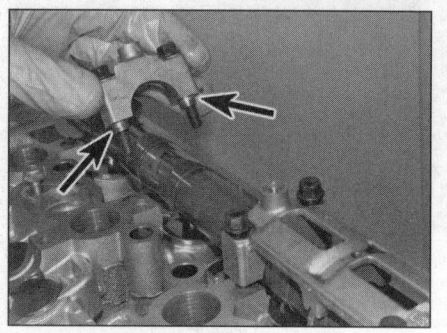

9.8 Remove the holders, noting the dowels (arrowed) where fitted

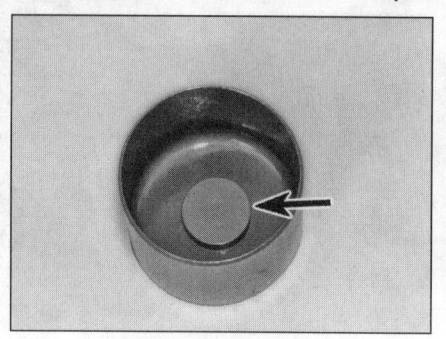

9.11 The shim (arrowed) usually sticks inside the follower

9.12 Remove the sprockets if required

Engine, clutch and transmission 2•17

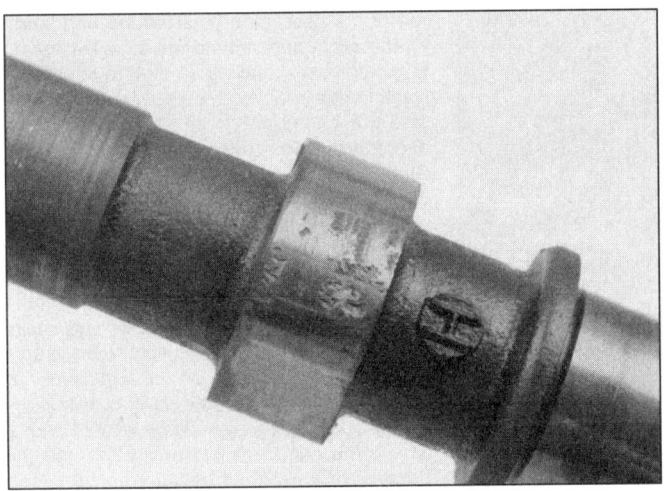

9.13 Check all related bearing surfaces for wear and damage

9.14 Checking camshaft lobe height

and are therefore interchangeable, so if not already done mark them according to their camshaft so they can be installed in their original position. Also make alignment marks between the sprocket and the camshaft so that the sprocket can be installed the correct way round to avoid confusion when setting up the timing.

Inspection

13 Inspect the bearing surfaces of the camshaft holders and cylinder heads and the corresponding journals and the lobes on the camshafts – look for score marks, deep scratches and evidence of spalling (a pitted appearance) **(see illustration)**. Check the oil passages for clogging.

14 Measure the height of each lobe with a micrometer **(see illustration)** and compare the results to the minimum height listed in this Chapter's Specifications. If damage is noted or wear is excessive, the camshaft must be replaced with a new one.

15 Check the amount of camshaft runout by supporting each end on V-blocks, and measuring any runout using a dial gauge. If the runout exceeds the specified limit the camshaft must be replaced with a new one.

> **HAYNES HiNT** *Refer to Tools and Workshop Tips in the Reference section for details of how to read a micrometer and dial gauge.*

16 Next, check the camshaft journal oil clearances. In order to negate the probability of the camshafts rotating (due to the fact that some of the lobes will be depressing their valves) as the holder bolts are tightened down, which will disturb the Plastigauge and lead to a false measurement, the valves should be removed from the cylinder head (if the cylinder head is being fully checked and overhauled due to wear you will be doing this anyway). To do this the head must be removed (see Sections 11 and 12). Clean the camshafts and the bearing surfaces in the cylinder head and camshaft holder with a clean lint-free cloth, then lay each camshaft in its correct location in the cylinder head (see Step 6).

17 Cut some strips of Plastigauge and lay one piece on each journal, parallel with the camshaft centreline **(see illustration)**. Make sure the camshaft holder dowels are installed **(see illustration 9.8)**. Fit the holders and tighten the bolts as described in Step 32. While doing this, don't let the camshafts rotate, or the Plastigauge will be disturbed and you will have to start again.

18 Now unscrew the camshaft holder bolts as described in Step 7, and lift off the holders.

19 To determine the oil clearance, compare the crushed Plastigauge (at its widest point) on each journal to the scale printed on the Plastigauge container **(see illustration)**. Compare the results to this Chapter's Specifications. If the oil clearance is greater than specified, measure the diameter of the camshaft journal with a micrometer. If it is within specifications, replace the cylinder head and camshaft holders with new ones (they come as a matched set). If the journal diameter is less than the specified limit, replace the camshaft with a new one and recheck the clearance. If the clearance is still too great, also replace the cylinder head and camshaft holders.

> **HAYNES HiNT** *Before replacing the camshafts or cylinder head and holders because of damage, check with motorcycle cylinder head specialists to see whether worn components can be renewed. Due to the cost of new components it is recommended that all options be explored before condemning them as trash!*

20 Except in cases of oil starvation, the cam chain should wear very little. If the chain has stretched excessively, which makes it difficult to maintain proper tension, or if it is stiff or the links are binding or kinking, replace it with a new one. Refer to Section 10 for replacement.

21 Check the sprockets for wear, cracks and other damage, and replace them with new ones if necessary (see Steps 12 and 24). If the sprockets are worn, the cam chain is also worn, and so probably is the sprocket on the crankshaft. If severe wear is apparent, the entire engine should be disassembled for inspection.

22 Inspect the cam chain guides and tensioner blade (see Section 10).

9.17 Plastigauge strip on journal

9.19 Measuring the crushed strip

2•18 Engine, clutch and transmission

9.25a Fit the shim into its recess...

9.25b ...then fit the follower

23 Inspect the outer surface of each cam follower for evidence of scoring or other damage. If a follower is in poor condition, it is probable that the bore in the cylinder head in which it works is also damaged.

Installation

24 If removed, fit the sprockets onto the camshafts. Make sure they are the correct way round and in their original location as shown and as identified by the marks made on removal (Step 12) **(see illustration 9.12)**. Clean the threads of the bolts and apply a suitable non-permanent thread locking compound, and tighten them to the torque setting specified at the beginning of the Chapter.

25 If removed, lubricate each shim with molybdenum disulphide oil (a 50/50 mixture of molybdenum disulphide grease and engine oil) and fit it into its recess on the top of the valve, with the size marking on the shim facing up **(see illustration)**. Make sure the shim is correctly seated, then lubricate each follower with molybdenum disulphide oil and fit it into its bore **(see illustration)**. **Note:** *It is most important that the shims and followers are returned to their original valves, otherwise the valve clearances will be inaccurate.*

26 Make sure the camshaft journals and the bearing surfaces in the cylinder head are clean, then apply molybdenum disulphide oil to them and to the camshaft lobes.

27 If removed, install the cam chain, the tensioner blade and the front guide blade (see Section 10).

28 Check that the 'T' mark on the timing rotor still faces back and aligns with the crankcase mating surfaces (see Step 4) **(see illustration 9.4b)**.

29 Fit the exhaust camshaft, with the punch mark on the right-hand end lobe facing up and the arrows on the sprocket parallel with the top of the head **(see illustrations and 9.4c)**. Fit the cam chain around the sprocket as you fit the camshaft, pulling up on it to remove all slack in the front run between the crankshaft and the camshaft. If you made your own alignment marks prior to disassembly (see Step 6), check that they align.

30 Now fit the intake camshaft, with the punch mark on the right-hand end lobe facing up and the lines on the sprocket parallel with the top of the head **(see illustrations and 9.4c)**. Fit the cam chain around the sprocket, aligning the marks (if made) between sprocket and chain. When fitting the chain, pull it tight to make sure there is no slack between the two camshaft sprockets – any slack in the chain must lie in the rear run, so that it is taken up by the tensioner.

31 Fit the camshaft holder dowels into the holders or cylinder head if removed **(see illustration 9.8)**. Make sure the bearing surfaces in the holders are clean, then lubricate them with molybdenum disulphide oil.

32 Clean the holder bolts, then lubricate the threads and under the heads with clean engine oil and fit them into the holders. Fit the holders in their correct position and way round (see Step 6). Tighten the bolts evenly and a little at a time in a criss-cross pattern, working from the centre of the head outwards (i.e. starting with the bolts that are above valves that will be opened when the camshafts are tightened down), to the torque setting specified at the beginning of this Chapter. Whilst tightening the bolts, make sure each holder is being pulled down squarely and is not binding on the dowels.

Caution: *The camshaft holder is likely to break if it is not tightened down evenly and squarely and the camshaft is likely to bend if it is tightened down onto the closed valves before the open ones.*

33 Using a piece of wooden dowel, press on the back of the cam chain tensioner blade via the tensioner bore in the cylinder head to take up any slack in the cam chain. Check that all the timing marks are still in **exact** alignment as described in Steps 4 and 6. If it is necessary to turn the engine slightly to align the marks with the engine mating surfaces keep the wooden dowel pressed onto the tensioner blade. Note that it is easy to be slightly out (by one tooth on a sprocket) without the marks appearing drastically out of alignment.

34 If the timing marks are out, unscrew the sprocket's bolts and slide it off the camshaft, then disengage it from the chain. Move the camshaft round as required, then fit the sprocket back into the chain and onto the camshaft, and check the marks again. With everything correctly aligned, clean the sprocket bolts and apply a suitable non-permanent thread locking compound, and tighten them to the torque setting specified at the beginning of the Chapter.

Caution: *If the marks are not aligned exactly as described, the valve timing will be incorrect and the valves may strike the pistons, causing extensive damage to the engine.*

9.29a Fit the exhaust camshaft...

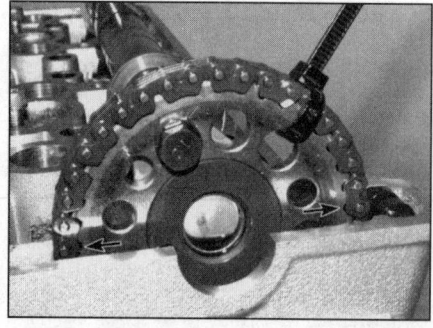

9.29b ...aligning the arrows with head

9.30a Fit the intake camshaft...

9.30b ...aligning the lines with head

Engine, clutch and transmission 2•19

35 With everything correctly aligned, release the screwdriver holding the cam chain tensioner and fit the cap bolt using a new sealing washer, or install the tensioner, as required (see Section 8). Turn the engine clockwise through two full turns and check again that all the timing marks still align (see Steps 4 and 6).
36 Check the valve clearances and adjust them if necessary (see Chapter 1).
37 Install the timing rotor cover (Section 14).
38 Install the valve cover (Section 7).
39 Install the spark plugs (see Chapter 1).

10 Cam chain, tensioner blade and guides

Tensioner blade and guides

1 Remove the valve cover (see Section 7), the timing rotor cover (see Section 14) and retract or remove the cam chain tensioner (see Section 9, Step 5, or Section 8, as required). The cam chain top guide is fixed in the valve cover and should not be removed.
2 Remove the camshafts (see Section 9).
3 Draw the front guide blade out of the top of the engine, noting which way round it fits **(see illustration)**.
4 Withdraw the pivot pin from the bottom of the tensioner blade, then draw the blade out of the top of the engine, noting which way round it fits **(see illustration)**.
5 Check the sliding surfaces of the tensioner blade and guides for excessive wear, deep grooves, cracking and other obvious damage, and replace them with new ones if necessary.
6 Installation is the reverse of removal. Apply some clean engine oil to the tensioner blade pivot pin. Make sure the guide blade seats correctly **(see illustrations)**.

Cam chain

7 Remove the front guide blade and tensioner blade (Steps 1 to 4). Remove the timing rotor (Section 14).

10.3 Lift the guide blade out

8 Disengage the cam chain and draw it out of the engine **(see illustration)**.
9 Except in cases of oil starvation, the cam chain wears very little. If the chain is stiff or the links are binding, or if the links are loose, discard the chain. A chain in poor condition will wear the sprocket teeth and ideally the chain and sprockets should be replaced as a set.
10 Installation is the reverse of removal.

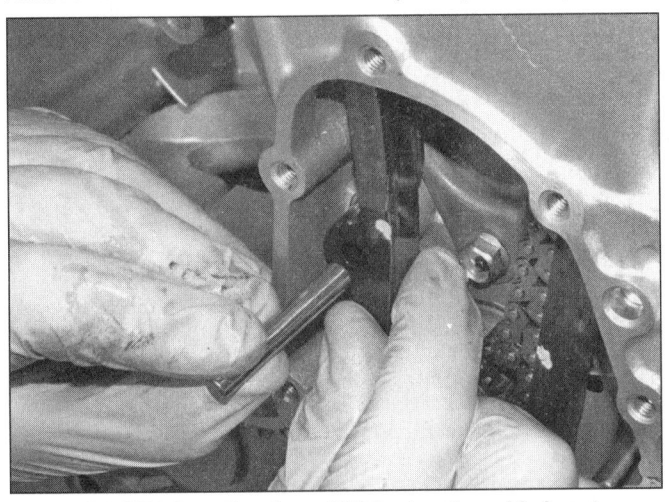

10.4 Withdraw the pin and lift the tensioner blade out

10.6a Locate the bottom end in its seat...

10.6b ...and the top end in the cut-outs

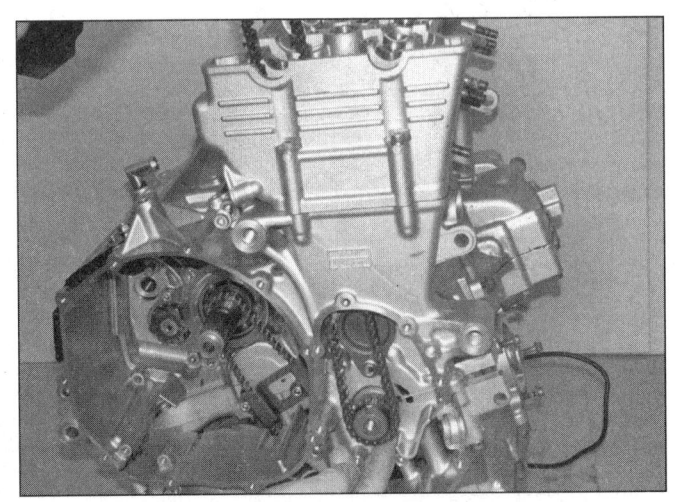

10.8 Slip the chain off the sprocket and remove it

2•20 Engine, clutch and transmission

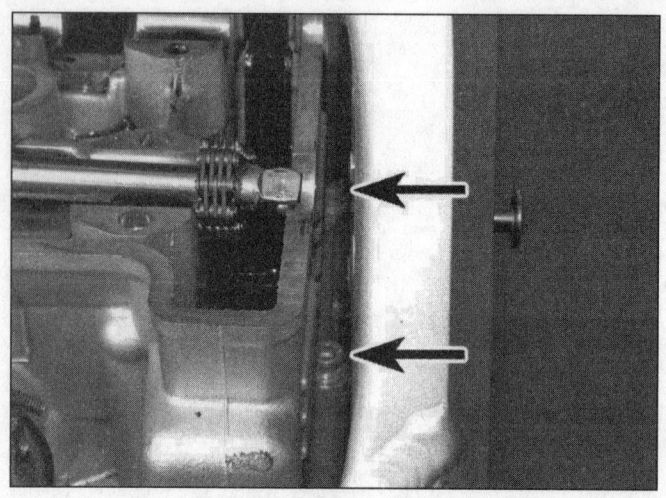

11.4a Cylinder head 6 mm bolts (arrowed)

11.4b Use a hex key and spanner if the engine is in the frame

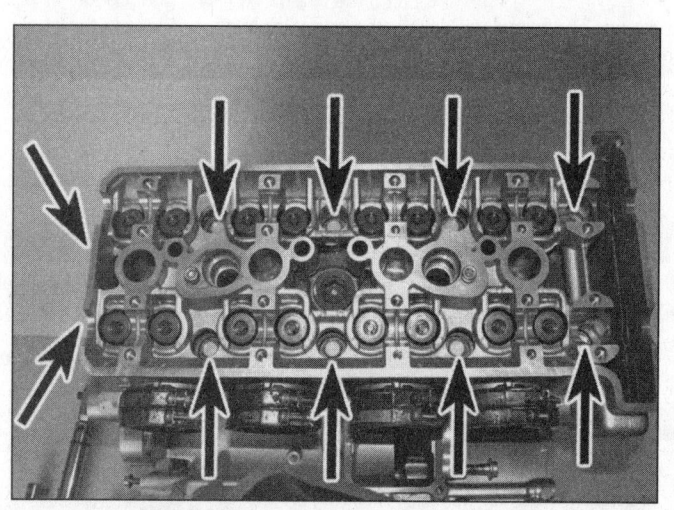

11.4c Cylinder head 10 mm bolts (arrowed)

11.5 Carefully lift the head up off the block

11 Cylinder head – removal and installation

Note: *New cylinder head bolts must be used when installing the head – it is best to order them in advance.*
Special tool: *A torque wrench and degree disc are needed.*

Removal

1 Remove the exhaust system and the throttle bodies (see Chapter 4).
2 Remove the valve cover (see Section 7).
3 Remove the camshafts, followers and shims (see Section 9).
4 The cylinder head is secured by two 6 mm bolts and ten 10 mm bolts with fitted washers (i.e. they can't be separated from the bolts). First unscrew the 6 mm bolts **(see illustration)** – if the engine is in the frame use a standard Allen key with a spanner on the end as shown **(see illustration)**, and remove the rear bolt, you can't remove the front bolt yet as the frame is in the way so leave it loose until the head has been removed. Now unscrew and remove the 10 mm bolts, slackening them evenly and a little at a time in a criss-cross pattern working from the outside to the middle until they are all loose **(see illustration)**. Note the bolts are stretch-type and can only be used once – new bolts must be used when installing the head.
5 Pull the cylinder head up off the block and pass the cam chain down through the tunnel, laying it over the front of the engine **(see illustration)**. If the head is stuck, tap around the joint faces with a soft-faced mallet. Do not attempt to free the head by inserting a screwdriver between the head and block mating surfaces – you'll damage them.
6 Remove the cylinder head gasket and discard it as a new one must be used **(see illustration 11.10)**. Remove the dowels from the cylinder block or the underside of the cylinder head if loose.
7 Check the cylinder head gasket and the mating surfaces on the cylinder head and block for signs of leakage, which could indicate warpage. Refer to Section 12 and check the cylinder head gasket surface for warpage.
8 Clean all traces of old gasket material from the cylinder head and block. If a scraper is used, take care not to scratch or gouge the soft aluminium. Be careful not to let any of the gasket material fall into the crankcase, the cylinder bore or the oil and coolant passages.

Installation

9 If removed, fit the dowels into the block **(see illustration 11.10)**. If the engine is in the frame fit one of the 6 mm bolts into the front hole in the right-hand side of the head.
10 Ensure both cylinder head and block mating surfaces are clean. Lay the new head gasket onto the block, locating it over the

Engine, clutch and transmission 2•21

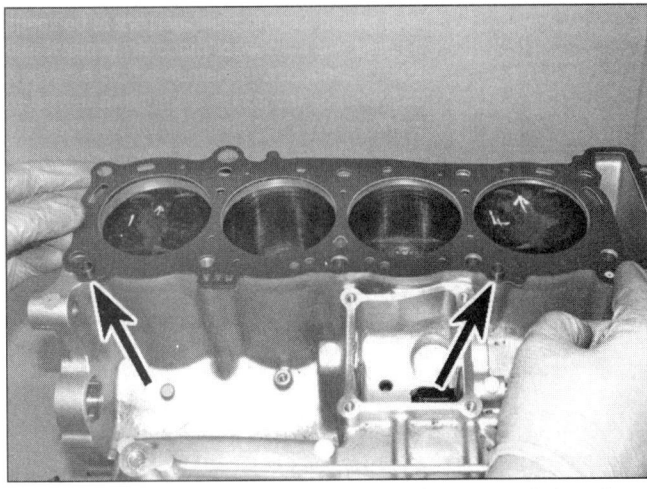

11.10 Fit the dowels (arrowed) then lay the new gasket on the cylinder

11.12 Lubricate the new bolts where described

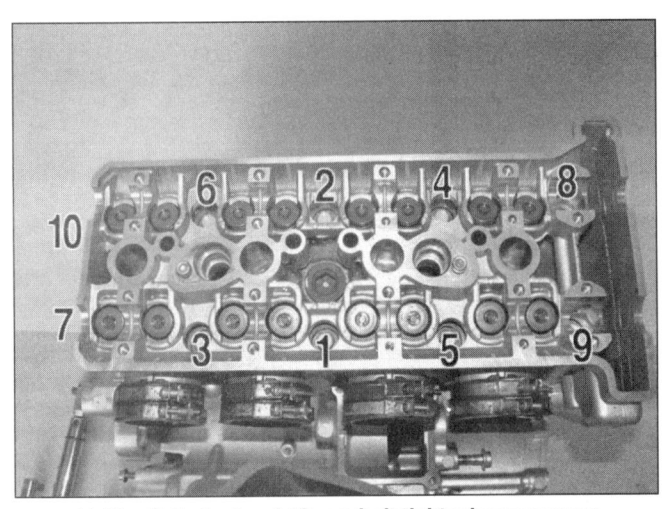

11.13a Cylinder head 10 mm bolt tightening sequence

11.13b Using a degree disc to angle-tighten the bolts

dowels and making sure all the holes are correctly aligned **(see illustration)**. Never reuse the old gasket.

11 Carefully fit the cylinder head onto the block, feeding the cam chain up the tunnel, and making sure the head locates correctly onto the dowels **(see illustration 11.5)**. Secure the chain to prevent it from falling back down.

12 Apply some engine oil to the threads and the seating surfaces of the heads and washers of all the 10 mm bolts, making sure you use new ones **(see illustration)**. Fit the bolts and tighten them all finger-tight.

13 The bolts must be tightened in four stages as follows: first, tighten them in the numerical sequence shown to the torque setting specified at the beginning of the Chapter **(see illustration)**. Second, loosen all the bolts in a reverse of the numerical sequence. Third, re-tighten them in the numerical sequence to the specified torque setting. Fourth, using a degree disc if available, tighten the bolts in the numerical sequence and in one go through 180° or ½ a turn **(see illustration)**. If you inadvertently tighten through more than the specified angle do not loosen the bolt off and retighten it – remove the bolt, replace it with a new one and repeat the four stage tightening sequence.

14 Tighten the 6 mm bolts to the specified torque setting **(see illustration)**.

15 Install the remaining components in a

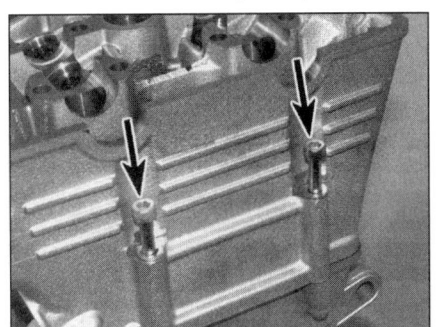

11.14 Tighten the 6 mm bolts (arrowed)

reverse of their removal sequence, referring to the relevant Sections or Chapters (see Steps 3 to 1).

12 Cylinder head and valves – overhaul

Special tool: A valve spring compressor is needed.

1 Because of the complex nature of this job and the special tools and equipment required, most owners leave servicing of the valves, valve seats and valve guides to a professional. However, you can make an initial assessment of whether the valves are seating correctly, and therefore sealing, by pouring a small amount of solvent into each of the valve ports. If the solvent leaks past any valve into the combustion chamber area the valve is not seating correctly and sealing.

2 With the correct tools (a valve spring compressor is essential – make sure it is

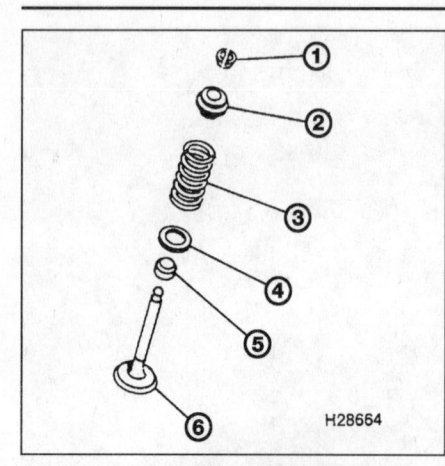

2•22 Engine, clutch and transmission

12.5 Valve components

1. Collets
2. Spring retainer
3. Spring
4. Spring seat
5. Valve stem oil seal
6. Valve

suitable for motorcycle work), you can also remove the valves and associated components from the cylinder head, clean them and check them for wear to assess the extent of the work needed, and, unless seat cutting or guide replacement is required, grind in the valves and reassemble them in the head.

3 A dealer service department or specialist can replace the guides and re-cut the valve seats.

4 After the valve service has been performed, be sure to clean it very thoroughly before installation on the engine to remove any metal particles or abrasive grit that may still be present from the valve service operations. Use compressed air, if available, to blow out all the holes and passages.

Disassembly

5 Before proceeding, arrange to label and store the valves along with their related components in such a way that they can be returned to their original locations without getting mixed up **(see illustration)**.

6 Compress the valve spring on the first valve with a spring compressor, making sure it is correctly located onto each end of the valve assembly **(see illustration)**. On the top of the valve the adaptor needs to be about the same size as the spring retainer – if it is too big it will contact the follower bore and mark it, and if it is too small it will be difficult to remove and install the collets **(see illustration)**. On the underside of the head make sure the plate (where present) on the compressor only contacts the valve and not the soft aluminium of the head **(see illustration)** – if the plate is too big for the valve, use a spacer between them. Do not compress the springs any more than is absolutely necessary.

Caution: Take great care not to mark the cam follower bore with the spring compressor.

7 Remove the collets, using a magnet or a screwdriver with a dab of grease on it **(see illustration)**. Carefully release the valve spring compressor and remove the spring retainer, noting which way up it fits, the spring and the valve **(see illustrations)**. If the valve binds in the guide and won't pull through, push it back

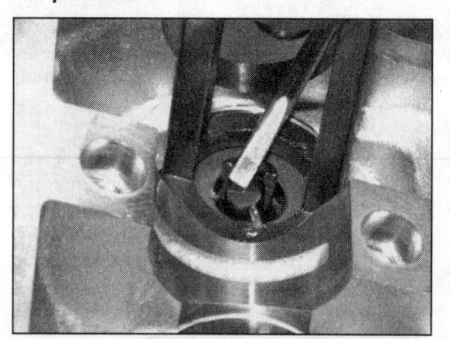

12.6a Compressing the valve springs using a valve spring compressor

12.6b Make sure the compressor locates correctly both on the top of the spring retainer...

12.6c ...and on the bottom of the valve

12.7a Remove the collets...

12.7b ...the spring retainer...

12.7c ...the spring...

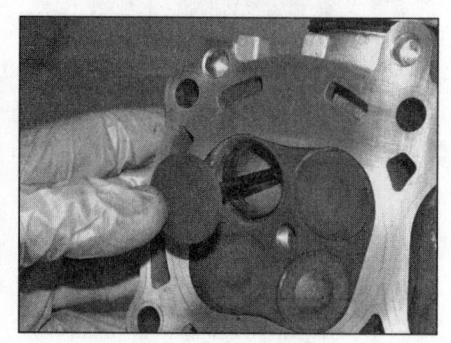

12.7d ...and the valve

> **HAYNES HINT**
>
> There is a quick way of removing valve components that avoids having to use a spring compressor: select a socket that seats on the valve retainer and give it a sharp tap with a soft hammer – this compresses the spring without moving the valve itself and unseats the collets. Note that a valve spring compressor has to be used when refitting the valve assembly.

Engine, clutch and transmission 2•23

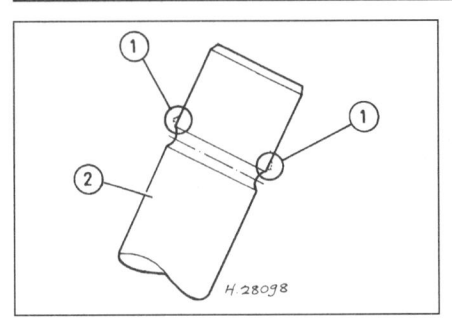

12.7e If the valve stem (2) won't pull through the guide, deburr the area (1) above the collet groove

12.8a Pull the seal off the valve stem...

12.8b ...then remove the spring seat

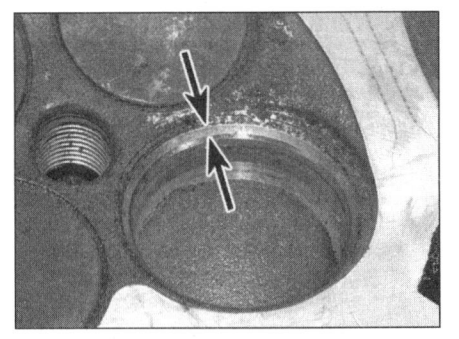

12.15 Measure the valve seat width

12.16a Measure the valve stem diameter with a micrometer

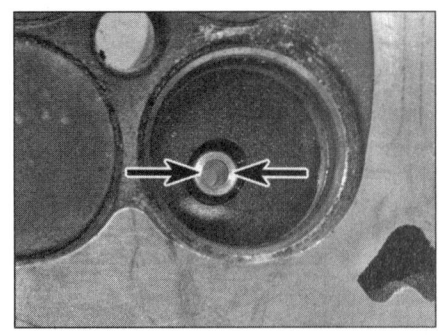

12.16b Measure the valve guide with a small bore gauge, then measure the bore gauge with a micrometer

into the head and deburr the area around the collet groove with a very fine file or whetstone **(see illustration)**.

8 Pull the valve stem seal off the top of the valve guide with pliers and discard it (the old seals should never be reused), then remove the spring seat noting which way up, it fits – using a magnet is the easiest way to remove the seat from the head **(see illustrations)**.

9 Repeat the procedure for the remaining valves. Remember to keep the parts for each valve together so they can be reinstalled in the same location.

10 Clean the cylinder head with solvent and dry it thoroughly. Compressed air will speed the drying process and ensure that all holes and recessed areas are clean. **Note:** *Do not use a wire brush mounted in a drill motor to clean the combustion chambers as the head material is soft and may be scratched or eroded away by the wire brush.*

11 Clean all of the valve springs, collets, retainers and spring seats with solvent and dry them thoroughly. Do the parts from one valve at a time so that no mixing of parts between valves occurs.

12 Scrape off any deposits that may have formed on the valve, then use a motorised wire brush to remove deposits from the valve heads and stems. Again, make sure the valves do not get mixed up.

Inspection

13 Inspect the head very carefully for cracks and other damage. If cracks are found, a new head is required. Check the camshaft bearing surfaces for wear and evidence of seizure. Check the camshafts and holders for wear as well (see Section 9).

14 Using a precision straight-edge and a feeler gauge set to the warpage limit listed in the specifications at the beginning of the Chapter, check the head gasket mating surface for warpage. Refer to *Tools and Workshop Tips* in the Reference section for details of how to use the straight-edge. If the head is warped beyond the limit specified at the beginning of this Chapter, consult a Yamaha dealer or take it to a specialist repair shop for an opinion, though be prepared to have to buy a new one.

15 Examine the valve seats in the combustion chamber. If they are pitted, cracked or burned, the head will require work beyond the scope of the home mechanic. Measure the valve seat width and compare it to this Chapter's Specifications **(see illustration)**. If it's outside of the specification or if it varies around its circumference, overhaul is required.

16 Working on one valve and guide at a time, measure the valve stem diameter **(see illustration)**. Clean the valve's guide using a guide reamer to remove any carbon build-up – insert the reamer from the underside of the head and turn it clockwise only. Now measure the inside diameter of the guide (at both ends and in the centre of the guide) with a small bore gauge, then measure the gauge with a micrometer **(see illustration)**. Measure the guide at the ends and at the centre to determine if they are worn in a bell-mouth pattern (more wear at the ends). Subtract the stem diameter from the valve guide diameter to obtain the valve stem-to-guide clearance. If the stem-to-guide clearance is greater than listed in this Chapter's Specifications, replace whichever component is beyond its specification limits with a new one. If the valve guide is within specifications, but is worn unevenly, it should be replaced with a new one. Repeat for the other valves.

17 Carefully inspect each valve face, stem and collet groove area for cracks, pits and burned spots.

18 Measure the various aspects of the valve head and compare them with the listed specifications **(see illustration)**. If the valve is worn it should be replaced with a new one.

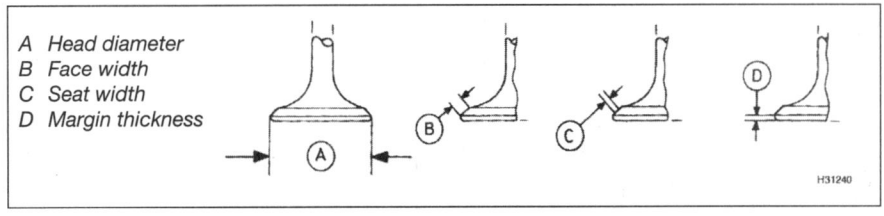

A Head diameter
B Face width
C Seat width
D Margin thickness

12.18 Valve head measurement points

2•24 Engine, clutch and transmission

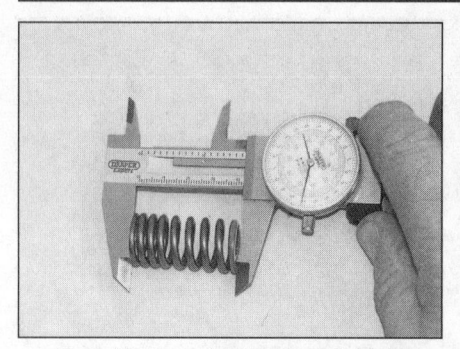

12.20 Measure the free length of the spring

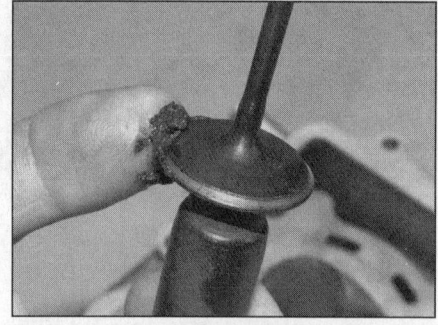

12.24 Apply dabs of paste around the valve face

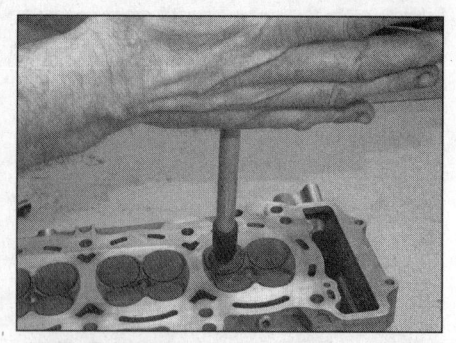

12.25 Rotate the valve grinding tool back and forth between the palms of your hands

19 Rotate the valve and check for any obvious indication that it is bent, in which case it must be replaced with a new one. Check the end of the stem for pitting and excessive wear. The presence of any of the above conditions indicates the need for valve servicing.

20 Check the end of each valve spring for wear and pitting. Measure the spring free lengths and compare them to the specifications **(see illustration)**. If any spring is shorter than specified it has sagged and must be replaced with a new one. Also place the spring upright on a flat surface and check it for bend by placing a ruler against it, or alternatively lay it against a set-square. If the bend in any spring is excessive, it must be replaced with a new one.

21 Check the spring seats, retainers and collets for obvious wear and cracks. Any questionable parts should not be reused, as extensive damage will occur in the event of failure during engine operation.

22 If the inspection indicates that no overhaul work is required, the valve components can be reinstalled in the head.

Reassembly

23 Unless a valve service has been performed, before installing the valves they should be ground in (lapped) to ensure a positive seal between the valves and seats. This procedure requires coarse and fine valve grinding compound and a valve grinding tool (either hand-held or drill driven – note that some drill-driven tools specify using only a fine grinding compound). If a grinding tool is not available, a piece of rubber or plastic hose can be slipped over the valve stem (after the valve has been installed in the guide) and used to turn the valve.

24 Apply a small amount of coarse grinding compound to the valve face **(see illustration)**. Smear some molybdenum disulphide oil (a 50/50 mixture of molybdenum disulphide grease and engine oil) to the valve stem, then slip the valve into the guide **(see illustration 12.7d)**. Note: *Make sure each valve is installed in its correct guide and be careful not to get any grinding compound on the valve stem.*

25 Attach the grinding tool to the valve and rotate the tool between the palms of your hands. Use a back-and-forth motion (as though rubbing your hands together) rather than a circular motion (i.e. so that the valve rotates alternately clockwise and anti-clockwise rather than in one direction only) **(see illustration)**. If a motorised tool is being used, take note of the correct drive speed for it – if your drill runs too fast and is not variable, use a hand tool instead. Lift the valve off the seat and turn it at regular intervals to distribute the grinding compound properly. Continue the grinding procedure until the valve face and seat contact area is of uniform width, and unbroken around the entire circumference.

26 Carefully remove the valve and wipe off all traces of grinding compound, making sure none gets in the guide. Use solvent to clean the valve and wipe the seat area thoroughly with a solvent soaked cloth.

27 Repeat the procedure with fine valve grinding compound, then use solvent to clean the valve and flush the guide, and wipe the seat area thoroughly with a solvent soaked cloth. Repeat the entire procedure for the remaining valves. On completion thoroughly clean the entire head again, then blow through all passages with compressed air. Make sure all traces of the grinding compound have been removed before assembling the head.

28 Working on one valve at a time, lay the spring seat in place in the cylinder head with its shouldered side facing up **(see illustration 12.8b)**. As it is easy to cock the seat on the top of the valve guide, and then tricky to get it to sit properly, fit it using a rod (such as a screwdriver) as a guide for it to slide down.

29 Fit a new valve stem seal onto the guide, again using a guide to locate it, then use finger pressure, a stem seal fitting tool or an appropriate size deep socket to push the seal squarely onto the end of the valve guide until it is felt to clip into place **(see illustration)**. Make sure the seal does not get cocked sideways as it could be damaged.

30 Coat the valve stem with molybdenum disulphide oil (a 50/50 mixture of molybdenum disulphide grease and engine oil), then slide it into its guide, rotating it slowly to avoid damaging the seal **(see illustration 12.7d)**. Check that the valve moves up-and-down freely in the guide.

31 Next, fit the spring, with the closer-wound coils facing down into the cylinder head **(see illustration 12.7c)**. Fit the spring retainer, with its shouldered side facing down so that it fits into the top of the spring **(see illustration 12.7b)**.

32 Apply a small amount of grease to the collets to help hold them in place. Compress the valve spring with a spring compressor, making sure it is correctly located onto each end of the valve assembly (see Step 6) **(see illustrations 12.6a, b and c)**. Do not compress the spring any more than is necessary to slip the collets into place. Locate each collet in turn into the groove in the valve stem using a screwdriver with a dab of grease on it **(see illustration)**. Carefully release the compressor, making sure the collets seat and lock in the retaining groove.

33 Repeat the procedure for the remaining valves. Remember to keep the parts for each

12.29 Fit a new valve stem seal and press it squarely into place

12.32 Locate each collet in its groove in the top of the valve stem

Engine, clutch and transmission 2•25

valve together and separate from the other valves so they can be reinstalled in the same location.

34 Support the cylinder head on blocks so the valves can't contact the work surface, then tap the end of each valve stem lightly to seat the collets in their grooves (see illustration).

> **HAYNES HiNT** *Check for proper sealing of the valves by pouring a small amount of solvent into each of the valve ports. If the solvent leaks past any valve into the combustion chamber the valve grinding operation on that valve should be repeated.*

35 After the cylinder head and camshaft have been installed, set the valve clearances (see Chapter 1).

13 Alternator rotor and starter clutch

Check

1 The operation of the starter clutch can be checked while it is in situ. Remove the starter motor (see Chapter 8). Check that the starter idle/reduction gear is able to rotate freely clockwise as you look at it via the starter motor aperture, but locks when rotated anti-clockwise (see illustration). If not, the starter clutch is faulty and should be removed for inspection.

Removal

Special tool: *A rotor holding strap and rotor puller will be required (see Steps 7 and 8).*

2 Remove the left-hand fairing side panel (see Chapter 7). On 2006 to 2012 models, note that to remove the alternator cover or stator completely you'll need to remove the air filter housing in order to feed the wiring back from the regulator/rectifier. This does however involve a lot of work, so if you can get away with just displacing the cover and supporting it to one side to gain access to the rotor/starter clutch then do so – to remove the air filter housing refer to Chapter 4. The stator is covered in Chapter 8.

3 Place the bike on the centrestand. Either drain the engine oil (see Chapter 1), or place a container under the engine to catch the oil that will come out when the cover is removed.

4 If you want to remove the alternator cover or stator completely, disconnect the alternator 3-pin wiring connector with the three white wires (see illustration 4.16a or b). Feed the wiring to the alternator cover, releasing it from the guides and noting its routing.

5 Working in a criss-cross pattern, evenly slacken the alternator cover bolts, noting the wiring guides, and the position of the shorter bolt (see illustration). Draw the cover off the engine, noting that it will be restrained by the force of the rotor magnets, and be prepared to catch any residual oil. Remove the gasket – a new one must be used on installation. Remove the dowels from either the cover or the crankcase if they are loose (see illustration 13.21a).

6 Withdraw the idle/reduction gear shaft from the crankcase and remove the gear, noting which way round it fits (see illustration).

7 To remove the rotor bolt it is necessary to stop the rotor from turning, using either the Yamaha rotor strap (part No. 90890-01701) or a commercially available equivalent (see illustration 13.19c). With the rotor held unscrew the bolt and remove the washer – note the bolt is very tight. Remove the wire piece from the bolt (see illustration 13.19a).

8 To remove the rotor from the shaft it is necessary to use a rotor puller – use either

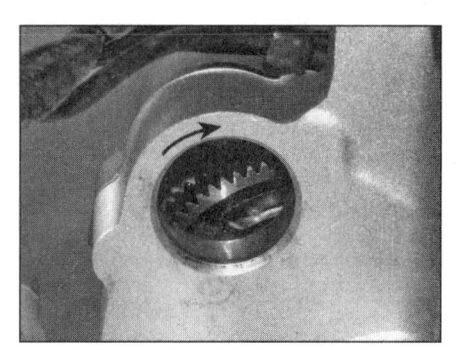

12.34a Seat the collets as described...

12.34b ...and check they are as shown

13.1 Check the starter clutch by turning the idle/reduction gear as described

13.5 Alternator cover bolts (arrowed)

13.6 Withdraw the shaft and remove the gear

2•26 Engine, clutch and transmission

13.8a Commercial equivalent to Yamaha's puller shown threaded into rotor holes – note the socket between the puller bolt and the crankshaft to protect the crank end as the bolt turns

13.8b Hold the rotor using the strap and turn the puller bolt

13.8c Withdraw the Woodruff key (arrowed)

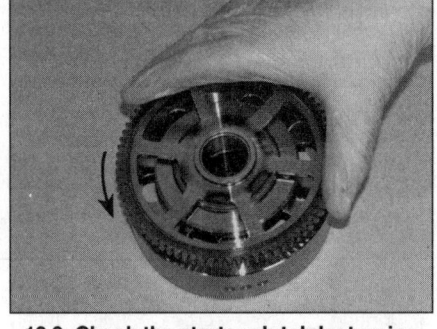

13.9 Check the starter clutch by turning the driven gear as described

13.10 Withdraw the driven gear

the Yamaha tool (part No. 90890-01362) or a commercially available equivalent designed for this bike **(see illustration)**. Fit the puller onto the rotor and turn it until the rotor is displaced from the shaft, holding the rotor to prevent the engine turning **(see illustration)**. If the rotor doesn't come off easily tap the end of the tool when it is tight, and if necessary heat the rotor hub using a hot air gun. Remove the Woodruff key from its slot in the crankshaft if loose **(see illustration)**.

Inspection and disassembly

9 With the alternator rotor face down on a workbench, check that the starter driven gear rotates freely when turned anti-clockwise and locks against the rotor clockwise **(see illustration)**. If it doesn't, the starter clutch should be dismantled for further investigation.
10 Withdraw the starter driven gear from the starter clutch **(see illustration)**. If the gear appears stuck, turn it anti-clockwise as you withdraw it to free it from the starter clutch.
11 Check the condition of the sprags inside the clutch body and the corresponding surface on the driven gear hub **(see illustration)**. If they are damaged, marked or flattened at any point, they should be replaced with new ones. To remove the sprag assembly, hold the rotor using a strap and unscrew the bolts inside it **(see illustration)**. Remove the sprag assembly from the rotor, noting how it fits. Install the sprag assembly in a reverse sequence. Apply clean engine oil to the sprags. Clean the bolts and apply a suitable non-permanent thread locking compound and tighten them to the torque setting specified at the beginning of the Chapter.
12 Check the bush in the starter driven gear and its corresponding surface on the crankshaft **(see illustration)**. If the bush has

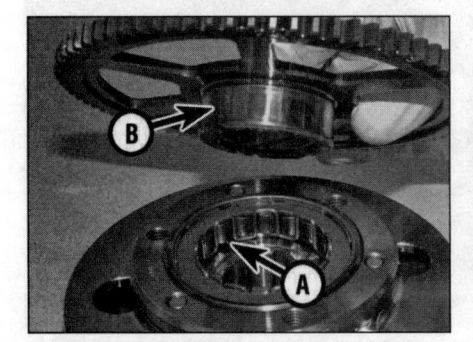

13.11a Check the sprag (A) and hub (B) mating surfaces

13.11b Sprag assembly bolts (arrowed)

13.12 Check the grooves (arrowed) for wear

Engine, clutch and transmission 2•27

13.18 Align the groove with the key and slide the rotor on

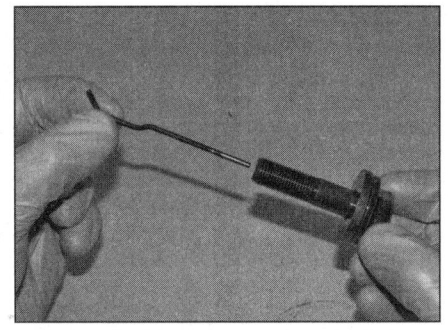

13.19a Fit the wire piece into the bolt...

13.19b ...then fit the bolt with its washer...

worn so the oil retention grooves are very shallow or no longer distinguishable replace the driven gear with a new one.

13 Check the teeth of the starter motor drive shaft, idle/reduction gear and starter driven gear. Replace the gears and/or starter motor if worn or chipped teeth are discovered on related gears. Also check the idle/reduction gear shaft for damage, and check that the gear is not a loose fit on the shaft.

Installation

14 Clean all traces of old gasket off the cover and crankcase mating surfaces and wipe them with a suitable solvent.
15 Clean the tapered end of the crankshaft and the corresponding mating surface on the inside of the rotor with a suitable solvent. Fit the Woodruff key into its slot in the crankshaft if removed **(see illustration 13.8c)**.
16 If separated, fit the starter clutch onto the back of the rotor (Step 11).
17 Fit the starter driven gear into the starter clutch, turning it anti-clockwise as you do **(see illustration 13.10)**.
18 Make sure that no metal objects have attached themselves to the magnet on the inside of the rotor. Slide the rotor onto the shaft, making sure the groove on the inside is aligned with and fits over the Woodruff key, and the key does not dislodge **(see illustration)**.
19 Apply some clean oil to the rotor bolt threads, the underside of the head, and the washer. Fit the wire piece into the bolt **(see illustration)**. Fit the bolt with its washer and tighten it to the torque setting specified at the beginning of the Chapter, holding the rotor as on removal **(see illustrations)**.
20 Lubricate the idle/reduction gear shaft with clean engine oil. Fit the gear and shaft in the crankcase, making sure the smaller pinion faces inwards and its teeth mesh correctly with the teeth of the starter driven gear **(see illustration 13.6)**.
21 Fit the dowels into the cover or crankcase if removed. Lay a new gasket over the dowels **(see illustration)**. Fit the cover, noting that the rotor magnets will forcibly draw the cover/stator on, making sure the dowels locate **(see illustration)**. Fit the cover bolts with the wiring guides, making sure the shorter bolt is in the correct place (if you are not sure where it should go check the amount it protrudes from the cover before the threads engage compared to the other bolts – if all are in the correct place

13.19c ...hold the rotor and tighten the bolt

the protrusion will be the same), and tighten them evenly in a criss-cross sequence to the specified torque **(see illustration 13.5)**.
22 If disconnected reconnect the wiring connector, making sure it is correctly routed and secured **(see illustration 4.16a or b)**. On 2006 to 2012 models install the air filter housing (see Chapter 4).
23 Fill the engine with oil, or top it up to the correct level, as required according to your removal method (see Chapter 1). Install the fairing side panel.

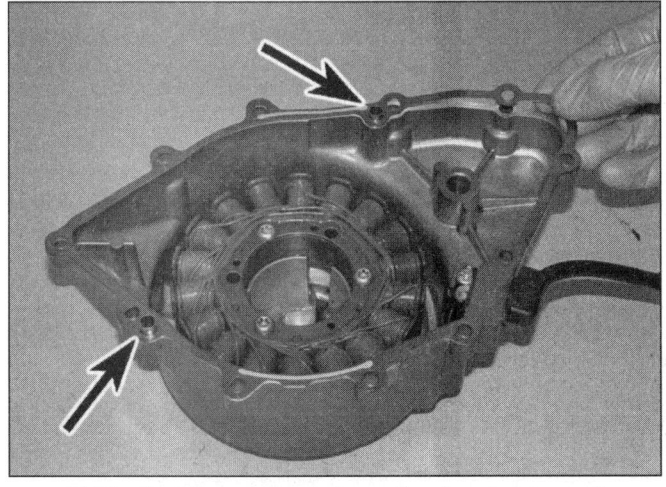

13.21a Seat the new gasket over the dowels (arrowed)

13.21b Carefully ease the cover into place

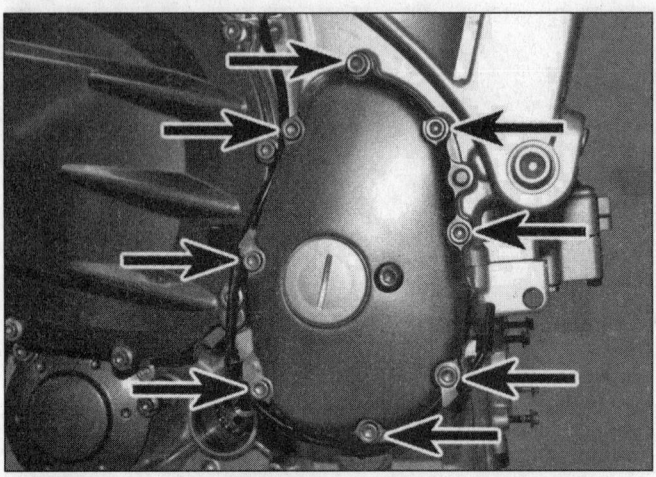

2•28 Engine, clutch and transmission

14.3a Timing rotor cover bolts (arrowed) – 2001 to 2012

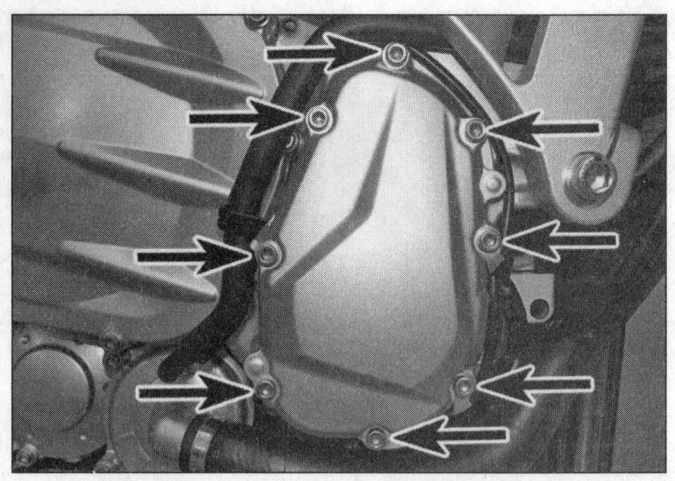

14.3b Timing rotor cover bolts (arrowed) – 2013-on

14 Timing rotor

Removal

1 Remove the right hand fairing side panel (see Chapter 7).
2 Place the bike on the sidestand. Place a container under the engine to catch any oil that may come out when the cover is removed.
3 Working in a criss-cross pattern, evenly slacken the timing rotor cover bolts, noting the wiring guides, and the positions of the longer bolts **(see illustrations)**. Draw the cover off the engine and be prepared to catch any residual oil. Remove the gasket – a new one must be used on installation. Remove the dowels from either the cover or the crankcase if they are loose **(see illustration 14.11a)**.
4 Displace the CKP sensor **(see illustration)**.
5 To unscrew the timing rotor bolt the crankshaft must be prevented from turning. To do this, either remove the alternator cover (Section 13) and counter-hold the crankshaft using a socket on the alternator rotor bolt (there is no danger of the bolt coming undone as it has a much higher torque setting than the timing rotor bolt), or use a rotor holder on the rotor **(see illustration 13.19c)**, or alternatively have an assistant sit on the bike, select a gear and apply the brakes. With the crankshaft locked, unscrew the bolt and remove the washer **(see illustration 14.9)**.
6 Remove the timing rotor, noting how it fits **(see illustration 14.8)**.

Inspection

7 Check the timing rotor triggers, and the locating tab on the back of the rotor and its slot in the end of the crankshaft for wear and damage.

Installation

8 Fit the timing rotor with the locating tab facing in, aligning it with and seating it in the cut-out in the crankshaft **(see illustration)**.
9 Fit the bolt with its washer and tighten it finger-tight **(see illustration)**. Lock the crankshaft using the same method as on removal – see Step 5, and tighten the bolt to the torque setting specified at the beginning of the Chapter for your model. Note that if you are using the alternator rotor bolt to counter-hold the crankshaft there should be no danger of it over-tightening as it is set to a much higher torque setting.
10 Clean the threads of the CKP sensor bolts and apply some threadlock, then fit the sensor **(see illustration 14.4)**.
11 Fit the dowels into the cover or crankcase if removed. Lay a new gasket over the dowels **(see illustration)**. Fit the cover, making sure the dowels locate **(see illustration)**. Fit the

14.4 Unscrew the bolts (A) and move the sensor out of the way. Timing rotor bolt (B)

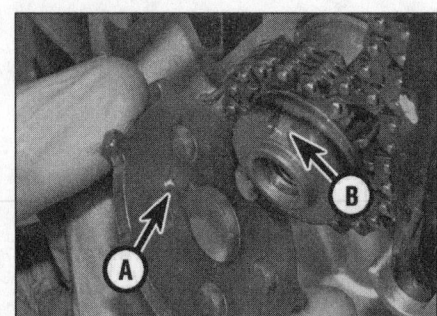

14.8 Locate the tab (A) in the cut-out (B)

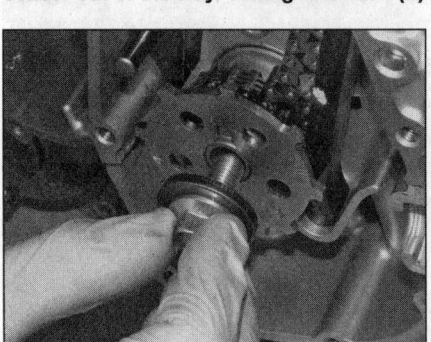

14.9 Fit the bolt with its washer

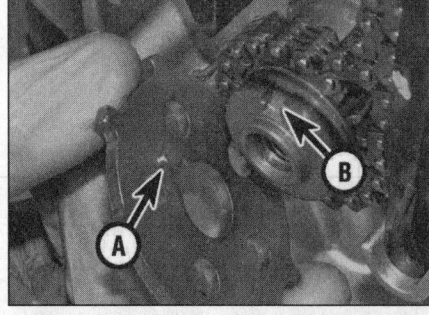

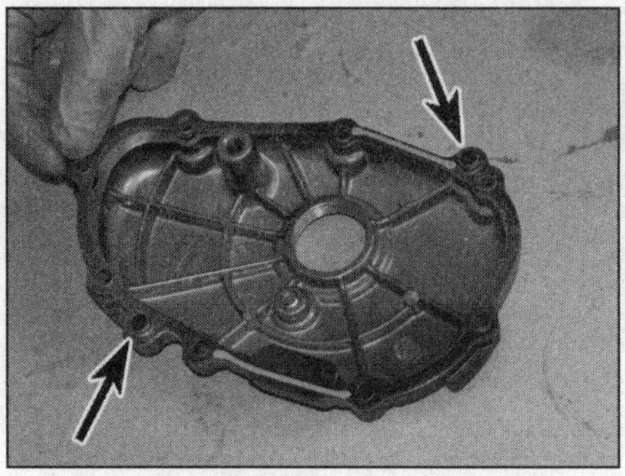

14.11a Seat the new gasket over the dowels (arrowed)…

14.11b …then fit the cover

Engine, clutch and transmission 2•29

15.3a Clutch cover bolts (arrowed)

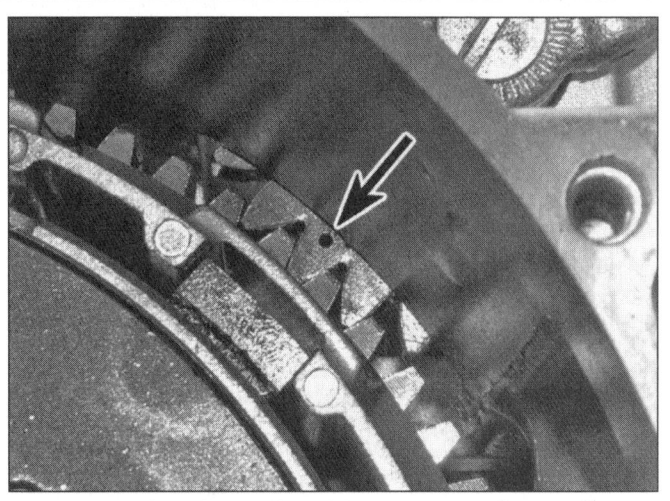

15.3b Note the position of the punch mark (arrowed)

cover bolts with the wiring guides, making sure the longer bolts are in the correct place (if you are not sure where they should go check the amount they protrude from the cover before the threads engage compared to the other bolts – if all are in the correct place the protrusion will be the same), and tighten them evenly in a criss-cross sequence to the specified torque **(see illustration 14.3a or b)**.
12 Check the oil level (see Chapter 1). Install the fairing side panel.

15 Clutch

Removal

Special tool: *A tool for holding the clutch centre will be required (see Step 10).*
1 Remove the right-hand fairing side panel (see Chapter 7). Drain the engine oil (see Chapter 1).
2 Remove the timing rotor cover (Section 14). Using a spanner or socket on the timing rotor bolt and rotating in a clockwise direction only, turn the engine until the 'T' mark on the rotor faces to the rear and aligns with the crankcase mating surfaces **(see illustrations 9.4a and b)**.

3 Working evenly in a criss-cross pattern, unscrew the clutch cover bolts, noting the idle speed adjuster holder on all except 2013-on models **(see illustration)**. Remove the cover, being prepared to catch any residual oil. Remove the gasket – a new one must be used. Remove the dowels from either the cover or the crankcase if they are loose **(see illustration 15.36a)**. Now note the position of the punch mark on the central of the three visible teeth on the rear balancer shaft gear **(see illustration)** – on installation the timing rotor mark and balancer mark must be in these same positions.
4 Counter-hold the clutch housing to prevent it turning and gradually slacken the diaphragm spring retainer bolts in a criss-cross pattern until spring pressure is released **(see illustration)**. Remove the bolts, retainer, diaphragm spring and spring seat, then remove the pressure plate **(see illustrations 15.35d, c, b and a)**.
5 On 2001 to 2005 models and 2009-on A (standard gearchange) models draw all but the innermost plain and friction plates out in pairs of one friction plate and one plain plate using a magnet on the plain plate teeth **(see illustration 15.6)**. Unless the plates are being replaced with new ones, keep them in their original order – note that the outermost friction plate is different to the rest, and must be installed in its correct position. Do not yet remove the inner plain and friction plates from the clutch centre that are behind the wire retainer and are part of the anti-judder assembly – refer to Step 20.
6 On 2006 to 2008 models and 2009-on AS (YCC-S) models draw the complete set of clutch plates out in pairs of one friction plate and one plain plate using a magnet on the plain plate **(see illustration)**. Unless the plates are being replaced with new ones, keep them in their original order – note that the outermost and innermost friction plates are different to the rest, and must be installed in their correct positions. Remove the anti-judder spring and spring seat **(see illustrations 15.34b and a)**.
7 If you are just replacing the clutch friction plates with new ones because they are worn now go to Steps 33-on to install the new plates and complete the clutch installation. If you need to remove the clutch centre and housing continue from the next step.
8 Remove the short pushrod and steel ball **(see illustration)**. The O-ring on the pushrod should be replaced with a new one. There's another, longer pushrod behind the steel ball that can be removed if required after displacing the release cylinder (see Section 16).

15.4 Diaphragm spring retainer bolts (arrowed)

15.6 Use a magnet to draw a pair of plates out

15.8 Remove the pushrod and ball – note the O-ring (arrowed)

2•30 Engine, clutch and transmission

15.9 Unscrew the bolts (arrowed) and remove the plate

15.10a Bend the tabs down

15.10b Hold the clutch centre and unscrew the nut

15.12a Thread the bolts in and use them to draw the sleeve out...

15.12b ...then remove the housing

15.13 Draw the sleeve out and remove the pump drive components

9 Remove the oil baffle plate **(see illustration)**.

10 Bend back the tab(s) on the clutch nut lockwasher **(see illustration)**. To remove the clutch nut the transmission input shaft must be locked – either use the Yamaha service tool (part. No. 90890-04086) or a commercially available equivalent as photographed (make sure the tool is a good fit in the splines of the clutch centre and that the tool handle doesn't mark the gasket surface on the crankcase) **(see illustration)**. Alternatively have an assistant sit on the bike, select a gear and apply the brakes. Unscrew the nut and remove the lockwasher, noting how it fits – a new nut must be used on installation.

11 Slide the clutch centre and the thrust washer off the shaft **(see illustrations 15.30a and 15.28)**.

12 Thread a pair of 5 mm bolts into the sleeve in the centre of the clutch housing **(see illustration)**. Support the clutch housing, then pull the bolt ends to pull the sleeve out, and remove the clutch housing **(see illustration)**.

13 If you need to remove the oil pump drive sprocket draw the sleeve out from its centre then disengage the chain and slide the sprocket off, followed by the collar, and on 2006-on models the spring washer, noting which way round they fit **(see illustration)**.

Inspection

14 After an extended period of service the clutch friction plates will wear and cause clutch slip. Measure the thickness of each friction plate using a Vernier caliper **(see**

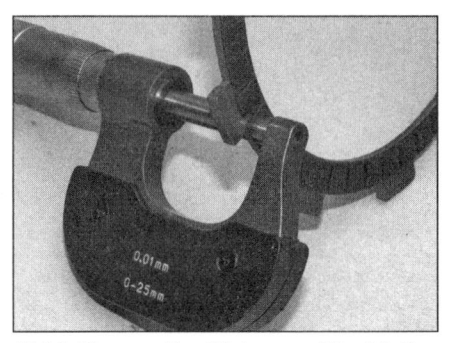

15.14 Measure the thickness of the friction plates

15.15 Check the plain plates for warpage

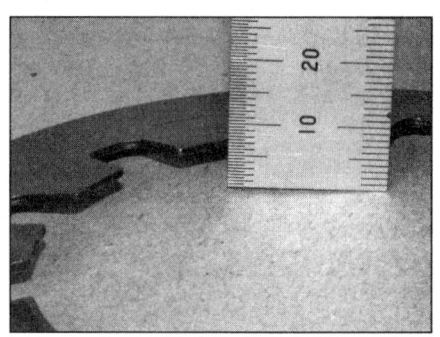

15.16 Measure the free height of the spring

illustration). If any plate has worn to or beyond the service limit given in the Specifications at the beginning of the Chapter, or if any of the plates smell burnt or are glazed, the friction plates must be replaced with a new set.

15 The plain plates should not show any signs of excess heating (bluing). Check for warpage using a flat surface and feeler gauges (see illustration). If any plate exceeds the maximum permissible amount of warpage, or shows signs of bluing, all plain plates must be replaced with a new set.

16 Check the clutch diaphragm spring and spring seat for wear, damage or deformation and replace them with new ones if necessary. Place the spring on a flat surface and measure its height at the centre rim (see illustration). If it is less than the minimum specified at the beginning of the Chapter, replace the spring with a new one.

17 Inspect the friction plate tabs and the clutch housing slots for burrs and indentations (see illustration). Similarly check for wear between the inner teeth of the plain plates and the slots in the clutch centre (see illustration). Wear of this nature will cause clutch drag and slow disengagement during gear changes as the plates will snag when the pressure plate is lifted. With care a small amount of wear can be corrected by dressing with a fine file, but if this is excessive the worn components should be replaced with new ones.

18 Check the needle roller bearing in the clutch housing and the surface of the sleeve it runs on (see illustration) – the bearing is part of the housing. Inspect the slots in the back

15.17a Check the friction plate tabs and housing slots...

15.17b ...and the plain plate teeth and centre slots as described

of the clutch housing and the drive dogs on the oil pump drive sprocket. If you removed the oil pump sprocket, check its bearing (see illustration). If there are any signs of wear or damage the parts must be replaced with new ones.

19 Check the pressure plate and its bearing for signs of wear or damage and roughness (see illustration).

20 On 2001 to 2005 models and 2009-on A (standard gearchange) models, if the clutch has been juddering, remove the wire retainer from the clutch centre, then remove the plain plate, friction plate, anti-judder spring and the spring seat. Check the spring and seat for wear, damage and deformation. If any is found, or the clutch has been juddering, replace them with new ones. Check the plain and friction plates as described in Steps 14 and 15. Check the wire retainer ring for

deformation – note that Yamaha specify to fit a new one whenever it is removed. Fit the spring seat, then fit the spring with the OUTSIDE mark facing out. Fit the friction plate over the spring and spring seat, then fit the plain plate. Secure the assembly with a new retainer ring, making sure it locates properly in its groove.

21 On 2006 to 2008 models and 2009-on AS (YCC-S) models check the anti-judder spring and seat for wear, damage and deformation. If any is found, or the clutch has been juddering, replace them with new ones.

22 Check the short pushrod and steel ball for wear or damage and replace them with new ones if defects are visible (see illustration 15.8). If you removed the long pushrod, make sure it isn't bent (roll it on a perfectly flat surface or use V-blocks and a dial gauge to measure run-out).

15.18a Check the bearing (arrowed) and the sleeve for wear

15.18b Check the bearing (arrowed) for wear

15.19 Check the bearing (arrowed) for wear

2•32 Engine, clutch and transmission

15.24a Fit the spring washer onto the collar...

15.24b ...as shown

15.24c Fit the collar...

15.24d ...and the sprocket...

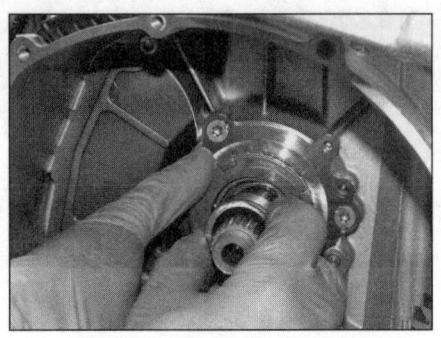

15.24e ...then slide the sleeve in

Installation

23 Remove all traces of old gasket from the crankcase and clutch cover surfaces.

24 If removed, on 2006-on models fit the spring washer onto the collar with the paint mark facing the collar so the outer rim is raised off as shown **(see illustrations)**. Fit the collar onto the shaft behind the chain, then fit the oil pump drive sprocket with its engagement dogs on the outside, and loop the chain around it **(see illustrations)**. Lubricate the sleeve with oil and slide it between the sprocket and shaft **(see illustration)**. Check the chain is still engaged around the driven sprocket on the pump.

25 The primary driven gear on the back of the clutch housing has a sprung inner section that eliminates backlash between it and the drive gear – insert a suitable pin or cross-head screwdriver through the holes in the housing and gears to hold the gears in alignment **(see illustrations)**.

26 Check the 'T' mark on the timing rotor faces to the rear and aligns with the crankcase mating surfaces, or turn the engine clockwise as required until it does **(see illustration 9.4b and a)**. Now turn the rear balancer shaft gear so the tooth with the punch mark is the central of the three visible teeth **(see illustration 15.3b)** – you will have to hold the gear in this position when fitting the clutch housing as the balancer weight will turn the gear out of position.

27 Lubricate the clutch housing needle roller bearing with clean engine oil. Fit the housing, making sure the gears engage correctly and the balancer gear mark is correct, and that the dogs on the oil pump drive gear locate into the slots in the back of the housing, then fit the sleeve into the centre of the housing with the holes on the outside **(see illustrations)**. Double-check engagement of the oil pump sprocket dogs by seeing whether the sleeve is flush with the housing rim **(see illustration)** – if the sleeve is recessed they are not engaged. There is no access to turn the pump chain or sprocket by hand, so you either have to try

15.25a Fit a suitable tool into the hole...

15.25b ...to align the gear teeth

15.27a Fit the housing, aligning and engaging it as described...

15.27b ...then slide the sleeve in

15.27c The sleeve and housing must be flush

Engine, clutch and transmission 2•33

15.27d Turn the water pump shaft to get the oil pump sprocket to move

15.28 Slide the thrust washer onto the shaft

again until you get them engaged, or remove the water pump (see Chapter 3) and turn the shaft tab while pressing on the clutch centre until they are felt to engage, at which point the housing will move in a bit, the sleeve will sit flush and you will no longer be able to turn the shaft **(see illustration)**. Remove the pin/screwdriver from the hole.

28 Lubricate the thrust washer with clean engine oil and fit it onto the shaft **(see illustration)**.
29 On 2001 to 2005 models and 2009-on A (standard gearchange) models, refer to Step 20 and check the anti-judder components are correctly fitted on the clutch centre.
30 Slide the clutch centre onto the shaft splines, then fit the new lockwasher **(see illustrations)**. Fit the clutch nut with its recessed side facing in and, using the method employed on removal to lock the input shaft (see Step 10), tighten the nut to the torque setting specified at the beginning of the Chapter **(see illustrations)**. Bend up the tabs of the lockwasher to secure the nut **(see illustration)**.

15.30a Fit the clutch centre...

15.30b ...and a new lockwasher

15.30c Fit the nut with the recessed side facing in...

15.30d ...then hold the centre and tighten the nut

15.30e Bend the tabs up against the nut

2•34 Engine, clutch and transmission

15.34a Fit the spring seat...

15.34b ...and the spring

15.34c Fit each red-dotted tab into the slot marked by triangles

31 Clean the threads of the oil baffle plate bolts and apply non-permanent threadlock. Fit the plate and tighten the bolts to the specified torque **(see illustration 15.9)**.

32 Fit a new O-ring onto the short pushrod **(see illustration 15.8)**. Lubricate the steel ball and the short pushrod with lithium grease. Push the steel ball into the shaft then slide the short pushrod in.

33 On 2001 to 2005 models and 2009-on A (standard gearchange) models coat each plain and friction plate with engine oil prior to installation. Build up the plates as follows: first fit a friction plate, then a plain plate, then alternate friction and plain plates until all are installed, making sure the outermost plate with the different friction face colour/pattern is fitted last.

34 On 2006 to 2008 models and 2009-on AS (YCC-S) models fit the anti-judder spring seat onto the clutch centre with the paint mark facing out, then fit the spring so its outer rim is raised off the seat **(see illustrations)**. Coat each plain and friction plate with engine oil prior to installation. Note the red dot on one of the tabs on each friction plate and fit that tab into the slot in the housing marked by triangles **(see illustration)**. Build up the plates as follows: fit the innermost friction plate (identifiable by its larger internal diameter) over the spring and spring seat, then fit a plain plate, then alternate friction and plain plates until all are installed, making sure the outermost plate with the different friction face colour/pattern is fitted last **(see illustrations)**.

35 Lubricate the bearing in the pressure plate

15.34d Locate the innermost friction plate over the anti-judder spring...

15.34e ...then fit a plain plate...

15.34f ...a standard friction plate and so on...

15.34g ...and finally the outermost plate that is darker

Engine, clutch and transmission 2•35

15.35a Fit the pressure plate...

15.35b ...the spring seat...

15.35c ...the diaphragm spring...

15.35d ...and its retainer

15.36a Seat the new gasket over the dowels (arrowed)...

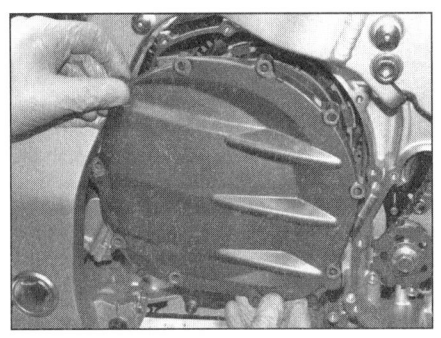

15.36b ...then fit the cover

with some clean oil **(see illustration 15.19)**. Fit the pressure plate onto the clutch, making sure it seats correctly with its inner rim castellations locating in the slots in the clutch centre **(see illustration)** – if there is any clearance between the clutch plates as you push on the pressure plate then it has not located properly. Fit the spring seat, diaphragm spring and spring retainer **(see illustrations)**. Fit the retainer bolts, then counter-hold the clutch housing and tighten them evenly and a little at a time in a criss-cross sequence to the specified torque setting **(see illustration 15.4)**.

36 Fit the dowels into the cover or crankcase if removed. Lay a new gasket over the dowels **(see illustration)**. Fit the cover, making sure the dowels locate **(see illustration)**. Fit the bolts and tighten them finger-tight at first, not forgetting to secure the idle speed adjuster bracket on all except 2013-on models **(see illustration 15.3a)**. Now tighten them in a clockwise rotation to the specified torque setting starting with the bolt shown, then go round them again in the same order.

37 Install the timing rotor cover (Section 14). Refill the engine with the specified quantity of oil (see Chapter 1). Install the right-hand fairing side panel (see Chapter 7).

38 On AS (YCC-S) models, if new friction plates have been fitted they must be broken in as follows: warm the engine up until at least three segments appear on the temperature gauge. Hold the rear brake on hard and select first gear. Open the throttle to one quarter of its travel for less than half a second then close it. Repeat this ten times. If the engine stalls,

select neutral, then restart the engine and let it idle for 90 seconds before starting the procedure again.

16 Clutch release mechanism – standard models

Master cylinder

Note: *If the master cylinder is being overhauled (usually due to sticking or poor action, or fluid leaks), a rebuild kit is available that includes the boot, circlip, washer, piston, seal, cup and spring. Some DOT 4 brake/clutch fluid is also required.*

Removal

Caution: Disassembly, overhaul and reassembly of the cylinder must be done

16.1 Clutch switch wiring connector (arrowed)

16.2 Master cylinder clamp bolts (arrowed)

in a spotlessly clean work area to avoid contamination and possible failure of the hydraulic system components. Do not, under any circumstances, use petroleum-based solvents to clean the parts. Use clean DOT 4 hydraulic fluid. To prevent damage from spilled fluid, always cover paintwork when working on the system.

1 Disconnect the wiring connector from the clutch switch **(see illustration)**.

2 If the master cylinder is just being displaced (e.g. for handlebar removal), follow this Step only: unscrew the clamp bolts and remove the clamp, then support the master cylinder assembly clear of the handlebar **(see illustration)**. Ensure no strain is placed on the hydraulic hose. Keep the reservoir upright to prevent air entering the system.

3 If the master cylinder is being overhauled, follow Steps 3 to 8, then remove the clutch lever (see Chapter 5).

2•36 Engine, clutch and transmission

16.4 Slacken the cover screws

16.5a Brake hose banjo bolt (arrowed)

16.5b Banjo union sealed with a nut and bolt and the washers

4 Slacken the reservoir cover screws **(see illustration)**.
5 Unscrew the clutch hose banjo bolt and detach the banjo union, noting its alignment with the master cylinder **(see illustration)**. Seal the banjo union – one way is to fit a suitable bolt and nut with the old sealing washers **(see illustration)**. Note that new sealing washers will be required later.
6 Unscrew the clamp bolts and remove the clamp, then lift the master cylinder away from the handlebar **(see illustration 16.2)**.
7 Remove the reservoir cover, diaphragm plate and diaphragm. Tip the brake fluid into a suitable container. Wipe any remaining fluid out of the reservoir with a clean rag.
8 If required, undo the clutch switch screw and remove the switch.

Overhaul

9 Carefully remove the pushrod and rubber boot from the master cylinder **(see illustration)**. Depress the piston and use circlip pliers to remove the circlip, then remove the washer, piston assembly and spring. If they are difficult to remove, apply low pressure compressed air to the fluid outlet. Lay the parts out in the proper order to prevent confusion during reassembly.
10 Clean the master cylinder bore and reservoir with clean brake/clutch fluid. If compressed air is available, blow it through the fluid galleries to ensure they are clear (make sure the air is filtered and unlubricated).
11 Check the master cylinder bore for corrosion, scratches, nicks and score marks. If damage or wear is evident, the master cylinder must be replaced with a new one. If the master cylinder is in poor condition, then the release cylinder should be checked as well.
12 Use all of the new parts included in the master cylinder rebuild kit, regardless of the apparent condition of the old ones.
13 Smear the cup and seal with new brake fluid. Fit the seal into its groove in the piston so the wide side will fit into the master cylinder first. Fit the cup over the narrow end of the spring so the flat side will sit against the piston.
14 Lubricate the master cylinder bore with new brake fluid. Fit the spring wide end first into the master cylinder. Make sure the lip of the cup does not turn inside out.
15 Lubricate the piston with clean brake fluid and slide it into the master cylinder and up against the spring. Make sure the lip of the cup seal does not turn inside out. Fit the washer onto the piston. Push the piston in to compress the spring and fit the new circlip, making sure it seats in its groove. Smear the pushrod and rubber boot with silicone grease. Fit the pushrod into the rubber boot so the rounded end will face the piston and seat the lip in the groove. Press the boot into place in the end of the cylinder.

Installation

16 If removed, fit the clutch switch onto the master cylinder.
17 Attach the master cylinder to the handlebar, aligning the inner side of the clamp joint with the punch mark on the top of the handlebar, then fit the clamp with its UP mark facing up **(see illustration)**. Tighten the upper bolt to the torque setting specified at the beginning of this Chapter, followed by the lower bolt.
18 Connect the clutch hose using new sealing washers, one on each side of the banjo fitting. Align the hose as noted on removal **(see illustration 16.5a)**. Tighten the banjo bolt to the torque setting specified at the beginning of this Chapter.
19 Install the clutch lever (see Chapter 5).
20 Connect the clutch switch wiring **(see illustration 16.1)**.

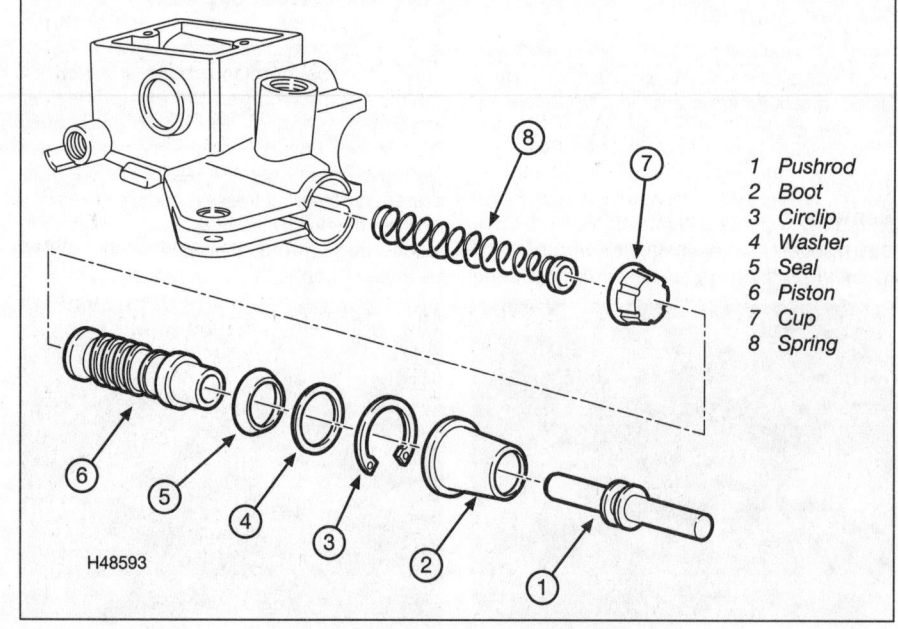

1 Pushrod
2 Boot
3 Circlip
4 Washer
5 Seal
6 Piston
7 Cup
8 Spring

16.9 Clutch master cylinder assembly

16.17 Align the clamp joint with the punch mark (arrowed)

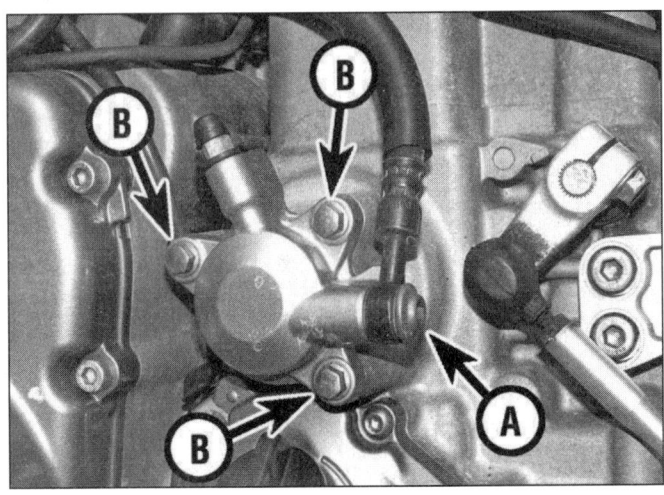

Engine, clutch and transmission 2•37

16.24 Clutch hose bolt (A), release cylinder bolts (B) – 2004 model shown

16.25a Remove the plate...

21 Fill the fluid reservoir with new DOT 4 brake/clutch fluid (see *Pre-ride* checks). Refer to Step 35 and bleed the air from the system. Inspect the reservoir diaphragm and fit a new one if it is damaged or deteriorated.

22 Check the operation of the clutch before riding the motorcycle.

Release cylinder

Removal

23 Remove the left-hand fairing side panel (see Chapter 7).

24 If the cylinder is being completely removed (rather than just being displaced – see Step 25), unscrew the clutch hose banjo bolt and detach the banjo union, noting its alignment with the release cylinder **(see illustration)**. Seal the banjo union – one way is to fit a suitable bolt and nut with the old sealing washers **(see illustration 16.5b)**. Note that new sealing washers will be required later.

25 Unscrew the release cylinder bolts and remove the cylinder **(see illustration 16.24)**. Remove the dowels if they are loose **(see illustration 16.30)**. Remove the shaped plate **(see illustration)**. If required withdraw

16.25b ...and withdraw the pushrod

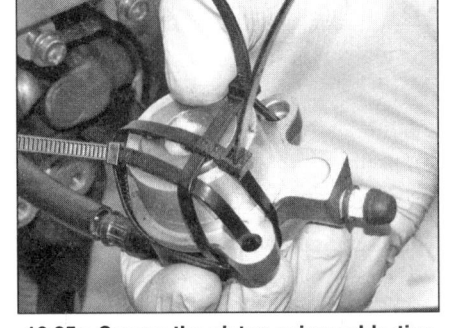

the pushrod **(see illustration)**. Fit cable-ties around the release cylinder as shown to prevent the piston creeping out **(see illustration)**.

Overhaul

26 The release cylinder comes as a complete unit – individual parts are not available. If the piston is sticking or there is fluid leakage from the seal replace the unit with a new one.

27 If required remove the pushrod seal from the crankcase using a seal hook and replace it with a new one **(see illustration)**. Fit the new pushrod seal with the marked side facing out,

16.25c Secure the piston using cable-ties

using finger pressure to set it flush with the rim **(see illustration)**.

28 Check the pushrod is straight by rolling it along a flat surface.

Installation

29 Clean the cylinder and crankcase mating surfaces.

30 If removed clean the pushrod and smear it with lithium grease, then slide it into place **(see illustration 16.25b)**. Fit the shaped plate **(see illustration 16.25a)**. Fit the dowels if removed **(see illustration)**.

31 Fit the release cylinder and tighten

16.27a Lever the old seal out...

16.27b ...and push the new one in

16.30 Make sure the dowels (arrowed) are fitted

2•38 Engine, clutch and transmission

16.31 Seat the cylinder onto the dowels

16.35 Bleed valve (arrowed)

the bolts to the torque setting specified at the beginning of the Chapter **(see illustration)**.

32 Connect the clutch hose using new sealing washers, one on each side of the banjo fitting. Align the hose as noted on removal **(see illustration 16.24)**. Tighten the banjo bolt to the torque setting specified at the beginning of this Chapter.

33 Fill the master cylinder with new DOT4 hydraulic fluid (see *Pre-ride checks*) and bleed the hydraulic system.

34 Check for leaks and thoroughly test the operation of the clutch before installing the fairing panel.

Clutch release mechanism bleeding

35 The procedure for bleeding the clutch and for changing the fluid or draining the system is the same as for the brake system – refer to Chapter 6, Section 11. The bleed valve is on the top of the release cylinder **(see illustration)**. To prevent the possibility of damage from spilled fluid cover the lower fairing and left-hand fairing side panel in rag, or remove them (see Chapter 7).

17 Clutch release mechanism – YCC-S models

1 The clutch release mechanism on models with YCC-S (Yamaha Chip Controlled Shift) consists of the clutch actuator (incorporating the master cylinder), and the clutch release cylinder **(see illustration)**. The mechanism functions in conjunction with the gearchange mechanism and is controlled electronically by the MCU (Motor Control Unit), but also with input from the engine management system ECU and the ABS control unit. The mechanical side of the system is covered in this Section. The electronic control side is covered in Section 20.

2 The system does require some maintenance, but not very often (see Chapter 1). However there is very little that can be done without opening the hydraulic side of the system, and bleeding the system afterwards is a complex and precise procedure requiring the use of specialised equipment. Therefore all work on the system should be carried out by a Yamaha dealer.

3 The only procedure that can be easily carried out is to displace the release cylinder from the engine, required for engine removal and for access to the clutch pushrod and its seal. The procedure is the same as for models with a standard gearchange – refer to Section 16, and do not detach the hydraulic hose.

18 Gearchange mechanism – standard models

Removal

1 Make sure the transmission is in neutral. Remove the clutch (see Section 15). Block the holes into the sump with clean rag to prevent anything falling in.

2 Remove the oil baffle plate **(see illustration)**.

3 On YCC-S models remove the gear position sensor (Section 20).

4 Unscrew the gearchange linkage arm pinch bolt and slide the arm off the shaft, noting the alignment of the punch mark on the shaft end with the slit in the clamp on standard gearchange models **(see illustration 4.13)**, or the alignment of the punch marks on YCC-S models **(see illustration 4.14a)**.

5 Remove the E-clip and washer from the shaft **(see illustration)**.

17.1 The clutch actuator (arrowed) sits in the frame between the engine and the swingarm

18.2 Unscrew the bolts (arrowed) and remove the plate

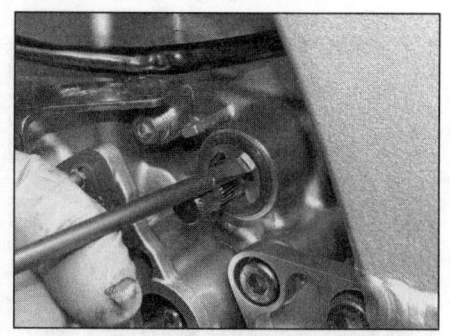

18.5 Lever the E-clip off and remove the washer

Engine, clutch and transmission 2•39

18.7 Withdraw the shaft/arm assembly, noting how it fits

18.8a Unhook the spring...

18.8b ...and remove the stopper arm and washer (arrowed)

18.9 Lever out the oil seal

18.10 Check the selector arm pawls and the pins...

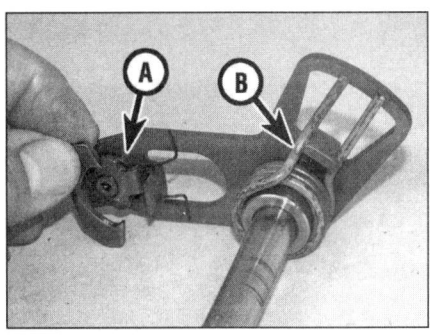

18.11a ...and check the action of the arm and its spring (A). Shaft centralising spring (B)

6 Note how the selector arm claw locates onto the selector drum pins, how the shaft centralising spring ends locate, and how the stopper arm roller locates in the neutral detent on the selector drum cam **(see illustration 18.18)**.
7 Withdraw the gearchange shaft from the engine **(see illustration)**.
8 Unhook the stopper arm spring **(see illustration)**. Withdraw the stopper arm from the engine **(see illustration)**. If the inner washer is not on the shaft retrieve it from the crankcase.
9 Whenever the shaft is removed a new oil seal should be fitted. Lever the old seal out with a screwdriver or seal hook **(see illustration)**.

Inspection

10 Inspect the selector arm claw and the pins in the end of the selector drum for wear and damage **(see illustration)**.
11 Check the selector arm spring and the shaft centralising spring for distortion and fatigue **(see illustration)**. Check that the centralising spring locating pin in the crankcase is securely tightened **(see illustration)**. If it is loose, remove it, clean its threads and apply a non-permanent thread locking compound to its threads, then tighten it to the torque setting specified at the beginning of the Chapter.
12 Check the gearchange shaft is straight and look for damage to the splines. If the shaft is bent you can attempt to straighten it, but if the splines are damaged the shaft must be replaced with a new one. Check the bearing in the crankcase **(see illustration)**. If necessary remove the bearing using an expanding internal puller with slide hammer attachment, but note that removal will damage it. Heat around the bearing housing with a hot air gun to ease removal. Press the new bearing in with the marked side facing out – do not drive it in.
13 Inspect the stopper arm roller and the detents in the camplate, and check the arm return spring **(see illustration)**. If they are worn or damaged they must be replaced with new ones.

Disassembly

14 If any parts are worn or damaged they can be replaced with new ones.
15 To disassemble the stopper arm shaft

18.11b Make sure the pin (arrowed) is tight

18.12 Gearchange shaft bearing (arrowed)

18.13 Check roller, detents and spring

2•40 Engine, clutch and transmission

18.15 Inner washer (A), circlip (B) and outer washer (C)

18.17 Stopper arm roller in neutral detent on YCC-S models

18.18 Check everything is correctly positioned

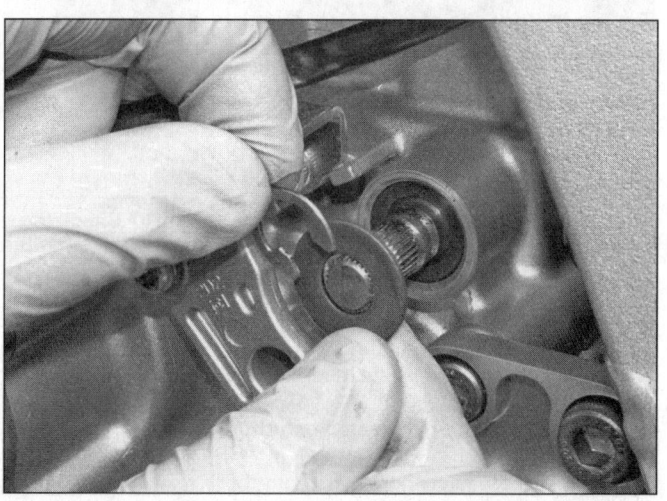

18.19a Fit the washer and clip...

18.19b ...using pliers to press the clip into the groove

slide the inner washer off, then release the circlip and slide it off, followed by the outer washer and the stopper arm (see illustration). Obtain new parts as required and reassemble in reverse order using a new circlip.

Installation

16 Press or drive a new shaft oil seal squarely into place, with its marked side facing out, using your fingers or a seal driver or suitable socket if necessary.

17 Make sure the inner washer is on the stopper arm shaft (see illustration 18.15). Slide the shaft into its hole (see illustration 18.8b). Seat the stopper arm roller in the neutral detent in the cam and hook up the spring (see illustration 18.8a) – note that on YCC-S models due to the different gear selection pattern the neutral detent is not the shallow one as it is for standard models, but the normal depth one above it (see illustration).

18 Smear some molybdenum disulphide oil (a 50/50 mixture of molybdenum disulphide grease and engine oil) onto the section of shaft that fits into the stopper arm. Wrap a single layer of thin insulating tape around the splines to protect the oil seal lips. Slide the gearchange shaft in, and locate the selector arm claw into position on the drum pins (see illustration 18.7). Ensure the centralising spring ends are correctly located on each side of the pins on the shaft and the crankcase (see illustration).

19 Remove the tape from the shaft splines. Fit the washer and the E-clip (see illustrations).

20 Slide the gearchange linkage arm onto the shaft, on standard gearchange models aligning the punch mark on the shaft end with the slit in the clamp (see illustration 4.13), or on YCC-S models aligning the punch marks (see illustration 14.4a). Tighten the pinch bolt. Check that the gearchange mechanism works correctly.

21 On YCC-S models install the gear position sensor (Section 20).

22 Clean the threads of the oil baffle plate bolts and apply non-permanent threadlock. Fit the plate and tighten the bolts to the specified torque (see illustration 18.2).

23 Install the clutch (see Section 15).

Engine, clutch and transmission 2•41

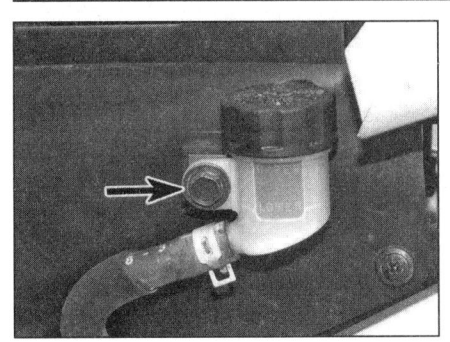

19.3a Unscrew the reservoir bolt (arrowed)

19.3b Release the trim clips, undo the screw and remove the shroud

19.3c Undo the screws and remove the duct

19 Gearchange mechanism – YCC-S models

General information

1 The gearchange actuator mechanism on models with YCC-S (Yamaha Chip Controlled Shift) consists of the shift actuator and the foot shift lever and switch and the hand shift switch. The mechanism functions in conjunction with the clutch release mechanism (Section 17) and is controlled electronically by the MCU (Motor Control Unit), but also with input from the engine management system ECU and the ABS control unit. The electronic control side of the YCC-S system is covered in Section 20.

Shift actuator

Removal

2 Make sure the transmission is in neutral. Remove the left-hand side cover (see Chapter 7).
3 Displace the clutch fluid reservoir, then release the air intake shroud trim clips, undo the screw and remove the shroud (see illustrations). Undo the air intake duct screws and remove the duct (see illustration).
4 Undo the gear position sensor cover screws, release the peg and remove the cover (see illustrations).
5 Fit a 5 mm pin through the hole in the actuator arm and into the actuator to lock the arm (see illustration). Pull the boot off each end of the linkage rod, unscrew the bolts and detach the rod from the arms. Remove the pin.
6 Disconnect the actuator wiring connectors (see illustration).
7 Slacken the rear sub-frame bolt (see illustration). Unscrew the front actuator bolt, then unscrew the rear bolt and remove the actuator (see illustration).

Inspection

8 The linkage rod has a damper mechanism – with the rod held upright on a worktop check the action of the damper by pressing the top of the rod – if the action is rough replace the rod with a new one. With the rod at rest check the index line on the rod is in line with the end

19.4a Undo the screws (arrowed)...

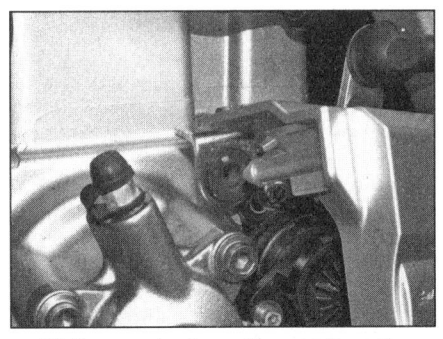

19.4b ...and release the peg from the grommet

19.5 Drill bit used as locking pin for actuator arm

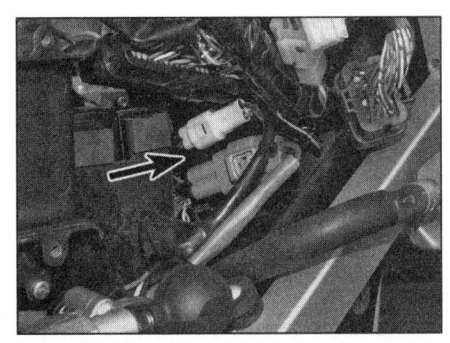

19.6 Actuator wiring connectors (arrowed)

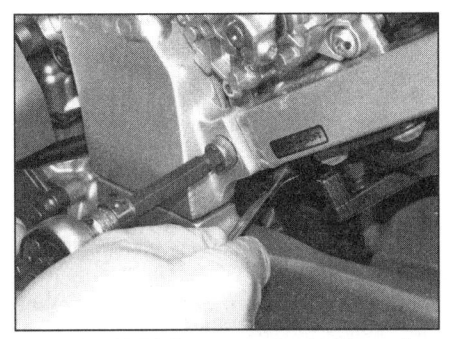

19.7a Hold the nut on the inside and slacken the bolt

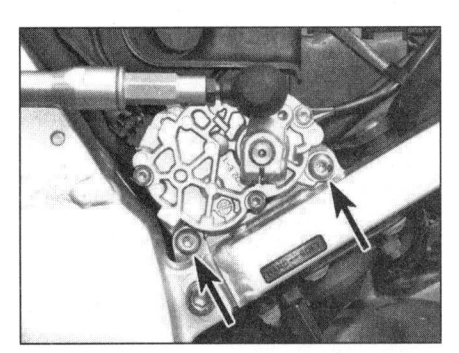

19.7b Actuator bolts (arrowed)

2•42 Engine, clutch and transmission

19.9 Locate the actuator and tighten the bolts as described

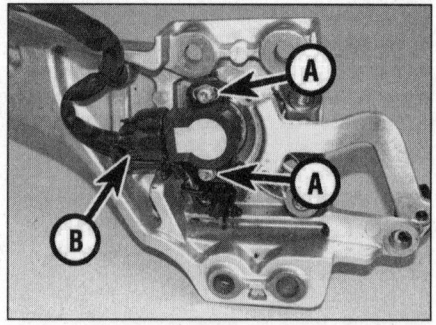

19.16 Shift switch screws (A) and wiring connector (B)

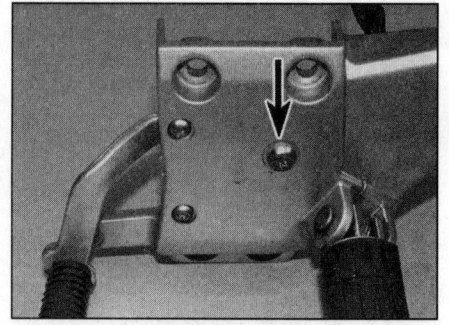

19.17 Gearchange lever pivot bolt (arrowed)

of the shroud – if not replace the rod with a new one.

Installation

9 Fit the actuator and finger-tighten the bolts **(see illustration)**. First tighten the rear bolt to the torque setting specified at the beginning of the Chapter, then tighten the front bolt. Tighten the sub-frame bolt **(see illustration 19.7a)**.
10 Connect the actuator wiring connectors **(see illustration 19.6)**.
11 Fit a 5 mm pin through the hole in the actuator arm and into the actuator to lock the arm **(see illustration 19.5)**. Fit the linkage rod onto the arms and tighten the bolts to the specified torque – when fitting the rod check that with it fitted onto the actuator arm the holes between the rod and the gearchange shaft arm are aligned. If not adjust the length of the rod by slackening the locknut on each end and turning the rod as required until the holes align, then tighten the locknuts. Do not move one of the arms to align the holes. Fit the boots. Remove the pin.
12 Install the remaining components in revers order of removal.

Foot shift switch and lever

Removal

13 Make sure the transmission is in neutral. Put the bike on the centrestand. Remove the left-hand side cover and fairing side panel (see Chapter 7).
14 Undo the gear position sensor cover screws, release the peg and remove the cover **(see illustrations 19.4a and b)**.
15 Unscrew the footrest bracket bolts and displace the footrest bracket/gearchange lever assembly and the sidestand assembly **(see illustrations 4.14c and d)**. Support the sidestand assembly so the wiring isn't strained.
16 Undo the switch screws and disconnect the wiring and remove the switch and the holder, noting how they fit **(see illustration)**.
17 If required unscrew the lever pivot bolt on the outside of the bracket and remove the pivot, the wave washer, plain washer, lever and washer, noting the ball and spring in the lever and how the pin locates between the centralising spring ends **(see illustration)**.

Inspection

18 Check the maximum resistance of the switch by connecting the positive (+) probe of an ohmmeter to the blue wire terminal in the switch and the negative (-) probe to the black/blue wire terminal. If the resistance is not 4.0 to 6.0 K-ohms replace it with a new one.

Installation

19 Clean the lever pivot bolt threads. Fit the washer onto the bracket, then fit the spring and ball into the lever and the lever onto the bracket, seating the pin between the return spring ends, then fit the plain washer, the wave washer and the pivot, locating the pins in the holes. Apply some fresh threadlock to the bolt and tighten it to the torque setting specified at the beginning of the Chapter.
20 Clean the switch screw threads. Fit the holder onto the pedal pivot, seating the forked ends around the projections. Offer up the footrest bracket/gearchange lever assembly, connect the wiring and fit the switch onto the holder, aligning them so the raised section on the holder located in the opening in the switch, then turn the switch anti-clockwise and finger-tighten the screws **(see illustration 19.16)**.
21 Now you need to adjust the position of the switch as follows: connect the positive (+) probe of a voltmeter to the orange/red wire terminal in the connector and the negative (-) probe to the black/blue wire terminal. Turn the ignition switch on and adjust the position of the switch until the voltage reading is 2.4 to 2.6 volts. Keeping the switch in this position remove each screw in turn, apply some non-permanent threadlock, then tighten the screw.
22 Fit and tighten the footrest bracket bolts as follows – first clean the bolt threads, then apply some fresh non-permanent threadlock. Fit all the bolts finger-tight at first, then tighten the lower (sidestand) bolts first, then the upper (M8) bolts, then the front (M10) bolt, applying the correct torque setting to each bolt as specified at the beginning of the Chapter **(see illustrations 4.14d and c)**.
23 Install the remaining components in the reverse order of removal.

Hand shift switch

24 The hand shift switch is part of the handlebar switch housing and is covered in Chapter 8.

20 YCC-S (Yamaha Chip Controlled Shift) system

Note: *At the time of writing no information was available on the YCC-S system fitted to 2013-on models.*

General information

1 The YCC-S (Yamaha Chip Controlled Shift) is a semi-automatic gearchange system that allows the rider to change gear using either a handlebar-mounted switch or a conventional gear lever without having to manually use a clutch. A signal is sent from either the handlebar switch or the shift switch to the MCU (Motor Control Unit). This in turn operates the clutch release mechanism actuator and the gearchange mechanism actuator, and controls the gearchange along with input from the engine management system ECU and the ABS control unit. The system automatically controls the clutch on start-up, when opening the throttle to pull away, and when coming to a stop. The system can override user input if gear changes up are made at engine revs lower than a specified minimum, delaying the change until revs are high enough, and if changes down are made at revs higher than a specified maximum, delaying the change until revs drop by closing the throttle, during which time the bike is effectively coasting.
2 The system consists of the control relay, the YCC-S indicator and warning light in the instrument cluster, a fuse, the hand shift switch and foot shift switch, the neutral switch, gear position sensor and speed sensor, the MCU (Motor Control Unit), the clutch actuator, and the gearchange actuator.
3 The mechanical parts of the system are covered in Sections 17 and 19. The electronic control side and fault diagnosis are covered in this Section. How to use the system is covered in your owner's handbook.

Engine, clutch and transmission 2•43

Fault diagnosis – 2006 to 2012 models

4 The system performs a self-diagnosis when the ignition switch is turned on, during which time the YCC-S indicator light and the warning light in the instrument cluster come on. The lights go out when the diagnosis is complete and no faults are found. If the lights stay on there is a fault.

5 The system also performs a self-diagnosis all the time the engine is running. If a fault occurs the indicator light and warning light come on and the system either operates under a 'limp-home' mode, or it shuts down and it is not possible to change gear. To engage neutral so the bike can be pushed, turn the ignition off and put the bike on the centrestand. Simultaneously turn the rear wheel forwards and push the gearchange linkage rod and arm on the engine until you find neutral – you cannot change gear by operating the gear lever.

6 If the indicator light and warning light on the instrument cluster stay on after initially turning the ignition on or come on when the motorcycle is running, the MCU will store the relevant fault code in its memory and this code (Sh followed by a number) will be shown on the instrument display after the engine has been stopped using the kill switch – if the engine is stopped using the ignition switch the code(s) may not be displayed when it is turned back on (it depends on the code). Stored fault codes can be retrieved in diagnostic mode – see Step 9. If both the YCC-S indicator light and the engine management indicator light come on with the warning light then faults have occurred in both systems – in this case after the engine has been stopped using the kill switch the engine management system fault code(s) will be displayed in preference to the YCC-S codes (see Chapter 4). After the engine management system has been rectified and the codes deleted the YCC-S code(s) will be displayed.

7 If the lights come stop the engine using the kill switch and note the fault code. The fault code table below tells you whether the bike can be started and gears can be changed or not.

8 If a fault appears, before taking the bike to a Yamaha dealer first ensure that the system wiring connectors are securely connected and free of corrosion – poor connections are the cause of

Fault code	Engine function	Gearchange function
SH--11	Engine does not start	Does not change gear
SH--12	Engine does not start	Does not change gear
SH--13	Engine does not start	Does not change gear
SH--14	Engine does not start	Does not change gear
SH--15	Engine does not start	Does not change gear
SH--16	Engine does not start	Does not change gear
SH--17	Engine does not start	Does not change gear
SH--18	Engine does not start	Does not change gear
SH--19	Engine does not start	Does not change gear
SH--21	Engine does not start	Does not change gear
SH--22	Engine starts	Does change gear
SH--23	Engine starts	Does change gear
SH--25	Engine does not start	Does not change gear
SH--26	Engine does not start	Does not change gear
SH--27	Engine starts	Does change gear
SH--31	Engine does not start	Does not change gear
SH--32	Engine does not start	Does not change gear
SH--34	Engine does not start	Does change gear
SH--35	Engine starts	Does change gear
SH--36	Engine does not start	Does not change gear
SH--37	Engine does not start	Does not change gear
SH--38	Engine starts	Does change gear
SH--39	Engine starts	Does change gear
SH--41	Engine starts	Does change gear
SH--42	Engine does not start	Does change gear
SH--43	Engine starts	Does change gear
SH--44	Engine does not start	Does not change gear
SH--45	Engine does not start	Does not change gear
SH--46	Engine does not start	Does not change gear
SH--47	Engine starts	Does change gear
SH--48	Engine does not start	Does not change gear
SH--49	Engine starts	Does change gear
SH--51	Engine does not start	Does not change gear
SH--52	Engine starts	Does change gear

the majority of problems. Also check the wiring itself for any obvious faults or breaks, and use a continuity tester to check the wiring between the component, its connectors and the MCU, referring to the wiring diagrams at the end of Chapter 8.

9 In the event of a fault that is not the result of a dodgy connector, and to retrieve any stored fault codes, take the bike to a Yamaha dealer – a special tool is needed to enter the system into diagnostic mode for code retrieval, fault repair and system reset.

Motor control unit (MCU)

10 Remove the seats and the right-hand side cover (see Chapter 7).

11 Disconnect the two wiring connectors on the right-hand side, then release the wiring clip (see illustration). Release the MCU strap and move the wiring aside (see illustrations).

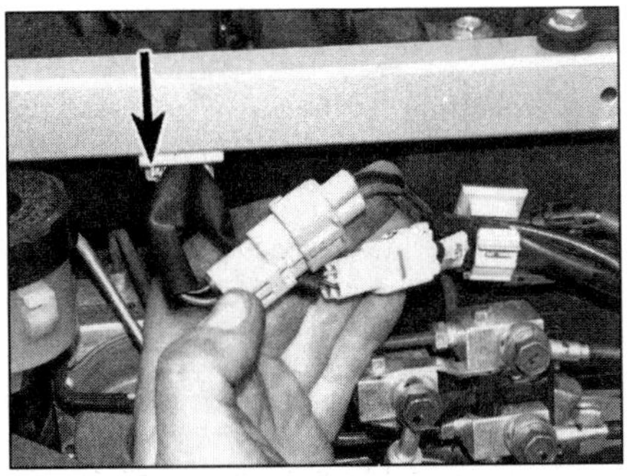

20.11a Disconnect the wiring and release the clip (arrowed)

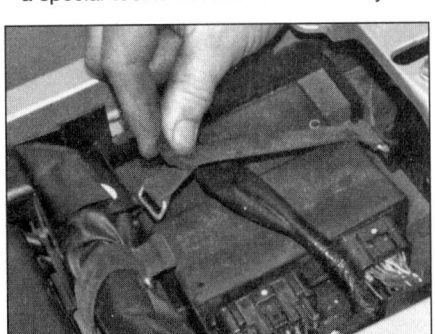

20.11b Unhook the strap...

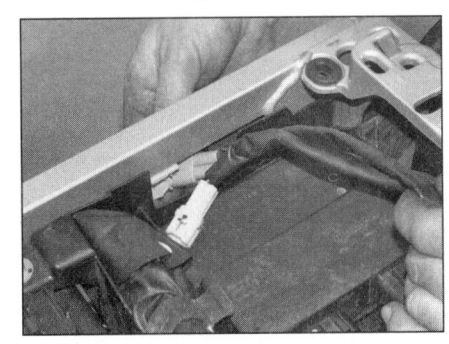

20.11c ...and draw the wiring out

2•44 Engine, clutch and transmission

12 Lift the MCU and disconnect the wiring connectors **(see illustration)**.
13 Installation is the reverse of removal.

Control relay

Check

14 Remove the relay (Steps 16 and 17).
15 Using an ohmmeter or continuity tester, connect its probes across the two blue/white wire terminals on the relay. There should be no continuity. Using a fully-charged 12V battery and some jumper leads, connect the positive (+) terminal of the battery to the yellow/green wire terminal on the relay, and the negative (–) terminal to the green wire terminal. There should now be continuity between the blue/white and blue/yellow wire terminals. If it does not test as described replace the relay with a new one.

Removal and installation

16 Remove the seats and the height adjuster piece (see Chapter 7). Remove the toolkit from its tray **(see illustration)**. Remove the motor control unit (see above). Disconnect the ECU wiring connector, then remove the tray **(see illustrations)**.
17 Displace the relay and disconnect the wiring connector **(see illustration)**.
18 Installation is the reverse of removal.

Speed sensor

19 The speed sensor is mounted in the back of the crankcase **(see illustration 20.21)**. To test the output from the sensor, place the motorcycle on the centrestand. Make sure the transmission is in neutral.
20 Remove the throttle bodies (see Chapter 4). Connect the positive (+) probe of a multimeter set to the DC20V scale to the white/yellow wire terminal in the connector (with it still connected), and connect the negative (–) probe to the black/blue wire terminal **(see illustration)**. Turn the ignition ON. Turn the rear wheel in its normal direction of rotation and check the reading on the multimeter – it should be seen to fluctuate between 0.6 and 4.8 volts as the wheel is turned. If not replace the sensor with a new one.
21 For best access to fit a new sensor remove the swingarm (see Chapter 5), though with the right tools and a bit of dexterity you may be OK with it in place. Unscrew the bolt and withdraw the sensor from the crankcase, noting the wiring clamp **(see illustration)**. Check the condition of the O-ring and replace it with a new one if it is damaged, deformed or deteriorated, but note that Yamaha do not list it as being available separately from the sensor, though they, or a good auto factor, should be able to supply one – take the old one along to match it up.
22 Smear the sensor O-ring with grease, then fit the sensor into the crankcase. Clean the bolt threads and apply some fresh threadlock then tighten the bolt, not forgetting to secure the wiring clamp with it **(see illustration 20.21)**. Connect the sensor wiring connector, then install the throttle bodies (see Chapter 4), and if removed the swingarm (see Chapter 5).

Gear position sensor

23 The gear position sensor is mounted in the left-hand side of the crankcase. Make sure the transmission is in neutral.

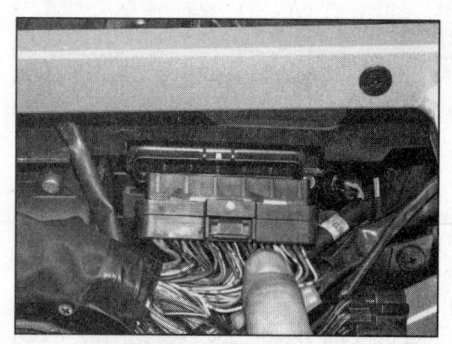

20.12 Lift the MCU and disconnect the wiring

20.16a Remove the toolkit

20.16b Disconnect the ECU

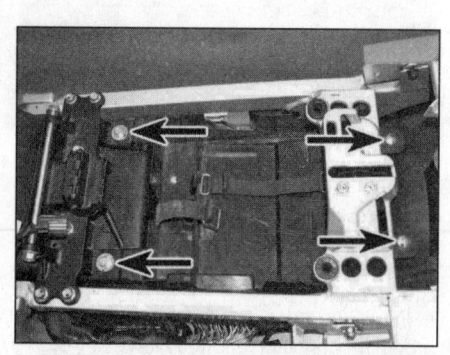

20.16c Undo the bolts and the screws (arrowed)...

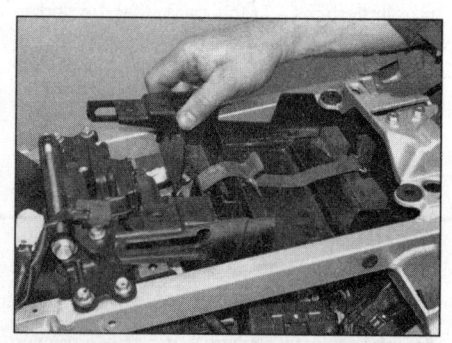

20.16d ...and remove the tray

20.17 YCC-S control relay (arrowed)

20.20 Speed sensor wiring connector (arrowed)

20.21 Speed sensor bolt (arrowed)

Engine, clutch and transmission 2•45

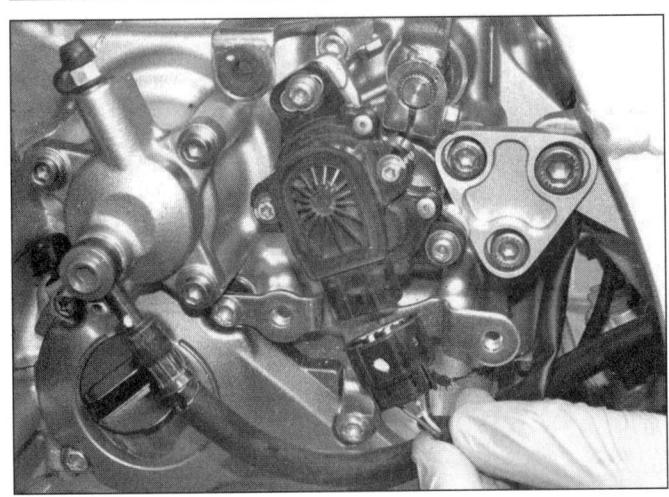

20.24 Disconnect the wiring

20.28 Gear position sensor screws (arrowed)

Check

24 Undo the gear position sensor cover screws, release the peg and remove the cover **(see illustrations 19.4a and b)**. Disconnect the wiring connector from the switch **(see illustration)**.
25 Check the maximum resistance of the switch by connecting the positive (+) probe of an ohmmeter to the blue wire terminal in the switch and the negative (-) probe to the black/blue wire terminal. If the resistance is not 4.0 to 6.0 K-ohms replace it with a new one.

Removal

26 Make sure the transmission is in neutral.
27 Undo the gear position sensor cover screws, release the peg and remove the cover **(see illustrations 19.4a and b)**. Disconnect the wiring connector from the switch **(see illustration 20.24)**.
28 Make an alignment mark of the position of the screws in their slots so the switch can be fitted in the same place. Undo the switch screws and remove the switch **(see illustration)** – do not undo the yellow painted screws.

Installation

29 Clean the switch screw threads. Fit the switch, aligning it so the tab locates in the slot in the switch, then turn the switch anti-clockwise and finger-tighten the screws, aligning them in the slots as marked on removal (unless a new switch is being fitted) **(see illustration)**. Connect the wiring connector **(see illustration 20.24)**.
30 Now you need to adjust the position of the switch as follows: connect the positive (+) probe of a voltmeter to the yellow wire terminal in the connector and the negative (-) probe to the black/blue wire terminal. Turn the ignition switch on and adjust the position of the switch until the voltage reading is 0.71 to 0.91 volts. Keeping the switch in this position remove each screw in turn, apply some non-permanent threadlock, then tighten the screw.
31 Fit the cover.

21 Oil sump, oil strainer and pressure relief valve

Removal

1 Remove the exhaust system (see Chapter 4).
2 Remove the sidestand assembly (see Chapter 5).
3 Drain the engine oil (see Chapter 1).
4 Remove the oil level sensor from the sump (see Chapter 8) – there is no need to disconnect the wiring connector, just release it from the clamp and guide on the sump and place it aside.
5 Unscrew the sump bolts, slackening them evenly in a criss-cross sequence to prevent distortion, and remove the wiring clamps and guide **(see illustration)**. Remove the sump – if it is stuck tap it gently around the perimeter using a soft-faced hammer. Remove the gasket, and the dowels if loose.

20.29 Locate the tab (A) in the slot (B)

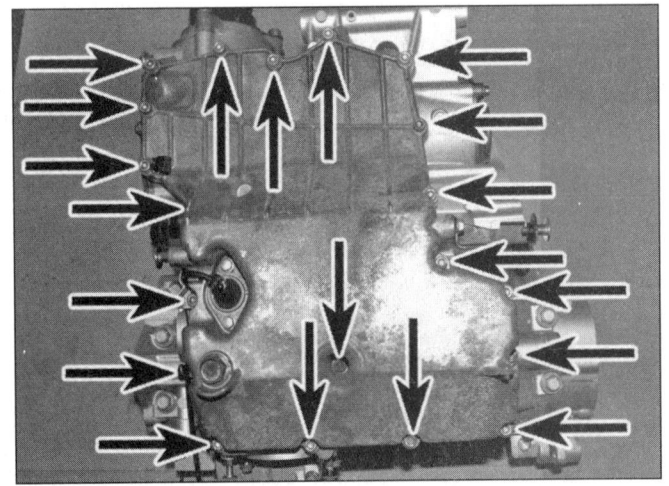

21.5 Sump bolts (arrowed)

2•46 Engine, clutch and transmission

21.6 Strainer bolts (arrowed)

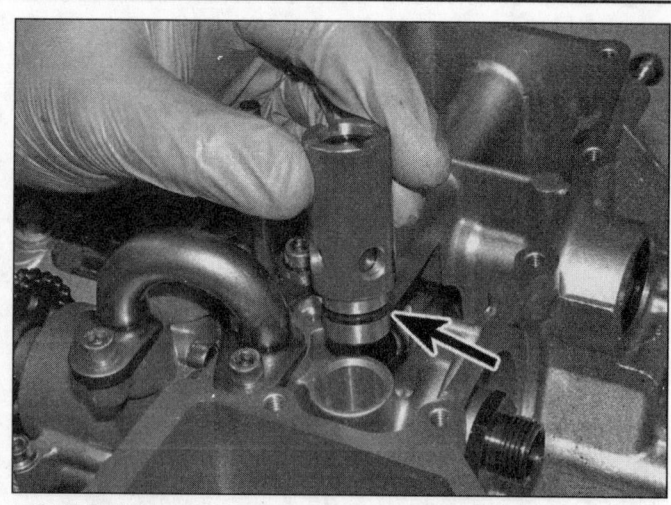

21.7 Pull the relief valve out and remove the O-ring (arrowed)

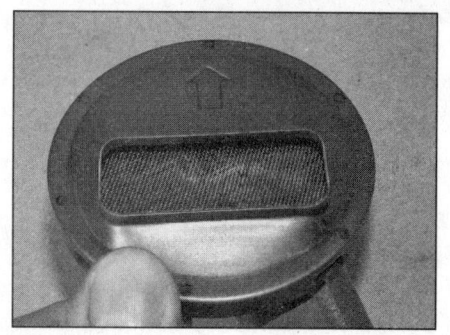

21.9 Clean the strainer mesh

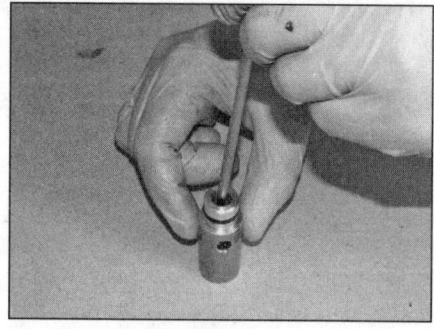

21.10 Check the plunger moves smoothly in the body

6 Unscrew the bolts and remove the strainer **(see illustration)**.
7 Pull the pressure relief valve out of its socket **(see illustration)**. Discard the O-ring – a new one must be used.

Inspection

8 Remove all traces of gasket from the sump and crankcase mating surfaces, and clean the inside of the sump with solvent. Blow the sump dry with compressed air if available.

9 Clean the oil strainer in solvent and remove any debris caught in the mesh **(see illustration)**. If the strainer gauze is damaged, replace the strainer with a new one.
10 Push the relief valve plunger into the valve body and check that it moves smoothly and freely against spring pressure **(see illustration)**. If not, remove the circlip, noting that it is under spring pressure, then remove the washer, spring and plunger. Clean all components in solvent, then check the plunger and the valve body for evidence of scoring, wear and any other damage. If any is found, replace the relief valve with a new one – individual components are not available. Otherwise, coat the plunger with oil and fit it closed end first back into the valve and recheck the movement. If it is good, fit the spring and washer and secure them with a new circlip.

Installation

11 Fit a new O-ring onto the relief valve and smear it with clean oil, then push the valve into its socket **(see illustration 21.7)**.
12 Clean the threads of the strainer bolts. Apply some non-permanent threadlock, then fit the strainer with the arrow pointing to the front and tighten the bolts to the torque setting specified at the beginning of the Chapter **(see illustration 21.6)**.
13 Clean the mating surfaces of the sump and crankcase with solvent. Fit the dowels if removed. Fit a new gasket onto the sump (or onto the crankcase if the engine is out of the frame). Position the sump onto the crankcase and fit the bolts finger-tight, not forgetting the wiring clamps and guide **(see illustration)**.

21.13a Lay a new gasket onto the dowels (arrowed)...

21.13b ...then fit the sump

Engine, clutch and transmission 2•47

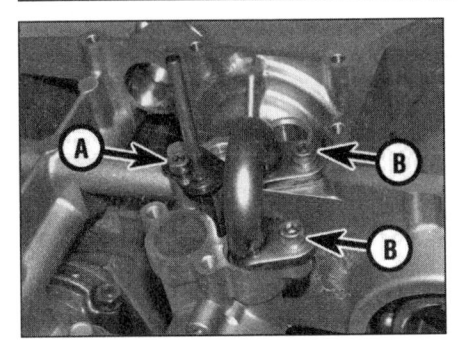

22.2 Oil return pipe bolt (A), oil delivery pipe bolts (B)

22.4a Unscrew the bolts (arrowed)...

22.4b ...withdraw the dowels...

Tighten the bolts evenly and a little at a time in a criss-cross pattern to the specified torque **(see illustration 21.5)**.
14 Install the oil level sensor (see Chapter 8).
15 Fill the engine with the correct type and quantity of oil as described in Chapter 1.
16 Install the exhaust system (see Chapter 4).
17 Install the sidestand assembly (see Chapter 5).
18 Start the engine and check that there are no leaks around the sump.

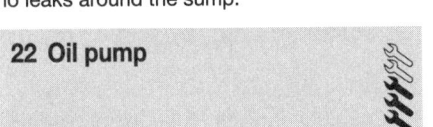

22 Oil pump

Removal

1 Remove the sump and the oil strainer (see Section 21).
2 Remove the oil return pipe **(see illustration)**.
3 Remove the oil delivery pipe **(see illustration 22.2)** – new O-rings must be used.
4 Unscrew the pump bolts, then withdraw the two long dowels **(see illustrations)**. Slide the pump in a bit and tilt it to disengage it from the water pump shaft and the chain **(see illustration)**.

Inspection

5 Unscrew the assembly bolts and detach the cover from the pump body **(see illustrations)**. Remove the locating pins if loose.
6 Remove the outer and inner rotors from the body, noting which way round they fit **(see illustrations 22.14e and d)**. Remove the drive pin and thrust washer then withdraw the shaft from the cover **(see illustrations 22.14c, b and a)**.
7 Clean all the components in solvent.
8 Inspect the pump body, shaft and rotors for scoring and wear. If any damage, scoring or uneven or excessive wear is evident, replace the pump with a new one (individual components are not available).
9 Fit the inner and outer rotors into the pump body, then slide the shaft through the inner rotor **(see illustrations 22.14e, d and a)**. Align the rotors as shown and measure the clearance between the inner rotor tip and the outer rotor with a feeler gauge and compare it to the service limit listed in the specifications at the beginning of the Chapter **(see illustration)**. If the clearance measured is greater than the maximum listed, replace the pump with a new one.
10 Measure the clearance between the outer rotor and the pump body with a feeler gauge and compare it to the maximum clearance listed in the specifications at the beginning of the Chapter **(see illustration)**. If the clearance measured is greater than the maximum listed, replace the pump with a new one.
11 Lay a straight-edge across the rotors and the pump body and, using a feeler gauge, measure the rotor end-float (the gap between the rotors and the straight-edge **(see**

22.4c ...and remove the pump as described

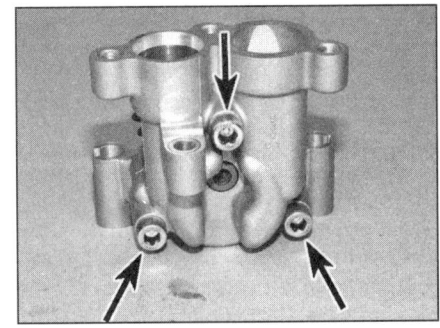

22.5a Unscrew the bolts (arrowed)...

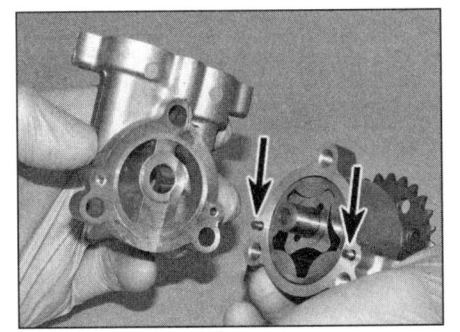

22.5b ...and draw the cover off the pump. Remove the pins (arrowed) if loose

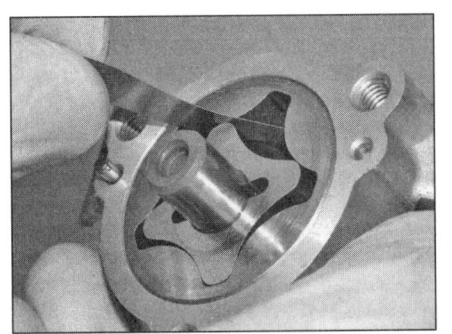

22.9 Measure the rotor tip clearance as shown

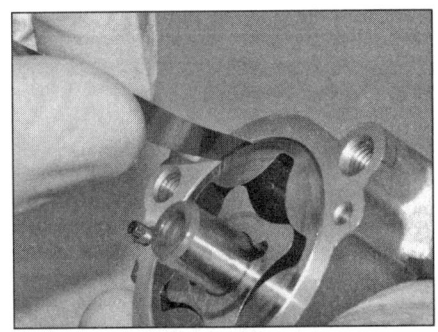

22.10 Measure the outer rotor to body clearance as shown

2•48 Engine, clutch and transmission

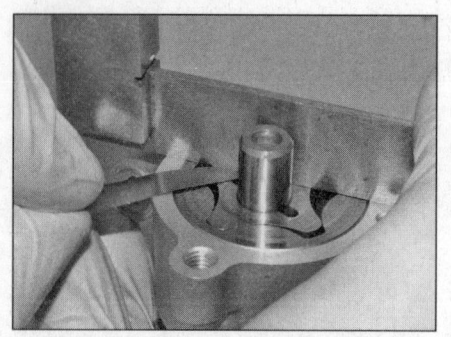

22.11 Measure the rotor end-float as shown

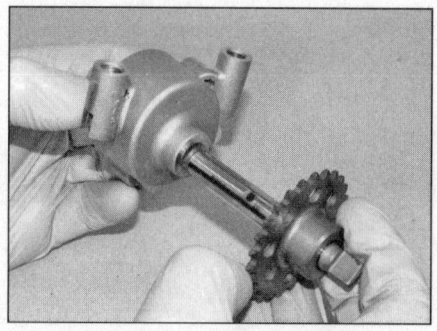

22.14a Slide the shaft through...

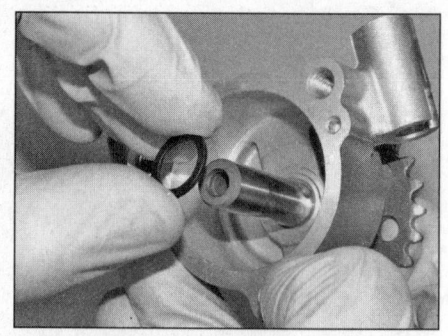

22.14b ...then fit the washer...

22.14c ...and the drive pin

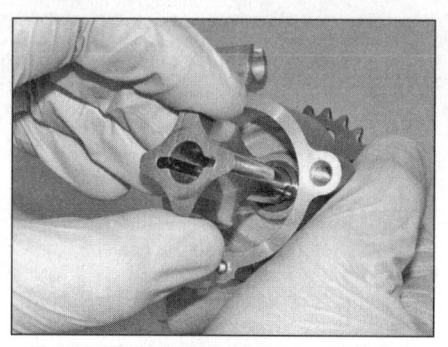

22.14d Fit the inner rotor recessed face over the washer...

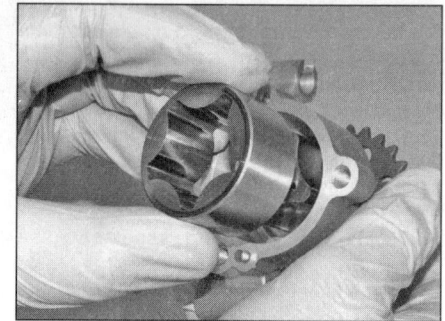

22.14e ...then fit the outer rotor

illustration). If the clearance measured is greater than the maximum listed, replace the pump with a new one.

12 Check the pump drive chain and driven sprocket for wear or damage, and replace them with a new set if necessary – remove the clutch to access the drive sprocket (Section 15).

13 If the pump is good, make sure all the components are clean, then lubricate them with new engine oil.

14 Slide the drive shaft through the body then fit the washer and the drive pin **(see illustrations)**. Fit the recessed face of the inner rotor into the body and seat the cut-outs over the drive pin **(see illustration)**. Fit the outer rotor **(see illustration)**.

15 Fit the locating pins if removed **(see illustration 22.5b)**. Fit the cover and tighten the bolts to the torque setting specified at the beginning of the Chapter **(see illustration 22.5a)**.

16 Rotate the pump shaft by hand and check it turns the rotors smoothly and freely.

Installation

17 Clean the threads of the pump mounting bolts and apply some non-permanent threadlock. Position the pump and engage the chain and shafts, then seat the pump and insert the dowels **(see illustrations 22.4c, b and a)**. Fit the bolts and tighten to the specified torque.

18 Fit new O-rings smeared with grease onto the oil delivery pipe **(see illustration)**. Clean the threads of the pipe bolts and apply some non-permanent threadlock. Fit the pipe and tighten the bolts to the specified torque **(see illustration)**.

19 Clean the threads of the return pipe bolt and apply some non-permanent threadlock. Fit the pipe and tighten the bolt to the specified torque **(see illustration)**.

20 Install the oil strainer and the sump (see Section 21).

23 Middle gear shafts

Note: *If there is oil leakage around the output shaft on the back of the engine the seal can be replaced with a new one with the shafts in place, but the engine must be removed from the frame to do so – see Step 12.*

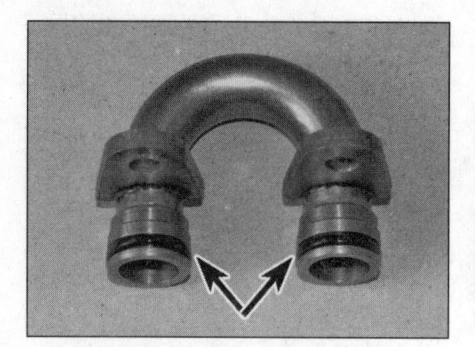

22.18a Fit new O-rings (arrowed)...

22.18b ...then fit the delivery pipe

22.19 Fit the pipe into its hole (arrowed) and seat the bracket

Engine, clutch and transmission 2•49

23.3 Middle gear shaft cover bolts (arrowed)

23.4 Drive shaft bearing housing bolts (arrowed)

Removal

1 Remove the engine from the frame (Section 4).
2 Remove the sump (Section 21) and oil pump (see Section 22). Leave the engine upside-down.
3 Working in a criss-cross pattern, evenly slacken the middle gear shaft cover bolts, noting the wiring guides, and on YCC-S models the bracket, and the positions of the different length bolts **(see illustration)**. Draw the cover off the engine and be prepared to catch any residual oil. Remove the gasket – a new one must be used on installation. Remove the dowels from either the cover or the crankcase if they are loose **(see illustration 23.18a)**.
4 Unscrew the input (drive) shaft bearing housing bolts and remove the housing **(see illustration)**. Remove the O-ring – a new one must be used **(see illustration 23.16)**.
5 Unscrew the output (driven) shaft end cover bolts and remove the cover **(see illustration)**. Grasp the bearing housing and draw the shaft out of the engine and remove the shims **(see illustrations 23.15b and c)**. Remove the O-ring **(see illustration 23.15a)** – a new one must be used.
6 Bend back the tabs on the drive gear nut **(see illustration)**. Counter-hold the right-hand end of the shaft using a 22 mm ring spanner **(see illustration)** and unscrew the nut. Remove the lockwasher then draw the bevel gear off the shaft **(see illustrations 23.14c and b)**. Withdraw the shaft from the right-hand side of the engine, sliding the spacer and the middle driven gear off the inner end as you do **(see illustration 23.14a)**.

Inspection

7 The middle gear shaft assemblies should last throughout the life of the motorcycle without the need for overhaul or component replacement.
8 Inspect the drive shaft bevel gear for signs of wear or damage. Check the shaft bearings – the outer one in the housing that was removed and the inner one in the crankcase. If any wear or damage is evident, or if the bearings show signs of roughness or play, replace the gear and/or bearings as necessary (see Step 11).
9 Inspect the driven shaft bevel gear for signs of wear or damage. Check the shaft bearings – the rear one in the housing on the shaft and the front one in the crankcase. If any wear or damage is evident, or if the bearings show signs of roughness or play, replace the gear and/or bearings as necessary (see Step 11).

10 Check the drive shaft damper cam surfaces for signs of wear or damage. If they are worn they can be replaced with new ones quite easily, but you need a spring compressor (Yamaha special tool part No. 90890-04090 or the commercial equivalent). If the cams are worn bear in mind that there could therefore be wear on the gears and in the bearings, in which case it is worth considering replacing both shafts as a set with new ones (Step 11). To replace the cams compress the damper spring and remove the retainers, noting how they fit **(see illustration)**. Slowly release the

23.5 Unscrew the bolts (arrowed) and remove the cover

23.6a Bend the tabs back

23.6b Counter-hold the shaft as shown and unscrew the nut

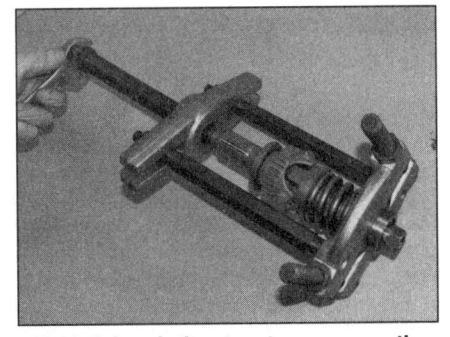

23.10 Drive shaft set up to compress the spring for shaft disassembly

2•50 Engine, clutch and transmission

23.12a Drill a small hole as shown...

23.12b ...then fit a self-tapping screw...

23.12c ...and remove the seal using suitable leverage on the screw

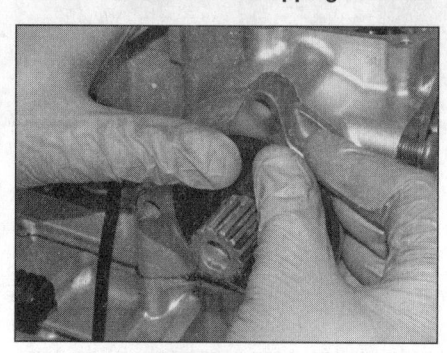

23.12d You should be able to fit the new seal using thumb pressure

compressor, and remove the spring seat, the spring, the driven cam and the drive cam. Replace the drive and driven cams with new ones, and the spring if required, then rebuild the shaft in reverse of the removal procedure.

11 If the bearings need to be removed or replaced, the shafts and engine should be taken to a Yamaha dealer as special tools are needed. If either of the bevel gears or shafts become worn or damaged, they are only available, and must be replaced, as a matched complete assembly, and again this should be carried out by a Yamaha dealer. If new shafts are fitted the driven shaft must be re-shimmed, and again this should be carried out by the dealer at the same time as it is a long and complicated process requiring special tools.

12 If there is any evidence of oil leakage around the output shaft the seal can be replaced with a new one – if not already done remove the end cover (Step 5). Drill a small hole into the seal as shown, then thread a medium-sized self-tapping screw into the hole **(see illustrations)**. Lever the seal out as shown **(see illustration)**. Lubricate the outer rim and lips of the new seal and press it squarely in with your fingers until it seats **(see illustration)**.

Installation

13 Lubricate all the bearings and the bevel gear teeth with oil. Smear some molybdenum disulphide oil (a 50/50 mixture of molybdenum disulphide grease and clean engine oil) onto the middle driven gear splines.

14 Slide the drive shaft into the engine, fitting the middle driven gear and spacer on as you do **(see illustration)**. Slide the bevel gear onto the end of the shaft **(see illustration)**. Fit a new lockwasher **(see illustration)**. Smear the threads of the nut with oil and fit it with its recessed side facing in **(see illustration)**. Counter-hold the right-hand end of the shaft using a ring spanner **(see illustration 23.6b)** and tighten the nut to the torque setting specified at the beginning of the Chapter **(see illustration)**. Bend the lockwasher tabs up against the nut **(see illustration)**.

15 Fit a new O-ring smeared with grease

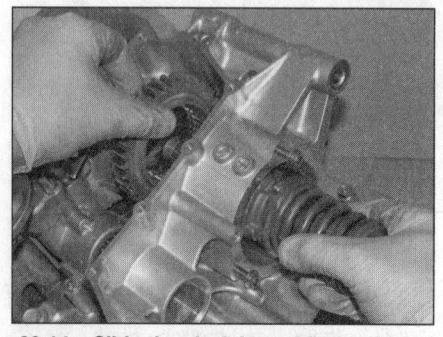

23.14a Slide the shaft in and fit the driven gear and spacer...

23.14b ...then fit the bevel gear...

23.14c ...a new lockwasher...

23.14d ...and the nut...

23.14e ...and tighten it to the specified torque

23.14f Bend the tabs up against the nut

Engine, clutch and transmission 2•51

23.15a Fit a new O-ring (arrowed)

23.15b Install the shaft with the notch (arrowed) to the bottom of the engine...

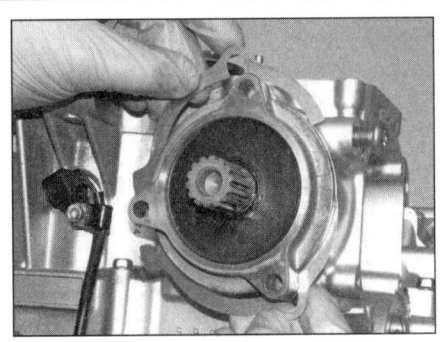

23.15c ...and fit the shims between the housing and crankcase

23.16 Fit a new O-ring (arrowed)

23.18a Fit the new gasket onto the dowels (arrowed)...

23.18b ...then fit the cover

onto the driven shaft bearing housing **(see illustration)**. Fit the shaft into the crankcase with the notch in the bearing housing facing the bottom of the engine **(see illustration)**. Fit the shims with the tabs facing the right-hand side of the engine **(see illustration)**. Clean the threads of the bolts then apply a non-permanent threadlock. Fit the end cover and tighten the bearing housing/end cover bolts finger-tight, then tighten them evenly and a little at a time to the specified torque setting **(see illustration 23.5)**.

16 Fit a new O-ring smeared with grease onto the drive shaft bearing housing **(see illustration)**. Fit the housing onto the crankcase. Fit the bolts and tighten them evenly and a little at a time to the specified torque setting **(see illustration 23.4)**.

17 Check the shafts rotate smoothly and freely (taking into account standard transmission drag).

18 Fit the dowels into the cover or crankcase if removed. Lay a new gasket over the dowels **(see illustration)**. Fit the cover, making sure the dowels locate **(see illustration)**. Clean the threads of the two top bolts and apply some non-permanent threadlock. Fit the cover bolts with the wiring guides and bracket where fitted, making sure the different length bolts are in the correct place (if you are not sure where they should go check the amount they protrude from the cover before the threads engage compared to the other bolts – if all are in the correct place the protrusion will be the same, if longer bolts are in the wrong place they will protrude more and other bolts will protrude less), and tighten them evenly in a criss-cross sequence to the specified torque **(see illustration 23.3)**.

19 Install the oil pump (Section 22) and sump (Section 21).

20 Install the engine (Section 4).

24 Crankcase separation and reassembly

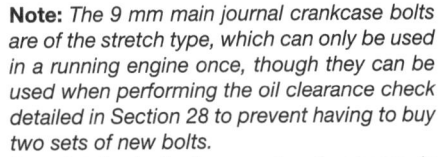

Note: *The 9 mm main journal crankcase bolts are of the stretch type, which can only be used in a running engine once, though they can be used when performing the oil clearance check detailed in Section 28 to prevent having to buy two sets of new bolts.*

Special tool: *A degree disc is shown in illustration 24.17 for tightening the crankshaft journal bolts; the procedure can however be performed without the tool.*

Separation

1 To access the pistons, connecting rods, crankshaft, balancer shafts, transmission shafts and the main and big-end bearings, the crankcase must be split into its two halves.

2 Before the crankcases can be separated the following components must be removed:
- Valve cover (Section 7)
- Camshafts (Section 9) – see Note
- Cam chain and blades (Section 10) – see Note
- Cylinder head (Section 11) – see Note
- Alternator rotor and starter clutch (Section 13)
- Gearchange mechanism (Section 18)
- Clutch (Section 15)
- Starter motor (Chapter 8)
- Water pump (Chapter 3)
- Oil pump (Section 22)
- Middle gear shafts (Section 23)
- Neutral switch/gear position switch (see Chapter 8) and speed sensor (Chapter 4 for 2001 to 2005 models or Section 20 for YCC-S models) as required according to model – if you don't remove the neutral switch from the back of the engine where fitted disconnect the wire from it **(see illustration)**.

Note: *If the crankcases are being separated to inspect the crankshaft without removing it, the camshafts and cylinder head can remain in situ. To remove the crankshaft without removing the connecting rods and pistons, the camshafts must be removed but the head can stay. However, if removal of the connecting rod assemblies is intended, full disassembly of the top-end*

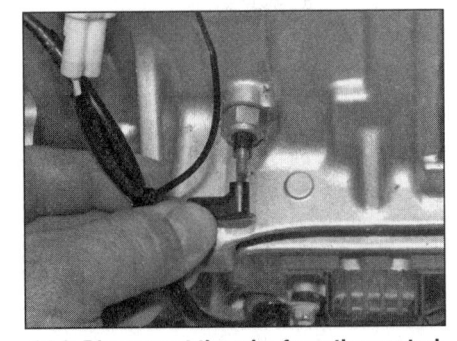

24.2 Disconnect the wire from the neutral switch

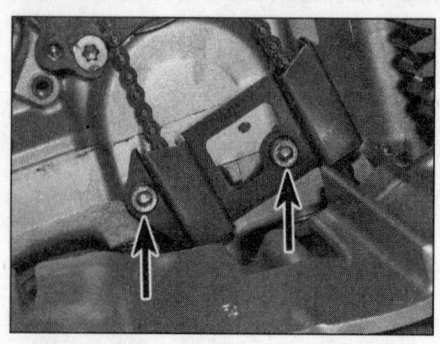

2•52 Engine, clutch and transmission

24.3 Unscrew the bolts (arrowed) and remove the guide and chain

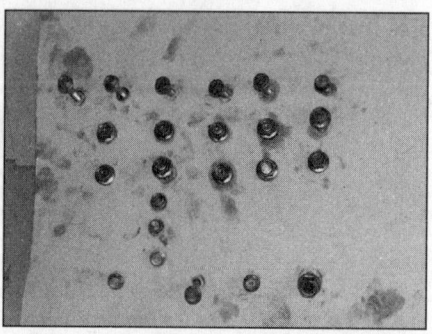

24.4 Example of a card template for storing crankcase bolts

is necessary. If you don't want to remove the timing rotor the cam chain can remain loose on the crankshaft after the camshafts have been removed, and can be taken off after the crankshaft has been removed.

3 Undo the oil pump drive chain guide bolts and remove the guide and the chain **(see illustration)**.

4 Place the engine upside down and support it on wooden blocks as required so it is level and stable. As there are many different sizes of bolt used to join the crankcases, draw an outline of the lower crankcase on a piece of cardboard, then punch a hole for each bolt – as each one is removed, store it in its relative position in the card **(see illustration)**. This will ensure all bolts and washers are installed in the correct location on reassembly.

5 Unscrew the 6 mm and 8 mm lower crankcase bolts evenly and a little at a time in reverse numerical order of the tightening sequence shown and as marked on the crankcase until they are finger-tight, then remove them **(see illustrations)**.

6 Now unscrew the ten 9 mm crankshaft journal bolts evenly and a little at a time and again in reverse of the tightening sequence **(see illustration 24.5a)**, i.e. starting from the outside and working to the centre, until they are finger-tight, then remove them.

7 Carefully lift the lower crankcase half off the upper half, using a soft-faced hammer to tap around the joint to initially separate the halves if necessary **(see illustration)**. **Note:** *If the halves do not separate easily, make sure all fasteners have been removed. Do not try and separate the halves by levering against the crankcase mating surfaces as they are easily scored and will leak oil in the future if damaged.*

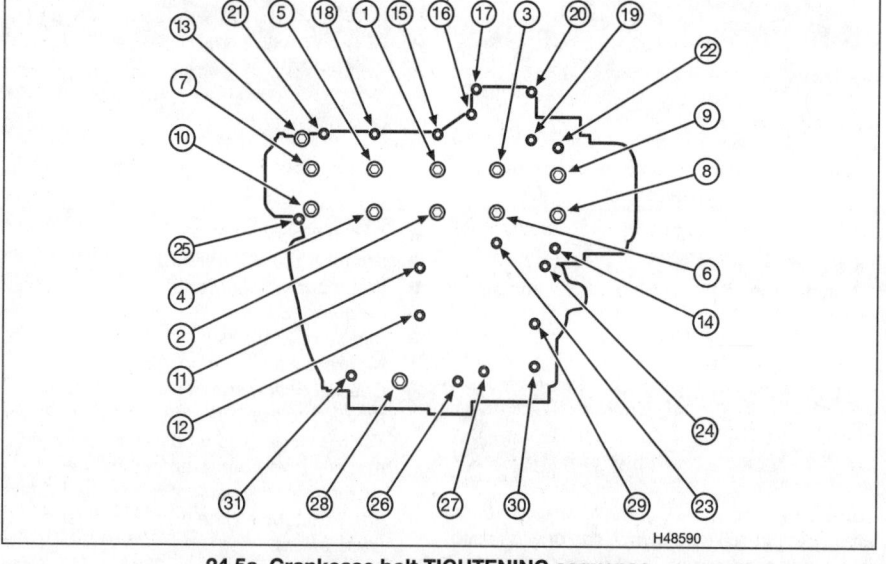

24.5a Crankcase bolt TIGHTENING sequence...

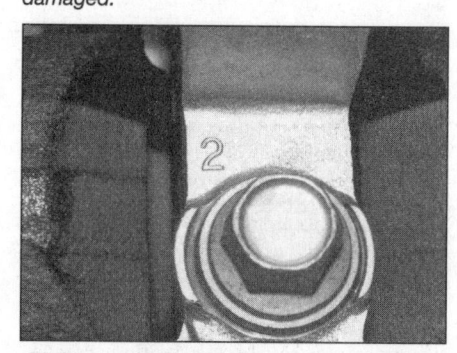

24.5b ...each bolt number is cast into the crankcase

24.5c A hole is provided for a socket extension for bolt 28

24.7 Lift the lower crankcase off the upper

Engine, clutch and transmission 2•53

24.13 Crankcase dowels (arrowed)

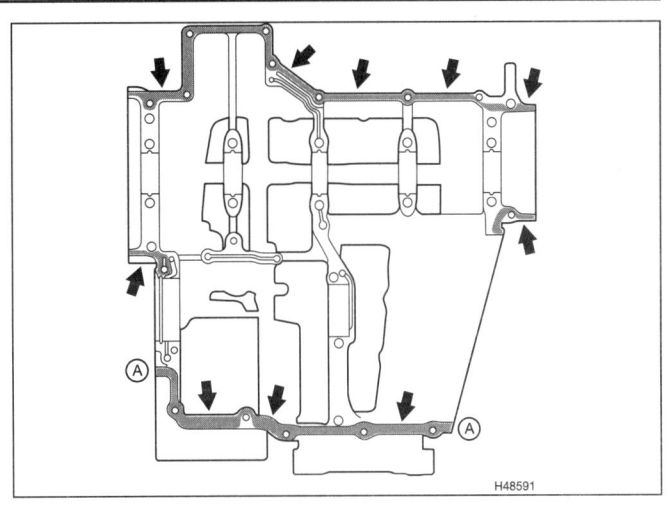

24.14 Crankcase sealant application
Note that the rear joint (A to A) should have two coats of sealant applied

8 Remove the three locating dowels from the crankcase if they are loose – they could be in either half (see illustration 24.13).
9 Refer to Sections 25 onwards for the removal, inspection and installation of the components housed within the crankcases.

Reassembly

10 Remove all traces of sealant from the crankcase mating surfaces.
11 Make sure the crankshaft, connecting rods and pistons and the balancer shafts and transmission shafts and all bearings are in place in the upper and lower crankcase halves.
12 Generously lubricate all bearings with clean engine oil, then use a rag soaked in high flash-point solvent to wipe over the mating surfaces of both crankcase halves to remove all traces of oil.
13 If removed, fit the three locating dowels in the upper crankcase half (see illustration).
14 Apply a small amount of suitable sealant (Three-Bond 1215 or equivalent RTV sealant – ask your dealer) to the shaded areas of the lower crankcase half as shown (see illustration). Note that the rear joint should have a second coating of sealant applied as shown in the illustration.

Caution: Apply the sealant only to the shaded areas. Do not apply an excessive amount as it will ooze out when the case halves are assembled and may obstruct oil passages. Do not apply the sealant within 2 to 3 mm of any of the bearing shells or surfaces, or oil passages.

15 Check again that all components are in position, and that the bearing shells are still correctly located in the lower crankcase half. Carefully fit the lower crankcase half down onto the upper crankcase half, making sure the dowels locate correctly (see illustration 24.7). Check that the lower crankcase half is correctly seated.

Caution: The crankcase halves should fit together without being forced. If the casings are not correctly seated, remove the lower crankcase half and investigate the problem. Do not attempt to pull them together using the crankcase bolts as the casing will crack and be ruined.

16 Lubricate the threads and washers of the ten NEW 9 mm crankshaft journal bolts, fit them and tighten them finger-tight (see illustration and 24.5a). Clean and lubricate the threads of the 6 mm and 8 mm crankcase bolts as you fit them in their original locations according to your template. Secure all bolts finger-tight.
17 The 9 mm crankshaft journal bolts must be tightened in four stages as follows: first, tighten them in the numerical sequence (1 to 10) shown to the torque setting specified at the beginning of the Chapter (see illustration 24.5a). Second, loosen all the bolts in a reverse of the numerical sequence. Third, re-tighten them in the numerical sequence to the specified torque setting. Fourth, using a degree disc if available, tighten the bolts in the numerical sequence and in one go

24.16 You must use new 9 mm crankshaft journal bolts

24.17 Using a degree disc to angle-tighten the 9 mm bolts

2•54 Engine, clutch and transmission

through 120° **(see illustration)**. If you do not have a degree disc mark some white paint on one of the corners of each bolt, then make a similar mark two corners clockwise from the first mark but on the crankcase, not the bolt – tighten the bolt until the mark on it aligns with the mark on the crankcase and it will have gone through the correct angle. If you inadvertently tighten through more than the specified angle do not loosen the bolt off and retighten it – remove the bolt, replace it with a new one and repeat the four stage tightening sequence.

18 Now tighten the 8 mm and 6 mm bolts evenly and a little at a time in correct numerical sequence to the torque setting specified at the beginning of the Chapter for each number bolt.

19 With all crankcase fasteners tightened, check that the crankshaft and balancer shafts rotate smoothly and easily, but at this stage do not worry about any noise from the gear teeth if the balancer backlash settings have been disturbed during the removal and installation procedure. Refer to Section 32 and adjust the backlash following the static adjustment procedure.

20 Clean the threads of the oil pump drive chain guide bolts and apply some fresh threadlock. Fit the chain and guide and tighten the bolts to the torque setting specified for your model **(see illustration 24.3)**.

21 Install all other removed assemblies in a reverse of the sequence given in Step 2.

25 Crankcases and cylinder bores

Crankcases

1 After the crankcases have been separated, remove the crankshaft and its bearing shells, connecting rods and pistons, transmission shafts, balancer shafts, neutral switch/gear position switch/gear position sensor/speed sensor according to model, referring to the relevant Sections of this Chapter, and to Chapters 4 and 8. If there are any other components or assemblies that have not been removed as part of your stripdown procedure, for example the starter motor or the coolant inlet union, remove these as well, referring to the relevant Chapter.

2 Withdraw the transmission shaft oil pipe **(see illustration)**. Remove the O-rings – new ones must be used **(see illustration)**. Remove the internal oil baffle plates and the crankcase damper plate if required **(see illustrations)**.

3 Clean the crankcases thoroughly with solvent and dry them with compressed air. Blow out all oil passages with compressed air. Clean the inside of the oil level inspection window. Clean and blow through the piston oil jets and holders.

4 Remove all traces of old gasket sealant from the mating surfaces. Clean up minor damage to the surfaces with a fine sharpening stone or grindstone.

Caution: Be very careful not to nick or gouge the crankcase mating surfaces or oil leaks will result. Check both crankcase halves very carefully for cracks and other damage.

5 Small cracks or holes in aluminium castings can be repaired with an epoxy resin adhesive as a temporary measure. Permanent repairs can only be done by argon-arc welding, and only a specialist in this process is in a position to advise on the economy or practical aspect of such a repair. If any damage is found that can't be repaired, replace the crankcase halves as a set.

6 Damaged threads can be economically reclaimed using a diamond section wire insert, for example of the Heli-Coil type (though there are other makes), which are easily fitted after drilling and re-tapping the affected thread.

7 Sheared studs or screws can usually be removed with extractors, which consist of a tapered, left-hand thread screw of very hard steel. These are inserted into a pre-drilled hole in the stud, and usually succeed in dislodging the most stubborn stud or screw. If a stud has sheared above its bore line, it can be removed using a conventional stud extractor that avoids the need for drilling.

> **HAYNES HINT**: *Refer to Tools and Workshop Tips for details of installing a thread insert and using screw extractors.*

25.2a Withdraw the oil pipe...

25.2b ...and retrieve the inner end O-ring if it is not on the pipe

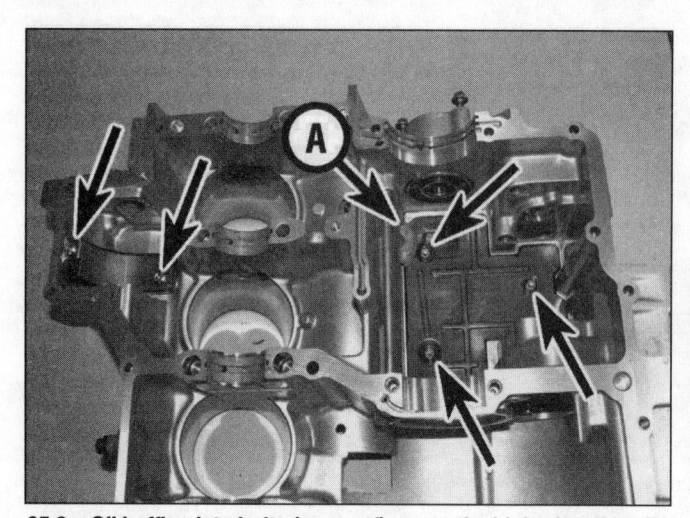

25.2c Oil baffle plate bolts (arrowed) – note the blob of sealant (A)

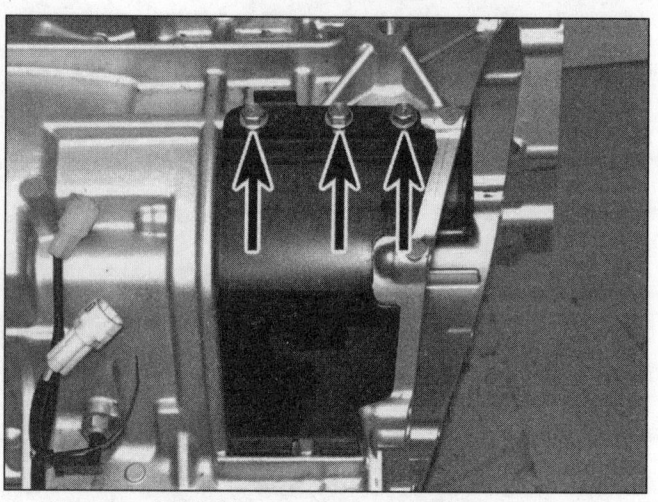

25.2d Damper plate bolts (arrowed)

Engine, clutch and transmission 2•55

8 Fit new O-rings smeared with grease onto the oil pipe **(see illustration)**. Slide the pipe into the crankcase **(see illustration 25.2a)** and locate the tab in the hole **(see illustration)**.

9 If the internal oil baffle plates and crankcase damper plate were removed clean the threads of the bolts and apply a suitable non-permanent threadlock, and tighten them to the torque setting specified at the beginning of the Chapter **(see illustrations 25.2c and d)**. Apply a blob of sealant to the front of the large baffle plate as shown.

10 Install all components and assemblies, referring to the relevant Sections of this and the other Chapters, before reassembling the crankcase halves.

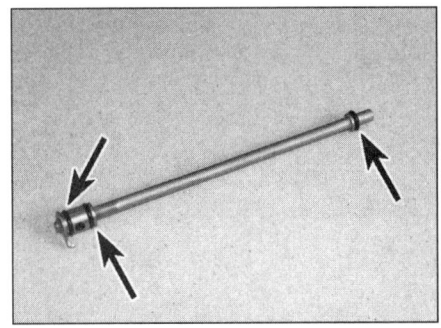

Cylinder bores

Note: *Do not attempt to separate the cylinder liners from the cylinder block. The liners are made of an aluminium/ceramic powdered metal composite and so great care must be taken not to scratch or gouge them.*

11 Check the cylinder walls carefully for scratches and score marks.

12 Using telescoping gauges and a micrometer (see *Tools and Workshop Tips*), check the dimensions of each cylinder to assess the amount of wear, taper and ovality. Measure near the top (but below the level of the top piston ring at TDC), centre and bottom (but above the level of the oil ring at BDC) of the bore, both parallel to and across the crankshaft axis **(see illustrations)**. Compare the results to the specifications at the beginning of the Chapter. If the cylinders are worn a new set of crankcases are required, along with new pistons and rings.

13 If the precision measuring tools are not available, take the upper crankcase to a Yamaha dealer or specialist motorcycle repair shop for assessment and advice.

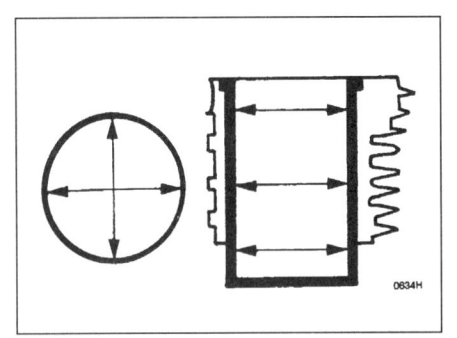

26 Connecting rod and main bearing information

1 Even though new main and connecting rod bearings are generally fitted during engine overhaul, the old bearings should be retained for close examination as they may reveal valuable information about the condition of the engine.

2 Bearing failure occurs mainly because of lack of lubrication, the presence of dirt or other foreign particles, overloading the engine and/or corrosion. Regardless of the cause of bearing failure, it must be corrected before the engine is reassembled to prevent it from happening again.

3 When examining the bearings, lay them out on a clean surface in the same general position as their location on the crankshaft journals.

25.8a Fit new O-rings (arrowed)

25.8b Seat the tab in the hole (arrowed)

25.12a Measure the cylinder bore in the directions shown...

25.12b ...using a telescoping gauge, then measure the gauge with a micrometer

This will enable you to match any noted bearing problems with the corresponding crankshaft journal.

4 Dirt and other foreign particles get into the engine in a variety of ways. They may be left in the engine during assembly or they may pass through filters or breathers, then get into the oil and from there into the bearings. Metal chips from machining operations and normal engine wear are often present. Abrasives are sometimes left in engine components after reconditioning operations, especially when parts are not thoroughly cleaned using the proper cleaning methods. Whatever the source, foreign objects often end up imbedded in the soft bearing material and are easily recognised. Large particles will not imbed in the bearing and will score or gouge the bearing and journal. The best prevention for this cause of bearing failure is to clean all parts thoroughly and keep everything spotlessly clean during engine reassembly. Regular oil and filter changes are also recommended.

5 Lack of lubrication or lubrication breakdown has a number of interrelated causes. Excessive heat (which thins the oil), overloading (which squeezes the oil from the bearing face) and oil leakage or throw off (from excessive bearing clearances, worn oil pump or high engine speeds) all contribute to lubrication breakdown. Blocked oil passages will starve a bearing of lubrication and destroy it. When lack of lubrication is the cause of bearing failure, the bearing material is wiped or extruded from the steel backing of the bearing. Temperatures may increase to the point where the steel backing and the journal turn blue from overheating.

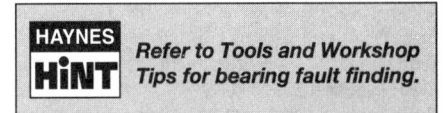

HAYNES HiNT *Refer to Tools and Workshop Tips for bearing fault finding.*

6 Riding habits can have a definite effect on bearing life. Full throttle low, speed operation, or labouring the engine, puts very high loads on bearings, which tend to squeeze out the oil film. These loads cause the bearings to flex, which produces fine cracks in the bearing face (fatigue failure). Eventually the bearing material will loosen in pieces and tear away from the steel backing. Short trip riding leads to corrosion of bearings, as insufficient engine heat is produced to drive off the condensed water and corrosive gases produced. These products collect in the engine oil, forming acid and sludge. As the oil is carried to the engine bearings, the acid attacks and corrodes the bearing material.

7 Incorrect bearing installation during engine assembly will lead to bearing failure as well. Tight fitting bearings which leave insufficient bearing oil clearances result in oil starvation. Dirt or foreign particles trapped behind a bearing shell result in high spots on the bearing which lead to failure.

8 To avoid bearing problems, clean all parts thoroughly before reassembly, double check all bearing clearance measurements and lubricate the new bearings with clean engine oil during installation.

2•56 Engine, clutch and transmission

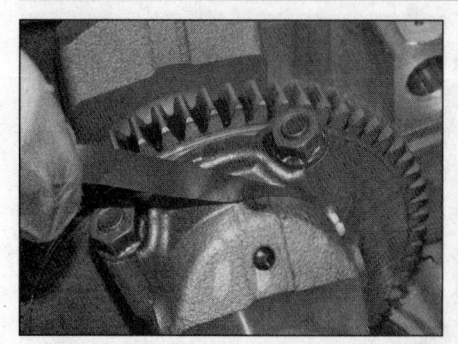

27.2 Measure the connecting rod side clearance

27.4a Unscrew the connecting rod cap nuts (arrowed)...

27.4b ...and remove the cap

27 Crankshaft and connecting rod removal and installation

Note: *The crankshaft journal bolts and the connecting rod bolts/nuts are of the stretch type and can only be used in a running engine once, though they can be used when performing the oil clearance check to prevent having to buy two sets of new bolts.*
Special tool: *A degree disc is shown in illustration 27.30b for tightening the connecting rod nuts; the procedure can however be performed without the tool.*

Removal

1 Remove the engine from the frame (see Section 4) and separate the crankcase halves (see Section 24). Remove the front balancer shaft (Section 32).
2 Before detaching the rods from the crankshaft, measure the side clearance (the gap between the connecting rod big-end and the crankshaft web) with a feeler gauge **(see illustration)**. If the clearance is greater than the service limit listed in this Chapter's Specifications, replace the rods with new ones, then check the clearance again. If the clearance is still excessive, replace the crankshaft with a new one.
3 Using paint or a felt marker pen, mark the relevant cylinder identity (1 to 4 from left to right) across the front face of each connecting rod and cap. Note that the number and letter already across the rear face of the rod and cap indicate rod size and weight grade **(see illustration 29.11)**. The piston crown is marked with a triangle pointing to the front of the engine, and there is a Y mark on each connecting rod that faces to the left-hand side. All these marks ensure everything can be easily installed in its correct location and way round on installation.
4 Unscrew the connecting rod cap nuts **(see illustration)**. Separate the caps from the crankpin **(see illustration)** – if they are difficult to remove tap the ends of the bolts with a soft-faced hammer. Push the rods and pistons up to the tops of the bores so that the bottom ends are clear of the crankshaft, taking care to keep the rods clear of the cylinder liners – it is best to protect the liners with some rag **(see illustration)**.
5 Lift the crankshaft out of the upper crankcase half, bringing the cam chain with it if it hasn't been removed, and taking care not to dislodge the main bearing shells **(see illustration)**. Wrap some rag around each connecting rod to protect the cylinder walls.
Caution: *Do not try to remove the piston/connecting rod from the bottom of the cylinder bore. The piston will not pass the crankcase main bearing webs. If the piston is pulled right to the bottom of the bore the oil control ring will expand and lock the piston in position. If this happens it is likely the ring will break.*
6 If you are doing a big-end oil clearance check leave the connecting rod assemblies installed and perform the check now (Section 29).
7 To remove the connecting rod assemblies turn the crankcase on its side. Push each piston/connecting rod assembly up its bore and remove it from the top making sure the connecting rod does not mark the cylinder walls **(see illustration)**. Keep the rod, cap, nuts and bolts (if they are to be used for an oil clearance check), and the bearing shells (if they are to be reused) together in their correct positions to ensure correct installation – fit the caps back onto the rods and finger-tighten the nuts to make sure.

HAYNES HiNT *To ease removal of the pistons, carefully remove any ridge of carbon built up on the top of each cylinder bore using a scraper, Stanley blade or scouring cloth. If there is a pronounced wear ridge, remove it using a ridge reamer.*

8 If necessary remove the main bearing shells from the crankcase halves using a small screwdriver inserted in the notch to lift them out, or by pushing the side out, but make sure you keep them in order **(see illustration 28.2)**. If they are being reused they must be returned to their original location.
9 Remove the pistons from the connecting rods if required (see Section 30).

27.4c Push the rod off the crank and up the bore

27.5 Lift the crankshaft out of the crankcase

27.7 Push the rod and remove the piston/rod assembly from the top of the bore

Engine, clutch and transmission 2•57

Crankshaft inspection

10 Clean the crankshaft with solvent, squirting it under pressure through all the oil passages. If available, blow the crank dry with compressed air, and also blow through the oil passages. Check the primary drive gear and the balancer drive gear for wear or damage **(see illustration)**. If any of the gear teeth are excessively worn, chipped or broken, the crankshaft must be replaced with a new one. If wear or damage is found, also inspect the primary driven gear on the back of the clutch housing (see Section 15), and the balancer shaft driven gears (see Section 32).

11 Refer to Section 26 and examine the main bearing shells. If they are scored, badly scuffed or appear to have been seized, a new set of shells must be installed, selected as described in Section 28. If they are badly damaged, check the corresponding crankshaft journals (Step 13). Evidence of extreme heat, such as discoloration, indicates that lubrication failure has occurred. Thoroughly check the oil pump and pressure relief valve as well as all oil holes and passages before reassembling the engine.

12 If the shells are not obviously damaged perform an oil clearance check to gauge the extent of wear (Section 28).

13 Give the crankshaft journals a close visual examination, paying particular attention where damaged bearings have been discovered. If the journals are scored or pitted in any way a new crankshaft will be required.

14 Place the crankshaft on V-blocks and check the runout at the main bearing journals using a dial gauge. Compare the reading to the maximum specified at the beginning of the Chapter. If the runout exceeds the limit, the crankshaft must be replaced with a new one.

Connecting rod inspection

15 Check the connecting rods for cracks and other obvious damage.

16 Apply clean engine oil to the piston pin, insert it into the connecting rod small-end and check for any freeplay between the two **(see illustration)**. Measure the pin external diameter at its centre, and the small-end bore diameter. Compare the result to the specifications at the beginning of the Chapter and replace the components that are worn with new ones.

17 Refer to Section 26 and examine the connecting rod bearing shells. If they are scored, badly scuffed, corroded, or appear to have seized, a new set of shells must be installed, selected as described in Section 29. If they are badly damaged, check the corresponding crankpin. Evidence of extreme heat, such as discoloration, indicates that lubrication failure has occurred. Be sure to thoroughly check the oil pump and pressure relief valve as well as all oil holes and passages before reassembling the engine.

18 If the shells are not obviously damaged perform an oil clearance check to gauge the extent of wear (Section 29).

19 Have the rods checked for twist and bend by a Yamaha dealer if you doubt they are straight.

Installation

20 Remove the shells from the rods and caps using a small screwdriver inserted in the notch to lift them out **(see illustration 29.2)**.

21 Knock the old bolts out of the connecting rods **(see illustrations)**. Lubricate the shanks of the NEW bolts with molybdenum disulphide oil (a 50/50 mixture of molybdenum disulphide grease and clean engine oil) and fit them into the rods – there are two ways to do this: if the pistons have been removed you can tap them in using a hammer until seated, making sure the oval heads are correctly aligned **(see illustrations)**; if the pistons have not been removed, or as an alternative to tapping them in if they have been removed, you can

27.10 Primary drive gear (A), balancer drive gear (B)

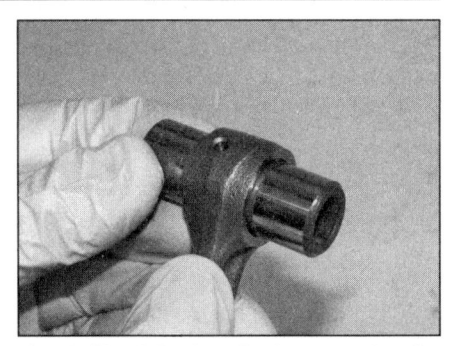

27.16 Check for freeplay between the pin and the rod

27.21a Fit a nut onto the end of the bolt and tap the bolt down...

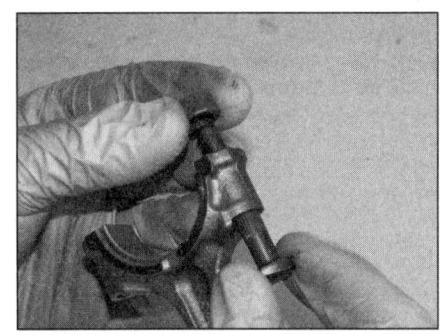

27.12b ...remove the nut and withdraw the bolt

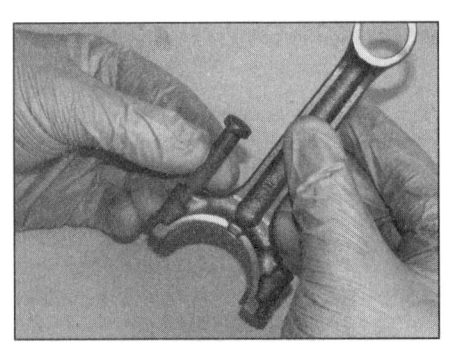

27.21c Fit the new bolt...

27.21d ...aligning the head correctly...

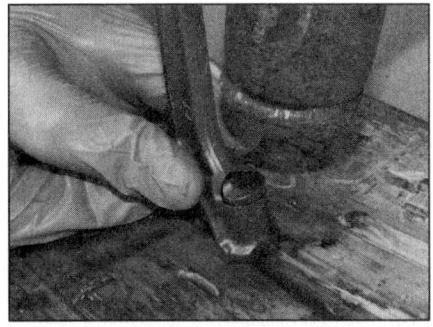

27.21e ...and tap it in until it seats

2•58 Engine, clutch and transmission

27.21f Offset the head slightly to counter the twist...

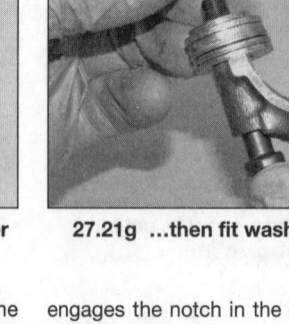

27.21g ...then fit washers and a nut...

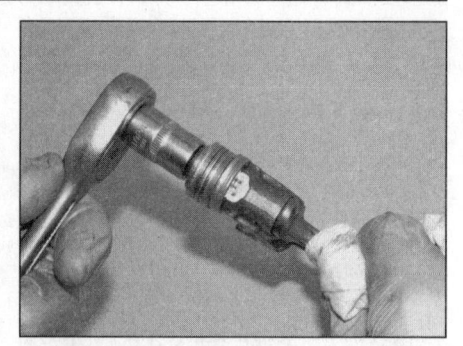

27.21h ...and tighten the nut to draw the bolt in

draw them in using the old nuts and some washers as spacers **(see illustrations)** – this is the better method as you know when the bolts are fully seated when the nuts go tight, but you have to counter the twisting effect by offsetting the bolt heads slightly clockwise (when viewed from the top) to ensure they align and seat correctly. If the head of any bolt is misaligned (whichever method used) tap the bolt out and reset it.

22 Fit the pistons onto the connecting rods if removed (see Section 30).

23 Clean the backs of the connecting rod bearing shells and the bearing housings in both cap and rod. If new shells are being fitted, clean all traces of any protective grease off using paraffin (kerosene). Wipe the shells, cap and rod dry with a clean lint free cloth. Fit the bearing shells in the connecting rods and caps, making sure the tab on each shell engages the notch in the connecting rod/cap **(see illustration)**. Lubricate the shells with clean engine oil.

24 Position the upper crankcase the correct way up. Lubricate the pistons, rings and cylinder bores with clean engine oil. Wrap some rag round the bottom of each connecting rod. Fit a piston ring compressor around the first piston being installed and tighten it to compress the rings – a compressor is required because there is very little lead-in for the rings to be easily fed in by hand **(see illustrations)**. Locate the piston/connecting assembly on the top of its bore with the triangle mark or your own mark on the piston crown pointing to the front of the engine, and tap the top of the piston using a wooden or plastic tool (such as the handle end of a hammer) until the piston is completely in the bore **(see illustrations)**. If resistance is felt a ring may be catching on the rim – do not try to force it in as rings are easily broken. Tighten the compressor a bit more to squash the ring. Install the other pistons/rods in the same way.

25 Carefully turn the crankcase upside down.

26 Clean the backs of the main bearing shells and the bearing housings in both crankcase halves. If new shells are being fitted, clean all traces of any protective grease off using paraffin (kerosene). Wipe the shells and crankcase halves dry with a lint-free cloth. Make sure all the oil passages and holes are clear, and blow them through with compressed air if it is available.

27 Press the bearing shells into their locations. Make sure the tab on each shell engages in the notch in the casing **(see illustration)**. Make sure the bearings are fitted in the correct locations and take care not to

27.23 Locate the tab in the notch

27.24a Fit the ring compressor over the piston...

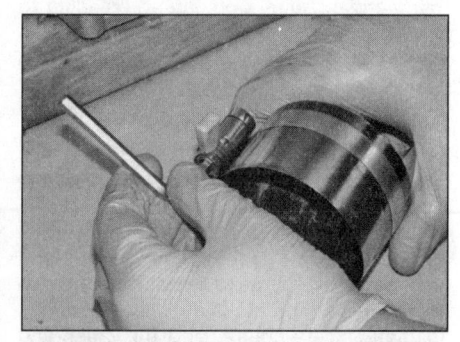

27.24b ...and tighten it to compress the rings

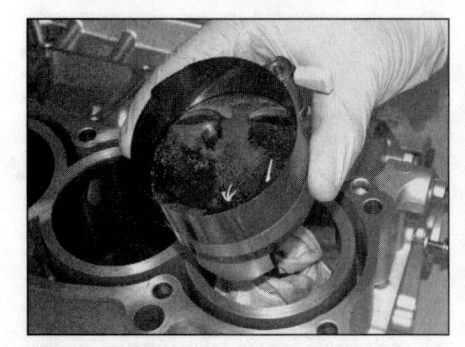

27.24c Fit the piston into its bore and seat the compressor on the block...

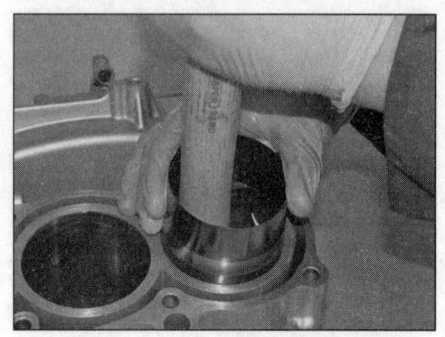

27.24d ...then tap the piston down

27.27 Locate the tab in the notch

Engine, clutch and transmission 2•59

27.30a Fit the new nuts

27.30b Using a degree disc to angle-tighten the connecting rod cap nuts

touch any shell's bearing surface with your fingers. Lubricate each shell with molybdenum disulphide oil (a 50/50 mixture of molybdenum disulphide grease and clean engine oil).

28 If the timing rotor has not been removed fit the cam chain around its sprocket on the crankshaft. Lower the crankshaft into position in the upper crankcase **(see illustration 27.5)**.

29 Lubricate the crankpins with clean engine oil. Remove the rag and carefully pull the connecting rods onto the crankpins, taking care not to mark the cylinders **(see illustration 27.4c)**. Fit the caps onto the rods **(see illustration 27.4b)** – make sure all previously made markings align, and that the rods are facing the right way (see Step 3).

30 Apply some clean oil to the threads and under the heads of the NEW connecting rod nuts, then fit them and tighten them finger-tight **(see illustration)**. The nuts must be tightened in two stages as follows: first, tighten them to the torque setting specified at the beginning of the Chapter. Second, using a degree disc if available, tighten the bolts in one go through 120° **(see illustrations)**. If you do not have a degree disc mark some white paint on one of the corners of each nut, them make a similar mark two corners clockwise from the first mark but on the connecting rod, not the nut, as shown – tighten the nut until the mark on it aligns with the mark on the rod and it will have gone through the correct angle. If you inadvertently tighten through more than the specified angle do not loosen the nut off and retighten it – remove the nut, connecting rod and bolt, replace the bolt with a new one and repeat the installation and tightening sequence using a new nut. It is highly advisable to have an assistant to hold the crankshaft down in the crankcase while tightening the bolts. Fit the other connecting rods in the same way.

31 Check to make sure that all components have been returned to their original locations using the marks made on disassembly. Check that the crankshaft is free to rotate easily. If there are any signs of roughness or tightness, remove the rods and recheck the bearing clearance. Sometimes tapping the bottom of the connecting rod cap will relieve tightness, but if in doubt, recheck the clearances.

32 Install the front balancer shaft (Section 32). Reassemble the crankcase halves (see Section 24).

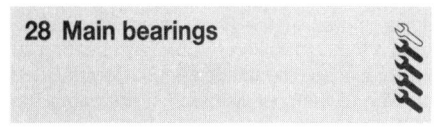

28 Main bearings

Oil clearance check

1 Whether new bearing shells are being fitted or the original ones are being reused, the main bearing oil clearance should be checked before the engine is reassembled. Main bearing oil clearance is measured with a product known as Plastigauge.

2 Remove the main bearing shells from the crankcase halves using a small screwdriver inserted in the notch to lift them out, or by pushing the side out, but make sure you keep them in order **(see illustration)**. Clean the backs of the shells and the bearing housings in both crankcase halves.

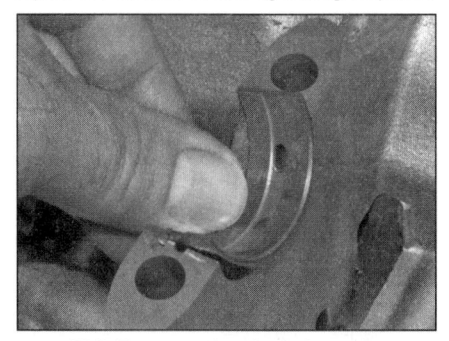

28.2 Remove the shells from the crankcases

28.13 Main bearing journal size code numbers (arrowed)

3 Press the bearing shells into their cut-outs, ensuring that the tab on each shell engages in the notch in the crankcase **(see illustration 27.27)**. Make sure the bearings are fitted in the correct locations and take care not to touch any shell's bearing surface with your fingers.

4 Ensure the shells and crankshaft are clean and dry. Lay the crankshaft in position in the upper crankcase **(see illustration 27.5)**. Fit the three crankcase dowels if removed **(see illustration 24.13)**.

5 Cut five lengths of the appropriate size Plastigauge (they should be slightly shorter than the width of the crankshaft journals). Place a strand of Plastigauge on each (cleaned) journal, avoiding the oil hole **(see illustration 9.17)**. During the procedure make sure the crankshaft is not rotated at all as this will disturb the Plastigauge and give false readings, in which case you must start again.

6 Carefully fit the lower crankcase half onto the upper half **(see illustration 24.7)**. Check that the lower half is correctly seated. **Note:** *Do not tighten the crankcase bolts if the casing is not correctly seated.* Fit the original 9 mm crankshaft journal bolts and tighten them finger-tight at first, then tighten them as described in Step 17 of Section 24.

7 Now slacken each bolt evenly and a little at a time in a reverse of the tightening sequence, i.e. starting from the outside and working to the centre, until they are all finger-tight, then remove the bolts. Carefully lift the lower crankcase off, making sure the Plastigauge is not disturbed.

8 Compare the width of the crushed Plastigauge on each crankshaft journal to the scale printed on the Plastigauge envelope to obtain the main bearing oil clearance **(see illustration 9.19)**. Compare the reading to the specifications at the beginning of the Chapter.

9 On completion carefully scrape away all traces of the Plastigauge material from the crankshaft journal and bearing shells using a fingernail or soft tool that will not score them.

10 If the clearance is within the range listed in this Chapter's Specifications and the bearings are in perfect condition, they can be reused.

11 If the clearance is beyond the service limit, replace the bearing shells with new ones (see below) and check the oil clearance once again. Always replace all of the shells as a set.

12 If the clearance is still greater than the service limit listed in this Chapter's Specifications, the crankshaft journal is worn and the crankshaft should be replaced with a new one.

Main bearing shell selection

13 Replacement main bearing shells are supplied on a selected fit basis according to the sizes of the crankshaft journals and their housings. The code numbers for the journals are the left-hand block of five numbers stamped on the outside of the left-hand crankshaft web **(see illustration)** (the right-hand block of four numbers are the

2•60 Engine, clutch and transmission

size codes for the connecting rod bearing journals). The first number of the block is for the left-hand (No. 1) journal, and so on.

14 The main bearing housing size code numbers are stamped on the back of the lower crankcase half **(see illustration)**. The first number of the five is for the left-hand (No. 1) bearing, and so on.

15 A range of bearing shells is available. To select the correct shells for a particular journal, subtract the crankshaft journal number from the crankcase number, and then add 2. Compare the result with the table below to find the colour coding of the replacement shells. For example, using the illustrations shown, for the left-hand main bearing the crankcase number 6 minus crankshaft number 2 plus 2 = 6; No. 6 bearing shells are colour coded pink. The colour code is marked on the side of each bearing shell **(see illustration)**.

Number	Colour
2	black
3	brown
4	green
5	yellow
6	pink
7	red
8	white

29 Connecting rod (big-end) bearings

Oil clearance check

1 Whether new bearing shells are being fitted or the original ones are being reused, the connecting rod bearing oil clearance should be checked prior to reassembly.

2 Remove the shells from the rods and caps **(see illustration)**. Clean the backs of the bearing shells and the bearing housings in both the connecting rod and cap.

3 Press the bearing shells into their housings, making sure the tab on each shell engages the notch in the connecting rod/cap **(see illustration 27.23)**. Make sure the bearings are fitted in the correct location and take care not to touch any shell's bearing surface with your fingers. Refer to Section 27 and lay the crankshaft in the upper crankcase half (make sure the main bearing shells are installed). Pull the connecting rods onto the crankpins **(see illustration 27.4c)**.

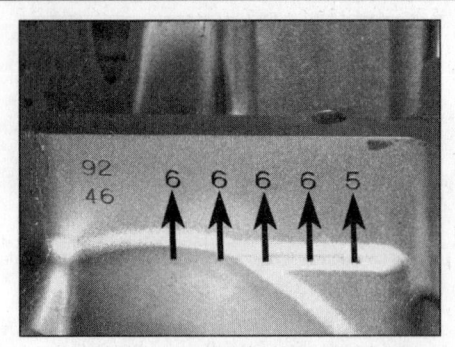

4 Cut a length of the appropriate size Plastigauge (it should be slightly shorter than the width of the crankpin). Place a strand of Plastigauge on each crankpin journal, making sure it is not over the oil hole **(see illustration 9.17)**. Fit the caps onto the rods **(see illustration 27.4b)**. Make sure each cap is fitted the correct way around so the previously made markings align. Fit the original nuts and tighten them as described in Step 30 of Section 27.

5 Now unscrew the nuts and remove the connecting rod caps. Compare the width of the crushed Plastigauge on the crankpin to the scale printed on the Plastigauge envelope to obtain the connecting rod big-end bearing oil clearance **(see illustration 9.19)**. Compare the reading to the specifications at the beginning of the Chapter.

6 On completion carefully scrape away all traces of the Plastigauge material from the crankpin and bearing shells using a fingernail or soft tool that will not score them.

7 If the clearance is within the range listed in this Chapter's Specifications and the bearings are in perfect condition, they can be reused.

8 If the clearance is beyond the service limit, replace the bearing shells with new ones (see below) and check the oil clearance once again. Always replace all of the shells as a set.

9 If the clearance is still greater than the service limit listed in this Chapter's Specifications, the crankpin journal is worn and the crankshaft should be replaced with a new one.

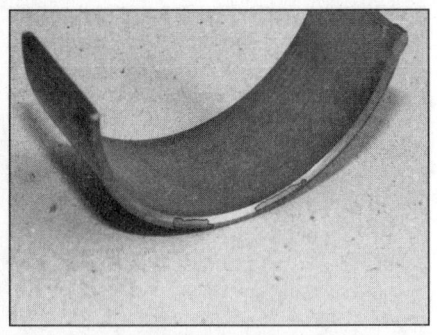

28.14 Main bearing housing size code numbers (arrowed)

28.15 Bearing shell colour code is on the side of the shell

Bearing shell selection

10 Replacement connecting rod bearing shells are supplied on a selected fit basis according to the sizes of the crankpin journals and their housings in the rod and cap. The code numbers for the big-end journals are the right-hand block of four numbers stamped on the outside of the left-hand crankshaft web **(see illustration)** (the left-hand block of five numbers are the size codes for the main bearing journals). The first number of the block is for the left-hand (No. 1) journal, and so on.

11 The connecting rod bearing housing size code number is marked on the rear face of the connecting rod and cap **(see illustration)**.

12 A range of bearing shells are available. To select the correct shells for a particular journal, subtract the crankpin journal number from the connecting rod number. Compare the result with the table below to find the colour coding of the replacement shells. For example, using the illustrations shown, for the left-hand (No. 1) crankpin journal the connecting rod number 6 minus journal number 1 = 5; No. 5 bearing shells are colour coded yellow. The colour code is marked on the side of each bearing shell **(see illustration 28.15)**.

Number	Colour
1	blue
2	black
3	brown
4	green
5	yellow
6	pink

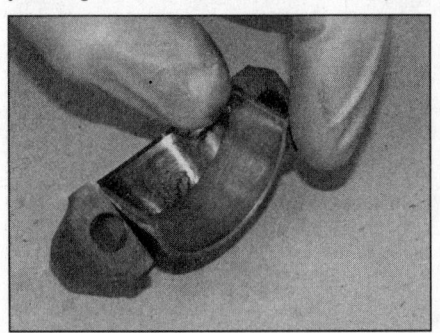

29.2 Remove the shells from the rods and caps

29.10 Crankpin journal size code numbers (arrowed)

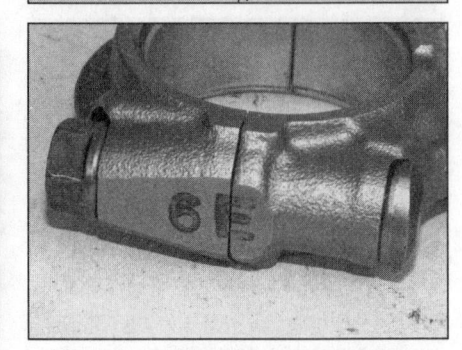

29.11 Connecting rod size number and weight letter

Engine, clutch and transmission 2•61

30 Pistons

Removal

1 Remove the crankshaft and connecting rods (see Section 27).
2 Before removing the piston from the connecting rod, use paint or a sharp scriber to write the cylinder identity and piston orientation on the crown of each piston (or on the inside of the skirt if the piston is dirty and going to be cleaned) **(see illustrations)**. Each piston crown is already marked with a triangle that points to the front of the engine (though it may be invisible until the piston is cleaned), and the Y mark on the connecting rod faces the left.
3 Carefully prise out the circlip on each side of the piston using needle-nose pliers or a small flat-bladed screwdriver inserted into the notch **(see illustration)**. Push the piston pin out and remove the piston from the connecting rod **(see illustration)**. Once removed the circlips must not be reused. Slide the pin back into its piston so that related parts do not get mixed up.

HAYNES HiNT *If a piston pin is a tight fit in the piston bosses, use a heat gun to heat the piston – this will expand the alloy piston sufficiently to release its grip on the pin. If the piston pin is particularly stubborn, extract it using a drawbolt tool, but be careful to protect the piston's working surfaces.*

4 Using your thumbs or a piston ring removal and installation tool, carefully remove the rings from the pistons **(see illustrations 31.10, 31.9a and b, 31.7c, b and a)**. Do not nick or gouge the pistons in the process. Carefully note which way up each ring fits and in which groove as they must be installed in their original positions if being reused. The upper surface of the top ring should be marked with the letter R or 1R at one end, and the second (middle) ring marked RN or 2R **(see illustration 31.9a)**. The top and second rings can also be identified by their different cross-section profiles.
5 Scrape all traces of carbon from the tops of the pistons. A hand-held wire brush or a piece of fine emery cloth can be used once most of the deposits have been scraped away. Do not, under any circumstances, use a wire brush mounted in a drill motor to remove deposits from the pistons; the piston material is soft and will be eroded away by the wire brush.
6 Use a piston ring groove cleaning tool to remove any carbon deposits from the ring grooves. If a tool is not available, a piece broken off an old ring will do the job. Be very careful to remove only the carbon deposits. Do not remove any metal and do not nick or gouge the sides of the ring grooves.

30.2a Make location and orientation markings on the piston

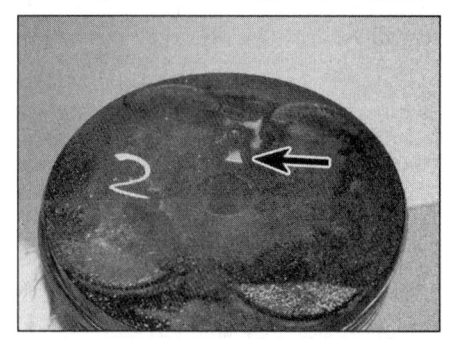

30.2b Triangle (arrowed) pointing to the front is visible after cleaning the carbon off

30.3a Prise out the circlip using a suitable tool in the notch...

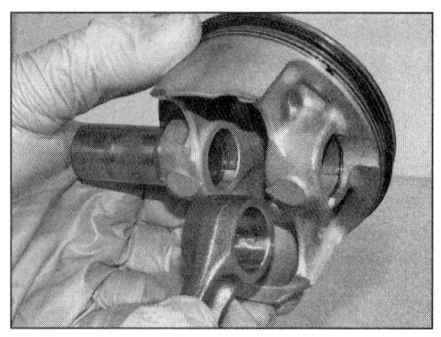

30.3b ...then push out the pin and separate the piston from the rod

7 Once the deposits have been removed, clean the pistons with solvent and dry them thoroughly. If the identification mark previously made on the piston is cleaned off, be sure to re-mark it with the correct identity. Make sure the oil return holes below the oil ring groove are clear.

Inspection

8 Carefully inspect each piston for cracks around the skirt, at the pin bosses and at the ring lands. Normal piston wear appears as even, vertical wear on the thrust surfaces of the piston. If the skirt is scored or scuffed, the engine may have been suffering from overheating and/or abnormal combustion, which causes excessively high operating temperatures. Also check that the circlip grooves are not damaged.
9 A hole in the top of the piston, in one extreme, or burned areas around the edge of the piston crown, indicate that pre-ignition or knocking under load have occurred. If you find evidence of any problems the cause must be corrected or the damage will occur again (see *Fault Finding* in the *Reference* section).
10 Measure the piston ring-to-groove clearance by laying each piston ring in its groove and slipping a feeler gauge in beside it **(see illustration)**. Make sure you have the correct ring for the groove (see Step 4). Check the clearance at three or four locations around the groove. If the clearance is greater than specified, replace both the piston and rings as a set. If new rings are being used, measure the clearance using the new rings. If the clearance is greater than that specified, the piston is worn and must be replaced with a new one.
11 Check the piston-to-bore clearance by measuring the bore (see Section 25), then measure the piston 5 mm up from the bottom of the skirt and at 90° to the piston pin axis **(see illustration)**. Make sure each piston is

30.10 Measure the piston ring-to-groove clearance with a feeler gauge

30.11 Measure the piston diameter with a micrometer at the specified distance from the bottom of the skirt

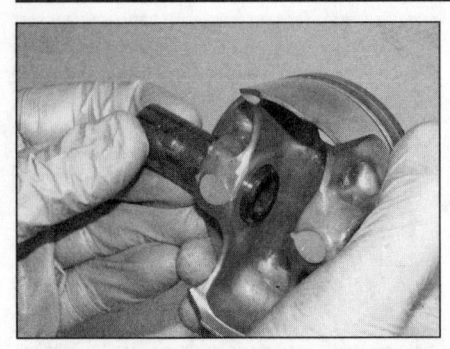

2•62 Engine, clutch and transmission

30.12a Check for freeplay between the pin and piston

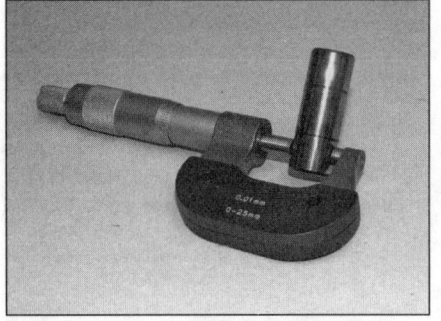

30.12b Measure the external diameter of the pin...

30.12c ...and the internal diameter of the bore in the piston

30.16 Secure the pin using a new circlip

matched to its correct cylinder. Refer to the Specifications at the beginning of the Chapter and subtract the piston diameter from the bore diameter to obtain the clearance. If it is greater than the specified figure, the piston must be replaced with a new one (assuming the bore itself is within limits).

12 Apply clean engine oil to the piston pin, insert it into the piston and check for any freeplay between the two **(see illustration)**. Measure the pin external diameter near each end, and the pin bores in the piston **(see illustrations)**. Calculate the difference to obtain the piston pin-to-piston pin bore clearance. Compare the result to the specifications at the beginning of the Chapter. If the clearance is greater than specified, replace the components that are worn beyond their specified limits. If not already done (see Section 27), repeat the measurements between the pin and the connecting rod small-end.

Installation

13 Inspect and install the piston rings (see Section 31).

14 Lubricate the piston pin, the piston pin bore and the connecting rod small-end bore with molybdenum disulphide oil (a 50/50 mixture of molybdenum disulphide grease and clean engine oil).

15 When fitting the pistons onto the connecting rods make sure that with the Y mark on the rod facing to the left the triangular mark on the piston crown points to the front **(see illustration 30.2)**.

16 Fit a *new* circlip into one side of the piston (do not reuse old circlips). Line up the piston on its correct connecting rod, and insert the piston pin from the other side **(see illustration 30.3b)**. Secure the pin with the other *new* circlip **(see illustration)**. When fitting the circlips, compress them only just enough to fit them in the piston, and make sure they are properly seated in their grooves with the open end away from the removal notch.

17 Install the connecting rods and crankshaft (see Section 27) and reassemble the crankcase halves (see Section 24).

31 Piston rings

Note: *It is good practice to replace the piston rings with new ones when an engine is being overhauled.*

Removal

1 See Section 30, Step 4.

Inspection

2 Whether reusing the old rings or fitting new ones, check the installed end gaps with the rings installed in the bore, as follows. Lay out each piston with its ring set and keep them together so the rings will be matched with the same piston and bore during the measurement procedure and engine assembly.

3 Insert the top ring into the top of the bore and square it up with the bore walls by pushing it in with the top of the piston **(see illustration)**. The ring should be at least 20 mm below the top edge of the bore, so it is within its area of travel in the bore. Slip a feeler gauge between the ends of the ring and compare the measurement to the specifications at the beginning of the Chapter **(see illustration)**.

4 If the gap is larger or smaller than specified, double check to make sure that you have the correct rings before proceeding; excess end gap is not critical unless it exceeds the service limit.

5 If the service limit is exceeded with new rings, check the bore for wear (see Section 25). If the gap is too small, the ring ends may come in contact with each other during engine operation, which can cause serious damage.

6 Repeat the procedure for the second ring and the oil control ring side-rails, but not the expander ring. Remember to keep the rings, pistons and bores matched up.

Installation

7 Fit the oil control ring (lowest on the piston) first. It is composed of three separate components, namely the expander and the upper and lower side-rails. Slip the expander into the groove, making sure the ends don't

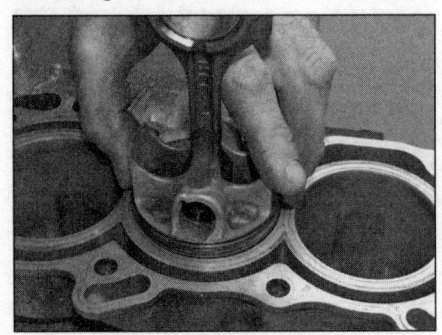

31.3a Fit the ring in its bore and set it square using the piston...

31.3b ...then measure the end gap using a feeler gauge

31.7a Fit the oil ring expander in its groove...

Engine, clutch and transmission 2•63

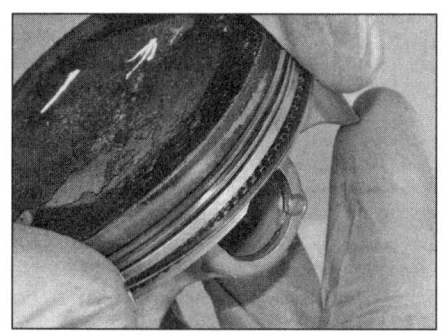

31.7b ...then fit the lower side rail...

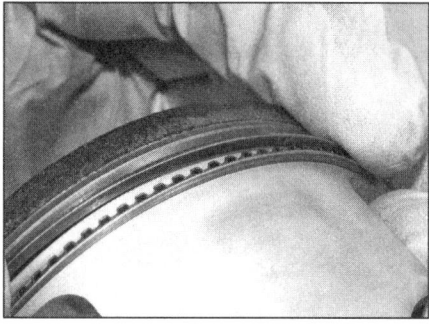

31.7c ...and the upper side rail on each side of it

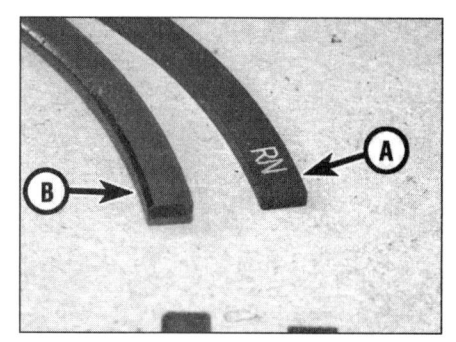

31.9a Second ring (A), top ring (B)

31.9b Fit the second ring – using a feeler gauge helps...

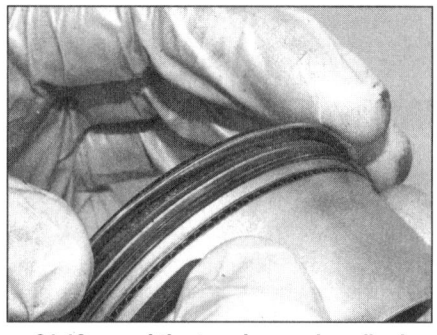

31.10 ...and the top ring as described

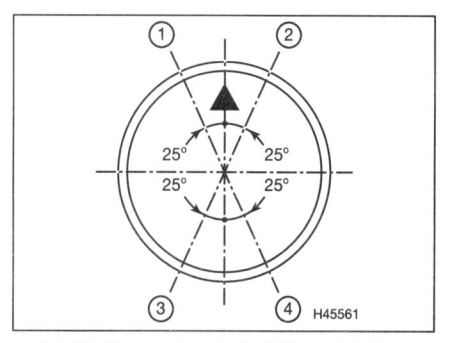

31.11 Piston ring installation details – stagger the ring end gaps as shown
1 Top ring
2 Oil ring lower side rail
3 Oil ring upper side rail
4 Second ring

overlap **(see illustration)**. Next fit the lower side-rail **(see illustration)**. Do not use a piston ring installation tool on the side-rails as they may be damaged. Instead, place one end of the side-rail into the groove between the expander and the ring land. Hold it firmly in place and slide a finger around the piston while pushing the rail into the groove. Next, fit the upper side-rail in the same manner **(see illustration)**. Check that the ends of the expander have not overlapped.

8 After the three oil ring components have been installed, check to make sure that both the upper and lower side-rails can be turned smoothly in the ring groove.

9 Fit the second (middle) ring next – it should be marked RN or 2R at one end, and it can also be identified by its square cross-section profile **(see illustration)**. Make sure that the ring is installed with the identification mark facing up. Fit the ring into the middle groove in the piston **(see illustration)**. Do not expand the ring any more than is necessary to slide it into place. To avoid breaking the ring, use a piston ring installation tool.

10 Finally, fit the top ring (it could be marked with the letter R or 1R, but on the engine photographed there were no markings), in the same manner into the top groove in the piston **(see illustration)**. Make sure the identification letter near the end gap is facing up.

11 Once the rings are correctly installed, check they move freely without snagging and stagger their end gaps as shown **(see illustration)**.

32 Balancer shafts

Removal

Front balancer shaft

1 Separate the crankcase halves (see Section 24) – the balancer shaft is in the upper half.
2 Make alignment marks between the balancer shaft holder and the slot on the end of the balancer shaft – this will give a good indication as to the starting point for resetting the backlash adjustment when the crankcases are reassembled **(see illustration)**. Note that if the relative positions of the shaft and holder are not disturbed, i.e. the pinch bolt is not slackened and the shaft is not turned in the holder and the holder is not removed from the shaft, there should be no reason to reset or adjust the backlash from its current position, unless it is suspected of not being correct. Unscrew the shaft holder mounting bolt.
3 Support the balancer gear/weight assembly, then withdraw the shaft, turning the holder/shaft if it appears stuck, and remove the gear/weight **(see illustration)**. Remove the shaft O-ring – a new one must be used.

Rear balancer shaft

4 Remove the throttle bodies (see Chapter 4).
5 Unscrew the balancer cover bolts and

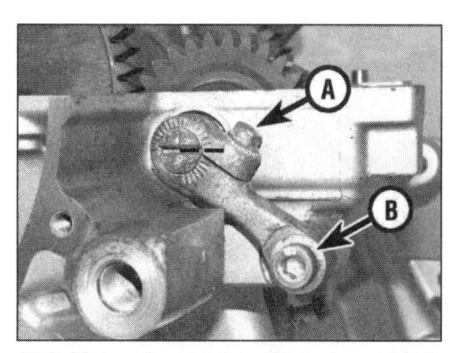

32.2 Make alignment marks between shaft and holder. Shaft holder pinch bolt (A) and mounting bolt (B)

32.3 Withdraw the shaft and remove the front balancer assembly

2•64 Engine, clutch and transmission

32.5 Rear balancer cover bolts (arrowed)

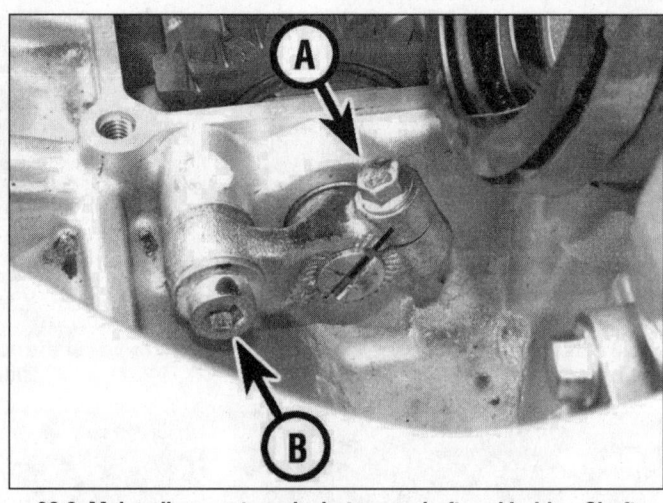

32.6 Make alignment marks between shaft and holder. Shaft holder pinch bolt (A) and mounting bolt (B)

remove the cover and the gasket **(see illustration)**. A new gasket must be used.

6 Make an alignment mark on the balancer shaft holder with the punch mark on the end of the balancer shaft – this will give a good indication as to the starting point for resetting the backlash adjustment when the crankcases are reassembled **(see illustration)**. Note that if the relative positions of the shaft and holder are not disturbed, i.e. the pinch bolt is not slackened and the shaft is not turned in the holder and the holder is not removed from the shaft, there should be no reason to reset or adjust the backlash from its current position,

unless it is suspected of not being correct. Unscrew the shaft holder mounting bolt.
7 Support the balancer gear/weight assembly, then withdraw the shaft, turning the holder/shaft if it appears stuck, and remove the gear/weight **(see illustration)**. Remove the shaft O-ring – a new one must be used.

Disassembly

8 Remove the shouldered washer and bearing from each end of the gear/weight **(see illustrations 32.12b and a)**. Separate the gear from the weight and remove the dampers **(see illustrations 32.11b and a)**.

Inspection

9 Clean, check and lubricate the bearings, then refit them. Slide the shaft back in and check that it runs freely and smoothly in the bearings. If there is any evidence of wear on the shaft, or it is a sloppy fit in the bearings, and the bearings are good, replace the shaft with a new one (first slacken the pinch bolt and remove the holder). If the bearings do not run smoothly and freely, or if there is any wear or damage evident, replace the gear/weight assembly with a new one – the bearings are not available separately.
10 Check the condition of the rubber dampers for damage, deformation and deterioration. Check the gear teeth, and if any damage or wear is evident also check the teeth on the drive gear on the crankshaft. The dampers and gear are not available separately – if there is wear or damage replace the gear/weight assembly with a new one.

Assembly

11 Smear the dampers with oil, then fit them back into the gear **(see illustration)**. Fit the gear onto the weight, aligning the marks on the inner rims, and making sure the dampers locate correctly **(see illustration)**.
12 Lubricate the bearings with clean oil and slide them in **(see illustration)**. Fit the shouldered washers **(see illustration)**.

32.7 Withdraw the rear shaft and remove the balancer assembly

32.11a Fit the dampers into the gear...

32.11b ...then fit the gear onto the weight, aligning the marks

32.12a Fit a bearing into each end...

32.12b ...and a washer onto each end

Engine, clutch and transmission 2•65

13 Fit a new O-ring smeared with grease onto the shaft **(see illustration)**. Fit the holder if removed, aligning it as shown relative to the slots and marks on the end of the shaft, and lightly tighten the pinch bolt.

Installation

Front balancer shaft

14 If the timing rotor has been removed fit it back onto the end of the crankshaft and finger-tighten the bolt **(see illustrations 14.8 and 14.9)**. If not already set, turn the crankshaft so the 'T' mark on the rotor faces to the rear and aligns with the crankcase mating surfaces **(see illustrations 9.4a and b)**.
15 Position the balancer gear/weight assembly in the crankcase, aligning the single punch mark on the weight with that on the crankcase **(see illustration)**. Slide the shaft in **(see illustration 32.3)**.
16 Clean the threads of the holder mounting bolt and apply some fresh threadlock. Fit the bolt and tighten it to the torque setting specified at the beginning of the Chapter **(see illustration 32.2)**.
17 Reassemble the crankcase halves (see Section 24).
18 If the relative positions of the shaft and holder have been disturbed carry out the static backlash adjustment procedure (see below).
19 Finish rebuilding the engine and install it (see Section 4).
20 Carry out the dynamic backlash adjustment procedure (see below).

Rear balancer shaft

21 Clean all old gasket off the balancer cover and crankcase mating surfaces.
22 Remove the timing rotor cover (Section 14). Turn the crankshaft so the 'T' mark on the rotor faces to the rear and aligns with the crankcase mating surfaces **(see illustrations 9.4a and b)**.
23 Position the balancer gear/weight assembly in the crankcase, aligning the double punch marks on the weight with the mark on the crankcase **(see illustration)**. Slide the shaft in **(see illustration 32.7)**.
24 Clean the threads of the holder mounting bolt and apply some fresh threadlock. Fit the bolt and tighten it to the torque setting specified at the beginning of the Chapter **(see illustration 32.6)**.
25 Fit the balancer cover using a new gasket with its UP mark facing up and tighten the bolts to the specified torque **(see illustration)**. Fit the timing rotor cover (Section 14).
26 If the relative positions of the shaft and holder have been disturbed carry out the static backlash adjustment procedure (see below).
27 Install the throttle bodies (see Chapter 4).
28 Carry out the dynamic backlash adjustment procedure (see below).

Backlash adjustment

Note: *A backlash adjustment is provided so that the gears mesh at their optimum point for quiet running with minimal wear. If the amount of backlash is too great, the shafts will clatter. If the gears are running tight, they will whine, and wear very quickly. At the optimum point the gears will run very quietly – it is easy to tell the difference with the engine running. Adjustment is possible due to the offset that allows eccentric movement of the balancer gear in relation to its drive gear when the shaft is turned. The static adjustment procedure allows the backlash to be set up in roughly the optimum position, but the dynamic procedure should always be carried out as well to fine tune the setting.*

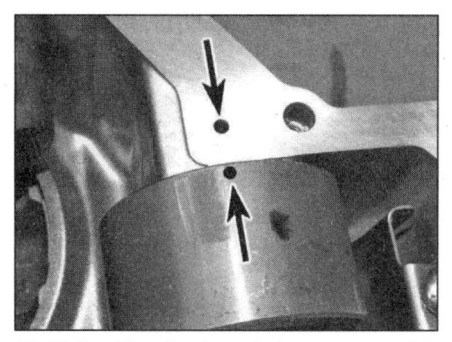

Static adjustment

Note: *This procedure must be carried out when the engine is cold. A torque wrench capable of accurately reading down to 0.4 Nm is required.*

29 Slacken the balancer shaft holder pinch bolt **(see illustration 32.2 or 32.6)**.
30 Turn the shaft slightly clockwise using a screwdriver in the slotted end, then turn it anti-clockwise until a torque of 0.4 Nm is reached – at this point backlash between the gears has been eliminated. Now turn the shaft clockwise so the slot moves one graduation as marked on the holder when doing the front balancer and two graduations when doing the rear, then tighten the pinch bolt.
31 Now carry out the dynamic adjustment procedure (see below).

Dynamic adjustment

Note: *This procedure must be carried out when the engine is warm.*

32 Start the engine and allow it to warm up, then let it idle.
33 Slacken the balancer shaft holder pinch bolt **(see illustration 32.2 or 32.6)**.

32.13 Fit a new O-ring (arrowed) into the groove

32.15 Position the front balancer assembly with the punch marks (arrowed) aligned

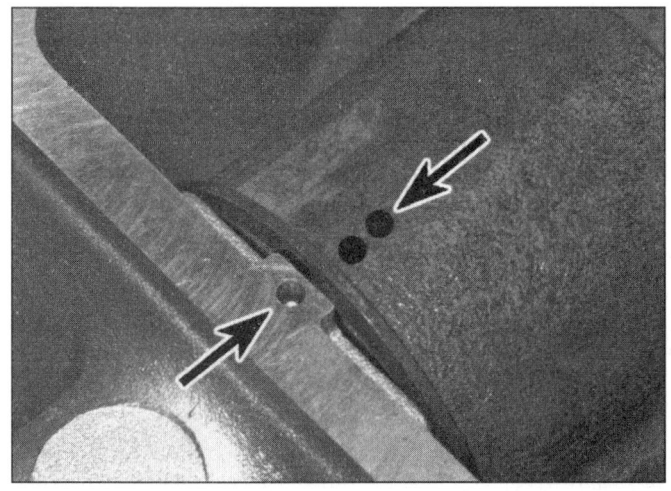

32.23 Position the rear balancer assembly with the punch marks (arrowed) aligned

32.25 Fit the gasket with the UP mark showing

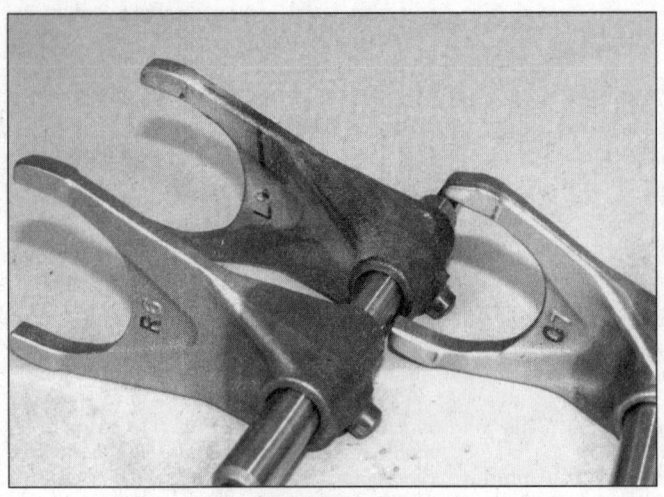

2•66 Engine, clutch and transmission

33.2 Note the identification letter on each fork

33.3 Retainer plate bolts (arrowed)

34 Turn the shaft slightly one way then the other to find the point at which the gears run at their quietest. Too far one way and the gears will whine (no backlash), too far the other and they will clatter (excessive backlash). Rev the engine and check that there is no unwanted noise at varying speeds.

35 On completion, tighten the pinch bolt.

33 Transmission assembly removal and installation

Removal

1 Remove the engine from the frame (Section 4) and separate the crankcase halves (Section 24).

2 Note that each selector fork is marked for identification. The left-hand fork is marked with an 'L', the middle fork is marked with a 'C', and the right-hand fork is marked with an 'R', all of which must face the right-hand crankcase half **(see illustration)**. The right and left-hand forks fit into the output shaft and the centre fork fits into the input shaft.

3 Unscrew the selector drum bearing and shaft retainer plate bolts and remove the plate, noting how it fits **(see illustration)**.

4 Withdraw the 'L' and 'R' fork shaft and remove the forks **(see illustration)**. Slide the forks back onto the shaft in their correct order and way round. The springs should stay in the shafts but take care in case they are loose and drop out.

5 Lift the output shaft out of the casing **(see illustration)**. If the shaft is stuck, use a soft-faced hammer and gently tap on the ends.

6 Withdraw the 'C' fork shaft and let the fork drop off the selector drum **(see illustration** **33.13)**. Withdraw the drum **(see illustration 33.12)**. Remove the fork. Slide the fork back onto the shaft the correct way round.

7 Undo the input shaft bearing housing screws **(see illustration)**. Thread two 6 mm bolts into the threaded holes in the housing (not the mounting screw holes) so they butt up against the crankcase, then tighten them evenly and a little at a time so the housing is pushed squarely out **(see illustration)**. When it is free withdraw the shaft **(see illustration 33.10a)**. Remove the bolts.

8 Refer to Section 34 for disassembly and inspection of the transmission shafts and bearings.

9 Refer to Section 35 for inspection of the selector drum and forks.

Installation

10 Clean the threads of the input shaft bearing housing screws – note that Yamaha specify to use new screws because of the indented rim. Slide the input shaft in the crankcase and fit the right-hand bearing

33.4 Withdraw the shaft and remove the L and R forks

33.5 Remove the output shaft

33.7a Undo the screws (arrowed)

33.7b Thread two bolts into the holes as shown and keep tightening to displace the housing

Engine, clutch and transmission 2•67

33.10a Slide the shaft in...

33.10b ...align the housing using a suitable rod as shown...

as far as it will go, using a rod or Allen key inserted through the hole in the housing rim and into that in the crankcase to ensure correct alignment (see illustrations). Now tap the housing squarely in using a soft hammer until the screws can be fitted, then use these to draw the housing in, tightening them a little at a time so the bearing is drawn in evenly all round (see illustrations). Now remove the screws, apply some threadlock, and tighten them to the torque setting specified at the beginning of the Chapter. Stake the rim of the screw against the indent in the housing (see illustration).

11 Apply clean engine oil to the 'C' selector fork ends and guide pin. Fit the fork, with its letter facing to the right-hand side of the engine, and locate it in the groove of its pinion on the input shaft, then allow it to sit on the crankcase (see illustration).

12 Apply clean engine oil to the journal on the left-hand end of the selector drum. Slide the drum into position in the crankcase (see illustration). Turn it so it is roughly in its neutral position (see illustration 33.3).

13 Lubricate the selector fork shaft with clean engine oil. Locate the guide pin on the end of the 'C' fork into its track in the selector drum and, then into its bore in the crankcase (see illustration).

14 Lower the output shaft into position in the upper crankcase (see illustration 33.5), making sure the bearing retainer locates in its

33.10c ...and tap the housing in...

33.10d ...until the screws can be used to draw it in the rest of the way

33.10e Stake the rim of each screw into the indent

33.11 Fit the fork into its pinion groove...

33.12 ...then slide the drum in

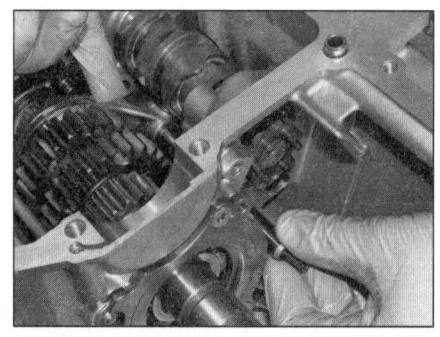

33.13 Seat the fork guide pin in its track and insert the shaft

2•68 Engine, clutch and transmission

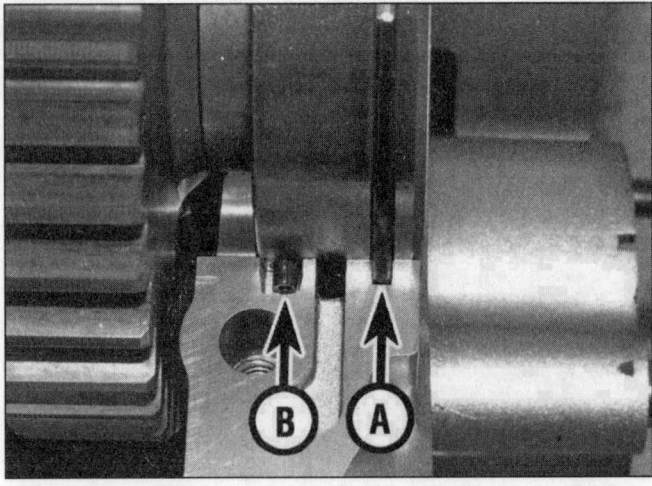

33.14 Make sure the retainer (A) and pin (B) seat correctly

33.15a Fit the R fork...

33.15b ...then insert the shaft...

33.15c ...then fit the L fork and slide the shaft all the way in

slot, and align the pin so it sits in the cut-out **(see illustration)**.
Caution: If the ring retainer and pin do not locate correctly, the crankcase halves will not seat properly.
15 Apply clean engine oil to the 'R' and 'L' selector fork ends and guide pins, and to their shaft. Fit the selector fork marked 'R', with its letter facing to the right-hand side of the engine, in the groove of its pinion on the output shaft, then seat the guide pin in its track in the drum and slide the shaft in and through the fork **(see illustrations)**. Fit the 'L' fork in the same way and slide the shaft into its bore in the crankcase **(see illustration)**.
16 With the selector drum in the neutral position check the transmission shafts are free to rotate easily and independently (i.e. the input shaft can turn whilst the output shaft is held stationary) before proceeding further. Also check that each gear can be selected by turning the input shaft with one hand and the selector drum cam with the other.
17 Clean the threads of the drum and shaft retainer plate bolts and apply a suitable thread locking compound. Fit the plate and tighten the bolts to the torque setting specified at the beginning of the Chapter **(see illustration 33.3)**.
18 Reassemble the crankcase halves (see Section 24).

34 Transmission shaft overhaul

1 Remove the transmission shafts from the crankcase (see Section 33). Always disassemble the transmission shafts separately to avoid mixing up the components.

HAYNES HiNT *When disassembling the transmission shafts, place the parts on a long rod or thread a wire through them to keep them in order and facing the proper direction.*

Input shaft disassembly
2 Mark the outer face of the 2nd gear pinion on the left-hand end of the shaft so it can re-fitted the same way round. Slide the pinion off the shaft **(see illustration 34.19)**.
3 Slide the tabbed lockwasher off the shaft, then turn the slotted splined washer to offset the splines and slide it off the shaft **(see illustrations 34.18c and a)**. Slide the 5th gear pinion and its splined bush off the shaft, followed by the splined washer **(see illustrations 34.17c, b and a)**.
4 Remove the circlip, then slide the 3rd gear pinion off the shaft **(see illustrations 34.16b and a)**.
5 Remove the circlip, then slide the splined washer, the 4th gear pinion and its bush off the shaft **(see illustrations 34.15d, c, b and a)**. The 1st gear pinion is integral with the shaft.

Input shaft inspection
6 Wash all of the components in clean solvent and dry them off.

Engine, clutch and transmission 2•69

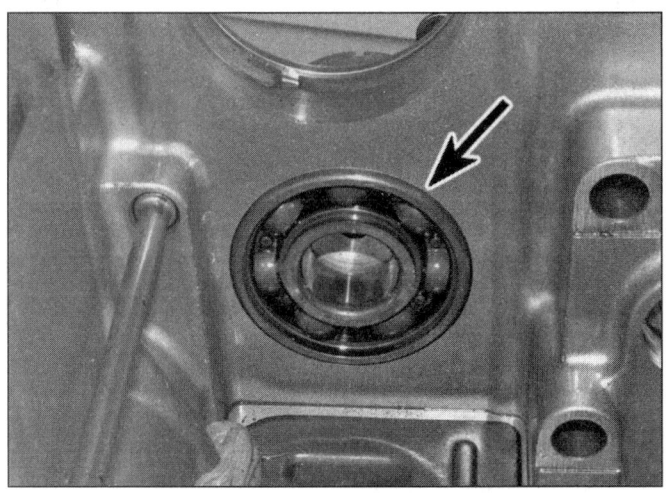

34.13a Input shaft left-hand bearing (arrowed)

34.13b Fit the puller bit behind the inner race and expand it...

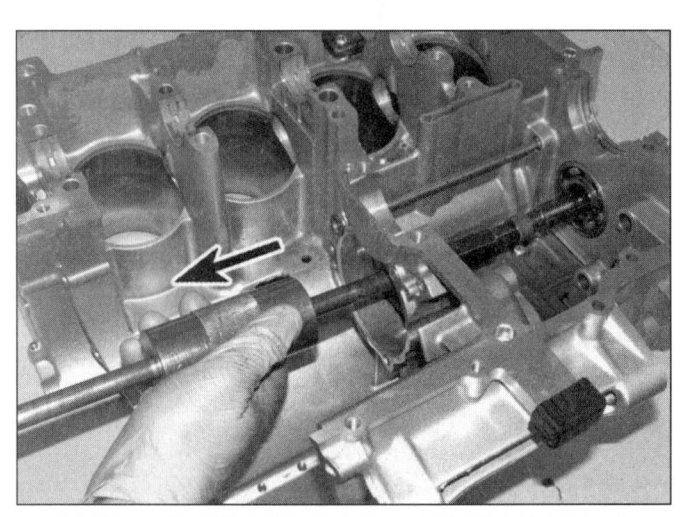

34.13c ...attach the slide-hammer and jar the bearing out

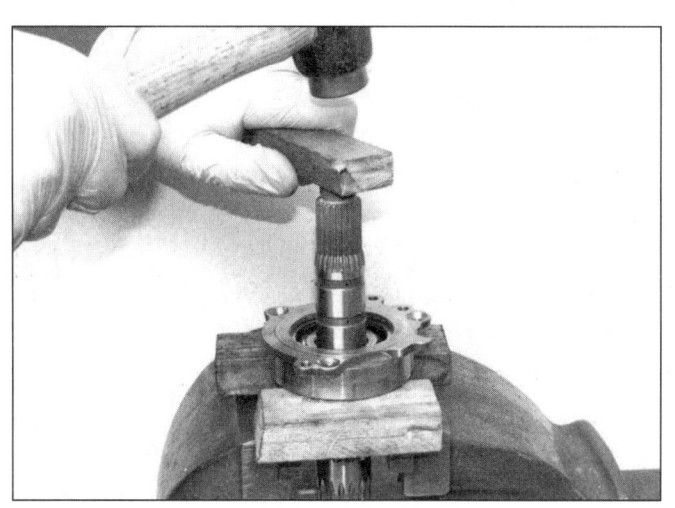

34.13d Tap the shaft out of the bearing as shown

7 Check the gear teeth for cracking, chipping, pitting and other obvious wear or damage. Any pinion that is damaged as such must be replaced with a new one.
8 Inspect the dogs and the dog holes in the gears for cracks, chips, and excessive wear especially in the form of rounded edges. Make sure mating gears engage properly. Replace the paired gears as a set if necessary.
9 Check for signs of scoring or bluing on the pinions, bushes and shaft. This could be caused by overheating due to inadequate lubrication. Check all the oil holes and passages are clear. Replace any damaged pinions or bushes.
10 Check that each pinion moves freely on the shaft or its bush but without undue freeplay. Check that each bush moves freely on the shaft but without undue freeplay.
11 The shaft is unlikely to sustain damage unless the engine has seized, placing an unusually high loading on the transmission, or the machine has covered a very high mileage. Check the surface of the shaft, especially where a pinion turns on it, and replace the shaft if it has scored or picked up, or if there are any cracks. Damage of any kind can only be cured by replacement.
12 Check the washers and replace any that are bent or appear weakened or worn. Use new ones if in any doubt. Note that you must use new circlips when overhauling gearshafts.
13 Check the transmission shaft bearings (the bearing for the left-hand end of the input shaft is in the crankcase) **(see illustration)**. The inner races should run smoothly and freely, and the outer races of the input shaft bearings should be tight in their housing – refer to *Tools and workshop Tips* in the Reference section for more information on bearings. To remove the bearing from the crankcase you will need an expanding puller to lock behind the bearing inner race and a slide-hammer attachment to jar the bearing out – heat around the bearing housing first **(see illustrations)**. Put the new bearing in the freezer for a while, and when cold heat the bearing housing with a hot air gun. Drive the new bearing in with the marked side facing up using a driver or socket that bears on the outer race until they seat. To remove the bearing from the right-hand end of the input shaft, seat the bearing in a vice as shown and drive the shaft out of the bearing using a piece of wood on the top of the shaft to protect it **(see illustration)**. Now support the housing rim, seating it high enough for the bearing to be driven out the bottom, then heat the housing and drive the bearing out using a bearing driver or socket. Put the new bearing in the freezer for a while, and when cold heat the bearing housing with a hot air gun. Drive the new bearing in until it seats using a bearing driver or socket on the outer race. Now put the shaft in the freezer for a while, and when cold heat the bearing with a hot air gun. Drive the new bearing onto the shaft until it seats using a piece of tubing over the shaft and located on the inner race.

Input shaft reassembly

14 During reassembly, apply molybdenum disulphide oil (a 50/50 mixture of molybdenum

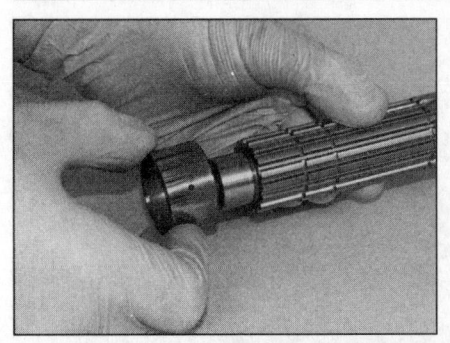

2•70 Engine, clutch and transmission

34.15a Slide the 4th gear bush...

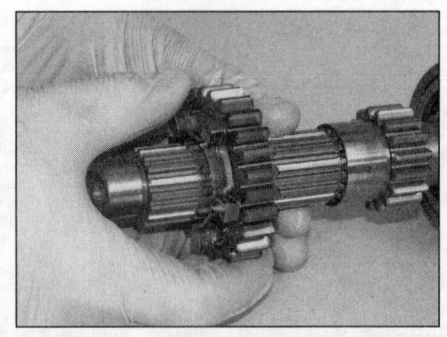

34.15b ...and the 4th gear pinion onto the shaft

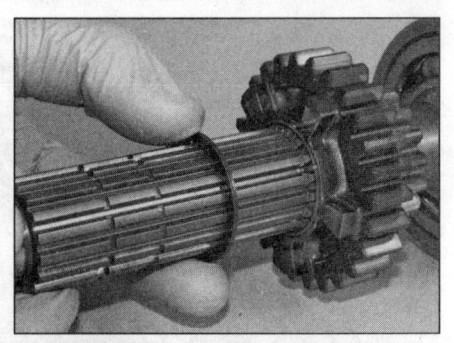

34.15c Slide on the splined washer...

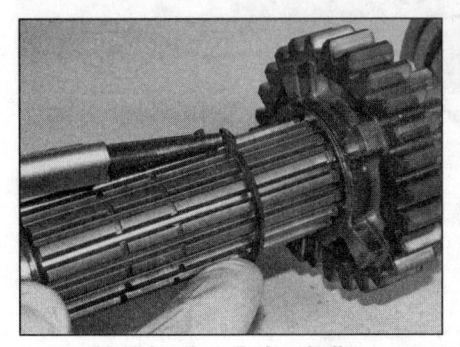

34.15d ...then fit the circlip...

34.15e ...making sure it locates correctly

disulphide grease and clean engine oil) to the mating surfaces of the shaft, pinions and bushes. When fitting the circlips, do not expand their ends any further than is necessary. Fit the stamped circlips and washers so that their chamfered side faces away from the thrust side.

15 Slide the 4th gear pinion bush onto the left-hand end of the shaft **(see illustration)**. Fit the 4th gear pinion onto the bush with its dogs facing away from the integral 1st gear **(see illustration)**. Slide the splined washer onto the shaft, then fit the circlip, making sure that it locates correctly in its groove **(see illustrations)**.

16 Slide the 3rd gear pinion onto the shaft with the selector fork groove facing away from the 4th gear pinion. Fit the circlip, making sure it is locates correctly in its groove **(see illustrations)**.

17 Slide the splined washer onto the shaft, followed by the 5th gear pinion splined bush, aligning the oil hole in the bush with the hole in the shaft. Slide the 5th gear pinion onto the bush, with its dogs facing the 3rd gear pinion **(see illustrations)**.

18 Slide the slotted splined washer onto the shaft and locate it in its groove, then turn it in the groove so that the splines on the washer align with the splines on the shaft and secure

34.16a Slide the 3rd gear pinion onto the shaft...

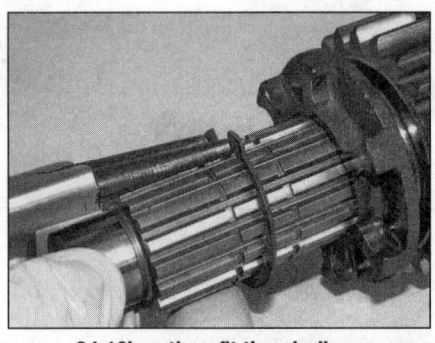

34.16b ...then fit the circlip...

34.16c ...making sure it locates correctly

34.17a Slide the splined washer...

34.17b ...the 5th gear splined bush...

34.17c ...the 5th gear pinion onto the shaft

Engine, clutch and transmission 2•71

34.18a Slide the slotted splined washer onto the shaft...

34.18b ...and locate it as shown

34.18c Slide the lockwasher onto the shaft and engage it with the slotted washer

34.19 Slide the 2nd gear pinion onto the shaft

34.20 The assembled input shaft should look like this

the washer in the groove **(see illustrations)**. Slide the tabbed lockwasher onto the shaft, aligning the tab that has the cut-outs on either side with the slot with the similar cut-out, locating the tabs in the slots **(see illustration)**.

19 Slide the 2nd gear pinion onto the shaft with the mark made on removal facing out **(see illustration)**.

20 Check that all components have been correctly installed **(see illustration)**.

Output shaft disassembly

21 Mark the outer face of the output drive gear on the right-hand end of the shaft so it can re-fitted the same way round. Slide the bearing, thrust washer and the output drive gear off the right-hand end of the shaft **(see illustrations 34.36c, b and a)**.

22 Slide the bearing, thrust washer, 2nd gear pinion, bush and thrust washer off the left-hand end of the shaft **(see illustrations 34.35e, d, c, b and a)**.

23 Slide the 5th gear pinion off the shaft **(see illustration 34.34)**.

24 Remove the circlip, then slide the splined washer, the 3rd gear pinion and its splined bush off the shaft **(see illustrations 34.33d, c, b and a)**.

25 Slide the tabbed lockwasher off the shaft, then turn the slotted splined washer to offset the splines and slide it off the shaft **(see illustrations 34.32c and a)**.

26 Slide the 4th gear pinion off the shaft **(see illustration 34.31)**.

27 Remove the circlip, then slide the splined washer, thrust washer, 1st gear pinion, needle bearing and thrust washer off the shaft **(see illustrations 34.30f, e, d, c, b and a)**.

Output shaft inspection

28 Refer to Steps 6 to 12 above.

Output shaft reassembly

29 During reassembly, apply molybdenum disulphide oil (a 50/50 mixture of molybdenum disulphide grease and clean engine oil) to the mating surfaces of the shaft, pinions and bushes. When fitting the circlips, do not expand their ends any further than is necessary. Fit the stamped circlips and washers so that their chamfered side faces away from the thrust side.

30 Slide the thrust washer and needle bearing onto the left-hand end of the shaft, then slide the 1st gear pinion onto the bearing with its flat face towards the thrust washer **(see illustrations)**. Slide the thrust washer and the splined washer

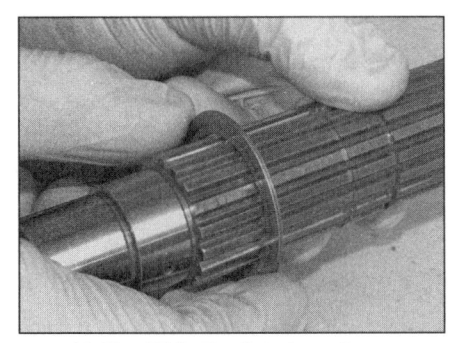

34.30a Slide the thrust washer...

34.30b ...and the bearing onto the shaft...

34.30c ...then fit the 1st gear pinion onto the bearing

2•72 Engine, clutch and transmission

34.30d Slide the thrust washer...

34.30e ...and the splined washer onto the shaft...

34.30f ...and secure them with the circlip...

on, then fit the circlip, making sure it locates correctly in its groove **(see illustrations)**.

31 Slide the 4th gear pinion onto the shaft with the selector fork groove facing away from the 1st gear pinion **(see illustration)**.

32 Slide the slotted splined washer onto the shaft and locate it in its groove, then turn it in the groove so that the splines on the washer align with the splines on the shaft and secure the washer in the groove **(see illustrations)**.

Slide the lockwasher onto the shaft, locating the tabs in the slots in the outer rim of the splined washer **(see illustration)**.

33 Slide the 3rd gear pinion splined bush onto the shaft **(see illustration)**. Slide the 3rd

34.30g ...making sure it locates in the groove

34.31 Slide the 4th gear pinion onto the shaft

34.32a Slide the slotted splined washer onto the shaft...

34.32b ...and locate it as shown

34.32c Slide the lockwasher onto the shaft and engage it with the slotted washer

34.33a Slide the 3rd gear pinion bush...

34.33b ...the 3rd gear pinion...

34.33c ...and the splined washer onto the shaft...

34.33d ...and secure them with the circlip...

Engine, clutch and transmission 2•73

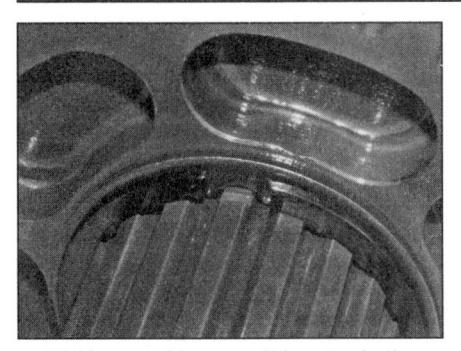

34.33e ...making sure it locates in the groove

34.34 Slide the 5th gear pinion onto the shaft

34.35a Slide the thrust washer...

gear pinion onto its bush with its dog holes facing away from the 4th gear pinion **(see illustration)**. Slide the splined washer on, then fit the circlip, making sure it is locates correctly in its groove **(see illustrations)**.

34 Slide the 5th gear pinion onto the shaft with its selector fork groove facing the 3rd gear pinion **(see illustration)**.

35 Slide the thrust washer and the bush onto the shaft, then slide the 2nd gear pinion onto the bush with its flat side facing out **(see illustrations)**. Fit the thrust washer, then the bearing, with the retaining ring outermost **(see illustrations)**.

36 Slide the output drive gear onto the right-hand end of the shaft, followed by the thrust washer with its chamfered side facing in, then fit the bearing **(see illustrations)**.

37 Check that all components have been correctly installed **(see illustration)**.

34.35b ...and bush onto the shaft...

34.35c ...then fit the 2nd gear pinion onto the bush

34.35d Fit the thrust washer...

34.35e ...and the bearing

34.36a Slide the output drive gear onto the shaft

34.36b Fit the chamfered side of the washer inwards...

34.36c ...then fit the bearing

34.37 The assembled shaft should be as shown

2•74 Engine, clutch and transmission

35.2 Check the fork ends and their pinion groove

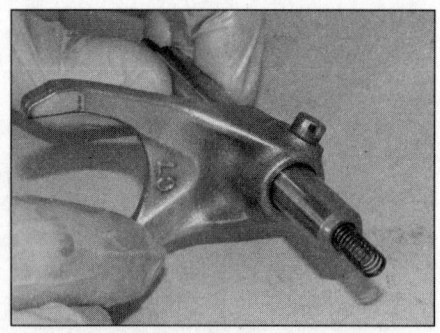

35.3 Check the fit of each fork on its shaft

35 Selector drum and forks

Note: *To access the selector drum and forks the engine must be removed from the frame and the crankcases separated.*

Removal and installation

1 See Section 33.

Inspection

2 Inspect the selector forks for any signs of wear or damage, especially around the fork ends where they engage with the groove in the pinion. Check that each fork fits correctly in its pinion groove **(see illustration)**. Check closely to see if the forks are bent. If the forks are in any way damaged they must be replaced with new ones.

3 Check that the forks fit correctly on their shaft – they should move freely with a light fit but no appreciable freeplay **(see illustration)**. Replace the forks and/or shaft with new ones if they are worn. Check that the fork shaft holes in the casing are neither worn nor damaged.

4 Check the selector fork shafts are straight by rolling them along a flat surface. A bent rod will cause difficulty in selecting gears and make the gearchange action heavy. Replace the shaft with a new one if it is bent.

5 Inspect the selector drum tracks and selector fork guide pins for signs of wear or damage **(see illustration)**. If either component shows signs of wear or damage the fork(s) and drum must be replaced with new ones.

6 Check that the selector drum bearing rotates freely and has no sign of freeplay between it and the casing **(see illustration)**. Replace the drum with a new one if necessary.

36 Running-in procedure

1 Make sure the engine oil and coolant levels are correct (see *Pre-ride checks*).
2 Make sure there is fuel in the tank.
3 Turn the ignition 'ON'. Check the transmission is in neutral.
4 Start the engine, then allow it to idle until it reaches normal operating temperature.
5 As no oil pressure warning light is fitted, an oil pressure check is advised (see Section 3), or at least the oil delivery check as described in Chapter 1, Section 8.
6 If a lubrication failure is suspected, stop the engine immediately and try to find the cause. If an engine is run without oil, even for a short period of time, severe damage will occur. Check carefully that there are no oil or coolant leaks and make sure the transmission and controls, especially the brakes and clutch, work properly before road testing the machine.
7 Treat the machine gently for the first few miles to allow the oil to circulate throughout the engine and any new parts installed to seat.
8 Great care is necessary if the engine has been extensively overhauled – the bike will have to be run in as when new. This means more use of the transmission and a restraining hand on the throttle until at least 600 miles (1000 km) have been covered. There is no point in keeping to any set road speed – the main idea is to keep from labouring the engine and to gradually increase performance up to the 1000 mile (1600 km) mark. These recommendations apply less when only a partial overhaul has been done, though it does depend to an extent on the nature of the work carried out and which components have been renewed. Experience is the best guide, since it is easy to tell when an engine is running freely. If in any doubt, consult a Yamaha dealer. The following maximum engine speed limitations, which Yamaha provide for new motorcycles, can be used as a guide.

Up to 600 miles (1000 km)
Do not exceed 4500 rpm for long periods

600 to 1000 miles (1000 to 1600 km)
Vary throttle position/speed. Do not exceed 5500 rpm

Over 1000 miles (1600 km)
Normal riding. Do not exceed tachometer red line

9 Upon completion of the road test, and after the engine has cooled down completely, recheck the valve clearances (see Chapter 1) and check the engine oil and coolant levels (see *Pre-ride checks*).
10 After running the rebuilt engine for 1000 miles (1600 km), change the engine oil and filter (see Chapter 1).

35.5 Check the tracks and guide pins

35.6 Check the bearing

Chapter 3
Cooling system

Contents

	Section number		Section number
Coolant change	see Chapter 1	General information	1
Coolant hoses, pipes and unions	8	Oil cooler	see Chapter 2
Coolant level check	see Pre-ride checks	Radiator	5
Coolant reservoir	7	Temperature display and ECT sensor	3
Cooling fan(s) and fan relay	2	Thermostat	4
Cooling system checks	see Chapter 1	Water pump	6

Degrees of difficulty

Easy, suitable for novice with little experience	Fairly easy, suitable for beginner with some experience	Fairly difficult, suitable for competent DIY mechanic	Difficult, suitable for experienced DIY mechanic	Very difficult, suitable for expert DIY or professional

Specifications

Coolant
Mixture type and capacity .... see Chapter 1

ECT sensor
Resistance @ 0°C .... 5.2 to 6.4 K-ohms
Resistance @ 20°C .... 2.45 K-ohms
Resistance @ 80°C .... 290 to 354 ohms

Thermostat
Opening temperature .... 69 to 73°C
Fully open .... 85°C
Valve lift .... 8 mm (min)

Radiator
Cap valve opening pressure .... 13.5 to 18 psi (0.9 to 1.25 Bar)

Torque settings
Coolant inlet union bolts .... 10 Nm
Coolant outlet pipe bolts .... 10 Nm
ECT sensor .... 18 Nm
Thermostat cover bolts .... 10 Nm
Water pump cover bolts .... 10 Nm
Water pump mounting bolts .... 12 Nm

1 General information

The cooling system uses a water/anti-freeze coolant to carry away excess heat from the engine and maintain as constant a temperature as possible. The cylinders are surrounded by a water jacket from which the heated coolant is circulated by thermo-syphonic action in conjunction with a water pump, which is driven by the oil pump. The hot coolant passes upwards to the thermostat and through to the radiator. The coolant then flows across the core of the radiator, then to the water pump and back to the engine. Coolant also circulates through the oil cooler on the front of the engine.

A thermostat is fitted in the system to prevent the coolant flowing through the

3•2 Cooling system

radiator when the engine is cold, therefore accelerating the speed at which the engine reaches normal operating temperature. An engine coolant temperature (ECT) sensor mounted in the end of the outlet pipe on the top of the engine provides information to the engine management system ECU (Electronic Control Unit), and to the temperature gauge on the instrument panel. A single cooling fan on 2001 to 2005 models and twin cooling fans from 2006-on, fitted to the back of the radiator, aid(s) cooling in extreme conditions by drawing extra air through. The fan motor(s) is/are controlled by a relay that receives a signal from the ECU, itself acting on information from the ECT sensor.

The complete cooling system is partially sealed and pressurised, the pressure being controlled by a valve contained in the spring-loaded filler cap. By pressurising the coolant the boiling point is raised, preventing premature boiling in adverse conditions. The overflow pipe from the system is connected to a reservoir into which excess coolant is expelled under pressure. The discharged coolant automatically returns to the radiator by the vacuum created when the engine cools.

⚠ **Warning: Do not remove the pressure cap from the filler neck when the engine is hot. Scalding hot coolant and steam may be blown out under pressure, which could cause serious injury. When the engine has cooled, place a thick rag, like a towel, over the pressure cap; slowly rotate the** cap anti-clockwise to the first stop. This procedure allows any residual pressure to escape. When the steam has stopped escaping, press down on the cap while turning it anti-clockwise and remove it.

Caution: Do not allow anti-freeze to come in contact with your skin or painted surfaces of the motorcycle. Rinse off any spills immediately with plenty of water. Anti-freeze is highly toxic if ingested. Never leave anti-freeze lying around in an open container or in puddles on the floor; children and pets are attracted by its sweet smell and may drink it. Check with the local authorities about disposing of used anti-freeze. Many communities will have collection centres which will see that anti-freeze is disposed of safely.

Caution: At all times use the specified type of anti-freeze, and always mix it with distilled water in the correct proportion. The anti-freeze contains corrosion inhibitors which are essential to avoid damage to the cooling system. A lack of these inhibitors could lead to a build-up of corrosion which would block the coolant passages, resulting in overheating and severe engine damage. Distilled water must be used as opposed to tap water to avoid a build-up of scale which would also block the passages.

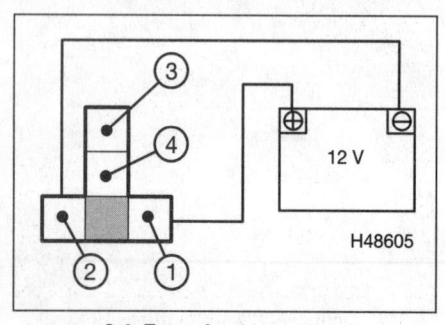

2 Cooling fan(s) and fan relay

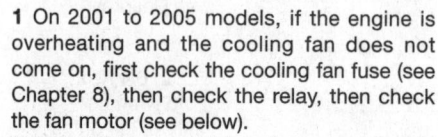

1 On 2001 to 2005 models, if the engine is overheating and the cooling fan does not come on, first check the cooling fan fuse (see Chapter 8), then check the relay, then check the fan motor (see below).

2 On 2006-on models, if the engine is overheating and one cooling fan does not come on, first check the cooling fan fuse (see Chapter 8), then check the fan motor (see below). If neither fan comes on check the relay, (see below), then the fuses (see Chapter 8), then the fan motors (see below).

Cooling fan relay

Check

3 Remove the relay (Step 8 or 9).
4 Set a multimeter to test continuity and connect it across terminals 3 and 4 on the relay (see illustration). There should be no continuity (infinite resistance). Using a fully-charged 12 volt battery and two insulated jumper wires, connect the positive (+) terminal of the battery to terminal 1 on the relay, and the negative (–) terminal to terminal 2. At this point the relay should be heard to click and the multimeter read 0 ohms (continuity). If so the relay is good. If not replace the relay with a new one.
5 If the relay is good, check the connector for loose or broken wires and terminals.
6 If the fan is on the whole time, refer to Step 8 or 9 and remove the relay – the fan should stop. If it does, the relay is defective and must be replaced with a new one.
7 If the fan works but is suspected of cutting in at the wrong temperature, check the ECT sensor (see Section 3).

Removal and installation

8 On 2001 to 2005 models remove the fairing (see Chapter 7). The relay is on the back of the instrument cluster (see illustration). Identify the relay using the wire colours in wiring diagram for your model at the end of the Chapter, displace it and disconnect its connector. If necessary (depending on the location of the relay), remove the windshield motor/instrument assembly from the fairing (see Chapter 8).
9 On 2006-on models remove the right-hand fairing side panel, and if required for best access the fairing (see Chapter 7). Displace the relay and disconnect the wiring (see illustration).
10 Installation is the reverse of removal.

Cooling fan(s)

Check

11 The cooling fan(s) is/are on the back of the radiator (2001 to 2005 models have a single fan, all later models have twin fans).
12 To test the cooling fan motor on 2001

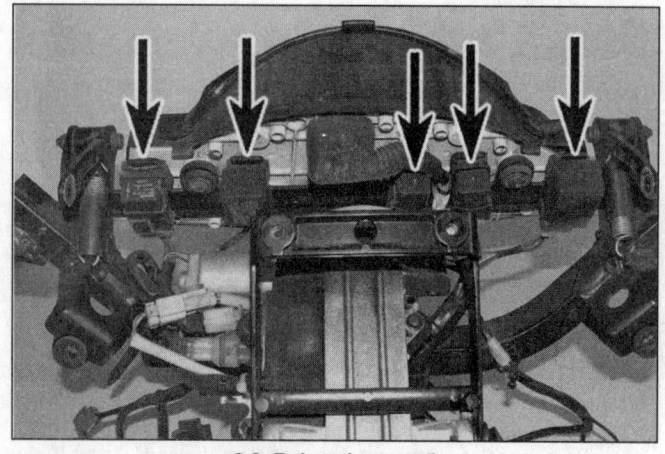

2.4 Fan relay test set-up

2.8 Relays (arrowed)

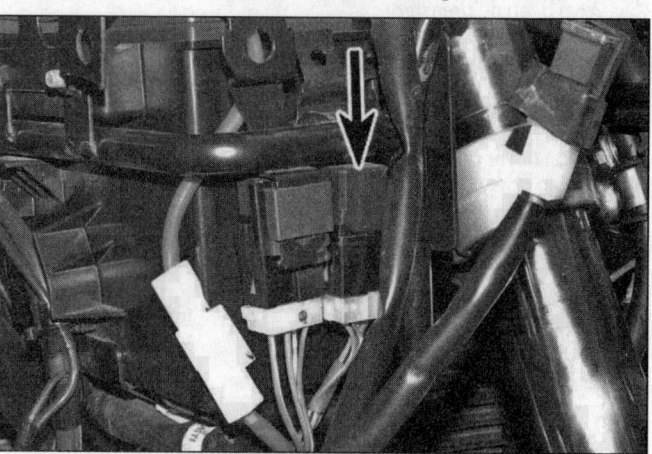

2.9 Fan relay (arrowed)

Cooling system 3•3

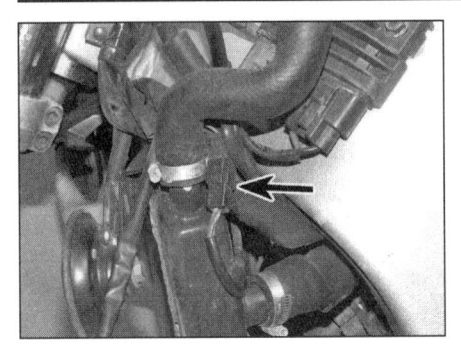

2.12a Cooling fan wiring connector (arrowed) – 2001 to 2005 models

2.12b Right-hand cooling fan wiring connector (arrowed) – 2006-on models

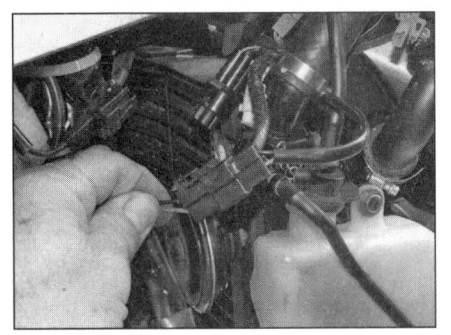

2.12c Left-hand cooling fan wiring connector (arrowed) – 2006-on models

to 2005 models remove the left-hand fairing side panel (see Chapter 7). On 2006-on models remove the right-hand fairing side panel to test the right-hand fan, and the left-hand panel to test the left-hand fan (see Chapter 7). Disconnect the fan wiring connector **(see illustrations)**. Using a 12 volt battery and two jumper wires with suitable connectors, connect the battery positive (+) lead to the blue wire terminal on the fan side of the wiring connector, and the battery negative (–) lead to the black wire terminal. Once connected the fan should operate. If it does not, and the connector and the wiring between it and the motor are good, then the fan motor is faulty. Individual components are not available for the fan assembly.

Removal and installation

⚠ *Warning: The engine must be completely cool before carrying out this procedure.*

13 Remove the radiator (see Section 5).
14 Unscrew the bolts and remove the fan assembly **(see illustration)**.
15 Installation is the reverse of removal.

3 Temperature display and ECT sensor

Temperature display

1 The circuit consists of the ECT sensor mounted in the coolant outlet pipe on the top of the valve cover, and the temperature display in the instrument cluster.
2 If the display does not work, check the ECT sensor and its connector (see below). If that is good check the wiring connector on the back of the instrument cluster, then check the wiring between the connectors (see Chapter 8). If no faults are found but there is still a problem the instrument display could be faulty. No information is available for testing the display – the best action is to take the instrument cluster to a Yamaha dealer for assessment.

ECT sensor

Check

3 The sensor is mounted in the outlet pipe on the top of the valve cover. The resistance of the sensor changes with changes in temperature – see the Specifications at the beginning of the chapter. While in theory it is possible to bench-test the sensor at those temperatures, in practice the test is difficult to set up and perform. However you can test the resistance of the sensor in the bike with the engine cold, warm and hot.
4 Remove the fuel tank (see Chapter 4).
5 On 2001 to 2005 models unscrew the AIS control valve holder bolt **(see illustration)**. On all models remove the T-bar **(see illustration)**. On 2006-on models remove the heat shield **(see illustrations)**.

2.14 Cooling fan bolts (arrowed)

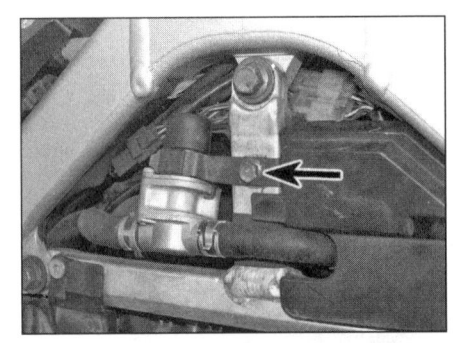

3.5a Unscrew the bolt (arrowed)

3.5b Unscrew the bolts (arrowed) and remove the T-bar

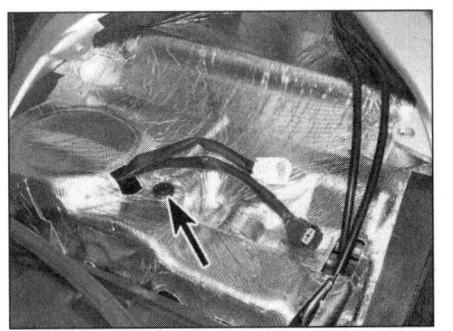

3.5c Release the trim clip (arrowed), thread the wiring through the hole and on 2013-on models slip the cables out of the slot...

3.5d ...and remove the heat shield

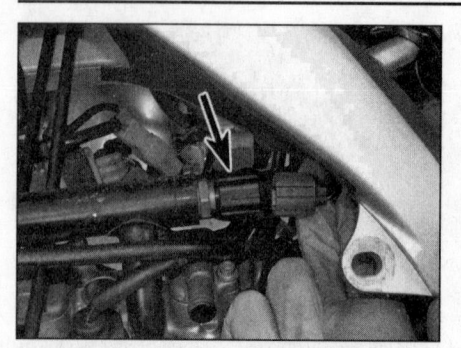

3•4 Cooling system

3.6 Disconnect the wiring connector from the sensor (arrowed)

6 Disconnect the ECT sensor wiring connector (see illustration).
7 Connect the probes of a multimeter set to read resistance to the terminals on the sensor and take several readings as the engine warms up. Resistance should decrease as temperature increases – if the sensor fails it is most likely to give a zero, constant, or infinite resistance reading at all temperatures.

Removal and installation

⚠️ **Warning: The engine must be completely cool before carrying out this procedure.**

8 The sensor is mounted in the outlet pipe on the top of the valve cover. Drain the cooling system (see Chapter 1).
9 Remove the fuel tank (see Chapter 4).
10 On 2001 to 2005 models unscrew the AIS control valve holder bolt (see illustration 3.5a). On all models remove the T-bar (see illustration 3.5b). On 2006-on models remove the heat shield (see illustrations 3.5c and d).
11 Disconnect the ECT sensor wiring connector (see illustration 3.6).
12 Unscrew and remove the sensor, and discard the sealing washer.
13 Fit a new sealing washer onto the sensor. Fit the sensor and tighten it to the torque setting specified at the beginning of the Chapter. Connect the wiring.
14 Fit the heat shield. Fit the T-bar and tighten the bolts to the torque setting specified in Chapter 4. On 2001 to 2005 models fit the AIS control valve holder bolt.
15 Refill the cooling system (see Chapter 1). Install the fuel tank.

4 Thermostat

1 The thermostat is automatic in operation and should give many years service without requiring attention. In the event of a failure, the valve will probably jam open, in which case the engine will take much longer than normal to warm up. Conversely, if the valve jams shut, the coolant will be unable to circulate and the engine will overheat. Neither condition is acceptable – the fault must be investigated promptly.

Removal

2 Drain the cooling system (see Chapter 1).

4.4a Unscrew the bolts (arrowed)...

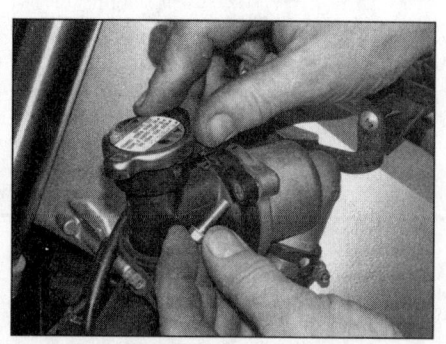

4.4b ...detach the cover...

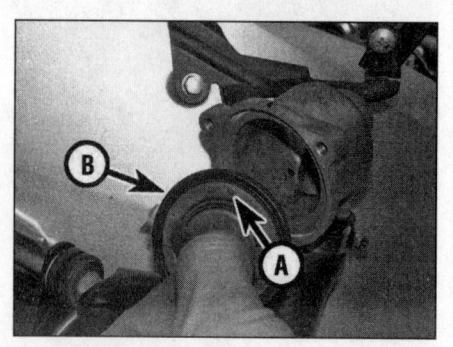

4.4c ...and remove the thermostat. Note the position of the hole (A). Check the seal (B)

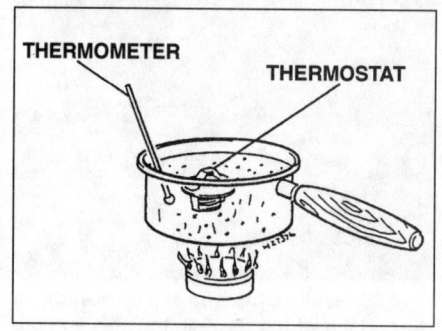

4.6 Thermostat testing set-up

3 On 2001 to 2005 models remove the AIS control valve and its hoses (see Chapter 4).
4 Unscrew the cover bolts and detach it from the housing (see illustrations). Withdraw the thermostat, noting how it fits (see illustration).

Thermostat check

5 Examine the thermostat visually before carrying out the test. If it remains in the open position at room temperature, it should be replaced with a new one. Also check the condition of the seal.
6 Suspend the thermostat by a piece of wire in a container of cold water. Place a thermometer capable of reading temperatures up to 110°C in the water so that the bulb is close to the thermostat (see illustration). Heat the water, noting the temperature when the thermostat opens, and compare the result with the specifications given at the beginning of the Chapter. Also check the amount the valve opens after it has been heated for a few minutes and compare the measurement to the specifications. If the readings obtained differ from those given, the thermostat is faulty and must be replaced with a new one.
7 In the event of thermostat failure, if the thermostat is permanently closed, as an emergency measure only it can be removed and the machine used without it (this is better than leaving it in as the engine will overheat). If it is permanently open you are better to leave it in. In both cases take care when starting the engine from cold as it will take much longer than usual to warm up. Ensure that a new unit is installed as soon as possible.

Installation

8 Installation is the reverse of removal, noting the following:
- Check the thermostat seal for signs of damage or deterioration and fit a new thermostat if necessary (see illustration 4.4c).
- Fit the thermostat into the housing with the hole at the top (see illustration 4.4c).
- Tighten the cover bolts to the torque setting specified at the beginning of the Chapter.
- On completion refill the cooling system (see Chapter 1).

5 Radiator

Note: *If the radiator is being removed as part of the engine removal procedure, detach the hoses from their unions on the engine rather than on the radiator and remove the radiator complete with its hoses. Note the routing of the hoses.*

Removal

⚠️ **Warning: The engine must be completely cool before carrying out this procedure.**

Cooling system 3•5

5.2 Horn wiring connectors (arrowed)

5.4a Radiator hoses (arrowed) – right-hand side

1 Drain the cooling system (see Chapter 1).
2 Disconnect the fan wiring connector(s) **(see illustration 2.12a or 2.12b and c)**. On 2001 to 2005 models disconnect the horn wiring connectors **(see illustration)**. On 2006-on models remove the horns (see Chapter 8).

3 Unscrew the coolant reservoir bolts, displace it from the radiator and support it clear and upright **(see illustration 7.2 or 7.6)**.
4 Slacken the clamps securing the hoses to the radiator and detach them **(see illustrations)**.

5 Unscrew the radiator mounting bolts, on 2001 to 2005 models remove the horns, and remove the radiator, taking care not to catch the fins on anything **(see illustrations)**.
6 If required remove the radiator bracket from the front of the engine **(see illustration)**.

5.4b Radiator hoses (arrowed) – left-hand side – 2004 model shown

5.5a Unscrew the bottom bolt (arrowed)...

5.5b ...and the top bolt (arrowed) on each side...

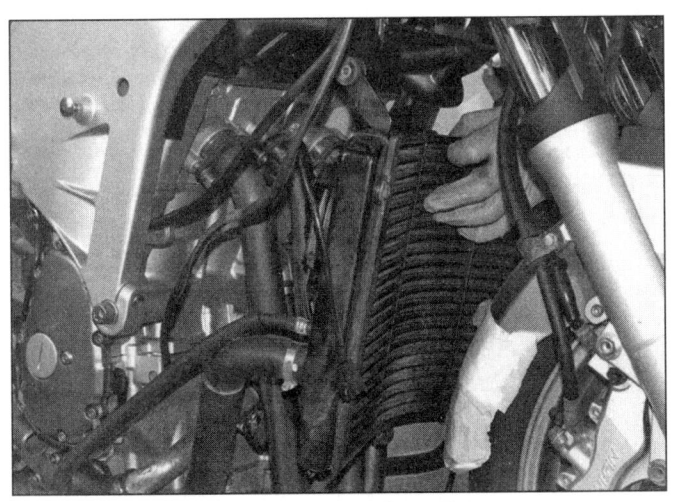

5.5c ...and remove the radiator

5.6 Radiator bracket bolt (arrowed)

3•6 Cooling system

5.8 Note the collars and check the condition of the grommets

7 If required remove the cooling fan(s) (see Section 2).
8 Note the arrangement of the collars and rubber grommets in the radiator mounts **(see illustration)**. Replace the grommets with new ones if they are damaged, deformed or deteriorated.
9 Check the radiator for signs of damage and clear any dirt or debris that might obstruct airflow and inhibit cooling. If the radiator fins are badly damaged or broken the radiator must be replaced with a new one.

Installation

10 Installation is the reverse of removal, noting the following.
● Make sure the rubber grommets are in place and the collars are fitted in them **(see illustration 5.8)**.
● Make sure the coolant hoses are in good condition (see Chapter 1), are pushed fully onto their unions and are securely retained by their clamps, using new ones if necessary **(see illustrations 5.4a and b)**.
● Make sure that the fan wiring is correctly connected **(see illustration 2.12a or 2.12b and c)**.
● On completion refill the cooling system (see Chapter 1).

Pressure cap check

11 If problems such as overheating or loss of coolant occur, check the entire system as described in Chapter 1. If there are no obvious problems and leaks the pressure cap should be checked by a Yamaha dealer with the special tester required to do the job. If the cap is defective, replace it with a new one.

6 Water pump

Check
1 Refer to Chapter 1, Section 10.

Removal
2 Drain the coolant (see Chapter 1).
3 Slacken the clamps securing the coolant hoses to the pump and detach the hoses, noting which fits where **(see illustration)**.
4 Unscrew the three mounting bolts and draw the pump from the crankcase **(see illustrations)**. It may be necessary to lever it out to overcome the O-ring on the rear of the pump body. Remove the O-ring – a new one must be used **(see illustration 6.22a)**.

Inspection
5 Unscrew the remaining two bolts and remove the cover **(see illustration)**. Remove the seal – a new one must be used **(see illustration 6.20a)**.
6 To check the pump impeller bearings, wiggle the impeller back-and-forth and spin it by hand. If there is excessive movement, or the bearings are noisy or rough when turned, they must be replaced with new ones.
7 Remove the circlip and withdraw the impeller from the pump body **(see illustrations 6.19b and a)**. Check that the shaft is at right-angles to the impeller.
8 Check the condition of the rubber damper and its holder on the rear face of the impeller **(see illustration)**. Do not remove them from the shaft unnecessarily, as they cannot be reused. If they are damaged or deteriorated, lever off the old ones with a flat-bladed screwdriver **(see illustrations)**. Apply coolant to the new ones and press them squarely down the shaft and into the back of the

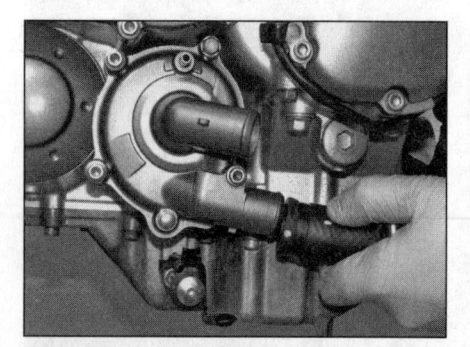

6.3 Slacken the clamps and detach the hoses

6.4a Unscrew the mounting bolts (arrowed)...

6.4b ...and remove the pump

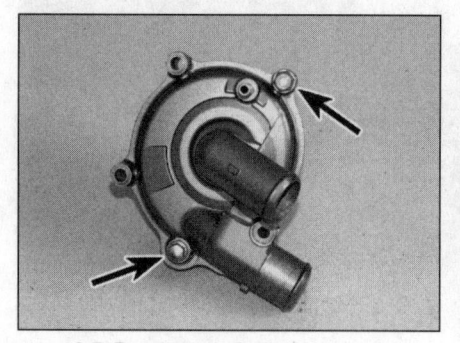

6.5 Pump cover bolts (arrowed)

6.8a Lever out the holder...

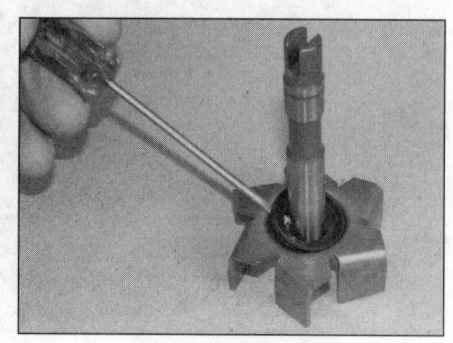

6.8b ...and the damper

Cooling system 3•7

6.8c Fit the new set with the white holder facing out and set them flush

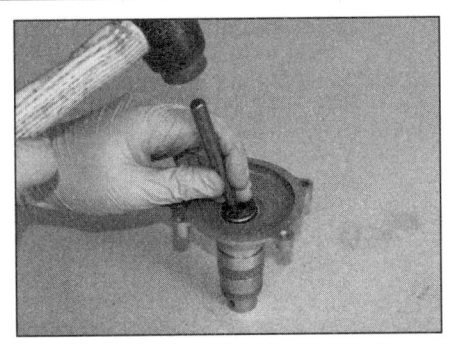

6.12 Drive the inner bearing out as shown

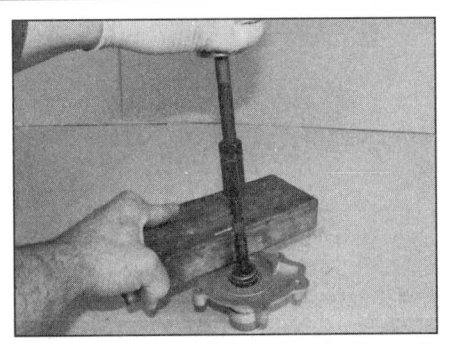

6.13 Using an expanding internal puller and slide-hammer to remove the mechanical seal

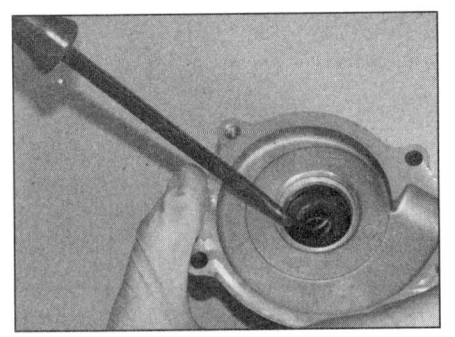

6.14 Lever out the oil seal

6.16a Use a socket to drive the inner bearing...

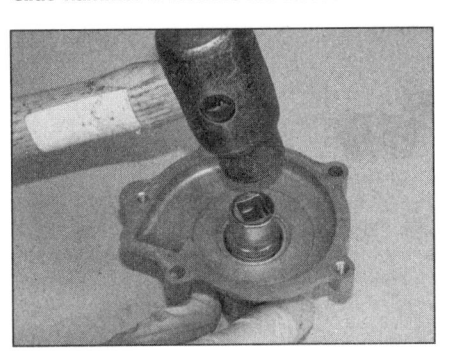

6.16b ...and the outer bearing in until they seat

impeller, setting them flush with the face **(see illustration)**.

9 Inspect the pump body for corrosion or a build-up of scale and clean with de-scaler and/or steel wool as necessary, then rinse the pump body in running clean water.

Seal and bearing removal and installation

10 If new bearings are required new seals must be fitted as they have to be removed in order to replace the outer bearing. The seals can be replaced without disturbing the bearings.

11 Remove the pump from the engine and the cover from the pump (Steps 4 and 5), then withdraw the impeller from the pump body (Step 7).

12 If the bearings are being replaced, support the inner end rim on a socket and drive the inner bearing out using a drift inserted from the outer side **(see illustration)**. Now drive the outer bearing, oil seal and mechanical seal out together using a drift inserted from the inner side.

13 To remove the mechanical seal with the bearings in place, use an expanding internal puller with slide-hammer attachment to jar it out **(see illustration)** – apply some heat to the hosing using a hot air gun to aid removal.

14 To remove the oil seal with the bearings in place, first remove the mechanical seal (see Step 13). Lever the oil seal out using a seal hook **(see illustration)**. Note which way round the seal fits.

15 Clean any traces of sealant from around the mechanical seal seat with a suitable solvent.

16 Drive each bearing into the pump body using a suitable socket on the outer race until it is seated **(see illustrations)**.

17 Apply a smear of coolant to the outside of the new oil seal. Use a socket to press or drive the seal into the body with the marked side facing out until it fits against the bearing, at which point the drain hole and the groove below it are visible **(see illustrations)**.

18 Smear Yamaha Bond 1215 or a suitable equivalent to the mechanical seal housing.

6.17a Fit the new seal with the marked side out...

6.17b ...so the groove and drain hole are exposed

3•8 Cooling system

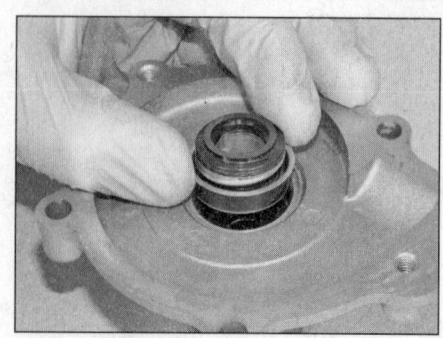

6.18a Fit the new seal...

6.18b ...using a suitable socket and preferably a press...

6.18c ...until the rim is seated

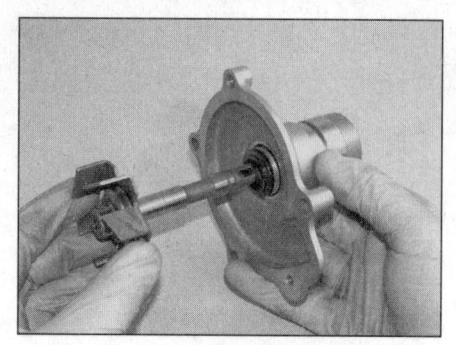

6.19a Insert the shaft...

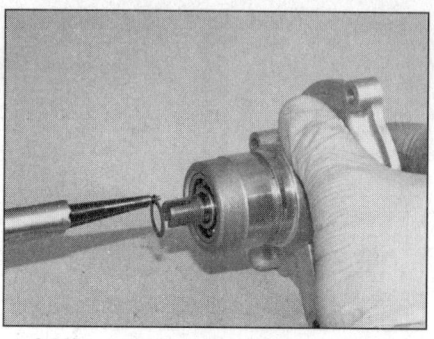

6.19b ...and push the impeller so the circlip can be fitted

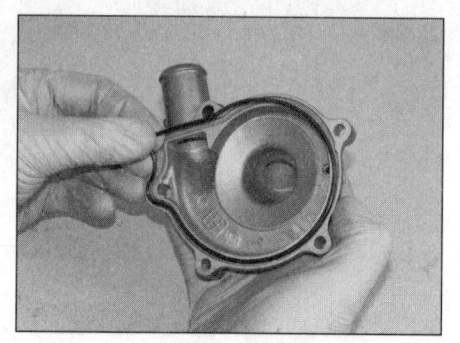

6.20a Fit a new seal into the groove...

6.20b ...then fit the cover

Press or carefully drive the new mechanical seal into the pump body using a suitable sized socket or seal driver that bears only on the outer rim of the seal and not on the centre (see illustrations). Yamaha produces a special tool, Part No. 90890-04078, for installing the seal if required. Make sure the seal rim is correctly seated (see illustration).

Assembly and installation

19 Lubricate the impeller shaft with coolant and slide it into the pump body (see illustration). Push the impeller against the seal to expose the circlip groove and fit a new circlip (see illustration).

20 Fit the new cover seal into its groove (see illustration). Fit the cover onto the pump and tighten the bolts to the torque setting specified at the beginning of the Chapter (see illustration).
21 Apply a smear of engine oil to the new pump body O-ring and fit it into its groove (see illustration). Slide the pump into the crankcase, aligning the slot in the shaft end with the tab on the oil pump shaft (see illustration). Make sure the mounting bolt holes are aligned then fit the bolts and tighten to the specified torque (see illustration 6.4a).
22 Fit the coolant hoses and secure with the clamps (see illustration 6.3).
23 Refill the cooling system (see Chapter 1).

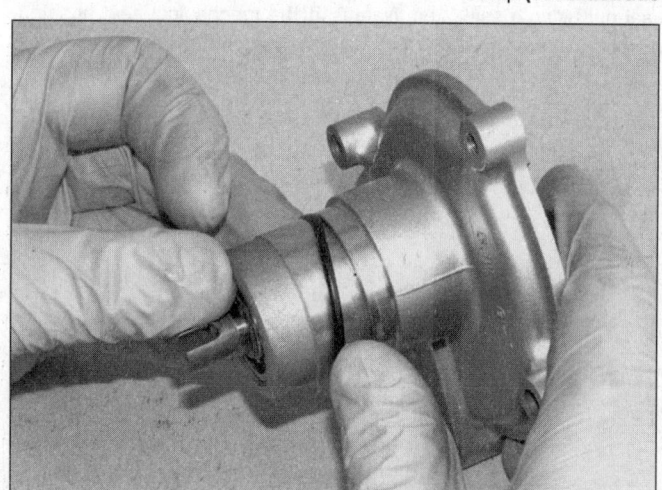

6.21a Fit the new O-ring

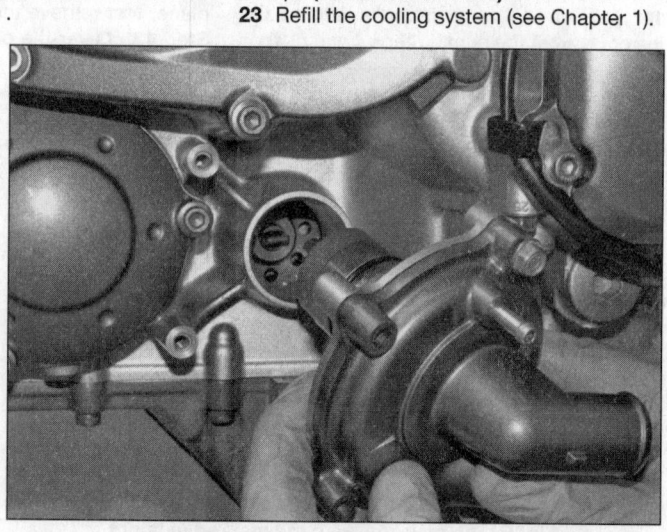

6.21b Align the slot with the drive tab

Cooling system 3•9

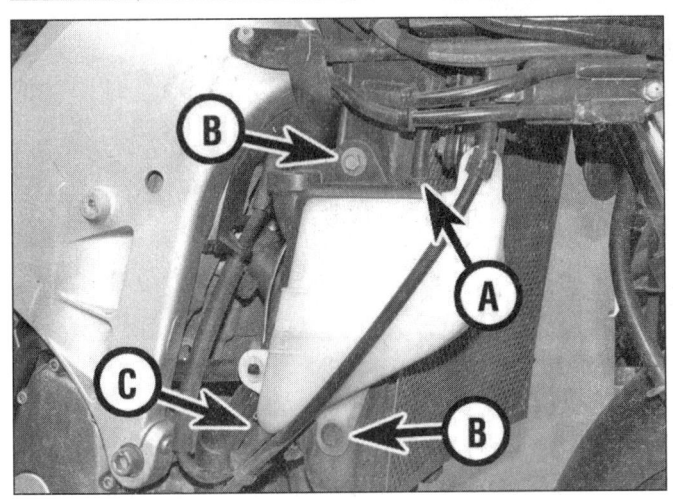

7.2 Breather hose (A), mounting bolts (B), overflow hose (C)

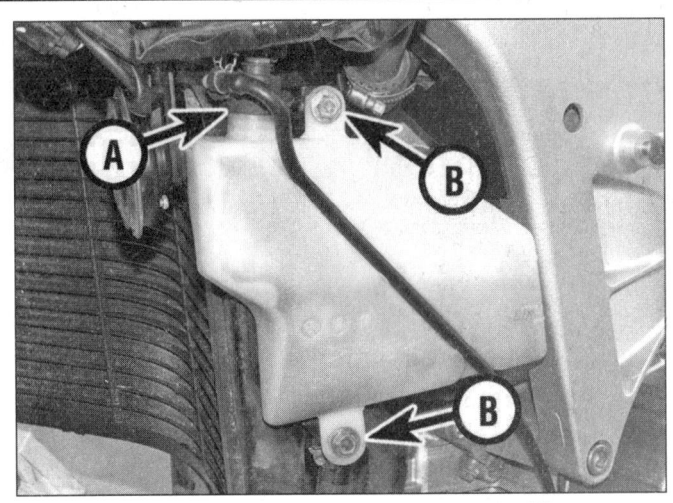

7.5 Release the cap (A). Mounting bolts (B)

7 Coolant reservoir

Removal

2001 to 2005 models

1 Remove the right-hand fairing side panel (see Chapter 7). Obtain a suitable container to drain the coolant into.
2 Detach the breather hose from the top of the reservoir **(see illustration)**.
3 Unscrew the bolts and displace the reservoir, then remove the cap and tip the coolant into the container. Detach the overflow hose from the bottom of the reservoir.

2006-on models

4 Remove the left-hand fairing side panel (see Chapter 7). Get a suitable container to drain the coolant into.

5 Release the cap from the top of the reservoir **(see illustration)**.
6 Unscrew the bolts and displace the reservoir, freeing the breather hose from its groove, and lowering it so the cap hose is clear, then tip the coolant into the container **(see illustration)**.

Installation

7 Installation is the reverse of removal. Refill the reservoir to the FULL level line with the specified coolant mixture (see *Pre-ride checks*).

8 Coolant hoses, pipes and unions

Removal

1 Before removing a hose, drain the coolant (see Chapter 1).

2 Use a screwdriver to slacken the larger-bore hose clamps, then slide them back along the hose and clear of the union spigot. The smaller-bore hoses are secured by spring clamps which can be expanded by squeezing their ears together with pliers.

Caution: The radiator unions are fragile. Do not use excessive force when attempting to remove the hoses.

3 If a hose proves stubborn, release it by rotating it on its union before working it off. If all else fails, cut the hose with a sharp knife. Whilst this means replacing the hose with a new one – it is preferable to buying a new radiator.
4 The inlet union on the front of the engine can be removed by unscrewing its bolts **(see illustration)**. Remove the O-ring – a new one must be used.
5 The outlet pipe on the top of the valve cover can only be removed after removing the AIS control valve and its hoses (see Chapter 4).

7.6 Displace the reservoir and free the hose

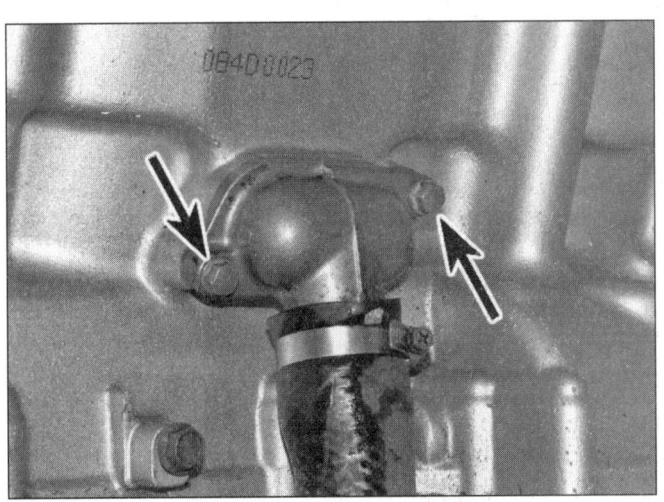

8.4 Inlet union bolts (arrowed)

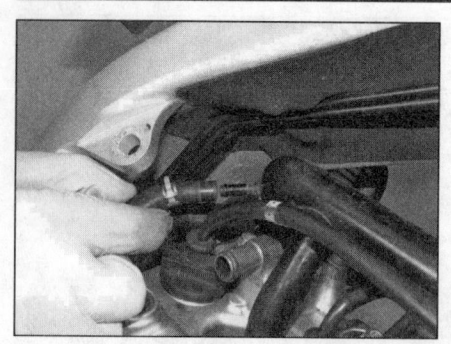

3•10 Cooling system

8.5a Detach the hose(s)...

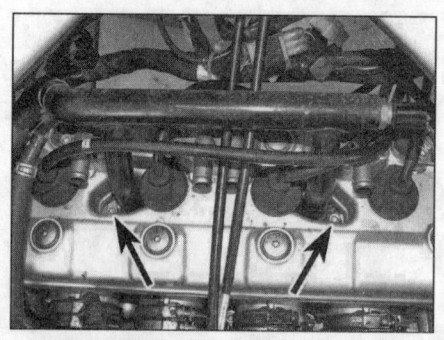

8.5b ...unscrew the bolts (arrowed)...

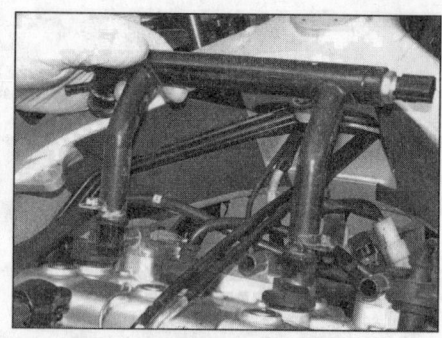

8.5c ...and remove the pipe

Disconnect the ECT sensor wiring connector **(see illustration 3.6)**. On 2001 to 2005 models undo the thermostat housing screw and pull the housing off the pipe. Detach the hose(s) **(see illustration)**. Unscrew the bolts and pull the union off **(see illustrations)**. Remove the O-rings – new ones must be used.

Installation

6 Slide the clamps onto the hose and then work the hose on to its union as far as the spigot where present.
7 Rotate the hose on its unions to settle it in

> **HAYNES HiNT** If the hose is difficult to push on its union, soften it by soaking it in very hot water, or alternatively a little soapy water on the union can be used as a lubricant.

position before sliding the clamps into place and tightening them securely.
8 To fit the inlet union, first clean the threads of the bolts. Smear a new O-ring with grease and fit it into its groove **(see illustration)**.

Apply some threadlock to the bolts, then fit the union and tighten the bolts to the torque setting specified at the beginning of the Chapter.
9 To fit the outlet pipe, smear new O-rings with grease and fit them **(see illustration)**. Fit the union, making sure it is seated, and tighten the bolts to the torque setting specified at the beginning of the Chapter. Connect the hose(s). On 2001 to 2005 models fit the thermostat housing using a new O-ring. Connect the ECT sensor wiring **(see illustration 3.6)**.
10 Refill the cooling system (see Chapter 1).

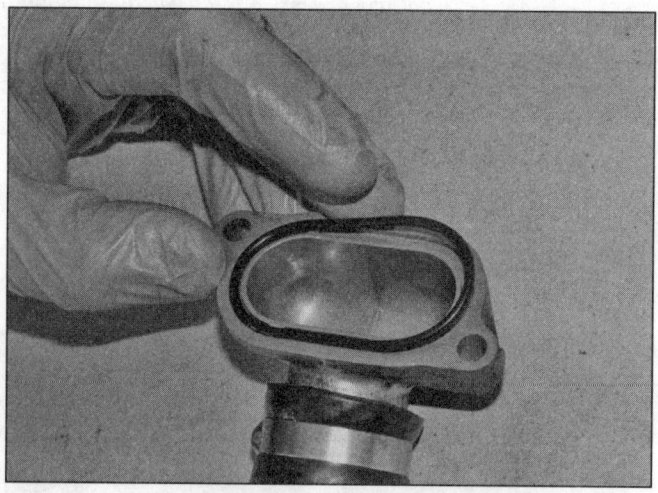

8.8 Use a new O-ring

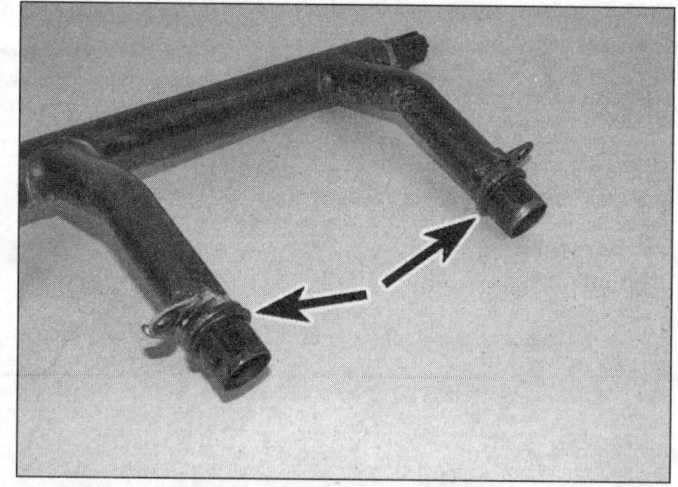

8.9 Use new O-rings (arrowed)

Chapter 4
Engine management system

Contents

	Section number
Air filter	see Chapter 1
Air filter housing	6
Air induction system (AIS)	19
Catalytic converter	18
Clutch switch	see Chapter 8
Electronic Control Unit (ECU)	15
Engine management system description	12
Engine management system fault diagnosis	13
Engine management system fuses	see Chapter 8
Engine management system relays	16
Engine management system sensors	14
Exhaust system	17
Fast idle system (2001 to 2012 models)	10
Fuel level sensor	5
Fuel rail and injectors	9
Fuel pressure	4

	Section number
Fuel pump	3
Fuel system check	see Chapter 1
Fuel tank	2
General information and precautions	1
Ignition coils	21
Ignition switch	see Chapter 8
Ignition system check	20
Ignition timing	22
Immobiliser system	23
Neutral switch	see Chapter 8
Sidestand switch	see Chapter 8
Spark plugs	see Chapter 1
Throttle bodies	7
Throttle cable check and adjustment	see Chapter 1
Throttle cables	8
YCC-T and cruise control systems (2013-on models)	11

Degrees of difficulty

Easy, suitable for novice with little experience	Fairly easy, suitable for beginner with some experience	Fairly difficult, suitable for competent DIY mechanic	Difficult, suitable for experienced DIY mechanic	Very difficult, suitable for expert DIY or professional

Specifications

General information
Cylinder numbering .... 1 to 4 from left to right
Spark plugs .... see Chapter 1

Fuel
Grade .... Regular unleaded, minimum 91 RON (Research Octane Number)
Fuel tank
  Capacity (including reserve) .... 25 litres
  Reserve volume
    2001 to 2005 models .... 5.0 litres
    2006-on models .... 5.5 litres

4•2 Engine management system

Fuel injection system

Fuel pressure
  2001 and 2002 models.................................. 250 kPa (36 psi)
  2003 model.. 294 kPa (43 psi)
  2004 to 2012 models.................................. 324 kPa (47 psi)
  2013-on models....................................... 300 to 390 kPa (44 to 57 psi)
Engine idle speed.. 1000 to 1100 rpm
Accelerator position sensor maximum resistance (2013-on models) .. 1.08 to 2.52 K-ohms @ 20°C
AIS control valve resistance.............................. 19 to 25 ohms
Atmospheric pressure sensor output voltage
  2001 to 2003 models.................................. 3.75 to 4.25 V
  2013-on models....................................... 3.57 to 3.71 V
Camshaft position sensor output voltage
  On .... 4.8 V or more
  Off .... 0.8 V or less
Crankshaft position (CKP) sensor
  Resistance .... 420 to 570 ohms
Engine coolant temperature (ECT) sensor resistance
  At 0°C.. 5.2 to 6.4 K-ohms
  At 20°C... 2.45 K-ohms
  At 80°C... 290 to 354 ohms
Fuel injector resistance................................. approx. 12 ohms
Intake air temperature (IAT) sensor resistance
  At 0°C.. 5.4 to 6.6 K-ohms
  At 80°C... 290 to 390 ohms
Intake air pressure (IAP) sensor output voltage
  2001 to 2012 models.................................. 3.75 to 4.25 V
  2013-on models....................................... 3.57 to 3.71 V
Throttle position sensor
  Maximum resistance
    2001 to 2007 models .... 4.0 to 6.0 K-ohms @ 20°C
    2008 to 2012 models .... 2.0 to 3.0 K-ohms @ 20°C
    2013-on models .... 1.2 to 2.8 K-ohms @ 20°C
  Voltage (for position adjustment on 2006 to 2012 models) .... 0.63 to 0.73 V
Tip-over sensor output voltage
  Sensor upright .... 0.4 to 1.4V
  Sensor tilted at specified angle .... 3.7 to 4.4V

Fuel level sensor

Resistance
  Full position .... 19 to 21 ohms
  Empty position .... 139 to 141 ohms

Ignition coils

2001 to 2012 models
  Primary winding resistance .... 1.5 to 2.5 ohms
  Secondary winding resistance
    With plug caps .... 32 to 38 K-ohms
    Without plug caps .... 12 to 18 K-ohms
  Plug cap resistance .... approximately 10 K-ohms
2013-on models
  Primary winding resistance .... 1.2 to 1.6 ohms
  Secondary winding resistance .... 8.5 to 11.5 K-ohms

Torque settings

AIS reed valve cover bolts .... 14 Nm
Exhaust system
  Downpipe flange nuts................................. 20 Nm
  Downpipe mounting bolts .... 17 Nm
  Silencer clamp bolt.................................. 20 Nm
  Silencer mounting bolt .... 25 Nm
Fuel pump bolts .... 4 Nm
Oxygen sensor .... 45 Nm
T-bar bolts
  2001 to 2005 models .... not available
  2006-on models .... 37 Nm

Engine management system 4•3

1 General information and precautions

General information

All models are fitted with a fully electronic engine management system that controls both the fuelling and ignition from one electronic control unit, or ECU.

Fuel system

The fuel system consists of the fuel tank with internal fuel pump assembly (incorporating the filter and fuel level sensor, and on 2004-on models the pressure regulator), the fuel supply hose, the fuel rail and injectors, the throttle body assembly, and the throttle cables. On 2001 to 2003 models the pressure regulator is on the end of the fuel rail, and there is a fuel return hose from it back to the tank. The system is switched on and off by the starter circuit cut-off relay and the fuel injection system relay. Fuel and air is supplied to the engine via 42 mm throttle bodies. The injectors are operated by the Electronic Control Unit (ECU), which uses information obtained from the various sensors it monitors to control the amount of fuel delivered.

All models have a fuel gauge incorporated in the instrument cluster, actuated by the level sensor inside the fuel tank.

Ignition system

The transistorised electronic ignition system is combined with the fuel injection system, both being controlled by the ECU. The ignition system comprises a timing rotor, crankshaft position sensor (CKP sensor), the ECU, the ignition coils and the spark plugs.

The triggers on the timing rotor, which is on the right-hand end of the crankshaft, generate a signal in the CKP sensor as the crankshaft rotates. The ECU calculates the ignition timing and supplies the ignition coils with the signals to produce a spark at the plugs. There is no provision for adjusting the ignition timing.

The system incorporates a starter safety circuit (see Section 14 in Chapter 1 for more information).

Note: *Individual engine management system components can be checked but not repaired. If system troubles occur, and the faulty component can be isolated, the only cure for the problem in most cases is to replace the part with a new one. Keep in mind that most electronic parts, once purchased, cannot be returned. To avoid unnecessary expense, make very sure the faulty component has been positively identified before buying a new part.*

Precautions

⚠ **Warning: Petrol (gasoline) is extremely flammable, so take extra precautions when you work on any part of the fuel system. Always remove the battery (see Chapter 8). Don't smoke or allow open flames or bare light bulbs near the work area, and don't work in a garage where a natural gas-type appliance is present. If you spill any fuel on your skin, rinse it off immediately with soap and water. When you perform any kind of work on the fuel system, wear safety glasses and have a fire extinguisher suitable for a class B type fire (flammable liquids) on hand.**

With a fuel injection system, some residual pressure will remain in the fuel hose and injectors after the motorcycle has been used. Before disconnecting the fuel hose, release fuel system pressure as described in Section 2. It is vital that no dirt or debris is allowed to enter the fuel tank or the fuel rail assembly whilst the fuel hoses are disconnected. Any foreign matter in the fuel system components could result in injector damage or malfunction. Ensure the ignition is switched OFF before disconnecting or reconnecting any fuel injection system wiring connector. If a connector is disconnected or reconnected with the ignition switched ON, the ECU may be damaged.

Always perform service procedures in a well-ventilated area to prevent a build-up of fumes.

Never work in a building containing a gas appliance with a pilot light, or any other form of naked flame. Ensure that there are no naked light bulbs or any sources of flame or sparks nearby.

Do not smoke (or allow anyone else to smoke) while in the vicinity of petrol (gasoline) or of components containing it. Remember the possible presence of vapour from these sources and move well clear before smoking.

Check all electrical equipment belonging to the house, garage or workshop where work is being undertaken (see the Safety first! section of this manual). Remember that certain electrical appliances such as drills, cutters etc, create sparks in the normal course of operation and must not be used near petrol (gasoline) or any component containing it. Again, remember the possible presence of fumes before using electrical equipment.

Always mop up any spilt fuel and safely dispose of the rag used.

Any stored fuel that is drained off during servicing work must be kept in sealed containers that are suitable for holding petrol (gasoline), and clearly marked as such; the containers themselves should be kept in a safe place. Note that this last point applies equally to the fuel tank if it is removed from the machine; also remember to keep its filler cap closed at all times.

Read the *Safety first!* section of this manual carefully before starting work.

2 Fuel tank

⚠ **Warning: Refer to the precautions given in Section 1 before starting work.**

Raise and removal

Note: *Removing the tank involves a small amount of unavoidable fuel spillage, which is obviously dangerous. Refer to the precautions given in Section 1 before starting work, and have plenty of rag to hand. Once the tank has been removed, rest it on some soft rag to prevent damaging the paintwork or hose unions. Try to time the removal procedure with a near empty tank, which makes it much easier to lift.*

1 Make sure the fuel cap is secure.
2 Remove the seats (see Chapter 7).
3 On 2001 to 2005 models release the trim clip (see Chapter 8) and undo the screw on each tank trim panel **(see illustration)**. Pull the peg out of the grommet and remove each panel **(see illustration)**.
4 On 2006-on models release the trim clip (see Chapter 8) and undo the screw on each side of the tank trim panel **(see illustration)**. Pull the peg out of the grommet on each side

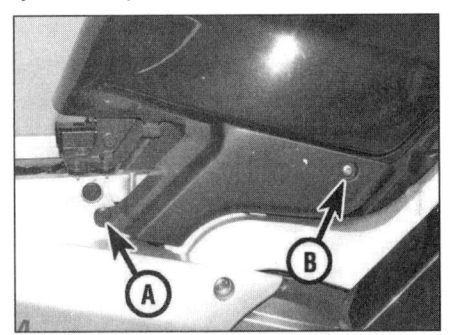

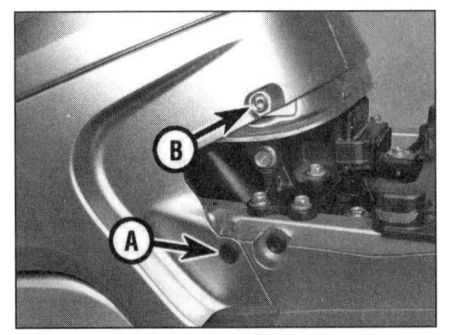

2.3a Release the trim clip (A) and undo the screw (B)...

2.3b ...then pull the peg out of the grommet

2.4a Release the trim clip (A) and undo the screw (B) on each side...

4•4 Engine management system

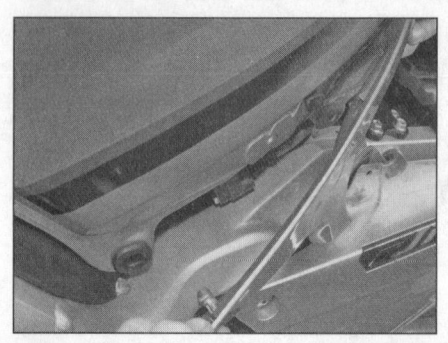

2.4b ...then pull the peg out of the grommet and draw the slot off the tab on each side

2.5 Slacken or unscrew the nut (arrowed)

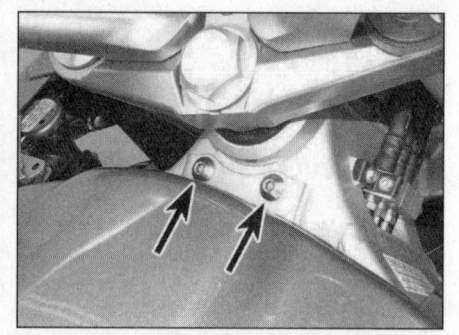

2.6 Unscrew the bolts (arrowed)

2.7 Tank supported using a piece of wood

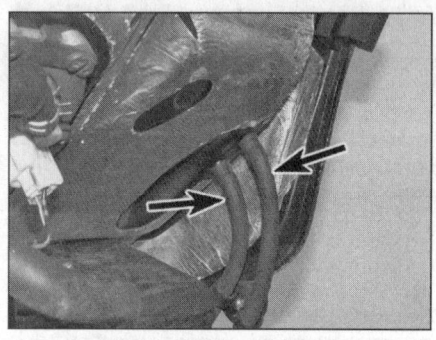

2.8a On 2001 to 2005 models detach both hoses (arrowed) from the tank

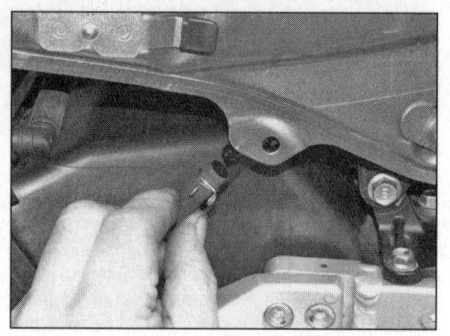

2.8b On 2006-on models detach the hose from the joint

and draw the panel back to disengage the slots from the tabs **(see illustration)**.

5 Slacken (if raising the tank) or unscrew (if removing the tank) the nut on the rear pivot bolt **(see illustration)**.

6 Unscrew the front mounting bolts **(see illustration)**.

7 Raise the front of the tank and fit a suitable piece of wood between the tank and the frame, making sure it is secure **(see illustration)**.

8 Disconnect the fuel tank drain and breather hoses **(see illustrations)**.

9 Disconnect the fuel pump and level sensor wiring connectors **(see illustration)**.

10 On 2001 to 2003 models disconnect the fuel return hose from the pressure regulator **(see illustration)**.

11 Place a wad of rag for catching any residual fuel in the hose under the connector

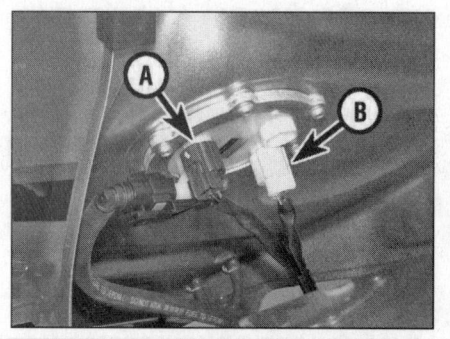

2.9 Fuel pump (green) wiring connector (A), fuel level sender (white) wiring connector (B)

on the fuel rail. Where fitted, remove the holder from the connector **(see illustration)**. Where

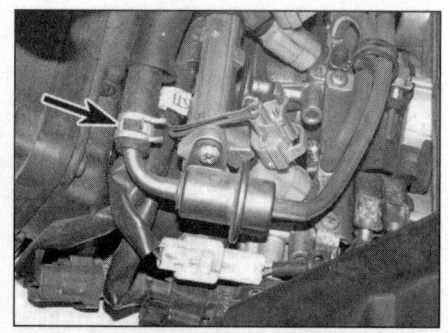

2.10 Release the clamp and detach the hose (arrowed)

no holder is fitted slide the cover across to reveal the retainer tabs **(see illustration)**.

2.11a Unclip the holder (arrowed)

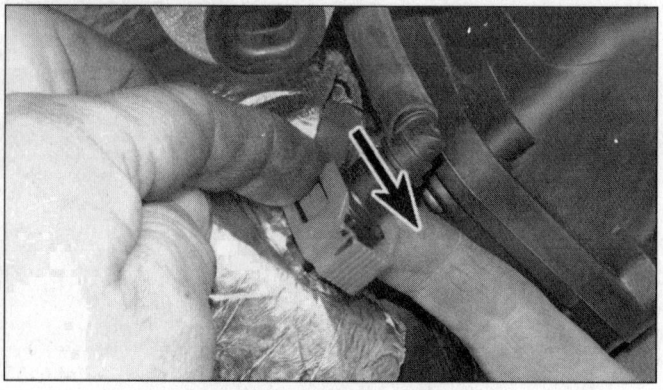

2.11b Slide the cover across

Engine management system 4•5

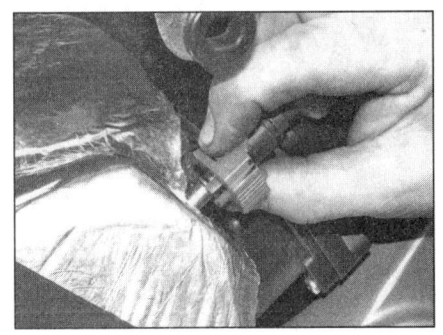

2.12a Press the tabs in...

2.12b ...and pull the connector off

2.14a Withdraw the bolt...

2.14b ...and remove the tank

2.19 Push the cover over the tabs

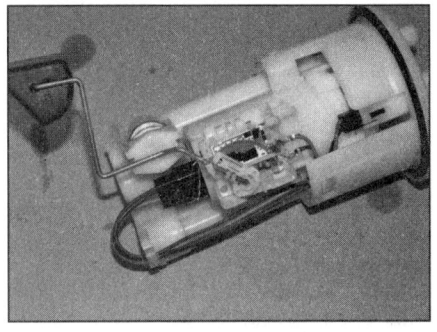

3.2 Check the pump wiring and connectors

12 Press the tabs in then pull the connector off the pipe (see illustrations). Seal the pipe and the hose connector with a piece from a plastic bag or the finger from a latex glove, secured with an elastic band, to prevent dirt getting in.
13 Remove the support and lower the tank.
14 Withdraw the pivot bolt (see illustration). Carefully lift the tank off the frame and remove it (see illustration).
15 Check all the tank rubbers and hoses for signs of damage or deterioration and replace them with new ones if necessary.

Installation

16 Fit any mounting rubbers that have been removed.
17 Depending on how the tank has been stood and how full it is there is the possibility of fuel having made its way into the breather pipe which could spurt out of the hose on the base when it is moved – be prepared with some rag for this.
18 Position the tank on the frame and insert the pivot bolt (see illustrations 2.14a). Fit the nut and tighten it finger-tight (see illustration 2.5). Raise and support the tank as before (see illustration 2.7).
19 Push the fuel hose connector onto the pipe until both retainer tabs click into place, then try to pull the connector off to make sure it has locked (see illustration 2.12b). Either push the cover across so the tabs cannot be pushed in (see illustration), or fit the holder onto the connector (see illustration 2.11a).
20 On 2001 to 2003 models connect the fuel return hose to the pressure regulator (see illustration 2.10).
21 Connect the fuel pump and level sensor wiring connectors (see illustration 2.9).
22 Connect the fuel tank drain and breather hoses (see illustration 2.8a or b). Make sure all the hoses and wiring are securely connected.
23 Remove the support and lower the tank – make sure the hoses do not get squashed or kinked. Fit and tighten the front mounting bolts, then tighten the nut on the pivot bolt (see illustrations 2.6 and 2.5).
24 Fit the tank trim panels (Step 3 or 4) and seats.

Repair

25 Repairs to the fuel tank should be carried out by a professional who has experience in this critical and potentially dangerous work. Even after cleaning and flushing of the fuel system, explosive fumes can remain and ignite during repair of the tank.
26 If the fuel tank is removed from the bike, it should not be placed in an area where sparks or open flames could ignite the fumes coming out of the tank. Be especially careful inside garages where a natural gas-type appliance is located – the pilot light could cause an explosion.

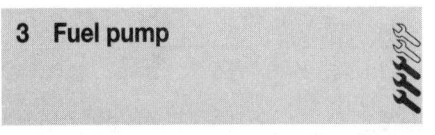

3 Fuel pump

Warning: *Refer to the precautions given in Section 1 before starting work.*

Check

1 The fuel pump is located inside the fuel tank. The fuel pump should run for a few seconds when the ignition is switched ON and the kill switch is set to RUN to pressurise the fuel system, and then cut out until the engine is started. Check that it does this – you can hear it run. If it doesn't, first raise the tank (Section 2, Steps 1 to 7), and check the pump (green) wiring connector is secure. Next check the main, ignition and fuel injection system fuses (see Chapter 8).
2 If the fuses are good make sure the ignition is OFF, then disconnect the pump (green) wiring connector (see illustration 2.9). Using a multimeter set to the ohms scale, connect the positive (+) probe to the red/blue wire terminal in the socket and the negative (-) probe to the black wire terminal and measure the resistance – there should be a small resistance (0.2 to 3.0 ohms is specified for 2001 to 2005 models, no data is available for later models). If there is zero or infinite resistance remove the pump (Steps 5 to 9) and make sure the wiring connectors and terminals are secure (see illustration). If the pump is faulty replace it with a new one it.
3 If the pump appears good, set the multimeter to the DC voltage scale and connect the positive (+) lead to the red/blue wire terminal in the wiring connector and the negative (–) lead to the black wire terminal. Switch the ignition ON and set the kill switch to RUN whilst noting the reading obtained on the meter. If battery voltage is present, the fuel pump circuit is operating correctly and the

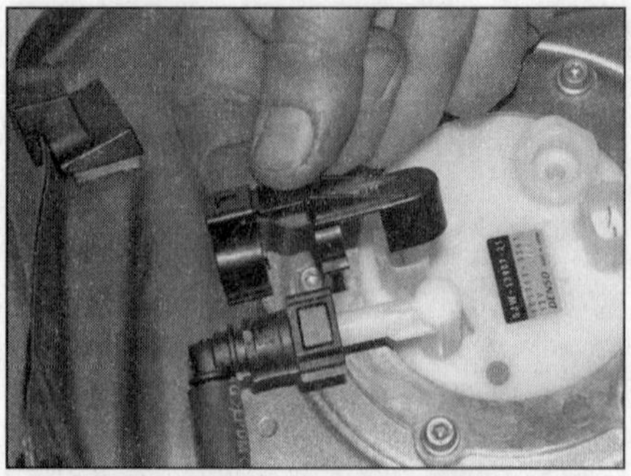

4•6 Engine management system

3.7a Remove the holder...

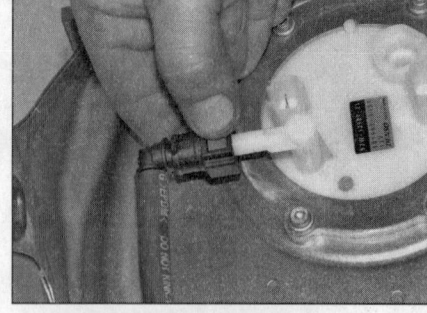

3.7b ...press the tabs in...

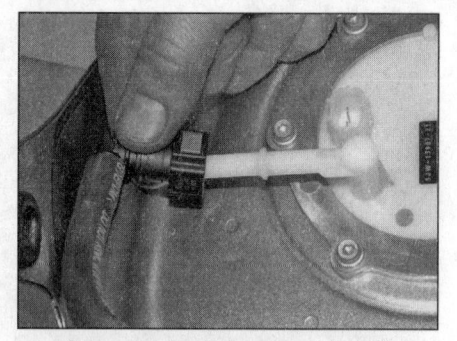

3.7c ...and pull the connector off

3.8a Lift the pump and carefully persuade the protrusion (arrowed) past the rim...

3.8b ...then tilt as shown and lift some more...

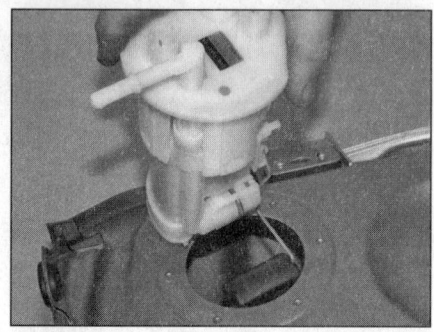

3.8c ...to get the level sensor float out

fuel pump itself is faulty and must be replaced with a new one.
4 If no reading is obtained, check the fuel injection system relay (Section 16).

Removal

5 Syphon as much fuel as possible from the tank into a suitable container, using a commercially available siphon pump. Remove the fuel tank (see Section 2). Make sure the fuel cap is secure, then place the tank upside down on plenty of rag.
6 On 2001 to 2003 models disconnect the fuel return hose.
7 Remove the holder from the fuel supply hose connector **(see illustration)**. Press the retainer tabs in then pull the connector off the pipe **(see illustrations)**. Seal the pipe and the hose connector with a piece from a plastic bag or the finger from a latex glove, secured with an elastic band, to prevent dirt getting in.
8 Unscrew the bolts and remove the pump retainer plate **(see illustrations 3.13b and a)**. Carefully manoeuvre the pump assembly from the tank – clearance is severly limited so take care **(see illustrations)**.
9 Remove the seal **(see illustration)** – a new one must be used on installation.

Installation

10 Make sure all wiring is securely connected.
11 Ensure the retainer plate and tank mating surfaces are clean and dry. Fit a new seal onto the pump with the flat side facing the base **(see illustration)**.
12 Carefully manoeuvre the pump assembly into the tank **(see illustrations 3.8c, b**

and a) – make sure it is positioned with the pipe pointing to the right-hand side of the tank (when the correct way up).
13 Fit the retainer plate, aligning the cut-out with the pin **(see illustration)**. Fit the bolts and

3.9 Remove the seal

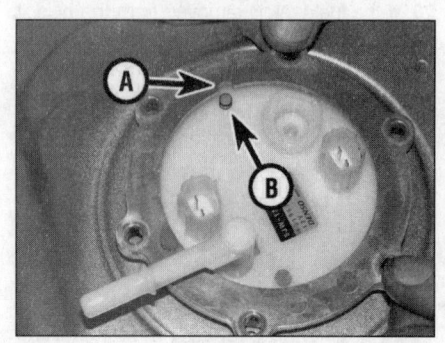

3.13a Seat the cut-out (A) around the pin (B)

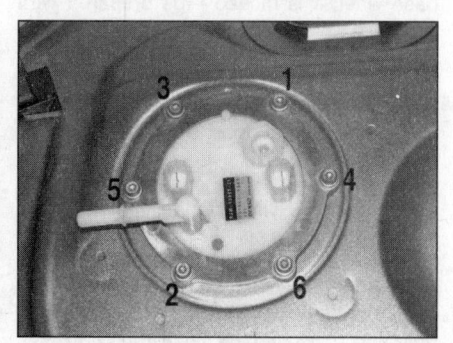

tighten them finger-tight. Now tighten them evenly and a little at a time in the numerical sequence shown to the torque setting specified at the beginning of the Chapter **(see illustration)**.

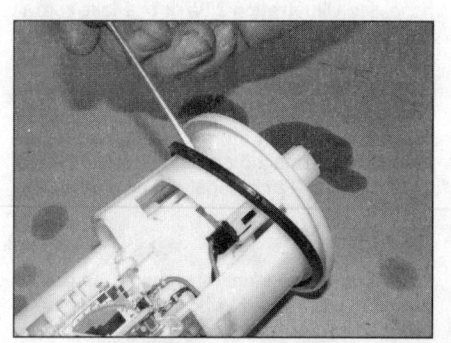

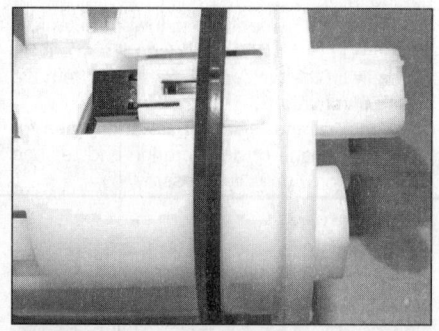

3.11 Make sure the new seal is the correct way round

3.13b Fuel pump bolt tightening sequence

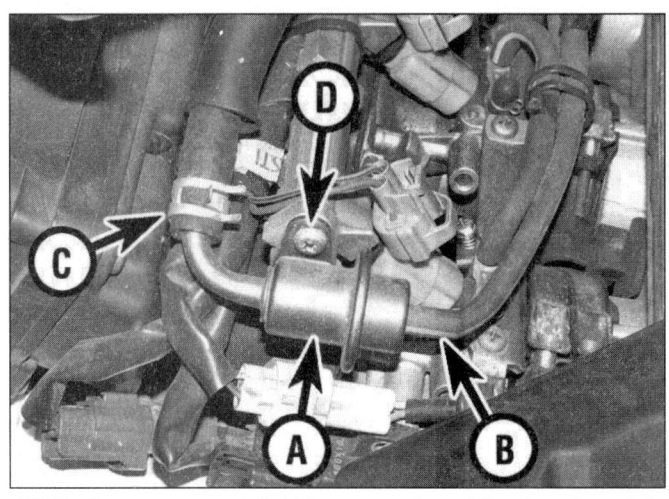

Engine management system 4•7

4.7 Fuel pressure regulator (A), vacuum hose (B), return hose (C), screw (D)

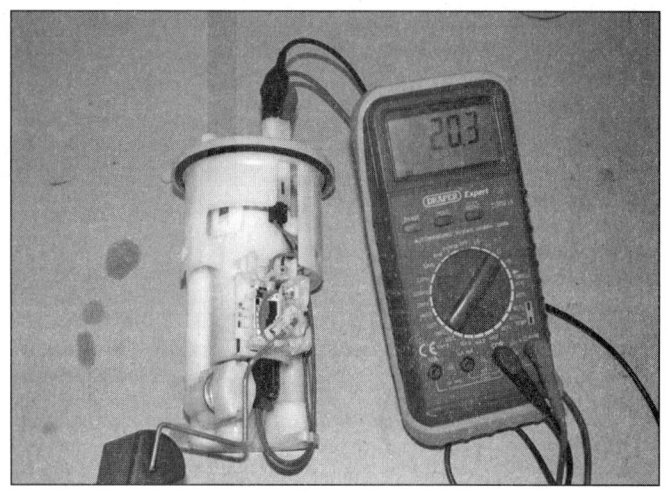

5.2a Check the resistance with the float arm in the full position...

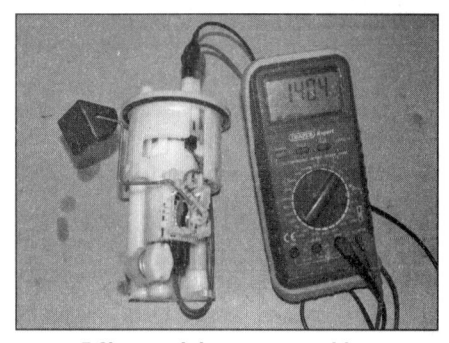

5.2b ...and the empty position

14 Push the fuel hose connector onto the pipe until both retainer tabs click into place, then try to pull the connector off to make sure it has locked. Push the cover across so the tabs cannot be pushed in **(see illustration 2.19)**. Fit the holder onto the connector. On 2001 to 2003 models connect the fuel return hose.
15 Install the fuel tank (see Section 2).

4 Fuel pressure

⚠ *Warning: Refer to the precautions given in Section 1 before starting work.*

Fuel pressure check

1 A pressure gauge along with some adapters and hoses that are compatible with the quick-release fittings of the bike's fuel hose are required for this check. Yamaha can supply the various parts required, but it may be cheaper to get a dealer to perform the check, especially as hopefully you will not need the equipment more than once.
2 If the fuel pressure is higher than specified, the pressure regulator or the fuel pump is faulty.
3 If the fuel pressure is lower than specified, first check for a leak, which should be obvious from the smell of fuel. If there are no leaks check for a pinched or blocked tank breather hose or fuel hose. Otherwise the fuel filter or pressure regulator or the pump itself, are faulty.
4 On all models the filter is incorporated in the fuel pump assembly, and is not available as a spare part. If the pump motor is faulty the complete assembly must be replaced with a new one.
5 On 2001 to 2003 models the pressure regulator is on the right-hand end of the fuel rail and is available separately. On all later models the regulator is incorporated in the fuel pump assembly, and is not available as a spare part.

Fuel pressure regulator (2001 to 2003 models)

6 Raise the fuel tank (Section 2, Steps 1 to 7).
7 Pull the vacuum hose off **(see illustration)**. Release the clamp on the fuel return hose and slide it back along the hose. Undo the screw and displace the regulator, and pull it out of the hose. Remove the O-ring.
8 Fit the regulator using a new O-ring. Make sure the hoses are secure.

5 Fuel level sensor

Check

1 If the gauge does not work, check the amount of fuel in the tank, then raise the tank (see Section 2, Steps 1 to 7). Disconnect the fuel level sensor (white) wiring connector **(see illustration 2.9)**. Connect an ohmmeter or multimeter set to the ohms scale to the terminals in the socket and measure the resistance. Compare the reading obtained to those given at the beginning of the Chapter for a full and empty tank, adjusting for the amount of fuel you estimate is there.
2 To accurately check the sensor remove the pump from the tank (Section 3). Check the float arm for damage and look for fuel inside the float, and check that the arm moves up and down smoothly and freely. Also check the wiring. Connect the meter to the socket terminals as above, then manually move the float up and down to simulate movement between the full and empty positions, and compare the resistance readings to those given **(see illustrations)**. If they are not as specified replace the pump assembly with a new one.
3 If the level sensor appears to be functioning correctly, connect the sensor wiring connector, turn the ignition ON and manually move the float up and down – if the gauge does not move in response to the movement of the float there is a fault in the wiring circuit or the instrument cluster (see Chapter 8).

Removal and installation

4 If the sensor is faulty remove the fuel pump and replace it with a new one (Section 3) – the level sensor is an integral component and not available separately.

6 Air filter housing

⚠ *Warning: Refer to the precautions given in Section 1 before starting work.*

1 Remove the throttle bodies (see Section 7).

4•8 Engine management system

6.2a Detach the hose...

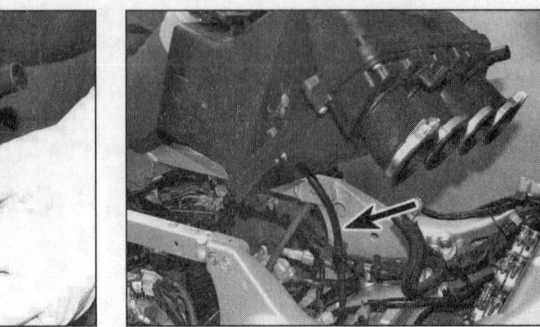

6.2b ...and remove the housing, bringing the drain hose (arrowed) with it

6.3 Feed the drain hose down the back of the engine and through the guide (arrowed)

2 Detach the crankcase breather hose and remove the housing **(see illustrations)**.
3 Installation is the reverse of removal, noting the following:
● Check the condition of all hoses and replace them with new ones if they are in any way damaged or deteriorated.
● Make sure the hoses are correctly routed **(see illustration)**.

7 Throttle bodies

Warning: Refer to the precautions given in Section 1 before starting work.

Removal

1 Remove the fuel tank (see Section 2).
2 Remove the air filter (see Chapter 1).
3 On 2001 to 2012 models drain the cooling system (see Chapter 3).
4 On 2001 to 2005 models unscrew the AIS control valve holder bolt **(see illustration)**. On all models remove the T-bar **(see illustration)**. On 2006-on models remove the heat shield **(see illustrations)**.
5 On 2006-on models remove the AIS control valve and hoses (Section 19).
6 Detach the throttle cables from the twistgrip (Section 8). Slacken the nuts or bolts holding the throttle cables in the bracket on the throttle bodies **(see illustration)**. Feed the cables through the frame, noting their routing – they are removed with the throttle bodies, and detached afterwards if required.
7 On 2001 to 2012 models disconnect the oxygen sensor wiring connector **(see illustration)**, the CMP sensor wiring connector **(see illustration)**, and the throttle body sub-loom wiring connector(s) **(see illustration)**. Displace the IAP sensor from the

7.4a Unscrew the bolt (arrowed)

7.4b Unscrew the bolts (arrowed) and remove the T-bar

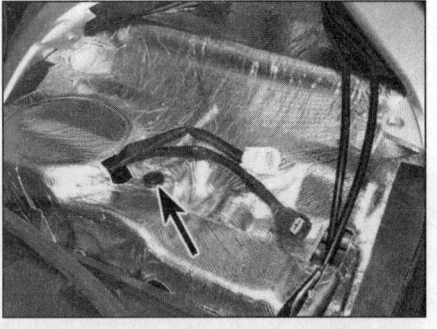

7.4c Release the trim clip (arrowed), thread the wiring through the hole and on 2013-on models slip the cables out of the slot...

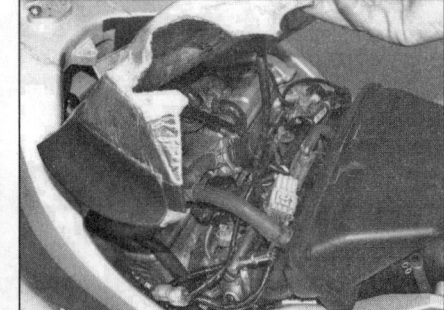

7.4d ...and remove the shield

7.6 Slacken the nuts (arrowed)

7.7a Disconnect the oxygen sensor connector...

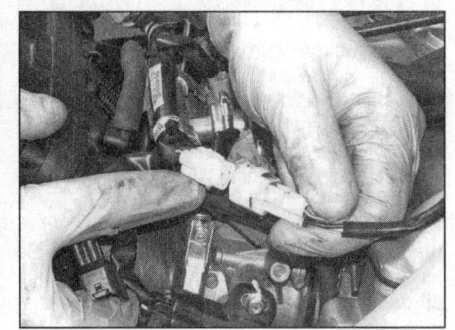

7.7b ...the CMP sensor connector...

Engine management system 4•9

7.7c ...and the throttle body connector(s) – 2010 model shown

7.7d Unscrew the bolts (arrowed)

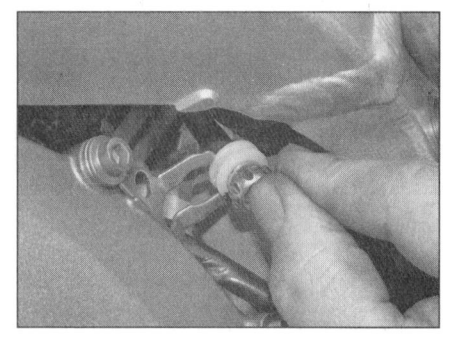

7.7e Release the adjuster

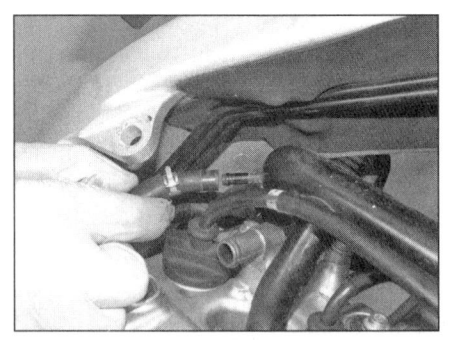

7.7f Detach the hose

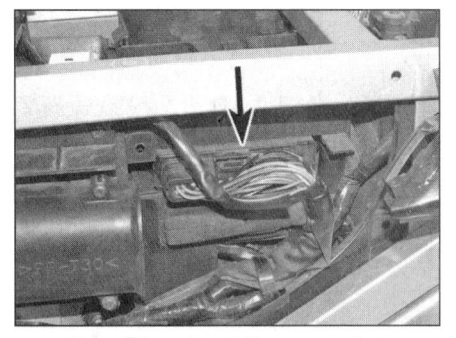

7.9a Disconnect the connector (arrowed)...

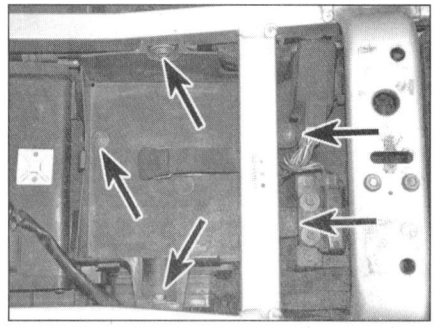

7.9b ...then undo the screws and bolts (arrowed)...

fuel rail for later access to the clamp screw **(see illustration)**. Release the idle speed adjuster from its holder **(see illustration)**. Detach the small-bore coolant hose for the fast idle system plunger unit from the right-hand end of the outlet pipe **(see illustration)**.

8 On 2013-on models disconnect the TP sensor wiring connector, the injector wiring connectors, the AP sensor wiring connector, the IAP sensor wiring connector, the grip cancel switch wiring connector. You will also need to disconnect the throttle servo motor wiring connector and the accelerator position sensor wiring connector, but do these after the air filter housing is displaced for better access.

9 On 2001 to 2005 models remove the toolkit from its tray. Disconnect the ECU wiring connector, then remove the tray **(see illustrations)**. Release the wiring tie and disconnect the IAT sensor wiring connector **(see illustration 14.37)**. Detach the AIS air supply hose from the air filter housing.

10 On 2006 to 2012 models remove the toolkit from its tray **(see illustration)**. On AS models, remove the motor control unit (see Section 20 in Chapter 2). Release the wiring from the clip on the right-hand side of the housing **(see illustration)**. Disconnect the ECU wiring connector, then remove the tray

7.9c ...and remove the tray

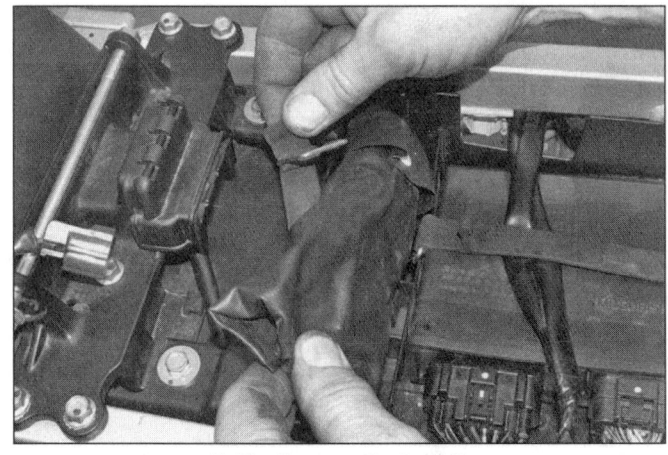

7.10a Remove the toolkit

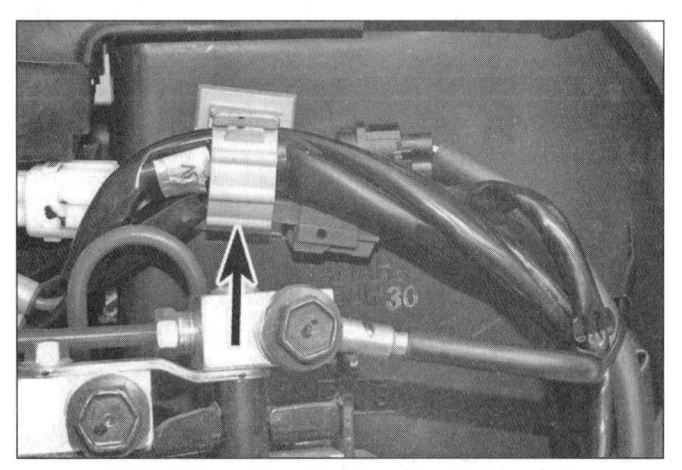

7.10b Release the wiring from the clip (arrowed)

4•10 Engine management system

7.10c Disconnect the connector...

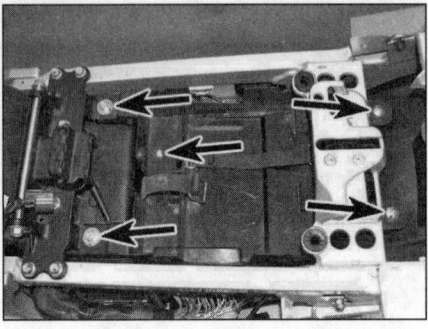

7.10d ...then undo the screws and bolts (arrowed)...

7.10e ...and remove the tray

(see illustrations). Release the wiring clip and disconnect the IAT sensor wiring connector (see illustration 14.37). Detach the bypass air unit hose from the air filter housing (see illustration).

11 On 2013-on models remove the toolkit from its tray. On AS models, remove the motor control unit (see Section 20 in Chapter 2). Release the wiring from the clip on the right-hand side of the housing. Remove the tray.

12 Unscrew the bolts securing the fuel tank bracket to the frame (see illustration).

13 Slacken the air intake duct clamp screws, then pull the air filter housing back off the throttle bodies (see illustrations).

14 Fully slacken the clamp on the throttle body side of each cylinder head intake duct

7.10f Detach the hose

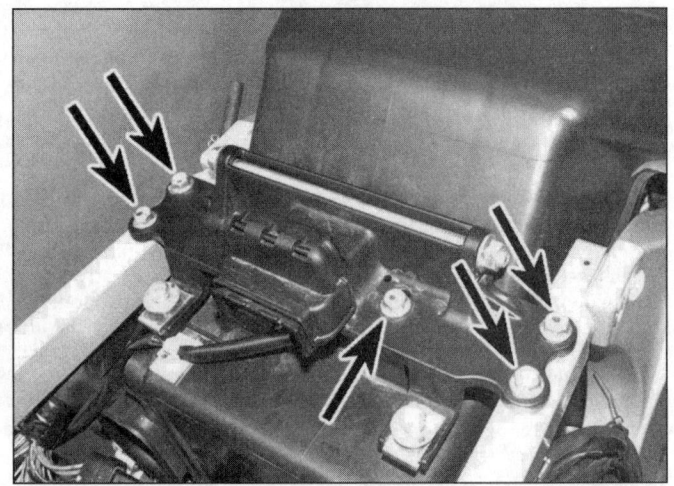

7.12 Unscrew the bolts (arrowed) and remove the bracket

7.13a Slacken the clamp screw (arrowed) securing each duct...

7.13b ...then pull the housing back

Engine management system 4•11

7.14a Slacken the clamp screws (arrowed)

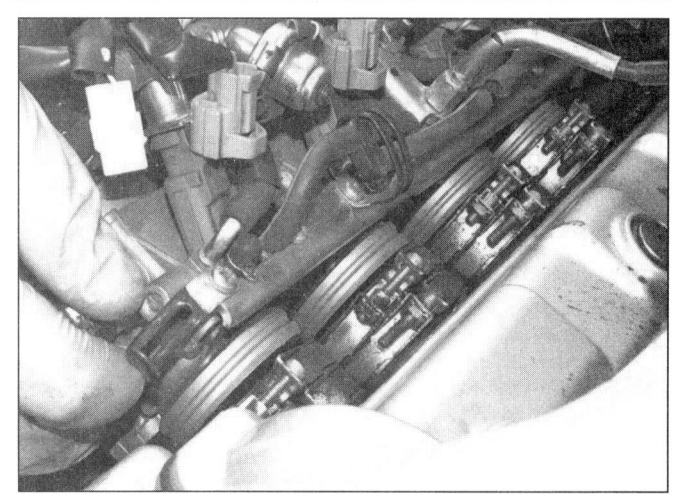

7.14b Displace the throttle bodies...

7.14c ...then detach the hose...

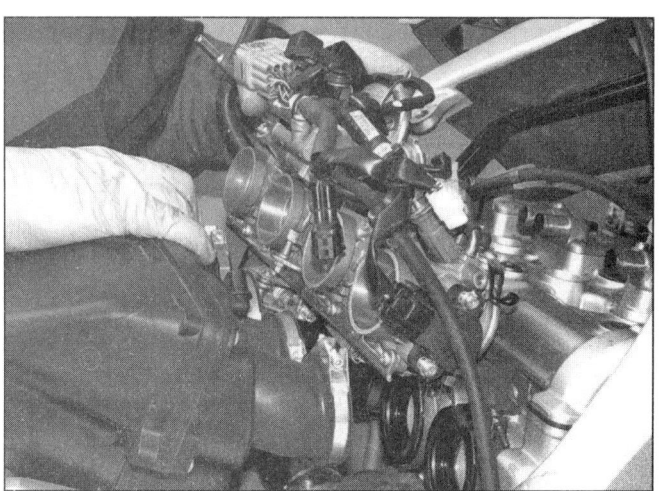

7.14d ...and remove the throttle bodies

(see illustration). Displace and lift the throttle body assembly, then on 2001 to 2012 models detach the bottom coolant hose from the plunger unit (see illustrations). Remove the throttle bodies, bringing the throttle cables, and on 2001 to 2012 models the top coolant hose, with it (see illustration).
15 If required detach the throttle cables from the pulley (Section 8).
16 If required unscrew the intake duct clamp screws and remove the ducts (see illustration).
Caution: Tape over or stuff clean rag into each cylinder head intake after removing the throttle body assembly to prevent anything getting in.

Inspection

17 Check over the entire assembly, looking for damaged or distorted components. Make sure the throttle valve linkage opens smoothly and returns under spring pressure (but do not let it snap forcibly closed). On 2001 to 2012 models check the fast idle system (Section 10).
Caution: Do not snap the throttle cam/valves from fully open to fully closed once the cables have been disconnected because this can lead to engine idle speed problems. Do not attempt to disassemble the throttle bodies any further than removal of the fuel rail and injectors (Section 9) and the sensors (Section 14).
18 On 2001 to 2003 models, if required remove the pressure regulator and fuel supply hose union from the fuel rail by undoing the screws. Use new O-rings when fitting them back on.
19 Check the condition of all hoses and replace them with new ones if they are in any way damaged or deteriorated.

Installation

20 Installation is the reverse of removal, noting the following:

- Do not forget to remove the covers or plugs from the intakes on the cylinder heads.
- If removed fit the intake ducts with the clamp screws at the top and locating the protrusions on each side of the rib on each port (see illustration 7.16).

7.16 Note how the ducts locate (arrow)

4•12 Engine management system

7.20 Note the routing of the throttle cables under the pipe (2001 to 2012 models) and through the frame

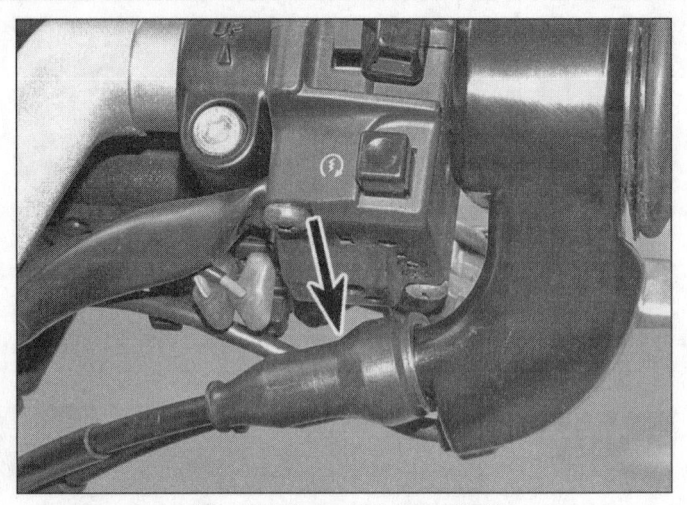

8.1a Pull the boot (arrowed) off

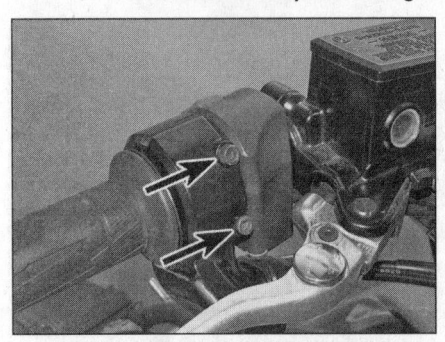

8.1b Undo the screws (arrowed)...

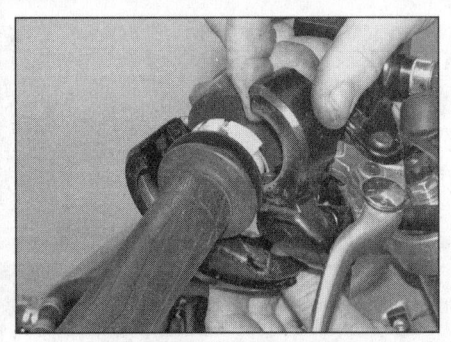

8.1c ...detach the housing...

8.1d ...remove the elbows...

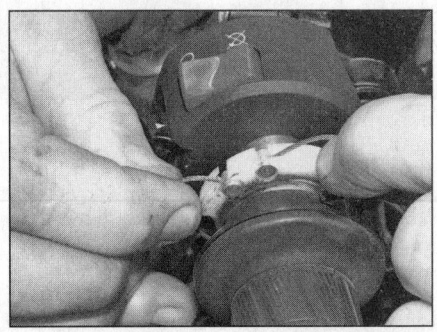

8.1e ...and detach the cable ends

8.3a Slip the cables out of the bracket...

8.3b ...and detach the ends from the pulley

- If removed, make sure the air filter housing is loosely positioned before installing the throttle bodies.
- Do not forget to connect the throttle cables before installing the throttle bodies.
- Lubricate the inside of the rubbers with a light smear of engine oil to aid installation.
- Make sure all cables, hoses and wiring are correctly routed (see illustration).
- Make sure all wiring connectors are securely connected.
- Tighten the T-bar bolts to the torque setting specified at the beginning of the Chapter.
- Check throttle cable freeplay at the twistgrip and adjust if necessary (see Chapter 1).

8 Throttle cables

⚠ *Warning: Refer to the precautions given in Section 1 before proceeding.*

Removal

1 Pull the rubber boot back off the throttle housing on the handlebar (see illustration). Undo the throttle housing screws and separate the halves (see illustrations). Displace the cable elbows from the housing, noting how they fit, and detach the cable nipples from the pulley (see illustrations). Mark each cable to ensure it is connected correctly on installation.

2 Remove the throttle bodies (see Section 7).

3 Mark each cable according to its location in the throttle bodies. On 2001 to 2012 models release the cables from the bracket and detach the ends from the pulley (see

Engine management system 4•13

8.3c Throttle cable arrangement – 2013-on models

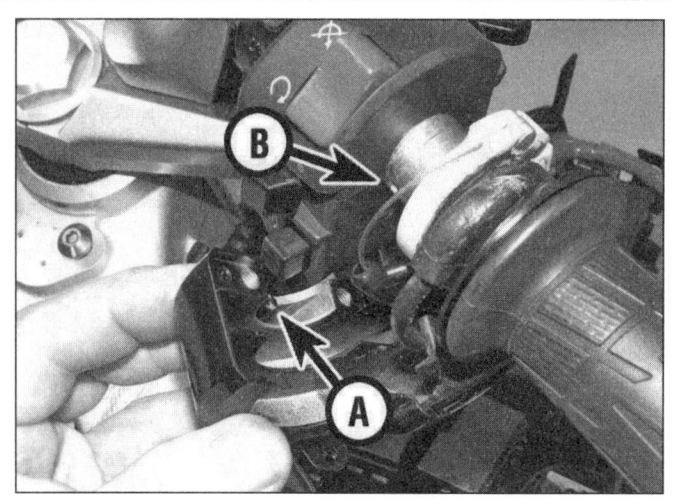

8.6 Locate the pin (A) in the hole (B)

illustrations). On 2013-on models unscrew the cable bracket bolts and detach the ends from the pulley (see illustration).

Installation

4 Lubricate the cable ends with multi-purpose grease and fit them into the throttle pulley, on 2001 to 2012 models making sure the opening cable is at the back (see illustration 8.3b). On 2001 to 2012 models fit the cable elbows into the bracket and lightly tighten the nuts (see illustration 8.3a). On 2013-on models fit the bracket and tighten the bolts.
5 Install the throttle bodies (see Section 7).
6 Lubricate the cable ends with multi-purpose grease and fit them into the throttle pulley at the handlebar, making sure the opening cable is at the front (see illustration 8.1e). Fit the cable elbows into the housing, making sure they locate correctly (see illustration 8.1d). Join the housing halves, making sure the pin locates in the hole in the handlebar, and tighten the screws (see illustration). Fit the rubber boot (see illustration 8.1a).

7 Check and adjust the cable freeplay (see Chapter 1).
8 Start the engine, then turn the handlebars from lock to lock and check that the idle speed does not rise as you do. If it does, the throttle cables are routed incorrectly. Correct the problem before riding the motorcycle.

9 Fuel rail and injectors

⚠ **Warning:** Refer to the precautions given in Section 1 before starting work.

Check

1 Raise the fuel tank (Section 2, Steps 1 to 7). On 2006-on models remove the T-bar and the heat shield (see illustrations 7.4b, c and d).
2 If the engine runs, start it and allow it to idle. Check the operation of each injector using a sounding rod held against it; an injector will emit a 'clicking' noise when functioning. If any injector is silent, either the injector or its wiring harness is faulty – see Step 4.
3 If the engine does not run, check the throttle body sub-loom connector (see illustration 7.7c), then check the wiring from it to each injector. Next check the fuel injection system relay (Section 16).
4 To check an individual injector disconnect the wiring connector (see illustration). Check the connector terminals and wires are secure. Connect an ohmmeter between the injector terminals and measure the resistance (see illustration). It should be as specified at the beginning of the Chapter. If the resistance differs greatly or measures zero or infinite resistance, replace the injector with a new one.

Removal

5 Remove the fuel tank (Section 2). Clean around the base of each injector using an air line and/or a soft brush.
6 Disconnect the TP sensor wiring connector (see illustration 14.27).

9.4a Disconnect the injector connector

9.4b Checking the resistance of an injector

4•14 Engine management system

9.7a Undo the screws (arrowed)...

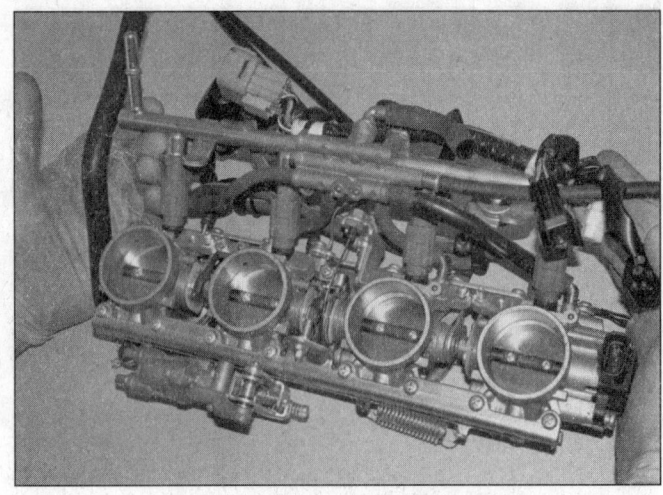

9.7b ...lift the rail and injectors off...

7 Undo the fuel rail screws, and on 2001 to 2012 models remove the spacers **(see illustration)**. Carefully lift off the rail, then remove the required injector(s) and disconnect the wiring connector(s) **(see illustrations)**.

8 Remove the seals, either from the injector seats in the throttle body, or from the injector nozzles **(see illustration)**. Remove the O-ring from the top of each removed injector **(see illustration 9.9)** – new ones must be used.

Installation

9 Fit a new O-ring lubricated with clean engine oil into the groove in the top of each removed injector **(see illustration)**.

10 Connect the wiring to the injector(s) **(see illustration 9.7d)**.

11 Fit the injector(s) into the rail, aligning the connector socket with the shaped side of the injector housing **(see illustration 9.7c)**.

12 Fit a new seal lubricated with clean engine oil onto all injector nozzles **(see illustration)**.

13 Seat the injector nozzles in the throttle bodies making sure the seals stay in place and locate correctly **(see illustration 9.7b)**. Fit the screws, and on 2001 to 2012 models the spacers, and tighten the screws **(see illustration)**.

14 On 2006-on models fit the heat shield and tighten the T-bar bolts to the specified torque setting **(see illustrations 7.4d, c and b)**. Install the fuel tank. Run the engine and check that the fuel system is working correctly before taking the machine out on the road.

10 Fast idle system (2001 to 2012 models)

⚠ *Warning: Refer to the precautions given in Section 1 before starting work.*

9.7c ...then remove the injector...

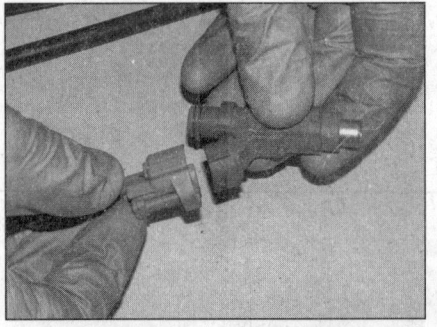

9.7d ...and disconnect the wiring

9.8 Remove the seals

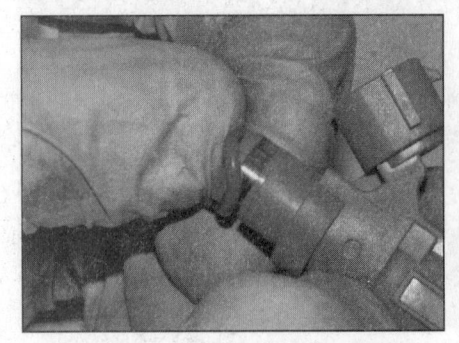

9.9 Fit a new O-ring into the groove

9.12 Fit a new seal onto each injector

9.13 Fit the spacers between the rail and the throttle bodies

Engine management system 4•15

10.1 Fast idle system wax unit (arrowed)

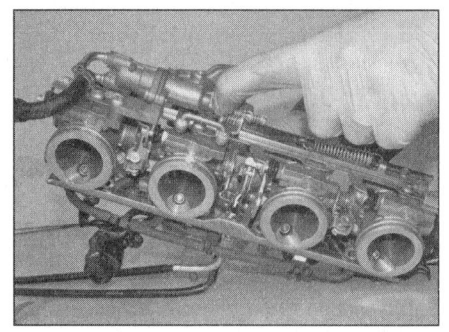

10.5a Check the movement of the linkage bar...

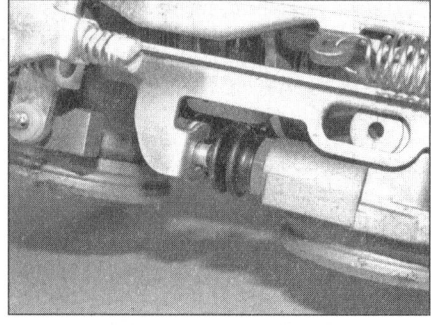

10.5b ...and the plungers

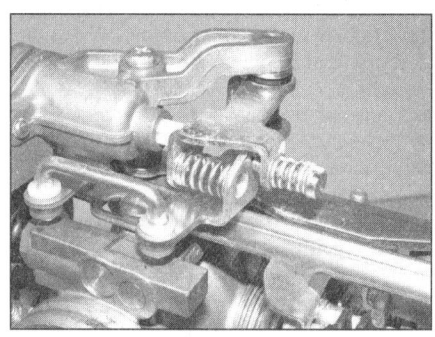

10.5c Clean and check all moving parts

1 The fast idle system works using a wax unit that is mounted in the middle of the throttle bodies (see illustration). The wax element inside the unit expands when hot and contracts when cold, reacting to the temperature of the coolant that flows around it. The wax unit pushrod actuates the linkage bar that is connected to the fast idle plungers on the throttle body.

2 The pushrod should be fully retracted and the plungers open when the engine is cold, and the pushrod extended and the plungers closed when the engine reaches normal operating temperature, which is usually reached after 10 to 15 minutes of stop-and-go riding. If a smooth, steady idle cannot be achieved, check that the unit is operating properly.

3 With the engine cold, raise the fuel tank (Section 2, Steps 1 to 7). On 2006-on models remove the T-bar and the heat shield (see illustrations 7.4b, c and d). Check the position of the pushrod and plungers. Run the engine until it reaches normal operating temperature, then check their position again.

4 If you suspect the unit is not working correctly, the fault lies in either the wax unit, the linkage or the plungers. Remove the throttle bodies (see Section 7).

5 Check the linkage bar assembly – the bar should move freely when the pushrod plate is moved and close the plungers, and return when released under tension from the return spring, opening the plungers (see illustrations). If the bar sticks, clean and check all parts of the linkage to identify the problem (see illustration). Also check the action of each individual plunger by pulling on its head – it should move smoothly and return under spring pressure.

6 If the linkage and plungers are all working, the wax unit is probably faulty – it can be tested as follows: note the position of the pushrod when the unit is cold – it should be fully retracted. Now gently heat it using a hair dryer and check that the pushrod extends. Now allow the unit to cool – as it does, the pushrod should retract.

7 No individual components are available for the fast idle system – if there is a problem that cannot be rectified, replace the throttle body assembly with a new one.

11 YCC-T and cruise control systems (2013-on models)

YCC-T (Yamaha Chip Controlled Throttle)

1 The YCC-T (Yamaha Chip Controlled Throttle) is a 'fly-by-wire' system that uses a servo motor to open and close the throttle butterfly valves in the throttle bodies. Throttle twistgrip operation appears as standard, with cables from it to the throttle bodies, but the cables are not connected directly to the butterfly valves. Instead they actuate an accelerator position sensor that, along with all the other sensors in the engine management system, sends information to the ECU. The ECU in turn calculates the ideal valve setting and controls the servo motor.

Accelerator position (TP) sensor
Check

2 The sensor is on the right-hand end of the throttle body assembly. Remove the sensor (Step 3). Using an ohmmeter or multimeter set to the K-ohms scale, connect the positive (+) probe to the blue wire terminal in the socket and the negative (-) probe to the black/blue wire terminal and measure the sensor maximum resistance. If it is not as specified at the beginning of the Chapter, replace the sensor with a new one.

Removal, installation and adjustment

3 Displace the throttle bodies, but leave the throttle cables attached (Section 7). Undo the screws and remove the sensor, noting how it fits. Check the actuating tab and the slot in the sensor it engages for wear and damage. Check the sensor rotor moves smoothly and freely.

4 Position the sensor and lightly tighten the screws. Check that the throttle butterfly valves are fully closed. Connect the sensor wiring connector. Simultaneously press and hold the TCS and RESET buttons on the instrument cluster, then turn the ignition ON and continue to hold the buttons for eight seconds or more until DIAG appears in the LCD display. Press and hold the TCS and RESET buttons for two seconds until the code 01 is displayed. Scroll through the codes and select code 14. Turn the throttle twistgrip fully closed. Carefully adjust the position of the sensor until 12-22 is displayed, then tighten the screws. Fully open the throttle – 97-107 should be displayed; if not readjust the sensor position. Select code 15. Turn the throttle twistgrip fully closed – 10-24 should be displayed; if not readjust the sensor position. Fully open the throttle – 95-109 should be displayed; if not readjust the sensor position. If you cannot get the correct numbers displayed however many times you try, fit a new sensor. Turn the ignition OFF.

Throttle servo motor

5 The motor is on the back the throttle body assembly. Remove the throttle bodies (Section 7).

6 To test the motor you need to apply 3 volts to its terminals – you can do this using two new 'C' (1.5 volt) batteries soldered together in series using short link wires, and with wires soldered to each open end preferably with small crocodile clips attached for connection to the terminals. DO NOT apply 12 volts to the motor. First connect the wire from the positive end of the batteries to the upper terminal and the negative to the lower – the motor should open the butterfly valves. Reverse the connection – the valves should close.

7 If the valves do not fully open and close replace the throttle body assembly with a new one – the motor is not available separately.

Cruise control

8 The cruise control system works in conjunction with the YCC-T system. Function

4•16 Engine management system

and operation of the system is covered in your owners Handbook. If there is a problem with the system this will be indicated by the cruise control indicator light and engine trouble warning light – plug-in diagnostic software is required to read fault and diagnostic codes, and this is only available at a Yamaha dealer.

12 Engine management system description

1 All models are equipped with a fuel injection system. It is controlled by the engine management system ECU that operates both the injection and ignition systems.
2 The ECU monitors signals from the following sensors.
- Camshaft position (CMP) sensor.
- Crankshaft position (CKP) sensor.
- Intake air pressure (IAP) sensor.
- Throttle position (TP) sensor.
- Engine coolant temperature (ECT) sensor (see Chapter 3).
- Intake air temperature (IAT) sensor.
- Atmospheric pressure (AP) sensor.
- Speed sensor.
- Oxygen sensor.
- Lean angle sensor.

3 Based on the information it receives, the ECU calculates the appropriate ignition and fuel requirements of the engine. By varying the length of the electronic pulse it sends to each injector, the ECU controls the length of time the injectors are held open and thereby the amount of fuel that is supplied to the engine. Fuel supply varies according to the engine's needs for starting, warming-up, idling, cruising and acceleration.
4 The engine trouble warning light should come on for 1.4 seconds when the ignition is switched ON, then go out – this serves as a check that the circuit is working correctly. If not, check the instrument cluster (see Chapter 8).
5 In the event of an abnormality in any of the sensor signals, the ECU will determine whether the engine can still be run safely. If it can, a back-up mode substitutes the sensor signal with a fixed signal, restricting performance but allowing the bike to be ridden home or to a dealer. When this occurs, the engine trouble warning light in the instrument cluster will come on and stay on. In some cases the engine will continue to run after the fault has been registered, but once stopped the engine will not be able to be restarted. If the fault is serious, the fuel injection system will be shut down and the engine will not run. When this occurs, the engine trouble warning light will flash while the start switch is being pressed.
6 After the engine has been stopped, the appropriate self-diagnostic fault code will appear on the clock LCD. See Section 13 for fault diagnosis.

13 Engine management system fault diagnosis

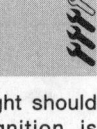

1 The engine trouble warning light should come on briefly when the ignition is switched ON, then go out – this serves as a check that the circuit is working correctly. If not, check the instrument cluster (see Chapter 8).
2 The system incorporates a self-diagnostic function whereby most faults, when they occur, are identified by a fault code that is displayed on the clock LCD after the engine has been stopped. The codes are stored in the ECU memory until a deletion operation is performed. In the case of a minor fault in the injection system, the engine trouble warning light in the instrument cluster will come on and stay on and the engine will continue to run, and may be able to be restarted, enabling the machine to be ridden, although performance will be significantly reduced. In the case of a major fault the warning light will flash and the engine will stop and not be able to be restarted. Certain faults will not activate the warning light and are not subject to a fault code, but will be recorded as a diagnostic code.

Fault code	Faulty component or circuit
11	Camshaft position sensor
12	Crankshaft position sensor
13	Intake air pressure sensor
14	Intake air pressure sensor hose system
15	Throttle position sensor circuit fault
16	Throttle position sensor sticking
19	Sidestand switch
20	Intake air pressure sensor/atmospheric pressure sensor
21	Coolant temperature sensor
22	Intake air temperature sensor
23 (2001 to 2003 and 2013-on models)	Atmospheric pressure sensor
24	Oxygen sensor
30	Lean angle sensor
31	Oxygen sensor (lean air:fuel mixture)
32	Oxygen sensor (rich air:fuel mixture)
33 (2001 to 2012 models)	Nos. 1/4 cylinder ignition coil
34 (2001 to 2012 models)	Nos. 2/3 cylinder ignition coil
33 (2013-on models)	No. 1 cylinder ignition coil
34 (2013-on models)	No. 2 cylinder ignition coil
35 (2013-on models)	No. 3 cylinder ignition coil
36 (2013-on models)	No. 4 cylinder ignition coil
39 (2013-on models)	Fuel injector
41	Lean angle sensor
42 (2001 to 2012 models)	Speed sensor/neutral switch/gear position sensor
42 (2013-on models)	Speed sensor/neutral switch/clutch switch
43	Battery voltage
44	EEPROM fault
46	Abnormal power supply
50	ECU malfunction
59 (2013-on models)	Accelerator position sensor
60 (2013-on models)	Throttle servo motor
69 (2013-on models)	Front wheel sensor
89 (2013-on models)	Err displayed on instruments – no signal between ECU and instruments
90 (2013-on models)	Front or rear brake light switch circuit fault
91 (2013-on models)	Cruise control switch or circuit fault
Er-1 Er-2 Er-3 Er-4	No information or unreadable communication from ECU

Engine management system 4•17

3 If a fault appears, first ensure that the relevant system wiring connectors are securely connected and free of corrosion – poor connections are the cause of the majority of problems. Also check the wiring itself for any obvious faults or breaks, and use a continuity tester to check the wiring between the component, its connectors and the ECU, referring to the wiring diagrams at the end of Chapter 8. Next refer to Section 8 to see if there are any other specific checks that can be made on that particular component using home equipment.

4 Also ensure that any fault is not due to poor maintenance – i.e. check that the air filter element is clean, that the spark plugs are in good condition, that the valve clearances are correctly adjusted, the cylinder compression pressures are correct, and the ignition timing is correct (refer to Chapters 1 and 2, and to Section 22). It is also worth removing the sensor(s) in question (see Section 14) and checking that the sensing tip or head is clean and not obstructed by anything. Where there is a vacuum hose to a sensor, make sure it is securely connected at both ends and has no cracks or splits.

5 If this fails to reveal the cause of the problem, or if there is a problem but no fault code is shown, the motorcycle should be taken to a Yamaha dealer for testing. They will have the special tools that should locate the fault quickly and simply.

14 Engine management system sensors

Caution: *Ensure the ignition is switched OFF before disconnecting/reconnecting any fuel injection system wiring connector. If a connector is disturbed with the ignition switched ON the ECU could be damaged.*

Camshaft position (CMP) sensor

Note: *The sensor can also be referred to as the cylinder identification sensor.*

Check

1 Support the bike on the centrestand. Remove the right-hand fairing side panel (Chapter 7). On 2001 to 2012 models remove the cap from the timing rotor cover **(see illustration)**. On 2013-on models remove the timing rotor cover (see Chapter 2).
2 Raise the fuel tank (Section 2, Steps 1 to 7).
3 Disconnect the sensor wiring connector **(see illustration 7.7b)**.
4 Using a voltmeter or multimeter set to the volts (DC) scale, insert the positive (+) probe of the meter into the white/black wire terminal in the back of the connector, with the connector still connected, and insert the negative (-) probe into the black/blue terminal. Turn the ignition switch ON. Using a socket on the timing rotor bolt turn the engine clockwise through 720° (two full turns), while keeping an eye on the meter **(see illustration)**. As the engine turns, the output voltage should fluctuate once from 0.6 volt or less to 4.8 volts or more as the trigger passes the sensor tip. Turn the ignition OFF. Fit the timing rotor cap or cover, according to model.
5 If the voltage does not rise as described, replace the sensor with a new one.

Removal

6 Remove the fuel tank (Section 2).
7 On 2001 to 2005 models unscrew the AIS control valve holder bolt **(see illustration 7.4a)**. On all models remove the T-bar **(see illustration 7.4b)**. On 2006-on models displace or remove the heat shield **(see illustrations 7.4c and d)**.
8 Disconnect the sensor wiring connector **(see illustration 7.7b)**. Undo the bolt and remove the sensor **(see illustration)**. Remove the O-ring – a new one must be used.

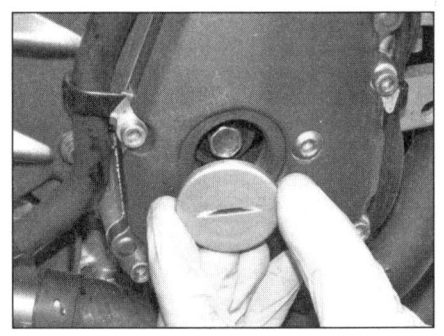

14.1 Remove the cap

Installation

9 Clean the sensor tip. Fit a new O-ring smeared with oil onto the sensor.
10 Fit the sensor and tighten the bolt **(see illustration 14.8)**. Connect the wiring **(see illustration 7.7b)**.
11 On 2006-on models fit the heat shield **(see illustrations 7.4d and c)**. Fit the T-bar and tighten the bolts to the torque setting specified at the beginning of the Chapter **(see illustration 7.4b)**. On 2001 to 2005 fit the AIS control valve holder bolt **(see illustration 7.4a)**.
12 Install the fuel tank.

Crankshaft position (CKP) sensor

13 Remove the right-hand fairing side panel (Chapter 7). Remove the throttle bodies (see Section 7). Make sure the ignition is OFF.

Check

14 The crankshaft position sensor is on the right-hand end of the crankshaft. Trace the wiring from the timing rotor cover and disconnect it at the off-white 2-pin connector **(see illustration)**. Using an ohmmeter or multimeter set to the ohms x 100 scale, measure the resistance between the terminals

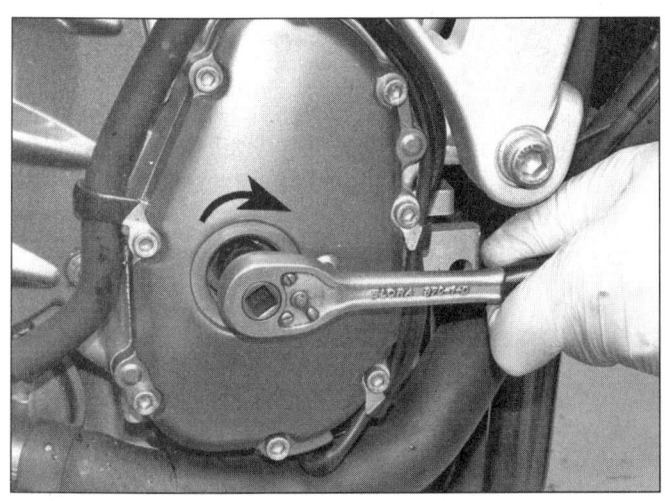

14.4 Turn the engine as described

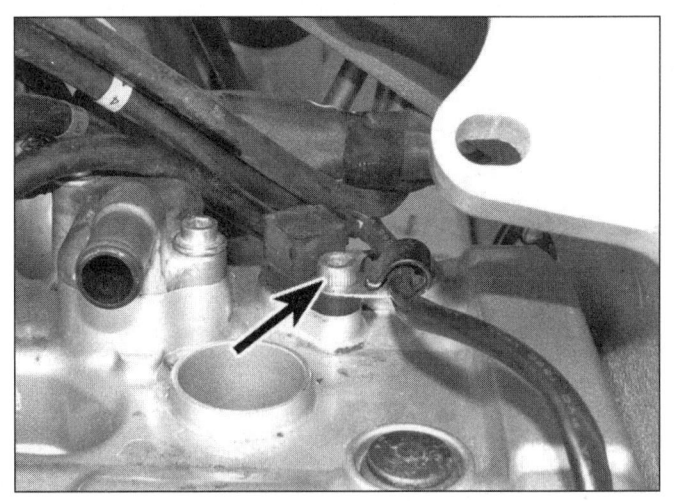

14.8 CMP sensor bolt (arrowed)

4•18 Engine management system

14.14 CKP sensor wiring connector

14.17a Unscrew the bolts (arrowed)...

14.17b ...free the grommet and remove the sensor

on the sensor side of the connector. If the result is not as specified at the beginning of the Chapter, replace the sensor with a new one.

Removal

15 Remove the timing rotor cover (see Chapter 2).
16 Trace the wiring from below the timing rotor cover and disconnect it at the off-white 2-pin connector **(see illustration 14.14)**. Feed the wiring back to the sensor, noting its routing and releasing it from any clips.
17 Undo the sensor mounting bolts, then free the wiring grommet and remove the sensor **(see illustrations)**.

Installation

18 Remove all traces of sealant from the sensor wiring grommet and clutch cover and apply a smear of fresh sealant to the grommet. Clean the sensor tip. Clean the threads of the sensor bolts and apply some fresh threadlock.
19 Locate the grommet and sensor and tighten the sensor bolts **(see illustration 14.17b)**.
20 Install the timing rotor cover (see Chapter 2).
21 Install the throttle bodies (see Section 4). Install the right-hand fairing side panel (Chapter 7).

Intake air pressure (IAP) sensor

22 The IAP sensor is mounted on the fuel rail **(see illustrations)**. Raise the fuel tank (Section 2, Steps 1 to 7). On 2006-on models remove the T-bar and the heat shield **(see illustrations 7.4b, c and d)**.

Check

23 Make sure that the vacuum hoses to the sensor are securely fixed at both ends, and have no cracks or splits.
24 Using a voltmeter or multimeter set to the volts (DC) scale, insert the positive (+) probe of the meter into the blue wire terminal (2001 to 2005 models), or pink/white wire terminal (2006 to 2012 models), or pink wire terminal (2013-on models) in the back of the connector according to model, with the connector still connected, and insert the negative (-) probe into the black/blue terminal. Turn the ignition ON and measure the sensor output voltage. Turn the ignition OFF. If the voltage is not as specified, replace the sensor with a new one.

Removal and installation

25 Disconnect the wiring connector **(see illustration 14.22)**. Undo the screw(s) and displace the sensor. Detach the vacuum hose **(see illustration)**.
26 Installation is the reverse of removal.

Throttle position (TP) sensor

27 The sensor is on the right-hand end of the throttle body assembly on 2001 to 2012 models, and on the left on 2013-on models **(see illustrations)**. Raise the fuel tank (Section 2, Steps 1 to 7). On 2006-on models remove the T-bar and the heat shield **(see illustrations 7.4b, c and d)**.

Check

28 Check the engine idle speed and make sure it is correctly set (see Chapter 1).
29 Disconnect the wiring connector. Using an ohmmeter or multimeter set to the K-ohms scale, connect the positive (+) probe to the blue

14.22a IAP sensor (arrowed) – 2001 to 2012 models

14.22b IAP sensor (arrowed) – 2013-on models

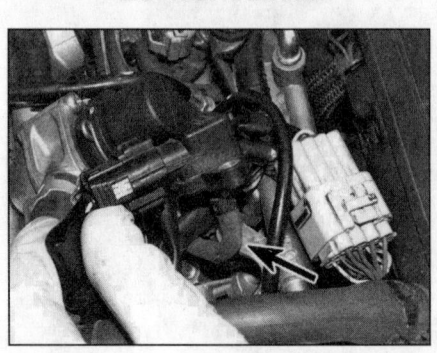

14.25 Detach the hose (arrowed) from the underside

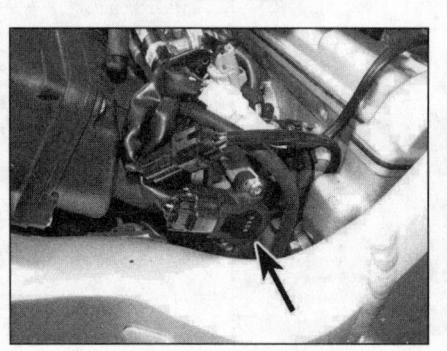

14.27a TP sensor (arrowed) – 2001 to 2012 models

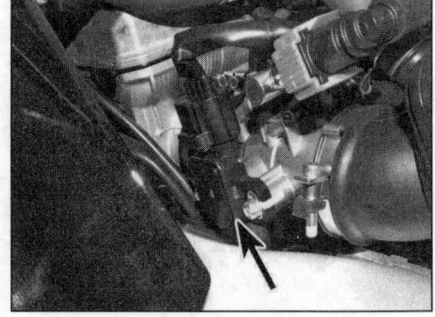

14.27b TP sensor (arrowed) – 2013-on models

Engine management system 4•19

wire terminal in the socket and the negative (-) probe to the black/blue wire terminal and measure the sensor maximum resistance. If it is not as specified at the beginning of the Chapter, replace the sensor with a new one.

Removal, installation and adjustment

30 Disconnect the sensor wiring connector **(see illustration 14.27)**. Undo the screws and remove the sensor, noting how it fits – if you don't have the correct tools to get on the bottom screw displace the throttle bodies (Section 7). Check the actuating tab and the slot in the sensor it engages for wear and damage. Check the sensor rotor moves smoothly and freely.

31 On 2001 to 2005 models, position the sensor and lightly tighten the screws. If not already done, refer to Step 29 and measure the sensor maximum resistance. Multiply the reading first by 0.13 and record the result, then by 0.15. The two results provide the required resistance range for the sensor. Now connect the positive (+) probe of the meter to the yellow wire terminal in the sensor and the negative (-) probe into the black/blue wire terminal. Carefully adjust the position of the sensor until the resistance is within the calculated range, then tighten the screws. Connect the wiring.

32 On 2006 to 2012 models, position the sensor and lightly tighten the screws. Connect the sensor wiring connector. Using a voltmeter or multimeter set to the volts (DC) scale, insert the positive (+) probe of the meter into the yellow wire terminal in back of the connector, with the connector still connected, and insert the negative (-) probe into the black/blue terminal. Turn the ignition ON and carefully adjust the position of the sensor until the voltage is within the range specified at the beginning of the Chapter, then tighten the screws. Turn the ignition OFF.

33 On 2013-on models, position the sensor and lightly tighten the screws. Connect the sensor wiring connector. Simultaneously press and hold the TCS and RESET buttons on the instrument cluster, then turn the ignition ON and continue to hold the buttons for eight seconds or more until DIAG appears in the LCD display. Press and hold the TCS and RESET buttons for two seconds until the code 01 is displayed. Carefully adjust the position of the sensor until 12-21 is displayed, then tighten the screws. Turn the ignition OFF.

Engine coolant temperature (ECT) sensor

34 see Chapter 3, Section 3.

Intake air temperature (IAT) sensor

35 On 2001 to 2012 models the sensor is mounted in the back of the air filter housing. Remove the seats, and on 2006 to 2012 models the height adjuster piece (see Chapter 7).

36 On 2013-on models the sensor is mounted on the windshield motor assembly **(see illustration)**. Remove the fairing (see Chapter 7), then remove the wiring connector board (see Chapter 8, Section 31); the sensor is next to the windshield motor.

14.36 IAT sensor – 2013-on models

Check

37 Disconnect the wiring connector **(see illustration)**. Connect an ohmmeter across the sensor terminals and measure its resistance. Compare the reading obtained to those given in the Specifications, allowing for ambient temperature difference. If the resistance reading differs greatly from that specified, especially if it is zero or infinite, the sensor is probably faulty.

Removal and installation

38 On 2001 to 2012 models disconnect the wiring connector **(see illustration 14.37)**. Unscrew and remove the sensor. Remove the seal and replace it with a new one.

39 On 2013-on models disconnect the wiring connector. Hold the nut on the underside, undo the screw and remove the sensor.

40 Installation is the reverse of removal.

Atmospheric pressure (AP) sensor

41 On 2001 to 2003 models the AP sensor is mounted on the underside of the rear sub-frame cross-member. Remove the seats (see Chapter 7).

42 On 2013-on models the AP sensor is mounted on the fuel rail **(see illustration)**. Raise the fuel tank (Section 2, Steps 1 to 7). Remove the T-bar and the heat shield **(see illustrations 7.4b, c and d)**.

14.42 Atmospheric pressure sensor – 2013-on models

14.37 Disconnect the wiring connector – 2001 to 2003 models

Check

43 Using a voltmeter or multimeter set to the volts (DC) scale, insert the positive (+) probe of the meter into the blue wire terminal (2001 to 2003 models) or pink wire terminal (2013-on models) in the back of the connector according to model, with the connector still connected, and insert the negative (-) probe into the black/blue terminal. Turn the ignition ON and measure the sensor output voltage. Turn the ignition OFF. If the voltage is not as specified, replace the sensor with a new one.

Removal and installation

44 Disconnect the wiring connector. Undo the screw(s) and remove the sensor.

45 Installation is the reverse of removal.

Speed sensor

2001 to 2005 models

46 The speed sensor is mounted in the back of the crankcase **(see illustration)**. To test the output from the sensor, place the motorcycle on the centrestand. Make sure the transmission is in neutral.

47 Remove the throttle bodies (Section 7). Connect the positive (+) probe of a multimeter set to the DC20V scale to the white wire terminal in the connector (with it still connected), and connect the negative (–) probe to the black/blue wire terminal. Turn the ignition ON. Turn the rear wheel in its normal direction of rotation and check the reading on the multimeter – it should be seen to fluctuate between 0.6 and 4.8 volts as the wheel is

14.46 Speed sensor (arrowed)

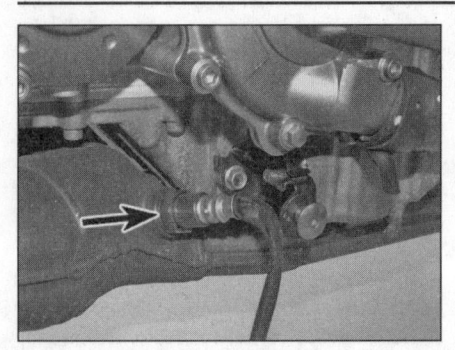

4•20 Engine management system

14.51 Oxygen sensor (arrowed) – 2001 to 2012 models

14.57a Tip-over sensor (arrowed) – 2001 to 2005 models

14.57b Tip-over sensor (arrowed) – 2006-on models

turned. If not replace the sensor with a new one.

48 For best access to fit a new sensor remove the swingarm (see Chapter 5), though with the right tools and a bit of dexterity you may be OK with it in place. Unscrew the bolt and withdraw the sensor from the crankcase, noting the wiring clamp **(see illustration 14.46)**. Check the condition of the O-ring and replace it with a new one if it is damaged, deformed or deteriorated, but note that Yamaha do not list it as being available separately from the sensor, though they, or a good auto factor, should be able to supply one – take the old one along to match it up.

49 Smear the sensor O-ring with grease, then fit the sensor into the crankcase. Clean the bolt threads and apply some fresh threadlock then tighten the bolt, not forgetting to secure the wiring clamp with it. Connect the sensor wiring connector, then install the throttle bodies (Section 7), and if removed the swingarm (Chapter 5).

2006-on models

50 The speed sensor function is taken from the signals produced by the rear wheel sensor, which is part of the ABS system – refer to Chapter 6.

Oxygen sensor

51 On 2001 to 2012 models the sensor is in the right-hand side of the collector box section of the exhaust **(see illustration)**. Remove the right-hand fairing side panel (see Chapter 7). To access the wiring connector, raise the fuel tank (Section 2, Steps 1 to 7). On 2006 to 2012 models remove the T-bar and the heat shield **(see illustrations 7.4b, c and d)**.

52 On 2013-on models the sensor is mounted in the back of the collector box section of the exhaust. Remove the right-hand fairing side panel (see Chapter 7). Trace the wiring from the sensor to the connector.

Check

53 Apart from wiring and connector checks, the operation of the oxygen sensor itself cannot be checked – if the sensor circuit is good (have this checked by a dealer for confirmation) and the sensor is thought to be faulty, replace it with a new one.

Removal and installation

Note: *The oxygen sensor is delicate and will not work if dropped or knocked, or if any cleaning materials are used on it. Ensure the exhaust system is cold before proceeding. A special socket to accommodate the sensor wiring can be bought if required, and enables the sensor to be tightened to the correct torque on installation.*

54 Disconnect the sensor wiring connector **(see illustration 7.7a)**. Feed the wiring to the sensor, noting its routing. On 2001 to 2012 models remove the fairing bracket from the sump.

55 Unscrew the sensor and remove it from the exhaust system **(see illustration 14.51)**.

56 Installation is the reverse of removal.

Tip-over sensor

57 The tip-over sensor is mounted on the top of the rear mudguard **(see illustrations)**. Remove the seats, and on 2006-on models the height adjuster piece (see Chapter 7).

58 On 2006-on models remove the toolkit from its tray **(see illustration 7.10a)**. On AS models, remove the motor control unit (see Section 20 in Chapter 2). Disconnect the ECU wiring connector, then remove the tray **(see illustrations 7.10c, d and e)**.

Check

59 Make sure the ignition is OFF. Displace the sensor (see Step 62) leaving the wiring connected.

60 Using a voltmeter or multimeter set to the volts (DC) scale, insert the positive (+) probe of the meter into the yellow/green wire terminal in back of the connector, with the connector still connected, and insert the negative (-) probe into the black/blue terminal. Turn the ignition ON. Hold the sensor in its normal position when the bike is upright with the UP mark facing up and note the voltage reading, then tilt it 65° to one side and then the other, again noting the readings. Turn the ignition OFF.

61 If the voltage is not as specified when the sensor is upright and tilted over, replace the sensor with a new one.

Removal and installation

62 Make sure the ignition is OFF. Undo the sensor bolts or screws (according to model), displace the sensor and disconnect the wiring connector **(see illustration 14.57a or b)**. Note the top surface of the sensor is marked UP – make sure this mark is on top when installing the sensor.

15 Electronic Control Unit (ECU)

Check

1 If the tests shown in the preceding Sections have failed to isolate the cause of a fault, and the engine management system fuses and relays and all wiring connectors are good, it is possible that the ECU itself is faulty. No details are available with which the unit can be tested. The best way to determine whether it is faulty or not is to substitute it with a known good one, having first checked all other components in the ignition system. Otherwise, take the unit to a Yamaha dealer for assessment.

Removal and installation

2 Make sure the ignition is OFF.

3 On 2001 to 2005 models remove the seats (see Chapter 7). Remove the toolkit from its tray. Disconnect the ECU wiring connector, then remove the tray **(see illustrations 7.9a, b and c)** – the ECU is on the underside **(see illustration)**. Undo the screws and remove the ECU.

4 On 2006 to 2012 models remove the

15.3 ECU screws (arrowed) – 2001 to 2005 models

Engine management system 4•21

seats and the height adjuster piece (see Chapter 7). Remove the toolkit from its tray **(see illustration 7.10a)**. On AS models, remove the YCC-S motor control unit (see Section 20 in Chapter 2). Disconnect the ECU wiring connector, then remove the tray **(see illustrations 7.10c, d and e)** – the ECU is on the underside **(see illustration)**. Undo the screws and remove the ECU.

5 On 2013-on models remove the right-hand fairing side panel (see Chapter 7). Remove the ECU cover; it is retained by a plastic plug at the base plus a screw next to it **(see illustrations)**. The headlight on/off relay and fan relay can remain attached to the cover. Release the ECU and disconnect its wiring connectors **(see illustration)**. When fitting the cover, hook its slots along the top edge over the tabs on the battery casing.

6 Installation is the reverse of removal.

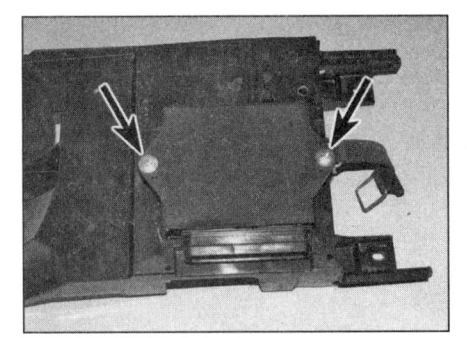

16 Engine management system relays

Fuel injection relay

1 The relay provides power to the fuel pump and fuel injectors.

2 On 2001 and 2002 models remove the fairing and detach it from its bracket (see Chapter 7). The relay is on the instrument cluster bracket – identify the relay from the colours of its wires, referring to the wiring diagrams at the end of Chapter 8. Displace the relay and disconnect the wiring.

3 On 2003-on models the relay is contained within the relay assembly – refer to Step 7 and remove it.

4 Using an ohmmeter or continuity tester, connect the positive (+) probe to the red (2001 to 2007 models) or brown/red (2008 to 2012 models) or brown/white (2013-on models) wire terminal on the relay and the negative (-) probe to the red/blue wire terminal. There should be no continuity. Using a fully-charged

15.4 ECU screws (arrowed) – 2006 to 2012 models

15.5a Prise out the plastic fastener (arrowed)...

15.5b ...remove the screw to free the ECU retainer...

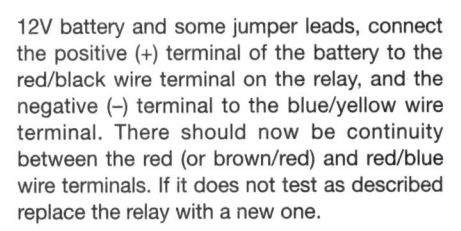

15.5c ...then disconnect the two multi-pin wiring connectors – 2013-on

12V battery and some jumper leads, connect the positive (+) terminal of the battery to the red/black wire terminal on the relay, and the negative (-) terminal to the blue/yellow wire terminal. There should now be continuity between the red (or brown/red) and red/blue wire terminals. If it does not test as described replace the relay with a new one.

Starter cut-off relay and diodes

5 The starter circuit cut-off relay and its associated diodes are part of the safety circuit (see Chapter 1 for more information on the circuit).

6 On 2001 to 2005 models the relay unit is mounted on the top of the rear mudguard **(see illustration)**. Remove the seats (see Chapter 7).

7 On 2006 to 2012 models the relay assembly is mounted behind the air filter housing **(see illustration)**. Remove the seats and the height adjuster piece (see Chapter 7). Remove the toolkit from its tray **(see illustration 7.10a)**. On AS models, remove the motor control unit (see Section 20 in Chapter 2). Disconnect the ECU wiring connector, then remove the tray **(see illustrations 7.10c, d and e)**.

8 On 2013-on models remove the instrument surround panel (see Chapter 7) – the relay unit

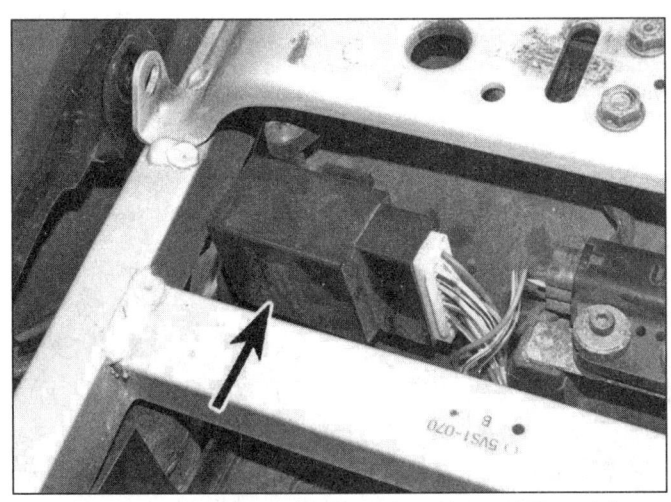

16.6 Starter cut-off relay (arrowed) – 2001 to 2005 models

16.7 Relay assembly (arrowed) – 2006 to 2012 models

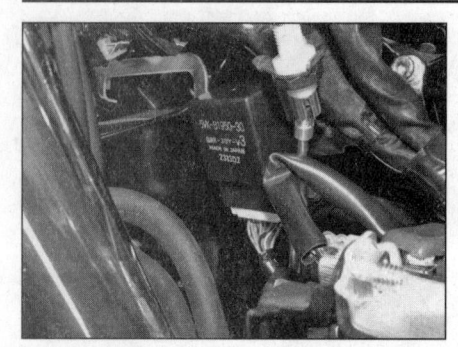

4•22 Engine management system

16.8 Relay assembly – 2013-on models

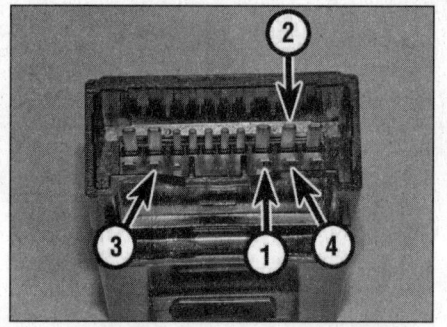

16.11 Starter cut-off relay test connections – 2006-on models
1 Battery positive to red/black terminal
2 Battery negative terminal to black/yellow terminal (black/red on AS model)
3 Ohmmeter positive probe to blue/white terminal
4 Ohmmeter negative probe to white/blue terminal

17.2 Slacken the clamp (arrowed)

is mounted to a bracket on the right-hand side **(see illustration)**.
9 Displace the relay and disconnect the wiring connector. Move the relay assembly to the bench for testing. Refer to the wiring diagram for your model (see end of Chapter 8) and the following procedures. Test the relay using an ohmmeter or continuity tester.
10 On 2001 and 2002 models, connect the positive (+) probe to the blue/white wire terminal on the relay and the negative (-) probe to the black wire terminal. There should be no continuity. Using a fully-charged 12V battery and some jumper leads, connect the positive (+) terminal of the battery to the red/black wire terminal on the relay, and the negative (–) terminal to the black/yellow wire terminal. There should now be continuity between the blue/white and black wire terminals. If it does not test as described replace the relay unit with a new one.
11 On 2003-on models, connect the positive (+) probe to the blue/white wire terminal on the relay and the negative (-) probe to the white/blue wire terminal. There should be no continuity. Using a fully-charged 12V battery and some jumper leads, connect the positive (+) terminal of the battery to the red/black wire terminal on the relay, and the negative (–) terminal to the black/yellow (A models) or black/red (AS models) wire terminal **(see illustration)**. There should now be continuity between the blue/white and white/blue wire terminals. If it does not test as described replace the relay unit with a new one.
12 The diodes contained within the relay assembly can be checked by performing a continuity test – diodes should show continuity in one direction and no continuity when the meter or tester probes are reversed. Connect the multimeter (set to ohms) or continuity tester across the wire terminals for the diode being tested – refer to the appropriate wiring diagram at the end of Chapter 8 for your model. If any diode shows the same condition in both directions it is faulty, and the relay unit must be replaced with a new one.
13 If the relay and diodes are good, but the starting system fault still exists, check all other components in the starting circuit (i.e. the neutral switch, sidestand switch, clutch switch, starter switch and starter relay) as described in the relevant Sections of Chapter 8. If all components are good, check the wiring between the various components (see *Wiring Diagrams* at the end of this Chapter).

17 Exhaust system

⚠ **Warning:** *If the engine has been running the exhaust system will be very hot. Allow the system to cool before carrying out any work.*

HAYNES HINT *Exhaust system clamp bolts tend to become corroded and seized. It is advisable to spray them with WD40 or a similar product before attempting to slacken them.*

Removal

Silencers
1 Remove the pannier if fitted.
2 Slacken the silencer clamp bolt **(see illustration)**.
3 Unscrew the silencer mounting bolt **(see illustration)**. Ease the silencer off the downpipes.
4 Check the condition of the sealing ring and replace with a new one if damaged or deformed or no longer sealing correctly – it could be in the end of the silencer or on the end of the collector box. If you do fit a new one, remove the clamp and expand the tangs on the end of the silencer pipes slightly to make them easier to fit.

Downpipes
5 Remove the radiator (see Chapter 3). Raise the fuel tank (Section 2, Steps 1 to 7). On 2006 to 2012 models remove the T-bar and the heat shield **(see illustrations 7.4b, c and d)**.
6 Remove the silencers (see above). Disconnect the oxygen sensor wiring connector **(see illustration 7.7a)**. Feed the wiring down to the sensor, noting its routing.
7 Unscrew the bolt on each side at the back **(see illustration)**. Unscrew the nuts securing

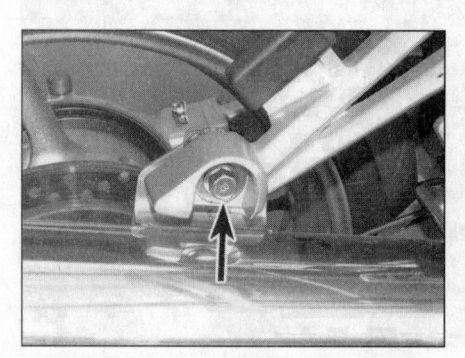

17.3 Silencer mounting bolt (arrowed)

17.7a Unscrew the bolts (arrowed)

17.7b Unscrew the nuts...

Engine management system 4•23

17.7c ...and remove the downpipe assembly

17.8 Remove the old sealing rings

the downpipe flanges to the cylinder heads, supporting the system as you remove the last nuts (see illustration). Draw the flanges off the studs and remove the downpipes (see illustration).

8 Remove the sealing ring from each port in the cylinder head and discard them as new ones must be used (see illustration).

Installation

9 Installation is the reverse of removal, noting the following:
- Replace any damaged, deformed or deteriorated mounting rubbers with new ones. Replace any badly corroded clamps, collars, nuts and bolts with new ones.
- Use a new sealing ring in each cylinder head port, and dab them with grease to stick them in place (see illustration).
- Apply a smear of copper grease to all screws, nuts and bolts to prevent them from seizing up. Fit and secure all mounts finger-tight before fully tightening them. Tighten the downpipe flange nuts before any mounting bolts. Tighten the nuts/bolts to the torque settings specified at the beginning of the Chapter where given.
- Do not forget to reconnect the oxygen sensor wiring connector, and make sure the wiring is correctly routed.
- Run the engine and check the system for leaks.

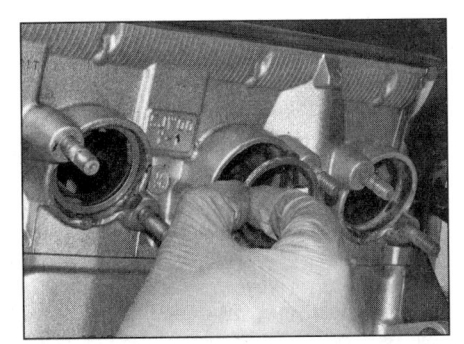

17.9 Fit a new sealing ring into each port

18 Catalytic converter

General information

1 There is a catalytic converter incorporated in the exhaust system to minimise the level of exhaust pollutants released into the atmosphere.
2 A catalytic converter consists of a canister containing a fine mesh impregnated with a catalyst material, over which the hot exhaust gases pass. The catalyst speeds up the oxidation of harmful carbon monoxide, unburned hydrocarbons and soot, effectively reducing the quantity of harmful products released into the atmosphere via the exhaust gases.
3 The catalytic converter is of the closed-loop type with exhaust gas oxygen content information being fed back to the ECU by the oxygen sensor.
4 Refer to Section 17 for exhaust system removal and installation, and Section 14 for oxygen sensor removal and installation information.

Precautions

5 A catalytic converter is a reliable and simple device which needs no maintenance in itself, but there are some facts of which an owner should be aware if the converter is to function properly for its full service life.
- DO NOT use leaded or lead replacement petrol (gasoline) – the additives will coat the precious metals, reducing their converting efficiency and will eventually destroy the catalytic converter.
- Always keep the ignition and fuel systems well-maintained in accordance with the manufacturer's schedule – if the fuel/air mixture is suspected of being incorrect have it checked on an exhaust gas analyser.
- If the engine develops a misfire, do not ride the bike at all (or at least as little as possible) until the fault is rectified.
- DO NOT use fuel or engine oil additives – these may contain substances harmful to the catalytic converter.
- DO NOT continue to use the bike if the engine burns oil to the extent of leaving a visible trail of blue smoke.
- Remember that the catalytic converter and oxygen sensor are FRAGILE – do not strike them with tools during servicing work.

19 Air induction system (AIS)

General information

1 To reduce the amount of unburned hydrocarbons released in the exhaust gases, an air induction system (AIS) is fitted. The system consists of the control valve (mounted under the fuel tank), the reed valves (fitted in the valve cover) and the hoses linking them (see illustration). The control valve is actuated electronically by the ECU.
2 When the valve is open it allows filtered air to be drawn through the reed valves and cylinder head passages and into the exhaust ports. The air mixes with the exhaust gases, causing any unburned particles of the fuel in the mixture to be burnt in the exhaust port/pipes. This process changes a considerable amount of hydrocarbons and carbon monoxide into

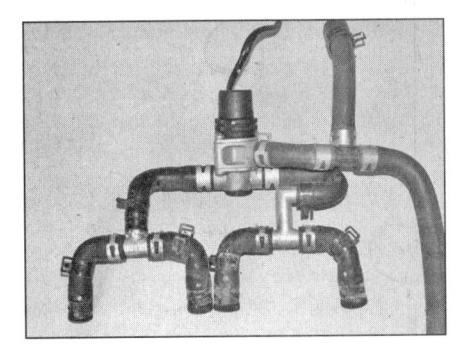

19.1 AIS control valve and hoses

4•24 Engine management system

19.4 Detach the hose

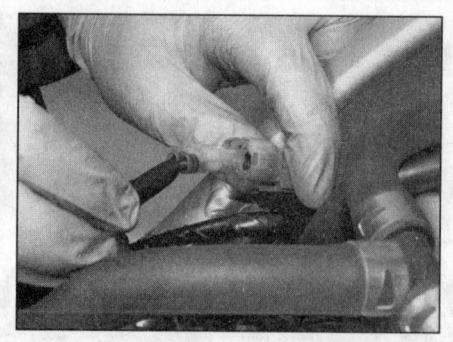

19.5 Disconnect the wiring

19.9 Detach the hoses and remove the valve

19.12a Remove the cover...

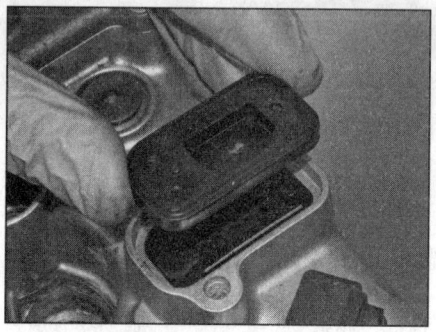

19.12b ...the reed valve...

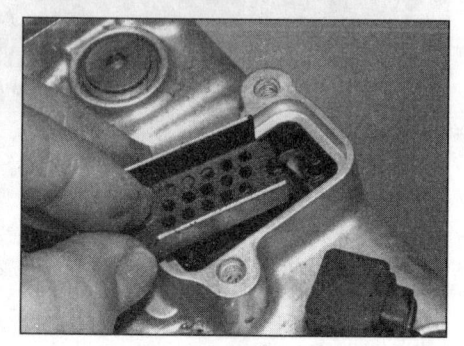

19.12c ...and the baseplate

relatively harmless carbon dioxide and water. The reed valves in the valve cover are fitted to prevent the flow of exhaust gases back up the cylinder head passages and into the air filter housing.

Testing

3 Raise the fuel tank (see Section 2, Steps 1 to 7). On 2006-on models remove the T-bar and the heat shield **(see illustrations 7.4b, c and d)**.
4 Detach the air supply hose from the air filter housing **(see illustration)**. Check that the hose is clean – the presence or carbon deposits indicates a faulty system. Start the engine again and allow it to idle, and check air is being sucked into the detached hose. Stop the engine.
5 If there is no air suction disconnect the control valve wiring connector **(see illustration)**. Clean the end of the air supply hose. Manually check the operation of the system by blowing through the hose – air should flow through the control valve and reed valves. Using a pair of auxiliary wires now apply battery voltage (12 volts) across the terminals in the control valve connector and repeat the check – no air should flow through the control valve. Disconnect the battery. If the valve does not behave as described check its resistance (Step 7).
6 Now suck on the hose – you should not be able to suck air back up, indicating the reed valves are closing and sealing correctly. If you can suck air through, remove the valves for cleaning (see below), then test again.
7 Check the resistance of the control valve solenoid by connecting an ohmmeter between its connector terminals and compare the reading obtained to that given in the Specifications. Replace the valve with a new one if faulty.

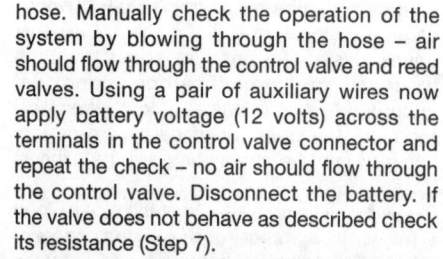

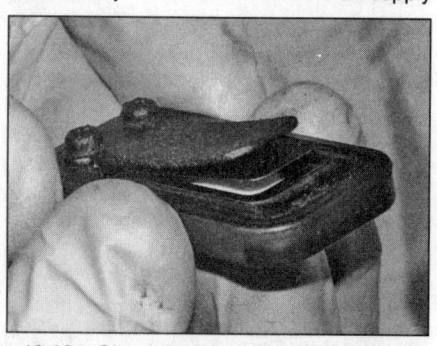

Component renewal

Control valve

8 Raise the fuel tank (see Section 2, Steps 1 to 7). On 2006-on models remove the T-bar and the heat shield **(see illustrations 7.4b, c and d)**.
9 Disconnect the wiring connector **(see illustration 19.5)**. On 2001 to 2005 models unscrew the holder bolt **(see illustration 7.4a)**. Release the clamps and detach the hoses as required, and remove the valve **(see illustration)**.
10 Installation is the reverse of removal. Tighten the T-bar bolts to the torque setting specified at the beginning of the Chapter.

Reed valves

11 Remove the control valve along with all the hoses. For best access remove the coolant outlet pipe from the valve cover (see Chapter 3).
12 Unscrew the bolts and remove the cover **(see illustration)**. Remove the reed valve, noting which way around it fits, then remove the baseplate **(see illustrations)**.
13 Lift the reed off its seat to check it is not stuck **(see illustration)**. Release it and make sure there is no gap between it and its seat **(see illustration)**. Check the condition of the rubber around the valve. If necessary replace the valve with a new one.
14 Installation is the reverse of removal. Make sure the baseplates, valves and housings are clean and free of carbon deposits, and that the baseplates and valves seat correctly. Tighten

19.13a Check the reed lifts off its seat...

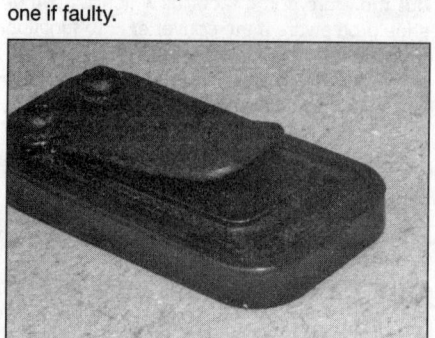

19.13b ...and seals correctly on it

Engine management system 4•25

20.5 Pull the cap off the plug

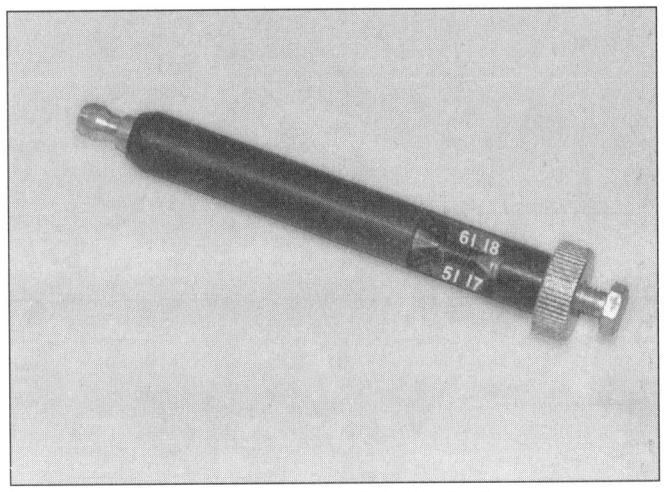

20.9 Ignition spark testing tool

the cover bolts to the torque setting specified at the beginning of the Chapter. Tighten the T-bar bolts to the torque setting specified at the beginning of the Chapter.

20 Ignition system check

⚠ **Warning:** *The energy levels in electronic systems can be very high. On no account should the ignition be switched on whilst the plugs or caps are being held. Shocks from the HT circuit can be most unpleasant. Secondly, it is vital that the engine is not turned over or run with any of the plug caps removed, and that the plugs are soundly earthed (grounded) when the system is checked for sparking. The ignition system components can be seriously damaged if the HT circuit becomes isolated.*

1 As no means of adjustment is available, any failure of the system can be traced to failure of a system component or a simple wiring fault. Of the two possibilities, the latter is by far the most likely. In the event of failure, check the system in a logical fashion, as described below.

2 Raise the fuel tank (Section 2, Steps 1 to 7).

3 On 2001 to 2005 models unscrew the AIS control valve holder bolt **(see illustration 7.4a)**. On all models remove the T-bar **(see illustration 7.4b)**. On 2006-on models remove the heat shield **(see illustrations 7.4c and d)**.

4 Make sure the ignition is OFF. Work on one cylinder at a time.

5 On 2001 to 2012 models pull the cap off the plug **(see illustration)**. Connect the cap to a spare spark plug (preferably use a new plug).

6 On 2013-on models disconnect the coil wiring connector and pull the coil off the spark plug. Reconnect the wiring connector. Connect the coil to a spare spark plug (preferably use a new plug).

7 Earth the plug against the cylinder head – do not earth the plug against the valve cover itself. If necessary, hold the spark plug with an insulated tool.

⚠ **Warning:** *Do not remove any of the spark plugs from the engine to perform this check – atomised fuel being pumped out of the open spark plug hole could ignite, causing severe injury! Make sure the plugs are securely held against the engine – if they are not earthed when the engine is turned over, the ECU could be damaged.*

8 Check that the kill switch is in the RUN position and the transmission is in neutral, then turn the ignition switch ON and turn the engine over on the starter motor. If the system is in good condition a regular, fat blue spark should be evident at the plug electrode. If the spark appears thin or yellowish, or is non-existent, further investigation is necessary. Turn the ignition OFF and repeat the check for each plug cap or coil.

9 The ignition system must be able to produce a spark that is capable of jumping at least a 6 mm gap. Simple ignition spark gap testing tools are commercially available **(see illustration)** – follow the manufacturer's instructions, and set the gap at 6 mm.

10 If the test results are good the entire ignition system can be considered good. If the spark appears thin or yellowish, or is non-existent, further investigation is necessary.

11 Ignition faults can be divided into two categories, namely those where the ignition system has failed completely, and those that are due to a partial failure. The likely faults are listed below, starting with the most probable source of failure. Work through the list systematically, referring to the subsequent sections for full details of the necessary checks and tests. **Note:** *Before checking the following items ensure that the battery is fully charged and that all fuses are in good condition.*

● On 2001 to 2012 models, loose spark plug cap or lead connection, faulty spark plug cap or HT lead, faulty spark plug, dirty, worn or corroded plug electrodes.
● On 2013-on models, loose coil, faulty spark plug, dirty, worn or corroded plug electrodes.
● Loose, corroded or damaged wiring connections, broken or shorted wiring between any of the component parts of the ignition system.
● Faulty neutral, clutch or sidestand switch (see Chapter 8).
● Faulty ignition coil(s) (Section 21).
● Faulty ignition switch or engine kill switch (see Chapter 8).
● Faulty crankshaft position (CKP) sensor (Section 14) or damaged triggers on timing rotor (Chapter 2).
● Faulty fuel injection relay (Section 16).
● Faulty ECU (Section 15).

12 If the above checks don't reveal the cause of the problem, have the ignition system tested by a Yamaha dealer. When refitting the T-bar tighten the bolts to the torque setting specified at the beginning of the Chapter.

21 Ignition coils

2001 to 2012 models

1 Remove the right-hand fairing side panel (see Chapter 7).

2 Raise the fuel tank (Section 2, Steps 1 to 7).

3 On 2001 to 2005 models unscrew the AIS control valve holder bolt **(see illustration 7.4a)**. On all models remove the T-bar **(see illustration 7.4b)**. On 2006 to 2012 models remove the heat shield **(see illustrations 7.4c and d)**.

Check

4 Check each coil visually for loose or damaged connectors and terminals, cracks and other damage.

4•26 Engine management system

21.5 Disconnect the primary wiring connectors

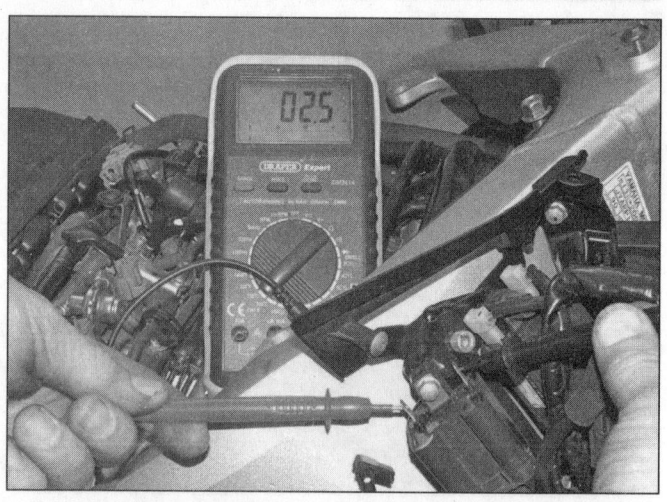

21.6 Coil primary resistance – connect the multimeter to the primary wiring terminals

21.7a Coil secondary resistance – connect the multimeter to the spark plug sockets

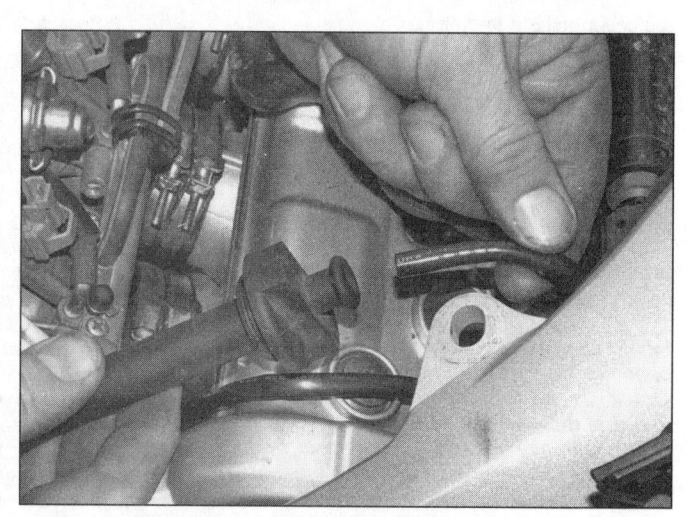

21.7b Unscrew the caps from the leads...

21.7c ...and test the coil again

21.7d Testing the plug cap

Engine management system 4•27

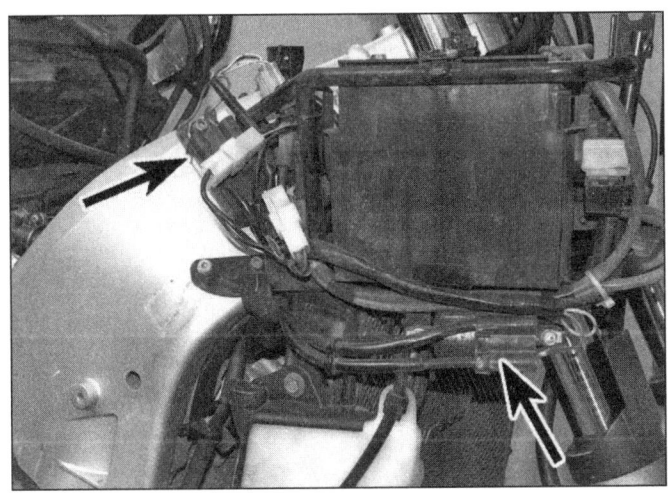

21.9a Ignition coils (arrowed) – 2001 to 2005 models

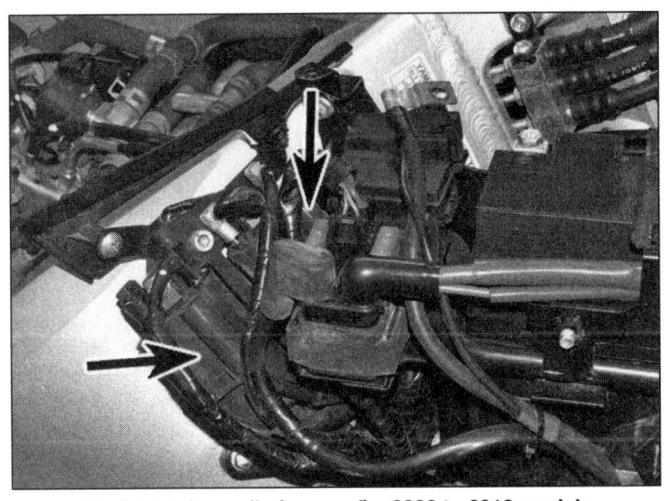

21.9b Ignition coils (arrowed) – 2006 to 2012 models

5 Disconnect the primary circuit wiring connectors from the coil **(see illustration)**. Pull the caps off the relevant spark plugs **(see illustration 20.5)**.

6 To check the condition of the primary windings, set a multimeter to the ohms x 1 scale. Connect the meter probes to the primary terminals on the coil and measure the resistance **(see illustration)**. If the reading obtained is not as given in the Specifications, it is likely that the coil is defective.

7 To check the resistance of the secondary windings, set the meter to the K-ohm scale. Connect one meter probe to the contact in one of the spark plug caps and the other probe to the other cap and measure the resistance **(see illustration)**. If the reading obtained is not as given in the Specifications, unscrew the plug caps and test the coil again, this time inserting the probes into the ends of the HT leads **(see illustrations)**. If the reading obtained is not as given in the Specifications (resistance without caps) it is likely the coil is defective. If the reading is good check the resistance of each plug cap, and if either is not as specified replace it with a new one **(see illustration)**.

> **HAYNES HiNT** Note if a fault exists in the ignition circuit for one pair of cylinders (e.g. 1 and 4), you can swap the coils over to check if the fault then appears on the other pair of cylinders (e.g. 2 and 3). If so, the coil is confirmed faulty.

Removal and installation

8 Disconnect the primary circuit wiring connectors from the coil, making a note of which fits where **(see illustration 21.5)**. Pull the caps off the spark plugs **(see illustration 20.5)**.

9 Move any wiring aside as required, then unscrew the bolts and remove the coil **(see illustrations)**.

10 Installation is the reverse of removal.

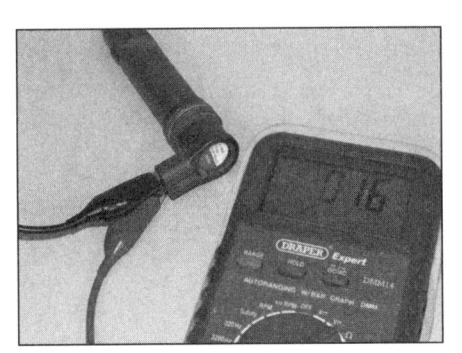

21.12 Coil primary resistance – connect the multimeter leads to the primary wiring terminals

2013-on models

Check

11 Remove the coil (Steps 15 and 16). Check it visually for cracks and other damage. Inspect the wiring terminals and the spark plug terminal.

12 Measure the primary circuit resistance with a multimeter as follows. Set the meter to the ohms x 1 scale and measure the resistance between the terminals on the coil **(see illustration)**. If the reading obtained is not within the range shown in the Specifications, it is likely that the coil is defective.

13 Measure the secondary circuit resistance with a multimeter as follows. Set the meter to the K-ohm scale. Connect one meter probe to one primary circuit terminal and the other probe to the spark plug terminal **(see illustration)**. If the reading obtained is not within the range shown in the Specifications, it is likely that the coil is defective.

14 If a coil is confirmed to be faulty, it must be replaced with a new one.

Removal and installation

15 Raise the fuel tank (Section 2, Steps 1 to 7).

16 Remove the T-bar **(see illustration 7.4b)**.

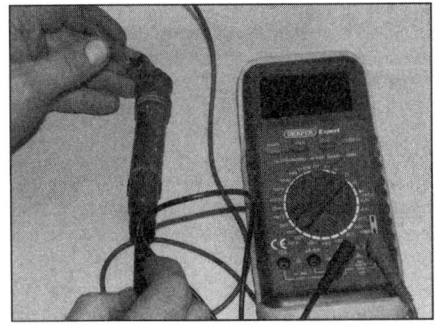

21.13 Coil secondary resistance – connect the multimeter leads between one terminal and the spark plug socket

Remove the heat shield **(see illustrations 7.4c and d)**.

17 Clean the area around the coil to prevent any dirt falling into the spark plug channels. Disconnect the wiring connector from the coil. Pull the coil off the spark plug.

18 Installation is the reverse of removal. Make sure the coils are pushed down firmly onto the spark plugs and that the wiring connectors are securely connected. Tighten the T-bar bolts to the torque setting specified at the beginning of the Chapter.

22 Ignition timing

General information

1 Since there is no way to adjust the ignition timing, and since no component is subject to mechanical wear, there is no need for regular checks; only if investigating a fault such as a loss of power or a misfire should the ignition timing be checked. Note that the timing can only be checked on 2001 to 2012 models – there is no provision for checking on later models.

4•28 Engine management system

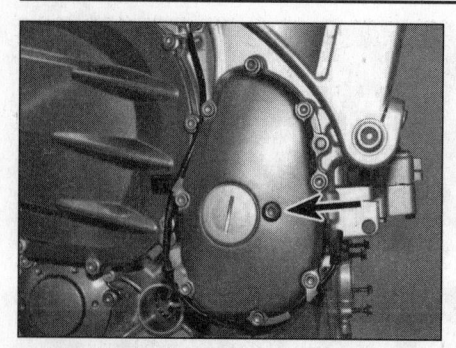

22.6 Timing inspection bolt (arrowed)

2 The ignition timing is checked dynamically (engine running) using a stroboscopic lamp. The inexpensive neon lamps should be adequate in theory, but in practice may produce a pulse of such low intensity that the timing mark remains indistinct. If possible, one of the more precise xenon tube lamps should be used, powered by an external source of the appropriate voltage. **Note:** *Do not use the machine's own battery as an incorrect reading may result from stray impulses within the machine's electrical system.*

Check

3 Warm the engine up to normal operating temperature then stop it.
4 Raise the fuel tank (Section 2, Steps 1 to 7).
5 On 2001 to 2005 models unscrew the AIS control valve holder bolt (see illustration 7.4a). On all models remove the T-bar (see illustration 7.4b). On 2006-on models remove the heat shield (see illustrations 7.4c and d).
6 Unscrew the timing inspection bolt from the timing rotor cover (see illustration). Remove the sealing washer – a new one must be used.
7 The dynamic timing mark on the rotor that indicates the firing point at idle speed for the No. 1 (left-hand) cylinder is an H on its side (see illustration).

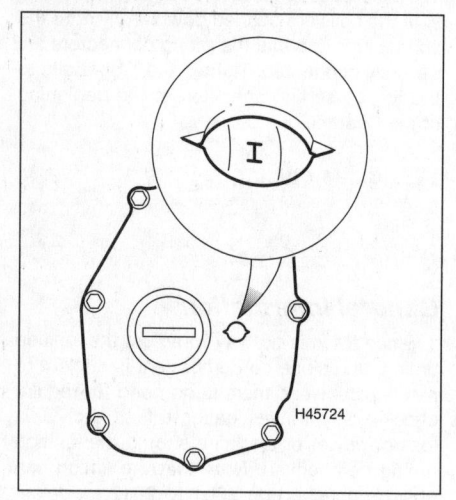

22.7 Timing mark alignment

> **HAYNES HINT** *Highlight the timing mark with white paint to make it more visible under the strobe light.*

8 Connect the timing light to the No. 1 (left-hand) cylinder coil HT lead.
9 Start the engine and aim the light through the hole in the timing rotor cover. The H mark or the white paint mark should be visible in line with the hole each time the light flashes. Now increase engine speed above 3000 rpm. The dynamic timing mark should appear to move anti-clockwise in relation to the static mark. This confirms the ignition is advancing.
10 As already stated, there is no means of adjustment of the ignition timing. If the ignition timing is incorrect, or suspected of being incorrect, one of the ignition system components is at fault, and the system must be tested as described in the preceding Sections of this Chapter.
11 When the check is complete, fit the timing inspection bolt using a new washer. Remove the strobe and fit all removed parts. Tighten the T-bar bolts to the torque setting specified at the beginning of the Chapter.

23 Immobiliser system

General information

Note: *2001 and 2002 models are not fitted with an immobiliser.*

1 The immobiliser system will only allow the machine to be started if the correct registered key is used to turn the ignition ON. The system consists of a transponder that is part of the ignition key, a receiver which is fitted around the ignition switch, and the ECU.
2 When the ignition is switched ON, the ECU sends power through the receiver to the transponder. The transponder sends a coded signal back through the receiver to the ECU. If the signal sent by the transponder matches the signal stored in the ECU memory, the immobiliser indicator light in the instrument cluster (marked by a key symbol) comes on for about a second, then goes out, and the ECU allows the engine to be started. If the key code signal is not recognised, or if there is a fault in the system, the indicator light flashes. If the light flashes, refer to the fault diagnosis and troubleshooting Sections below. Likewise if the light does not come on at all. When the ignition is switched OFF the immobiliser light will start to flash after thirty seconds, indicating the system is enabled. The light will stop flashing after 24 hours but the system remains enabled.
3 The ECU can store the codes for up to three registered keys, two of which are standard use keys with black casings, and one is a code re-registering key with a red casing. They keys should be kept separately (i.e. not on the same key-ring) as the proximity of another key to the one being used in the switch can lead to the signal from it being jammed, and the bike will not start. The key has a built-in transponder which can be damaged if the key is dropped or knocked, gets too hot, is too close to a magnetic object, or is submerged in water. If all the keys are lost, the ECU must be replaced with a new one, so always make sure you have one spare key. If a new key is obtained, it must be registered into the system before the bike can be started.

> **HAYNES HINT** *If you lose a key, or suspect it has been stolen, immediately re-register your code re-registering key and your remaining key – this will cancel the registration of the key that has been lost (or possibly stolen) which means that it will not be possible to start the bike using that key.*
> *If all three keys are lost, or if the ignition switch is faulty, a new ECU, immobiliser unit and lock set must be fitted. If either the immobiliser or ECU is faulty either unit can be replaced on its own.*

Standard key registration procedure

Note: *This must be done when a key is lost (so that it cannot be used) and when a new one is obtained, or when a new 'code re-registering key' has been registered.*

4 Obtain a new key from a Yamaha dealer, and have it cut to match the original key.
5 Turn the ignition switch ON using the code re-registering key, then turn it OFF and remove the key within 5 seconds Now insert the key you wish to register and turn it ON within 5 seconds. The immobiliser indicator light should flash on and off every half second. This indicates that the system is in registration mode. At this point the registration of the other existing standard key will have been cancelled, so this will also have to be registered. If the light stops flashing, more than 5 seconds have elapsed and the system is no longer in registration mode, in which case start again.
6 To register the second key, turn the ignition OFF and remove the first key, placing it well away from the receiver, and within 5 seconds insert the second key into the switch and turn it ON. When the light stops flashing the second key is registered and the system is no longer in registration mode.
7 On completion turn the ignition OFF and remove the key.
8 Check that both registered keys can start the motorcycle.

Code re-registering key registration procedure

Note: *This must be done when a new ECU or immobiliser receiver is fitted.*

Engine management system 4•29

9 Obtain a new key from a Yamaha dealer, and have it cut to match the original key.
10 Turn the ignition switch ON using the new code re-registering key. The immobiliser light will come on for about one second, then go out, indicating that the key has been registered.
11 Check that the key can start the motorcycle.
12 Now register the standard keys as described in Steps 4 to 8.

Installing a new ECU

13 Install the ECU (see Section 15).
14 Turn the ignition switch ON using the code re-registering key. This registers the key to the new ECU.
15 Check that the key can start the motorcycle.
16 Now register the standard keys as described in Steps 4 to 8.

Installing a new immobiliser

17 Remove the old immobiliser receiver from the ignition switch and fit the new one (see Step 27).
18 Turn the ignition switch ON using the code re-registering key. This registers the key to the new immobiliser.
19 Check that the key can start the motorcycle.
20 Now register the standard keys as described in Steps 4 to 8.

Fault diagnosis

21 If there is a fault in the system, the immobiliser indicator light in the instrument cluster (marked by a key symbol and located in the tachometer face) flashes and a fault code is shown in the LCD display.

Troubleshooting procedure

22 If fault code 51 or 52 is shown, first check that none of the other registered keys are close to the receiver. If they are, remove them and try the ignition again.
23 If any fault code is shown, first check the fuses and the wiring and connectors between the immobiliser receiver, ignition switch and the ECU (see *Wiring diagrams* at the end of Chapter 8). A continuity test of all wires will locate a break or short in any circuit. Inspect the terminals inside the wiring connectors and ensure they are not loose, bent or corroded. Spray the inside of the connectors with a proprietary electrical terminal cleaner before reconnection. Also make sure the battery is in good condition and that the ignition switch is not faulty (see Chapter 8).
24 If the immobiliser LED or the LCD display in the instrument cluster do not come on, refer to Chapter 8 and check the instrument cluster.
25 If all indications are that either the immobiliser or the ECU are faulty, it is worth having them checked by a Yamaha dealer before buying replacements.

Replacement

26 To replace the receiver, raise the fuel tank (Section 2, Steps 1 to 7).
27 On 2003 to 2005 models unscrew the AIS control valve holder bolt **(see illustration 7.4a)**. On all models remove the T-bar **(see illustration 7.4b)**. On 2006-on models remove the heat shield **(see illustrations 7.4c and d)**.
28 Trace the wiring from the receiver and disconnect the wiring connector. Feed the wiring back to the receiver, freeing it from any ties and noting its routing. Undo the screws and remove the receiver, noting how it fits **(see illustration)**. Turn the handlebars as required to access the screws, or remove the fairing if required (see Chapter 7).
29 To replace the ECU see Section 15.

Fault code	Symptoms	Possible causes
51	Signal from key not being received by immobiliser	Interference from other keys or magnet Faulty key transponder Faulty immobiliser receiver
52	Code from key not recognised by receiver	Interference from other key Unregistered key being used
53	Signal from immobiliser not being received by ECU	Faulty wiring or wiring connector Faulty immobiliser receiver Faulty ECU
54	Code from immobiliser not recognised by ECU	Faulty wiring or wiring connector Immobiliser unregistered to ECU – code re-registering key not registered Faulty immobiliser receiver Faulty ECU
55	Key registration error	Same key being registered twice
56	Code from immobiliser not recognised by ECU	Faulty wiring or wiring connector Faulty immobiliser receiver Faulty ECU

23.28 Immobiliser receiver screws (arrowed)

Notes

Chapter 5
Frame and suspension

Contents

	Section number
Footrests, brake pedal and gearchange lever	3
Fork oil change	7
Fork overhaul	8
Fork removal and installation	6
Frame inspection and repair	2
General information	1
Handlebar switches	see Chapter 8
Handlebars and levers	5
Rear shock absorber	11
Rear suspension linkage	12

	Section number
Sidestand and centrestand	4
Sidestand switch	see Chapter 8
Stand lubrication	see Chapter 1
Steering head bearing check and adjustment	see Chapter 1
Steering head bearings	10
Steering stem	9
Suspension adjustment	14
Suspension check	see Chapter 1
Swingarm	13

Degrees of difficulty

| **Easy,** suitable for novice with little experience | **Fairly easy,** suitable for beginner with some experience | **Fairly difficult,** suitable for competent DIY mechanic | **Difficult,** suitable for experienced DIY mechanic | **Very difficult,** suitable for expert DIY or professional |

Specifications

Front forks
Fork oil type
  2001 to 2005 models .... 10W fork oil (Yamaha suspension oil 01)
  2006-on models .... Yamaha suspension oil M1 or Öhlins R&T43
Fork oil capacity (per fork)
  2001 and 2002 models.. 670 cc
  2003 to 2005 models... 664 cc
  2006 to 2012 models... 696 cc
  2013-on models
    Right-hand fork... 694 cc
    Left-hand fork.. 716 cc
Fork oil level*
  2001 and 2002 models.. 100 mm
  2003 to 2005 models... 104 mm
  2006 to 2012 models... 92 mm
  2013-on models
    Right-hand fork... 90 mm
    Left-hand fork.. 106 mm
Fork spring free length (min)
  2001 and 2002 models
    Standard.. 261 mm
    Service limit .... 256 mm
  2003 to 2005 models
    Standard.. 264 mm
    Service limit .... 259 mm
  2006 to 2012 models
    Standard.. 262 mm
    Service limit .... 257 mm
  2013-on models
    Standard.. 345 mm
    Service limit .... 340 mm
Fork tube runout limit... 0.2 mm
*Oil level is measured from the top of the tube with the fork spring removed and the leg fully compressed.

5•2 Frame and suspension

Torque settings

Centrestand pivot and bracket bolts/nuts	55 Nm
Clutch master cylinder clamp bolts	10 Nm
Footrest bracket bolts (left-hand side)	
Lower (sidestand) bolts	65 Nm
Upper (M8) bolts	28 Nm
Front (M10) bolt	49 Nm
Footrest bracket bolts (right-hand side)	28 Nm
Fork damper bolt	35 Nm
Fork top bolt	25 Nm
Fork clamp bolts – 2001 to 2005 models	
Top yoke	34 Nm
Bottom yoke	39 Nm
Fork clamp bolts – 2006-on models	
Top yoke	26 Nm
Bottom yoke	23 Nm
Front brake master cylinder clamp bolts	10 Nm
Handlebar bolts – 2001 to 2005 models	23 Nm
Handlebar bolt – 2006-on models	23 Nm
Handlebar nut – 2006-on models	65 Nm
Shock absorber	
Top bolt/nut	64 Nm
Bottom bolt/nut	40 Nm
Sidestand pivot bolt nut	58 Nm
Steering head bearing adjuster nut	
Initial setting	52 Nm
Final setting	18 Nm
Steering stem nut	115 Nm
Suspension linkage	
Linkage arm-to-frame	40 Nm
Linkage rods-to-linkage arm and swingarm	48 Nm
Swingarm pivot bolt	
2001 to 2005 models	7 Nm
2006-on models	23 Nm
Swingarm pivot bolt locknut	115 Nm
Swingarm pivot bolt nut	125 Nm

1 General information

All models have an aluminium frame using the engine as a stressed member.

Front suspension is by a pair of 48 mm oil-damped telescopic forks with adjustable spring pre-load and both rebound and compression damping (on 2013 and later models only the right-hand fork has the adjustable damping).

Rear suspension is by steel swingarm and a single shock absorber, via a rising rate linkage, with adjustable spring pre-load and rebound damping.

The swingarm pivots through the frame and houses the final driveshaft in its left-hand arm.

2 Frame inspection and repair

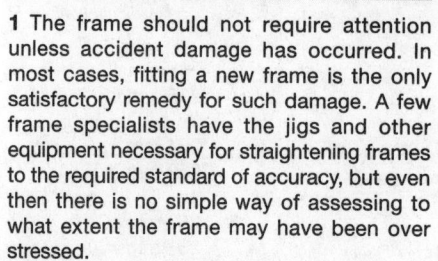

1 The frame should not require attention unless accident damage has occurred. In most cases, fitting a new frame is the only satisfactory remedy for such damage. A few frame specialists have the jigs and other equipment necessary for straightening frames to the required standard of accuracy, but even then there is no simple way of assessing to what extent the frame may have been over stressed.

2 After a high mileage, the frame should be examined closely for signs of cracking or splitting at the welded joints. Loose engine mounting bolts can cause ovaling or fracturing of the mounting points. Minor damage can often be repaired by welding, depending on the extent and nature of the damage.

3 Remember that a frame that is out of alignment will cause handling problems. If, as the result of an accident, misalignment is suspected, it will be necessary to strip the machine completely so the frame can be thoroughly checked.

3 Footrests, brake pedal and gearchange lever

Footrests

1 To remove a front footrest remove the split pin from the bottom of the pivot pin, then withdraw the pin and remove the footrest

Frame and suspension 5•3

3.1 Remove the split pin (arrowed), then draw the pivot pin out the top

3.2 Unscrew the nut (arrowed), then draw the pivot bolt out the top

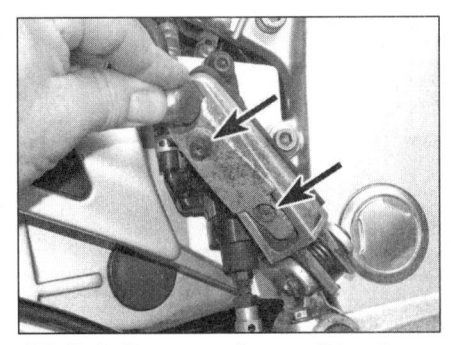

3.3 Undo the screws (arrowed) to release the rubber

(see illustration). Note the fitting of the return spring.

2 To remove a rear footrest, unscrew the nut on the bottom of the pivot bolt, then withdraw the bolt and remove the footrest (see illustration). Note the fitting of the detent plate, ball and spring, and the sleeve for the bolt

3 If necessary you can replace the footrest rubbers with new ones – undo the screws on the underside to release the rubber, and note the washer with the outer bolt (except 2013-on models) and the fitting of the setting plate on the front footrest (see illustration).

4 Installation is the reverse of removal. Apply a small amount of grease to the pivot pin.

Brake pedal

5 Note the alignment of the punch mark on the pedal with that on the shaft (see illustration). Unscrew the pinch bolt and slide the pedal off.

6 Installation is the reverse of removal. Smear some grease onto the shaft splines, and make sure the punch marks align.

Gearchange lever and linkage – standard gearchange models

Removal

7 Put the bike on the centrestand. Note the alignment of the slit in the gearchange linkage arm with the punch mark on the shaft, then unscrew the pinch bolt and slide the arm off (see illustration).

8 Unscrew the footrest bracket bolts and remove the footrest bracket/gearchange lever assembly, and support the sidestand assembly so the wiring is not strained.

9 Unscrew the lever pivot bolt, noting the wave washer and the plain washers behind the lever.

10 If you want to disassemble the linkage note how far the rod is threaded onto the lever and arm as this determines the height of the lever relative to the footrest. Slacken the locknut on each end of the linkage rod – it has left-hand threads on one end (mark that end of the rod as a guide for refitting it) then thread the lever and arm off the rod. If required pull the boot back off the linkage arm pivot, unscrew the bolt and detach the arm, noting the washer between the arm and the pivot eye.

11 Check all components for wear and damage – all are available separately.

Installation

12 Installation is the reverse of removal, noting the following:
- Clean off all old grease from the pivot components and apply fresh grease.
- If the linkage was disassembled leave the locknuts loose for the time being so the height of the lever can be adjusted.
- Fit the plain washer with the smaller internal diameter between the lever pivot and the footrest bracket, and fit the wave washer against the pivot bolt head, then the other plain washer.
- Fit and tighten the footrest bracket bolts as follows – first clean the bolt threads, then apply some fresh non-permanent threadlock. Fit all the bolts finger-tight at first, then tighten the lower (sidestand) bolts first, then the upper (M8) bolts, then the front (M10) bolt, applying the correct torque setting to each bolt as specified at the beginning of the Chapter.
- Align the slit in the linkage arm clamp with the punch mark on the gearchange shaft (see illustration 3.7).
- Adjust the gear lever height by screwing the linkage rod in or out of the lever and arm so the line on the lever lies between the lines on the footrest bracket, with its exact position determined by rider preference (see illustration). Tighten the locknuts on completion.

Gearchange lever and linkage – YCC-S models

13 See Chapter 2, Section 19.

4 Sidestand and centrestand

Sidestand

Removal

1 Support the bike on the centrestand. Remove the left-hand fairing side panel (see Chapter 7). Disconnect the sidestand switch

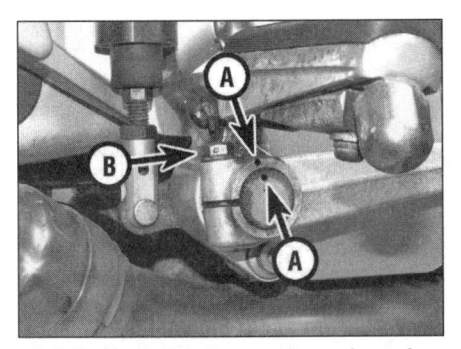

3.5 Brake pedal alignment punch marks (A), pinch bolt (B)

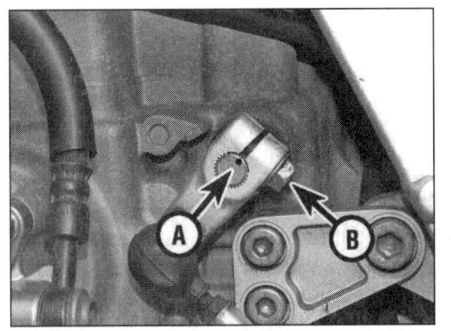

3.7 Gearchange lever alignment punch mark (A), clamp bolt (B)

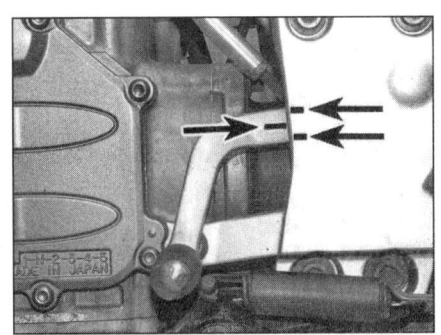

3.12 The line on the lever must be between those on the bracket

5•4 Frame and suspension

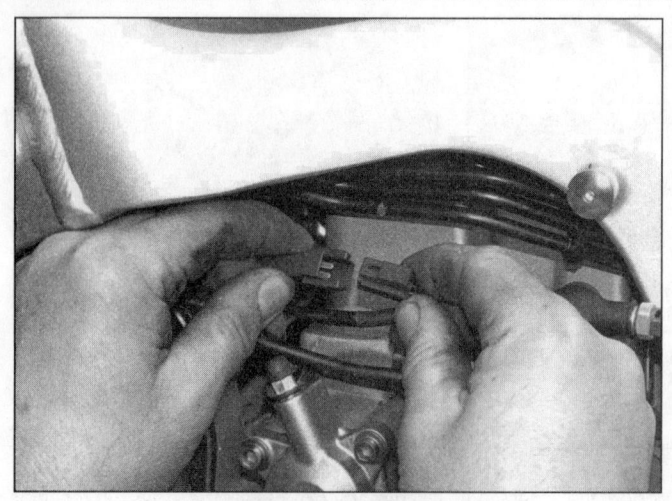

4.1 Disconnect the wiring

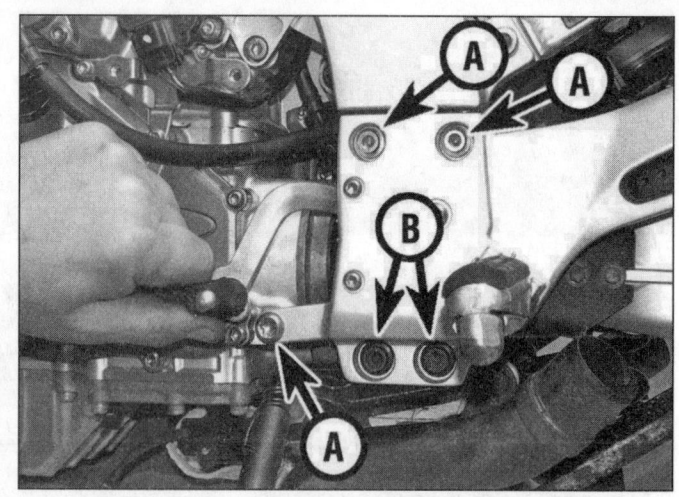

4.2a Slacken the bolts (A) and unscrew the bolts (B)...

4.2b ...and remove the stand assembly

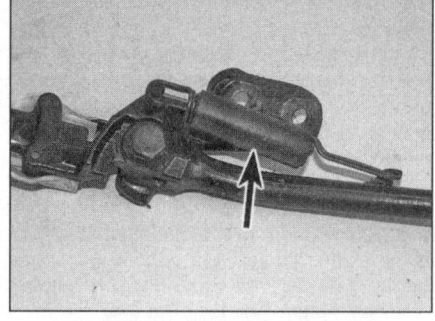

4.3 Sidestand springs (arrowed)

wiring connector **(see illustration)**. Feed the wiring down to the switch, releasing it from the guides and noting its routing.
2 Slacken the footrest bracket bolts, then unscrew the bottom bolts securing the sidestand bracket and draw the stand assembly out **(see illustrations)**.
3 With the stand in the retracted position carefully unhook and remove the springs **(see illustration)**.
4 Unscrew the nut and remove the washer from the pivot bolt **(see illustration)**. Remove the pivot bolt and sleeve, then remove the stand.

Installation

5 Apply grease to the sleeve and pivot bolt shank. Position the stand and fit the sleeve and bolt. Fit the washer and tighten the nut to the torque setting specified at the beginning of the Chapter **(see illustration 4.4)**.

6 Reconnect the springs **(see illustration 4.3)**.
7 Clean the sidestand bolt threads, then apply some fresh non-permanent threadlock. Fit the sidestand bracket and tighten the lower (sidestand) bolts first, then the upper (M8) bolts, then the front (M10) bolt, applying the correct torque setting to each bolt as specified at the beginning of the Chapter.
8 Check the operation of the stand and switch (see Chapter 1). Check the springs hold the stand securely up when not in use – an accident is almost certain to occur if the stand extends while the machine is in motion.

Centrestand

9 If necessary remove the exhaust system (see Chapter 4) – whether you need to or not will depend from which side the bolts have been fitted; if both bolts have been fitted from the inside with the nuts on the outside you will be OK. On the model photographed there was one on the inside and one on the outside **(see illustration)**.

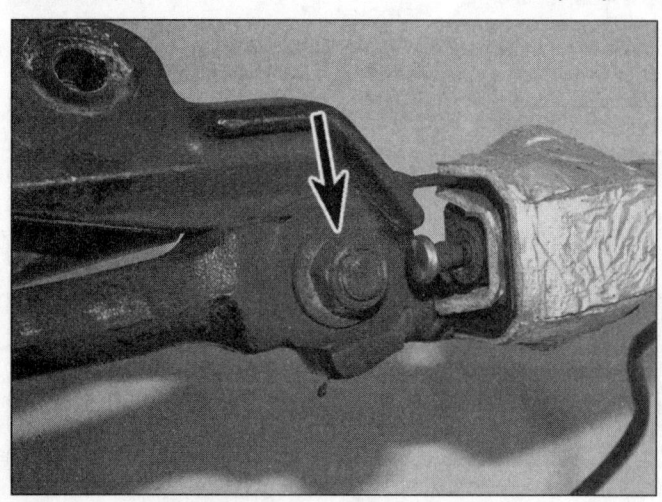

4.4 Sidestand pivot bolt nut (arrowed)

4.9 Centrestand springs (A), nuts (B) and bolts (C)

Frame and suspension 5•5

10 Support the bike on the sidestand. Retract the stand so the springs are more relaxed. Carefully unhook and remove the stand springs.
11 Unscrew the nut from each pivot bolt. Support the stand, withdraw the pivot bolts and remove the stand.
12 Installation is the reverse of removal. Apply grease to the pivot bolts and tighten the nuts to the torque setting specified at the beginning of the Chapter.

5 Handlebars and levers

Handlebar

Removal

Note: *The handlebars can be displaced from the top yoke without detaching any of the assemblies from them – follow Step 1 and 9 or 10 (according to model) only. Rest the assembly on some rag.*

1 As a precaution, raise the fuel tank (see Chapter 4) and remove the fairing side panels (see Chapter 7) – though not actually necessary, this will prevent the possibility of any damage in case a tool slips or you drop something. On 2001 to 2005 models, if the handlebars are being displaced with the assemblies still attached, detach the wiring/hose/cable guides from the top yoke.

2 On 2001 to 2012 models disconnect the wires from the brake light switch or clutch switch, according to side and model **(see illustrations)**. On 2013-on models undo the screw and displace the switch. Unscrew the two brake or clutch (except AS models) master cylinder assembly clamp bolts and position the assembly clear of the handlebar, making sure no strain is placed on the hydraulic hose **(see illustrations)**. Keep the master cylinder reservoir upright to prevent possible fluid leakage.

3 Disconnect the throttle cables (see Chapter 4).

4 Undo the switch housing screws and displace the housing(s) **(see illustrations)** – there is no need to disconnect the wiring, but on 2006-on models release all wiring from the retainers on the underside of the handlebar, or do this afterwards for best access to the bottom screw **(see illustration)**.

5 Undo the handlebar end-weight retaining

5.2a Brake light switch connectors (arrowed)

5.2b Clutch switch connector (arrowed)

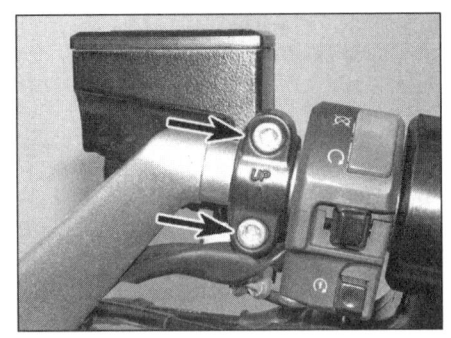

5.2c Brake master cylinder clamp bolts (arrowed)

5.2d Clutch master cylinder clamp bolts (arrowed)

5.4a Left-hand switch housing screws (arrowed) – 2001 to 2005 models

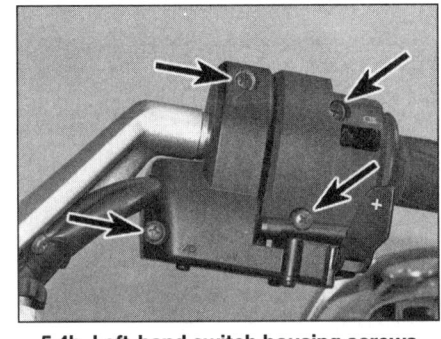

5.4b Left-hand switch housing screws (arrowed) – AS models

5.4c Right-hand switch housing screws (arrowed) – 2001 to 2005 models

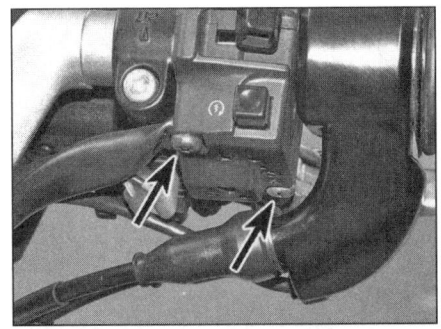

5.4d Right-hand switch housing screws (arrowed) – AS models

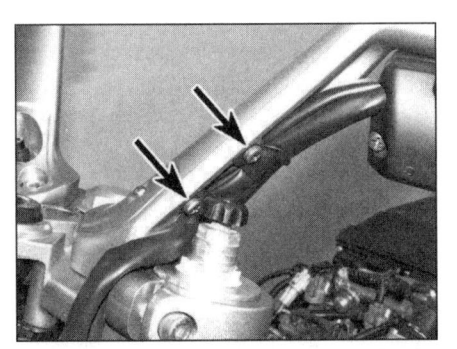

5.4e Handlebar wiring retainer screws (arrowed)

5•6 Frame and suspension

5.5 Handlebar end-weight screw (arrowed)

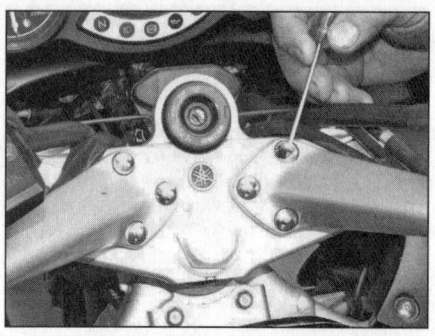

5.8 Remove the blanking caps, then unscrew the bolts

screw and remove the weight **(see illustration)**.

6 On 2008 to 2012 models remove the left-hand fairing side panel, and on 2013-on models remove the fairing (see Chapter 7). Trace the heated grip wiring and disconnect it at the connectors, then feed it out of the frame so there is plenty of slack.

7 Slide the throttle twistgrip off the right handlebar. Remove the grip from the left handlebar if required – you may need to insert a suitable tool (that won't scratch the handlebar or damage the grip) between the grip and the handlebar from the inner end, then squirt some lubricant (such as WD40) or compressed air in the gap and allow it to work its way round.

8 On 2001 to 2005 models remove the blanking caps from the handlebar bolts, then unscrew the bolts and remove the handlebar **(see illustration)**.

9 On 2006-on models, remove the mounting cover **(see illustration)**. Unscrew the nut and the bolt and remove the handlebar, noting its set position **(see illustration)** – there are three positions it can be fitted in.

Installation

10 Installation is the reverse of removal, noting the following.
- On 2001 to 2005 models tighten the handlebar bolts to the torque setting specified at the beginning of the Chapter.
- On 2006-on models make sure both handlebars are set in the same position – there are three to choose from. Fit the washers and tighten the nuts finger-tight only so the holders can be aligned with the handlebars. Fit the bolt and the nut, then tighten the bolt first, then the nut, to the torque settings specified at the beginning of the Chapter.

- Smear some grease onto the throttle twistgrip sliding surface.
- Fit the brake and clutch master cylinder clamps with the UP mark facing up **(see illustrations 5.2c and d)** and either with the clamp mating surfaces aligned with the punch mark on the top of the handlebar **(see illustration)**, or locating the pin in the clamp in the hole in the handlebar, according to side and model. Tighten the top bolt first, then the bottom, to the specified torque setting.
- Refer to Chapter 4 for installation of the throttle cables.
- Make sure the pin in each switch housing locates in its hole in the handlebar.
- Do not forget to reconnect the front brake light switch and clutch switch wiring connectors **(see illustrations 5.2a and b)**.
- Check the operation of the throttle, brake and clutch, and adjust throttle cable freeplay if required (see Chapter 1).

Levers

11 Undo the lever pivot screw locknut, then undo the pivot screw and remove the lever **(see illustrations)**. Note the pushrod bush in the clutch lever – make sure it does not drop out.

12 Installation is the reverse of removal. Apply silicone grease to the contact area between the master cylinder pushrod tip and the lever and to the pivot screw shaft. Make sure the clutch lever bush is in place, and when fitting the lever locate the pushrod tip in the hole in the bush. Tighten the pivot screw lightly, then hold it and tighten the locknut.

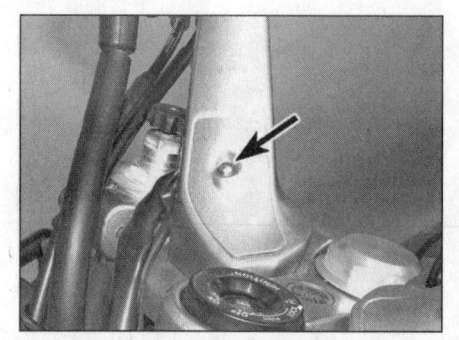

5.9a Undo the screw (arrowed) and remove the cover...

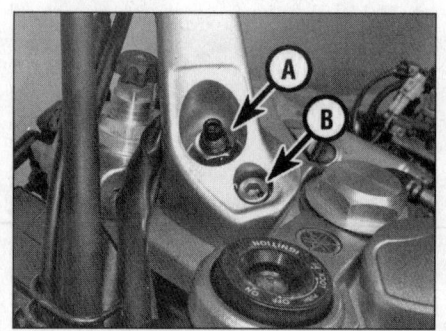

5.9b ...to access the nut (A) and the bolt (B)

5.10 Align the clamp mating surfaces with the punch mark (arrowed)

5.11a Unscrew the nut...

5.11b ...then undo the screw...

5.11c ...and remove the lever

Frame and suspension

6 Fork removal and installation

Removal

1 Remove the fairing side panels (see Chapter 7).
2 Remove the front mudguard (see Chapter 7).
3 Remove the front wheel (see Chapter 6). Tie the front brake calipers back so that they are out of the way.
4 Note the routing of all cables, hoses and wiring around the forks.
5 Working on one fork at a time, slacken the fork clamp bolt in the top yoke (see illustration). If the fork oil is being changed, or if the fork is to be disassembled, slacken the fork top bolt (see illustration).
6 Slacken the fork clamp bolts in the bottom yoke, and remove the fork by twisting it and pulling it downwards (see illustrations).

HAYNES HiNT *If the fork legs are seized in the yokes, spray the area with penetrating oil and allow time for it to soak in before trying again.*

Installation

7 Remove any traces of corrosion from the fork tube and the yokes. As you fit each fork make sure all cables, hoses and wiring are routed on the correct side of the fork.
8 Slide the fork up through the bottom yoke and into the top yoke and set the top of the fork tube (not the top bolt) flush with the upper surface of the yoke (see illustration 6.5a), then tighten the fork clamp bolts in the bottom yoke to the torque setting specified at the beginning of the Chapter (see illustration 6.6a).
9 If the fork oil was changed or if the fork has been dismantled, tighten the fork top bolt to the specified torque setting (see illustration 6.5b).
10 Now tighten the fork clamp bolt in the top yoke to the specified torque.
11 Install the front wheel (see Chapter 6) and the front mudguard (see Chapter 7).
12 Install the fairing side panels (see Chapter 7). Check the operation of the front forks and brakes before taking the machine out on the road.

7 Fork oil change

1 After a high mileage the fork oil will deteriorate and its damping and lubrication qualities will be impaired. Always change the oil in both fork legs.
2 Remove the fork – make sure you loosen the top bolt while the leg is still clamped in the bottom yoke (see Section 6).

Left-hand fork – 2013-on models

3 Unscrew the fork top bolt from the top of the inner tube – the bolt is under pressure from the fork spring, so use a ratchet tool so it does not need to be removed from the bolt as you unscrew it, and maintain some downward pressure on it, particularly as you come to the end of the threads, or alternatively hold the tool still and twist the fork tube to unthread it from the bolt.
4 Slide the inner tube down and remove the washer, spacer, washer and spring.
5 Invert the fork leg over a suitable container and pump it several times to expel as much oil as possible (see illustration 7.15). Support the fork upside down in the container for a while to allow it to drain, then pump the fork again. If the fork oil contains metal particles inspect the fork bushes for wear (see Section 8). Wipe any excess oil off the spring and the spacer.
6 Stand the fork upright. Slowly pour in the specified quantity of the specified grade of fork oil (see illustration 7.16a). Now pump the fork slowly at least ten times to distribute the oil evenly and expel all air from the damper. Leave the fork to stand for ten minutes to allow the oil to settle and any air to rise.
7 Slide the inner tube down gently until it seats on the bottom. Measure the oil level from the top of the tube (see illustration 7.17). Add or subtract oil until it is at the level specified at the beginning of this Chapter.
8 Pull the inner tube out, then fit the spring with the narrow half at the bottom, then fit the washer, spacer and washer.
9 If the top bolt O-ring is damaged or deteriorated fit a new one (see illustration 7.21). Smear some fork oil onto the O-ring. Extend the inner tube and fit the top bolt into it, compressing the spring as you do, and thread it in, making sure it does not cross-thread, keeping downward pressure on the spring, using a ratchet tool or by turning the tube while holding the bolt still, and tighten it as much as possible holding the inner tube by hand. **Note:** *Tighten the top bolt to the specified torque setting when the fork has been installed in the bike and is held in the bottom yoke, but before the top yoke clamp bolt is tightened.*
10 Install the fork (see Section 6).

Both forks – 2001 to 2012 models, right-hand fork – 2013-on models

11 Unscrew the fork top bolt from the top of the inner tube (see illustration). The bolt will remain on the damper rod.

6.5a Top yoke fork clamp bolt (arrowed)

6.5b Slacken the top bolt now if required

6.6a Bottom yoke fork clamp bolts (arrowed)

6.6b Draw the fork down and out of the yokes

7.11 Thread the top bolt out of the tube

5•8 Frame and suspension

7.12 Hold the locknut and unscrew the top bolt

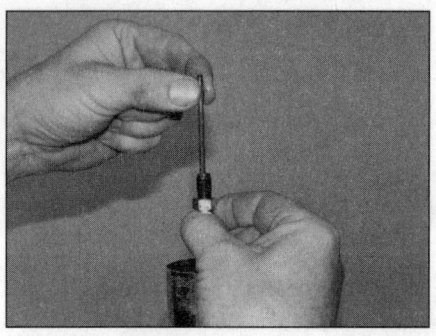

7.13 Remove the rod

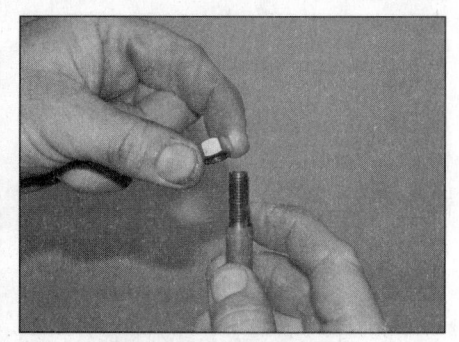

7.14a Unscrew the nut...

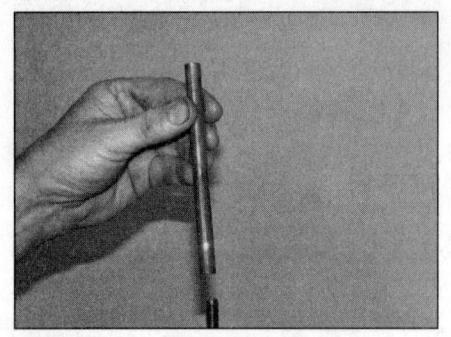

7.14b ...and remove the spacer...

7.14c ...and the washer and spring

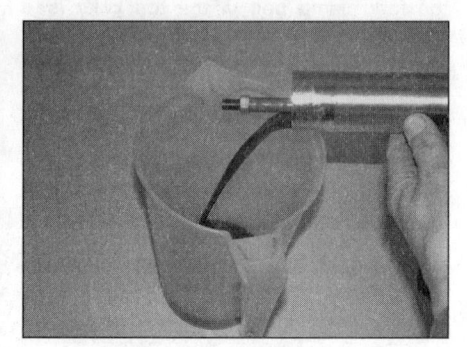

7.15 Drain the oil as described

12 Slide the inner tube down gently until it seats on the bottom. Counter-hold the locknut and unscrew the top bolt using a spanner on the pre-load adjuster hex **(see illustration)**.

13 Withdraw the damping adjuster rod **(see illustration)** – on 2013 models there is a damping valve and spring that may also come out, but if they don't they will probably come out with the oil when you drain it, so retrieve them from the oil.

14 Thread the nut off the damper rod and remove the spacer **(see illustrations)**. Hook the washer and spring out of the tube **(see illustration)**.

15 Invert the fork leg over a suitable container and pump the fork and damper rod several times to expel as much fork oil as possible **(see illustration)**. Support the fork upside down in the container for a while to allow as much oil as possible to drain, then pump the fork and rod again. If the fork oil contains metal particles inspect the fork bushes for wear (see Section 8). Wipe any excess oil off the spring.

16 Stand the fork upright. Slowly pour in the specified quantity of the specified grade of fork oil **(see illustration)**. Now pump the fork and damper rod slowly at least ten times each to distribute the oil evenly and expel all air from the damper **(see illustration)**. Leave the fork to stand for ten minutes to allow the oil to settle and any air to rise.

7.16a Fill the fork slowly to prevent air bubbles and overfilling

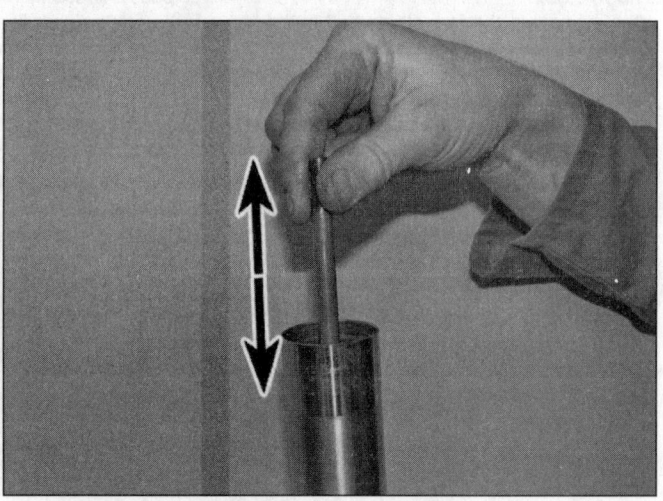

7.16b Pump the fork and rod

Frame and suspension 5•9

7.17 Measure the distance from the top of the tube to the oil

7.18a Fit the spring...

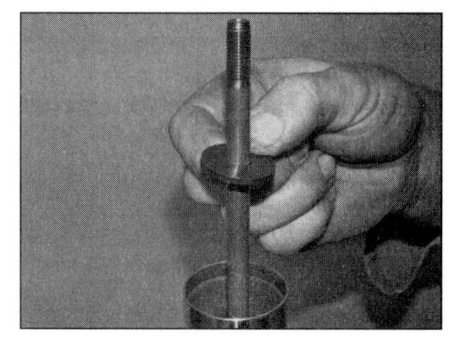

7.18b ...the washer...

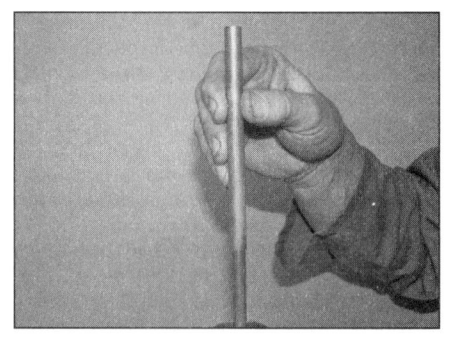

7.18c ...and the spacer

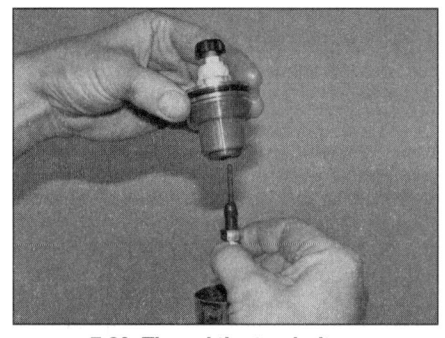

7.20 Thread the top bolt on

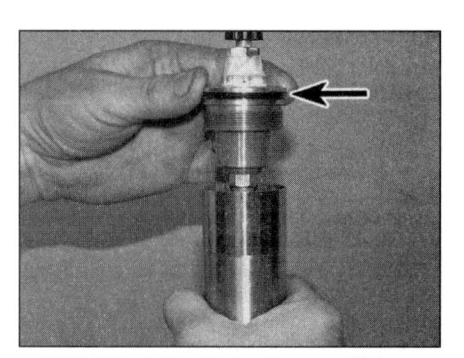

7.21 Check the O-ring (arrowed) then thread the top bolt into the tube

17 Slide the inner tube down gently until it seats on the bottom. Measure the oil level from the top of the tube **(see illustration)**. Add or subtract oil until it is at the level specified at the beginning of this Chapter.

18 Pull the damper rod and inner tube out as far as possible, then fit the spring with the narrow half at the bottom **(see illustration)**. Keeping the damper rod extended, fit the washer and spacer **(see illustrations)**. Thread the nut onto the rod and down to the bottom of the threads, leaving it loose **(see illustration 7.14a)**.

19 On 2013-on models fit the spring and damping valve. On all models fit the damping adjuster rod **(see illustration 7.13)**.

20 Thread the top bolt onto the damper rod until it becomes finger tight **(see illustration)**. Counter-hold the pre-load adjuster hex using a spanner as before and tighten the locknut securely against it **(see illustration 7.12)**.

21 If the top bolt O-ring is damaged or deteriorated fit a new one. Smear some fork oil onto the O-ring. Extend the inner tube and thread the top bolt into it, making sure it does not cross-thread, and tighten it as much as possible holding the inner tube by hand **(see illustration)**. **Note:** *Tighten the top bolt to the specified torque setting when the fork has been installed in the bike and is held in the bottom yoke, but before the top yoke clamp bolt is tightened.*

22 Install the fork (see Section 6).

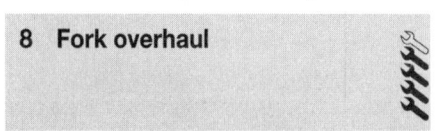

8 Fork overhaul

1 Remove the fork – make sure you loosen the top bolt while the leg is still clamped in the bottom yoke (see Section 6). Always dismantle the fork legs separately to avoid interchanging parts and thus causing an accelerated rate of wear. Store all components in separate, clearly marked containers.

Disassembly

2 Remove the axle clamp bolts **(see illustration)**. If required remove the fork protector, but only do so if necessary as it is retained by a small tab which may break off, meaning you will have to fit a new one **(see illustration)**.

3 Lay the fork flat on the bench with the caliper mounting lugs to the left. Hold the fork down and slacken then lightly retighten the damper bolt in the base of the fork **(see illustration)**. If the damper rotates inside the fork whilst attempting to unscrew the bolt, compress the fork so that the spring exerts pressure on its head whilst the bolt is

8.2a Remove the axle clamp bolts

8.2b Tap the protector off using a soft drift such as a piece of wood

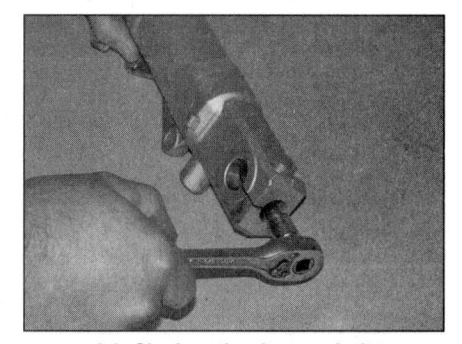

8.3 Slacken the damper bolt

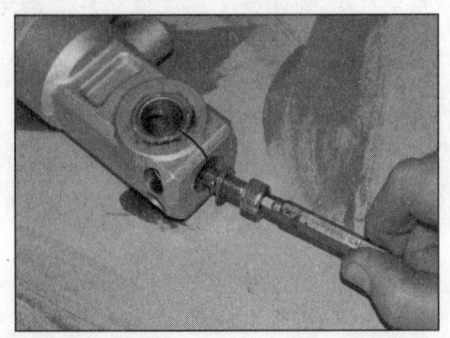

5•10 Frame and suspension

8.5 Remove the bolt and its washer

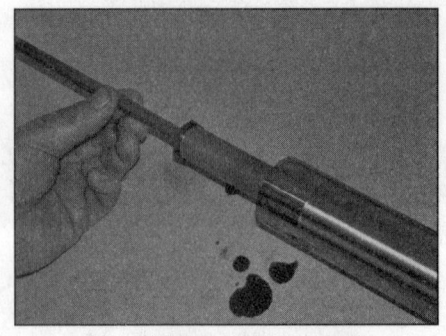

8.6a Withdraw the damper...

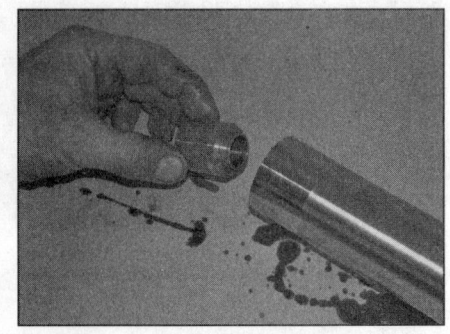

8.6b ...and tip the oil lock piece out

unscrewed. Alternatively, if available use an air wrench.
4 Refer to the Section 7, Steps 3 to 5 or 11 to 15 and drain the oil from the fork.
5 Remove the damper bolt and its sealing washer from the bottom of the fork **(see illustration)**. A new sealing washer must be used on reassembly.
6 Withdraw the damper **(see illustration)**. On all except 2013-on models tip the oil lock piece out **(see illustration)**
7 Carefully prise out the dust seal from the top of the outer tube **(see illustration)**.
8 Carefully prise out the oil seal retaining clip, taking care not to scratch the surface of the inner tube **(see illustration)**.
9 To separate the inner and outer tubes it is necessary to displace the top bush, on 2006-on models the middle bush, and the oil seal from the outer tube. To do this grasp the inner tube in one hand and the outer tube in the other and compress them slightly, then pull them apart repeatedly until the bush(es) and seal are tapped out **(see illustrations)**.
10 Slide the oil seal, the washer, the top bush, and on 2006-on models the middle bush, off the inner tube, noting which way up they fit **(see illustration 8.9b)**. Discard the oil seal and the dust seal as new ones must be used. Do not remove the bottom bush from the inner tube unless it is being replaced with a new one – to remove it carefully lever its ends apart using a screwdriver and slide it out of its recess **(see illustration)**.

Inspection

11 Clean all parts in solvent and blow them dry with compressed air, if available.
12 Check the fork inner tube for score marks, dents, pitting, scratches, flaking of its surface and excessive or abnormal wear. If corrosion damage is excessive the inner tubes can be re-chromed using hard chrome. Otherwise fit a new tube. Check the tube for runout using V-blocks and a dial gauge. If the amount of runout exceeds the service limit specified, a new tube should be fitted.

⚠ **Warning: If the inner tube is bent or exceeds the runout limit, it should not be straightened; replace it with a new one.**

13 Check the fork outer tube for cracks. Check the fork seal seat and housing for nicks, gouges and scratches. If damage is evident, leaks will occur. Also check the oil seal washer for damage or distortion and fit a new one if necessary.
14 Check the spring for cracks and other damage. Measure the spring free length and compare the measurement to the specifications at the beginning of the Chapter **(see illustration)**. If it is defective or sagged below the service limit, replace the springs in

8.7 Prise out the dust seal using a flat-bladed screwdriver

8.8 Prise out the retaining clip using a flat-bladed screwdriver

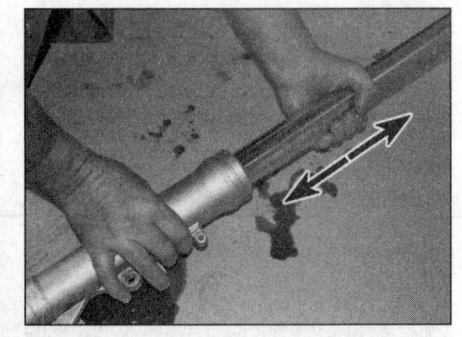

8.9a To separate the tubes pull them apart firmly several times...

8.9b ...the slide-hammer effect will displace the oil seal, washer and bush(es)

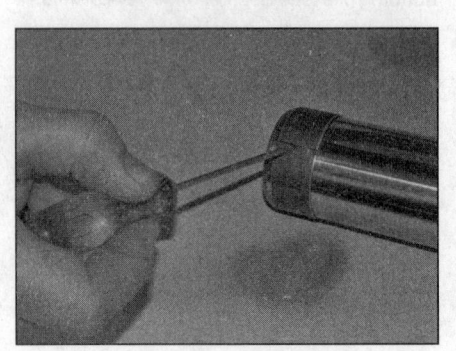

8.10 Carefully lever the ends of the bush apart to expand it

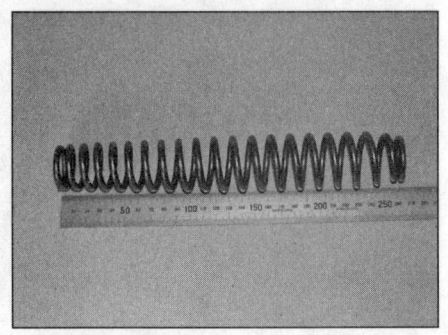

8.14 Check the free length of the spring

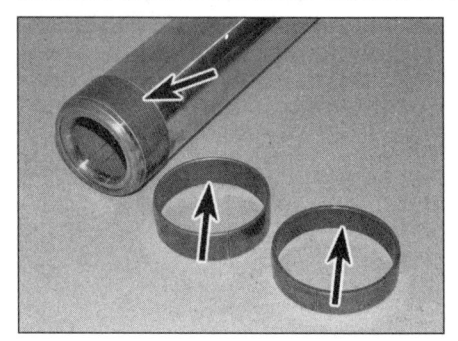

Frame and suspension 5•11

8.15 Check the working surface (arrowed) of each bush for wear

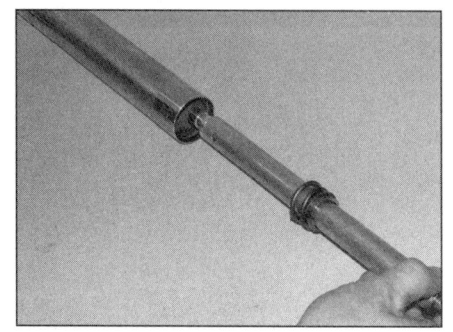

8.18a Fit the damper into the tube...

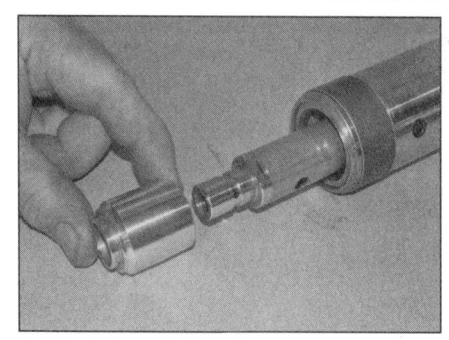

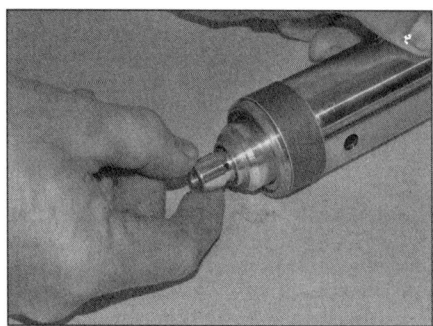

8.18b ...then fit the oil lock piece onto the protruding end...

8.18c ...and push it into the tube

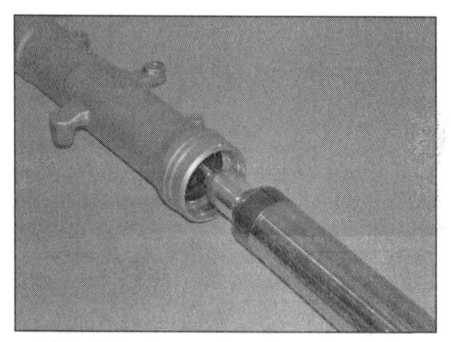

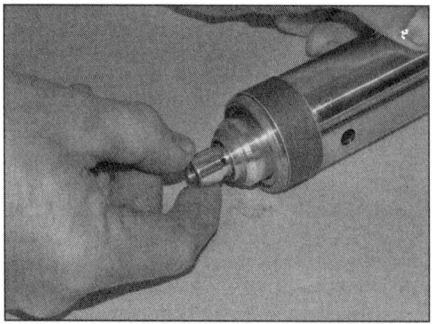

8.19 Slide the inner tube into the outer tube

both forks with new ones. Never renew only one spring.

15 Examine the working surfaces of the bushes (i.e. the outer surface of the bottom bush and the inner surface of the top bush, and on 2006-on models the middle bush) **(see illustration)**; if the grey Teflon outer surface has been worn away to reveal the copper inner surface over more than 75% of the surface area, or if the bushes are scored or badly scuffed (which can easily occur during the tube separation process), they must be replaced with new ones. Note that it is a good idea to replace the bushes with new ones as a matter of course as part of a fork overhaul, and Yamaha specify to do this.

16 Check the damper and the rebound spring fitted on it for damage and wear.

Reassembly

17 If necessary, fit a new bottom bush into its recess in the bottom of the inner tube **(see illustration 8.10)**.

18 Slide the damper into the top of the inner tube and all the way down so it protrudes from the bottom **(see illustration)**. On 2001 to 2012 models fit the oil lock piece onto the bottom of the damper, then push the damper back into the tube so the oil lock piece fits into the bottom of the tube **(see illustrations)**.

19 Apply a smear of the specified clean fork oil to the surface of the bottom bush. Slide the inner tube fully into the outer tube **(see illustration)**.

20 Clean the threads of the damper bolt. Lay the fork flat on the bench with the caliper mounting lugs to the right. Fit a new sealing washer onto the bolt and apply a few drops of a suitable non-permanent thread locking compound **(see illustration)**. Fit the bolt into the bottom of the outer tube and thread it into the damper, tightening it to the torque setting specified at the beginning of the Chapter **(see illustration)**. If the rod rotates inside the tube as you tighten the bolt, wait until the fork is fully reassembled and tighten it then (the pressure of the spring on the head of the damper will prevent it from turning).

21 On 2006-on models you need to find a suitable piece of plastic tubing to drive the middle bush down into the fork – it needs to have a 50 mm diameter and be 2 mm thick, though you can use a narrower and thinner piece and slit it lengthways so it expands to

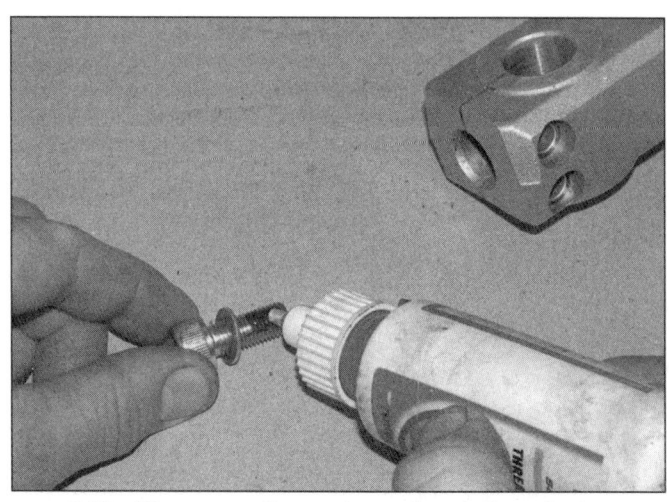

8.20a Fit a new sealing washer and apply threadlock...

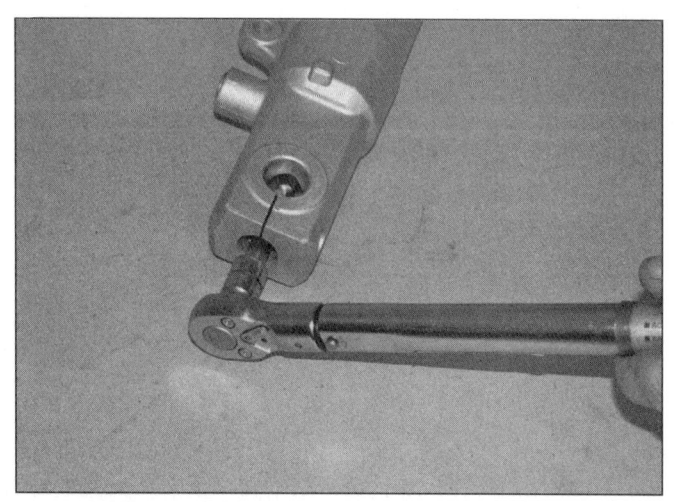

8.20b ...and tighten the bolt to the specified torque

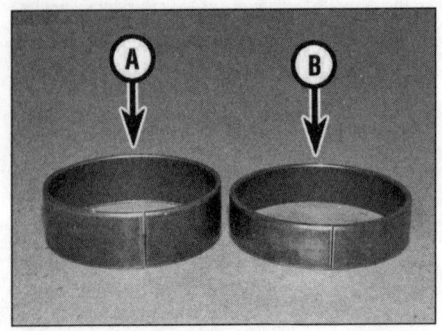

5•12 Frame and suspension

8.21a Middle bush (A), top bush (B)

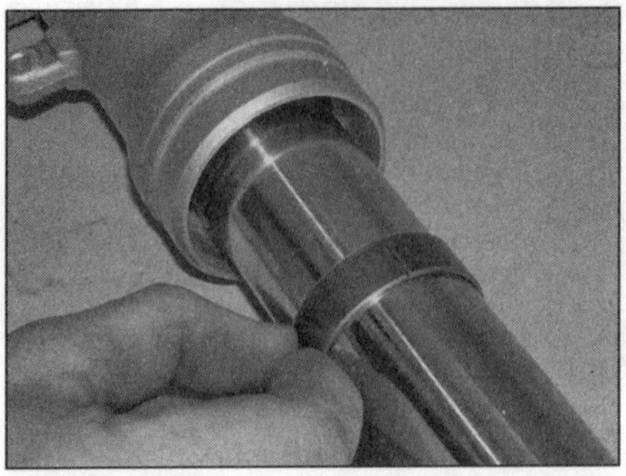

8.21b Slide the bush down into the outer tube

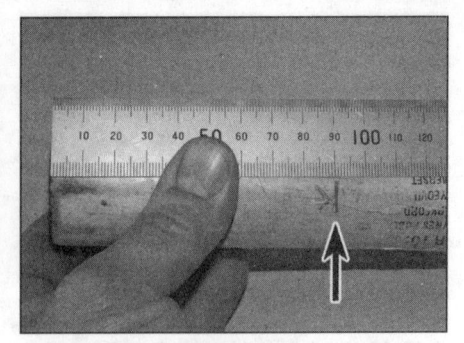

8.21c Make a depth mark on your tube

fit around the tube. We did just that using a piece of tube that welding rods come packed in **(see illustration 8.21d)**. It must also be long enough to extend about 120 mm above the top of the inner tube. Apply a smear of the specified clean fork oil to the inner surface of the middle bush (it has a diameter of 51 mm and a height of 15 mm **(see illustration)** – do not mix it up with the top bush, which has a diameter of 52 mm and a height of 12 mm).

Slide the bush down the inner tube and seat it in the top of the outer tube **(see illustration)**. Tape over the top of the inner tube to prevent any debris dropping in. Make a mark on your tube 90 mm from the bottom **(see illustration)** – this represents the set depth of the top of the middle bush, and when this is flush with the top of the fork outer tube you know the bush is seated in the correct place. Slide your tube over the fork inner tube and onto the bush, place a piece of wood over the top of your tube and tap it with a mallet until the bush is seated and your mark is level with the top of the fork outer tube **(see illustrations)**.

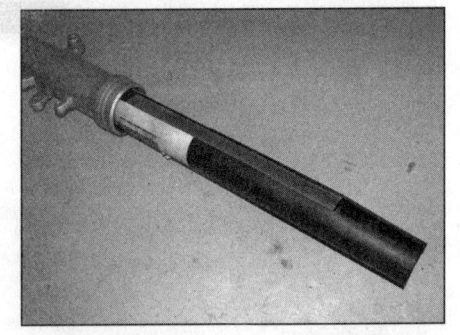

22 Apply a smear of the specified clean fork oil to the inner surface of the top bush. Slide the bush down the inner tube and seat it in the top of the outer tube **(see illustration)**. On 2006-on models use the same piece of tubing as in Step 21 to drive the top bush fully into its recess. On 2001 to 2005 models either use the same method as in Step 21, or use a suitable flat-end punch (i.e. not a centre-punch) as a drift, with the oil seal washer in place **(see illustration 8.23)** as an interface to prevent damaging the edges of the bush **(see illustration)**. Wrap tape around the drift to prevent scratching the inner tube. Tap evenly around the rim of the bush – make sure it enters the recess square, and tap it in until it seats **(see illustration)**. It is best to make sure that the inner tube is withdrawn as much as possible from the outer tube so that any accidental scratching is confined to the area that does not affect the oil seal.

23 Fit the oil seal washer **(see illustration)**.

8.21d Fit your tube over the fork...

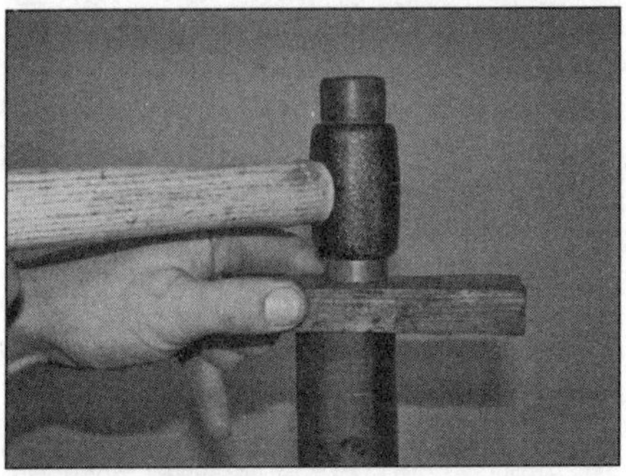

8.21e ...then tap on a piece of wood placed on the top...

8.21f ...until your marker is flush with the top of the outer tube

8.22a Slide the top bush down and into the outer tube

8.22b Using a punch to fit the top bush

8.22c Make sure the bush (arrowed) has been fully driven in

8.23 Fit the washer

Frame and suspension 5•13

8.24a Slide the seal down and into the outer tube...

8.24b ...then fit the old seal on top...

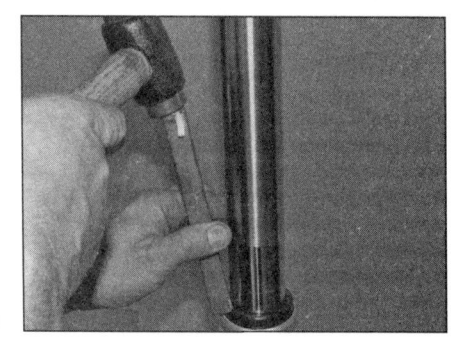

8.24c ...and drive the new seal in and onto its seat using the old seal as an interface

8.24d Lift the old seal...

8.24e ...and make sure the retaining clip groove (arrowed) is fully exposed

8.25 Fit the retaining clip in its groove...

24 Apply a smear of the clean fork oil to the lips of the new oil seal. Slide the seal onto the tube with its marked side facing up **(see illustration)**. Fit the old seal above it to act as an interface to avoid damaging the new seal and drive the seal squarely into place using a piece of wood until the retaining clip groove is visible **(see illustrations)**. The new seal is seated when the old seal is just about flush with the rim of the outer tube – at this point lift it and check that the retaining clip groove is fully exposed **(see illustration)**. Remove the old seal.

25 Fit the retaining clip, making sure it is correctly located in its groove **(see illustration)**.
26 Press the dust seal into the top of the outer tube **(see illustration)**.
27 Refer to Section 7, Steps 6 to 9 or 16 to 21 and fill the fork with oil and finish reassembly.
28 If the damper bolt requires tightening (see Step 20), place the fork upside down on the floor, using a rag to protect it, then have an assistant compress the fork so that maximum spring pressure is placed on the damper rod head while tightening the bolt to the specified torque setting.

29 Fit the fork protector if removed, using a new one if necessary, and aligning the tab with the cut-out **(see illustration)**.
30 Install the fork (see Section 6).

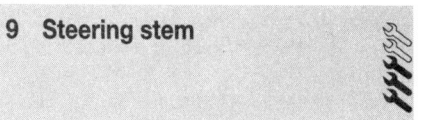

9 Steering stem

Special tool: *Either the Yamaha special tool (part No. 90890-01403), equivalent peg spanner, or a suitably sized C-spanner is necessary for this procedure.*

8.26 ...then press the dust seal in

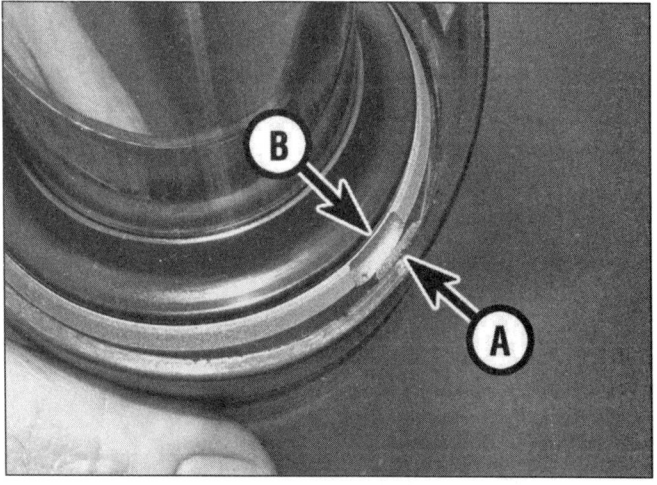

8.29 Align the tab (A) with the cut-out (B)

5•14 Frame and suspension

9.4 Displace the hoses/pipes and shield from the bottom yoke as required according to model

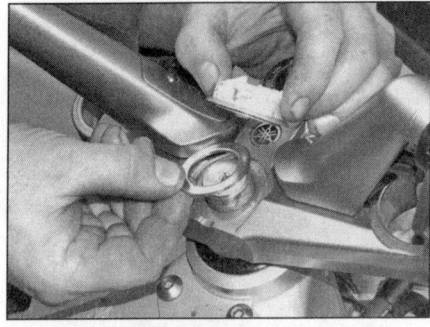

9.5a Unscrew the steering stem nut and remove the washer...

9.5b ...and lift the handlebar/yoke assembly off

9.6a Remove the lockwasher...

9.6b ...then unscrew the locknut...

9.6c ...and remove the rubber washer

Removal

1 Remove the fairing side panels and the fairing (see Chapter 7).
2 As a precaution, remove the fuel tank (see Chapter 4) – though not actually essential, this will prevent the possibility of damage should a tool slip.
3 Remove the front forks (see Section 6).
4 Displace the brake hose assembly and shield from the bottom yoke (see illustration).
5 Wrap a layer of masking tape around the steering stem nut to prevent marking it. Unscrew the nut and remove the washer (see illustration). Gently ease the top yoke/handlebar assembly up off the steering stem and position it clear, using rag to protect other components (see illustration).
6 Remove the tabbed lockwasher, noting how it fits, then unscrew and remove the locknut using either a C-spanner or a peg spanner, though it should only be finger-tight (see illustrations). Remove the rubber washer (see illustration).
7 If the Yamaha tool is not available, make an alignment mark between the adjuster nut and the frame – this can serve as a rough guide for the tightness of the adjuster nut on installation.

As you unscrew the nut count the number of turns.
8 Support the bottom yoke and unscrew the adjuster nut using a peg-spanner or a C-spanner (see illustration 9.14). Gently lower the bottom yoke and steering stem out of the frame (see illustration 9.12a).
9 Remove the grease seal, inner race and bearing from the top of the steering head (see illustration). Remove the bearing and grease seal from the base of the steering stem (see illustration).
10 Remove all traces of old grease from the bearings and races and check them for wear

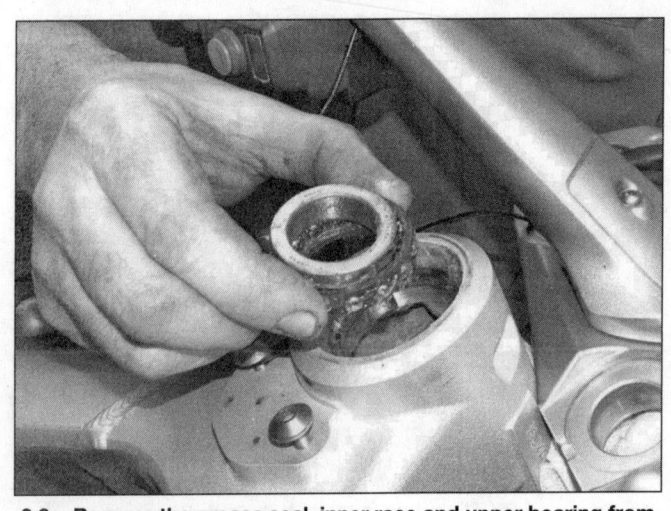

9.9a Remove the grease seal, inner race and upper bearing from the head...

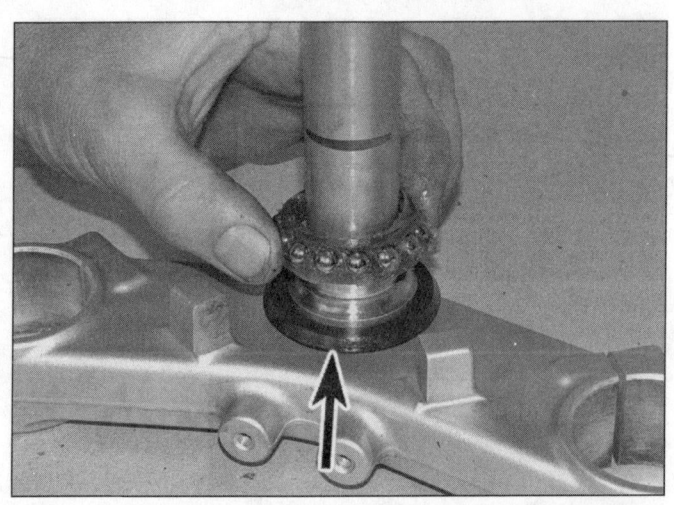

9.9b ...and the lower bearing and seal (arrowed) from the stem

Frame and suspension 5•15

9.11a Fit the lower seal...

9.11b ...making sure it is the correct way round and is seated over the race

9.12a Fit the stem up through the head

9.12b Fit the bearing...

9.12c ...the inner race...

9.12d ...and the seal...

or damage as described in Section 10. **Note:** *Do not attempt to remove the races from the steering head or the steering stem unless they are to be replaced with new ones (see Section 10).*

Installation

11 Smear a liberal quantity of lithium based multi-purpose grease onto the bearing races, and work some grease well into both the upper and lower bearings and over the grease seals; fit new seals if necessary. Fit the lower bearing seal over the race **(see illustrations)**. Fit the bearing **(see illustration 9.9b)**.

12 Carefully lift the steering stem/bottom yoke up through the steering head and support it there **(see illustration)**. Fit the upper bearing, the inner race and the grease seal **(see illustrations)**. Thread the adjuster nut onto the steering stem and tighten it finger-tight **(see illustration)**.

13 If the Yamaha service tool is available, tighten the nut to the initial torque setting specified at the beginning of this Chapter. Make sure the torque wrench handle is at right-angles (90°) to the centre line between the adjuster nut and the service tool wrench socket **(see illustration)**. Now slacken the nut one turn, then tighten it to the final torque setting specified. Check that the steering stem is able to move smoothly (though it may feel a bit tight, but this is normal as the weight of the forks and wheel is not influencing the feel) from lock-to-lock following adjustment – note that it is best to check and if necessary reset the bearing adjustment as described in Chapter 1 after the forks and front wheel and all other components have been installed.

14 If the Yamaha tool is not available, tighten the nut the number of turns recorded on removal using a C-spanner until the marks align **(see illustration)**. Turn the steering from lock-to-lock five times, then slacken the nut, and tighten it again until the marks align. Install the forks and wheel, then refer to the procedure in Chapter 1 and check the feel of the bearings as described, and adjust if necessary.

Caution: Take great care not to apply excessive pressure because this will cause premature failure of the bearings.

15 With the bearings correctly adjusted, fit the rubber washer and the locknut **(see illustrations 9.6c and b)**. Tighten the locknut

9.12e ...then thread the adjuster nut on

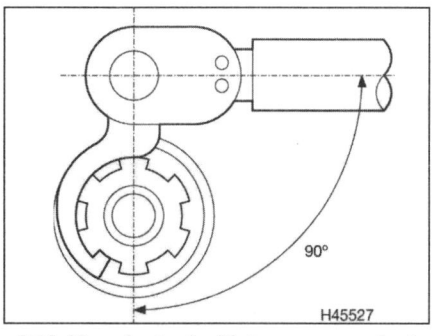

9.13 Yamaha tool with torque wrench at correct angle to tool

9.14 Tightening the nut using a C-spanner

5•16 Frame and suspension

9.16a Align the yokes by fitting one fork

9.16b Tighten the stem nut to the specified torque

10.4 Drive the bearing races out with a brass drift, locating it on the rim

finger-tight, then tighten it further until its notches align with those in the adjuster nut, making sure it does not turn as well. Fit the lockwasher so that the tabs fit into the notches in both the locknut and adjuster nut **(see illustration 9.6a)**.

16 Fit the top yoke/handlebar assembly onto the steering stem and forks **(see illustration 9.5b)**. Fit the washer and the steering stem nut finger-tight **(see illustration 9.5a)**. Fit one fork up into the yokes to align them and tighten the bottom yoke clamp bolts to secure the fork **(see illustration)**. Tighten the steering stem nut to the torque setting specified at the beginning of the Chapter **(see illustration)**.

17 Install the remaining components in a reverse of the removal procedure, referring to the relevant Sections or Chapters, and to the torque settings specified at the beginning of the Chapter.

18 Carry out a final check of the steering head bearing freeplay as described in Chapter 1, and if necessary re-adjust.

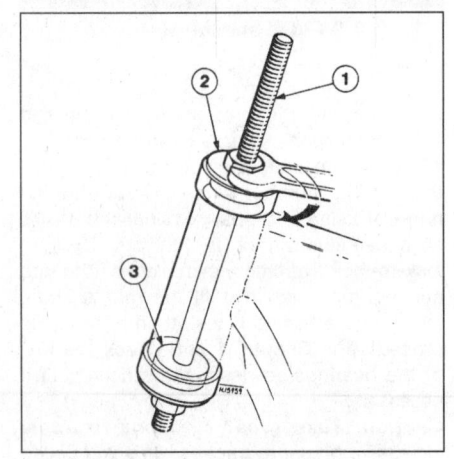

10 Steering head bearings

Inspection

1 Remove the steering stem (see Section 9).
2 Remove all traces of old grease from the bearings and races.
3 Inspect the races – they should be polished and free from indentations. Inspect the bearing balls for signs of wear, damage or discoloration, and examine the ball retainer cage for signs of cracks or splits. If there are any signs of wear on any of the above components both upper and lower bearing assemblies must be renewed as a set. Only remove the outer races in the steering head and the lower bearing inner race on the steering stem if they need to be replaced with new ones – do not re-use them once they have been removed.

Replacement

4 The outer races are an interference fit in the steering head – tap them from position using a suitable drift, locating it in the notches that expose the inner rim of the race, and moving from notch to notch so the race is driven out square **(see illustration)**. Tap firmly and evenly between the recesses to ensure the race is driven out squarely.

5 Press the new outer races into the head using a drawbolt arrangement **(see illustration)**, or drive them in using a large diameter tubular drift. Ensure that the drawbolt washer or drift (as applicable) bears only on the outer edge of the race and does not contact the working surface. Alternatively, have the races installed by a Yamaha dealer equipped with the bearing race installation tools.

HAYNES HiNT *Installation of new bearing outer races is made much easier if the races are left overnight in the freezer. This causes them to contract slightly making them a looser fit. Alternatively, use a freeze spray.*

6 Only remove the lower bearing inner race from the steering stem if a new one is being fitted. To remove the race, position the yoke on its front with the stem resting on a piece of wood so the threads are clear to prevent damage. Tap under the race using a cold chisel to displace it, and if required use two screwdrivers placed on opposite sides to work it free, using blocks of wood to improve leverage and protect the yoke **(see illustrations)**. If the race is firmly in place it will be necessary to use a puller **(see illustration)**. Take the steering stem to a Yamaha dealer if required.

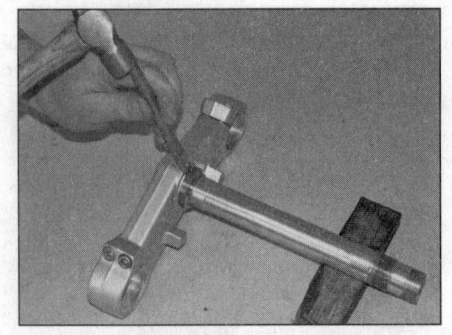

10.5 Drawbolt arrangement for fitting steering stem bearing races
1 Long bolt or threaded bar
2 Thick washer
3 Guide for lower race

10.6a Remove the lower bearing race using a cold chisel...

10.6b ...and/or screwdrivers...

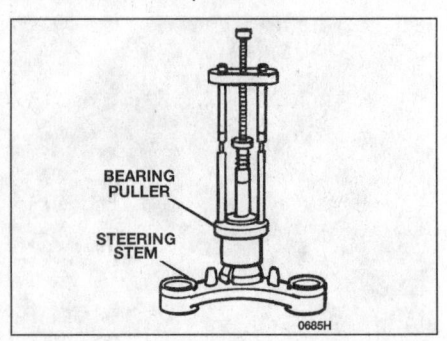

10.6c ...or using a puller if necessary

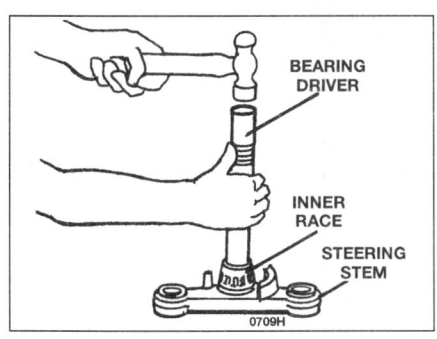

Frame and suspension 5•17

10.7 Drive the new inner race on using a suitable bearing driver or a length of pipe that bears only against the inner rim and not the bearing surface

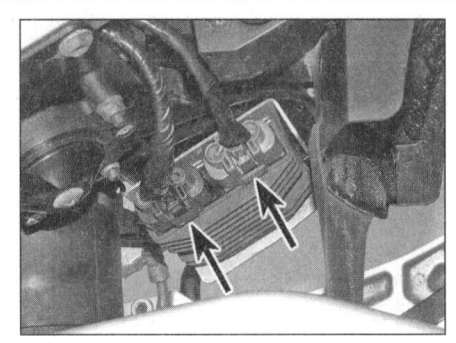

11.5a Regulator/rectifier wiring connectors (arrowed)

11.5b Pre-load adjuster nuts (arrowed)

7 Fit the new lower race onto the steering stem. Drive the race into position using a length of tubing with an internal diameter slightly larger than the steering stem, and make sure that it bears only on the inner rim of the race and does not contact the working surface **(see illustration)** – heating the race and cooling the steering stem will make installation easier, or use an hydraulic press if necessary.

8 Install the steering stem (see Section 9).

11 Rear shock absorber

Warning: Do not attempt to disassemble the shock absorber in the home workshop. It is nitrogen-charged under high pressure. Improper disassembly could result in serious injury.

Removal

1 Support the bike on the centrestand. Tie the front brake lever to the handlebar to ensure the bike can't roll forward.
2 Remove the seats and side covers (see Chapter 7).
3 Remove the rear wheel (see Chapter 6).
4 On AS models displace the YCC-S shift actuator (see Chapter 2, Section 19).
5 On 2006-on models disconnect the regulator/rectifier wiring connectors **(see illustration)**. On all models undo the remote pre-load adjuster nuts and displace the adjuster **(see illustration)**.
6 Where fitted undo the brake hose guide bolt on the right-hand side and slide the guide down the hose **(see illustration)**.

7 Unscrew the nut, remove the washer and withdraw the bolt securing the linkage rods to the swingarm and move the rods down **(see illustration)**.
8 Unscrew the nut, remove the washer and withdraw the bolt securing the bottom of the shock absorber and move the linkage arm down **(see illustration)**.
9 Unscrew the nut on the bolt securing the top of the shock absorber **(see illustration)**. Support the shock and withdraw the bolt, noting the spacer, then remove the shock absorber, feeding the adjuster down and noting the routing of the cables **(see illustrations)**.

Inspection

10 Check the shock absorber for obvious physical damage and oil leakage, and the spring for looseness, cracks or signs of fatigue.

11.6 Unscrew the bolt (arrowed) and move the guide down

11.7 Detach the linkage rods from the swingarm

11.8 Detach the linkage arm from the shock absorber

11.9a Unscrew the top bolt nut...

11.9b ...withdraw the bolt with its spacer...

11.9c ...and remove the shock absorber

5•18 Frame and suspension

11.11 Check the bush (arrowed)

11.12 Check the adjuster cables and lever

11 Check the bush in the top of the shock absorber for wear or damage (see illustration).
12 Check the adjuster cables for damage (see illustration). Make sure the adjuster lever moves smoothly.
13 With the exception of the adjuster and its cables (that come as an assembly), parts are not available for the shock absorber itself. If it is worn or damaged, it must be replaced with a new one. Before disposing of an old shock absorber, you should release the nitrogen gas from the top. To do this, make a drill point 15 to 20 mm below the bottom of the top mount using a centre punch. Mount the shock in a vice. Drill a hole using a sharp 2 or 3 mm drill bit to release the gas – it is best to cover the shock and drill and avert your face to prevent the possibility of injury, making sure the material used does not get caught in the chuck as it spins.

⚠ *Warning: Wear protective eyewear and be very careful when releasing the gas pressure – it is possible for fine debris particles to be released with it, and as the pressure is high these could damage your eyes if done carelessly.*

Installation

14 Installation is the reverse of removal, noting the following:
- Apply the recommended grease (see Chapter 1) to the shock absorber pivot points.
- Fit the shock absorber with the remote pre-load adjuster cables facing the right-hand side of the bike where they exit the shock.
- Tighten the nuts/bolts to the torque settings specified at the beginning of the Chapter.
- On AS models refer to Chapter 2, Section 19 for installation of the shift actuator.
- Do not forget to refit the brake hose guide on the right-hand side where removed, and to reconnect the regulator/rectifier wiring connectors on 2006-on models (see illustrations 11.6 and 11.5a).

12 Rear suspension linkage

Removal

1 Support the bike on the sidestand, then place a support (such as an axle stand or jack) on the right-hand side so that no weight is transmitted through any part of the rear suspension. Tie the front brake lever to the handlebar to ensure the bike can't roll forward.
2 Unscrew the nut, remove the washer and withdraw the bolt securing the linkage rods to the swingarm and move the rods down (see illustration 11.7).
3 Unscrew the nut and withdraw the bolt securing the bottom of the shock absorber to the linkage arm (see illustration 11.8).
4 If required remove the exhaust system (see Chapter 4) – whether you need to or not will depend primarily on whether the exhaust/centrestand bracket front bolts are inserted from the inside of the bracket or the outside, and the degree of access required. If you don't remove the system, unscrew the downpipe assembly bolt on each side (see illustration). Unscrew the centrestand bracket bolts and remove the stand assembly (see Section 4).
5 Unscrew the nut and withdraw bolt securing the linkage arm to the frame, noting the spacer, and remove the linkage assembly (see illustration).
6 Unscrew the nut, remove the washer and withdraw the bolt securing the linkage rods to the linkage arm and separate them.

Inspection

7 Withdraw the sleeves from the linkage arm and from the rod's pivot in the swingarm (see illustrations).
8 Thoroughly clean all components, removing all traces of dirt, corrosion and grease.
9 Check the linkage rods and arm closely, looking for obvious signs of wear such as heavy scoring, or for damage such as cracks or distortion. Replace worn or damaged components with new ones as required.
10 Check the condition of the grease seals and bearings. Fit the sleeves back in and check for play between them and the bearings. Refer to *Tools and Workshop Tips* in the Reference

12.4 Exhaust downpipe bolts (A), exhaust/centrestand bracket nuts/bolts (B)

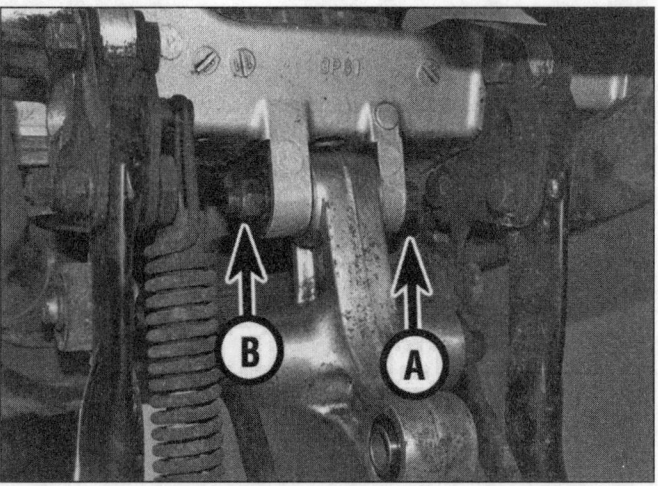

12.5 Linkage arm-to-frame bolt (A) and nut (B)

Frame and suspension 5•19

12.7a Withdraw the sleeves from the linkage arm...

12.7b ...and swingarm (shown removed and upside down)

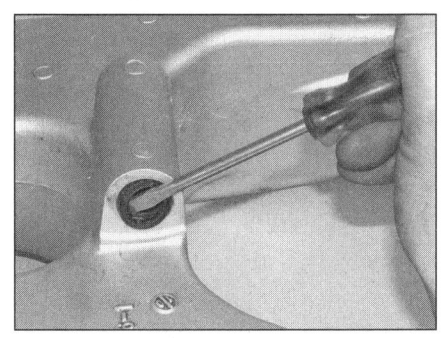

12.11 If necessary lever the seals out using a screwdriver

section for more information on bearings. Inspect all components closely, looking for obvious signs of wear such as heavy scoring, or for damage such as cracks or distortion. Replace worn or damaged components with new ones as required.

11 If required lever out the grease seals using a seal hook or screwdriver **(see illustration)**. Discard them – new ones must be used.

12 Worn bearings can be driven or drawn out of their bores, but note that removal will destroy them; new bearings should be obtained before work commences. The new bearings should be packed with lithium-based multi purpose grease, then pressed or drawn into their bores rather than driven into position. In the absence of a press, a suitable drawbolt tool can be made up as described in *Tools and Workshop Tips* in the Reference section. When fitting the new bearings into the front and rear pivots in the linkage arm, make sure they are central in their bores (i.e. the depth of the recess for the grease seal is the same on each side). When fitting the new bearings into the middle pivot press them in until they seat. When fitting the new bearings into the swingarm press them in until the depth of the recess for the grease seal is 4 mm on each side.

13 Lubricate the needle bearings, sleeves and seals with a lithium-based multi-purpose grease.

14 Fit the new seals squarely into place with the marked flat side facing out **(see illustration)**. Fit the sleeves **(see illustrations 12.7a and b)**.

Installation

15 Installation is the reverse of removal, noting the following:
● Make sure the 5JW mark on the linkage arm faces to the left-hand side.
● Tighten the suspension linkage bolt nuts to the torque settings specified at the beginning of the Chapter.

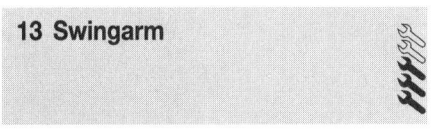

13 Swingarm

Removal

1 Support the bike on the centrestand. Tie the front brake lever to the handlebar to ensure the bike can't roll forward.
2 Remove the silencers (see Chapter 4).

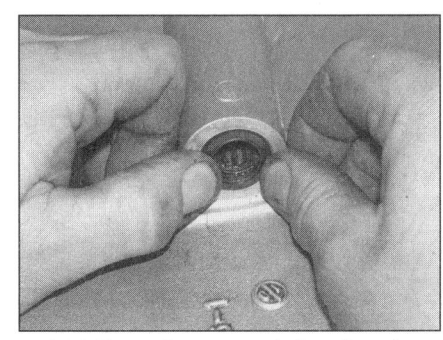

12.14 Press the new seals in using your fingers, or lay a piece of wood across and tap them in

3 Remove the rear wheel (see Chapter 6).
4 Remove the final drive housing and driveshaft, and the universal joint (see Chapter 6).
5 Remove the rear shock absorber (Section 11).
6 Unscrew the right-hand footrest bracket bolts **(see illustration)**.
7 Undo the brake hose guide bolts **(see illustration)**. Tie the brake caliper assembly up out of the way.

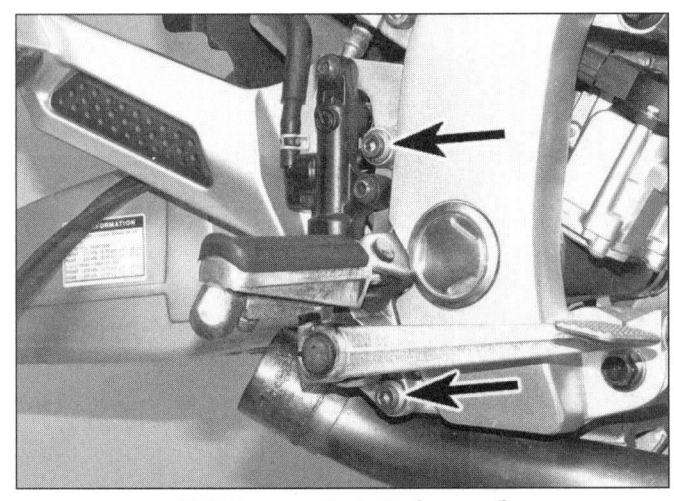

13.6 Unscrew the bolts (arrowed)

13.7 Hose guide bolts (arrowed)

5•20 Frame and suspension

13.8a Remove the pivot cap

13.8b Unscrew the nut and remove the washer

13.9a Unscrew the bolt (arrowed) and remove the plate (AS model type shown)

13.9b Unscrew the locknut (arrowed)

13.10a Use a large hex bit to unscrew the pivot bolt

13.10b Withdraw the bolt and remove the swingarm

Frame and suspension 5•21

13.11a Remove the collar...

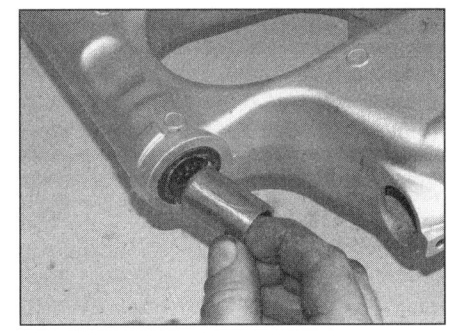

13.11b ...and the sleeve

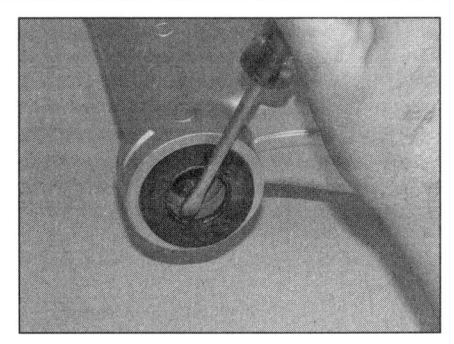

13.15 Lever the seals out

8 Remove the swingarm pivot cap from the right-hand side **(see illustration)**. Unscrew the pivot bolt nut and remove the washer **(see illustration)**.
9 Remove the locking plate from the left-hand side **(see illustration)**. Unscrew the swingarm pivot locknut **(see illustration)**.
10 Unscrew the pivot bolt using a large hex bit **(see illustration)**. Withdraw the bolt and manoeuvre the swingarm back out of the frame, holding the right-hand footrest assembly out of the way **(see illustration)**.

Inspection

11 Remove the collar from the right-hand side and the sleeve from the left **(see illustrations)**.
12 Thoroughly clean all pivot components, removing all traces of dirt, corrosion and old grease.
13 Check the swingarm closely, looking for obvious signs of wear such as heavy scoring, or for damage such as cracks or distortion.
14 Check the condition of the grease seals and bearings – there is a ball bearing in the right-hand side of the arm and a needle bearing in the left. Check the ball bearing runs smoothly. Fit the sleeve back in the needle bearing and check for play between them. Refer to *Tools and Workshop Tips* in the Reference section for more information on bearings. Inspect all components closely, looking for obvious signs of wear such as heavy scoring, or for damage such as cracks

or distortion. Replace worn or damaged components with new ones as required.
15 If required lever out the grease seals using a seal hook or screwdriver **(see illustration)**. Discard them – new ones must be used.
16 Worn bearings can be pulled out of their bores using an expanding internal puller with slide-hammer attachment, but note that removal will damage them. Remove the circlip from the right-hand side before removing the ball bearing, and heat around the bearing housing with a hot air gun to ease removal **(see illustration)**. Remove the inner sleeve that sits between the bearings, and clean it. Fit the new needle bearing first, pack it with lithium-based multi purpose grease, and press or draw it in – do not drive it in. In the absence of a press, a suitable drawbolt tool can be made up as described in *Tools and Workshop Tips* in the Reference section. Fit the inner sleeve. Fit the new ball bearing into the right-hand side with the marked side facing, and use a bearing driver or socket that seats on the outer race to drive it in until it seats – freezing the bearing and heating the housing will ease installation. Secure it with a new circlip. When fitting the needle bearing into the left-hand side make sure the marked side faces out and the set depth of the outer end below the rim of the bore is 7 mm.
17 Lubricate the new seals with a smear of grease. Fit them squarely into place, with the marked flat side facing out **(see illustration)**.
18 Lubricate the collar and sleeve with grease. Fit the collar into the right-hand

side and the sleeve into the left **(see illustrations 13.11a and b)**.
19 Refer to Chapter 6 to check the driveshaft, final drive housing and universal joint.

Installation

20 Clean the swingarm pivot bolt and smear it with grease, including the threads.
21 Offer up the swingarm and slide the pivot bolt through from the left-hand side **(see illustration 13.10b)**. Tighten it to the torque setting specified at the beginning of the Chapter for your model **(see illustration 13.10a)**. Fit the locknut and tighten to the specified torque **(see illustration 13.9b)**. Fit the locking plate **(see illustration 13.9a)**.
22 Fit the washer and nut onto the pivot bolt and tighten the nut to the torque setting specified at the beginning of the Chapter **(see illustration 13.8b)**. Check the swingarm moves up and down smoothly and freely. Fit the pivot cap **(see illustration 13.8a)**.
23 Fit the brake hose guides **(see illustration 13.7)**. Clean the threads of the footrest bracket bolts and apply some fresh threadlock, and tighten them to the specified torque **(see illustration 13.6)**.
24 Install the remaining components in reverse order. Check the operation of the rear suspension and brake before taking the bike on the road.

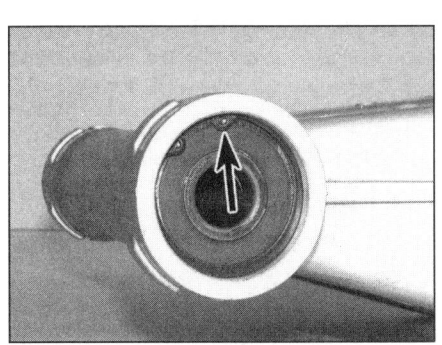

14 Suspension adjustment

13.16 Ball bearing is secured by a circlip (arrowed)

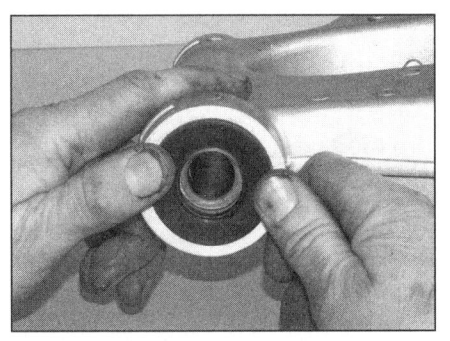

13.17 Press the new seals in using your fingers, or lay a piece of wood across and tap them in

Front forks

2001 to 2012 models

1 The forks have adjustable spring pre-load, rebound damping and compression damping.
2 Pre-load is adjusted by turning the adjuster in the fork top bolt **(see illustration)**. There are 6 settings, identified by lines on the adjuster. To increase the pre-load, turn the adjuster clockwise. To decrease the pre-load, turn the adjuster anti-clockwise. The standard position is with the third line from the top level with the top bolt hex on 2001 to 2005 models, and the fourth line from the top on 2006 to 2012 models.

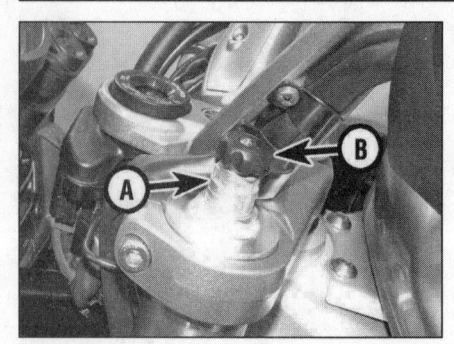

5•22 Frame and suspension

14.2 Spring pre-load adjuster (A) and rebound damping adjuster (B) – 2001 to 2012

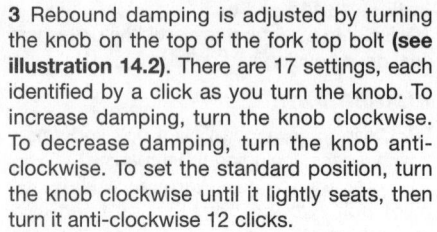

14.4 Compression damping adjuster (arrowed)

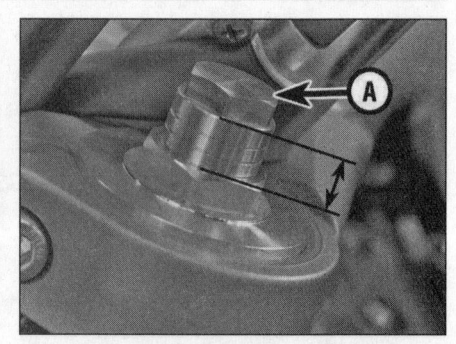

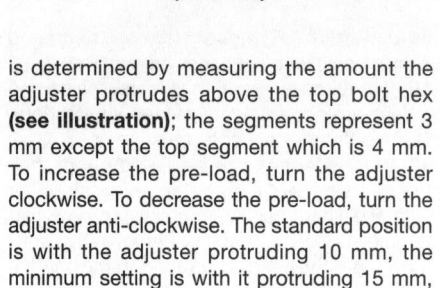

14.6 Spring pre-load adjuster (A) showing standard setting on left-hand fork – 2013-on

3 Rebound damping is adjusted by turning the knob on the top of the fork top bolt **(see illustration 14.2)**. There are 17 settings, each identified by a click as you turn the knob. To increase damping, turn the knob clockwise. To decrease damping, turn the knob anti-clockwise. To set the standard position, turn the knob clockwise until it lightly seats, then turn it anti-clockwise 12 clicks.

4 Compression damping is adjusted by turning the screw in the base of the fork **(see illustration)**. There are 21 settings, each identified by a click as you turn the screw. To increase damping, turn the screw clockwise. To decrease damping, turn the screw anti-clockwise. To set the standard position, turn the screw clockwise until it lightly seats, then turn it anti-clockwise 12 clicks.

2013-on models

5 The forks have adjustable spring pre-load in each fork, and adjustable rebound damping and compression damping in the right-hand fork.

6 Pre-load is adjusted by turning the adjuster in the fork top bolt. The amount of pre-load is determined by measuring the amount the adjuster protrudes above the top bolt hex **(see illustration)**; the segments represent 3 mm except the top segment which is 4 mm. To increase the pre-load, turn the adjuster clockwise. To decrease the pre-load, turn the adjuster anti-clockwise. The standard position is with the adjuster protruding 10 mm, the minimum setting is with it protruding 15 mm, and the maximum is with zero protrusion.

7 Rebound damping is adjusted by turning the knob on the top of the right-hand fork top bolt **(see illustration)**. There are 16 settings, each identified by a click as you turn the knob. To increase damping, turn the knob clockwise. To decrease damping, turn the knob anti-clockwise. To set the standard position, turn the knob clockwise until it lightly seats, then turn it anti-clockwise 12 clicks.

8 Compression damping is adjusted by turning the screw in the base of the right-hand fork **(see illustration 14.4)**. There are 21 settings, each identified by a click as you turn the screw. To increase damping, turn the screw clockwise. To decrease damping, turn the screw anti-clockwise. To set the standard position, turn the screw clockwise until it lightly seats, then turn it anti-clockwise 11 clicks.

Rear shock absorber

9 The shock absorber has adjustable spring pre-load and rebound damping.

10 Pre-load is adjusted by moving the lever on the left-hand side of the bike **(see illustration)**. Moving the lever towards the front of the bike increases pre-load, and moving it to the rear decreases it.

11 Rebound damping is adjusted by turning the knob on the bottom of the shock absorber **(see illustration)**. There are 18 settings, each identified by a click as you turn the knob. To increase damping, turn the knob anti-clockwise. To decrease damping, turn the knob clockwise. To set the standard position, turn the knob anti-clockwise until it lightly seats, then turn it clockwise 10 clicks on 2001 to 2005 models, and 12 clicks on all other models – the maximum setting is 3 clicks clockwise from its seat, and the minimum is 20 clicks clockwise.

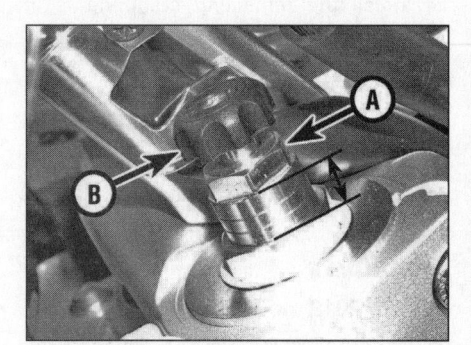

14.7 Spring pre-load adjuster (A) showing standard setting, and damping adjuster (B) on right-hand fork – 2013-on

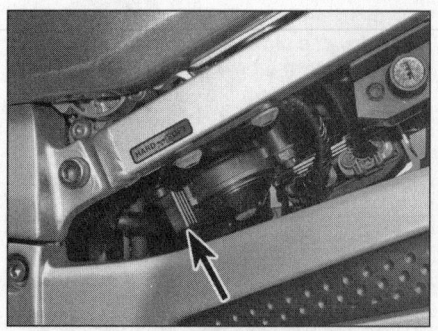

14.10 Spring pre-load adjuster lever (arrowed)

14.11 Rebound damping adjuster (arrowed)

Chapter 6
Brakes, wheels and final drive

Contents

	Section number		Section number
ABS components	14	Front wheel	17
ABS fault diagnosis	13	General information	1
ABS operation	12	Rear brake caliper	7
Brake fluid level check	see *Pre-ride checks*	Rear brake disc	8
Brake hoses and fittings	10	Rear brake master cylinder	9
Brake light switches	see Chapter 8	Rear brake pads	6
Brake pad wear check	see Chapter 1	Rear wheel	18
Brake system bleeding and fluid change	11	Rear wheel drive coupling	22
Brake system check	see Chapter 1	Tyre pressure, tread depth and condition	see *Pre-ride checks*
Final drive housing, driveshaft and universal joint	21	Tyres	20
Final drive gear oil change	see Chapter 1	Wheel alignment check	16
Final drive gear oil level check	see Chapter 1	Wheel bearing check	see Chapter 1
Front brake calipers	3	Wheel bearings	19
Front brake discs	4	Wheel check	see Chapter 1
Front brake master cylinder	5	Wheel inspection and repair	15
Front brake pads	2		

Degrees of difficulty

Easy, suitable for novice with little experience	**Fairly easy,** suitable for beginner with some experience	**Fairly difficult,** suitable for competent DIY mechanic	**Difficult,** suitable for experienced DIY mechanic	**Very difficult,** suitable for expert DIY or professional

Specifications

Brake fluid
Brake fluid type .... DOT 4

Front brake pads
Friction material thickness
  New .... 5.5 mm
  Service limit .... 0.5 mm

Rear brake pads
Friction material thickness
  New .... 6.3 mm
  Service limit .... 0.8 mm

Front brake discs
Diameter
  2001 and 2002 models .... 298 mm
  2003-on models .... 320 mm
Thickness
  2001 and 2002 models
    Standard .... 5.0 mm
    Service limit .... 4.5 mm
  2003-on models
    Standard .... 4.5 mm
    Service limit .... 4.0 mm
Maximum runout .... 0.1 mm

Rear brake disc
Diameter .... 282 mm
Thickness
  2001 to 2005 models
    Standard .... 6.0 mm
    Service limit .... 5.5 mm
  2006-on models
    Standard .... 5.0 mm
    Service limit .... 4.5 mm
Maximum runout .... 0.15 mm

Master cylinders
Bore diameter
  Front
    2001 and 2002 models .... 14 mm
    2003 to 2005 non-ABS models .... 15 mm
    2003 to 2005 ABS models .... 16 mm
    2006-on models .... 15 mm
  Rear
    2001 to 2005 models .... 14 mm
    2006-on models .... 15 mm

Wheels
Maximum wheel runout (front and rear)
  Axial (side-to-side) .... 0.5 mm
  Radial (out-of-round) .... 1.0 mm

Tyres
Tyre pressures .... see *Pre-ride* checks
Tyres
  Front 120/70-ZR17M/C (58W)
  Rear 180/55-ZR17M/C (73W)
*Refer to the owners handbook or the tyre information label on the swingarm for approved tyre brands.

Final drive
Final drive oil .... see Chapter 1

Torque settings
Brake caliper bleed valves .... 6 Nm
Brake disc bolts (front and rear) .... 18 Nm
Brake hose banjo bolts .... 30 Nm
Brake pipe gland nuts (ABS models) .... 16 Nm
Brake torque arm bolt nuts .... 30 Nm
Final drive housing nuts .... 42 Nm
Footrest bracket bolts (left-hand side)
  Lower (sidestand) bolts .... 65 Nm
  Upper (M8) bolts .... 28 Nm
  Front (M10) bolt .... 49 Nm
Front axle (2001 to 2005 models) .... 72 Nm
Front axle bolt (2006-on models) .... 91 Nm
Front axle clamp bolt(s)
  2001 to 2005 models .... 23 Nm
  2006-on models .... 21 Nm
Front brake caliper mounting bolts .... 40 Nm
Front brake master cylinder clamp bolts .... 10 Nm
Front brake pad retaining pins (2006-on models) .. 17 Nm
Front wheel sensor rotor screws .... 8 Nm
Rear axle clamp bolt
  2001 to 2005 models .... 16 Nm
  2006-on models .... 23 Nm
Rear axle nut .... 125 Nm
Rear brake caliper mounting bolts
  2001 models .... 26 Nm
  2002-on models .... 27 Nm
Rear brake master cylinder mounting bolts .... 18 Nm
Rear wheel ball bearing retainer (2008-on models) .. 80 Nm
Rear wheel drive coupling retainer screws .... 5 Nm
Rear wheel sensor rotor screws .... 8 Nm

Brakes, wheels and final drive 6•3

1 General information

All models covered in this manual are fitted with cast alloy wheels designed for tubeless tyres only. Both front and rear brakes are hydraulically operated disc brakes.

The hydraulic braking system has two twin-opposed piston calipers at the front, and a single piston sliding caliper at the rear.

An ABS system is fitted on A models from 2003 to 2005 and on all models as standard from 2006. Linked brakes are also a feature from 2006 onwards – when the front brake lever is applied the system actuates both pairs of pistons in the left-hand front caliper but only one pair in the right-hand front caliper. When the rear brake pedal is applied the system actuates the rear caliper and the other pair of pistons in the right-hand caliper via a proportional control valve and a metering valve.

Caution: *Disc brake components rarely require disassembly. Do not disassemble components unless absolutely necessary. If an hydraulic brake hose is loosened or disconnected, the banjo union sealing washers must be replaced with new ones and the system must be bled upon reassembly. Do not use solvents on internal brake components. Solvents will cause the seals to swell and distort. Use only clean DOT 4 brake fluid for cleaning. Use care when working with brake fluid as it can injure your eyes and it will damage painted surfaces and plastic parts.*

2 Front brake pads

Caution: *Do not operate the brakes while a caliper is off the disc.*

1 Displace the brake hose holder from the fork **(see illustration)**. Lay some rag over the mudguard to prevent the loose guides scratching it.

2 On 2001 to 2005 models, unscrew the caliper mounting bolts and slide the caliper off the disc **(see illustration)**. Remove the R-clip from each end of the pad pin, then withdraw the pin and remove the pad spring and the pads **(see illustration)**. Check the clips for corrosion and distortion and replace them with new ones if necessary.

3 On 2006 models onward, slacken the pad retaining pins **(see illustration)**. Unscrew the caliper mounting bolts and slide the caliper assembly off the disc. Unscrew and remove the pad pin for one pair of pads, then remove the pad spring and the pads **(see illustrations)**. Repeat for the other pair of pads.

4 On 2001 to 2005 models, if required remove the shim from the back of each pad, noting how it fits – note that new pads should come with new shims where applicable, but make sure they do, especially if fitting after-market pads, before discarding the old ones.

2.1 Brake hose holder bolt (arrowed)

5 Inspect the surface of each pad for contamination and check that the friction material has not worn to or beyond its service limit (see Chapter 1, Section 1). If any pad is worn, fouled with oil or grease, or heavily scored or damaged, fit a complete set of new pads. Also check that wear is even across each pad on 2001 to 2005 models, on each pad in the left-hand caliper on 2006-on models, and on each opposed pad in the right-hand caliper (you can expect a wear rate difference between each pair of pads in this caliper due to the linked braking system). Uneven wear is indicative of a sticking or seized piston (see Steps 7 and 8). **Note:** *It is not possible to degrease the friction material; if the pads are contaminated in any way they must be replaced with new ones.*

6 If the pads are in good condition clean them carefully, using a fine wire brush that is completely

2.2a Caliper mounting bolts (arrowed)

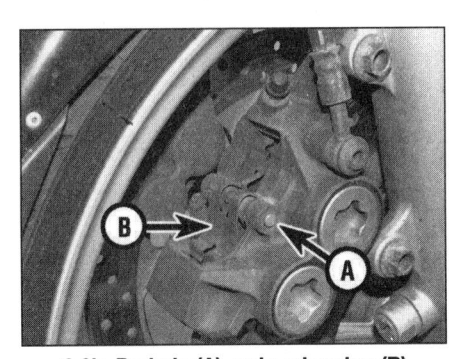

2.2b Pad pin (A) and pad spring (B)

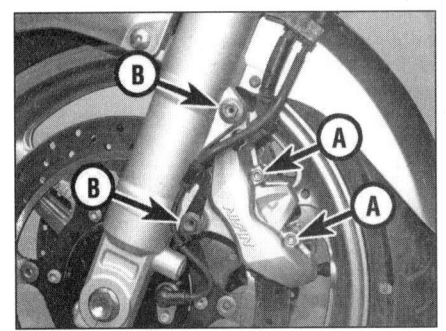

2.3a Pad pins (A), caliper mounting bolts (B)

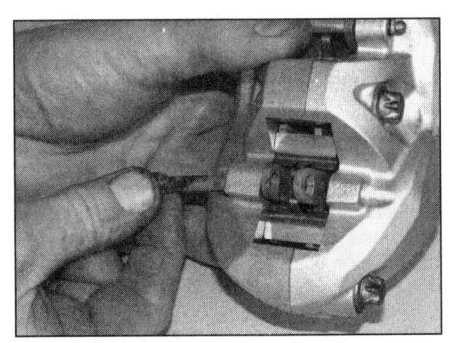

2.3b Remove the pin...

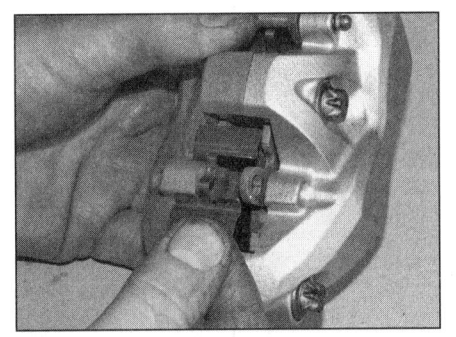

2.3c ...the spring...

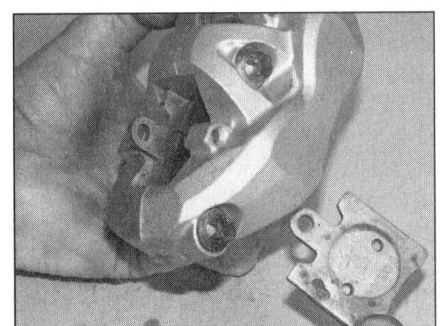

2.3d ...and the pads

6•4 Brakes, wheels and final drive

2.7 Press the pistons in using one of the methods described

2.14 Slide the caliper onto the disc and fit the bolts

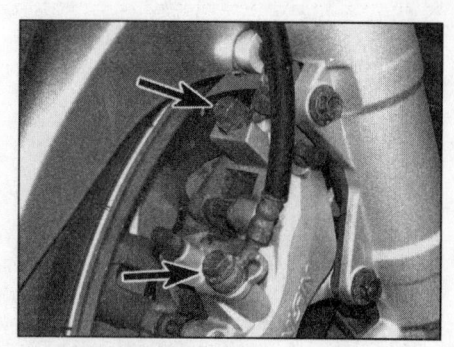

3.2a Brake hose banjo bolts (arrowed) – RH caliper on 2006-on models

3.2b Seal the banjo using a nut and bolt and the sealing washers

free of oil and grease to remove all traces of road dirt and corrosion. Using a pointed instrument, dig out any embedded particles of foreign matter. Spray with a dedicated brake cleaner.

7 Clean around the exposed section of each piston to remove any dirt or debris that could cause the seals to be damaged. If new pads are being fitted check the fluid level in the reservoir before pushing the pistons in to create room for them (see *Pre-ride checks*) – if the fluid level is not near the LOWER level line it may be necessary to remove the master cylinder reservoir cover, plate and diaphragm and remove some fluid. To push the pistons back use finger pressure or a piece of wood or metal as leverage, or place the old pads back in the caliper and use a metal bar or a screwdriver inserted between them (but take care not to damage the friction surface if the pads are being re-used), or use grips or a G-clamp and a piece of wood, with rag or card to protect the caliper body **(see illustration)**. Alternatively obtain a proper piston-pushing tool from a good tool supplier **(see illustration 6.6)**. If new pads are being fitted push the pistons all the way back into the caliper; if the old pads are still serviceable push the pistons in a little way. If the pistons are difficult to push back, remove the bleed valve cap, then attach a length of clear hose to the bleed valve and place the open end in a suitable container, then open the valve and try again (see Section 11). Take great care not to draw any air into the system. If in doubt, bleed the brakes afterwards.

8 If a piston appears seized, first block or hold the other piston(s) using wood or cable-ties, then apply the brake lever, or on 2006-on models the brake pedal, and check whether the piston in question moves at all. If it moves out but can't be pushed back in the chances are there is some hidden corrosion stopping it. If it doesn't move at all, or to fully clean and inspect the pistons, disassemble the caliper and overhaul it (see Section 3).

9 Remove all traces of corrosion from the pad pin(s) and check for wear and damage. On 2006-on models check the condition of the stopper ring on each pin and replace it with a new one if it is damaged or deformed.

10 Check the condition of the brake disc (see Section 4).

11 On 2001 to 2005 models, if removed fit the shim onto the back of each pad, making sure it locates correctly. Clean the outer face of each shim so it is shiny.

12 On pads without shims lightly smear the back of the pad backing material with copper-based grease, making sure that none gets on the friction material. Also smear the pad pin, but not the stopper ring where fitted.

13 On 2001 to 2005 models fit the pads into the caliper so the friction material on each pad faces the other. Fit the pad spring with the arrow pointing in the direction of forward rotation, then insert the pad pin and fit the R-clip into the hole **(see illustration 2.2b)**. Slide the caliper onto the disc making sure the pads locate correctly on each side. Fit the caliper mounting bolts and tighten them to the torque setting specified at the beginning of the Chapter.

14 On 2006-on models fit one pair of pads into the caliper so the friction material on each pad faces the other **(see illustration 2.3d)**. Fit the pad spring, then insert the pad pin and tighten it finger-tight **(see illustrations 2.3c and b)**. Repeat for the other pair of pads. Slide the caliper onto the disc making sure the pads locate correctly on each side **(see illustration)**. Fit the caliper mounting bolts and tighten them to the torque setting specified at the beginning of the Chapter. Tighten the pad pins to the specified torque setting **(see illustration 2.3a)**.

15 Fit the brake hose holder onto the fork **(see illustration 2.1)**.

16 Operate the brake lever until the pads contact the discs. On 2006-on models also operate the brake pedal until the lower pads in the right-hand caliper contact the disc. Check the level of fluid in each reservoir and top-up if necessary (see *Pre-ride checks*).

17 Check the operation of the brakes before riding the motorcycle.

3 Front brake calipers

Warning: Overhaul of the brake calipers must be done in a spotlessly clean work area to avoid contamination and possible failure of the brake hydraulic system components. Do not, under any circumstances, use petroleum-based solvents to clean brake parts. Use clean DOT 4 brake fluid, dedicated brake cleaner or denatured alcohol only, as described. To prevent damage from spilled brake fluid, always cover paintwork when working on the braking system, and have plenty of absorbent rag to hand to catch and wipe off any spilled fluid.

Removal

Note: *If the caliper is being overhauled (usually due to sticking pistons or fluid leaks) read through the entire procedure first and make sure that you have obtained all the new parts required, including some new DOT 4 brake fluid.*

Caution: *Do not operate the brakes while a caliper is off the disc.*

1 If you just want to displace the calipers for front wheel or fork removal, displace the brake hose holders from the forks **(see illustration 2.1)**. Lay some rag over the mudguard to prevent the loose guides scratching it. Unscrew the caliper mounting bolts and slide the caliper assembly off the disc **(see illustration 2.2a or 2.3a)**. Tie the front brake calipers and hoses back so that they are out of the way.

2 If the caliper is being completely removed or overhauled, stuff some rag around the brake hose banjo union. Note the alignment of the brake hose(s) **(see illustration)**. Unscrew the hose banjo bolt(s) and detach the union(s), catching the brake fluid. Seal the union(s) – one way of doing this is to fit a suitable bolt and nut with the old sealing washers **(see illustration)**. Note that new sealing washers will be required later.

Brakes, wheels and final drive 6•5

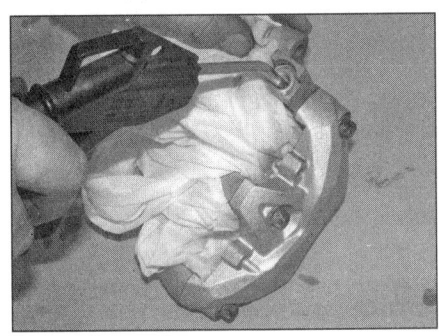

3.6a Use rag to protect the pistons and caliper then apply compressed air...

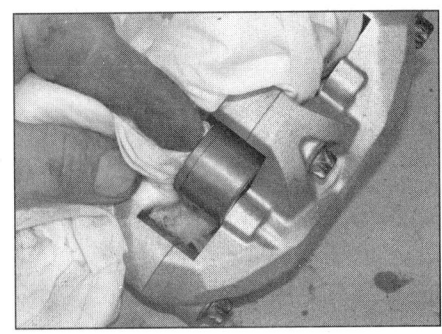

3.6b ...to force the pistons out

3.7 Removing a piston using circlip pliers

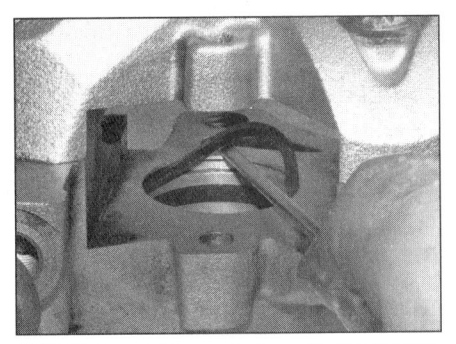

3.10 Remove the seals from their grooves

3.13a Lubricate the new piston seals with brake fluid...

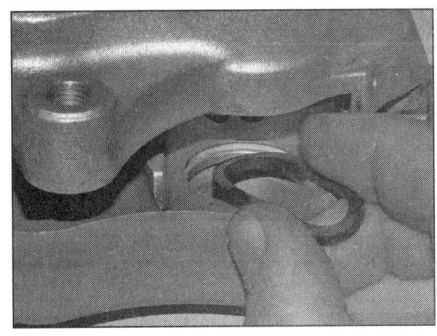

3.13b ...then fit them into their grooves

3 If the caliper is being overhauled, follow the procedure for your model in Section 2 and remove the brake pads – this involves removing the caliper from the disc.

Overhaul

4 Clean the exterior of the caliper with denatured alcohol or brake system cleaner. Have some clean rag ready to catch any spilled brake fluid.

5 To remove the pistons you need either a supply of compressed air, or a piston removal tool, or if neither are available a good pair of external circlip removal pliers.

6 If you use compressed air wedge some rag or a piece of wood between the pistons, then gradually and progressively apply the compressed air, starting with a fairly low pressure, to the fluid passage and allow the pistons to ease out of their bores **(see illustrations)**. Make sure the pistons are displaced evenly, using a piece of wood to block one while another moves if necessary.

7 If you are using a dedicated tool or the circlip pliers, grip the inner wall then twist and pull the piston out, keeping it square to the bore wall **(see illustration)**. Do not try to remove a piston by levering it out or by using pliers or other grips that may scratch the outer wall, unless you are prepared to fit a new piston, and possibly a new caliper.

8 If a piston is stuck in its bore due to corrosion the caliper should be replaced with a new one.

9 Mark each piston and the caliper body to ensure that the pistons can be matched to their original bores on reassembly.

10 Remove the dust seals and the piston seals from the bores using a plastic tool to avoid scratching the bores **(see illustration)**. Discard the seals – new ones must be fitted on reassembly.

11 Clean the pistons and bores with clean brake fluid. If compressed air is available, blow it through the fluid passages to ensure they are clear (make sure it is filtered and unlubricated).

Caution: Do not, under any circumstances, use a petroleum-based solvent to clean brake parts.

12 Inspect the caliper bores and pistons for signs of corrosion, nicks and burrs and loss of plating. If surface defects are present, the pistons and/or the caliper assembly must be replaced with new ones.

13 Lubricate the new piston seals with clean brake fluid and fit them into the inner grooves in the caliper bores **(see illustrations)**. On 2006-on models note that there are two sizes of bore in the right-hand caliper and care must therefore be taken to ensure that the correct size seals are fitted to the correct bores. The same applies when fitting the new dust seals and pistons.

14 Lubricate the new dust seals with silicone grease and fit them into the outer grooves in the caliper bores **(see illustration)**.

15 Lubricate the pistons with clean brake fluid and fit them, closed-end first, into the caliper bores, taking care not to displace the seals **(see illustration)**. Using your thumbs, push the pistons all the way in, making sure they enter the bore square.

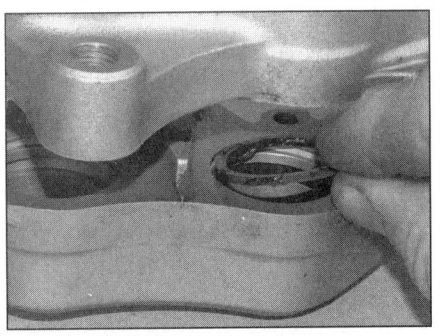

3.14 Lubricate the new dust seals with silicone grease then fit them into their grooves

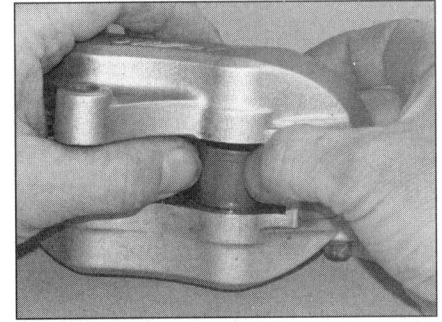

3.15 Fit the pistons and push them all the way in

6•6 Brakes, wheels and final drive

Installation

16 If the caliper was overhauled refer to Section 2 and if not already done clean and check the pads, pad pin(s), and spring(s). Fit the brake pads into the caliper and the caliper onto the disc.

17 If the caliper was just displaced slide it onto the disc making sure the pads locate correctly on each side (see illustration 2.14). Fit the caliper mounting bolts and tighten them to the torque setting specified at the beginning of the Chapter.

18 If detached, connect the brake hose(s) to the caliper, using new sealing washers on each side of the banjo union(s), and align it/them as noted on removal (see illustration). Tighten the banjo bolts to the specified torque setting.

19 Fit the brake hose holder onto the fork (see illustration 2.1).

20 Refer to Section 11 and bleed the system.

21 Operate the brake lever until the pads contact the discs. On 2006-on models also operate the brake pedal until the lower pads in the right-hand caliper contact the disc. Check the level of fluid in each reservoir and top-up if necessary (see *Pre-ride checks*).

22 Check that there are no fluid leaks and test the operation of the brakes before riding the motorcycle.

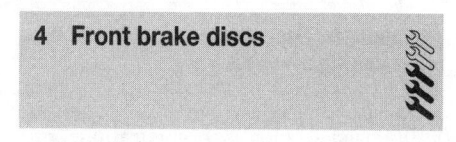

4 Front brake discs

Inspection

1 Inspect the surface of the disc for score marks and other damage. Light scratches are normal after use and won't affect brake operation, but deep grooves and heavy score marks will reduce braking efficiency and accelerate pad wear. If a disc is badly grooved it must be replaced with a new one.

2 The disc must not be allowed to wear down to a thickness less than the service limit listed in this Chapter's Specifications. The minimum thickness is also stamped on the disc. Check the thickness of the disc in the middle of the pad contact area using a micrometer (see illustration) – do not measure across the rim of the disc with a ruler. Replace the disc with a new one if necessary.

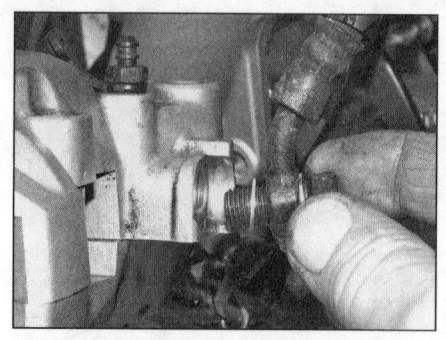

3 To check if the disc is warped, position the bike on the centrestand and support it so the front wheel is off the ground. Mount a dial gauge to the fork leg, with the gauge plunger touching the surface of the disc about 1.5 mm from its outer edge (see illustration). Rotate the wheel and watch the gauge needle, comparing the reading with the limit listed in the Specifications at the beginning of this Chapter. If the runout is greater than the maximum limit, check the wheel bearings for play (see Chapter 1). If the bearings are worn, install new ones (see Section 19) and repeat this check. If the disc runout is still excessive, remove the disc and check for corrosion where it seats on the hub and clean it up if necessary. You can also try moving the disc around the wheel one bolt hole at a time and after each movement rechecking for runout. In most cases a new disc will have to be fitted.

Removal

4 Remove the wheel (see Section 17).

Caution: *Don't lay the wheel down and allow it to rest on either disc – the disc could become warped. Set the wheel on wood blocks so the wheel rim supports the weight of the wheel.*

5 If you are not replacing the disc with a new one, mark the relationship of the disc to the wheel, so it can be installed in the same position and on the same side as originally fitted. Unscrew the disc bolts, loosening them evenly and a little at a time in a criss-cross pattern to avoid distorting the disc, then remove the disc (see illustration).

Installation

6 Before fitting the disc, make sure there is no dirt or corrosion where the disc seats on the hub. If the disc does not sit flat when it is bolted down, it will appear to be warped when checked or when the front brake is used.

7 Fit the disc on the wheel with its marked side facing out, aligning the previously applied matchmarks (if you're reinstalling the original disc), and making sure the arrow points in the direction of normal rotation.

8 Clean the threads of the bolts and apply fresh thread locking compound, and tighten them evenly and a little at a time in a criss-cross pattern to the torque setting specified at the beginning of this Chapter. Clean the disc using acetone or brake system cleaner. If a new disc has been installed, remove any protective coating from its working surfaces and fit new brake pads.

9 Install the front wheel (see Section 17).

10 Operate the brake lever until the pads contact the discs. On 2006-on models also operate the brake pedal until the lower pads in the right-hand caliper contact the disc. Check the level of fluid in each reservoir and top-up if necessary (see *Pre-ride checks*).

11 Check the operation of the brakes before riding the motorcycle.

5 Front brake master cylinder

⚠ **Warning:** *Overhaul must be done in a spotlessly clean work area to avoid contamination and possible failure of the brake hydraulic system components. Do not, under any circumstances, use petroleum-based solvents to clean brake parts. Use clean DOT 4 brake fluid, dedicated brake cleaner or denatured alcohol only, as described. To prevent damage from spilled brake fluid, always cover paintwork when working on the braking system, and have plenty of absorbent rag to hand to catch and wipe off any spilled fluid.*

3.18 Always use new sealing washers

4.2 Check disc thickness using a micrometer

4.3 Checking disc runout with a dial gauge

4.5 Brake disc bolts (arrowed)

Brakes, wheels and final drive 6•7

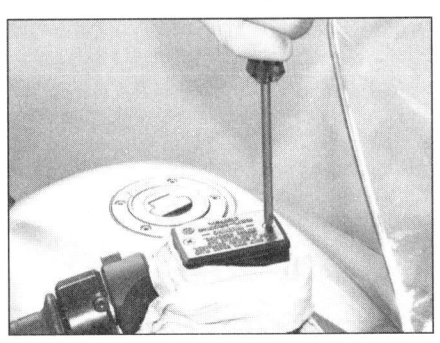

5.3 Slacken the cover screws

5.4 Brake hose banjo bolt (arrowed)

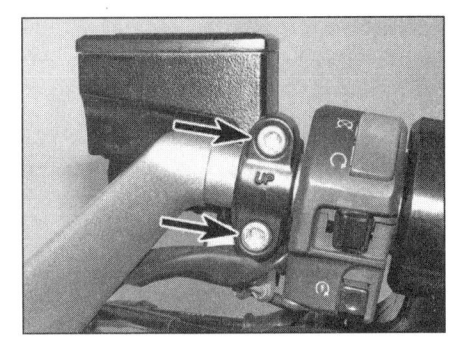

5.5 Master cylinder bolts (arrowed)

Note: *If the master cylinder is being overhauled (usually due to sticking or poor action, or fluid leaks), a rebuild kit is available that includes the boot, pushrod (ABS models), circlip, piston, seal, cup and spring. Some DOT 4 brake/clutch fluid is also required. The master cylinder can be overhauled with it still mounted on the handlebar if required (start at Step 7), and on 2003 to 2005 models with ABS and all 2006-on models there is an advantage in doing it this way as you can leave the brake hose connected, making it possible to bleed the air from the master cylinder from the top only (bleeding air through the ABS modulator requires a special tool – see Section 11).*

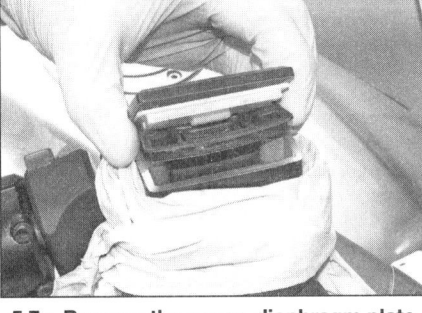

5.7a Remove the cover, diaphragm plate and diaphragm

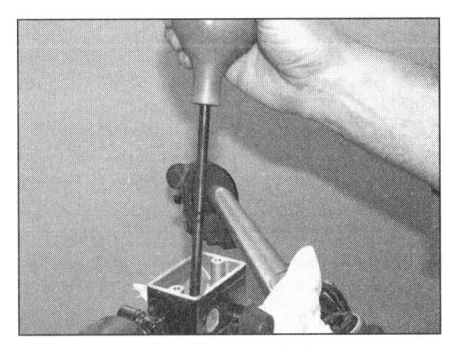

5.7b Sucking the fluid out

Removal

1 Remove the brake light switch (see Chapter 8).
2 Remove the brake lever (see Chapter 5).
3 Slacken the reservoir cover screws **(see illustration)**.
4 Stuff some rag under the master cylinder. Note the alignment of the brake hose. Unscrew the hose banjo bolt and detach the banjo union, catching the brake fluid **(see illustration)**. Seal the union – one way of doing this is to fit a suitable bolt and nut with the old sealing washers **(see illustration 3.2b)**. Note that new sealing washers will be required later.
5 Unscrew the master cylinder clamp bolts and remove the back of the clamp, noting how it fits, then lift the master cylinder away from the handlebar **(see illustration)**.
6 Remove the reservoir cover, diaphragm plate and the diaphragm and tip the fluid from the master cylinder and reservoir into a suitable container. Wipe any remaining fluid out of the reservoir with a clean rag.

Overhaul

7 If you are overhauling the master cylinder in situ remove the brake lever (see Chapter 5). Displace the throttle cable housing (see Chapter 4 – you can leave the cables themselves connected), and if required for best access the switch housing (see Chapter 8 – there is no need to disconnect the wiring connector). Stuff some rag under the master cylinder. Remove the reservoir cover, diaphragm plate and the diaphragm **(see illustration)**. Remove the fluid from the reservoir into a suitable container, either by sucking it up using a tool as shown, drawing it out into a syringe, or soaking it up in some paper towel **(see illustration)**. Wipe any remaining fluid out of the reservoir with a clean rag. Refit the cover.
8 Remove the rubber boot from the master cylinder **(see illustration)**.
9 Push the piston in and use circlip pliers to remove the circlip, then slide out the piston assembly and spring, noting how they fit **(see illustrations)**.
10 Clean the master cylinder and reservoir with clean brake fluid.
Caution: Do not, under any circumstances, use a petroleum-based solvent to clean brake parts.
11 Check the master cylinder bore for corrosion, scratches, nicks and score marks. If damage or wear is evident, the master cylinder must be replaced with a new one.

5.8 Remove the boot from the end of the master cylinder piston...

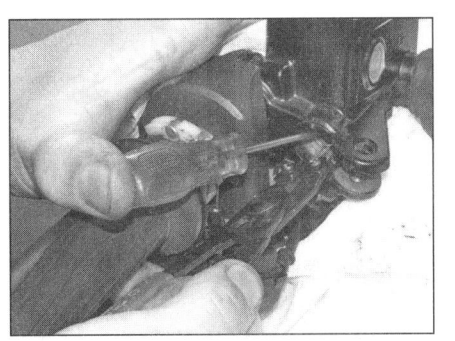

5.9a ...then depress the piston, release the circlip...

5.9b ...and draw out the piston and spring

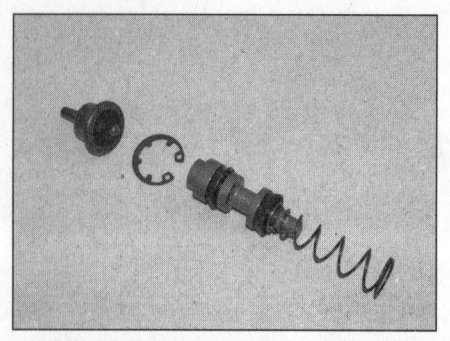

6•8 Brakes, wheels and final drive

5.12a Rebuild kit contents – AS model type shown

5.12b Make sure the cup (A) and seal (B) are correctly installed

12 The dust boot, pushrod (ABS models), circlip, piston and its cup and seal, and the spring are all included in a master cylinder rebuild kit, and all other components are available individually **(see illustrations)**. Use all of the new parts, regardless of the apparent condition of the old ones. Lubricate the master cylinder bore with new brake fluid.

13 On models without ABS lubricate the piston, cup, seal and master cylinder bore with clean brake fluid. If not already done fit the cup onto the spring, locating the peg in the hole. Fit the spring into the master cylinder, making sure the lips on the cup do not turn inside out. Slide the piston into the master cylinder, making sure the lips on the seal do not turn inside out. Push the piston in to compress the spring and fit the new circlip, making sure it locates in the groove **(see illustration 5.14b)**.

14 On models with ABS lubricate the piston, cup, seal and master cylinder bore with clean brake fluid. Slide the spring and piston assembly into the master cylinder **(see illustration)**. Make sure the lips on the cup and seal do not turn inside out. Push the piston in to compress the spring and fit the new circlip, making sure it locates in the groove **(see illustration)**.

15 Smear the outer end of the piston and the inside of the boot, and on ABS models the pushrod, with silicone grease **(see illustration)**. Carefully push the wide rim of the boot onto its seat in the master cylinder **(see illustrations)**. On models without ABS locate the narrow end lips in the groove in the piston.

16 Inspect the reservoir diaphragm and fit a new one if it is damaged or deteriorated.

17 If you have overhauled the master cylinder in situ fit the switch housing (if removed), throttle cable housing and brake lever.

Installation

18 Attach the master cylinder to the handlebar and fit the back of the clamp with its UP mark facing up, either with the clamp mating surfaces aligned with the punch mark on the top of the handlebar, or locating the pin in the clamp in the hole in the handlebar, according to model **(see illustration)**. Tighten the upper bolt to the torque setting specified at the beginning of this Chapter, followed by the lower bolt.

19 Connect the brake hose to the master cylinder, using new sealing washers on each side of the banjo fitting **(see illustration 3.18)**. Align the hose as noted on removal **(see illustration 5.4)**. Tighten the banjo bolt to the torque setting specified at the beginning of this Chapter.

20 Install the brake lever (see Chapter 5).
21 Install the brake light switch (see Chapter 8).
22 Refer to Section 11 and bleed the system – if you have overhauled the master cylinder in situ only bleed the top of the system as described in Step 5. Check that there are no fluid leaks and test the operation of the brakes before riding the motorcycle.

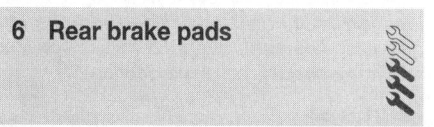

6 Rear brake pads

Caution: Do not operate the brake pedal with the pads removed or the caliper off the disc.

5.14a Slide the spring and piston assembly in...

5.14b ...then push the pushrod in and fit the circlip, helping it in with a screwdriver

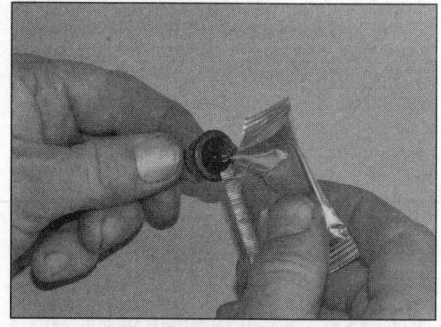

5.15a Lubricate the rubber boot...

5.15b ...fit it into the cylinder...

5.15c ...and use a 13mm socket to push the rim in

5.18 Where appropriate align the mating surface with the punch mark (arrowed)

Brakes, wheels and final drive 6•9

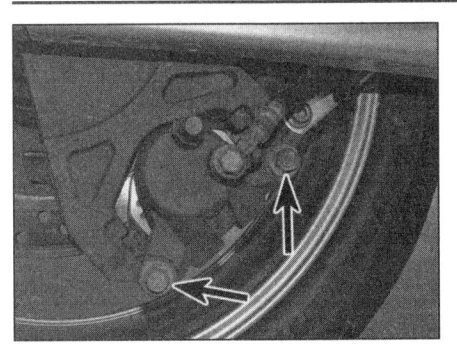

6.1 Caliper mounting bolts (arrowed)

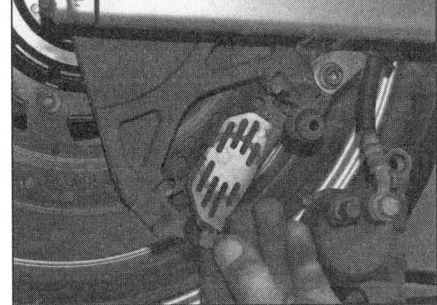

6.2 Remove the pads, noting how the ends seat

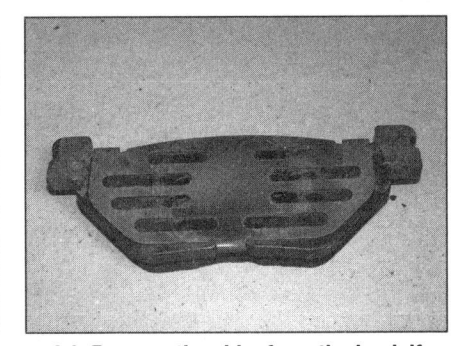

6.3 Remove the shim from the back if required

1 Unscrew the caliper mounting bolts and slide the caliper off the disc **(see illustration)**.
2 Remove the pads from the caliper bracket **(see illustration)**.
3 Where fitted and if required remove the shim from the back of each pad, noting how it fits **(see illustration)** – note that new pads may not come with new shims, but make sure they do, especially if fitting after-market pads, before discarding the old ones.
4 Inspect the surface of each pad for contamination and check that the friction material has not worn beyond its service limit (see Chapter 1, Section 1). If either pad is worn, fouled with oil or grease, or heavily scored or damaged, fit a set of new pads. **Note:** *It is not possible to degrease the friction material; if the pads are contaminated in any way they must be replaced with new ones.*
5 If the pads are in good condition clean them carefully, using a fine wire brush that is completely free of oil and grease to remove all traces of road dirt and corrosion. Using a pointed instrument, dig out any embedded particles of foreign matter. Spray with a dedicated brake cleaner to remove any dust.
6 Clean around the exposed section of the piston to remove any dirt or debris that could cause the seals to be damaged. If new pads are being fitted check the fluid level in the reservoir before pushing the piston in to create room for them (see *Pre-ride checks*) – if the fluid level is not near the LOWER level line it may be necessary to remove the master cylinder reservoir cap, plate and diaphragm and remove some fluid. To push the piston back use finger pressure or a piece of wood or metal as leverage, or place the old pads back in the caliper and use a metal bar or a screwdriver inserted between them (but take care not to damage the friction surface if the pads are being re-used), or use grips or a G-clamp and a piece of wood, with rag or card to protect the caliper body **(see illustration 2.7)**. Alternatively obtain a proper piston-pushing tool from a good tool supplier **(see illustration)**. If new pads are being fitted push the piston all the way back into the caliper; if the old pads are still serviceable push the piston in a little way. If the piston is difficult to push back, remove the bleed valve cap, then attach a length of clear hose to the bleed valve and place the open end in a suitable container, then open the valve and try again (see Section 11). Take great care not to draw any air into the system. If in doubt, bleed the brakes afterwards.
7 Clean all old grease off the sliding sections of the mounting bolts. Check the condition of the rubber boots and replace them with new ones if necessary **(see illustration)**.

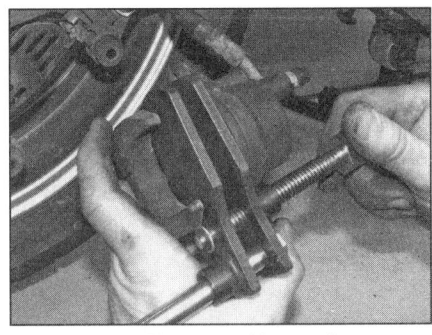

6.6 Piston pushing tool

8 Check the condition of the brake disc (see Section 8).
9 If removed fit the shim onto the back of each pad, making sure it locates correctly **(see illustration 6.3)**. Clean the outer face of each shim so it is shiny. Also clean the pad guides in the bracket so they are shiny – remove them from the bracket if required, and if necessary replace them with new ones.
10 Smear the sliding sections of the mounting bolts and inside the rubber boots with silicone grease.
11 Fit the pads into the caliper bracket with the friction material facing the disc **(see illustration)**.

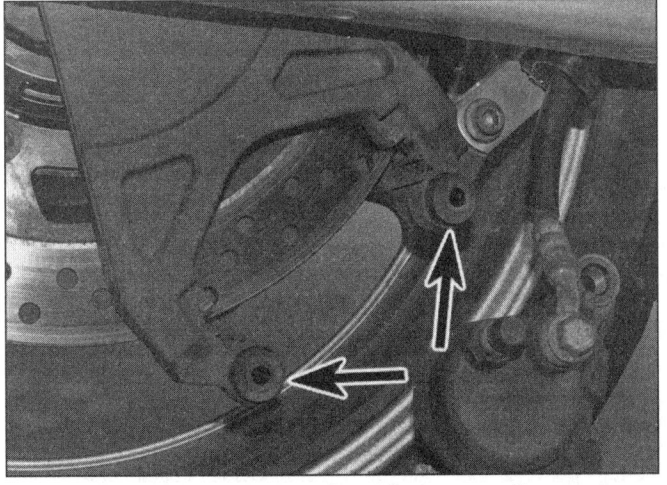

6.7 Check the boots (arrowed) and fit new ones if necessary

6.11 Make sure each end of the pad seats correctly against the guide

6•10 Brakes, wheels and final drive

6.12 Slide the caliper over the pads and fit the bolts

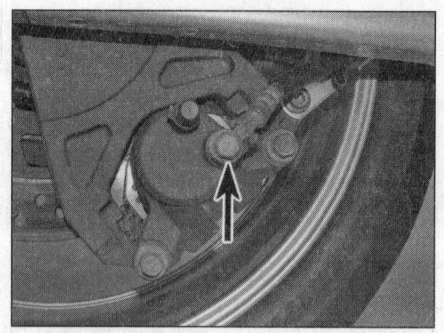

7.1 Brake hose banjo bolt (arrowed)

8.3 Rear brake disc bolts (arrowed)

12 Slide the caliper onto the disc and tighten the mounting bolts to the torque setting specified at the beginning of the Chapter **(see illustration)**.

13 Operate the brake pedal until the pads contact the disc. Check the level of fluid in each reservoir and top-up if necessary (see *Pre-ride checks*).

14 Check the operation of the brakes before riding the motorcycle.

7 Rear brake caliper

⚠ **Warning:** *Overhaul must be done in a spotlessly clean work area to avoid contamination and possible failure of the brake hydraulic system components. Do not, under any circumstances, use petroleum-based solvents to clean brake parts. Use clean DOT 4 brake fluid, dedicated brake cleaner or denatured alcohol only, as described. To prevent damage from spilled brake fluid, always cover paintwork when working on the braking system, and have plenty of absorbent rag to hand to catch and wipe off any spilled fluid.*

Removal

Note: *If the caliper is being overhauled (usually due to a sticking piston or fluid leak) read through the entire procedure first and make sure that you have obtained all the new parts required, including some new DOT 4 brake fluid.*

Caution: *Do not operate the brake pedal while the caliper is off the disc.*

1 If the caliper is being completely removed or overhauled, stuff some rag around the brake hose banjo union. Note the alignment of the brake hose. Unscrew the hose banjo bolt and detach the union, catching the brake fluid **(see illustration)**. Seal the union – one way of doing this is to fit a suitable bolt and nut with the old sealing washers **(see illustration 3.2b)**. Note that new sealing washers will be required later.

2 Unscrew the caliper mounting bolts and slide the caliper off the disc **(see illustration 6.1)**.

Overhaul

3 Clean the exterior of the caliper with denatured alcohol or brake system cleaner. Have some clean rag ready to catch any spilled brake fluid.

4 To remove the piston you need either a supply of compressed air, or a piston removal tool, or if neither are available a good pair of external circlip removal pliers.

5 If you use compressed air wedge some rag or a piece of wood between the piston and the inner side of the caliper **(see illustration 3.6a)**. Gradually and progressively apply the compressed air, starting with a fairly low pressure, to the fluid passage and allow the piston to ease out of the bore **(see illustration 3.6b)**.

6 If you are using a dedicated tool or the circlip pliers grip the inner wall, then twist and pull the piston out, keeping it square to the bore wall. Do not try to remove the piston by levering it out or by using pliers or other grips that may scratch the outer wall, unless you are prepared to fit a new piston, and possibly a new caliper.

7 If the piston is stuck in its bore due to corrosion the caliper should be replaced with a new one.

8 Remove the dust seal and the piston seal from the bore using a plastic tool to avoid scratching **(see illustration 3.10)**. Discard the seals – new ones must be fitted on reassembly.

9 Clean the piston and bore with clean brake fluid. If compressed air is available, blow it through the fluid passages to ensure they are clear (make sure it is filtered and unlubricated).

Caution: *Do not, under any circumstances, use a petroleum-based solvent to clean brake parts.*

10 Inspect the caliper bore and piston for signs of corrosion, nicks and burrs and loss of plating. If surface defects are present, the piston and/or the caliper assembly must be replaced with new ones.

11 Lubricate the new piston seal with clean brake fluid and fit it into the inner groove in the caliper bore **(see illustrations 3.13a and b)**.

12 Lubricate the new dust seal with silicone grease and fit it into the outer groove in the caliper bore **(see illustration 3.14)**.

13 Lubricate the piston with clean brake fluid and fit it, closed-end first, into the caliper bore, taking care not to displace the seals **(see illustration 3.15)**. Using your thumbs, push the piston all the way in, making sure it enters the bore square.

Installation

14 Refer to Section 6 and clean and check the pads, pad guides, caliper mounting bolts and rubber boots, then fit the pads in the caliper bracket.

15 Slide the caliper onto the disc and tighten the mounting bolts to the torque setting specified at the beginning of the Chapter **(see illustration 6.12)**.

16 If detached connect the brake hose to the caliper, using new sealing washers on each side of the banjo fitting **(see illustration 3.18)**. Align the fitting as noted on removal **(see illustration 7.1)**. Tighten the banjo bolt to the specified torque setting.

17 Refer to Section 11 and bleed the system. Check that there are no fluid leaks and test the operation of the brakes before riding the bike.

8 Rear brake disc

Inspection

1 Refer to Section 4 of this Chapter, noting that the dial gauge should be attached to the swingarm.

Removal

2 Remove the rear wheel (see Section 18).

3 If you are not replacing the disc with a new one, mark the relationship of the disc to the wheel or stub axle so it can be installed in the same position. Unscrew the disc bolts, loosening them evenly and a little at a time in a criss-cross pattern to avoid distorting the disc, then remove the disc **(see illustration)**.

Installation

4 Before fitting the disc, make sure there is no dirt or corrosion where the disc seats on the hub. If the disc does not sit flat when it is bolted down, it will appear to be warped when checked or when the rear brake is used.

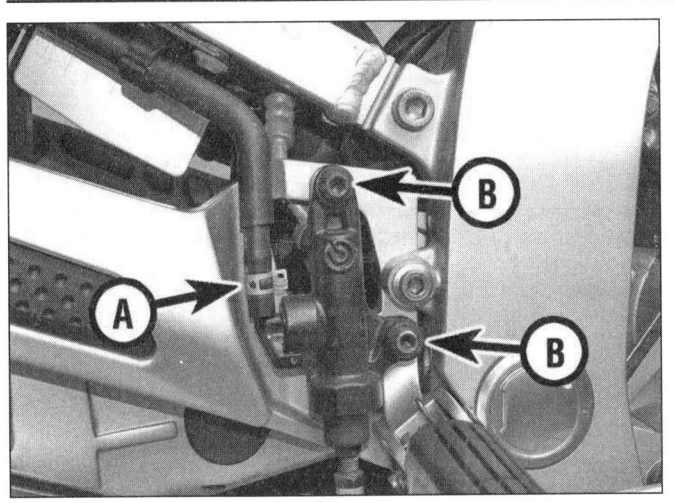

Brakes, wheels and final drive 6•11

9.2 Release the clamp and detach the hose (A). Master cylinder mounting bolts (B)

9.3 Brake hose banjo bolt (arrowed) – AS models

5 Fit the disc on the wheel with its marked side facing out, aligning the previously applied matchmarks (if you're reinstalling the original disc).
6 Either fit the new bolts, or clean the threads of the original bolts and apply fresh thread locking compound. Tighten the bolts evenly and a little at a time in a criss-cross pattern to the torque setting specified at the beginning of this Chapter. Clean the disc using acetone or brake system cleaner. If a new disc has been installed, remove any protective coating from its working surfaces and fit new brake pads.
7 Install the rear wheel (see Section 18).
8 Operate the brake pedal several times to bring the pads into contact with the disc. Check the operation of the brakes before riding the motorcycle.

9 Rear brake master cylinder

Warning: *Overhaul must be done in a spotlessly clean work area to avoid contamination and possible failure of the brake hydraulic system components. Do not, under any circumstances, use petroleum-based solvents to clean brake parts. Use clean DOT 4 brake fluid, dedicated brake cleaner or denatured alcohol only, as described. To prevent damage from spilled brake fluid, always cover paintwork when working on the braking system, and have plenty of absorbent rag to hand to catch and wipe off any spilled fluid.*

Removal

Note: *If the master cylinder is being overhauled (usually due to sticking or poor action, or fluid leaks) read through the entire procedure first and make sure that you have obtained all the new parts required, including some new DOT 4 brake fluid.*

1 Remove the right-hand side cover (see Chapter 7).
2 Support a container suitable for draining the brake fluid from the reservoir next to the master cylinder. Place some rag around the master cylinder. Detach the reservoir hose from its union and place it in the container to allow the fluid to drain **(see illustration)**.
3 Note the alignment of the brake hose on the back of the master cylinder – the banjo bolt is difficult to access, so if you can't get onto it with the tools you have available detach the hose from the caliper **(see illustration 7.1)** and free it from the swingarm on non-ABS models, or from the pipe union on ABS models **(see illustration)**. Unscrew the required banjo bolt and detach the union, catching the brake fluid. Seal the union – one way of doing this is to fit a suitable bolt and nut with the old sealing washers **(see illustration 3.2b)**. Note that new sealing washers will be required later.
4 Straighten the ends of the split pin and withdraw it from the master cylinder pushrod pin, then remove the washer **(see illustration)**. Withdraw the pin.
5 Unscrew the master cylinder bolts and remove the master cylinder **(see illustration 9.2)**.

Overhaul

6 If required, undo the reservoir hose union screw and detach it from the master cylinder. Remove the O-ring – a new one must be used.
7 Dislodge the rubber boot from the base of the master cylinder and from around the pushrod, noting how it locates. Push the pushrod in and use circlip pliers to remove the circlip from its groove and slide out the pushrod, piston and spring. Lay the parts out in order as you remove them to prevent confusion during reassembly **(see illustration 9.10)**.
8 Clean the master cylinder with clean brake fluid.

Caution: *Do not, under any circumstances, use a petroleum-based solvent to clean brake parts.*

9 Check the master cylinder bore for corrosion, scratches, nicks and score marks. If damage or wear is evident, the master cylinder must be replaced with a new one. If the master cylinder is in poor condition, then the caliper should be checked as well.
10 The dust boot, circlip, piston, seal, cup and spring are all included in the master cylinder rebuild kit **(see illustration)**. Use all of the new parts, regardless of the apparent condition of the old ones. Slacken the locknut holding the pedal joint piece on the old pushrod and transfer it to the new one, setting

9.4 Remove the split pin (arrowed) and withdraw the pivot pin

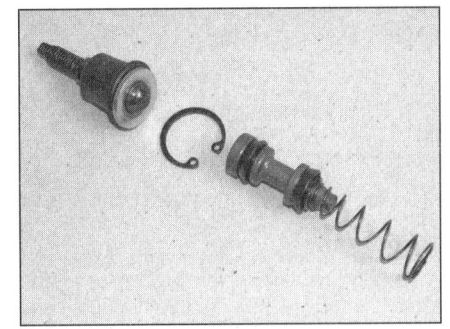

9.10 Rebuild kit contents

it in the same place – count the number of exposed threads between the locknut and the pushrod hex to be exact **(see illustration 9.4)**.

11 Fit the new circlip onto the pushrod between the rubber boot and the washer. Lubricate the piston, cup, seal and master cylinder bore with clean brake fluid. Slide the spring and piston assembly into the master cylinder. Make sure the lips on the cup and seal do not turn inside out. Smear some silicone grease onto the rounded end of the pushrod and around the lips of the boot. Push the piston in using the pushrod until the washer is beyond the circlip groove, then locate the circlip in the groove. Fit the rubber boot, making sure the lips are seated correctly in the master cylinder and around the pushrod.

12 If removed fit a new fluid reservoir hose union O-ring smeared with brake fluid, then press the union into the master cylinder and secure it with the screw.

Installation

13 Fit the master cylinder onto the bracket and tighten the bolts to the torque setting specified at the beginning of the Chapter **(see illustration 9.2)**.

14 Align the pushrod with the brake pedal, then insert the pin **(see illustration 9.4)**. Fit the washer and a new split pin, bending the ends round to lock it.

15 Connect the brake hose to the master cylinder, caliper or pipe union, using new sealing washers on each side of the banjo fitting **(see illustration 3.18)**. Align the fitting as noted on removal **(see illustration 9.2)**. Tighten the banjo bolt to the specified torque setting. Secure the brake hose to the swingarm if detached.

16 Check the reservoir hose for cracks or splits and replace it with a new one if necessary. Connect the hose to the union on the master cylinder and secure it with the clip **(see illustration 9.2)**. Check that the hose is secured with a clip at the reservoir end as well. If the clips have weakened, use new ones.

17 Refer to Section 11 and bleed the system. Check that there are no fluid leaks and test the operation of the brakes before riding the motorcycle.

18 Install the right-hand side cover (see Chapter 7).

10 Brake hoses and fittings

Inspection

1 To fully inspect all the brake hoses and pipes on ABS models remove the right-hand side cover (see Chapter 7) and raise the fuel tank (see Chapter 4).

2 Check brake hose condition according to the brake system check interval in the service schedule (see Chapter 1). Twist and flex the hoses while looking for cracks, bulges and seeping hydraulic fluid. Check extra carefully around the areas where the hoses connect with the banjo fittings, as these are common areas for hose failure.

3 On ABS models also check the brake pipes, the hose and pipe joints, the modulator, and on 2006–on models the proportional control valve and the metering valve referring to the relevant Sections of this Chapter, for signs of fluid leakage and for any dents or cracks in the pipes.

Removal and installation

4 Drain all old brake fluid from the system (see Section 11).

5 The brake hoses, and some of the pipes on 2006-on ABS models, have banjo fittings on each end. Cover the surrounding area with plenty of rags and unscrew the banjo bolt at each end of the hose, noting the alignment of the fitting with the master cylinder or brake caliper **(see illustrations 3.2a, 5.4, 7.1, and 9.3)**. Free the hose from any clips or guides and remove it, noting its routing. Discard the sealing washers. **Note:** *Do not operate the brake lever or pedal while a brake hose is disconnected.*

6 Position the new hose, making sure it isn't twisted or otherwise strained, and ensure that it is correctly routed through any clips or guides and is clear of all moving components.

7 Check that the fittings align correctly, then install the banjo bolts, using new sealing washers on both sides of the fittings **(see illustration 3.18)**. Tighten the banjo bolts to the torque setting specified at the beginning of this Chapter.

8 The brake pipes (with the exception of those on the metering valve on 2006-on models) are held by gland nuts. There are no sealing washers. Unscrew the nuts and detach the pipes. Make sure the pipe is correctly positioned, fitted into any clips, and with any joint blocks secured, before tightening the nuts. If the correct tools are available tighten the gland nuts to the torque setting specified at the beginning of this Chapter for your model.

9 Refill the system with new DOT 4 brake fluid (see *Pre-ride checks*) and bleed the air from it (see Section 11).

10 Check the operation of the brakes before riding the motorcycle.

11 Brake system bleeding and fluid change

Note: *On models with ABS a test adaptor that plugs into the wiring loom is required to pulse test the ABS system after any work, including bleeding the system, is carried out. The test adaptor is available from Yamaha, part No. 90890-03149.*

Bleeding

1 Bleeding a brake is the process of removing aerated brake fluid from the master cylinder, the hose(s)/pipe(s) and the brake caliper(s). Bleeding is necessary whenever a brake system hydraulic connection is loosened, after a component or hose is replaced with a new one, when a master cylinder or caliper is overhauled, or when there is a spongy feel to the lever and it travels all the way back to the handlebar, and where braking force is less than it should be, and it is not due to any mechanical fault in the system (i.e. a sticking piston in the caliper, or a pad that is not moving as it should due to corrosion, for example on the pad pin). Leaks in the system may also allow air to enter, but leaking brake fluid will reveal their presence and warn you of the need for repair.

2 Brake bleeding is considered by some as a bit of a black art – seasoned professionals sometimes have trouble getting a good firm feel in the brake lever, while a first timer may have no trouble at all. One of the problems, particularly with the front brakes, is that you are working against natural principles – science dictates that air bubbles in a liquid will rise to the top, but the process entails pumping the brake fluid and any air bubbles it contains down, from the master cylinder at the top to the bleed valve in the caliper at the bottom, so while the fluid is moving down the air bubbles will want to rise. Air bubbles can also get trapped, particularly where there are high points in its path, and when there are extra components and pipes such as on ABS models.

3 To bleed the brakes using the conventional method, you will need some new DOT 4 brake fluid, a length of clear flexible hose, a small container partially filled with clean brake fluid, some rags, and a spanner to fit the brake caliper bleed valve. Bleeding kits that include the hose, a one-way valve and a container are available relatively cheaply from a good auto store, and simplify the task. You also need a block of wood as a support for the fluid container **(see illustration 11.6c)**.

4 Cover painted components to prevent damage in the event that brake fluid is spilled. **Caution: Brake fluid attacks painted finishes and plastics – to prevent damage from spilled fluid, always cover paintwork when working on the braking system, and clean up any spills immediately using brake cleaner.**

Front brake system

5 Turn the handlebars so the reservoir is level. Undo the reservoir cover screws and remove the cover, diaphragm plate and diaphragm **(see illustration 5.7a)**. Slowly pump the brake lever a few times to dislodge any fine air bubbles from the small hole in the bottom of

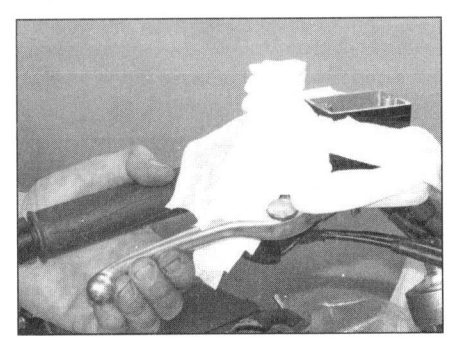

Brakes, wheels and final drive 6•13

11.5a Pump the lever...

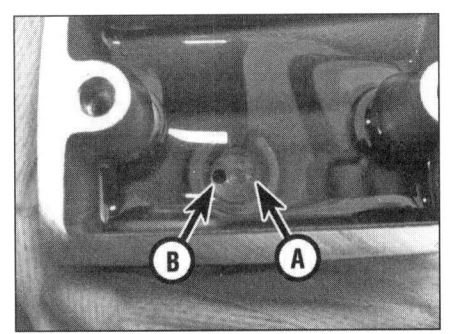

11.5b ...and check for fine air bubbles from the small hole (A). Large hole (B)

11.5c Air bubble rising from the large hole

11.6a Pull the cap off the valve (arrowed)...

11.6b ...fit the ring spanner onto the valve hex and connect the bleed hose

11.6c Use a block of wood to rest the fluid container on

the reservoir **(see illustrations)**. Now hold the lever in to force the large air bubbles out of the large hole **(see illustration)** – you can tie the lever to the handlebar and leave it pressurised for a while to prevent having to hold it, then release it and slowly pump it a few times, then tie it back again. It can take a while to bleed all the air in this way, particularly if the master cylinder was overhauled in situ, but it is worth the perseverance to prevent having to bleed via the calipers, especially on ABS models as it means pushing the air all the way through the system and then having to pulse the ABS modulator using the special tool. You can tell when all the air is gone as the large hole appears completely dark, whereas if there is any air left it will appear to have a silvery rim that is actually the edge of an air bubble.

6 Pull the dust cap off the bleed valve on the left-hand caliper **(see illustration)**. If using a ring spanner (which is preferable to an open-ended one) fit it onto the valve **(see illustration)**. Attach one end of the bleeding hose to the bleed valve and, if not using a kit, submerge the other end in the clean brake fluid in the container **(see illustration)**.

7 Check the fluid level in the reservoir – keep it topped up and do not allow the level to drop below the bottom of the window during the procedure **(see illustration)**.

8 Slowly squeeze the brake lever and open the bleed valve a quarter turn **(see illustration)**. When the valve is opened, brake fluid will flow out of the master cylinder into the clear tubing, and the lever will move to the handlebar. If there is air in the system there will be air bubbles in the brake fluid coming out of the caliper.

9 Tighten the bleed valve, then release the

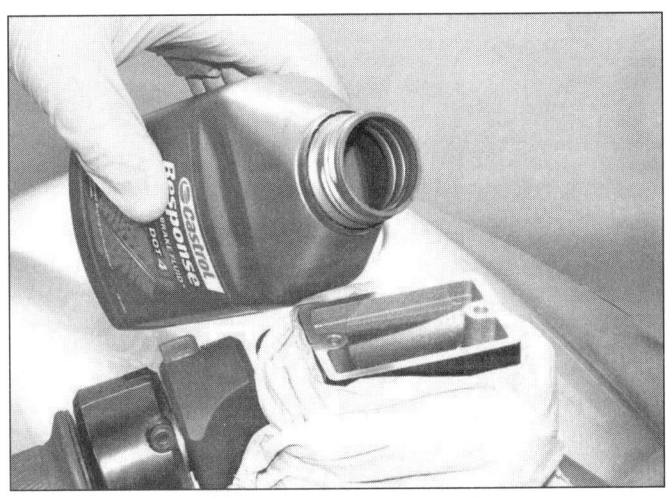

11.7 Keep the reservoir topped up

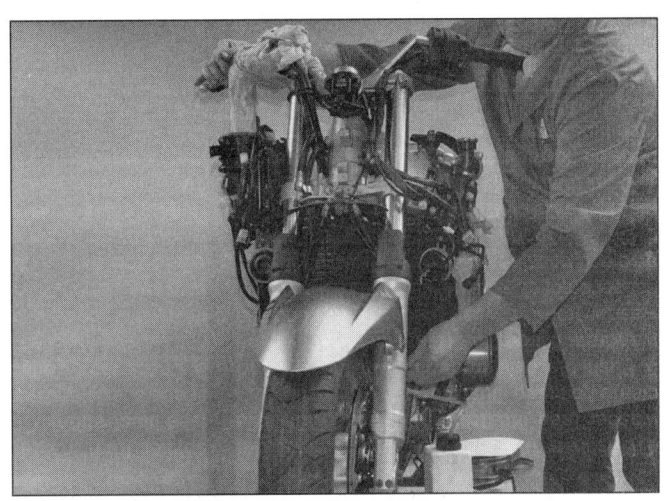

11.8 Bleeding the front brake system

6•14 Brakes, wheels and final drive

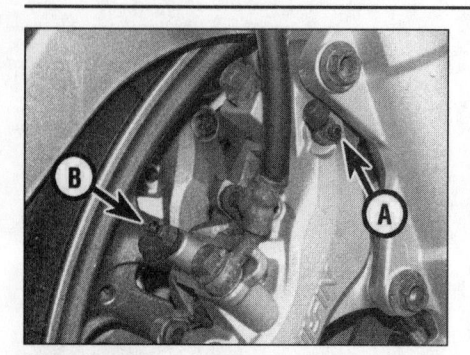

11.10 Right-hand caliper upper bleed valve (A), lower bleed valve (B) – 2006-on models

11.13 Remove the cap, diaphragm plate and diaphragm

11.15a Pull the cap off the valve...

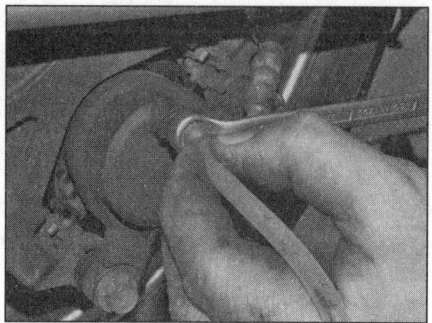

11.15b ...fit the ring spanner onto the valve hex and connect the bleed hose

brake lever. Repeat the process until no air bubbles are visible in the brake fluid leaving the caliper, and the lever is firm when applied, topping the reservoir up when necessary. On completion tighten the bleed valve.

10 Now transfer the equipment to the bleed valve on the right-hand caliper – on 2006-on models bleed via the upper valve **(see illustration)**. Repeat the bleeding procedure.

11 On ABS models refer to the procedure at the end of this section and pulse test the system (unless you have overhauled the master cylinder in situ and bled it as described in Step 5 only – if the system has been bled via the calipers you must carry out the test).

Rear brake system

12 Remove the right-hand side cover (see Chapter 7).

13 Unscrew the reservoir cap, and remove the diaphragm plate and diaphragm **(see illustration)**. Slowly pump the brake pedal a few times to dislodge any air bubbles from the holes in the bottom of the reservoir.

14 On 2006-on models bleed the front portion of the system first using the lower bleed valve on the right-hand caliper **(see illustration 11.10)**, then bleed the rear portion using the bleed valve on the rear caliper as described below. Note that the rear brake pedal may have some resistance to it as you push it down – this is due to the proportional control valve and is normal, but make sure you push the pedal all the way down

15 Pull the dust cap off the caliper bleed valve **(see illustration)**. If using a ring spanner (which is preferable to an open-ended one) fit it onto the valve. Attach one end of the bleeding hose to the bleed valve **(see illustration)** and, if not using a kit, submerge the other end in the clean brake fluid in the container.

16 Check the fluid level in the reservoir – keep it topped up and do not allow the level to drop below the lower level line during the procedure **(see illustration)**.

17 Slowly press the brake pedal and open the bleed valve a quarter turn **(see illustration)**. When the valve is opened, brake fluid will flow out of the master cylinder into the clear tubing, and the pedal will move down. If there is air in the system there will be air bubbles in the brake fluid coming out of the caliper.

18 Tighten the bleed valve, then release the brake pedal. Repeat the process until no air bubbles are visible in the brake fluid leaving the caliper, and the pedal is firm when applied, topping the reservoir up when necessary. On completion tighten the bleed valve.

19 On ABS models refer to the procedure at the end of this section and pulse test the system.

Both systems

20 If it is not possible to produce a firm feel to the lever or pedal, the fluid may be full of many tiny air bubbles rather than a few big ones. To remedy this apply some pressure to the system, for the front brake by tying the front brake lever lightly back to the handlebar, and for the rear by tying a weight to the brake pedal – do not apply too much pressure or the cup and seals in the master cylinder and caliper may fail. Let the fluid stabilise for a few hours, after which the tiny bubbles should either have risen to the top in the reservoir, or have formed into one or more big bubbles that can be more easily bled out by repeating the bleeding procedure.

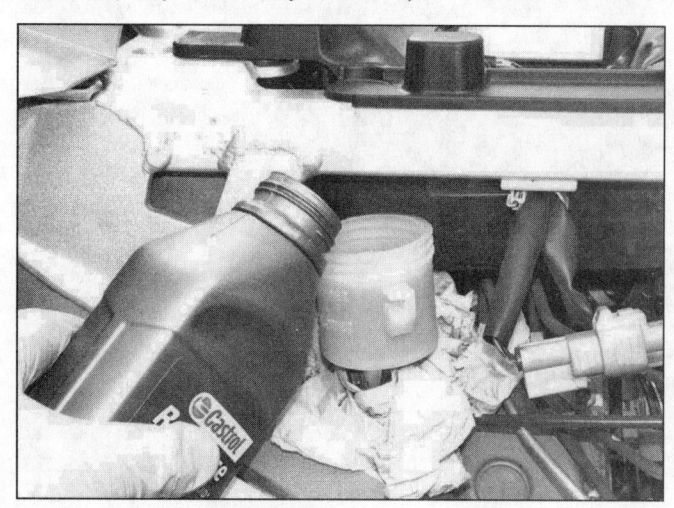

11.16 Keep the reservoir topped up

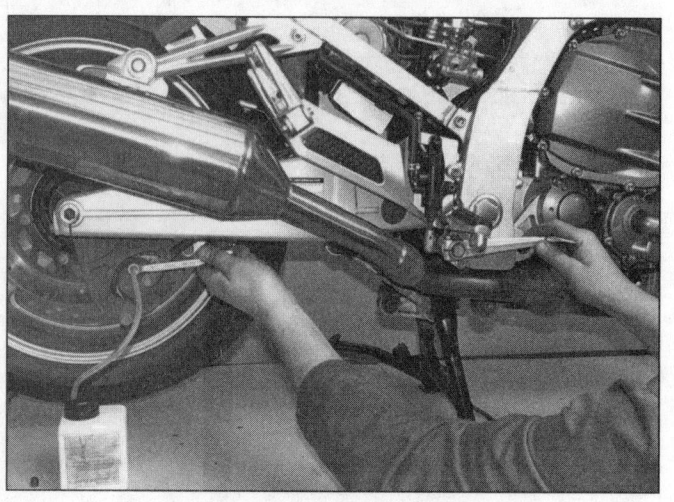

11.17 Bleeding the rear brake system

Brakes, wheels and final drive 6•15

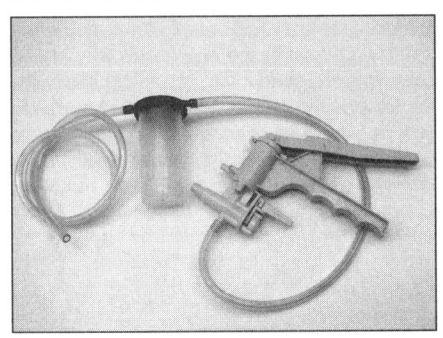

11.22 A vacuum-operated brake bleeding tool

11.37a ABS test adapter (arrowed) – 2003 to 2005 models

11.37b ABS test adapter (arrowed) is tucked in next to the battery positive terminal – 2006-on models

21 If you are still having trouble look for any high point in the system in which a pocket of air may become trapped. Displace and agitate the hose or pipe so the bubble can be dislodged (but take care not to bend a pipe) – tapping it may help. If necessary displace the master cylinder and/or the caliper(s), and free the brake hose(s) from guides and move the parts around to dislodge the air and encourage it towards a bleed valve – refer to the relevant Sections as required to displace components. On models with ABS it is not practical to disturb the modulator or proportional control valve as the pipes have to be detached, allowing more air to enter the system – if you cannot get the system to bleed correctly take the bike to a Yamaha dealer.

22 If bleeding the system using the conventional tools and methods stated does not give satisfactory results, or if otherwise preferred, you can use a commercially available vacuum-type brake bleeding tool, such as the Mity-vac, following the manufacturer's instructions **(see illustration)**. This type of tool literally sucks the fluid out by creating a vacuum at the bleed valve. Users of such tools often get confused by the amount of air that appears to be in the brake fluid – more often than not this is caused by the vacuum sucking air past the bleed valve threads (air provides less resistance to the vacuum than the brake fluid) where it mixes with the fluid being drawn out. If this is the case the vacuum applied may be too great, or the bleed valve may have been loosened too much. One way to get round this is to remove the bleed valve and thread some PTFE tape around its threads, but note that doing so will be a bit messy, so have some rag to hand.

23 When the system has been successfully bled there should be a good and progressively firm feel as the lever or pedal is applied, and the lever or pedal should not be able to travel all the way back to the handlebar or down to its stop.

24 On completion remove the equipment used and make sure the bleed valve is tight (to the torque setting specified at the beginning of the Chapter if you have a suitable torque wrench), then fit the dust cap. Top-up the reservoir, then fit the diaphragm, diaphragm plate, and cover or cap **(see illustration 5.7a and 11.13)**. Check for spilled brake fluid and clean up as required. Check the entire system for fluid leaks.

25 On ABS models refer to the procedure below and pulse test the system.

26 Check the operation of the brake before riding the motorcycle.

Fluid change

27 Changing the brake fluid is a similar process to bleeding the brakes and requires the same materials plus a suitable tool (such as a syringe, or alternatively lots of absorbent rag or paper) for siphoning the fluid out of the reservoir.

28 Cover painted components and fit the equipment to the relevant caliper following the appropriate Steps in the bleeding procedure given above. Remove the reservoir cover or cap, diaphragm plate and diaphragm **(see illustrations 5.7a and 11.13)**. Remove the fluid from the reservoir into a suitable container, either by sucking it up using a tool as shown, drawing it out into a syringe, or soaking it up in some paper towel **(see illustration 5.7b)**. Wipe the reservoir clean. Fill the reservoir with new brake fluid **(see illustration 11.7 or 11.16)**. Squeeze or press the brake lever or pedal and open the bleed valve **(see illustrations 11.8 and 11.17)**. When the valve is opened, brake fluid will flow out of the caliper into the clear tubing, and the lever will move toward the handlebar, or the pedal will move down.

29 Tighten the bleed valve, then slowly release the brake lever or pedal. Keep the reservoir topped-up with new fluid at all times or air may enter the system and greatly increase the length of the task. Repeat the process until new fluid can be seen emerging from the caliper bleed valve.

> **HAYNES HiNT** Old brake fluid is invariably much darker in colour than new fluid, making it easy to see when all old fluid has been expelled from the system.

30 On completion remove the equipment used and make sure the bleed valve is tight (to the torque setting specified at the beginning of the Chapter if you have a suitable torque wrench), then fit the dust cap. Top-up the reservoir, then fit the diaphragm, diaphragm plate, and cover or cap. Check for spilled brake fluid and clean up as required. Check the entire system for fluid leaks.

31 On ABS models refer to the procedure below and pulse test the system.

32 Check the operation of the brakes before riding the motorcycle.

Draining the system for overhaul

33 Draining the brake fluid is again a similar process to bleeding the brakes. The quickest and easiest way is to use a commercially available vacuum-type brake bleeding tool (see Step 22) – follow the manufacturer's instructions. Otherwise follow the procedure described above for changing the fluid, but quite simply do not put any new fluid into the reservoir – the system fills itself with air instead.

34 When it comes to refilling the system start by adding new fluid from a sealed container to the reservoir, then perform the bleeding procedure as described above until the fluid comes out of the bleed valve, and keep at it until you are certain there is no more air left in the system. When doing the rear circuit via the rear brake pedal on 2006-on models, start with the lower bleed valve on the right-hand front caliper, and transfer to the rear caliper when it is obvious that there is mostly fluid coming out, even though there may still be some air – this is normal as the rear portion of the circuit is still full of air and some may be working its way to the front. When the rear portion is mostly filled with fluid bleed the system as described above, front first.

Pulse test procedure

Special tool: A test adaptor, available from Yamaha, part No. 90890-03149, is required.

2003 to 2012 models

35 Put the bike on the centrestand. Remove the battery access panel (see Chapter 7).

36 Check battery voltage (see Chapter 8) – it needs to be fully charged (12.8 volts or higher).

37 Remove the blanking cover from the test adapter connector next to the battery and plug the test adapter in **(see illustrations)**.

38 Make sure the kill switch is set to OFF, then turn the ignition switch ON, and wait

6•16 Brakes, wheels and final drive

until the ABS light goes out – do not apply the brake lever or pedal. Push the start button for at least 4 seconds, then release it.

39 Simultaneously apply the brake lever and pedal and keep them applied – quick pulses should be felt briefly first in the lever, then in the pedal, then again in the lever (if they do not occur in that order, and the hoses were disconnected from the modulator, they have been reconnected incorrectly).

40 Turn the ignition OFF and remove the test adapter, then turn the ignition ON and set the kill switch to RUN. Turn the ignition OFF.

2013-on models

41 Put the bike on the centrestand. Remove the battery access panel (see Chapter 7).

42 Check battery voltage (see Chapter 8) – it needs to be fully charged (12.8 volts or higher).

43 Remove the blanking cover from the test adapter connector next to the battery and plug the test adapter in **(see illustration 11.37b)**.

44 Put the sidestand down and select a gear. Turn the ignition switch ON, then push the start button for at least 4 seconds, then release it.

45 Simultaneously apply the brake lever and pedal and keep them applied – quick pulses should be felt briefly first in the lever, then in the pedal, then again in the lever (if they do not occur in that order, and the hoses were disconnected from the modulator, they have been reconnected incorrectly).

46 Turn the ignition OFF and remove the test adapter, then turn the ignition ON, select neutral and retract the sidestand. Turn the ignition OFF.

12 ABS operation

1 The anti-lock brake system (ABS) prevents the wheels from locking up under hard braking or on uneven road surfaces. A sensor on each wheel transmits information about the speed of rotation to the ABS control unit; if the unit senses that a wheel is about to lock, it releases brake pressure to that wheel momentarily, preventing a skid.

2 The anti-lock system is self-checking and is activated when the ignition switch is turned on – the ABS indicator light in the instrument cluster will come on for 2 seconds, and if the ABS is normal, the light will go off. **Note:** *If the ABS indicator light does not come on initially there is a fault in the system – see Section 13.*

3 If the indicator light remains on, flashes, or does either while the machine is being ridden, there is a fault in the system and the ABS function will be switched off – the brakes will still function but in normal mode. A fault code will be registered and stored in the ECU.

4 To retrieve any stored fault codes, a test adaptor, available from Yamaha, part No. 90890-03149, is required. Remove the battery cover (see Chapter 7). Remove the blanking cover from the test adapter connector next to the battery and plug the test adapter in **(see illustration 11.37a or b)**. The warning light will flash and the fault code(s) will be displayed in the instrument cluster.

5 Remove the test adaptor when the code or codes have been recorded.

6 Once the fault has been corrected, erase the fault code(s) as follows. Follow Step 4 and connect the test adapter. Turn the ignition on – the fault code(s) will be displayed. On 2003 to 2012 models make sure the kill switch is set to OFF. On 2013-on models extend the sidestand and select a gear. Push the starter button at

Fault codes	Faulty component or system	Possible causes
11, 13, 15, 17, 25, 26, 45	Front wheel speed sensor circuit Front wheel speed sensor Front wheel sensor rotor	Faulty wiring or wiring connector Faulty sensor Damaged sensor rotor
12, 14, 16, 18, 27, 46	Rear wheel speed sensor circuit Rear wheel speed sensor Rear wheel sensor rotor	Faulty wiring or wiring connector Faulty sensor Damaged sensor rotor
21	Modulator solenoid	Faulty modulator Faulty wiring or wiring connector
22	Starter circuit	Faulty wiring or wiring connector
23, 24	Brake light circuit	Faulty wiring or wiring connector Faulty bulb Faulty switch Faulty relay
31, 32	Modulator relay	ABS solenoid fuse Faulty wiring or wiring connector Faulty relay Faulty modulator
33, 34	Modulator motor	ABS motor fuse Faulty wiring or wiring connector Faulty relay Faulty modulator
41	Front wheel can lock	Brake drag Brake fluid or hose problem Pulse test result incorrect Faulty modulator
42, 47 (2013-on models)	Rear wheel can lock	Brake drag Brake fluid or hose problem Pulse test result incorrect Faulty modulator
51 (2003 to 2005 models)	Front wheel can lock	Battery voltage low Brake drag Brake fluid or hose problem Pulse test result incorrect Faulty modulator
52 (2003 to 2005 models)	Rear wheel can lock	Battery voltage low Brake drag Brake fluid or hose problem Pulse test result incorrect Faulty modulator
43	Front wheel speed sensor signal	Incorrect sensor installation Faulty wiring or wiring connector Damaged sensor rotor
44	Rear wheel speed sensor signal	Incorrect sensor installation Faulty wiring or wiring connector Damaged sensor rotor
51 and 52 (2006-on models)	Power supply voltage high	Battery Charging system
53 and 54 (2006-on models)	Power supply voltage low	Battery Charging system Faulty wiring or wiring connector
56	Modulator power circuit	Faulty modulator
63	Front wheel speed sensor power	Faulty wiring or wiring connector Faulty modulator
64	Rear wheel speed sensor power	Faulty wiring or wiring connector Faulty modulator

Brakes, wheels and final drive 6•17

least ten times within 4 seconds. The display should revert to normal and the ABS light flashes while the codes are being deleted. When the light stops flashing turn the ignition off then on again – no codes should be displayed. If they are, there is still a fault. On 2003 to 2005 models the warning should come on for 2 seconds, then go out for 3 seconds, then flash – this confirms the codes are deleted.

7 Turn the ignition switch OFF and remove the test adapter when the code or codes have been erased. Check that the ABS is operating normally (see Step 2).

Note: *The ABS indicator may diagnose a fault if tyre sizes other than those specified by Yamaha are fitted, if the tyre pressures are incorrect, if the machine has been run continuously over bumpy roads, if the front wheel comes off the ground whilst riding (wheelie) or if the machine is on an auxiliary stand with the engine running and the rear wheel turning.*

13 ABS fault diagnosis

1 If a fault is indicated in the ABS, first check that the battery is fully charged, then check the ABS fuses (see Chapter 8).

2 If a fault appears, identify the cause using the fault code table opposite and first make sure that the relevant system wiring connectors are securely connected and free of corrosion – poor connections are the cause of the majority of problems. Also check the wiring itself for any obvious faults or breaks, referring to the wiring diagrams at the end of Chapter 8. Refer to Chapter 8, Section 2, for general electrical fault finding procedures and equipment. In the case of a wheel speed sensor related problem also check the sensor tip and rotor are not dirty or damaged (Section 14).

3 If after a thorough check, the source of a fault has not been identified, have the system tested by a Yamaha dealer.

14 ABS components

Note: *A test adaptor that plugs into the wiring loom is required to pulse test the ABS system following any work involving the hydraulic side of the system. The test adaptor is available from Yamaha, part No. 90890-03149. Due to the complexity of the system, particularly on 2006-on models, it is recommended that work is carried out by a Yamaha dealer.*

Front wheel sensor

1 Raise the fuel tank (see Chapter 4). On 2003 to 2005 models unscrew the AIS control valve holder bolt **(see illustration)**. On all models remove the T-bar **(see illustration)**. On 2006-on models remove the heat shield **(see illustrations)**. Trace the wheel sensor wiring to the connector and disconnect it.

2 Release the sensor wiring guides and feed the wire down to the sensor, noting its routing. Unscrew the sensor bolt and remove the sensor **(see illustration)**.

3 Make sure the tip of the sensor, its mounting surfaces, and the sensor rotor are clean and show no signs of damage. Fit the sensor and tighten the bolt. Feed the wiring up to the connector, routing and securing it as noted on removal.

Front sensor rotor

Note: *On 2003 to 2007 models the rotor is part of the wheel and cannot be replaced separately – if it is damaged a new wheel must be fitted. On 2008 to 2012 models the rotor can be removed from the wheel but is not listed as a spare part, so check with your dealer as to availability. On 2013-on models the rotor is listed as a spare part. On 2008-on models take great care not to damage the rotor or use magnetic tools near it, do not clean it using solvent, and take care not to subject it to any sort of impact, and replace the bolts with new ones if removed.*

4 Remove the front wheel (see Section 17).

5 Undo the screws securing the rotor and lift it off **(see illustration)**.

6 Make sure there is no dirt or corrosion where the ring seats on the hub – if the ring does not sit flat the signals from the sensor could be distorted. Fit new bolts and apply a non-permanent thread locking compound and tighten them to the torque setting specified at the beginning of the Chapter.

7 Install the front wheel (see Section 17).

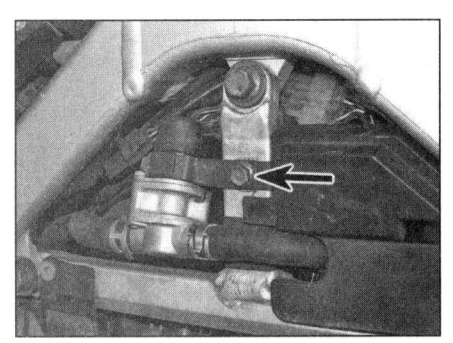

14.1a Unscrew the bolt (arrowed)

14.1b Unscrew the bolts (arrowed) and remove the T-bar

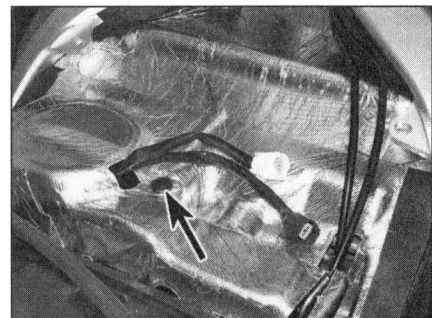

14.1c Release the trim clip (arrowed), thread the wiring through the hole and on 2013-on models slip the cables out of the slot...

14.1d ...and remove the shield

14.2 Front wheel sensor bolt (arrowed)

14.5 Front sensor rotor screws (arrowed)

6•18 Brakes, wheels and final drive

14.8a Rear wheel sensor connector (arrowed) – 2003 to 2005 models

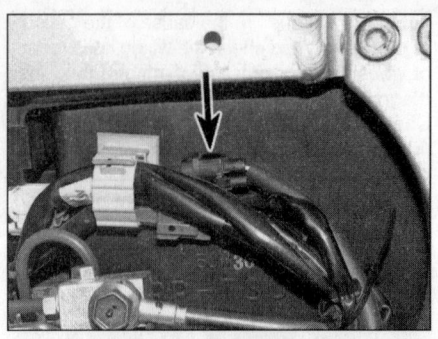

14.8b Rear wheel sensor connector (arrowed) – 2006-on models

Rear wheel sensor

8 On 2003 to 2005 models remove the ABS control unit (see below). On 2006-on models remove the right-hand side cover (see Chapter 7). Disconnect the wheel sensor wiring connector **(see illustrations)**.
9 Release the sensor wiring guides and feed the wire down to the sensor, noting its routing. Unscrew the sensor bolt and remove the sensor **(see illustration)**.
10 Make sure the tip of the sensor, its mounting surfaces, and the sensor rotor are clean. Fit the sensor and tighten the bolt. Feed the wiring up to the connector, routing and securing it as noted on removal.
11 Install the ABS control unit or side cover according to model.

Rear sensor rotor

Note: *On 2003 to 2007 models the rotor is part of the wheel and cannot be replaced separately – if it is damaged a new wheel must be fitted. On 2008 to 2012 models the rotor can be removed from the wheel but is not listed as a spare part, so check with your dealer as to availability. On 2013-on models the rotor is listed as a spare part. On 2008-on models take great care not to damage the rotor or use magnetic tools near it, do not clean it using solvent, and take care not to subject it to any sort of impact, and replace the bolts with new ones if removed.*

12 Remove the rear wheel (see Section 18).
13 Undo the screws securing the rotor and lift it off **(see illustration 14.5)**.
14 Make sure there is no dirt or corrosion where the ring seats on the hub – if the ring does not sit flat the signals from the sensor could be distorted. Fit new bolts and apply a non-permanent thread locking compound and tighten them to the torque setting specified at the beginning of the Chapter.
15 Install the rear wheel (see Section 18).

Modulator

2003 to 2005 models

Note: *Before removing the modulator drain all old brake fluid from the brake system, then fill with new fluid on installation (see Section 11). The modulator cannot be dismantled for overhaul, and no component parts are available. If it fails, it must be replaced with a new one.*

16 Remove the air filter housing (see Chapter 4).
17 Disconnect the modulator wiring connectors **(see illustration)**.
18 Cover the area around the modulator with clean rag to prevent damage to paintwork in the event that brake fluid is spilled.
19 Mark each brake hose according to its location on the modulator. Unscrew the brake hose bolts and detach the hoses. Seal the unions – one way of doing this is to fit a suitable bolt and nut with the old sealing washers **(see illustration 3.2b)**. Note that new sealing washers will be required later. Plug the holes in the modulator using rubber bungs or loosely fit M10 x 1.25 bolts to prevent dirt entering the system.
20 Unscrew the six nuts and remove the brackets and modulator assembly.

14.9 Rear wheel sensor bolt (arrowed)

14.17 ABS modulator (arrowed) – 2003 to 2005 models

21 Installation is the reverse of removal, noting the following:
● Connect the brake hoses using new sealing washers on each side of the banjo fitting **(see illustration 3.18)**. Align the fittings as noted on removal **(see illustration 14.17)**. Tighten the banjo bolts to the specified torque setting.
● Make sure the wiring connectors are secure.
● Follow the procedure in Section 11 to refill and bleed the brake system. Check that there are no fluid leaks and test the operation of the brakes before riding the motorcycle.

2006 to 2007 models

Note: *Before removing the modulator drain all old brake fluid from the brake system, then fill with new fluid on installation (see Section 11). The modulator cannot be dismantled for overhaul, and no component parts are available. If it fails, it must be replaced with a new one.*

22 Remove the right-hand side cover (see Chapter 7).
23 Remove the ABS control unit (see below).
24 Cover the area around the modulator with clean rag to prevent damage to paintwork in the event that brake fluid is spilled.
25 Mark each brake hose according to its location on the modulator. Unscrew the brake hose bolts and detach the hoses. Seal the unions – one way of doing this is to fit a suitable bolt and nut with the old sealing washers **(see illustration 3.2b)**. Note that new sealing washers will be required later. Plug the holes in the modulator using rubber bungs or loosely fit M10 x 1.25 bolts to prevent dirt entering the system.
26 Disconnect the modulator wiring connectors.
27 Unscrew the nuts and remove the modulator assembly – access to the inner nuts is restricted by the rear mudguard, so if necessary release the trim clips and undo the screws securing the mudguard so it can be lowered to provide better access, or if preferred remove it completely after first removing the tail light assembly.
28 Installation is the reverse of removal, noting the following:
● Connect the brake hoses using new sealing washers on each side of the banjo fitting **(see illustration 3.18)**. Align the fittings as noted on removal. Tighten the banjo bolts to the specified torque setting.
● Make sure the wiring connectors are secure.
● Follow the procedure in Section 11 to refill and bleed the brake system. Check that there are no fluid leaks and test the operation of the brakes before riding the motorcycle.

2008-on models

Note: *Before removing the modulator drain all old brake fluid from the brake system, then fill with new fluid on installation (see Section 11).*

Brakes, wheels and final drive 6•19

Note the alignment of the pipes and hoses before detaching them. Take great care not too bend the pipes – detach both ends of a pipe and remove it completely rather than only one end and risk it bending. The modulator cannot be dismantled for overhaul, and no component parts are available. If either valve fails, it must be replaced with a new one.

29 Remove the air filter housing (see Chapter 4).
30 Remove the tail light (see Chapter 8).
31 Displace the rear brake fluid reservoir and all electrical components from the rear mudguard
32 Cover the area around the modulator with clean rag to prevent damage to paintwork in the event that brake fluid is spilled. Remove the metering valve and proportional control valve (see below) **(see illustration)**. Remove the brake pipes from the modulator and pipe/hose joints. Plug the ends of the pipes or wrap something tightly around them. Plug the holes in the modulator using rubber bungs or loosely fit M10 x 1.0 bolts to prevent dirt entering the system.
33 Pull up the release clip on the top of the modulator wiring connector and disconnect it.
34 Release the trim clips and undo the screws securing the mudguard so it can be lowered, or if preferred remove it completely.
35 Unscrew the nuts and remove the modulator assembly.
36 Installation is the reverse of removal, noting the following:
● Do not tighten any of the pipe nuts or banjo bolts until all pipes are loosely connected at each end to ensure correct alignment.
● Connect the brake hoses using new sealing washers on each side of the banjo fitting **(see illustration 3.18)**. Align the fittings as noted on removal. Tighten the banjo bolts to the specified torque setting.
● Make sure the wiring connectors are secure.

● Follow the procedure in Section 11 to refill and bleed the brake system. Check that there are no fluid leaks and test the operation of the brakes before riding the motorcycle.
Caution: Brake fluid attacks painted finishes and plastics – to prevent damage from spilled fluid, always cover paintwork when working on the braking system, and clean up any spills immediately using brake cleaner.

Metering valve (2006-on models)

Note: Before removing the valve drain all old brake fluid from the brake system, then fill with new fluid on installation (see Section 11). The valve cannot be dismantled for overhaul, and no component parts are available. If either valve fails, it must be replaced with a new one.

37 Remove the right-hand side cover (see Chapter 7).
38 Cover the area around the valve with clean rag to prevent damage to paintwork in the event that brake fluid is spilled **(see illustration 14.32)**.
39 Note the alignment of the brake hoses on the valve. Unscrew the brake hose bolts and detach the hoses. Seal the unions – one way of doing this is to fit a suitable bolt and nut with the old sealing washers **(see illustration 3.2b)**. Note that new sealing washers will be required later.
40 Unscrew the bolts and remove the valve.
41 Installation is the reverse of removal, noting the following:
● Connect the brake hoses using new sealing washers on each side of the banjo fitting **(see illustration 3.18)**. Align the fittings as noted on removal. Tighten the banjo bolts to the specified torque setting.
● Follow the procedure in Section 11 to refill and bleed the brake system. Check

that there are no fluid leaks and test the operation of the brakes before riding the motorcycle.

Proportional control valve (2006-on models)

Note: Before removing the valve drain all old brake fluid from the brake system, then fill with new fluid on installation (see Section 11). Note the alignment of the pipes and hoses before detaching them. Take great care not too bend the pipes – detach both ends of a pipe and remove it completely rather than only one end and risk it bending. The valve cannot be dismantled for overhaul, and no component parts are available. If either valve fails, it must be replaced with a new one.

42 Remove the metering valve (see above)
43 Unscrew the pipe joint nuts and detach pipes from the valve **(see illustration 14.32)**. Plug the ends of the pipes or wrap something tightly around them. Remove the holder from the pipe/hose connection.
44 Unscrew the bolts and remove the valve.
45 Installation is the reverse of removal, noting the following:
● Make sure all pipes and hoses are correctly aligned and abutted, and are loosely fitted at each end before .
● Refer to Section 11 and fill and/or bleed the system as required. Check that there are no fluid leaks and test the operation of the brakes before riding the motorcycle.

ABS control unit

Note: On 2008-on models the control unit is integrated in the modulator.

46 On 2001 to 2005 models remove the seats (see Chapter 7). Remove the toolkit from its tray. Disconnect the ECU wiring connector, then remove the tray **(see illustrations)**.

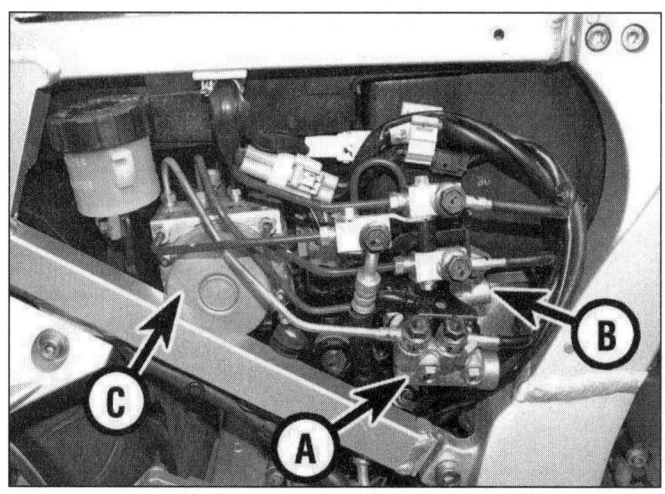

14.32 Metering valve (A), proportional control valve (B), modulator (C) – 2008-on models

14.46a Disconnect the connector (arrowed)...

6•20 Brakes, wheels and final drive

14.46b ...then undo the screws and bolts (arrowed)...

14.46c ...and remove the tray

14.46d Remove the padding...

14.46e ...lift the control unit...

Remove the padding **(see illustration)**. Lift the ABS control unit, remove the cover and disconnect the wiring **(see illustrations)**.
47 On 2006 and 2007 models remove the seats and the height adjuster piece (see Chapter 7). Remove the toolkit from its tray **(see illustration)**. On AS models, remove the motor control unit (see Section 20 in Chapter 2). Disconnect the ECU wiring connector, then remove the tray **(see illustrations)**. Lift the ABS control unit, remove the cover and disconnect the wiring.
48 Installation is the reverse of removal.

ABS relay(s)

Note: *On 2008-on models the relay is integrated in the modulator.*
49 Remove the right-hand side cover (see Chapter 7). Displace the relay and disconnect the wiring **(see illustration)**.
50 To test the relays on 2001 to 2005 models (there are two relays within the one unit) refer to the illustration and check there is continuity between the terminals indicated by the connected circles first with no battery connected (normal condition),

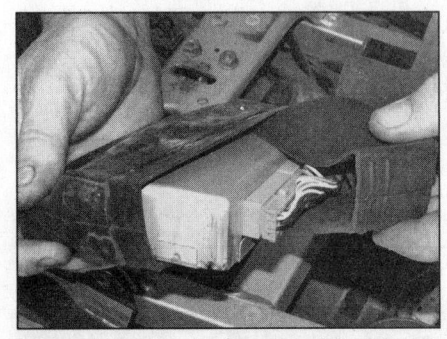

14.46f ...remove the cover and disconnect the wiring

14.47a Remove the toolkit

14.47b Disconnect the connector...

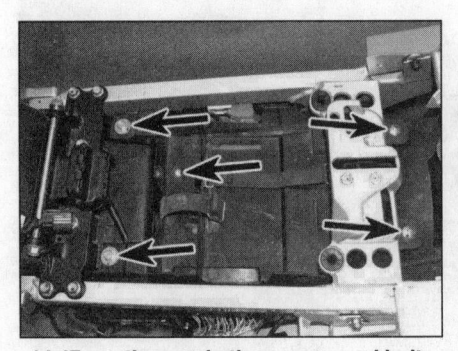

14.47c ...then undo the screws and bolts (arrowed)...

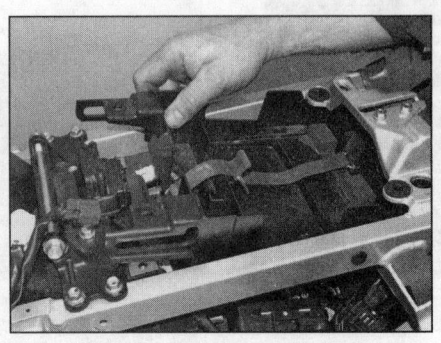

14.47d ...and remove the tray

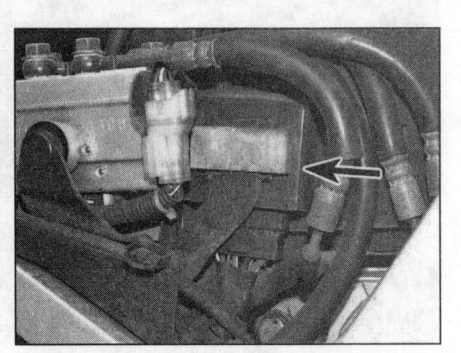

14.49 ABS relay (arrowed) – 2001 to 2005 models

Brakes, wheels and final drive 6•21

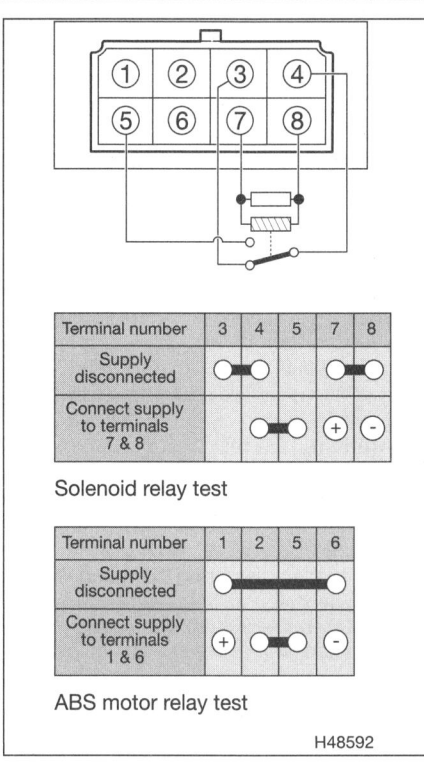

14.50 ABS relay tests

Terminal number	3	4	5	7	8
Supply disconnected		○─○		○─○	
Connect supply to terminals 7 & 8		○ ○		(+)	(−)

Solenoid relay test

Terminal number	1	2	5	6
Supply disconnected	○────	────○		
Connect supply to terminals 1 & 6	(+)	○─○		(−)

ABS motor relay test

then with the battery connected as directed **(see illustration)**. Also check the resistance between terminals 7 and 8 – there should be 150 to 450 ohms. If the relay fails any of the checks replace it with a new one.
51 To test the relay on 2006 and 2007 models check there is a resistance of 50 to 150 ohms between the red/white and white/black wire terminals on the relay. Now connect a battery to those terminals (positive lead to red/white) and check there is continuity between the other two terminals. If the relay fails either of the checks replace it with a new one.
52 Installation is the reverse of removal.

15 Wheel inspection and repair

1 In order to carry out a proper inspection of the wheels, support the bike on the centrestand. Clean the wheels thoroughly to remove mud and dirt that may interfere with the inspection procedure or mask defects. Make a general check of the wheels (see Chapter 1) and tyres (see *Pre-ride checks*).
2 Inspect the wheels for cracks, flat spots on the rim and other damage. Look very closely for dents in the area where the tyre bead contacts the rim. Dents in this area may prevent complete sealing of the tyre against the rim, which leads to deflation of the tyre over a period of time. If damage is evident, or if runout in either direction is excessive, the wheel will have to be replaced with a new one. Never attempt to repair a damaged alloy wheel.
3 To check axial (side-to-side) runout of the wheel rim attach a dial gauge to the fork or the swingarm and position its tip against the side of the wheel rim. Spin the wheel slowly and check the amount of run-out, comparing it to the specification listed at the beginning of the Chapter **(see illustration)**.
4 In order to accurately check radial (out of round) runout with the dial gauge, remove the wheel from the machine, and the tyre from the wheel. With the axle clamped in a vice and the dial gauge positioned on the top of the rim, the wheel can be rotated to check the runout **(see illustration 15.3)**.
5 An easier, though slightly less accurate,

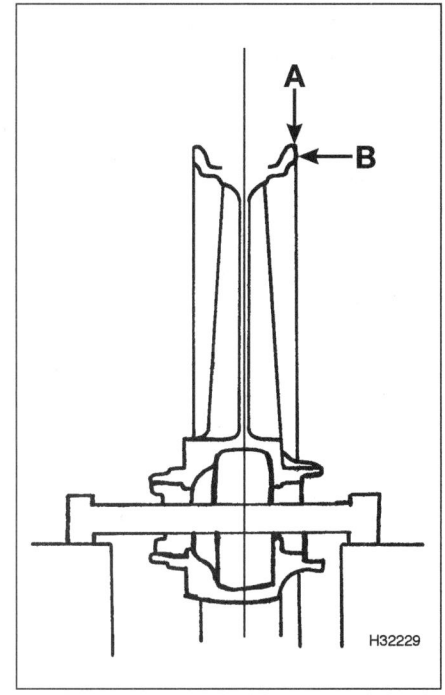

15.3 Check the wheel for radial (out-of-round) runout (A) and axial (side-to-side) runout (B)

method is to attach a stiff wire pointer to the fork or the swingarm and position the end a fraction of an inch from the wheel rim where the wheel and tyre join. If the wheel is true, the distance from the pointer to the rim will be constant as the wheel is rotated. **Note:** *If wheel runout is excessive, check the wheel bearings very carefully before renewing the wheel.*

16 Wheel alignment check

1 Misalignment of the wheels due to a bent frame or forks can cause strange and possibly serious handling problems. If the frame or forks are at fault, repair by a frame specialist or renewal are the only options.
2 To check wheel alignment you will need an assistant, a length of string or a perfectly straight piece of wood and a ruler. A plumb bob or spirit level for checking that the wheels are vertical will also be required.
3 Support the bike on the centrestand. Measure the width of both tyres at their widest points. Subtract the smaller measurement from the larger measurement, then divide the difference by two. The result is the amount of offset that should exist between the front and rear tyres on both sides of the machine.
4 If the string method is used, have your assistant hold one end of it about halfway between the floor and the rear axle, with the string touching the back edge of the rear tyre sidewall.
5 Run the other end of the string forward and pull it tight so that it is roughly parallel to the floor **(see illustration)**. Slowly bring the string into contact with the front edge of the rear tyre sidewall, then turn the front wheel until it is parallel with the string. Measure the distance from the front tyre sidewall to the string.
6 Repeat the procedure on the other side of the motorcycle. The distance from the front tyre sidewall to the string should be equal on both sides.
7 As previously mentioned, a perfectly

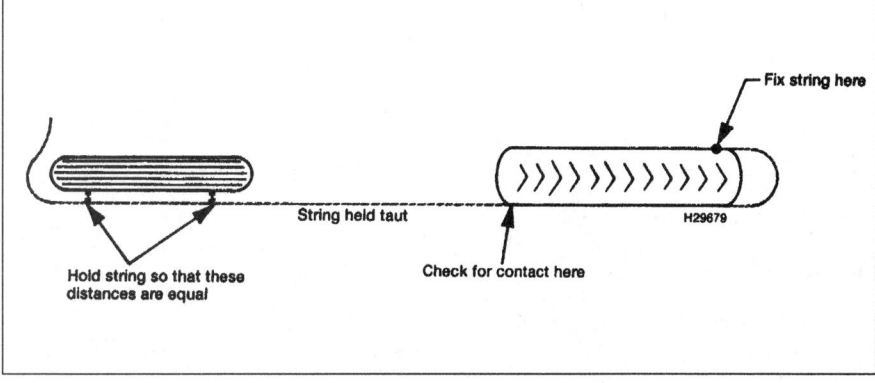

16.5 Wheel alignment check using string

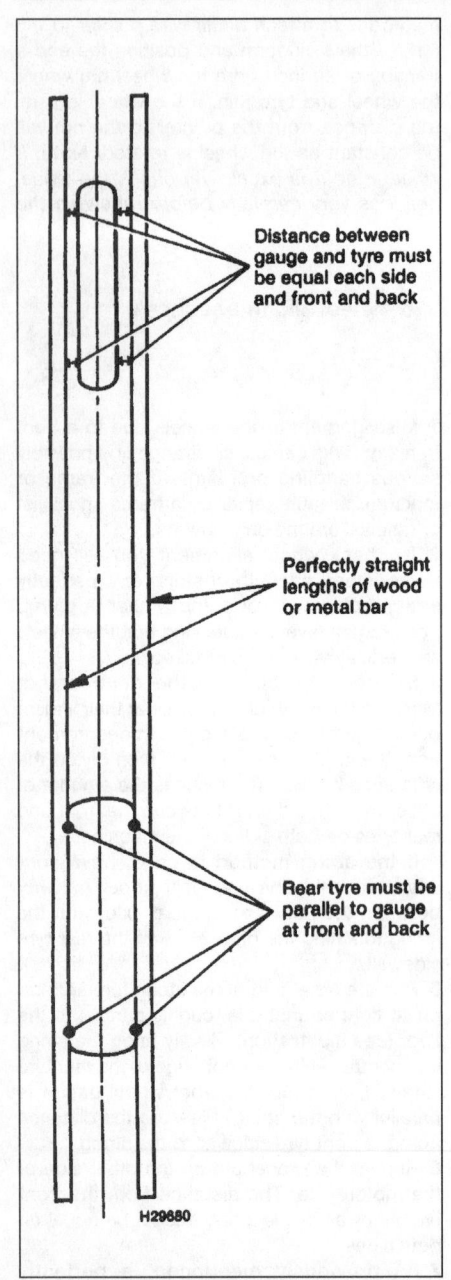

6•22 Brakes, wheels and final drive

straight length of wood or metal bar may be substituted for the string (see illustration).

8 If the distance between the string and tyre is greater on one side, or if the rear wheel appears to be out of alignment, have your machine checked by a Yamaha dealer or frame specialist.

9 If the front-to-back alignment is correct, the wheels still may be out of alignment vertically.

10 Using a plumb bob or spirit level, check the rear wheel to make sure it is vertical. To do this, hold the string of the plumb bob against the tyre upper sidewall and allow the weight to settle just off the floor. If the string touches both the upper and lower tyre sidewalls and is perfectly straight, the wheel is vertical. If it is not, adjust the stand until it is.

11 Once the rear wheel is vertical, check the front wheel in the same manner. If both wheels are not perfectly vertical, the frame and/or major suspension components are bent.

17 Front wheel

Removal

1 Position the motorcycle on the centrestand, and support it so that the front wheel is just off the ground. If a jack is being placed under the exhaust, place a piece of wood on the jack head to spread the load. Always make sure the motorcycle is properly supported.

2 Displace the front brake calipers (see Section 3). Support the calipers with a cable-tie or a bungee cord so that no strain is placed on the hydraulic hoses. There is no need to disconnect the hoses from the calipers. Note: *Do not operate the front brake lever with the calipers removed.*

3 Remove the mudguard (see Chapter 7).

4 On 2001 to 2005 models slacken the axle clamp bolt on the bottom of the right-hand fork. Unscrew the axle. Take the weight of the wheel, then withdraw the axle. Carefully lower the wheel. On ABS models draw the wheel back a bit and displace the wheel sensor plate (see illustration 17.5d). Remove the wheel from between the forks.

5 On 2006-on models slacken the axle clamp bolts on the bottom of the left-hand fork (see illustration). Unscrew the axle bolt most of the way out of the left-hand end of the axle. Slacken the axle clamp bolts on the bottom of the right-hand fork (see illustration). Take the weight of the wheel, then push the axle through from the left using the axle bolt, then remove the bolt and withdraw the axle from the right (see illustration). Carefully lower the wheel. Draw the wheel back a bit and displace the wheel sensor plate (see illustration). Remove the wheel from between the forks.

6 Note the collar in the right-hand side of the wheel, and on non-ABS models in the left-hand side, and remove it/them, on non-ABS models noting which fits where (see illustration). On ABS models there is a collar in the wheel sensor plate. Clean all old grease off the collars, axle and seals.

Caution: *Don't lay the wheel down and allow it to rest on a disc – the disc could*

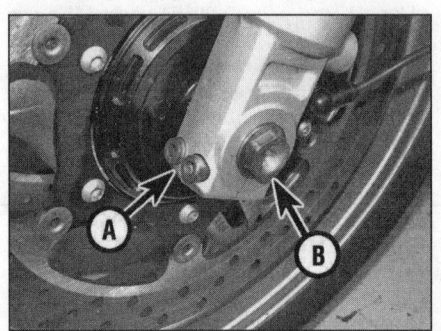

16.7 Wheel alignment check using a straight-edge

17.5a Slacken the axle clamp bolts (A), then partially unscrew the axle bolt (B)

17.5b Slacken the axle clamp bolts (arrowed)

17.5c Displace and withdraw the axle as described...

17.5d ...then move the wheel back and displace the wheel sensor plate

17.6 Right-hand side collar

Brakes, wheels and final drive 6•23

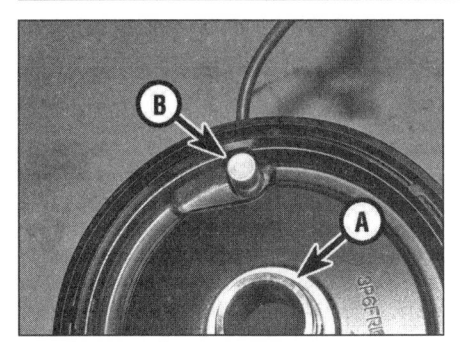

17.9 Check the collar (A) and the wheel sensor tip (B)

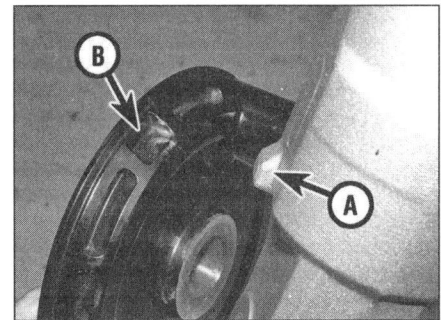

17.11 Seat the lug (A) in the cut-out (B)

17.13a Fit and tighten the axle bolt...

17.13b ...using a hex bit to counter-hold the axle head if necessary

17.18 Measuring the depth from the rim of the speed sensor housing to the rotor

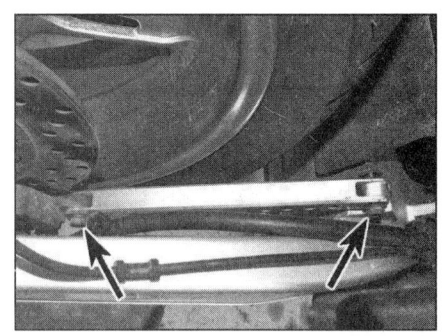

18.3 Brake torque arm bolts (arrowed)

become warped. Set the wheel on wood blocks so the disc doesn't support the weight of the wheel.

7 Check the axle is straight by rolling it on a flat surface such as a piece of plate glass (first remove any corrosion using steel wool). If the equipment is available, place the axle in V-blocks and check for runout using a dial gauge. If the axle is bent replace it with a new one.
8 Check the condition of the grease seals and wheel bearings (see Section 19).

Installation

9 Apply a smear of grease to the inside of the wheel collars, and also to the outside where they fit into the seals. On non-ABS models fit the short collar into the right-hand side of the wheel and the long collar into the left-hand side. On ABS models fit the collar into the right-hand side of the wheel **(see illustration 17.6)**. Also make sure the collar is seated correctly in the wheel sensor plate and the head of the sensor is clean **(see illustration)**.
10 Each side of the wheel can be identified using the directional arrow (denoting the normal direction of wheel rotation) on the tyre and on the brake disc. Manoeuvre the wheel into position between the forks – check it is the correct way round using the directional arrows. On ABS models locate the wheel sensor plate **(see illustration 17.5d)**.
11 Apply a thin coat of grease to the axle. Lift the wheel into place, making sure the collar(s)/

sensor plate remain in position, and seating the lug on the fork in the cut-out in the sensor plate **(see illustration)**. Slide the axle through from the right-hand side **(see illustration 17.5c)**.
12 On 2001 to 2005 models tighten the axle to the torque setting specified at the beginning of the Chapter.
13 On 2006-on models fit the axle bolt and tighten it to the torque setting specified at the beginning of the Chapter **(see illustration)**. If the axle turns when tightening the bolt counter-hold it using a large hex bit in the right-hand end **(see illustration)**. Tighten the axle clamp bolts on the bottom of the left-hand fork to the specified torque setting **(see illustration 17.5b)**.
14 Lower the front wheel to the ground. Install the brake calipers (see Section 3, and the Note therein regarding the mounting bolts).
15 Apply the brake lever, and on 2006-on models the pedal, a few times to bring the pads back into contact with the discs, then with the front brake applied pump the front forks a few times to settle all components in position. On 2006-on models check the head of the axle is flush with the outer surface of the fork, and if not align the fork so it is.
16 On 2001 to 2005 models tighten the axle clamp bolt on the right-hand fork to the specified torque.
17 On 2006-on models tighten the axle clamp bolts on the bottom of the right-hand fork to the specified torque, tightening the outer bolt

first, then the inner, then the outer again **(see illustration 17.5a)**.
18 On 2008-on models, if new wheel bearings have been fitted remove the wheel sensor (Section 14), and check the distance from the speed sensor housing rim to the rotor is 28.89 to 29.41 mm on 2008 to 2012 models, or 28.82 to 29.66 mm on 2013-on models – take the measurement using the depth facility in the handle end of a Vernier caliper **(see illustration)**. If it isn't correct the bearings may not be correctly seated and the sensor head gap will be incorrect which could lead to incorrect operation of the ABS.
19 Clean the discs using brake system cleaner. Check for correct operation of the brakes before riding the motorcycle.

18 Rear wheel

Removal

1 Position the bike on the centrestand. Tie the front brake lever to the handlebar.
2 Remove the panniers if fitted.
3 Unscrew the brake torque arm nuts, withdraw the bolts and displace the arm **(see illustration)**. Release the brake hose clip using a screwdriver inserted up the end of the arm **(see illustration 18.16b)**.

6•24 Brakes, wheels and final drive

18.4a Unscrew the nut and remove the washer

18.4b Slacken the clamp bolt (arrowed)

18.5a Withdraw the axle…

18.5b …collecting the washer…

18.5c …and displace the caliper/bracket assembly

18.6 Draw the wheel sensor plate off

4 Unscrew the axle nut and remove the washer (see illustration). Slacken the axle clamp bolt (see illustration).
5 Push the axle through from the left and withdraw it from the right, then remove the washer from between the swingarm and the caliper bracket, slide the caliper/bracket off the disc and position it clear (see illustrations).
6 On ABS models displace the wheel sensor plate (see illustration).
7 Draw the wheel to the right off the final drive housing, lower it to the ground and remove it (see illustration).
Caution: Do not lay the wheel down and allow it to rest on the disc – it could become warped. Set the wheel on wood blocks so the disc doesn't support the weight of the wheel. Do not operate the brake pedal with the wheel removed.
8 On non-ABS models remove the collar from the right-hand side of the wheel. Remove the spacer from inside the final drive housing (see illustration). Clean all old grease off the spacers, axle and seals.
9 Check the axle is straight by rolling it on a flat surface such as a piece of plate glass (if the axle is corroded, first remove the corrosion with steel wool). If the equipment is available, place the axle in V-blocks and check for runout using a dial gauge. If the axle is bent replace it with a new one.
10 Check the condition of the grease seals and wheel bearings (see Section 19). Check the condition of the drive coupling (see Section 22). Check the condition of the drive coupling seal and replace it with a new one if it is damaged or deformed (see illustration 18.11).

Installation

11 Apply a smear of grease to the inside of the final drive housing spacer, and the inside and outside of the collar for the right-hand side, that on ABS models is in the wheel sensor plate. Fit the long spacer into the final drive housing, making sure it locates correctly (see illustration 18.8). Make sure the drive coupling seal is in place (see illustration). Apply some molybdenum disulphide paste or grease to the drive coupling splines.
12 Manoeuvre the wheel into position between the ends of the swingarm, then lift it onto the final drive housing, engaging the splines and pushing it to the left (see illustration 18.7).
13 On ABS models locate the wheel sensor plate with the sensor in the 1 o'clock position (see illustration 18.6).
14 Slide the brake caliper onto the disc locating the bracket between the wheel and the swingarm (see illustration 18.5c) – on non-ABS models make sure the collar stays in place, and

18.7 Draw the wheel off the housing and remove it

18.8 Remove the spacer from the final drive housing

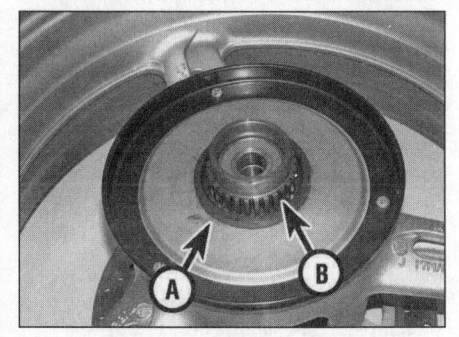

18.11 Check the seal (A) and grease the splines (B)

Brakes, wheels and final drive 6•25

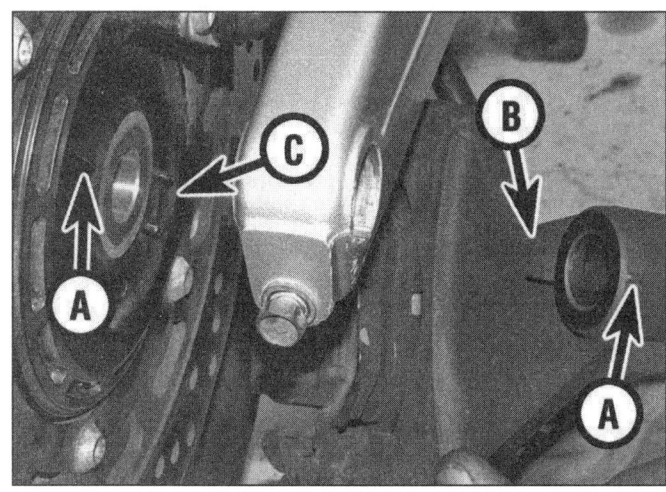

18.14 Align the marks (A) so the lug (B) sits between the ribs (C)

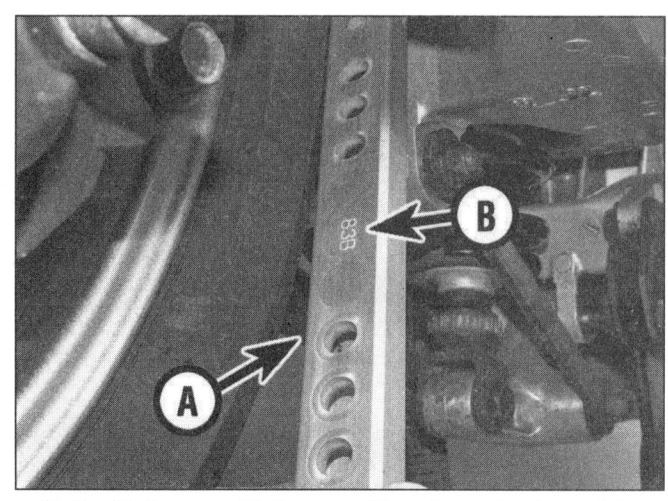

18.16a Fit the arm with the seam (A) on the underside and the mark (B) facing in

on ABS models align the marks on the bracket and sensor plate so the lug on the bracket sits between the ribs on the plate **(see illustration)**.
15 Apply a thin coat of grease to the axle. Slide the axle in from the right, fitting the washer between the swingarm and caliper bracket **(see illustrations 18.5b and a)**. Fit the washer and the axle nut and tighten them finger-tight **(see illustration 18.4a)**. Check that everything is correctly aligned.
16 Fit the brake torque arm with the seam on the underside and the marked side facing in and tighten the nuts to the torque setting specified at the beginning of the Chapter **(see illustration)**. Fit the brake hose clip **(see illustration)**.
17 Tighten the axle nut to the torque setting specified at the beginning of the Chapter, counter-holding the axle head if required using a large hex bit.
18 Tighten the axle clamp bolt to the specified torque for your model **(see illustration 18.4b)**.
19 On 2008-on models, if new wheel bearings have been fitted remove the wheel sensor (Section 14), and check the distance from the sensor housing rim to the rotor is 28.89 to 29.41 mm on 2008 to 2012 models, or 28.84 to 29.64 mm on 2013-on models – take the measurement using the depth facility in the handle end of a Vernier caliper **(see illustration 17.18)**. If it isn't correct the bearings may not be correctly seated and the sensor head gap will be too wide which could lead to incorrect operation of the ABS.
20 Clean the disc using brake system cleaner. Check the operation of the brakes carefully before riding the bike.

19 Wheel bearings

Note: *Always renew the wheel bearings in sets, never individually. Applying some heat to the bearing housing using a hot air gun will make removal and installation easier, and chilling the new bearings in a fridge or freezer before fitting them also helps.*

Front wheel bearings

1 Remove the wheel (see Section 17). Support the wheel on wood blocks so that the wheel rim supports the weight of the wheel.
2 Inspect the seals and bearings – check that the bearing inner race turns smoothly and that the outer race is a tight fit in the hub (see *Tools and Workshop Tips* in the Reference Section).
Note: *Do not remove the bearings unless they are going to be replaced with new ones.*
3 If new components are needed, it is best to remove the discs (see Section 4), and on ABS models the sensor rotor (Section 14), to prevent them being damaged or distorted during bearing removal. Lever the bearing seal out from each side of the hub using a flat-bladed screwdriver or a seal hook **(see illustration)**. Take care not to damage the hub. New seals must be fitted on reassembly.

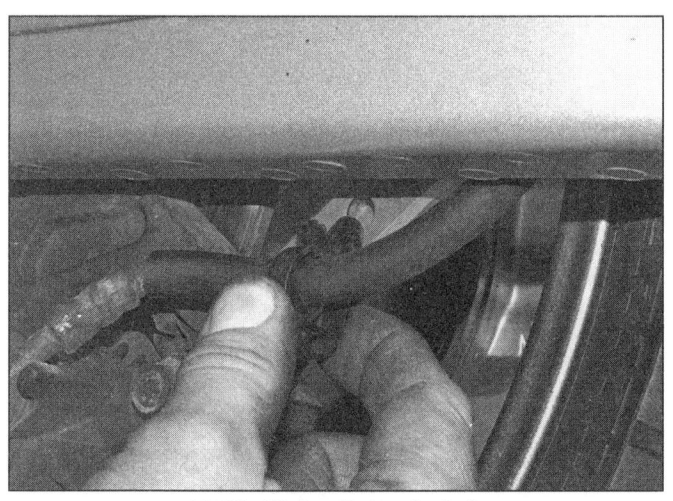

18.16b Fit the clip into its hole

19.3 Lever out the bearing seals

6•26 Brakes, wheels and final drive

19.4a Fit the attachment under the bearing (arrowed)...

19.4b ...then fit the slide-hammer and jar the bearing out

19.7 Using a socket to drive the bearing in

19.9 Fit the seal, setting it flush with the rim

4 Remove the bearing from one side using an internal expanding puller, either of the screw-type or with slide-hammer attachment, which can be obtained commercially – select the correct attachment and locate it between the inner race of the upper bearing and the spacer, then tighten the inner bolt to expand and lock the puller **(see illustration)**. Either tighten the puller bolt to draw the bearing out, or attach the slide hammer, hold the wheel firmly down and jar the bearing out **(see illustration)**. Having removed the first bearing, remove the spacer that fits between the bearings.
5 Remove the other bearing in the same way, or drive it out using a suitable drift (such as a socket on an extension) inserted from the opposite side and located on the inner race.
6 Thoroughly clean the hub area of the wheel with a suitable solvent and inspect the bearing housing for scoring and wear.
7 Fit the new bearings with the marked side facing outwards. Drive them into the hub using a bearing driver or suitable socket that seats on the outer race **(see illustration)**. Make sure the bearing fits squarely and all the way onto its seat.
8 Turn the wheel over and fit the bearing spacer. Fit the second bearing in the same way as the first.
9 Fit the new seals into the hub using finger pressure or a suitable driver that bears on the outer rim, setting them flush with the hub **(see illustration)**. Smear the seal lips with grease.
10 Install the brake discs and sensor rotor if removed (see Sections 4 and 14). Clean the discs using brake system cleaner, then install the wheel (see Section 17).

Rear wheel bearings

11 Remove the wheel (see Section 18). Support the wheel on wood blocks so that the wheel rim supports the weight of the wheel.
12 Remove the drive coupling and rubber dampers (Section 22).
13 Withdraw the sleeve from the needle bearing in the left-hand side **(see illustration)**.
14 Inspect the seals and bearings in both sides of the hub – check that the inner race of the ball bearing in the right-hand side turns smoothly and that the outer race is a tight fit in the hub (see *Tools and Workshop Tips* in the Reference section). **Note:** *Do not remove the bearings unless they are going to be replaced with new ones.*
15 If new components are needed it is best to remove the disc (see Section 8), and on ABS models the sensor rotor (Section 14), to prevent them being damaged or distorted during bearing removal. Lever the bearing seal out from each side of the hub using a flat-bladed screwdriver or a seal hook **(see illustration)**. Take care not to damage the hub. Discard the seal as a new one should be fitted on reassembly.
16 Remove the needle bearing using an internal expanding puller, either of the screw-type or with slide-hammer attachment,

19.13 Withdraw the sleeve

19.15 Lever out the bearing seal

Brakes, wheels and final drive 6•27

19.16a Fit the attachment...

19.16b ...under the bearing (arrowed)...

19.16c ...then fit the slide-hammer and jar the bearing out

which can be obtained commercially – select the correct attachment and locate it between the bearing and the spacer, then tighten the inner bolt to expand and lock the puller (see illustrations). Either tighten the puller bolt to draw the bearing out, or attach the slide-hammer, hold the wheel firmly down and jar the bearing out (see illustration). Having removed the bearing, remove the spacer that fits between the bearings.

17 Turn the wheel over. On 2001 to 2007 models remove the circlip securing the ball bearing. On 2008-on models remove the bearing retainer using either the Yamaha tool (part No. 90890-01525), or a deep 41 mm nut onto which you fit a socket, and turning it CLOCKWISE to undo it (it has left-hand threads) (see illustrations). Remove the ball bearing in the same way as the needle bearing using a puller, or turn the wheel back over and drive it out using a suitable drift (such as a socket on an extension) inserted from the opposite side and located on the inner race.

18 Thoroughly clean the hub area of the wheel with a suitable solvent and inspect the bearing housing for scoring and wear.

19 Fit the new ball bearing with its marked side facing outwards. Drive into the hub using a bearing driver or suitable socket that seats on the outer race (see illustration 19.7). Make sure the bearing fits squarely and all the way onto its seat. On 2001 to 2007 models fit a new circlip into the groove. On 2008-on models clean the threads of the bearing retainer and apply some fresh threadlock, and tighten it to the torque setting specified at the beginning of the Chapter, turning it ANTI-CLOCKWISE.

20 Turn the wheel over and fit the bearing spacer. Press or draw the needle bearing in – do not drive it in or it will be ruined. Set it so the depth of the outer rim is 3.5 to 4.5 mm below the rim of its bore.

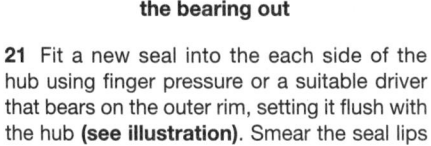

21 Fit a new seal into the each side of the hub using finger pressure or a suitable driver that bears on the outer rim, setting it flush with the hub (see illustration). Smear the seal lips with grease.

22 Fit the sleeve into the needle bearing (see illustration 19.13).

23 Check the drive coupling and its bearings and the damper segments, then fit them onto the wheel (Section 22). Install the brake disc and sensor rotor if removed (see Sections 8 and 14). Clean the brake disc using acetone or brake system cleaner. Install the wheel (see Section 18).

Drive coupling bearing

24 Remove the wheel (see Section 18), then remove the coupling and rubber dampers from the wheel (Section 22).

25 Check that the bearing inner race turns smoothly and that the outer race is a tight fit in the coupling (see *Tools and Workshop Tips* in the Reference Section). **Note:** *Do not remove the bearing unless it is being replaced with a new one.*

26 If a new bearing is needed support the coupling on blocks of wood and drive the bearing out from the inside using a bearing driver or socket (see illustration).

27 Thoroughly clean the coupling with a suitable solvent and inspect the bearing housing for scoring and wear.

28 Fit the new bearing with its marked side facing outwards. Drive into the coupling using a bearing driver or suitable socket that seats on the outer race (see illustration). Make sure

19.17a Fit a deep 41 mm nut into the retainer...

19.17b ...then fit a socket onto the nut

19.21 Fit the seal, setting it flush with the rim

19.26 Drive the bearing out from the inside

19.28 Drive the bearing in from the outside

6•28 Brakes, wheels and final drive

the bearing fits squarely and all the way onto its seat.

29 Check the condition of the seal and clean it or replace it with a new one if necessary **(see illustration)**. Fit the coupling (Section 22), then install the wheel (see Section 18).

20 Tyres

General information

1 The wheels are designed to take tubeless tyres only. Tyre sizes are given in the Specifications at the beginning of this chapter.

2 Refer to the *Pre-ride checks* listed at the beginning of this manual for tyre maintenance.

Fitting new tyres

3 When selecting new tyres, refer to the tyre information in the Owner's Handbook. Ensure that front and rear tyre types are compatible, the correct size and correct speed rating; if necessary seek advice from a Yamaha dealer or tyre fitting specialist **(see illustration)**.

4 It is recommended that tyres are fitted by a motorcycle tyre specialist rather than attempted in the home workshop. This is particularly relevant in the case of tubeless tyres because the force required to break the seal between the wheel rim and tyre bead is substantial, and is usually beyond the capabilities of an individual working with normal tyre levers. Additionally, the specialist will be able to balance the wheels after tyre fitting.

19.29 Check the seal

5 Note that punctured tubeless tyres can in some cases be repaired. External repairs made using a repair kit should only ever be considered as a temporary measure to get you to a dealer for a new tyre, and riding at speed or with any extra load should be avoided. Internal repairs carried out by a motorcycle tyre fitting specialist are better. Make sure a wheel with a repaired tyre is balanced before it is fitted back on the bike. Seek advise from the repairer regarding the speed and load capabilities of a repaired tyre.

21 Final drive housing, driveshaft and universal joint

Final drive housing and driveshaft

Removal

1 If required drain the final drive gear oil (see Chapter 1).

2 Remove the rear wheel (see Section 18).

3 Support the final drive housing, then unscrew the four nuts and remove the washers securing it to the swingarm **(see illustration)**.

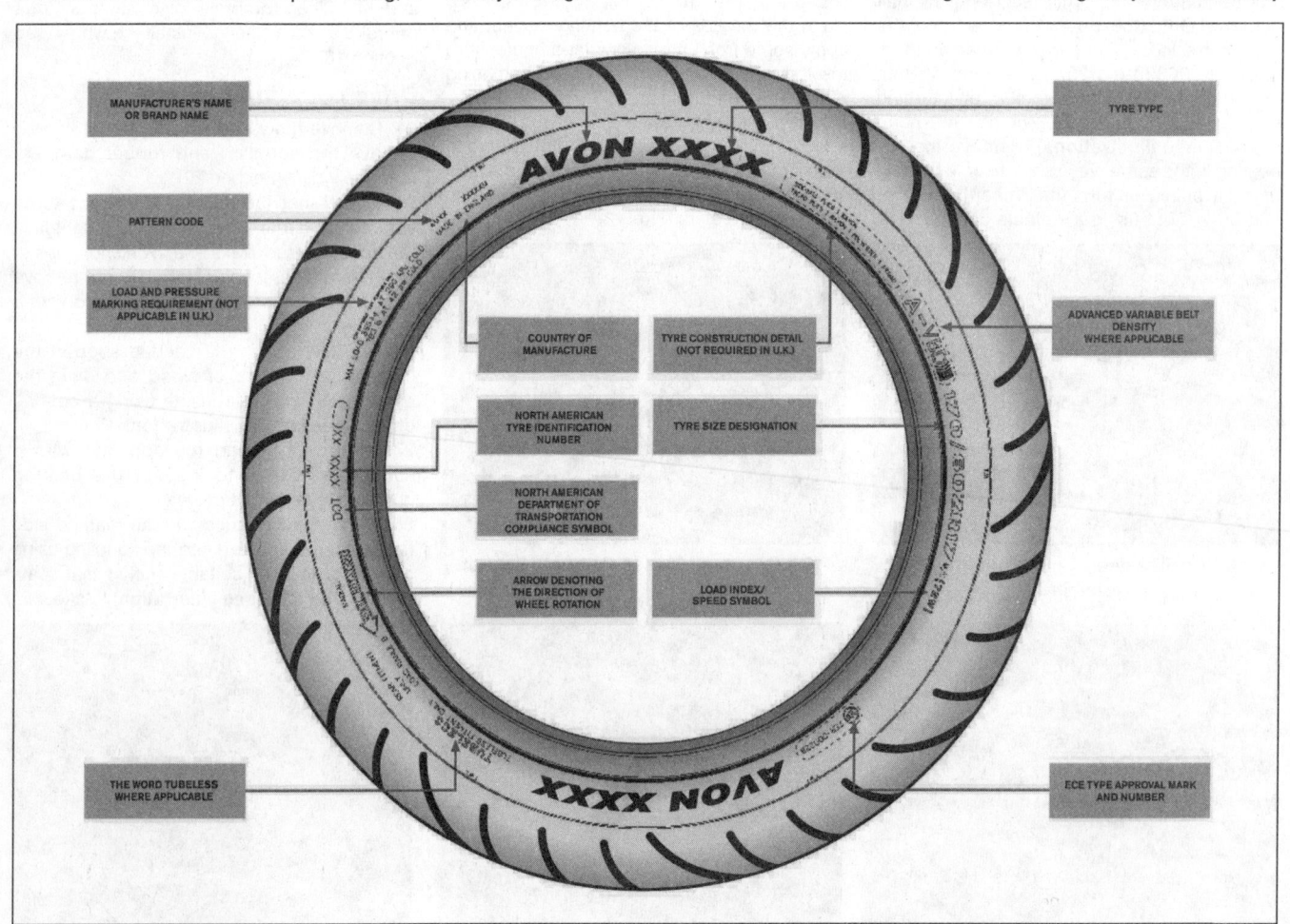

20.3 Common tyre sidewall markings

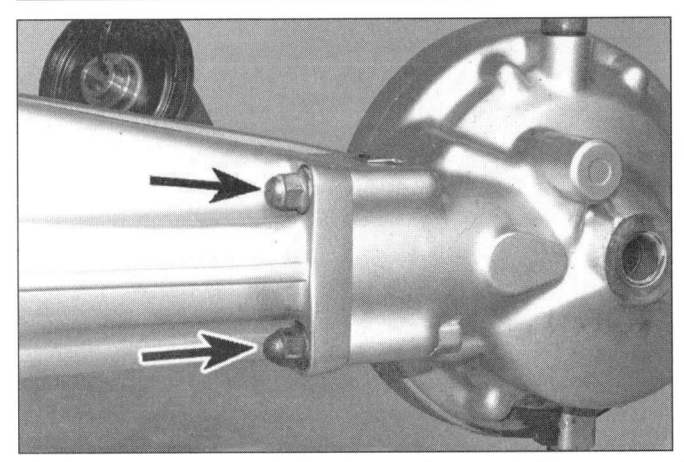

Brakes, wheels and final drive 6•29

21.3a Unscrew the nuts (arrowed) on each side...

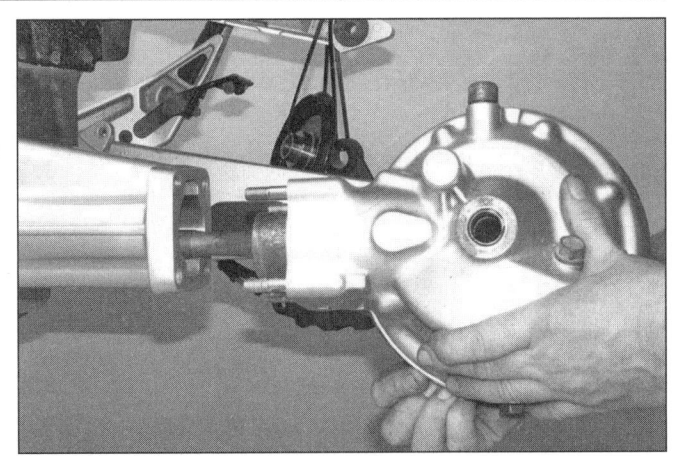

21.3b ...and remove the housing and driveshaft

21.4a Drive the housing off the shaft as shown

21.4b Remove the front circlip...

Draw the housing off – the driveshaft will come with it **(see illustration)**.

4 If required remove the driveshaft from the final drive housing, but note that a new oil seal will be needed when you refit it: to remove the shaft secure it in a vice and have an assistant hold the housing, then tap the housing off the shaft using a mallet and piece of wood as shown **(see illustration)**. Note that oil can now leak out if the housing is not supported upright. Remove the circlip from the front of the shaft **(see illustration)**. Remove the circlip and washer from the bottom of the shaft **(see illustrations)**. Use a cold chisel to dislodge the oil seal and slide it off **(see illustration)**. Remove the spring from the housing only if it is loose **(see illustration)**.

Inspection

5 Rotate the driveshaft joint in the front of the final drive housing – check it rotates smoothly and freely and that the power is transmitted correctly through the bevel gear assembly to the output boss. If there are any signs of roughness or notchiness or any evidence of wear or excessive backlash, the unit must be disassembled and examined further.

6 Check the housing for any evidence of oil leakage from the seals. If there is leakage from around the driveshaft seal remove the shaft

21.4c ...the rear circlip...

21.4d ...and the washer

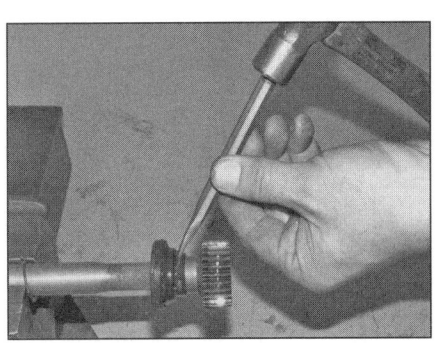

21.4e Drive the seal off

21.4f The spring (arrowed) should be secure

6•30 Brakes, wheels and final drive

21.7 Check all related splines for wear and damage

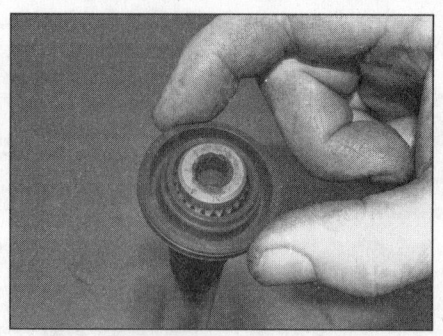

21.9a Make sure the seal is the correct way round

21.9b Fit the old seal onto the new one to act as an interface...

21.9c ...then use a suitable nut...

21.9d ...and/or piece of tube to drive the seal on...

21.9e ...until it is seated

and replace the seal with a new one – see Steps 4 and 9/10.

7 Check the splines on each end of the driveshaft and those in the final drive housing for wear and damage **(see illustration)**. If any is evident on the front splines also check the universal joint (see below). Replace worn or damaged components with new ones.

8 If attention to the final drive housing is required, the complete unit should be taken to a Yamaha dealer or service agent who will have the necessary special tools and expertise to carry out the complicated inspection and overhaul procedure.

Installation

9 Smear the inner lip of the new oil seal with lithium-based grease. Slide the seal all the way down the shaft, making sure it is the correct way round as shown **(see illustration)**. Now slide the old seal onto the new one, then find a suitable nut or spacer and/or a piece of tubing that will fit around the inner lip of the seal to drive the seal on until it seats **(see illustrations)**. Remove the old seal **(see illustration)**. Fit the washer, then fit a new circlip into its groove **(see illustration 21.4d and c)**. Fit a new circlip into the front groove in the shaft **(see illustration 21.4b)**.

10 Make sure the spring is in the housing **(see illustration 21.4f)**. Smear the driveshaft and final drive housing splines with molybdenum disulphide grease. Smear the outer lip of the seal with lithium-based grease. Fit the shaft into the housing, then drive the seal in using a piece of tubing that locates only on the outer lip until it seats **(see illustrations)**.

11 Fit the final drive housing onto the swingarm, making sure the driveshaft engages correctly with the universal joint **(see illustration 21.3b)** – you can remove the UJ

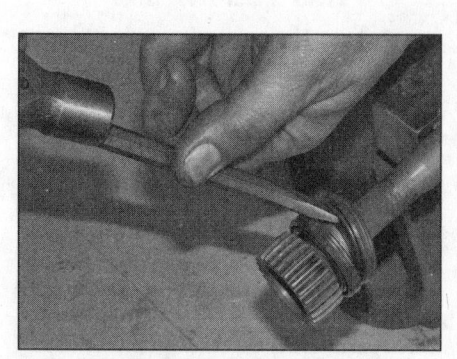

21.9f Remove the old seal

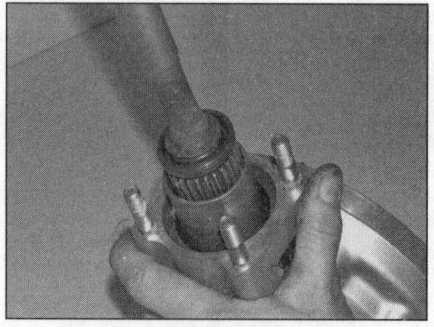

21.10a Fit the shaft into the housing...

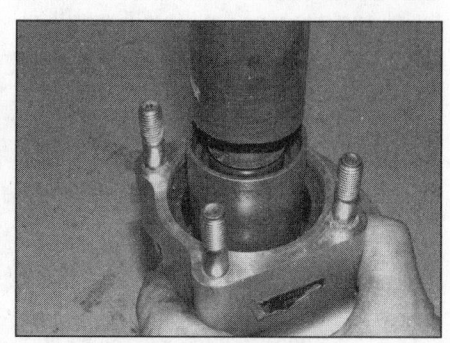

21.10b ...and drive the seal in

Brakes, wheels and final drive 6•31

21.11a Remove the cover and guide the shaft into the UJ

21.11b Fit the washers and the nuts

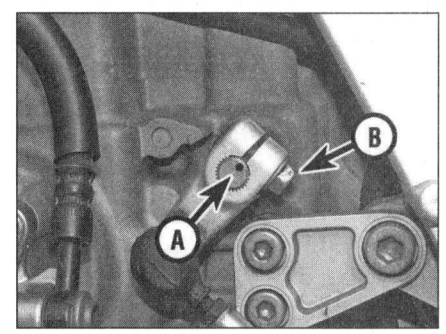

21.15 Note the alignment of the punch mark (A) then unscrew the bolt (B) and slide the arm off the shaft

cover **(see illustrations 21.17a to d)** and guide the shaft in if required, or turn the output boss on the housing to confirm engagement **(see illustration)**. Fit the washers and nuts and tighten them evenly in a criss-cross pattern to the torque setting specified at the beginning of the Chapter **(see illustration)**.

12 Install the rear wheel (see Section 18). Go around the final drive housing nuts again, tightening them to the specified torque.

13 If drained fill the final drive housing with the correct grade and quantity of oil (see Chapter 1).

Universal joint

Removal

14 Remove the final drive housing and driveshaft (see above).

15 On models with a standard gearchange, note the alignment of the slit in the gearchange linkage arm with the punch mark on the shaft, then unscrew the pinch bolt and slide the arm off **(see illustration)**. Unscrew the footrest bracket bolts and remove the footrest bracket/gearchange lever assembly, and support the sidestand assembly so the wiring is not strained **(see illustrations 21.16a and b)**.

16 On YCC-S models unscrew the footrest bracket bolts and displace the footrest bracket/gearchange lever assembly and the sidestand assembly, supporting them so they are clear of the UJ with no strain on the wiring **(see illustrations)**.

17 Remove the UJ covers **(see illustrations)**.

18 Remove the UJ **(see illustration)**.

21.16a Unscrew the bolts (arrowed)...

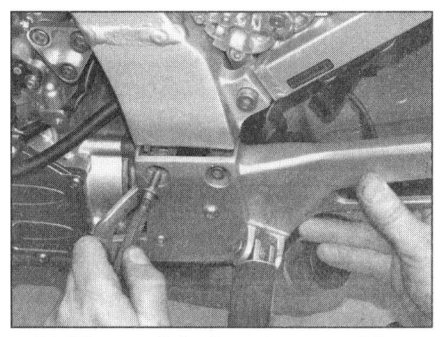

21.16b ...and displace the assemblies

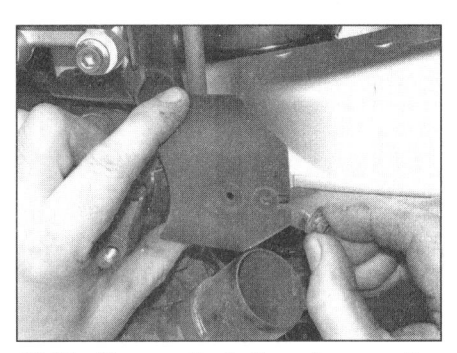

21.17a Unscrew the bolts and remove the outer cover

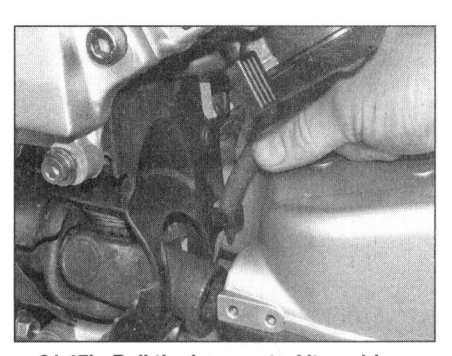

21.17b Pull the hose out of its guide...

21.17c ...release the trim clip...

21.17d ...and remove the inner cover

21.18 Slide the UJ off the shaft

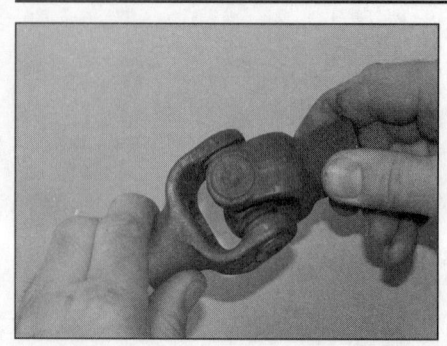

6•32 Brakes, wheels and final drive

21.19 Check for any play and rough movement

22.3a Undo the screws (arrowed), remove the retainer...

22.3b ...and lift the coupling out

Inspection

19 Check the splines in each end of the UJ, on the front of the driveshaft and on the output shaft on the engine for wear and damage. Check for any play or roughness in the joint coupling **(see illustration)**. Replace worn or damaged components with new ones.

Installation

20 Installation is the reverse of removal, noting the following:
- Smear the UJ and output shaft splines with molybdenum disulphide grease.
- Fit and tighten the footrest bracket bolts as follows – first clean the bolt threads, then apply some fresh non-permanent threadlock. Fit all the bolts finger-tight at first, then tighten the lower (sidestand) bolts first, then the upper (M8) bolts, then the front (M10) bolt, applying the correct torque setting to each bolt as specified at the beginning of the Chapter.
- On models with a standard gearchange align the slit in the linkage arm clamp with the punch mark on the gearchange shaft **(see illustration 21.15)**.

22 Rear wheel drive coupling

1 Remove the rear wheel (see Section 18).
2 Check for play between the drive coupling and the wheel hub. Any play indicates worn rubber damper segments.
3 Undo the drive coupling retainer screws, remove the retainer and lift the coupling out of the hub **(see illustrations)**.
Caution: Do not lay the wheel down on the disc as it could become warped. Lay the wheel on wooden blocks so that the disc is off the ground.
4 Check the condition of the splines on the drive coupling and those in the final drive housing for wear and damage. Replace the coupling with a new one if necessary. If the splines in the final drive housing are worn or damaged refer to Section 21.

22.5 Check the rubber dampers

5 Lift the rubber damper segments from the wheel and check them for cracks, hardening and general deterioration **(see illustration)**. Replace them with a new set if necessary.
6 Fit the drive coupling. Clean the threads of the retainer screws and apply some fresh threadlock. Fit the retainer and tighten the screws.
7 Install the wheel (see Section 18).

Chapter 7
Bodywork

Contents

	Section number		Section number
General information	1	Bodywork (2006 to 2012 models)	4
Trim clips	2	Bodywork (2013-on models)	5
Bodywork (2001 to 2005 models)	3		

Degrees of difficulty

Easy, suitable for novice with little experience	**Fairly easy,** suitable for beginner with some experience	**Fairly difficult,** suitable for competent DIY mechanic	**Difficult,** suitable for experienced DIY mechanic	**Very difficult,** suitable for expert DIY or professional

1 General information

This Chapter covers the procedures necessary to remove and install the bodywork. Since many service and repair operations on these motorcycles require the removal of the body panels, the procedures are grouped here and referred to from other Chapters.

In the case of damage to the bodywork, it is usually necessary to remove the broken component and replace it with a new (or used) one. Note that there are however some companies that specialise in 'plastic welding' and there are a number of bodywork repair kits now available for motorcycles.

When attempting to remove any body panel, first study it closely, noting any fasteners and associated fittings, to be sure of returning everything to its correct place on installation. Refer to Section 2 for more information on the types of trim clip used and how to release and refit them. In some cases the aid of an assistant will be required when removing panels, to help avoid the risk of damage to paintwork. Once the evident fasteners have been removed, try to withdraw the panel as described but DO NOT FORCE IT – if it will not release, check that all fasteners have been removed and try again.

When installing a body panel, first study it closely, noting any fasteners and associated fittings removed with it, to be sure of returning everything to its correct place. Check that all fasteners are in good condition, including the trim clips and damping/rubber mounts; replace any faulty fasteners with new ones before the panel is reassembled. Check also that all mounting brackets are straight and repair them or replace them with new ones if necessary before attempting to install the panel.

Tighten the fasteners securely, but be careful not to overtighten any of them or the panel may break (not always immediately) due to the uneven stress.

7•2 Bodywork

2.2a Push the centre pin (arrowed)...

2.2b ...into the body to release the clip

2.2c Push the centre pin out before installing the clip, then push it in when installed to lock it

2.3 Pull the centre pin (arrowed) out to release the clip, and push it back in to lock it

2.4a Undo the centre screw then pull the clip out

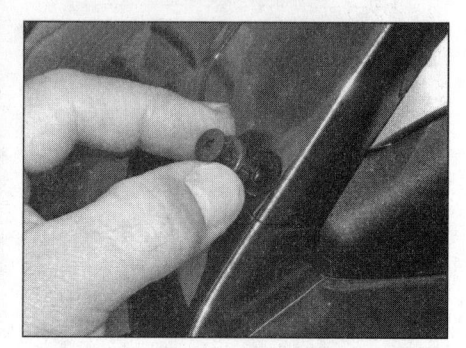

2.4b Fit the clip in the hole then push the centre in to lock it

2 Trim clips

1 Three types of plastic trim clip may be used, so carefully note which fits where when removing the body panels.

2 The first and most widely used type has a centre pin that you push into the body of the clip to allow the clip to be drawn out of the panel **(see illustrations)**. To install the clip, first expand the pawls of the clip body and push the centre pin back out **(see illustration)**. Now fit the clip body into its hole, then push the centre pin in so that it is flush with the clip head. The clip should now be locked in place.

3 The second type has a protruding centre pin that you pull out of the body of the clip to allow the clip to be drawn out of the panel **(see illustration)**. To install the clip, fit the clip body into its hole, then push the centre pin in. The clip should now be locked in place.

4 The third type of trim clip has a Phillips screw head in the centre that you unscrew, then pull the body of the clip out of the panel **(see illustration)**. When installing the clip, insert it in the panel then push the centre fully into the body **(see illustration)**. As they are made of plastic, the threads easily become worn in which case the centres may not unscrew. If this happens, lever the centre out of the body using a small screwdriver and replace the trim clip with a new one.

3 Bodywork (2001 to 2005 models)

Seats

1 Remove the rider's seat first – unlock the seat using the ignition key, turning it clockwise, then draw the seat back and up, noting how the tab at the front locates **(see illustration)**.

2 Draw the passenger seat forward and up, noting how the pegs at the front sit in the holes in the cross-beam and how it locates over the tab at the back **(see illustration)**.

3 Installation is the reverse of removal. Make sure the seats locate correctly. Push down

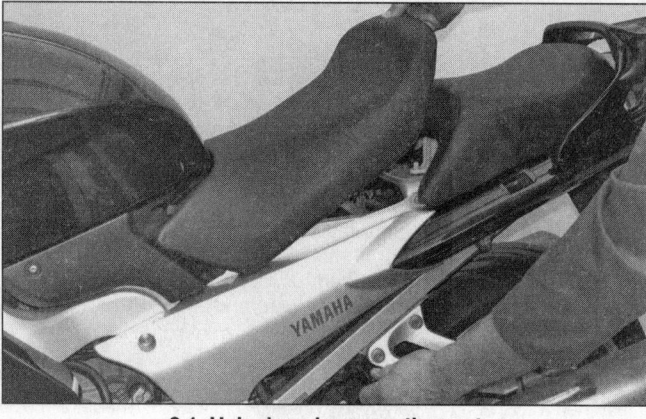

3.1 Unlock and remove the seat

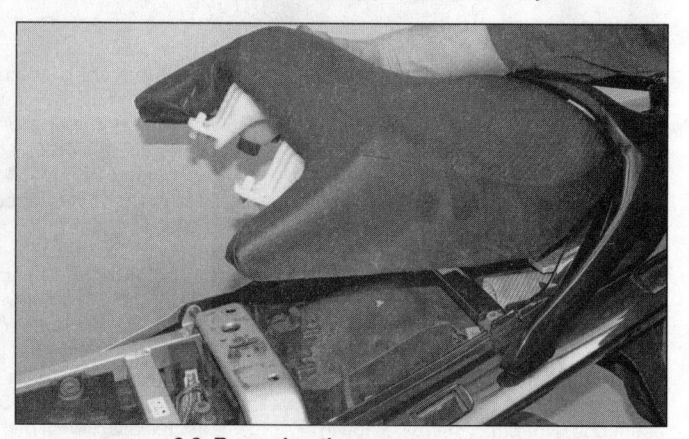

3.2 Removing the passenger seat

Bodywork 7•3

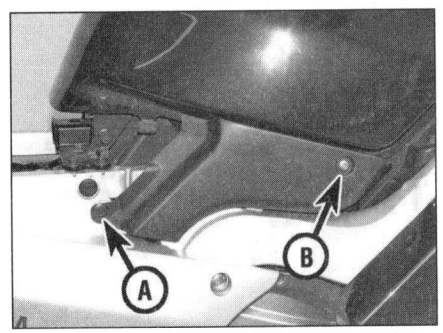

3.4a Release the trim clip (A) and undo the screw (B)...

3.4b ...then release the peg and remove the cover

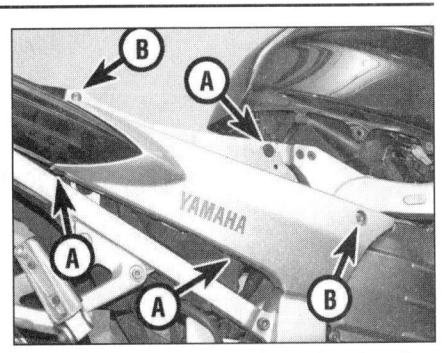

3.5a Release the trim clips (A) and undo the screws (B)...

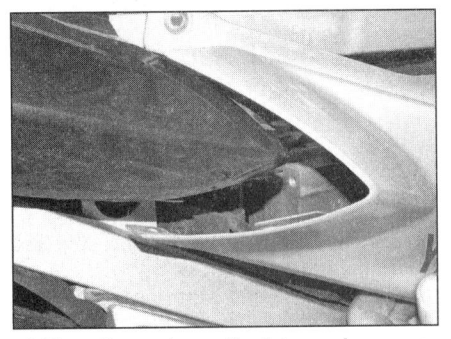

3.5b ...then release the tabs and remove the cover

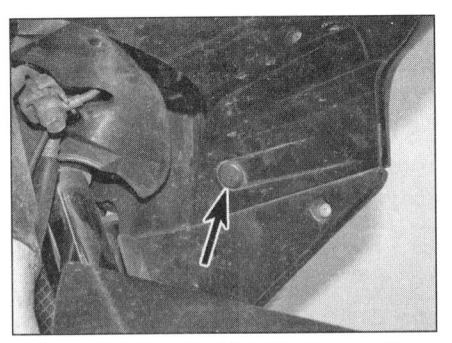

3.11a Release the trim clip (arrowed)...

3.11b ...and the trim clip (arrowed)

on the back of the rider's seat to engage the latch.

Side covers

4 Remove the seats. Remove the fuel tank trim piece **(see illustrations)**.
5 Release the three trim clips, then undo the two screws and remove the cover, noting how the tabs at the back locate **(see illustrations)**.
6 Installation is the reverse of removal.

Grab-rack and rear cover

7 Remove the seats and side covers.

8 Unscrew the five grab-rack bolts, noting the collars with the front ones, and lift the grab-rack off.
9 Release the two trim clips on each underside and the one on the top at the back and remove the rear cover.
10 Installation is the reverse of removal.

Fairing side panels

11 To remove the left-hand panel release the trim clips, one at the front and one in the cockpit **(see illustrations)**. If the other panel

has not already been removed undo the two centre panel screws and the joining screw on the underside **(see illustration)**. Undo the side panel screws, displace the panel and disconnect the turn signal wiring connector **(see illustrations 3.12b and c)**.
12 To remove the right-hand panel release the trim clip at the front **(see illustration)**. If the other panel has not already been removed undo the two centre panel screws and the joining screw on the underside **(see illustration 3.11c)**. Undo the side panel screws, displace the panel and disconnect the

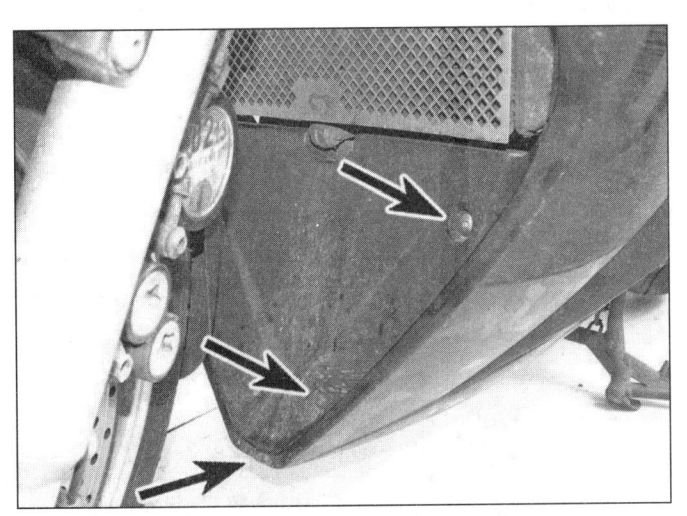

3.11c Undo the screws (arrowed)

3.11d Left-hand fairing side panel screws (arrowed)

7•4 Bodywork

3.12a Release the trim clip (arrowed)

3.12b Undo the screws (arrowed), displace the panel...

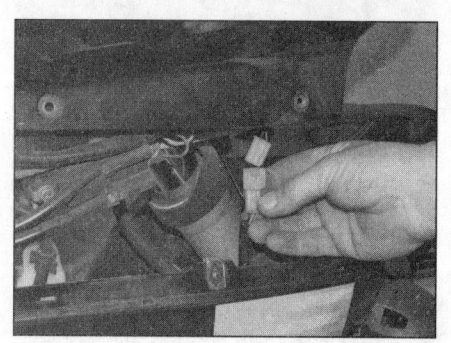

3.12c ...and disconnect the wiring

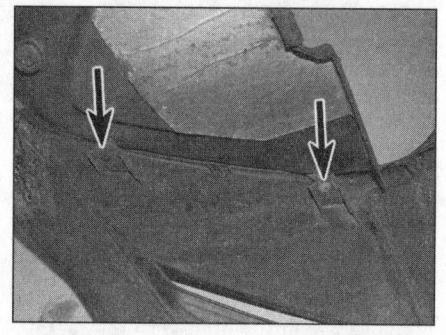

3.12d Centre panel screws (arrowed)

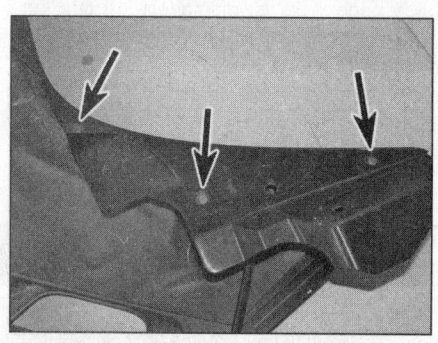

3.13 Inner panel screws (arrowed)

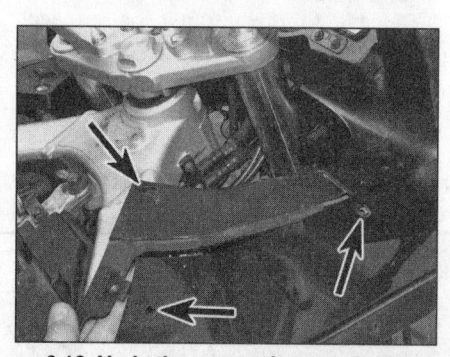

3.16 Undo the screws (arrowed) and remove the panel

3.18a Release the trim clip (arrowed)...

3.18b ...and undo the screws (arrowed)

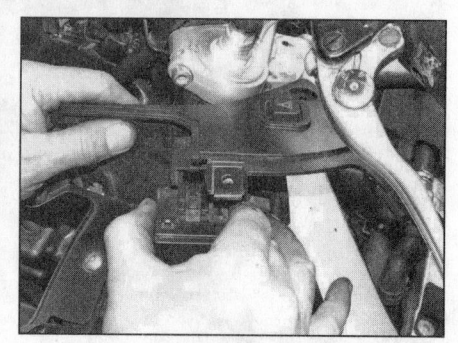

3.18c Displace the fusebox...

turn signal wiring connector **(see illustrations)** – the centre panel comes away with the side panel, and can be detached if required by undoing the two screws on the inner side **(see illustration)**.

13 If required detach the inner panel by undoing the screws **(see illustration)**.

14 If required remove the turn signal (see Chapter 8).

15 Installation is the reverse of removal.

Battery access panel

16 Undo the three screws and remove the panel **(see illustration)**.

17 Installation is the reverse of removal. Make sure the tab locates correctly.

Hazard switch panel

18 Release the trim clip and undo the screws **(see illustration)**. Carefully release the panel, then displace the fusebox and disconnect the hazard switch wiring connector **(see illustrations)**.

19 Installation is the reverse of removal.

Fairing pocket (2003 to 2005 models)

20 Remove the hazard switch panel and the left-hand instrument surround panel.

Bodywork 7•5

3.18d ...and disconnect the wiring

3.21a Undo the screws (arrowed), displace the pocket...

21 Undo the three screws, displace the pocket and disconnect the release switch wiring connector **(see illustrations)**.

22 Installation is the reverse of removal.

Instrument surround panels

23 Remove the battery access panel and hazard switch panel.

24 Remove the right-hand surround panel first – release the trim clip, then undo the two screws and remove the panel **(see illustrations)**.

25 Undo the two screws and remove the left-hand panel.

26 Installation is the reverse of removal.

Windshield

27 Undo the screws and remove the outer bracket and the windshield **(see illustration)**.

28 If required undo the inner bracket screws, then unscrew the nut on each side bolt and lift the inner bracket off **(see illustrations)**. Remove the bolts from the bracket, noting the collars and washers **(see illustration)**.

29 The windshield motor is covered in Chapter 8.

30 Installation is the reverse of removal.

Fairing

31 Remove the fairing side panels.

32 Remove the instrument surround panels.

33 Raise the fuel tank (see Chapter 4).

3.21b ...and disconnect the wiring

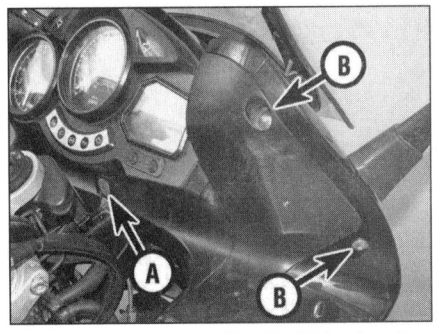

3.24a Release the trim clip (A) and undo the screws (B)...

3.24b ...then release and remove the panel

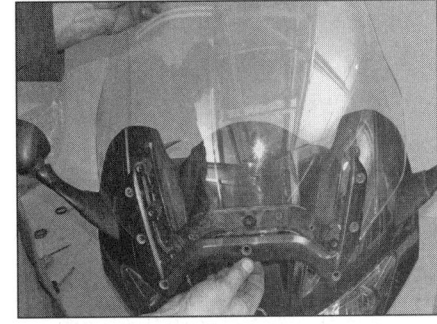

3.27 Seven screws secure the outer bracket and windshield

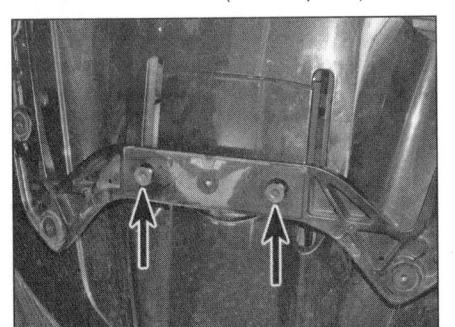

3.28a Undo the screws (arrowed)...

3.28b ...and the nut on each side to release the inner bracket

3.28c Remove each bolt with its washer and collar

7•6 Bodywork

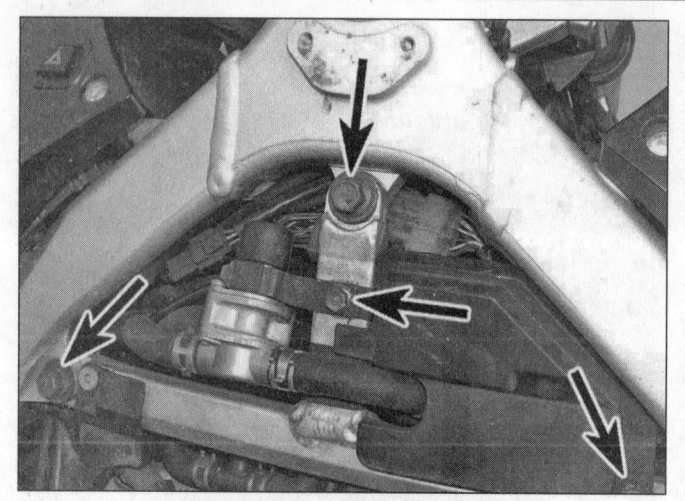

3.34a Unscrew the bolts (arrowed)...

3.34b ...and remove the T-bar

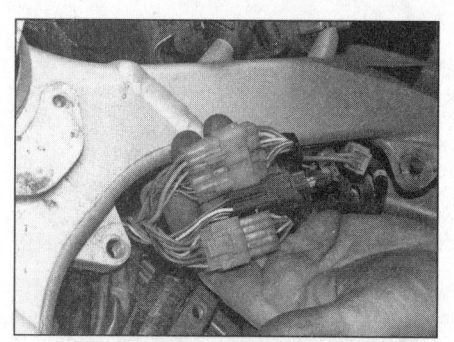

3.35a Disconnect the wiring

3.35b Release the clip (arrowed)

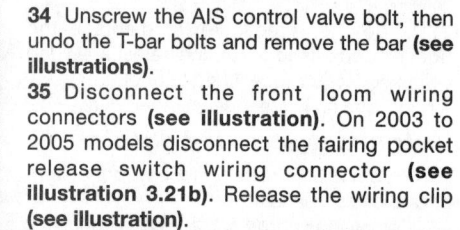

34 Unscrew the AIS control valve bolt, then undo the T-bar bolts and remove the bar **(see illustrations)**.
35 Disconnect the front loom wiring connectors **(see illustration)**. On 2003 to 2005 models disconnect the fairing pocket release switch wiring connector **(see illustration 3.21b)**. Release the wiring clip **(see illustration)**.
36 Unscrew the bolt on the right-hand side **(see illustration)**.
37 Unscrew the fairing bracket nuts, then withdraw the bracket **(see illustrations)**. Lift the fairing assembly (including the headlight and

3.36 Unscrew the bolt (arrowed)

3.37a Unscrew the nuts (arrowed)...

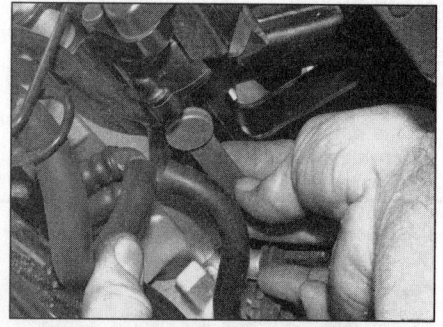

3.37b ...and withdraw the bracket

3.37c Lift the fairing bracket off the peg (arrowed)...

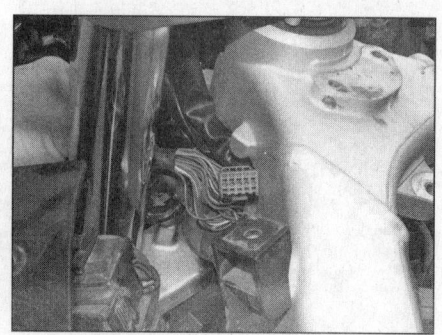

3.37d ...draw the wiring out...

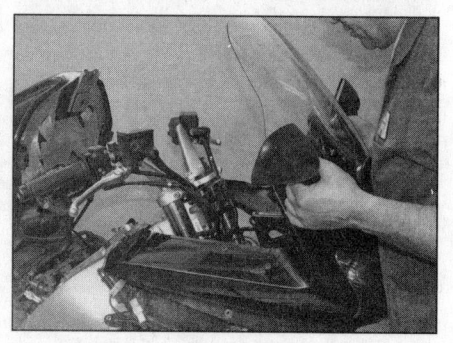

3.37e ...and remove the fairing

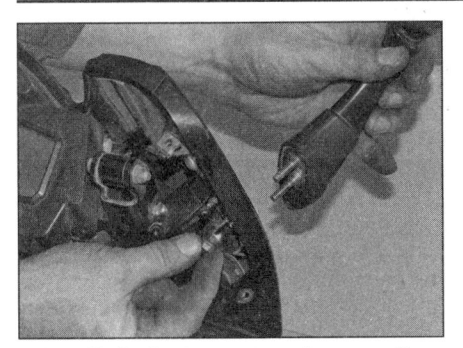

Bodywork 7•7

3.44 Undo the two nuts and remove the mirror

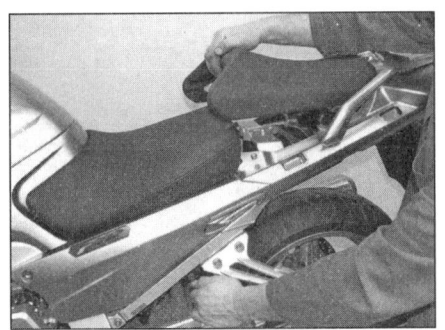

4.1 Unlock and remove the seat

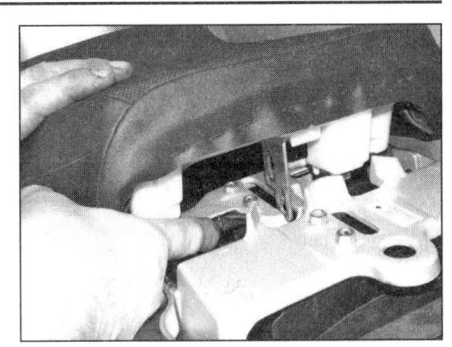

4.2 Removing the rider's seat

instruments) to release the hole in the bracket from the peg on the top mounting lug and draw the assembly forwards off the frame, drawing the wiring through the frame **(see illustrations)**.

38 If required remove the windshield and its inner bracket (see above), the mirrors (see below), the windshield motor and instrument assembly, and the headlight (see Chapter 8). Having done that you can detach the side sections of the fairing from the centre section by undoing the screws.

39 Installation is the reverse of removal. Tighten the T-bar bolts to the torque setting specified at the beginning of Chapter 4.

Front mudguard

40 Unscrew the brake hose holder bolt on each side **(see illustration 4.46)**.
41 Unscrew the two bolts on each side, then draw the mudguard forwards **(see illustrations 4.47a and b)**.
42 Installation is the reverse of removal.

Mirrors

43 Remove the instrument surround panels.
44 Undo the nuts and remove the mirror **(see illustration)**.
45 Installation is the reverse of removal.

4 Bodywork (2006 to 2012 models)

Seats

1 Remove the passenger seat first – unlock the seat using the ignition key, turning it clockwise, then draw the seat up and forwards, noting how the tabs at the back locate **(see illustration)**.
2 Move the rider's seat release lever to the left, then draw the seat up back, noting how the tab at the front locates **(see illustration)**.
3 If required remove the height adjuster plate, noting how it locates **(see illustration)**.
4 Installation is the reverse of removal. Fit the height adjuster plate in the desired position, identified by the H and L (high and low) alignment marks **(see illustration)** – if you adjust the position also move the seat tab locater cover on the tank bracket accordingly. Make sure the seats locate correctly. Push down on the back of the rider's seat and the front of the passenger seat to engage the latches.

Side covers

5 Remove the seats. Remove the fuel tank trim piece **(see illustrations)**.

4.3 Remove the seat height adjuster

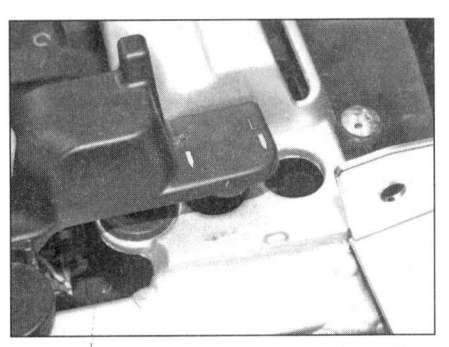

4.4 Set the adjuster in the desired position according to the H and L marks

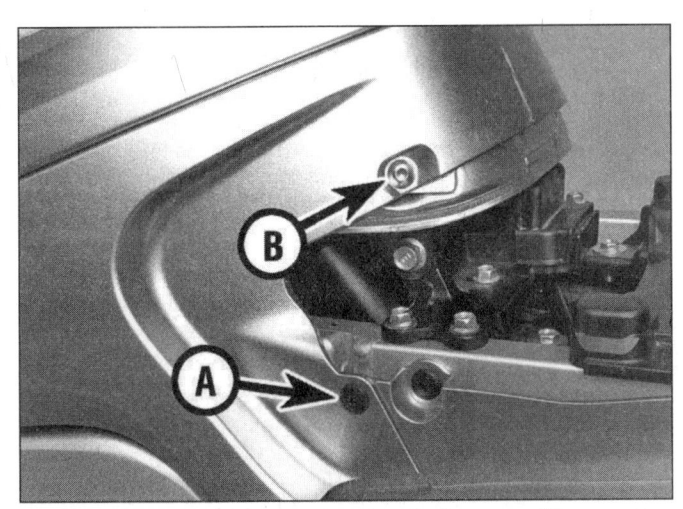

4.5a Release the trim clip (A) and undo the screw (B) on each side...

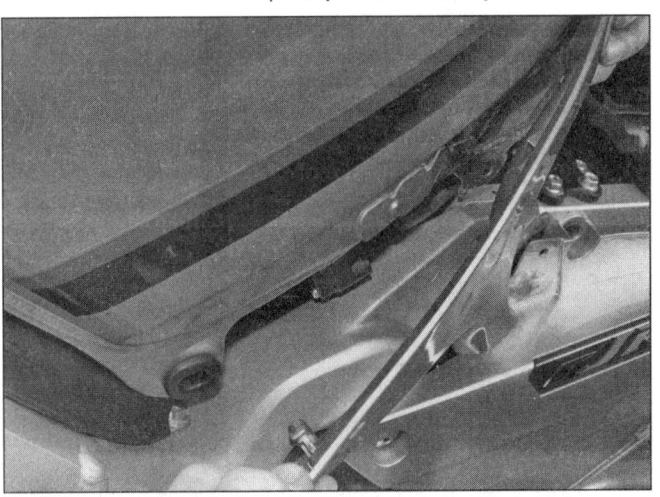

4.5b ...then pull the peg out of the grommet and draw the slot off the tab on each side

7•8 Bodywork

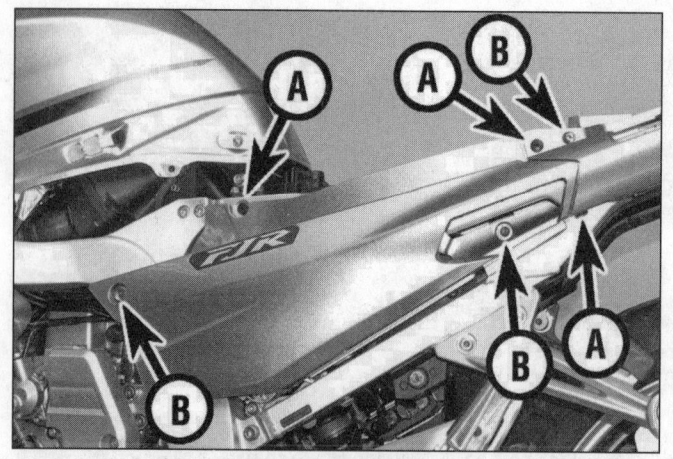

4.6a Release the trim clips (A) and undo the screws (B)...

4.6b ...then release the bottom edge...

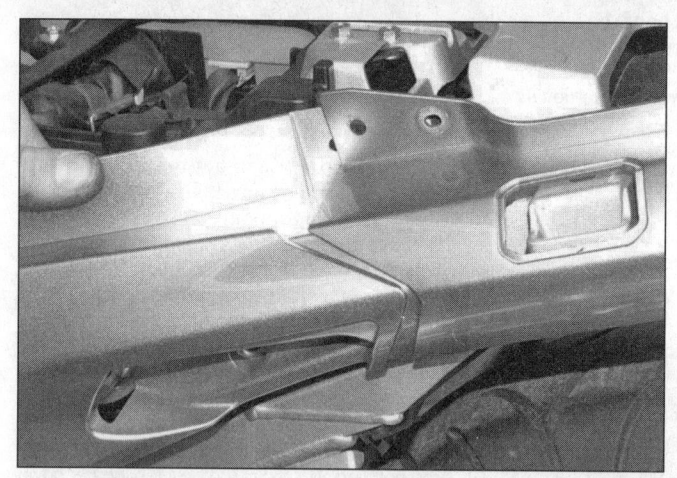

4.6c ...and the rear edge of the left-hand cover

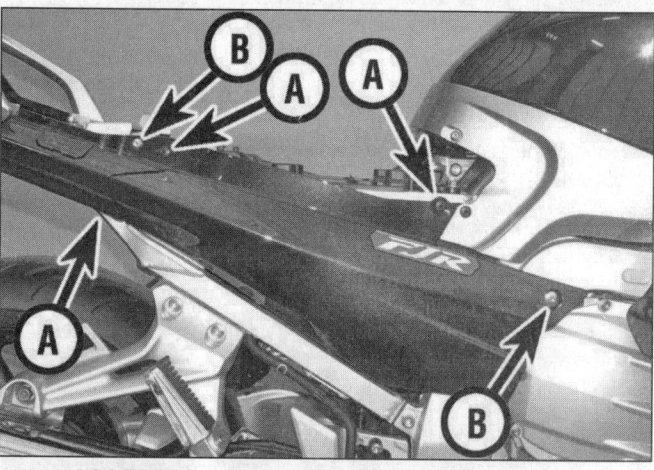

4.6d Right-hand cover trim clips (A) and screws (B)

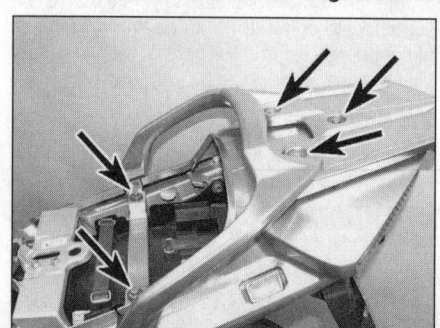

4.9 Grab-rack bolts (arrowed)

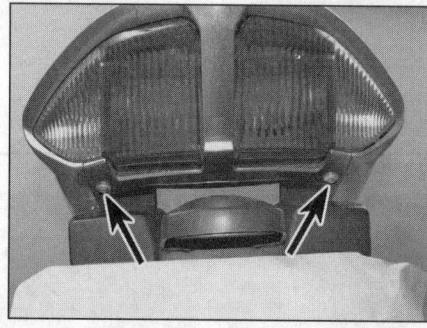

4.10a Undo the screws (arrowed)...

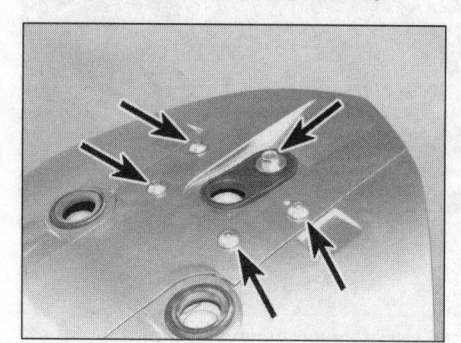

4.10b ...and the screws and bolt (arrowed)...

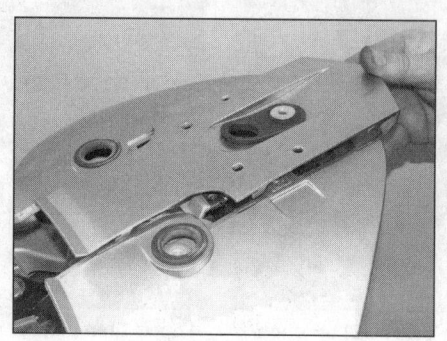

4.10c ...then draw the centre section off

6 Release the trim clips, then undo the screws (see illustration). Carefully pull the bottom edge of the cover away to release it from the grommet, then draw it forwards to release it from the rear cover (see illustrations).
7 Installation is the reverse of removal.

Grab-rack and rear covers

8 Remove the seats.
9 Unscrew the five grab-rack bolts, noting the collars with the front ones, and lift the grab-rack off (see illustration).
10 Undo the two screws on the underside of the centre section of the rear cover and the four screws and bolt on the top, then draw the cover back to release the hooks from the slots (see illustrations).
11 Release the trim clips on the underside of the side section of the rear cover (see illustration). Release the trim clip and undo the screw at the front at the front. Carefully pull the bottom edge away to release the cut-out from the grommet and remove the cover (see illustration).
12 Installation is the reverse of removal.

Fairing side panels

13 Remove the adjustable wing panel from the side panel being removed (see illustrations).

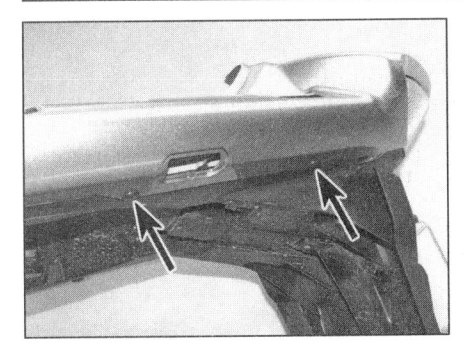

Bodywork 7•9

4.11a Release the trim clips (arrowed)

4.11b Release the cover from the grommet (arrowed)

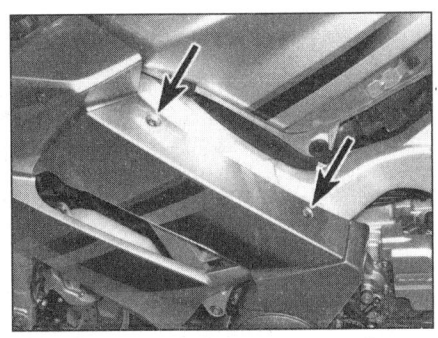

4.13a Undo the screws (arrowed)...

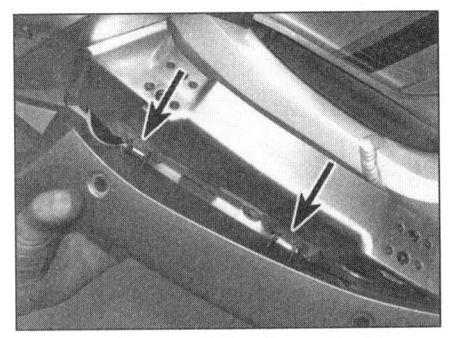

4.13b ...then carefully release the hinges from the clips

4.14a Release the trim clips (arrowed)...

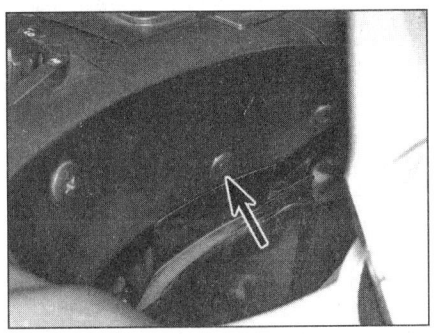

4.14b ...and the trim clip (arrowed)

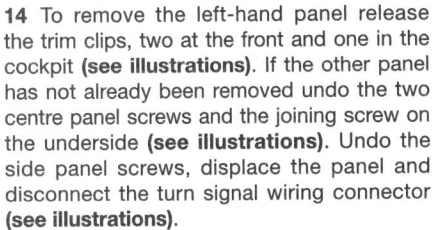

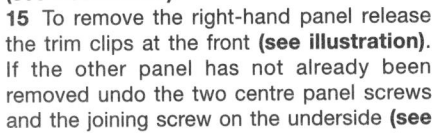

14 To remove the left-hand panel release the trim clips, two at the front and one in the cockpit (see illustrations). If the other panel has not already been removed undo the two centre panel screws and the joining screw on the underside (see illustrations). Undo the side panel screws, displace the panel and disconnect the turn signal wiring connector (see illustrations).

15 To remove the right-hand panel release the trim clips at the front (see illustration). If the other panel has not already been removed undo the two centre panel screws and the joining screw on the underside (see

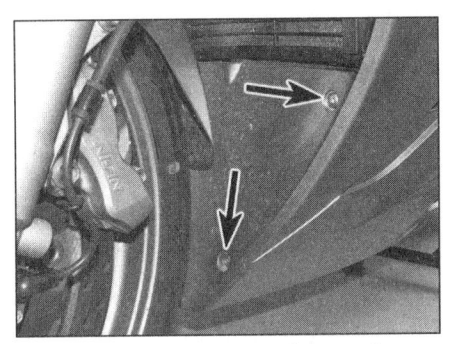

4.14c Undo the screws (arrowed)...

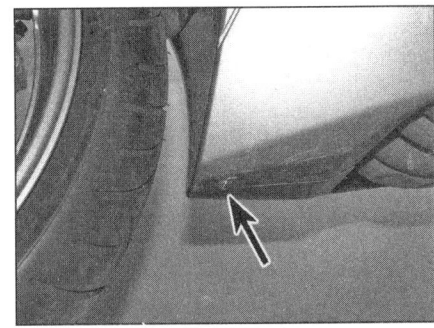

4.14d ...and the screw (arrowed)

4.14e Undo the screws (arrowed), displace the panel...

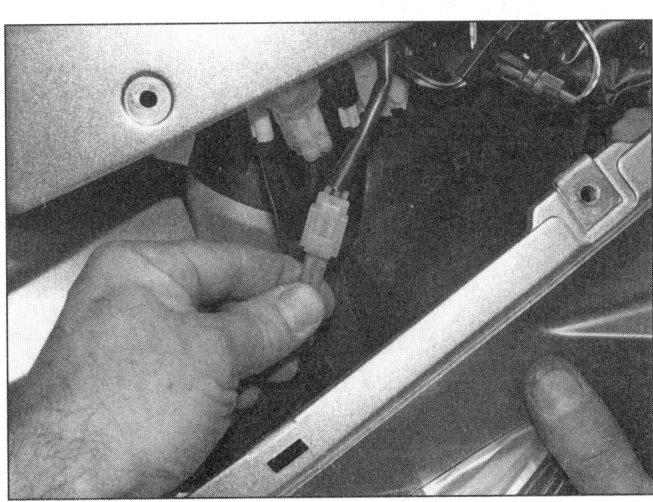

4.14f ...and disconnect the wiring

7•10 Bodywork

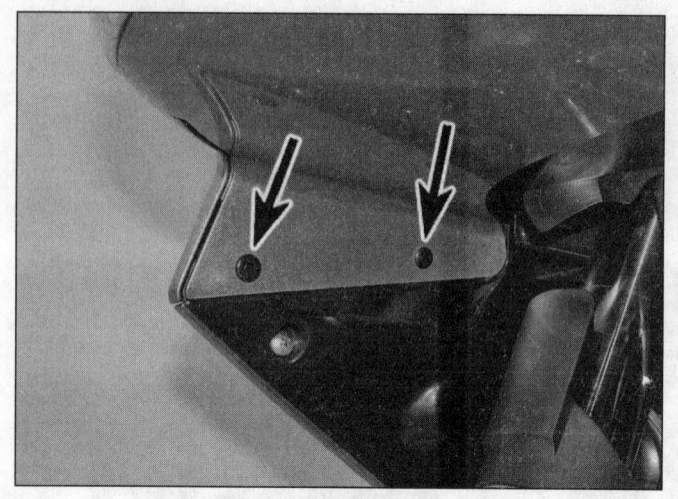

4.15a Release the trim clips (arrowed)

4.15b Undo the screws (arrowed), displace the panel...

illustrations 4.14c and d). Undo the side panel screws, displace the panel and disconnect the turn signal wiring connector (see illustrations) – the centre panel comes away with the side panel, and can be detached if required by undoing the two screws on the inner side.

16 If required detach the inner panel by undoing the screws (see illustration).

17 If required remove the turn signal (see Chapter 8).

18 Installation is the reverse of removal. There are two positions for the adjustable wing panel – fit it in the desired position.

Battery access panel

19 Release the trim clip, then undo the two screws and remove the panel (see illustrations).

20 Installation is the reverse of removal. Make sure the tab locates correctly.

Left-hand cockpit trim panel (2006 and 2007 models)

21 Open the fairing pocket. Release the trim clips and undo the two screws and remove the panel (see illustration 4.23a and b).

22 Installation is the reverse of removal.

Heated grip control panel (2008 to 2012 models)

23 Open the fairing pocket. Release the trim clips and undo the two screws (see illustration). Carefully displace the panel and disconnect the wiring connector (see illustration).

24 Installation is the reverse of removal.

Fairing pocket

25 Remove the left-hand cockpit trim panel or heated grip control panel (according to model), and the left-hand instrument surround panel.

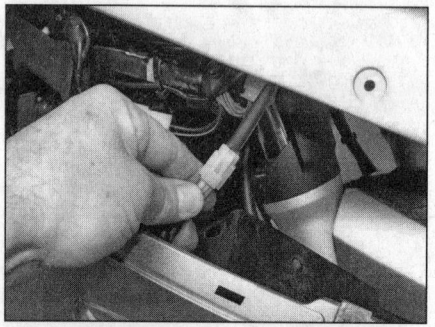

4.15c ...and disconnect the wiring

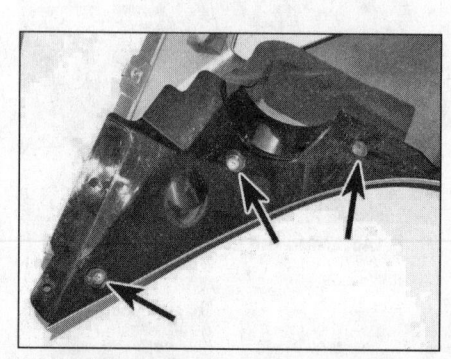

4.16 Inner panel screws (arrowed)

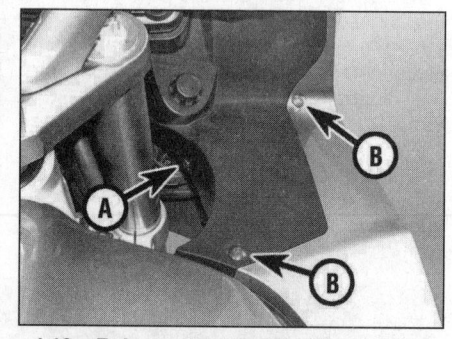

4.19a Release the trim clip (A), undo the screws (B)...

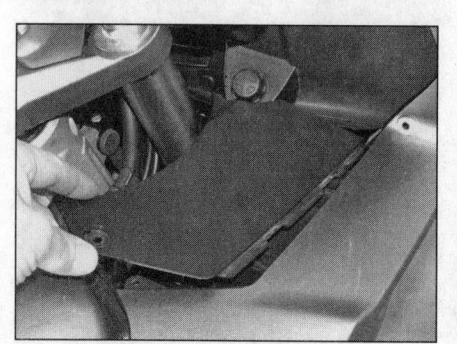

4.19b ...and remove the panel

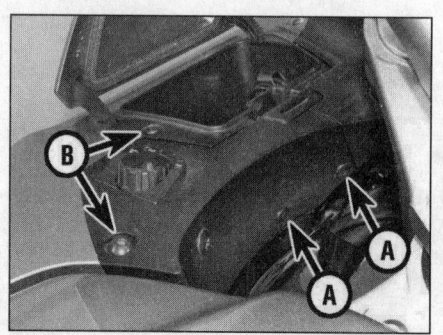

4.23a Release the trim clips (A), undo the screws (B)...

4.23b ...displace the panel and disconnect the wiring

Bodywork 7•11

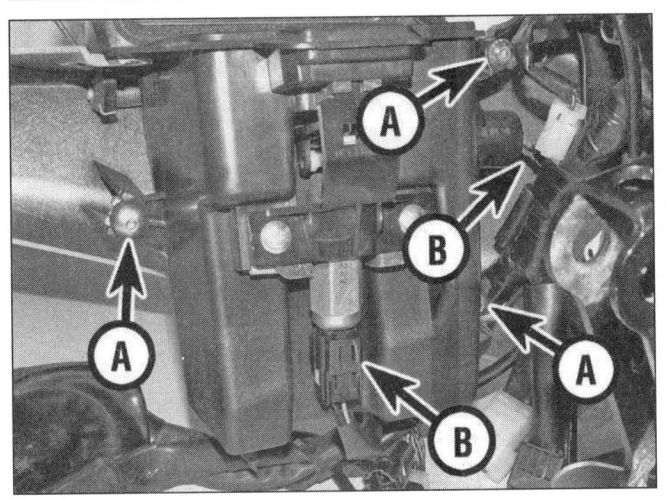

4.26 Fairing pocket screws (A) and wiring connectors (B – aux socket connector hidden)

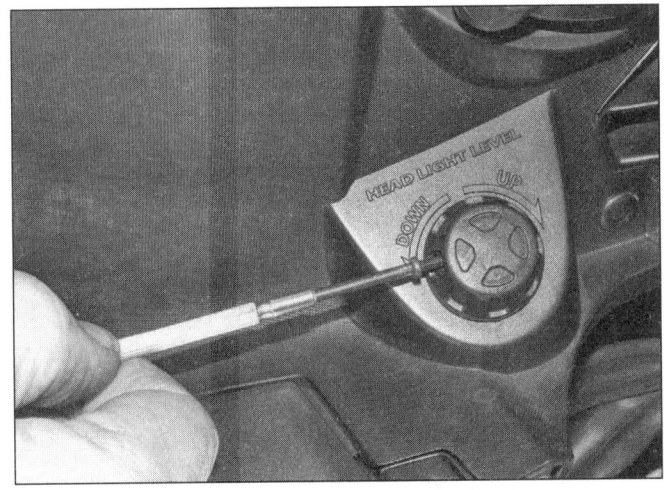

4.29a Undo the screw...

26 Undo the three screws, displace the pocket and disconnect the release switch and auxiliary socket wiring connectors (**see illustration**).

27 Installation is the reverse of removal.

Instrument surround panels

28 Remove the battery access panel, and the left-hand cockpit trim panel or heated grip control panel (according to model).

29 Undo the headlight beam adjuster knob screw and pull the knob off (**see illustrations**). Undo the adjuster nut (**see illustration**).

30 Release the trim clip, undo the screw(s) and remove the panel (**see illustrations**).

31 Installation is the reverse of removal – pull the headlight adjuster into the panel as you fit it, aligning the tab with the cut-out (**see illustration 4.30b**).

Windshield

32 Undo the screws, then lift the cover and slide it up to release the hooks from the windshield (**see illustrations**).

33 Undo the screws and remove the windshield (**see illustration**).

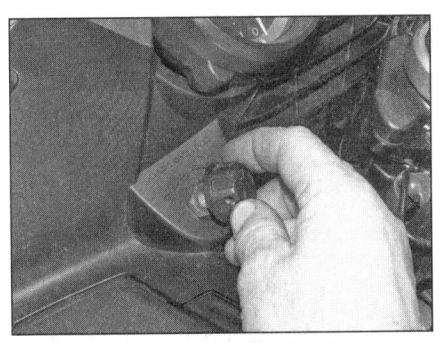

4.29b ...pull the knob off...

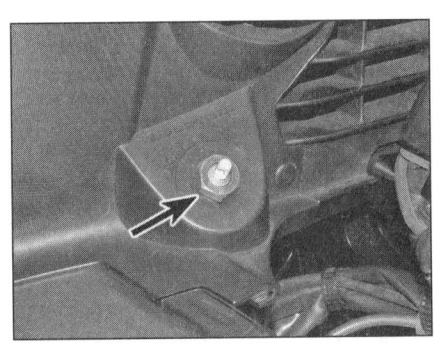

4.29c ...then unscrew the nut (arrowed)

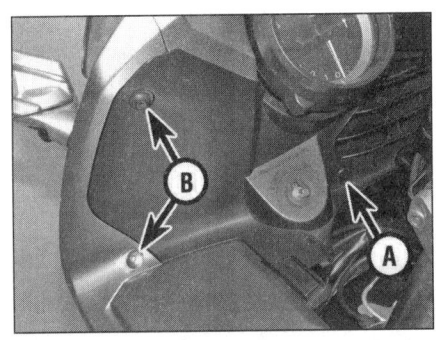

4.30a Release the trim clip (A) and undo the screws (B)...

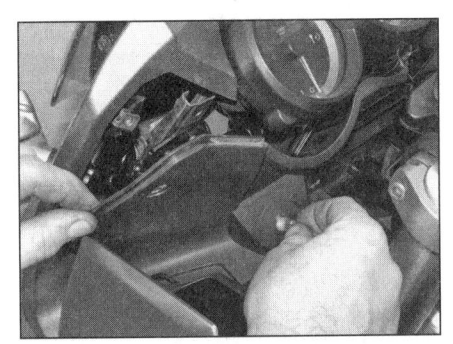

4.30b ...then release and remove the panel

4.32a Undo the screws (arrowed)...

4.32b ...lift the bottom edge and slide it up

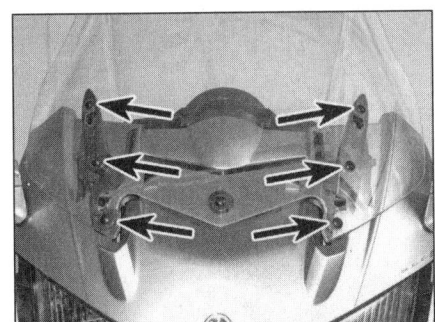

4.33 Windshield screws (arrowed)

4.34 Undo the screws (arrowed) on each side

4.40a Release the clip (arrowed)...

4.40b ...and the ties (arrowed)

34 Undo the two screws on each side and remove the bracket **(see illustration)**.
35 The windshield motor is covered in Chapter 8.
36 Installation is the reverse of removal.

Fairing

37 Remove the fairing side panels.
38 Remove the instrument surround panels.
39 Raise the fuel tank (see Chapter 4).
40 Release the wiring clip and the two wiring ties **(see illustrations)**.
41 Disconnect the front loom and horn wiring connectors **(see illustrations)**.
42 Unscrew the bolt on the right-hand side **(see illustration)**.
43 Unscrew the fairing bracket nuts, then withdraw the bracket **(see illustrations)**. Lift the fairing assembly (including the headlight and instruments) to release the hole in the bracket from the peg on the top mounting lug and draw the assembly forwards off the frame **(see illustrations)**.

44 If required remove the windshield and its bracket (see above), the mirrors (see below), the windshield motor and instrument assembly, and the headlight (see Chapter 8). Having done that you can detach the side sections of the fairing from the centre section by undoing the screws.

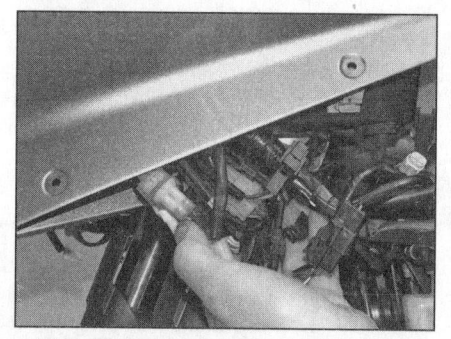

4.41a Disconnect all the relevant wiring connectors...

45 Installation is the reverse of removal. Make sure all wiring connectors are connected.

Front mudguard

46 Unscrew the brake hose holder bolt on each side **(see illustration)**.
47 Unscrew the two bolts on each side,

4.41b ...and the horn connectors (arrowed) on each side

4.42 Unscrew the bolt (arrowed)

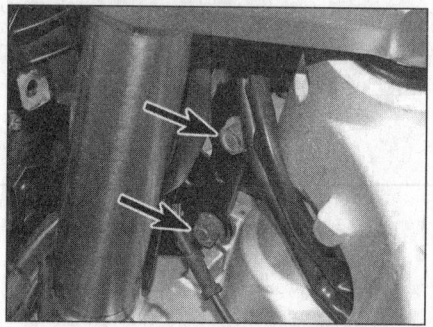

4.43a Unscrew the nuts (arrowed)...

4.43b ...and withdraw the bracket (arrowed)

4.43c Lift the fairing bracket off the peg (arrowed)...

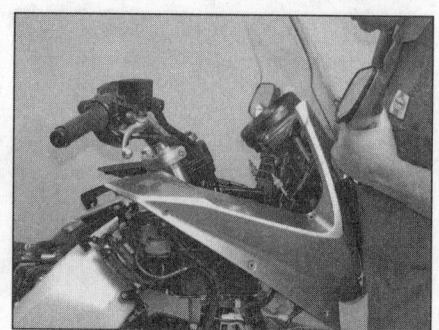

4.43d ...and remove the fairing

4.46 Brake hose holder bolt (arrowed)

Bodywork 7•13

4.47a Unscrew the bolts (arrowed) on each side...

4.47b ...and remove the mudguard

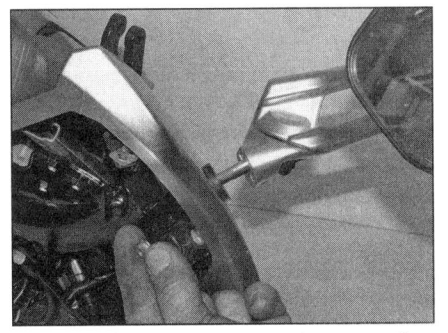

4.50a Undo the two nuts and remove the mirror...

4.50b ...and the mirror pad

then draw the mudguard forwards **(see illustrations)**.

48 Installation is the reverse of removal.

Mirrors

49 Remove the instrument surround panels.

50 Undo the nuts and remove the mirror **(see illustration)**. If required remove the mirror pad **(see illustration)**.

51 Installation is the reverse of removal. Make sure the mirror pad is in place.

5 Bodywork (2013-on models)

Seats, side covers, grab-rack and rear covers

Removal and installation

1 Refer to Section 4.

Instrument surround panel

2 Slacken off the grub screw in each headlight beam adjuster knob and pull the knobs off the adjuster rod ends **(see illustration)**.

3 Release the trim clips and two screws from each side of the panel **(see illustrations)**, then carefully release the top edge of the panel from the fairing and manoeuvre it past the steering head.

4 Installation is the reverse of removal. Be careful to clip the top edge of the panel under the fairing, engaging the tabs correctly **(see illustration)**. Pull the headlight adjuster into the panel as you fit it and align the tab with the cut-out when fitting the knobs. Check the beam height adjustment if the setting has been disturbed.

Battery access panel

5 Remove the instrument surround panel.

6 Release the trim clip from the inner edge, then undo the two screws **(see illustrations)**. Slide the panel forwards to disengage its

5.2 Headlight adjuster knob grub screw (arrowed)

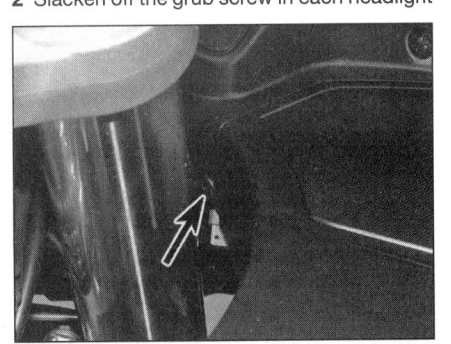

5.3a Instrument panel surround trim clip (arrowed)...

5.3b ...screw on each side of inner edge (arrowed)...

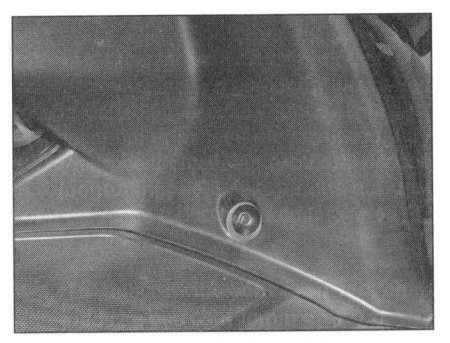

5.3c ...and outer edge

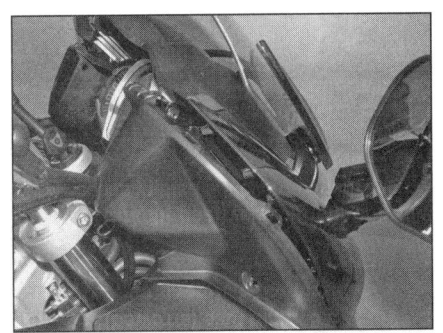

5.4 Tabs on panel edges engage with those on fairing

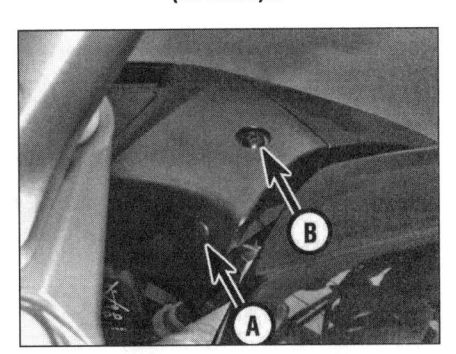

5.6a Trim clip (A), screw (B)...

7•14 Bodywork

slot from the fairing side panel slot **(see illustration)**.

7 Installation is the reverse of removal. Make sure the tab locates correctly and the edges of the panel locate under those of the fairing side panel.

Left-hand cockpit trim panel

8 Remove the instrument surround panel.
9 Open the fairing pocket and remove the screw from the rim of the box **(see illustration)**. Release the trim clips and undo the screw and remove the panel **(see illustration)**.
10 Installation is the reverse of removal.

Left-hand fairing side panel and fairing pocket

11 Remove the instrument surround panel and left-hand cockpit trim panel.
12 Remove the adjustable wing panel by releasing the fastener at the back, then sliding the panel up to release the hooks **(see illustrations)**.
13 Release the two trim clips from the front inside face of the panel **(see illustration)**. Remove the single screw from the front edge of the fairing pocket trim **(see illustration)**.

5.6b ...and screw at front secure access panel

5.6c Slot on rear edge engages tab on fairing side panel

Remove the screw from the air intake grille at the front **(see illustration)**. Undo the two centre panel screws and the joining screw on the underside **(see illustrations)**. Undo the two main side panel screws, displace the panel and disconnect the wiring connectors

5.9a Remove screw in fairing pocket rim (arrowed)...

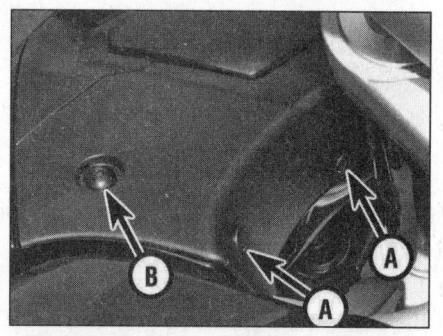

5.9b ...trim clips (A) and screw (B) to free cockpit panel

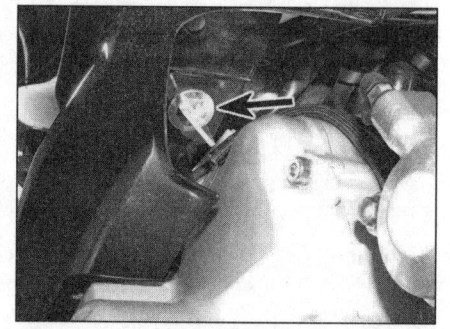

5.12a Quick release fastener (arrowed)...

5.12b ...and tabs secure wing panel

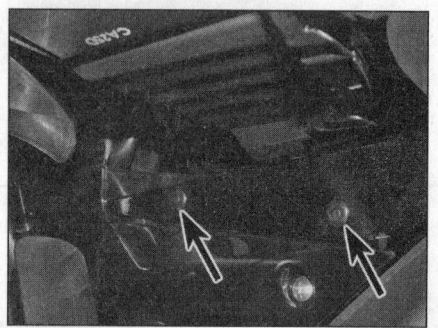

5.13a Two trim clips on inner face

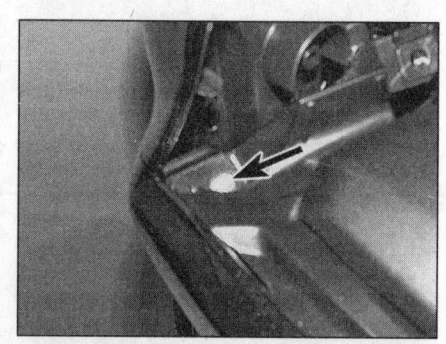

5.13b Single screw from inside top corner

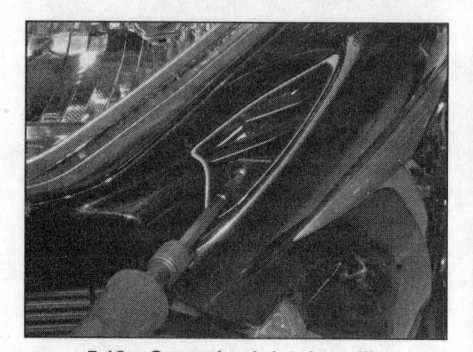

5.13c Screw in air intake grille

5.13d Two screws retain centre panel...

5.13e ...and single screw joins left and right side panels

Bodywork 7•15

5.13f Two main side panel screws (arrowed)

5.13g Disconnect the three wire connectors

for the turn signal, DC power socket and fairing pocket lock **(see illustrations)**.

14 Remove the inner panel to access the LED turn signal unit and fairing pocket **(see illustrations)**. With the fairing pocket removed, access is available to the trim panel at the top of the side panel **(see illustration)**.

15 Installation is the reverse of removal. There are two positions for the adjustable wing panel – fit it in the desired position.

Right-hand fairing side panel

16 Remove the instrument surround panel and battery access panel.

17 Remove the adjustable wing panel by releasing the fastener at the back, then sliding the panel up to release the hooks **(see illustrations)**.

18 To remove the right-hand panel release the two trim clips from the front inside face of the panel **(see illustration)**. Remove the screw from the air intake grille at the front **(see illustration)**. Undo the two centre panel screws on the left-hand side and the joining screw on the underside **(see illustrations 5.13d and e)**. Remove the single screw from the front top edge of the panel and disconnect the turn signal wiring connector

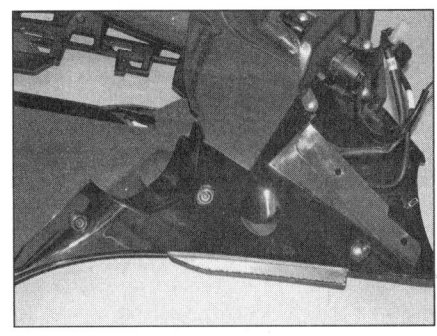

5.14a Remove the inner panel...

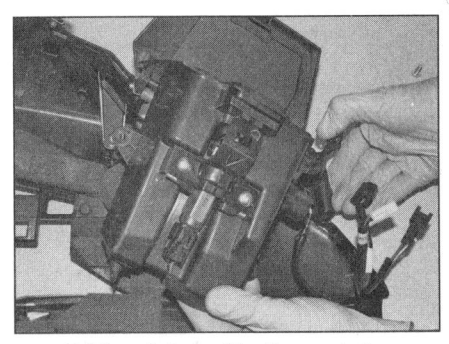

5.14b ...followed by the pocket...

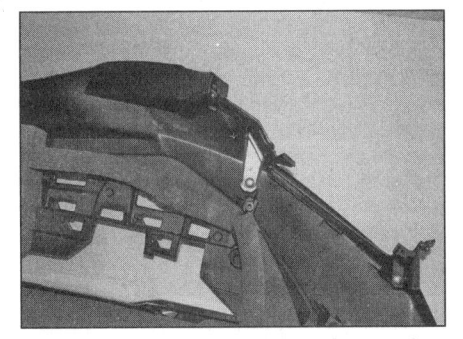

5.14c ...and the remaining trim panel

5.17a Quick release fastener (arrowed)...

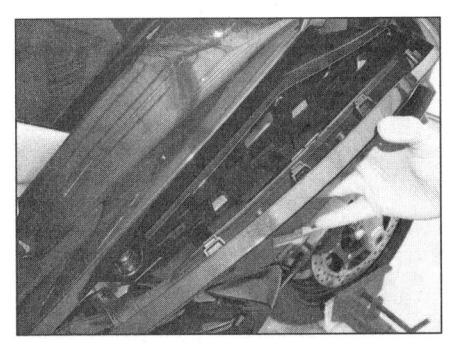

5.17b ...and tabs secure wing panel

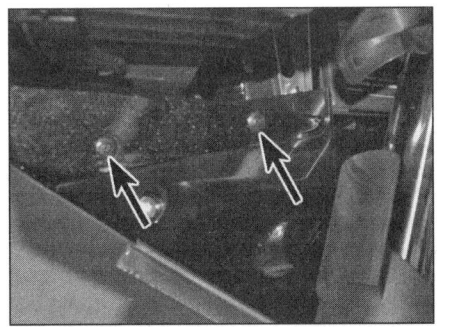

5.18a Two trim clips on inner face

5.18b Screw in air intake grille

7•16 Bodywork

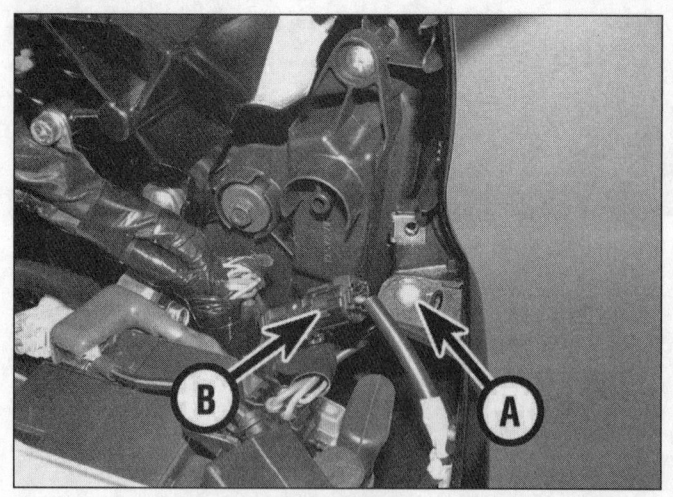

5.18c Single screw from inside top corner (A) and turn signal wire connector (B)

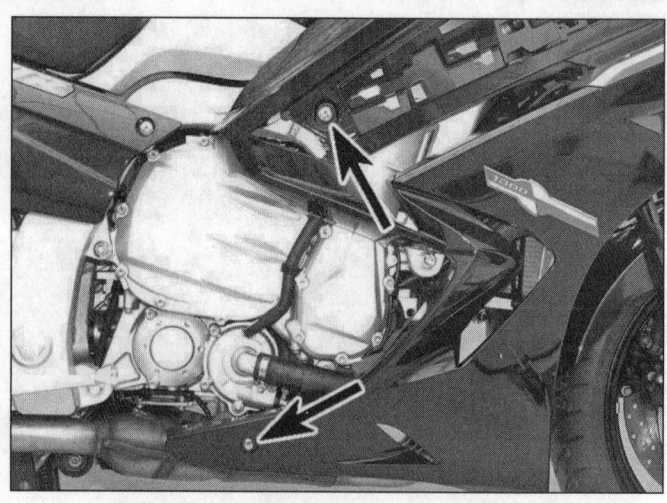

5.18d Two main side panel screws (arrowed)

(see illustration). Undo the side panel screws and displace the panel (see illustration). The centre panel comes away with the side panel, and can be detached if required by undoing the two screws on the inner side (see illustration).

19 For access to the LED turn signal unit detach the inner panel by undoing the screws (see illustration).

20 Installation is the reverse of removal. There are two positions for the adjustable wing panel – fit it in the desired position.

Windshield

21 Remove the screw from the underside of each cover, then slide the covers up to remove them from the slots in the screen (see illustrations).

22 Undo the six screws and remove the windshield (see illustration). Note that the screws thread into rubber-bodied wellnuts which should remain captive in the windshield brackets.

23 Undo the two bolts to free each bracket (see illustration).

24 The windshield motor and relays are covered in Chapter 8.

25 Installation is the reverse of removal.

Fairing

26 Remove the instrument surround panel, battery access panel, left-hand cockpit trim panel, both side panels and the windshield and its brackets.

27 Remove the centre cover assembly from the fairing; it is retained by two screws in the

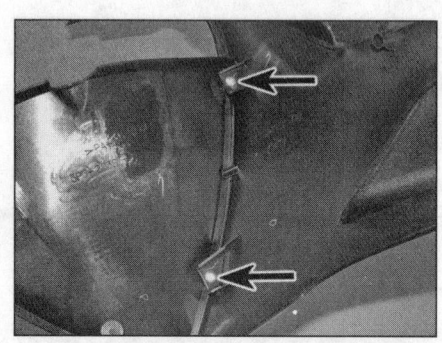

5.18e Centre panel screws (arrowed)

5.19 Remove the inner panel to access the turn signal

5.21a Remove the screw...

5.21b ...and disengage the cover

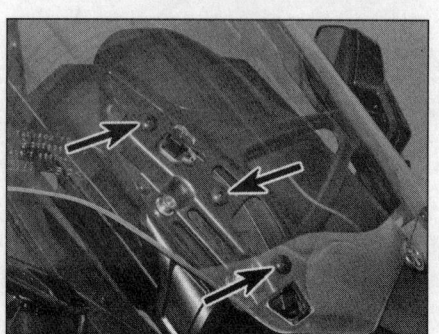

5.22 Screen is held by three screws (arrowed) on each side

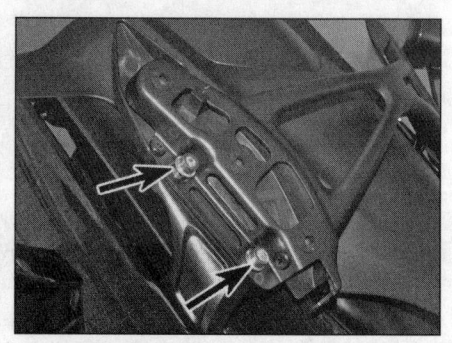

5.23 Fairing bracket bolts (arrowed)

Bodywork 7•17

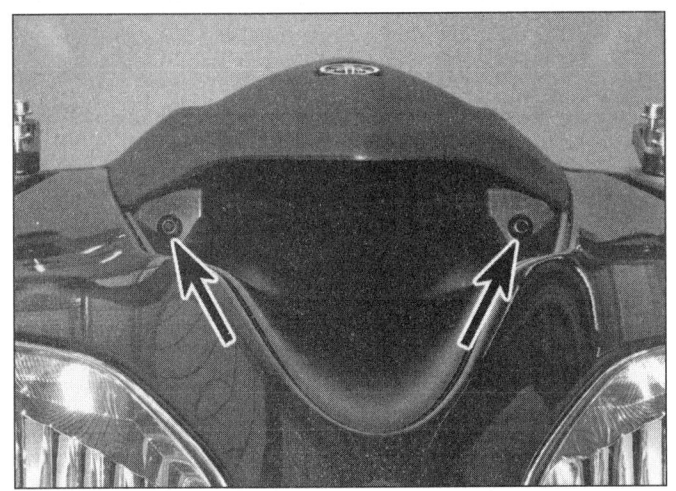

5.27a Centre cover is retained by two screws (arrowed)...

5.27b ...and tabs along all edges

centre, a tab at the lower point and clips all along the edges **(see illustrations)**.

28 Remove the mirrors. Each mirror is retained by two nuts on the inner side **(see illustration)**. Collect the rubber damper pad from the outer mounting **(see illustration)**.

29 The following procedure describes removal of the fairing without the headlights. Note that it is also possible to remove the fairing complete with headlights, although this will require the headlight wiring to be detached and the vertical beam adjuster rods to be disconnected.

30 Working from the inside of the fairing, remove the two screws from each side and the central screw **(see illustrations)**. Now carefully ease the fairing off the headlights.

31 Installation is the reverse of removal.

Front mudguard

32 Unscrew the brake hose holder bolt on each side **(see illustration 4.46)**.

33 Unscrew the two bolts on each side, then draw the mudguard forwards **(see illustrations 4.47a and b)**.

34 Installation is the reverse of removal.

Mirrors

35 Remove the instrument surround panel.

36 Undo the nuts and remove the mirror **(see illustrations 5.28a and b)**. If required remove the outer mirror pad **(see illustration 5.28c)**.

37 Installation is the reverse of removal. Make sure the outer mirror pad is in place.

5.28a Remove the two nuts...

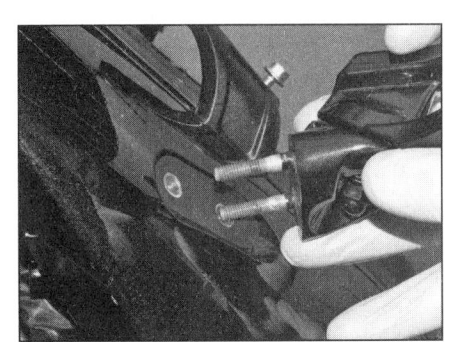

5.28b ...and free the mirror...

5.28c ...collecting the rubber damper pad

5.30a Fairing is retained to headlight by a screw on each side at the bottom...

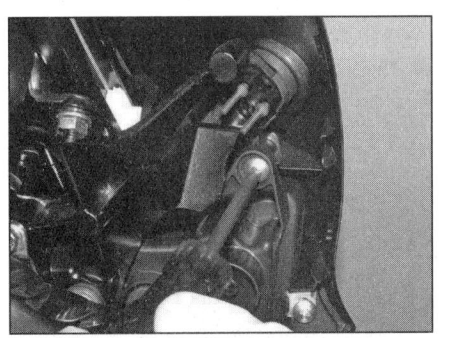

5.30b ...and top of headlight casing...

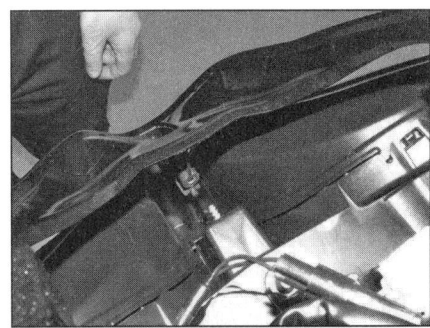

5.30c ...and by a single screw between the headlight units

Notes

Chapter 8
Electrical system

Contents

	Section number		Section number
Alternator rotor	see Chapter 2	Ignition switch	18
Alternator stator	29	Ignition system components	see Chapter 4
Battery charging	4	Instrument check and disassembly	16
Battery removal and maintenance	3	Instrument removal and installation	15
Brake light switches	14	Lighting system check	6
Brake/tail/licence plate light bulbs	9	Neutral switch/gear position switch	20
Charging system testing	28	Oil level sensor	17
Clutch switch	22	Regulator/rectifier	30
Cooling fans and relay	see Chapter 3	Sidestand switch	21
Electrical system fault finding	2	Starter circuit cut-off relay and diodes	see Chapter 4
Fuel injection system relay	see Chapter 4	Starter motor overhaul	27
Fuses	5	Starter motor removal and installation	26
General information	1	Starter relay	25
Handlebar switches	19	Tail light	10
Headlight	8	Turn signal assemblies	13
Headlight and sidelight bulbs	7	Turn signal bulbs	12
Heated grips	23	Turn signal circuit check	11
Horn(s)	24	Windshield motor	31

Degrees of difficulty

Easy, suitable for novice with little experience	Fairly easy, suitable for beginner with some experience	Fairly difficult, suitable for competent DIY mechanic	Difficult, suitable for experienced DIY mechanic	Very difficult, suitable for expert DIY or professional

Specifications

Battery
Type	GT14B-4
Capacity	12 V, 12 Ah
Voltage	
Fully-charged	12.8 V
Discharged	12.0 V
Charging rate	1.2 A for 5 to 10 hrs

Charging system
Alternator stator coil resistance	
2001 to 2005 models	0.15 to 0.23 ohms
2006-on models	0.13 to 0.19 ohms
Nominal output	
2001 to 2005 models	490 W @ 5000 rpm
2006-on models	590 W @ 5000 rpm
Regulated voltage (no load)	
2001 to 2005 models	14.1 to 14.9 V
2006 to 2012 models	14.2 to 14.8 V
2013-on models	14.3 to 14.7 V
Current leakage	around 2 mA (max)

Starter motor
Brush length	
New	10.8 mm
Service limit (min)	3.5 mm
Mica undercut	1.5 mm
Commutator diameter	
New	24.5 mm
Service limit (min)	23.5 mm

8•2 Electrical system

Fuses
See Section 5 and fusebox lid for fuse location and identification

Main	50A
Fuel injection system	15A
Headlight	25A
Radiator fan	
2001 to 2005 models	15A
2006 to 2012 models	15A x 2
2013-on models	10A x 2
Cooling system (2013-on models)	30A
Signalling system	
2001 to 2012 models	15A
2013-on models	10A
Ignition	
2001 to 2012 models	10A
2013-on models	20A
Hazard lights	
2001 to 2005, and 2013-on models	7.5A
2006 to 2012 models	10A
Parking lights (2001 to 2005 models)	10A
Power back-up (instruments)	
2001 to 2012 models	10A
2013-on models	7.5A
Windshield motor	
2001 to 2005 models	2A
2013-on models	20A
ABS system	
2003 to 2005 models	
Control unit	7.5A
Motor	30A
2006 and 2007 models	
Control unit	10A
Motor	30A
2008 to 2012 models	
Motor	30A
Solenoid	20A
Control unit	10A
2013-on models	
Motor	30A
Solenoid	20A
Control unit	7.5A
YCC-S	30A
YCC-T (2013-on models)	7.5A
Cruise control (2013-on models)	1A
Auxiliary DC jack	3A
Brake light (2013-on models)	1A

Bulbs

Headlights	60/55W x 2 H4
Sidelights	
2001 to 2012 models	5W x 2
2013-on models	LED
Brake/tail lights	21/5W x 2
Licence plate light	5W
Turn signal lights	
2001 to 2012 models	21W x 4
2013-on models	
Front	LED
Rear	21W x 2
Instrument illumination	
2001 to 2005 models	1.12W
2006-on models	LED
Instrument warning lights	
2001 to 2005 models	
Turn signals	1.4W
All others	1.12W
2006-on models	LED

Torque settings

Alternator stator screws	10 Nm
Footrest bracket bolts (right-hand side)	28 Nm
Neutral switch	20 Nm
Oil level sensor bolts	10 Nm
Starter motor bolts	10 Nm

1 General information

All models have a 12 volt electrical system charged by a three-phase alternator with a separate regulator/rectifier.

The regulator maintains the charging system output within the specified range to prevent overcharging, and the rectifier converts the ac (alternating current) output of the alternator to dc (direct current) to power the lights and other components and to charge the battery. The alternator rotor is mounted on the left-hand end of the crankshaft with the stator in the cover.

The starter motor is mounted on the top of the crankcase behind the cylinders. The starting system includes the motor, the battery, the relay and the various wires and switches. Some of the switches are part of a starter interlock system that prevents the engine from being started under certain conditions (see Chapter 1).

Note: *Keep in mind that electrical parts, once purchased, often cannot be returned. To avoid unnecessary expense, make very sure the faulty component has been positively identified before buying a replacement part.*

2 Electrical system fault finding

1 A typical electrical circuit consists of an electrical component, the switches, relays, etc, related to that component and the wiring and connectors that link the component to the battery and the frame.

2 Before tackling any troublesome electrical circuit, first study the wiring diagram thoroughly to get a complete picture of what makes up that individual circuit. Trouble spots, for instance, can often be narrowed down by noting if other components related to that circuit are operating properly or not. If several components or circuits fail at one time, chances are the fault lies either in the fuse or in a common earth (ground) connection, as several circuits are often routed through the same fuse and earth (ground) connections.

3 Electrical problems often stem from simple causes, such as loose or corroded connections or a blown fuse. Prior to any electrical fault finding, always visually check the condition of the fuse, wires and connections in the problem circuit. Intermittent failures can be especially frustrating, since you can't always duplicate the failure when it's convenient to test. In such situations, a good practice is to clean all connections in the affected circuit, whether or not they appear to be good – where possible use a dedicated electrical cleaning spray along with sandpaper, wire wool or other abrasive material to remove corrosion, and a dedicated electrical protection spray to prevent further problems. All of the connections and wires should also be wiggled to check for looseness which can cause intermittent failure.

4 If you don't have a multimeter it is highly advisable to obtain one – they are not expensive and will enable a full range of electrical tests to be made **(see illustration)**. Go for a modern digital one with LCD display as they are easier to use. A continuity tester and/or test light are useful for certain electrical checks as an alternative, though are limited in their usefulness compared to a multimeter **(see illustrations)**.

Continuity checks

5 The term continuity describes the uninterrupted flow of electricity through an electrical circuit. Continuity can be checked with a multimeter set either to its continuity function (a beep is emitted when continuity is found), or to the resistance (ohms / Ω) function, or with a dedicated continuity tester. Both instruments are powered by an internal battery, therefore the checks are made with the ignition OFF. As a safety precaution, always disconnect the battery negative (-) lead before making continuity checks, particularly if ignition switch checks are being made.

6 If using a multimeter, select the continuity function if it has one, or the resistance (ohms) function. Touch the meter probes together and check that a beep is emitted or the meter reads zero, which indicates continuity. If there is no continuity there will be no beep or the meter will show infinite resistance. After using the meter, always switch it OFF to conserve its battery.

7 A continuity tester can be used in the same way – its light should come on or it should beep to indicate continuity in the switch ON position, but should be off or silent in the OFF position.

8 Note that the polarity of the test probes doesn't matter for continuity checks, although care should be taken to follow specific test procedures if a diode or solid-state component is being checked.

Switch continuity checks

9 If a switch is at fault, trace its wiring to the wiring connectors. Separate the connectors and inspect them for security and condition. A build-up of dirt or corrosion here will most likely be the cause of the problem – clean up and apply a water dispersant such as WD40, or alternatively use a dedicated contact cleaner and protection spray.

10 If using a multimeter, select the continuity function if it has one, or the resistance (ohms) function, and connect its probes to the terminals

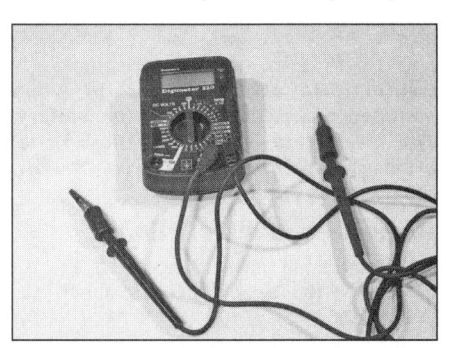

2.4a A digital multimeter can be used for all electrical tests

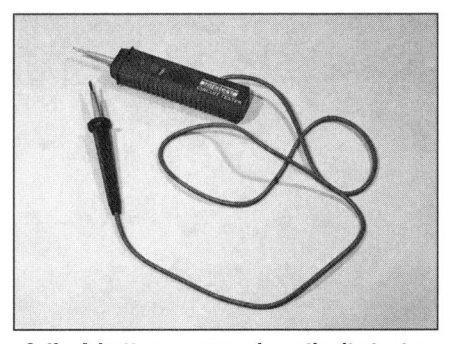

2.4b A battery-powered continuity tester

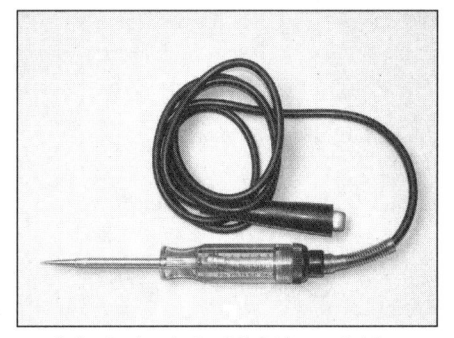

2.4c A simple test light is useful for voltage tests

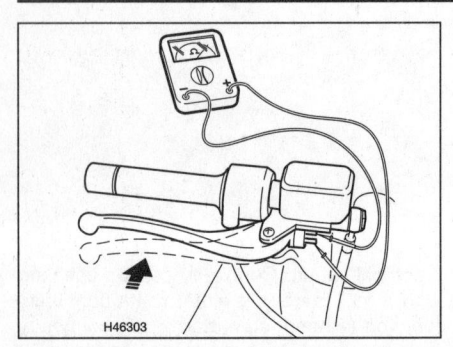

8•4 Electrical system

2.10 Continuity should be indicated across switch terminals when lever is operated

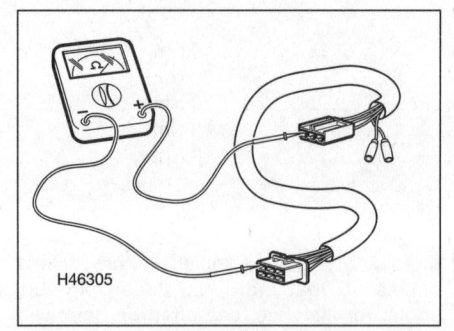

2.12 Wiring continuity check. Connect the meter probes across each end of the same wire

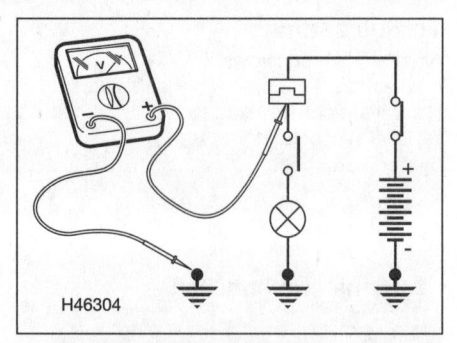

2.15 Voltage check. Connect the meter positive probe to the component and the negative probe to earth

in the connector **(see illustration)**. Simple ON/OFF type switches, such as brake light switches, only have two wires whereas combination switches, like the handlebar switches, have many wires. Study the wiring diagram to ensure that you are connecting to the correct pair of wires. Continuity should be indicated with the switch ON and no continuity with it OFF.

Wiring continuity checks

11 Many electrical faults are caused by damaged wiring, often due to incorrect routing or chaffing on frame components. Loose, wet or corroded wire connectors can also be the cause of electrical problems.
12 A continuity check can be made on a single length of wire by disconnecting it at each end and connecting the meter or continuity tester probes to each end of the wire **(see illustration)**. Continuity (low or no resistance – 0 ohms) should be indicated if the wire is good. If no continuity (high resistance) is shown, suspect a broken wire.
13 To check for continuity to earth in any earth wire connect one probe of your meter or tester to the earth wire terminal in the connector and the other to the frame, engine, or battery earth (-) terminal. Continuity (low or no resistance – 0 ohms) should be indicated if the wire is good. If no continuity (high resistance) is shown, suspect a broken wire or corroded or loose earth point (see below).

Voltage checks

14 A voltage check can determine whether power is reaching a component. Use a multimeter set to the dc voltage scale, or a test light. The test light is the cheaper component, but the meter has the advantage of being able to give a voltage reading.
15 Connect the meter or test light in parallel, i.e. across the load **(see illustration)**.
16 First identify the relevant wiring circuit by referring to the wiring diagram at the end of this manual. If other electrical components share the same power supply (i.e. are fed from the same fuse), take note whether they are working correctly – this is useful information in deciding where to start checking the circuit.
17 If using a meter, check first that the meter leads are plugged into the correct terminals on the meter (red to positive (+), black to negative (-). Set the meter to the dc volts function, where necessary at a range suitable for the battery voltage – 0 to 20 vdc. Connect the meter red probe (+) to the power supply wire and the black probe to a good metal earth (ground) on the bike's frame or directly to the battery negative terminal. Battery voltage should be shown on the meter with the ignition switch, and if necessary any other relevant switch, ON.
18 If using a test light, connect its positive (+) probe to the power supply terminal and its negative (-) probe to a good earth (ground) on the bike's frame. With the switch, and if necessary any other relevant switch, ON, the test light should illuminate.
19 If no voltage is indicated, work back towards the fuse continuing to check for voltage. When you reach a point where there is voltage, you know the problem lies between that point and your last check point.

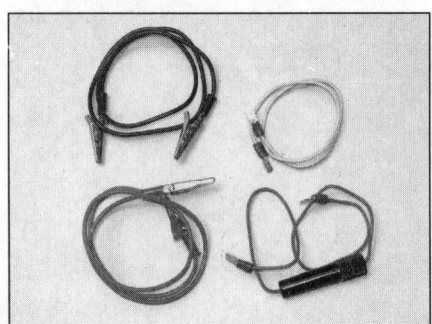

Earth (ground) checks

20 Earth connections are made either directly to the engine or frame via the mounting of the component, or by a separate wire into the earth circuit of the wiring harness. Alternatively a short earth wire is sometimes run from the component directly to the bike's frame.
21 Corrosion is a common cause of a poor earth connection, as is a loose earth terminal fastener.
22 If total or multiple component failure is experienced, check the security of the main earth lead from the negative (-) terminal of the battery, the earth lead bolted to the engine, and the main earth point(s) on the frame. If corroded, dismantle the connection and clean all surfaces back to bare metal. Remake the connection and prevent further corrosion from forming by smearing battery terminal grease over the connection.
23 To check the earth of a component, use an insulated jumper wire to temporarily bypass its earth connection **(see illustration)** – connect one end of the jumper wire to the earth terminal or metal body of the component and the other end to the bike's frame. If the circuit works with the jumper wire installed, the earth circuit is faulty.
24 To check an earth wire first check for corroded or loose connections, then check the wiring for continuity (Step 13) between each connector in the circuit in turn, and then to its earth point, to locate the break.

3 Battery removal and maintenance

Caution: Be extremely careful when handling or working around the battery. The electrolyte is very caustic and an explosive gas (hydrogen) is given off when the battery is charging.

Removal and installation

1 Make sure the ignition is switched OFF.
2 Remove the battery access panel (see Chapter 7).
3 Unscrew the negative (–) terminal bolt first and disconnect the lead from the battery **(see illustration)**. Lift up the red insulating cover to

2.23 A selection of insulated jumper wires

3.3 Disconnect the negative lead first then disconnect the positive lead (arrowed)

Electrical system 8•5

access the positive (+) terminal, then unscrew the bolt and disconnect the lead.
4 On 2006 to 2012 models release the trim clips and move the cover aside **(see illustration)**.
5 Unscrew the battery retainer bolt and remove the retainers **(see illustrations)**. Lift the battery out **(see illustration)**.
6 Installation is the reverse of removal. Clean the battery terminals and lead ends with a wire brush, emery paper or steel wool. Reconnect the leads, connecting the positive (+) terminal first.

HAYNES HiNT *Battery corrosion can be kept to a minimum by applying a layer of battery terminal grease or petroleum jelly (Vaseline) to the terminals after the leads have been connected. DO NOT use a mineral based grease.*

Inspection and maintenance

7 The battery on all models is of the maintenance free (sealed) type, therefore requiring no regular maintenance. However, the following checks should still be performed. **Note:** *Do not attempt to remove the battery caps to check the electrolyte level or battery specific gravity. Removal will damage the caps, resulting in electrolyte leakage and battery damage.*
8 Check the state of charge by measuring the voltage at the battery terminals **(see illustration)**. Connect the voltmeter positive (+) probe to the battery positive (+) terminal, and the negative (–) probe to the battery negative (–) terminal. When fully-charged there should be 12.8 volts (or more) present. If the voltage falls below 12 volts remove the battery (see above), and recharge it as described in Section 4.
9 Check the battery terminals and leads are tight and free of corrosion. If corrosion is evident, clean the terminals as described above, then protect them from further corrosion (see **Haynes Hint**).
10 Keep the battery case clean to prevent current leakage, which can discharge the battery over a period of time (especially when it sits unused). Wash the outside of the case

3.4 Release the trim clips (arrowed)

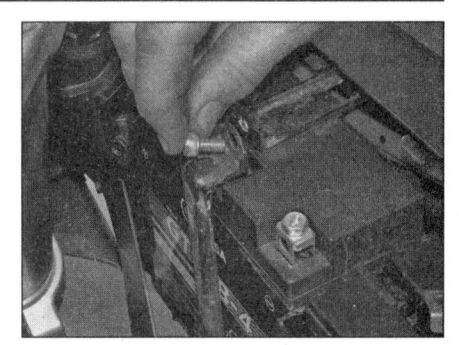

3.5a Unscrew the bolt...

3.5b ...and remove the retainer...

3.5c ...then remove the battery

with a solution of baking soda and water. Rinse the battery thoroughly, then dry it.
11 Look for cracks in the case and replace the battery with a new one if any are found. If acid has been spilled on the frame or battery box, neutralise it with a baking soda and water solution, dry it thoroughly, then touch up any damaged paint.
12 If the motorcycle sits unused for long periods of time, disconnect the leads from the battery terminals, negative (–) terminal first. Refer to Section 4 and charge the battery once every month to six weeks.

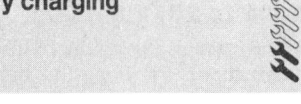

4 Battery charging

Caution: Be extremely careful when handling or working around the battery. The electrolyte is very caustic and an explosive gas (hydrogen) is given off when the battery is charging.

1 Remove the battery (see Section 3). Connect the charger to the battery, making sure that the positive (+) lead on the charger is connected to the positive (+) terminal on the battery, and the negative (–) lead is connected to the negative (–) terminal.
2 Yamaha recommend that the battery is charged at the rate specified at the beginning of the Chapter. A higher 'quick charge' rate can be used if absolutely necessary (but Yamaha specify not to) for a short time only – excess use could cause damage to the battery. If a normal domestic charger is used check that after a possible initial peak, the charge rate falls to a safe level **(see illustration)**. If the battery becomes hot during charging **stop**. Further charging will cause damage. Note that there are many bike-specific chargers available from good suppliers that are designed for the maintenance and recovery of motorcycle batteries, in particular catering for the requirements of heavily discharged MF batteries. They are not expensive, and are a worthwhile investment, especially if the bike is not used over winter. Follow the manufacturer's instructions.
3 If the recharged battery discharges rapidly if left disconnected it is likely that an internal short caused by physical damage or sulphation has occurred. A new battery will be required. A sound item will tend to lose its charge at about 1% per day.
4 Install the battery (see Section 3).
5 If the motorcycle sits unused for long periods of time, charge the battery once every month to six weeks and leave it disconnected.

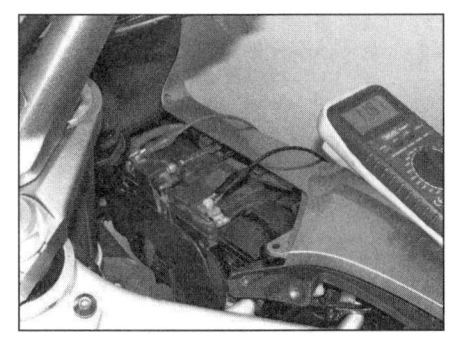

3.8 Checking battery voltage

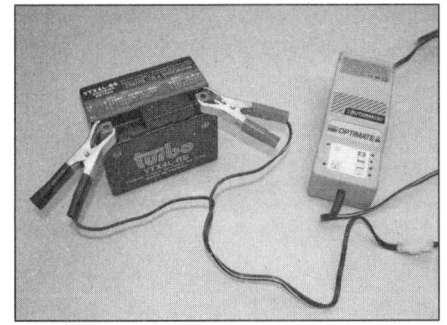

4.2 Battery connected to a charger

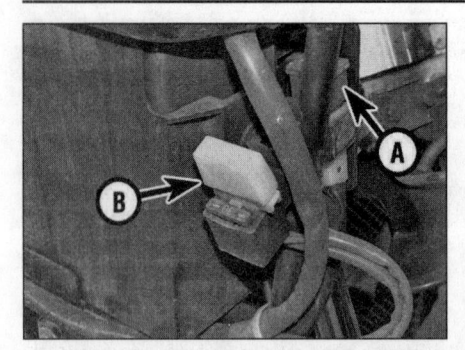

8•6 Electrical system

5.2 Main fuse (A), ABS motor fuse (B) and its spare

5.3 Fuel injection system fuse (arrowed) and its spare

5.4a Fuseboxes (arrowed)

5.4b Unclip the lids to access the fuses

5.6 Main fuse (arrowed)

5.7 ABS motor fuse and its spare

5 Fuses

1 The electrical system as a whole is protected by the main fuse, and individual circuits are protected by other fuses of different ratings.

2001 to 2005 models

2 The main fuse, and on 2003 to 2005 A models the ABS motor fuse and a spare, are in front of the battery **(see illustration)** – to access them remove the battery access panel (see Chapter 7).

3 The fuel injection fuse and a spare are fitted with the starter relay **(see illustration)** – to access them remove the battery access panel (see Chapter 7).

4 All other fuses are housed in the fuseboxes, located under the hazard switch panel **(see illustration)**. Remove the panel for access (see Chapter 7). The location, identity and rating of each fuse is marked on the box or holder lid. Unclip the lid to access the fuses **(see illustration)**.

5 A spare fuse of each rating is provided.

2006 to 2012 models

6 The main fuse is in front of the battery **(see illustration)** – remove the battery access panel, and for best access the fairing (see Chapter 7).

7 The ABS motor fuse and a spare are fitted with the starter relay **(see illustration)** – to access it remove the fairing (see Chapter 7). All other fuses are housed in the fuseboxes **(see illustration)** – remove the battery access panel (see Chapter 7). The location, identity and rating of each fuse is marked on the box lid. Unclip the lid to access the fuses **(see illustration)**. A spare fuse of each rating is provided.

2013-on models

8 Remove the battery access panel to inspect the fuses (see Chapter 7).

9 The main fuse is in front of the battery **(see illustration)**. The cooling system fuse and a spare are fitted with the starter relay **(see**

5.8a Fuseboxes (arrowed)

5.8b Unclip the lids to access the fuses

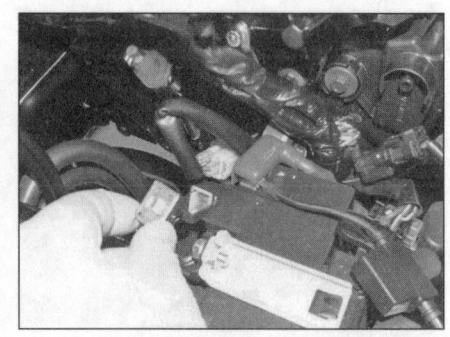

5.9a Main fuse is a push fit in its holder and secured with rubber strap

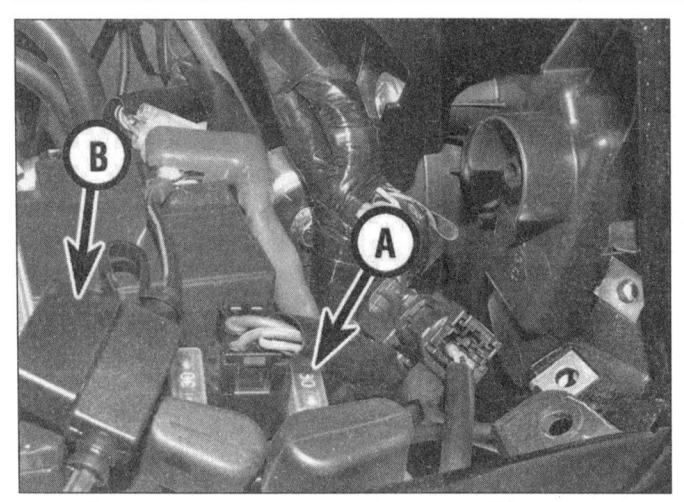

Electrical system 8•7

5.9b Cooling system fuse (A). The in-line fuse (B) is for a trickle charger adaptor

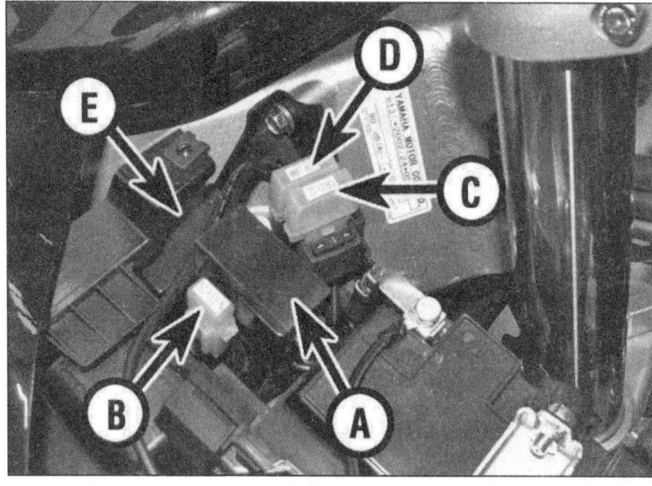

5.9c Front fusebox (A) and external windshield fuse (B), cruise control fuse (C), brake light fuse (D) – rear fusebox and external hazard fuse (E) hidden from view

illustration). There are two fuseboxes to the rear of the battery, with separate holders next to them for the cruise control, brake light, hazard and windshield motor fuses **(see illustration)**. Note that the rear fusebox is obscured by the fairing bracket; it may be necessary to remove the fairing side panel for full access.

All models

10 The fuses can be removed and checked visually – use the tool provided in the toolkit, your fingers, or a suitable pair of pliers **(see illustration)**. Note that main 50A fuse is housed in a red casing with transparent lid; in the event of it failing, the complete casing is renewed – it is not possible to open it to extract the fuse element.

11 A blown fuse is easily identified by a break in the element **(see illustration)**, but if there is any doubt check the fuse for continuity (see Section 2). Each fuse is clearly marked with its rating and must only be replaced by a fuse of the correct rating. If a spare fuse is used, always replace it with a new one so that a spare of each rating is carried on the bike at all times.

⚠ **Warning: Never put in a fuse of a higher rating or bridge the terminals with any other** substitute, however temporary it may be. Serious damage may be done to the circuit, or a fire may start.

12 If the new fuse blows immediately check the wiring circuit very carefully for evidence of a short-circuit. Look for bare wires and chafed, melted or burned insulation.

13 Occasionally a fuse will blow or cause an open-circuit for no obvious reason. Corrosion of the fuse ends and fusebox terminals may occur and cause poor fuse contact. If this happens, remove the corrosion with a wire brush or emery paper, then spray the fuse end and terminals with electrical contact cleaner.

6 Lighting system check

Note: *Refer to electrical system fault finding in Section 2 and to the wiring diagram for your model at the end of this Chapter.*

1 If a light fails first check the bulb (see relevant Section), and the bulb terminals in the holder. If none of the lights work, check the battery (see Section 3). Low battery voltage indicates either a faulty battery or a defective charging system. Refer to Section 3 for battery checks and Section 28 for charging system tests. Also check the relevant fuse (Section 5) – if there is more than one problem at the same time, it is likely to be a fault relating to a multi-function component, such as one of the fuses governing more than one circuit, or the ignition switch. When checking for a blown filament in a bulb, it is advisable to back up a visual check with a continuity test of the filament as it is not always apparent that a bulb has blown **(see illustration)**.

Headlight

2 All models have two twin filament bulbs. If one headlight beam fails to work, first check the bulb (see Section 7). If all headlight beams fail to work, first check the fuse (see Section 5), and then the relays (the ON/OFF relay has overall control of the headlights, and the dimmer relay controls switching between the HI and LO beam circuits – Step 3 or 4). If they are good, the problem lies in the wiring or connectors, or the dimmer switch. Refer to Section 19 for the switch testing procedures, and to Section 2 and the wiring diagrams at the end of this Chapter.

3 To access the relays, on 2001 to 2005 models remove the fairing (see Chapter 7). The relay is on the back of the instrument

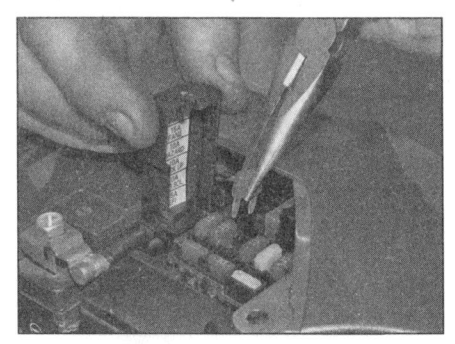

5.10 Pull the fuse out

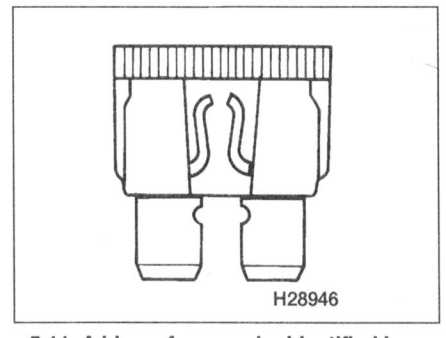

5.11 A blown fuse can be identified by a break in its element

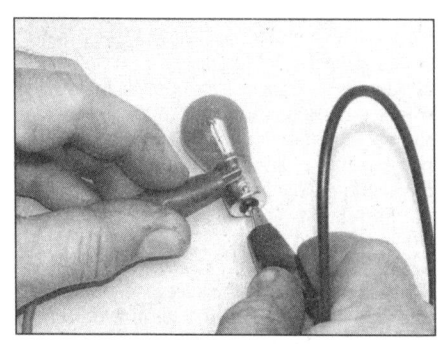

6.1 Checking a bulb filament for continuity

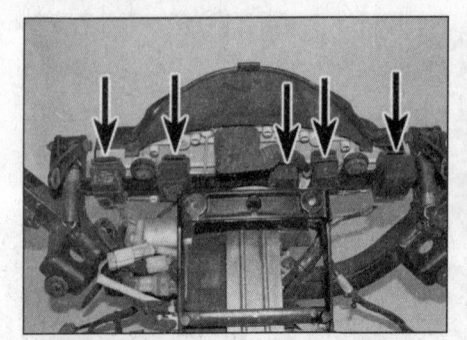

8•8 Electrical system

6.3a Relays (arrowed) – 2001-2005 models

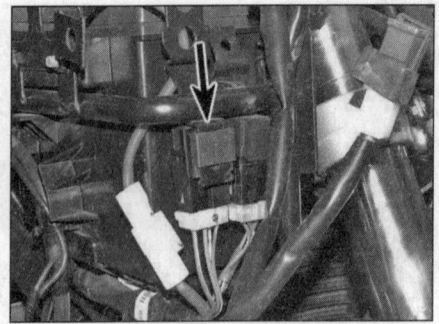

6.3b Headlight ON/OFF relay (arrowed) – 2006-2012 models

6.3c Headlight dimmer relay (arrowed) – 2006-2012 models

6.3d Headlight ON/OFF relay (arrowed) – 2013-on models

6.3e Headlight dimmer relay (arrowed) – 2013-on models

cluster **(see illustration)**. Identify the relay using the wiring diagram for your model at the end of the Chapter, displace it and disconnect its connector. If necessary (depending on the location of the relay), remove the windshield motor/instrument assembly from the fairing (Section 31). On 2006 to 2012 models to access the ON/OFF relay remove the right-hand fairing side panel, and if required for best access the fairing, and to access the dimmer relay remove the left-hand instrument surround panel (see Chapter 7). Displace the relay and disconnect the wiring **(see illustrations)**. On 2013-on models the on/off relay is mounted on the ECU bracket and the dimmer relay is behind the headlight on the left-hand side; remove the fairing right-hand side panel and instrument surround panel for access **(see illustrations)**.

4 Test the ON/OFF relay as follows **(see illustration)**: set a multimeter to test continuity and connect it across terminals 3 and 4 on the relay – there should be no continuity. Using a fully-charged 12 volt battery and two insulated jumper wires, connect the positive (+) terminal of the battery to terminal 1 on the relay, and the negative (–) terminal to terminal 2. At this point the relay should be heard to click and there should be continuity across 3 and 4. If so the relay is good. If not replace the relay with a new one.

5 Test the dimmer relay as follows **(see illustration)**: set a multimeter to test continuity and connect it across the terminals 3 and 4 on the relay – there should be continuity. Now connect across terminals 3 and 5 – there should be no continuity. Using a fully-charged

12 volt battery and two insulated jumper wires, connect the positive (+) terminal of the battery to terminal 1 on the relay, and the negative (–) terminal to terminal 2. Now there should be no continuity across 3 and 4, and there should be continuity across 3 and 5. If so the

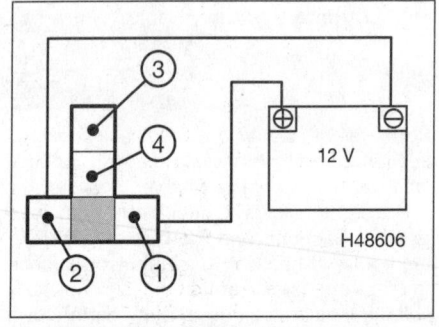

6.4 On/off relay terminal numbers

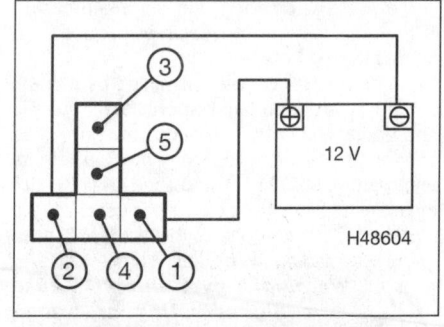

6.5 Dimmer relay terminal numbers

relay is good. If not replace the relay with a new one.

Brake lights

6 If one brake light fails to work, check the bulb (see Section 9). If both bulbs fail to work, if the fuse is good, refer to Section 14 for the switch testing procedures. On 2006-on models next check the relay(s) – Steps 7 to 10. If the switches and relays are good check the wiring and connectors in the circuit.

7 The 2006 to 2012 models have a brake light relay, and 2013-on models also have a brake switch relay. To access the relay(s), remove the seats and the height adjuster piece (see Chapter 7). Remove the toolkit from its tray **(see illustration)**. On AS models, remove the YCC-S motor control unit (see Section 20 in Chapter 2). Disconnect the ECU wiring connector, then remove the tray **(see illustrations)**. Displace the relay

6.7a Remove the toolkit

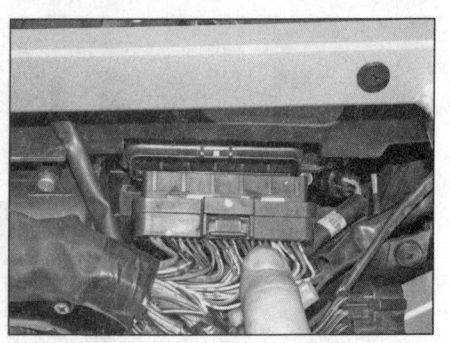

6.7b Disconnect the connector...

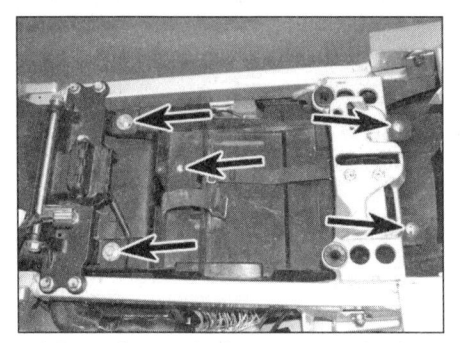

Electrical system 8•9

6.7c ...then undo the screws and bolts (arrowed)...

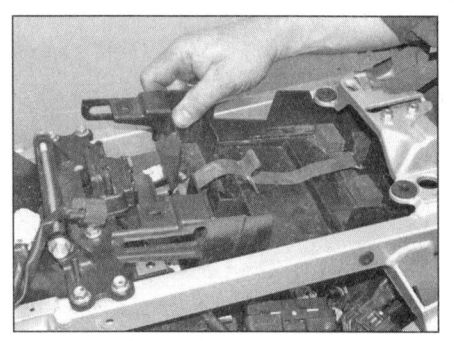

6.7d ...and remove the tray

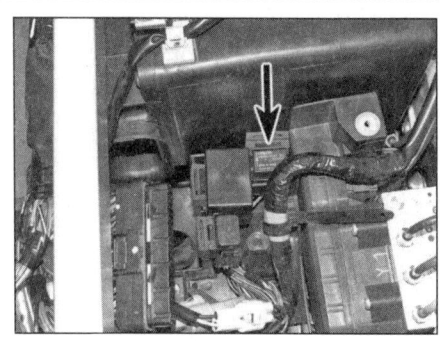

6.7e Brake light relay (arrowed) – 2006 to 2012

and disconnect the wiring connector **(see illustration)**.

8 The 2013-on models have a brake light relay and a brake switch relay. To access the relay(s), remove the left-hand side cover (see Chapter 7). Reach in through the cut-out in the inner panel to access the relays **(see illustration)**. Displace the relay and disconnect the wiring connector.

9 Test the brake light relay as follows **(see illustration)**: set a multimeter to test continuity and connect it across terminals 3 and 4 on the relay – there should be continuity. Using a fully-charged 12 volt battery and two insulated jumper wires, connect the positive (+) terminal of the battery to terminal 1 on the relay, and the negative (–) terminal to terminal 2. At this point the relay should be heard to click and there should be no continuity across 3 and 4. If this is the case the relay is good. If not replace the relay with a new one.

10 On 2013 models test the brake switch relay as follows **(see illustration 6.4)**: set a multimeter to test continuity and connect it across terminals 3 and 4 on the relay – there should be no continuity. Using a fully-charged 12 volt battery and two insulated jumper wires, connect the positive (+) terminal of the battery to terminal 1 on the relay, and the negative (–) terminal to terminal 2. At this point the relay should be heard to click and there should be continuity across 3 and 4. If so the relay is good. If not replace the relay with a new one.

Turn signals

11 See Section 11.

Instrument and warning lights

12 See Section 16.

7 Headlight and sidelight bulbs

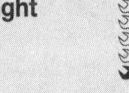

Note: *The headlight bulbs are of the H4 halogen type. Do not touch the bulb glass as skin acids will shorten the bulb's service life. If the bulb is accidentally touched, it should be wiped carefully when cold with a rag soaked in methylated spirit and dried before fitting. Always use a paper towel or dry cloth when handling new bulbs to prevent injury if the bulb should break and to increase bulb life.*

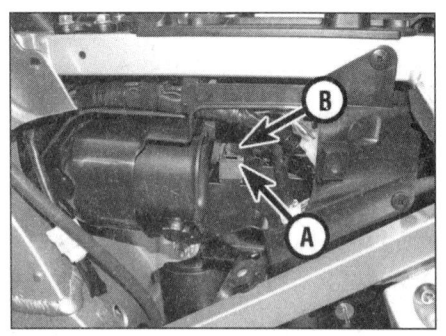

6.8 Brake switch relay (A) and brake light relay (B) – 2013-on

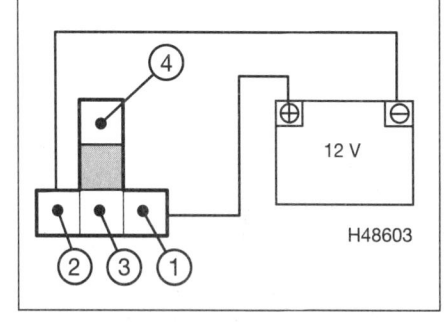

Headlights

1 Remove the instrument surround panel(s) (see Chapter 7). Turn the handlebars as required to aid access.

2 Disconnect the wiring connector from the bulb **(see illustration)**.

7.2 Disconnect the wiring connector...

7.4a Release the clip...

6.9 Brake light relay terminal numbers

3 Remove the rubber cover **(see illustration)**.
4 Release the retaining clip and remove the bulb **(see illustrations)**.
5 Fit the new bulb bearing in mind the information in the **Note** above. Make sure the bulb locates correctly and secure it with the retaining clip **(see illustrations 7.4b and a)**.

7.3 ...then remove the cover

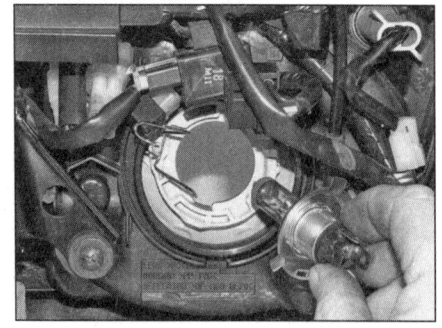

7.4b ...and remove the bulb

8•10 Electrical system

7.10 Release the bulbholder...

7.11 ...then pull the bulb out

6 Fit the rubber cover **(see illustration 7.3)**.
7 Connect the wiring connector **(see illustration 7.2)**.
8 Check the headlight works. Install the instrument surround.

Sidelights – 2001 to 2012 models

9 Remove the instrument surround panel(s) (see Chapter 7).

10 Turn the bulbholder a quarter turn anti-clockwise and draw it out of the headlight **(see illustration)**.
11 Carefully pull the bulb out of the holder **(see illustration)**.
12 Fit the new bulb in the bulbholder, then fit the bulbholder into the headlight – make sure it locates and locks correctly.

13 Check the sidelight works then install the instrument surround.

8 Headlight

Removal

1 Remove the fairing (see Chapter 7).
2 On 2001 to 2012 models remove the windshield motor and instrument assembly (Section 31). Undo the screws and remove the headlight **(see illustrations)**. Note the collars in the grommets. Make sure the grommets are in good condition – replace them with new ones if necessary.
3 On 2013-on models remove the bolts which retain the headlight unit to the mounting bracket **(see illustrations)**. Disconnect the vertical beam adjuster rods from the back of the headlight. Ease the headlight forwards to disconnect the wiring connectors from the back of the unit.

8.2a Headlight screws (arrowed) – 2001 to 2005 models

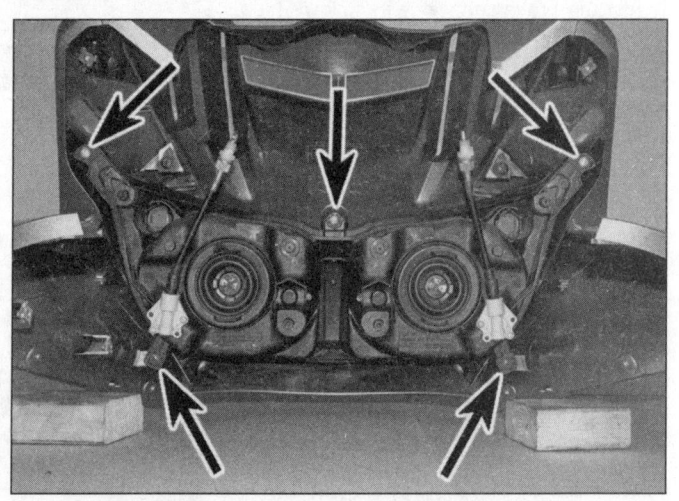

8.2b Headlight screws (arrowed) – 2006 to 2012 models

8.3a Headlight unit is retained by screws...

8.3b ...to the mounting bracket – 2013-on models

Electrical system 8•11

4 If required remove the headlight bulbs and sidelight bulbholders (see Section 7).

Installation

5 Installation is the reverse of removal. Make sure are the collars are fitted in the grommets. Check the operation of the headlights and sidelights. Check the headlight aim.

Aim

Note: *An improperly adjusted headlight may cause problems for oncoming traffic or provide poor, unsafe illumination of the road ahead. Before adjusting the headlight aim, be sure to consult with local traffic laws and regulations – for UK models refer to MOT Test Checks in the Reference section.*

6 Each headlight beam can adjusted separately both horizontally and vertically. Before making any adjustment, check that the tyre pressures are correct and the suspension is adjusted as required. Make any adjustments to the headlight aim with the machine off its stand and on level ground, with the fuel tank half full and with an assistant sitting on the seat. If the bike is usually ridden with a passenger on the back, have a second assistant to do this.

7 On 2001 to 2005 models the vertical alignment adjusters are accessible by reaching down between the fork and the instrument surround, or up from under the fairing, as preferred **(see illustration)** – turn the handlebars to improve access. To move a beam up turn the relevant vertical alignment adjuster anti-clockwise, to move a beam down turn the adjuster clockwise.

8 On 2006-on models the vertical alignment adjuster knobs are on the instrument surround panel(s) **(see illustration)**. To move a beam up turn the adjuster clockwise, to move a beam down turn the adjuster anti-clockwise.

9 To move a beam to the right or left remove the instrument surround panel(s) (see Chapter 7) – the adjuster for each beam is on the top inner corner of the light on 2001 to 2012 models **(see illustration)**, and on the outer sides on 2013-on models **(see illustration)**. Turn the relevant adjuster as required.

9 Brake/tail/licence plate light bulbs

Note: *It is a good idea to use a paper towel or dry cloth when handling bulbs to prevent injury if it breaks, and to increase bulb life.*

Brake/tail lights

1 Remove the passenger seat (see Chapter 7).

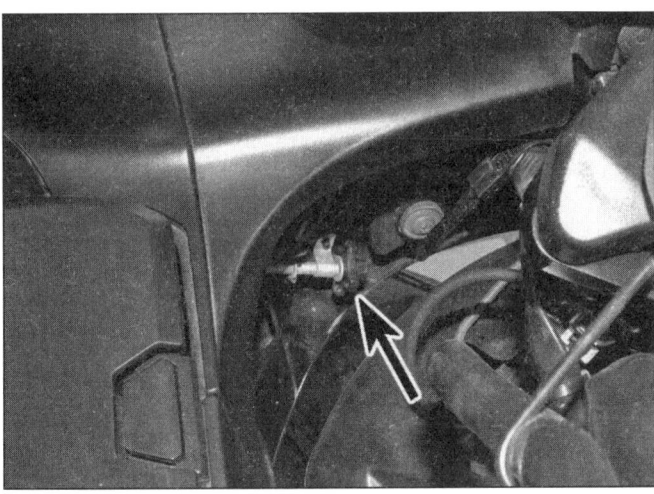

8.7 Vertical adjuster (arrowed) for left-hand beam – 2001 to 2005 models

8.8 Vertical adjuster (arrowed) for left-hand beam – 2006-on models

8.9a Horizontal adjusters (arrowed) – 2001 to 2012 models

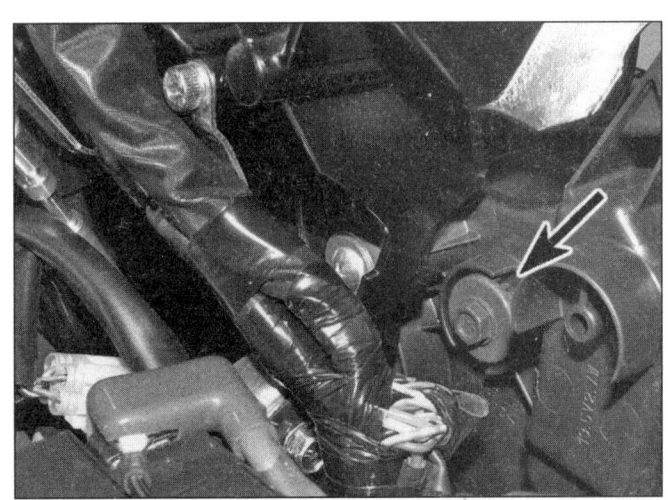

8.9b Horizontal adjuster on each side can be turned either by the bolt head or by engaging a Philips head screwdriver in the cut-out (arrowed) – 2013-on models

8•12 Electrical system

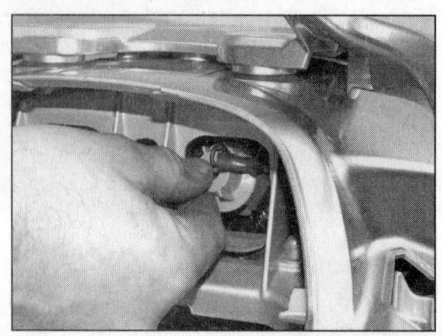

9.2 Release the bulbholder...

9.3 ...then remove the bulb from it

9.7 Undo the screws (arrowed)...

9.8 ...remove the bulbholder...

9.9 ...and pull the bulb out

2 Turn the bulbholder anti-clockwise to release it **(see illustration)**.
3 Carefully push the bulb in and turn it anti-clockwise to release it **(see illustration)**.
4 Check the socket terminals for corrosion and clean them if necessary.
5 Line up the pins of the new bulb with the slots in the socket, then push the bulb in and turn it clockwise until it locks into place.
6 Fit the bulbholder and turn it clockwise.

Licence plate light (2006-on models)

7 Undo the screws and detach the licence plate light **(see illustration)**.
8 Carefully pull the bulbholder out **(see illustration)**.
9 Carefully pull the bulb out of the holder **(see illustration)**.
10 Fit the new bulb in the bulbholder, then fit the bulbholder into the light – make sure the rubber seal is in good condition and correctly seated.
11 Fit the licence plate light.

10 Tail light

1 Remove the grab-rack and rear cover(s) (see Chapter 7).
2 Either remove the bulbholders or disconnect the tail light wiring connector.
3 Unscrew the bolt(s) and remove the tail light **(see illustration)**.
4 Installation is the reverse of removal. Make sure the grommets are in good condition – replace them with new ones if necessary. Check the operation of the tail and brake lights.

11 Turn signal circuit check

1 Most turn signal problems are the result of a burned out bulb or corroded socket. This is especially true when the turn signals function properly in one direction (although possibly too quickly), but fail to flash in the other direction. If this is the case, first check the bulbs, the sockets and the wiring connectors (see Sections 12 and 13). If all the turn signals fail to work, check the fuse (see Section 5), and on 2001 to 2012 models then check the relay (see Steps 2 to 4). If they are good, the problem lies in the wiring or connectors, or the switch. Refer to Section 19 for the switch testing procedures, and to Section 2 and the wiring diagrams at the end of this Chapter to check the wiring. On 2013-on models the turn signal relay (flasher unit) is incorporated in the instrument cluster – if no fault can be found in the rest of the circuit the instrument cluster could be faulty (Section 16).
2 To check the relay on 2001 to 2012 models remove the fairing (see Chapter 7).
3 Displace the relay and disconnect the wiring connector **(see illustrations)** – for best access on 2001 to 2005 models remove the windshield motor/instrument assembly from the fairing (Section 31).
4 Check for battery voltage at the brown/green (2001 to 2005 models) or blue/red (2006 to 2012 models) wire terminal on the

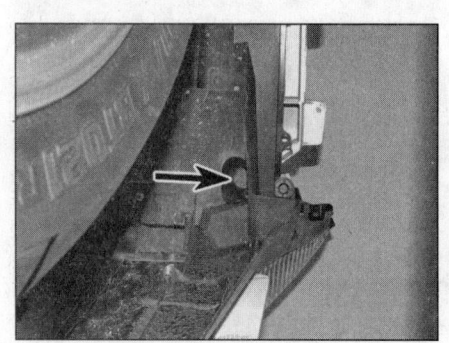

10.3 On 2006-on models there is a bolt (arrowed) underneath on each side

11.3a Turn signal relay (arrowed) – 2001 to 2005 models

11.3b Turn signal relay (arrowed) – 2006 to 2012 models

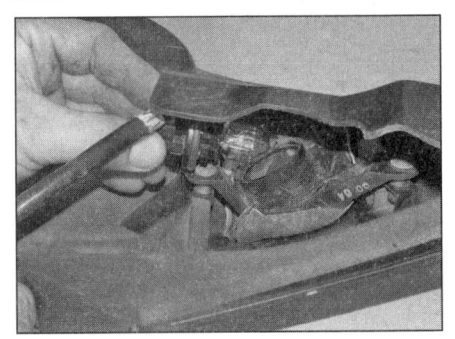

Electrical system 8•13

12.6 Release the front bulbholder...

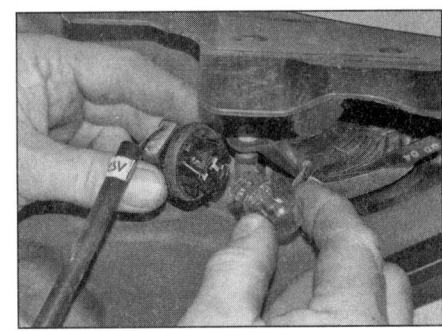

12.7 ...then remove the bulb from it

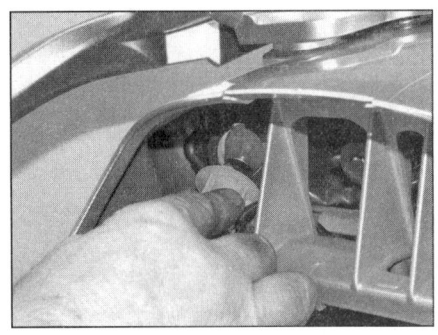

12.13 Release the rear bulbholder...

loom side of the connector with the ignition ON. If no voltage is present, check the wire from the relay to the fuse for continuity. Refer to electrical system fault finding in Section 2 and to the wiring diagrams at the end of this Chapter. If voltage was present, short between the brown/green and brown/white (2001 to 2005 models) or blue/red and brown/green (2006 to 2012 models) wire terminals on the loom side of the connector using a jumper wire. Turn the ignition ON and operate the turn signal switch. If the lights come on (they won't flash), the relay is faulty and must be replaced with a new one.

5 If the lights do not come on, check the brown/white (2001 to 2005 models) or brown/green (2006 to 2012 models) wire for continuity to the left-hand switch housing, and repair or renew the wiring or connectors as required.

6 If all is good so far, or if the lights came on one side but not the other, check the wiring between the left-hand switch housing and the turn signals themselves. Repair or renew the wiring or connectors as necessary.

12 Turn signal bulbs

Note: *It is a good idea to use a paper towel or dry cloth when handling bulbs to prevent injury if the bulb should break and to increase bulb life.*

Front turn signals

2001 and 2002 models

1 Undo the screw securing the lens and detach it from the housing.
2 Push the bulb in and twist it anti-clockwise to release it. Check the socket terminals for corrosion and clean them if necessary.
3 Line up the pins of the new bulb with the slots in the socket, then push the bulb in and turn it clockwise until it locks into place.
4 Fit the lens onto the housing and fit the screw – do not overtighten it as it is easy to strip the threads or crack the lens. Check the turn signal works.

2003 to 2012 models

5 Remove the fairing side panel (see Chapter 7).
6 Turn the bulbholder anti-clockwise to release it **(see illustration)**.
7 Carefully pull the bulb out **(see illustration)**.
8 Check the socket terminals for corrosion and clean them if necessary.
9 Push the new bulb in.
10 Fit the bulbholder and turn it clockwise.
11 Install the fairing side panel. Check the turn signal works.

Rear turn signals

12 Remove the passenger seat (see Chapter 7).
13 Turn the bulbholder anti-clockwise to release it **(see illustration)**.
14 Carefully push the bulb in and turn it anti-clockwise to release it **(see illustration)**.

15 Check the socket terminals for corrosion and clean them if necessary.
16 Line up the pins of the new bulb with the slots in the socket, then push the bulb in and turn it clockwise until it locks into place.
17 Fit the bulbholder and turn it clockwise.

13 Turn signal assemblies

Front turn signals

1 Remove the fairing side panel, then remove the inner panel from it (see Chapter 7).
2 On 2001 and 2002 models remove the plate on the inner side of the panel then remove the turn signal from the outer side, taking care as you draw the wire through.
3 On 2003 to 2012 models undo the screws and remove the turn signal **(see illustration)**. If required turn the bulbholder anti-clockwise to release it **(see illustration 12.6)**.
4 On 2013-on models, undo the fasteners securing the LED unit to the fairing side panel **(see illustration)**. Note that the individual LEDs are not available separately.
5 Installation is the reverse of removal. Check the operation of the turn signal.

Rear turn signals

6 The rear turn signals are incorporated in the tail light assembly (Section 10).

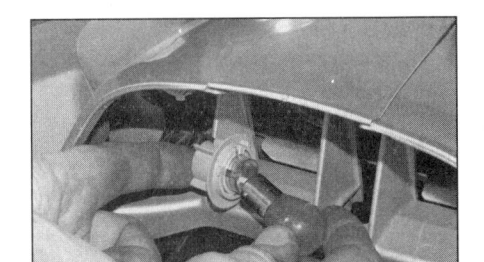

12.14 ...then remove the bulb from it

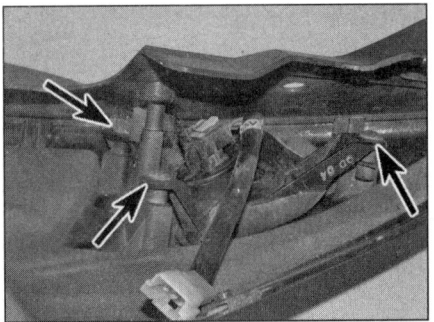

13.3 Turn signal screws (arrowed) – 2004 model shown

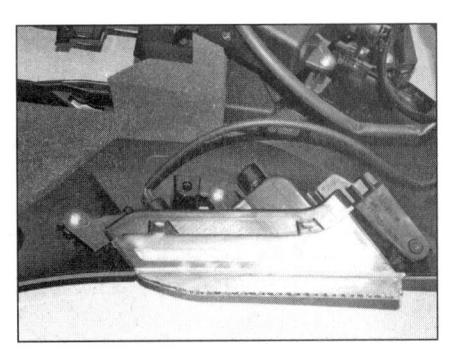

13.4 LED turn signal mounts to inside of fairing side panel – 2013-on

8•14 Electrical system

14.2 Front brake switch wiring connectors (arrowed)

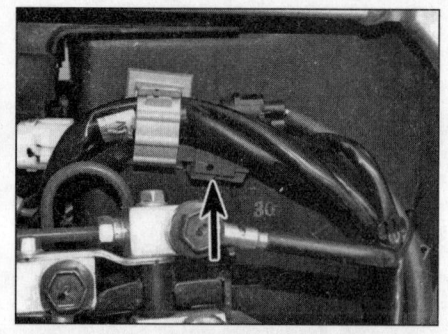

14.3 Rear brake switch wiring connector (arrowed)

14 Brake light switches

Circuit check

Note: *Refer to electrical system fault finding in Section 2 and to the wiring diagram for your model at the end of this Chapter.*

1 Before checking the switches, and if not already done, check the brake light circuit (see Section 6).
2 The front brake light switch is mounted on the underside of the brake master cylinder. On 2001 to 2012 models disconnect the wiring connectors from the switch **(see illustration)**. On 2013-on models remove the fairing (see Chapter 7), then trace the wiring from the switch and disconnect it at the connector. Using a continuity tester, connect the probes to the terminals of the switch. With the brake lever at rest, there should be no continuity. With the brake lever applied, there should be continuity. If the switch does not behave as described, replace it with a new one.
3 The rear brake light switch is mounted on the inside of the rider's right-hand footrest bracket. Remove the right-hand side cover (see Chapter 7). Disconnect the switch wiring connector **(see illustrations)**. Using a continuity tester, connect the probes to the terminals on the switch side of the wiring connector. With the brake pedal at rest, there should be no continuity. With the brake pedal applied, there should be continuity. If the switch does not behave as described, replace it with a new one, although check first that the spring has not become detached or broken, and the switch is adjusted correctly (see Chapter 1).
4 If the switches are good, check the wiring between the connector and the fusebox and the brake light, referring to Section 2 and the relevant wiring diagram at the end of this Chapter.

Switch replacement

Front brake lever switch

5 The switch is mounted on the underside of the brake master cylinder. On 2001 to 2012 models disconnect the wiring connectors from the switch **(see illustration 14.2)**. On 2013-on models remove the fairing (see Chapter 7), then trace the wiring from the switch and disconnect it at the connector – feed the wiring back to the switch, releasing it from any ties and guides and noting its routing.
6 Undo the single screw securing the switch to the master cylinder and remove the switch.
7 Installation is the reverse of removal. Make sure the peg on the switch is correctly located in its hole before tightening the screw. The switch isn't adjustable.

Rear brake pedal switch

8 The rear brake light switch is mounted on the inside of the right-hand footrest bracket. Remove the right-hand side cover (see Chapter 7). Disconnect the switch wiring connector **(see illustration 14.3)**. Feed the wiring down to the switch, noting its routing and releasing it from any ties.
9 Unscrew the footrest bracket bolts and displace the bracket **(see illustration)**.
10 Detach the end of the switch spring from the brake pedal **(see illustration)**. Press the tabs on the nut in and pull the switch out of the bracket.
11 Installation is the reverse of removal. Make sure the brake light is activated just before the rear brake pedal takes effect. If adjustment is necessary, refer to Chapter 1, Section 1. Tighten the footrest bracket bolts to the torque setting specified at the beginning of the Chapter.

15 Instrument removal and installation

2001 to 2012 models

1 Remove the fairing (see Chapter 7). Remove the windshield motor/instrument assembly from the fairing (Section 31).
2 Undo the screws, noting the washers where fitted, and displace the instrument cluster,

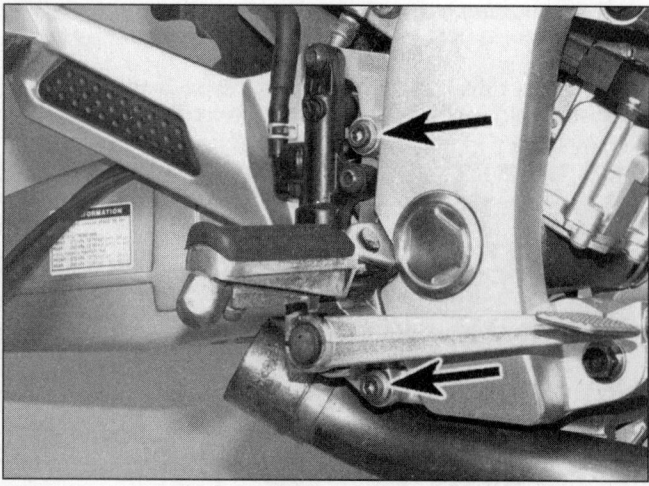

14.9 Footrest bracket bolts (arrowed)

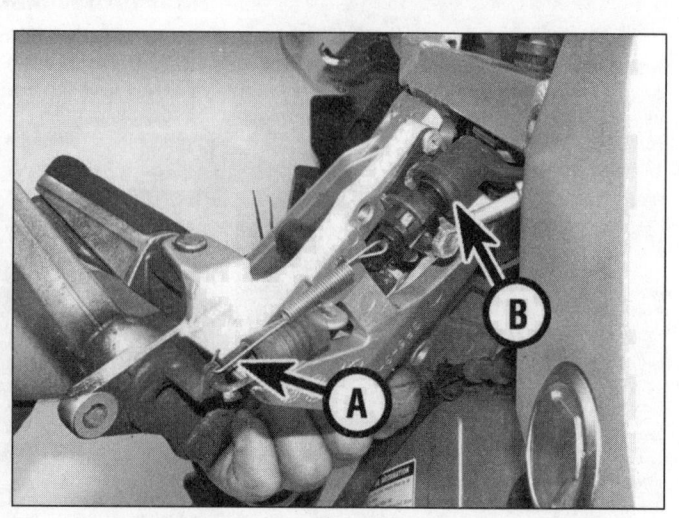

14.10 Detach the spring (A) and remove the switch (B)

Electrical system 8•15

15.2a Instrument cluster screws (arrowed) – 2001 to 2005

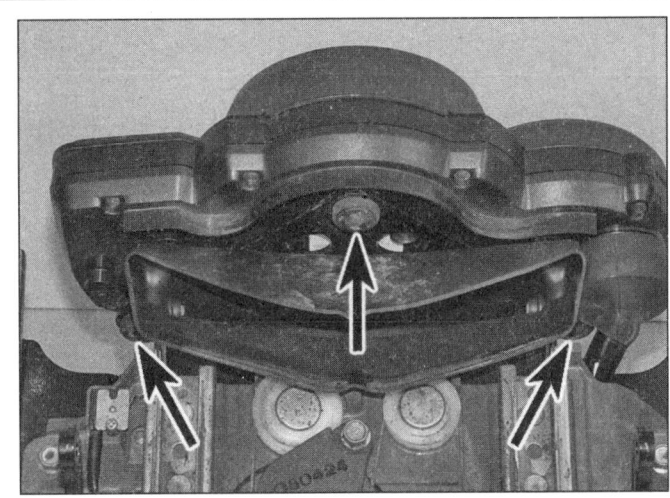

15.2b Instrument cluster screws (arrowed) – 2006 to 2012

15.2c Lift the instruments off and disconnect the wiring

then disconnect the wiring connector **(see illustrations)**.

3 Installation is the reverse of removal. Check the rubber grommets and replace them with new ones if necessary.

2013-on models

4 Remove the fairing (see Chapter 7).

5 Disconnect the wiring connectors which run across the front of the connector board **(see illustration 31.6a)**. Remove the two bolts (retained by nuts on the back) and displace the connector board **(see illustration 31.6b)**. Hold the board to one side and remove the three mounting screws, then disconnect the wiring plug to free the instruments **(see illustrations)**.

6 Installation is the reverse of removal. Check the rubber grommets and replace them with new ones if necessary.

16 Instrument check and disassembly

Note: *Refer to electrical system fault finding in Section 2 and to the wiring diagram for your model at the end of this Chapter.*

Check

1 If all instrument and display functions fail at the same time, check the circuit fuse and the wiring and connectors, referring to the *Wiring Diagrams* at the end of the Chapter.

Tachometer

2 No test details are available for the tachometer. If it fails a new printed circuit board must be installed (see Steps 8 and 9).

Oil level display

3 The oil level display is controlled by the oil level sensor – refer to Section 17 for test details.

Coolant temperature display

4 The coolant temperature display is controlled by the coolant temperature sensor – refer to Chapter 3 for test details.

Speedometer

5 No test details are available for the speedometer. The speedometer is controlled by the ECU. If the speedometer does not work have the bike tested by a Yamaha dealer

15.5a Instrument cluster screws (arrowed) – 2013-on

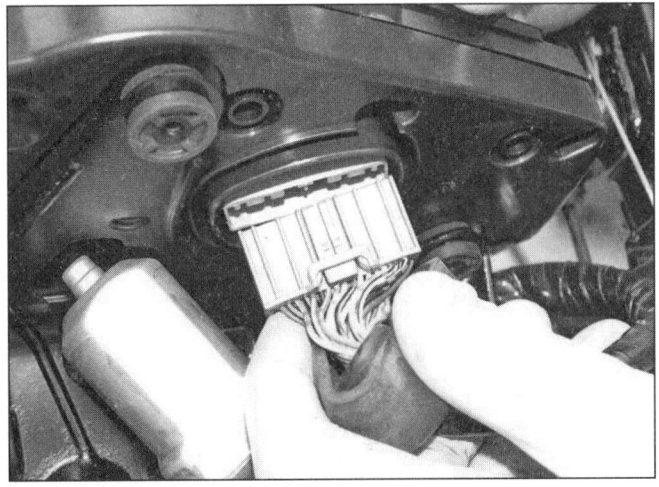

15.5b Disconnecting the instrument wiring

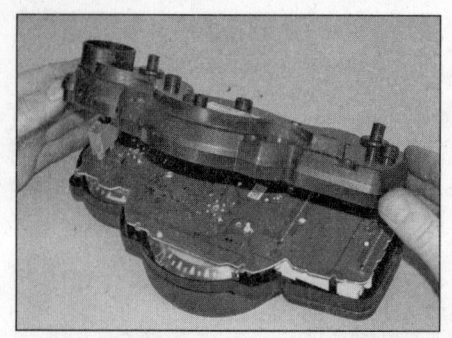

8•16 Electrical system

16.9a Undo the screws and remove the cover...

16.9b ...then lift the PCB out

Instrument illumination and warning lights

6 On 2001 to 2005 models all instrument illumination and warning lights have conventional bulbs.

7 On 2006-on models all instrument illumination and warning lights are LEDs that cannot be replaced with new ones – if one fails a new instrument cluster must be fitted.

Replacement

8 Only the front and rear covers are available separately – if the instrument board is faulty a complete new instrument cluster must be fitted.

9 To replace a cover undo the screws on the rear cover, then remove the cover (see illustration). Lift the instrument board out of the front cover (see illustration). When reassembling it make sure the rubber seal is correctly seated.

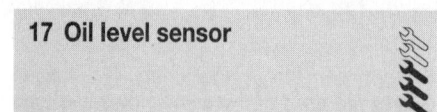

17 Oil level sensor

Note: Refer to electrical system fault finding in Section 2 and to the wiring diagram for your model at the end of this Chapter.

Check

1 The oil level warning light will come on for a few seconds when the ignition is switched ON as a check of the warning light. It should then go out and the motorcycle can be started. If the warning light remains on or comes on while riding, check the oil level as described in *Pre-ride checks*. If the oil level is correct, check the sensor as described below.

2 To check the sensor, remove it from the sump (see Steps 4 to 6). Make sure the sensor float is not stuck and moves freely between its top and bottom positions. Connect the positive probe of a multimeter set to test continuity to the sensor wire and the other probe to the base of the sensor. With the sensor upright (i.e. in its normal installed position with the wiring at the bottom), there should be no continuity (see illustration). Turn the sensor upside down (see illustration) – there should now be continuity. If either condition does not occur, replace the sensor with a new one.

3 If the sensor is working check the wiring and connectors between it and the instrument cluster. On 2001 to 2005 models also refer to Section 16 regarding the warning light. If no faults can be found it is possible the instrument cluster is faulty.

> **HAYNES HINT** On all models the warning light may flicker during sudden acceleration or deceleration or when riding up or down hill. Note that this is a characteristic of the system and provided the oil level is correct, does not indicate a fault.

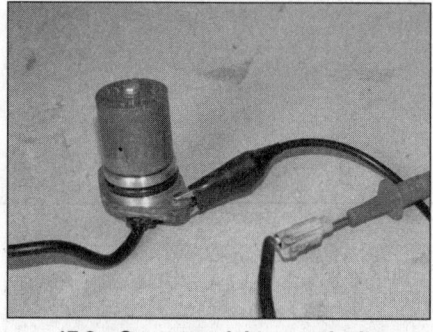

Removal

4 Remove the left-hand fairing side panel (see Chapter 7). Drain the engine oil (see Chapter 1).

5 Remove the throttle bodies (see Chapter 4), then trace the wire back from the sensor and disconnect it at the connector (see illustration). Release the wire from any ties and clamps and the guide secured by one sump bolt (see illustration 17.6), and feed it back to the sensor noting the correct routing.

6 Unscrew the sensor bolts and withdraw the sensor from the sump, being prepared to catch any residual oil (see illustrations). Inspect the O-ring and fit a new if it is damaged or leakage has been noticed (see illustration 17.7). Note that the O-ring is not listed as a spare for 2001 to 2008 models, but is for 2009-on – check with a Yamaha dealer whether their size is the same.

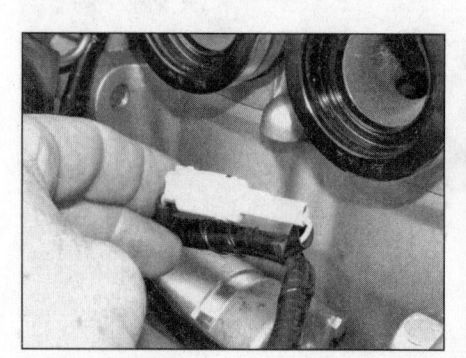

17.2a Sensor upright – continuity

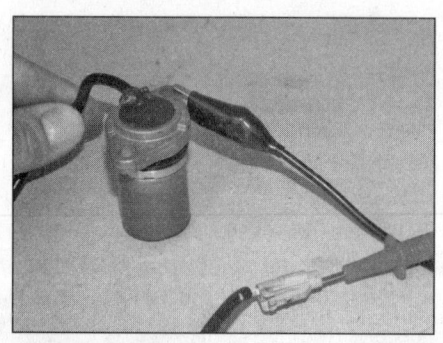

17.2b Sensor upside down – no continuity

17.5 Oil level sensor wiring connector

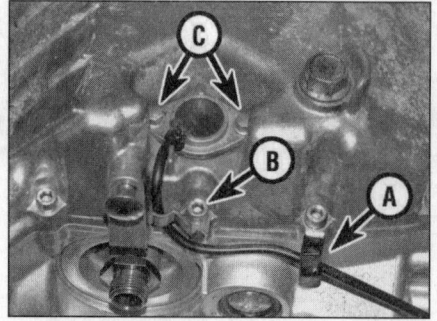

17.6a Oil level sensor wiring clamp (A), wiring guide bolt (B) and mounting bolts (C)

17.6b Lever the sensor out if necessary

Electrical system 8•17

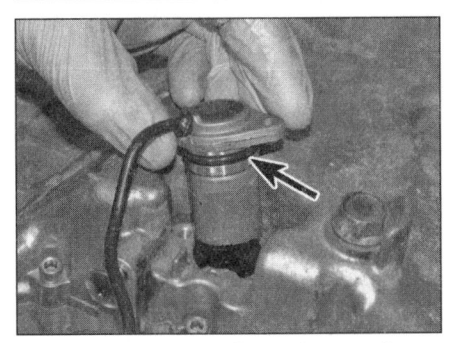

17.7 Grease the O-ring (arrowed)

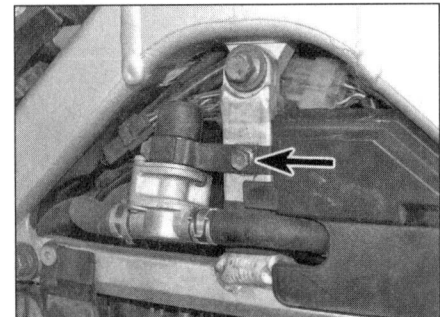

18.2a Unscrew the bolt (arrowed)

18.2b Unscrew the bolts (arrowed) and remove the T-bar

Installation

7 Smear the sensor O-ring with lithium grease **(see illustration)**. Fit the sensor into the sump and tighten the bolts to the torque setting specified at the beginning of this Chapter.
8 Feed the wiring to the connector and secure it with the guide and clamp(s) and any ties previously released **(see illustration 17.6a)**.
9 Fill the engine with the specified amount of oil (see Chapter 1) and check the operation of the sensor. Install all disturbed components.

18 Ignition switch

> **Warning: To prevent the risk of short circuits, disconnect the battery negative (–) lead before making any ignition switch checks.**

Note: *Refer to electrical system fault finding in Section 2 and to the wiring diagram for your model at the end of this Chapter.*

Check

1 The switch can be checked for continuity using an ohmmeter or a continuity test light. Always disconnect the battery negative (–) lead, which will prevent the possibility of a short circuit, before making the checks (see Section 3). Before checking the switch check the main fuse (Section 5).
2 To access the connector raise the fuel tank (see Chapter 4). On 2001 to 2005 models unscrew the AIS control valve holder bolt **(see illustration)**. On all models remove the T-bar **(see illustration)**. On 2006-on models remove the heat shield **(see illustrations)**. Trace the wiring from the switch to the connector and disconnect it. Check for loose or broken connections.
3 Using an ohmmeter or a continuity tester connected to the switch side of the connector, check the continuity of the connector terminal pairs shown with linked circles in the table for the ignition switch shown in the wiring diagram for your model at the end of this Chapter. Continuity should exist between those terminals when the switch is in the ON position.

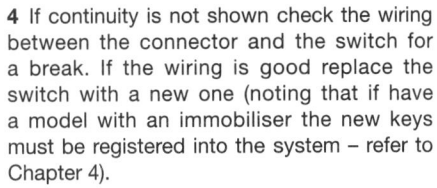

4 If continuity is not shown check the wiring between the connector and the switch for a break. If the wiring is good replace the switch with a new one (noting that if have a model with an immobiliser the new keys must be registered into the system – refer to Chapter 4).
5 If the switch is good, reconnect the battery. Check there is battery voltage at the red wire terminal in the loom side of the connector. If not, there is a break in the wire between the connector and the battery. If there is voltage check all other wires for continuity to the fusebox.

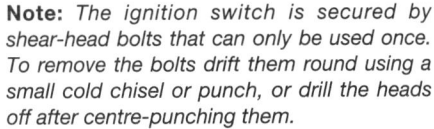

Removal

Note: *The ignition switch is secured by shear-head bolts that can only be used once. To remove the bolts drift them round using a small cold chisel or punch, or drill the heads off after centre-punching them.*

6 Disconnect the battery negative (–) lead (see Section 3).
7 Refer to Step 2 to access the switch wiring connector. Trace the wiring from the switch to the connector and disconnect it, and where fitted the immobiliser receiver connector. Feed the wiring back to the switch, freeing it from any clips and ties and noting the routing.
8 Displace the handlebars from the top yoke, then remove the yoke (see Chapter 5).
9 Protect and secure the yoke sufficiently, then undo the security bolts (see **Note**), and remove the switch **(see illustration)**.
10 Where fitted separate the immobiliser receiver from the switch.

18.2d ...and remove the shield

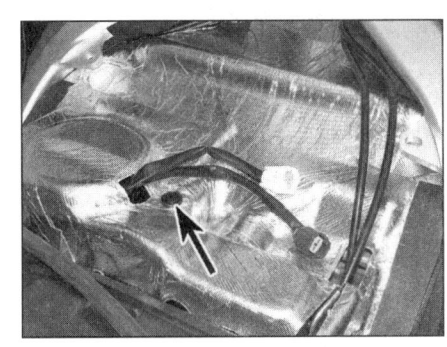

18.2c Release the trim clip (arrowed), thread the wiring through the hole and on 2013-on models slip the cables out of the slot...

Installation

11 Installation is the reverse of removal. Use new ignition switch bolts and tighten them until the heads shear off. Refer to Chapter 5 to install the top yoke and handlebars. Make sure the wiring is correctly routed and securely connected.

19 Handlebar switches

1 Generally speaking, the switches are reliable and trouble-free. Most troubles, when they do occur, are caused by dirty or corroded contacts, but wear and breakage of internal parts is a possibility that should not be

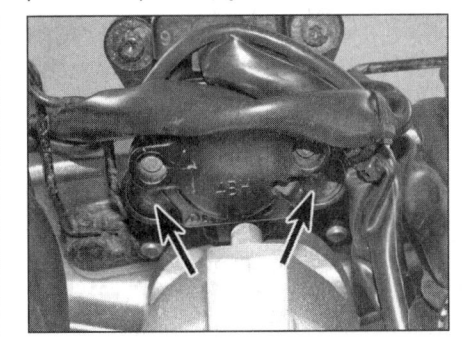

18.9 Ignition switch bolts (arrowed)

8•18 Electrical system

19.8a Left-hand switch housing screws (arrowed) – 2001 to 2005 models

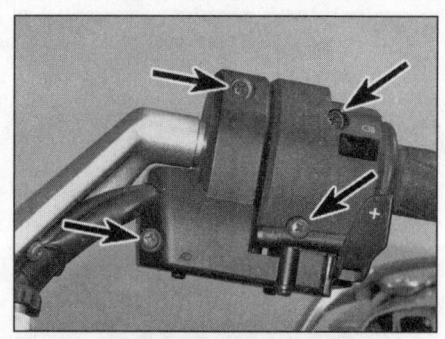

19.8b Left-hand switch housing screws (arrowed) – AS models

19.8c Right-hand switch housing screws (arrowed) – 2001 to 2005 models

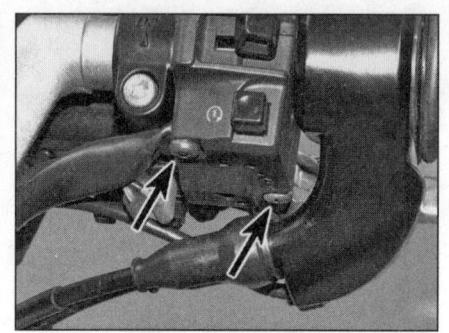

19.8d Right-hand switch housing screws (arrowed) – AS models

overlooked. If breakage does occur, the entire switch and related wiring harness will have to be replaced with a new one, as individual parts are not available.

Check

Note: *Refer to electrical system fault finding in Section 2 and to the wiring diagram for your model at the end of this Chapter.*

2 The switches can be checked for continuity using an ohmmeter or a continuity test light. Always disconnect the battery negative (–) lead, which will prevent the possibility of a short circuit, before making the checks (see Section 3).

3 To access the connectors, on 2001 to 2012 models raise the fuel tank (see Chapter 4), then on 2003 to 2005 models unscrew the AIS control valve holder bolt **(see illustration 18.2a)**, on all models remove the T-bar **(see illustration 18.2b)** and heat shield **(see illustrations 18.2c and d)**. Trace the wiring from the switch to the connector(s) and disconnect it/them. Check for loose or broken connections.

4 Using an ohmmeter or a continuity tester connected to the switch side of the connector, check the continuity of the connector terminal pairs shown with linked circles in the tables for the individual switches shown in the wiring diagram for your model at the end of this Chapter. Continuity should exist between the terminals connected by a solid line on the diagram when the switch is in the indicated position.

5 If the continuity check indicates a problem exists, displace the switch housing, and spray the switch contacts with electrical contact cleaner (there is no need to remove the switch completely). If they are accessible, the contacts can be scraped clean with a knife or polished with crocus cloth. If switch components are damaged or broken, it should be obvious when the switch is disassembled.

Removal and installation

6 Refer to Step 3 to access the switch wiring connectors. Feed the wiring back to the switch, freeing it from any clips and ties and noting the routing.

7 If removing the right-hand switch on 2001 to 2012 models disconnect the wires from the brake light switch **(see illustration 14.2)**. If removing the left-hand switch on 2001 to 2012 models (except on YCC-S models) disconnect the wires from the clutch switch **(see illustration 22.2)**.

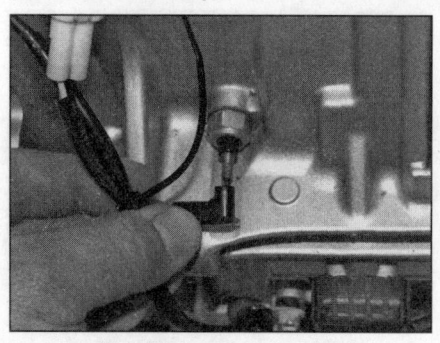

20.3 Disconnect the wire

8 Undo the screws and free the switch from the handlebar by separating the halves **(see illustrations)** – on 2006 to 2012 models you need to displace the throttle cable housing to get on the front screw for the right-hand housing (see Chapter 4).

9 Installation is the reverse of removal. Locate the pin in the switch housing in the hole in the handlebar. Do not over-tighten the screws.

20 Neutral switch/gear position switch

Note: *Refer to electrical system fault finding in Section 2 and to the wiring diagram for your model at the end of this Chapter.*

1 All 2001 to 2005 models and 2006-on AS models have a neutral switch in the back of the engine. The 2006-on A models have a gear position switch on the left-hand side of the engine. The 2006-on AS models, as well as the neutral switch, have a gear position sensor for the YCC-S – this is covered in Chapter 2, Section 20.

2 The neutral light should come whenever the ignition switch is ON and the transmission is in neutral. The switch is part of the starter interlock safety circuit which prevents or stops the engine running if the transmission is in gear whilst the sidestand is down, and prevents the engine from starting if the transmission is in gear unless the sidestand is up and the clutch is pulled in.

Neutral switch

Check

3 If the light does not come on when it should, but all other instrument functions work, remove the throttle bodies (see Chapter 4). Pull the wiring connector off the switch **(see illustration)**.

4 Check for continuity between the switch terminal and the crankcase. With the transmission in neutral, there should be continuity. With the transmission in gear, there should be no continuity. If not, remove the switch (Step 8) and check whether the plunger is bent or damaged, or just stuck **(see illustration)**. Replace the switch with a new one if necessary.

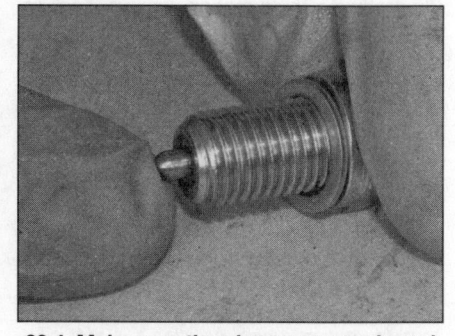

20.4 Make sure the plunger moves in and out smoothly and freely

Electrical system 8•19

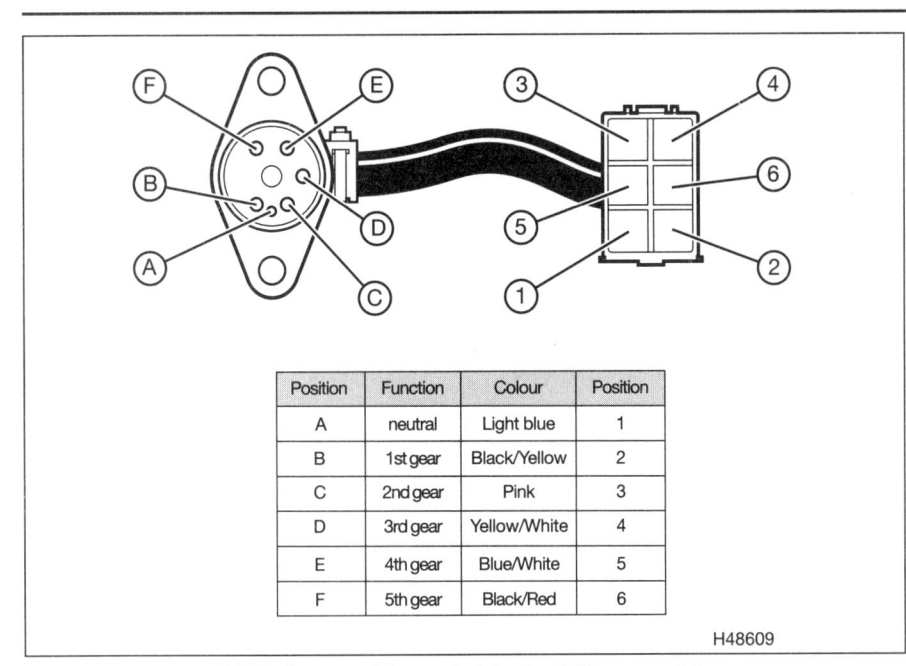

Position	Function	Colour	Position
A	neutral	Light blue	1
B	1st gear	Black/Yellow	2
C	2nd gear	Pink	3
D	3rd gear	Yellow/White	4
E	4th gear	Blue/White	5
F	5th gear	Black/Red	6

20.13 Gear position switch test – 2013-on models

5 If the switch is good check for continuity in the wire from the connector to the starter circuit cut-off relay (see Chapter 4). Next check the diodes in the relay, then check the wire from the relay to the instrument cluster. On 2001 to 2005 models also refer to Section 16 regarding the warning light. If no faults can be found check the other components (clutch switch, sidestand switch, starter circuit cut-off relay) in the starter safety circuit, and check the wiring between them for continuity, and the connectors for loose or broken connections. On 2006-on models, if no faults can be found, it is possible the instrument cluster is faulty.

Removal and installation

6 Remove the throttle bodies (see Chapter 4).
7 Pull the wiring connector off the switch **(see illustration 20.3)**.
8 Clean the area around the switch, then unscrew it from the crankcase. Remove the sealing washer – a new one should be used.
9 Fit the switch using a new washer and tighten it to the torque setting specified at the beginning of the Chapter.

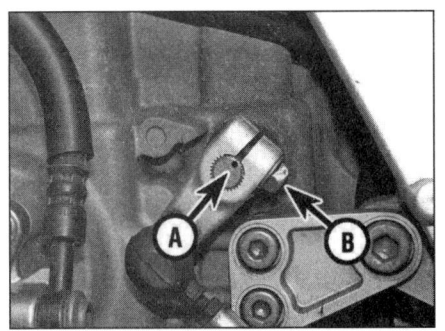

20.15 Alignment punch mark (A), clamp bolt (B)

10 Connect the wiring connector and check the operation of the neutral light. Install the throttle bodies (see Chapter 4).

Gear position switch

Check

11 If the neutral light does not come on when it should, but all other instrument functions work, remove the left-hand side cover (see Chapter 7). Trace the wiring from the switch and disconnect the wiring connector. Check for loose or broken connections. Check for continuity between the black (2006 to 2012 models) or light blue (2013-on models) terminal and the crankcase. With the transmission in neutral, there should be continuity. With the transmission in gear, there should be no continuity. If the switch is good, check for continuity in the light blue wire from the connector to the starter circuit cut-off relay (see Chapter 4). Next check the diodes in the relay, then check the wire from the relay to the instrument cluster. If no faults can be found check the other components (clutch switch,

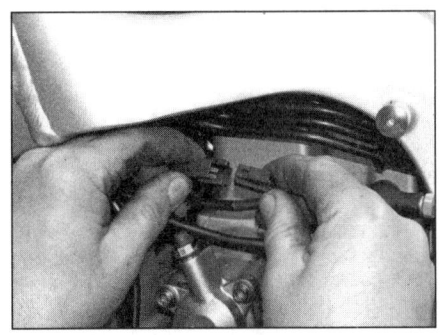

21.2 Disconnect the wiring

sidestand switch, starter circuit cut-off relay) in the starter safety circuit, and check the wiring between them for continuity, and the connectors for loose or broken connections. If no faults can be found, it is possible the instrument cluster is faulty.

12 Remove the switch and check the condition of the contact points on its inner face. Replace the switch with a new one if necessary.

13 Each contact point on the switch face should have continuity with one of the terminals in the connector. Information for which contact is connected to which terminal is given for 2013-on models **(see illustration)**; test information is not available for 2006 to 2012 models although the test pattern is likely to be the same. Test the switch accordingly. If the terminals differ on 2006 to 2012 models, the testing principle applies. If any contact does not show continuity with one of the terminals fit a new switch.

Removal and installation

14 Remove the left-hand side cover. Trace the wiring from the switch and disconnect the wiring connector. Feed the wiring back to the switch, releasing it from any ties and guides and noting its routing.
15 Note the alignment of the slit in the gearchange linkage arm with the punch mark on the shaft, then unscrew the pinch bolt and slide the arm off **(see illustration)**.
16 Undo the screws and remove the switch. Remove the O-ring – a new one should be used.
17 Fit the switch using a new O-ring smeared with grease and tighten the screws.
18 Connect the wiring connector and check the operation of the neutral light.

21 Sidestand switch

1 The sidestand switch is mounted on the stand bracket. The switch is part of the starter interlock safety circuit that prevents or stops the engine running if the transmission is in gear whilst the sidestand is down, and prevents the engine from starting if the transmission is in gear unless the sidestand is up and the clutch is pulled in.

Check

Note: *Refer to electrical system fault finding in Section 2 and to the wiring diagram for your model at the end of this Chapter.*

2 Remove the left-hand fairing side panel (see Chapter 7). Disconnect the sidestand switch wiring connector **(see illustration)**.
3 Check the operation of the switch using an ohmmeter or continuity test light. Connect the meter between the wire terminals on the switch side of the connector. With the sidestand up there should be continuity (zero resistance) between the terminals, and with the stand down there should be no continuity (infinite resistance).

8•20 Electrical system

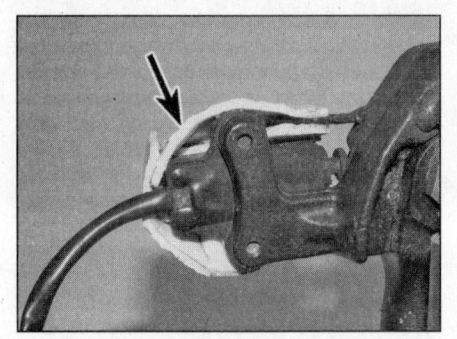

21.6 Where fitted remove the heat shield (arrowed)

22.2 Clutch switch wiring connector (arrowed)

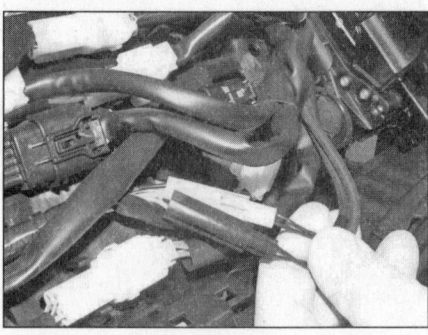

23.2 On 2013-on models grip wiring connectors are colour-coded grey (right) and black (left)

4 If the switch does not perform as described, check the wiring between the connector and the switch for a break. If the wiring is good replace the switch with a new one.
5 If the switch is good, check the other components (clutch switch, neutral switch, starter circuit cut-off relay and diodes) in the starter safety circuit, and check the wiring between them for continuity, and the connectors for loose or broken connections – refer to Chapter 4 for the starter circuit cut-off relay and diodes.

Removal and installation

6 Remove the sidestand assembly (see Chapter 5). Where fitted remove the heat shield from the switch **(see illustration)**.
7 Undo the screws and remove the cover and the switch from the stand bracket, noting how it fits.
8 Clean the threads of the screws and apply some fresh threadlock. Fit the switch and cover onto the bracket and tighten the screws. Where removed fit the heat shield.
9 Feed the wiring up to its connector, making sure it is correctly routed and secured by any clips.
10 Reconnect the wiring connector and check the operation of the switch.

22 Clutch switch

1 The clutch switch is mounted on the underside of the clutch master cylinder. The switch is part of the starter interlock safety circuit which prevents or stops the engine running if the transmission is in gear whilst the sidestand is down, and prevents the engine from starting if the transmission is in gear unless the sidestand is up and the clutch lever is pulled in. The switch isn't adjustable.

Check

Note: Refer to electrical system fault finding in Section 2 and to the wiring diagram for your model at the end of this Chapter.
2 On 2001 to 2012 models disconnect the wiring connector from the switch **(see illustration)**. On 2013-on models remove the fairing (see Chapter 7), then trace the wiring from the switch and disconnect it at the connector. Connect the probes of an ohmmeter or a continuity tester to the two switch terminals. With the clutch lever pulled in, continuity should be indicated. With the clutch lever out, no continuity (infinite resistance) should be indicated.
3 If the switch is good, check the other components (sidestand switch, neutral switch, starter circuit cut-off relay and diodes) in the starter safety circuit, and check the wiring between them for continuity, and the connectors for loose or broken connections – refer to Chapter 4 for the starter circuit cut-off relay and diodes.

Removal and installation

4 The clutch switch is mounted on the underside of the master cylinder.
5 On 2001 to 2012 models disconnect the wiring connector from the switch **(see illustration 22.2)**. On 2013-on models remove the fairing (see Chapter 7), then trace the wiring from the switch and disconnect it at the connector – feed the wiring back to the switch, releasing it from any ties and guides and noting its routing.
6 Undo the screw securing the switch and remove it, noting how it fits.
7 Installation is the reverse of removal. Make sure the switch is correctly located before tightening its screw.

23 Heated grips

Note: Refer to electrical system fault finding in Section 2 and to the wiring diagram for your model at the end of this Chapter.
1 On 2006 to 2012 models remove the left-hand fairing side panel, and on 2013-on models remove the fairing centre cover (see Chapter 7).
2 To test the grips trace the wiring from the grip and disconnect it at the connector **(see illustration)**. Check for loose or broken connections. Using an ohmmeter, connect the probes to the terminals in the grip side of the connector and measure the resistance – the right-hand grip should show 1.17 to 1.43 ohms, and the left-hand grip should show 1.21 to 1.48 ohms. If not, refer to the relevant Steps in Section 5 of Chapter 5 and replace the grips with new ones.
3 To test the heated grip control knob on 2006 to 2012 models disconnect the wiring connectors. Check for loose or broken connections. Check there is continuity between the brown wire terminal in the control knob side of the blue connector and the black/green wire terminal in the white connector with the knob turned ON, and no continuity in the OFF position. If not remove the heated grip control panel (see Chapter 7) and replace the control knob with a new one. If all is good so far test the headlight ON/OFF relay (Section 6) – the relay also switches the power to the heated grip system.
4 On 2013-on models check the left-hand switch housing on the handlebar and all wiring and connectors. If no fault can be found have the system tested by a Yamaha dealer.

24 Horn(s)

1 On 2001 to 2012 models a horn is mounted on each top corner of the radiator, on 2013-on models there is one horn on the left-hand end.

Check

Note: Refer to electrical system fault finding in Section 2 and to the wiring diagram for your model at the end of this Chapter.
2 If both horns fail on 2001 to 2012 models and if the horn fails on 2013-on models first check the signalling system fuse (Section 5).
3 Remove the fairing side panel(s) for access to the horn(s) (see Chapter 7). Disconnect the wiring connectors from the horn **(see illustration)**. Check them for loose wires. Using two jumper wires, apply voltage from a fully-charged 12V battery directly to the terminals on the horn. If the horn doesn't sound, replace it with a new one.

Electrical system 8•21

24.3 Horn wiring connectors (arrowed)

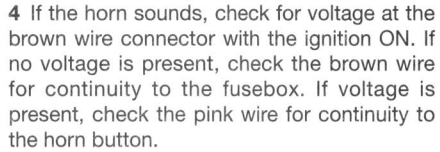

25.2a Starter relay (arrowed) – 2001 to 2005 models

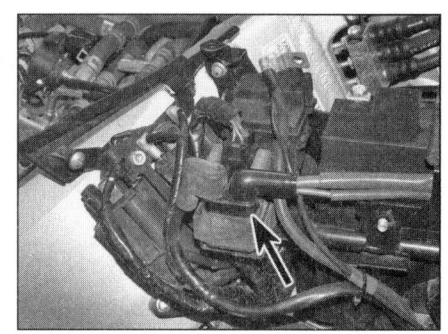

25.2b Starter relay (arrowed) – 2006-on models

4 If the horn sounds, check for voltage at the brown wire connector with the ignition ON. If no voltage is present, check the brown wire for continuity to the fusebox. If voltage is present, check the pink wire for continuity to the horn button.

5 If all is good check the button contacts in the switch housing (see Section 19).

Replacement

6 Remove the fairing side panel(s) for access to the horn(s) (see Chapter 7).

7 Disconnect the wiring connectors from the horn **(see illustration 24.3)**. Unscrew the bolt securing the horn.

8 Fit the horn and tighten the bolt. Connect the wiring to the horn. Check that it works.

25 Starter relay

Note: *Refer to electrical system fault finding in Section 2 and to the wiring diagram for your model at the end of this Chapter.*

Check

1 If the starter circuit is faulty, first check the fuse (see Section 5).

2 To access the relay, on 2001 to 2005 models and 2013-on models remove the battery access panel, and on 2006 to 2012 models remove the fairing (see Chapter 7) **(see illustrations)**.

3 Lift the rubber terminal cover and unscrew the bolt securing the starter motor lead, identified by the letter M (the other lead, marked B, is the battery lead) **(see illustration)**; position the lead away from the relay.

4 With the bike on the centrestand and the sidestand up, the ignition switch ON, the engine kill switch in the RUN position, and the transmission in neutral, press the starter switch. The relay should be heard to click.

5 If the relay doesn't click, switch off the ignition and remove the relay as described below; test it as follows:

6 Set a multimeter to the ohms x 1 scale and connect it across the relay's battery (B) and starter motor (M) terminals **(see illustration)**. There should be no continuity. Using a fully-charged 12 volt battery and two insulated jumper wires, connect the positive (+) terminal of the battery to the red/white wire (C) terminal of the relay, and the negative (–) terminal to the blue/white wire (D) terminal of the relay. At this point the relay should be heard to click and the multimeter read 0 ohms (continuity). If this is the case the relay is proved good. If the relay does not click when battery voltage is applied and indicates no continuity (infinite resistance) across its terminals, it is faulty and must be replaced with a new one.

7 If the relay is good, check for continuity in the red lead from the battery to the relay, and in the black lead from the relay to the starter motor. Check that the terminals at each end of the lead are tight and corrosion-free.

8 Next check the red/white and blue/white wires to the relay and the other components in the starter circuit.

Replacement

9 To access the relay, on 2001 to 2005 models remove the battery access panel, and on all other models remove the fairing (see Chapter 7) **(see illustration 25.2a or b)**.

10 Disconnect the battery (see Section 3).

11 Disconnect the relay wiring connector **(see illustration)**. Unscrew the bolts securing the starter motor and battery leads to the relay and detach the leads **(see illustration 25.3)**. If the relay is being replaced with a new one, remove the fuses and fit them into the new relay.

12 Installation is the reverse of removal. Connect the lead from the battery to the terminal marked B and the lead from the starter motor to the terminal marked M, and make sure the terminal bolts are securely tightened. Do not forget to fit the fuses into the relay if removed. Connect the negative (–) lead last when reconnecting the battery.

26 Starter motor removal and installation

Removal

1 The starter motor is mounted on the crankcase behind the cylinders. Remove the throttle bodies (see Chapter 4).

2 Peel back the rubber terminal cover on

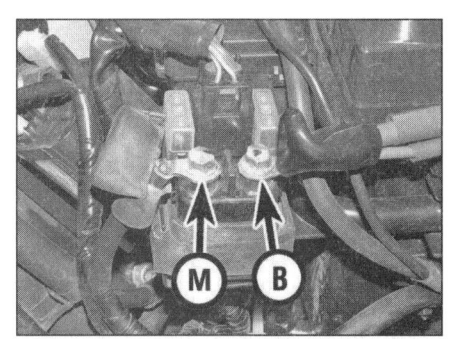

25.3 Lift the rubber covers to access the starter motor lead terminal (M) and battery lead terminal (B)

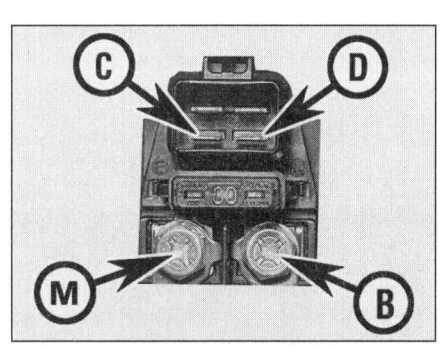

25.6 Starter relay test terminal identification

25.11 Disconnect the wiring connector then detach the leads

8•22 Electrical system

26.2 Pull back the terminal cover then unscrew the nut and detach the lead

26.3a Unscrew the two bolts (arrowed), noting the earth lead...

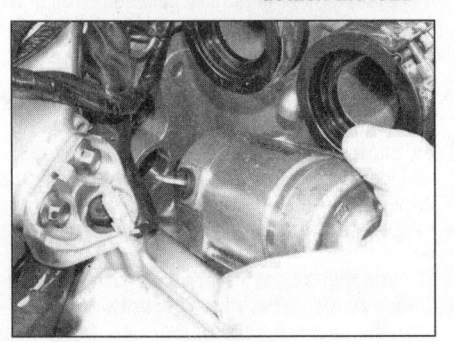

26.3b ...and remove the motor

26.5 Fit a new O-ring (arrowed)

the starter motor **(see illustration)**. Unscrew the nut, remove the screw and detach the lead.
3 Unscrew the two bolts securing the starter motor to the crankcase **(see illustration)**. Slide the starter motor out, using a screwdriver as leverage if required **(see illustration)**.
4 Remove the O-ring on the end of the starter motor – a new one must be used **(see illustration 26.5)**.

Installation

5 Fit a new O-ring smeared with grease onto the end of the starter motor, making sure it is seated in its groove **(see illustration)**.
6 Manoeuvre the motor into position, meshing starter motor teeth with those of the starter idle/reduction gear **(see illustration 26.3b)**. Fit the bolts and tighten them to the torque setting specified at the beginning of the Chapter **(see illustration 26.3a)**.
7 Connect the starter lead to the motor **(see illustration 26.2)**. Fit the rubber cover over the terminal.
8 Install the throttle bodies (see Chapter 4).

27 Starter motor overhaul

Check

1 Remove the starter motor (see Section 26). Cover the body in some rag and clamp the motor mounting lugs in a soft-jawed vice – do not overtighten it.
2 Using a fully-charged 12 volt battery and two insulated jumper wires, connect the positive (+) terminal of the battery to the protruding terminal on the starter motor, and the negative (–) terminal to one of the motor's mounting lugs. At this point the starter motor should spin. If this is the case the motor is proved good, though it is worth disassembling it and checking it if you suspect it of not working properly under load. If the motor does not spin, disassemble it for inspection.

Disassembly

3 Remove the starter motor (see Section 26).
4 Note any alignment marks between the main housing and the front and rear covers, or make your own if they aren't clear **(see illustration)**.
5 Unscrew the two long bolts and remove the rear cover **(see illustrations)**.

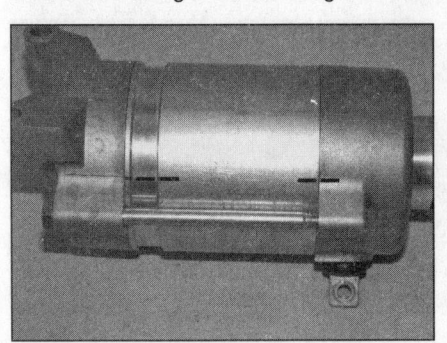

27.4 Note the alignment marks (highlighted) between the housing and the covers, or make your own

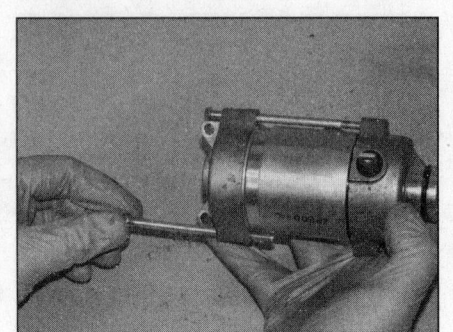

27.5a Unscrew the bolts...

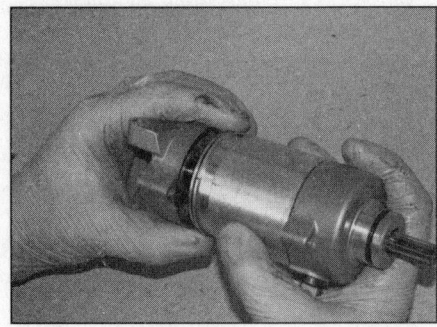

27.5b ...and remove the rear cover

Electrical system 8•23

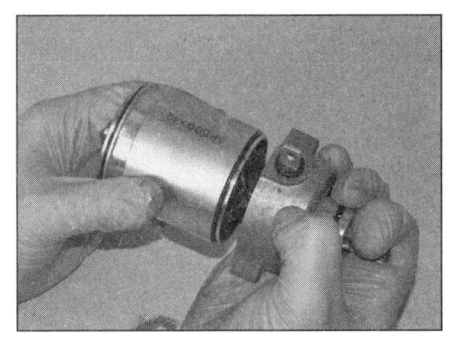

27.6 Draw the housing off

27.7a Withdraw the armature...

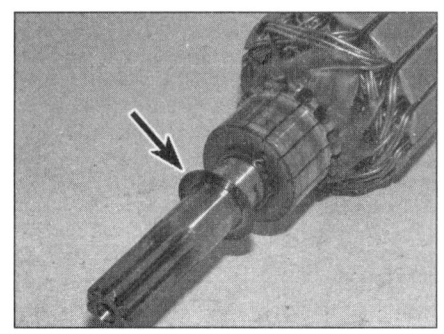

27.7b ...noting the washer (arrowed)

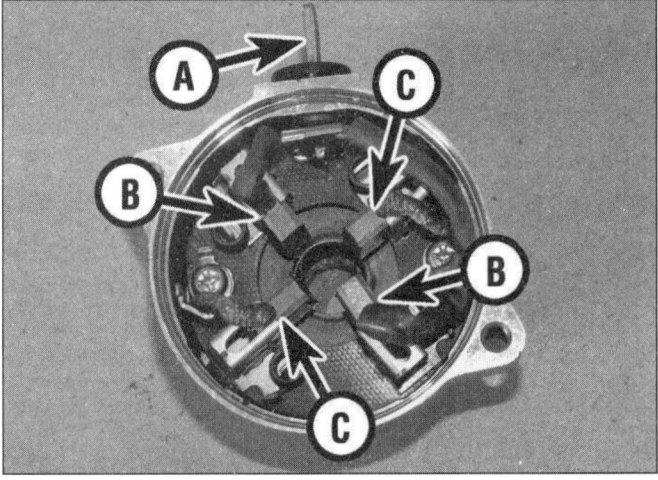

27.8 Terminal bolt (A), positive brushes (B), negative brushes (C)

27.9 Brushplate screws (arrowed)

6 Hold the shaft and draw the housing off the armature **(see illustration)** – it is held in by the attraction of the magnets, so take care not to lose your grip before the magnets lose theirs.
7 Withdraw the armature from the front cover, noting the washer **(see illustrations)**.
8 At this stage check for continuity between the terminal bolt and the positive brushes **(see illustration)** – there should be continuity (zero resistance). Check for continuity between the terminal bolt and the cover – there should be no continuity (infinite resistance). Also check for continuity between the negative and positive brushes – there should be no continuity (infinite resistance). If there is no continuity when there should be or *vice versa*, identify the faulty component and replace it with a new one.
9 If required slide the brushes out of their housings, then undo the brushplate screws and remove the negative brushes and the plate, and where fitted the tabbed washer **(see illustration)**.

10 To remove the positive brushes you must unsolder the wire plate from the terminal **(see illustration)**.

Inspection

11 The parts of the starter motor that are most likely to require attention are the brushes. Measure the length of each brush and compare the results to the length listed in this Chapter's Specifications **(see illustration)**. If worn replace the brushes with a new set

27.10 Unsolder the terminal (arrowed) to release the positive brushplate

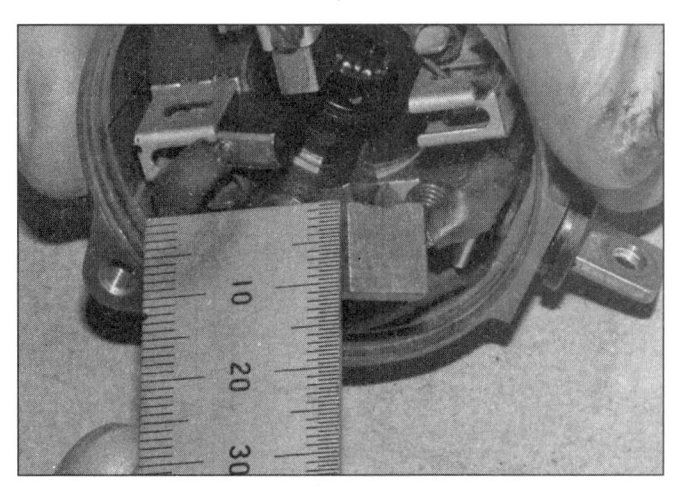

27.11 Measure the length of each brush

8•24 Electrical system

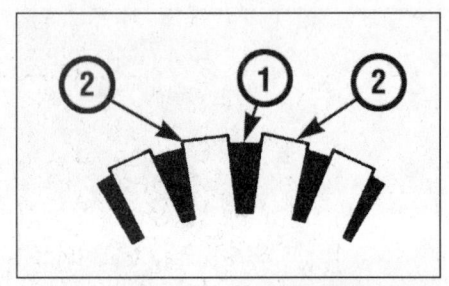

27.12 Check the depth of the Mica (1) between each pair of bars (2)

– see Steps 9 and 10. If the brushes are not worn excessively, nor cracked, chipped, or otherwise damaged, they can be reused.

12 Inspect the commutator bars on the armature for scoring, scratches and discoloration. The commutator can be cleaned and polished with crocus cloth or 600 grit sandpaper, but do not use anything coarser. After cleaning, blow and wipe away any residue with a cloth soaked in electrical system cleaner or denatured alcohol. Check the depth of the insulating Mica between each bar – it should be 1.5 mm below the surface **(see illustration)**. As the bars wear the Mica should be gently scratched away using a hacksaw blade to maintain the correct depth.

13 Measure the commutator diameter and replace the armature with a new one if worn to or beyond the service limit specified at the beginning of the Chapter. Using an ohmmeter or a continuity test light, check for continuity between the commutator bars **(see illustration)**. Continuity should exist between each bar and all of the others. Also, check for continuity between the commutator bars and the armature shaft **(see illustration)**. There should be no continuity (infinite resistance) between the commutator and the shaft. If not, the armature is faulty and a new starter motor must be obtained – the armature is not available separately.

14 Check the front end of the armature shaft for worn, cracked, chipped and broken teeth. If the shaft is damaged or worn, a new starter motor must be obtained – the armature is not available separately.

15 Inspect the front and rear covers for signs of cracks or wear. Check the oil seal and the bearing in the front cover and the bush in the rear cover for wear and damage **(see illustrations)** – the seal, bearing, bush and covers are not listed as being available separately so if necessary a new starter motor must be fitted.

16 Inspect the magnets in the main housing and the housing itself for cracks.

17 Inspect the terminal and its insulator for signs of looseness, damage or deformation and replace the front cover with a new one if necessary.

Reassembly

18 If removed locate the positive brushes in the front cover, making sure each is correctly

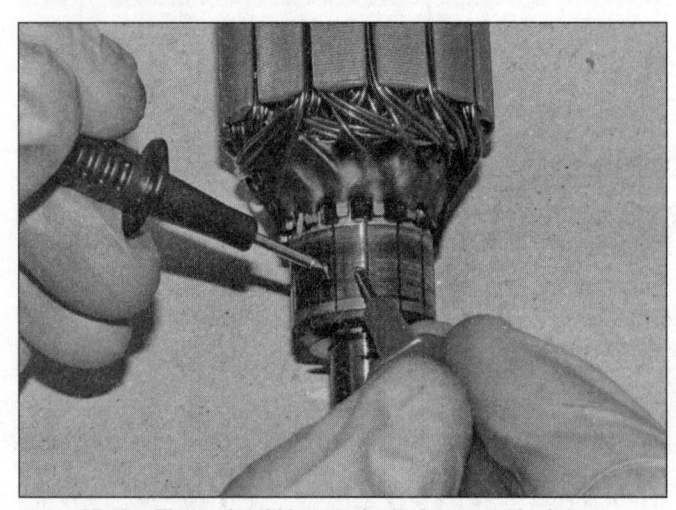

27.13a There should be continuity between the bars...

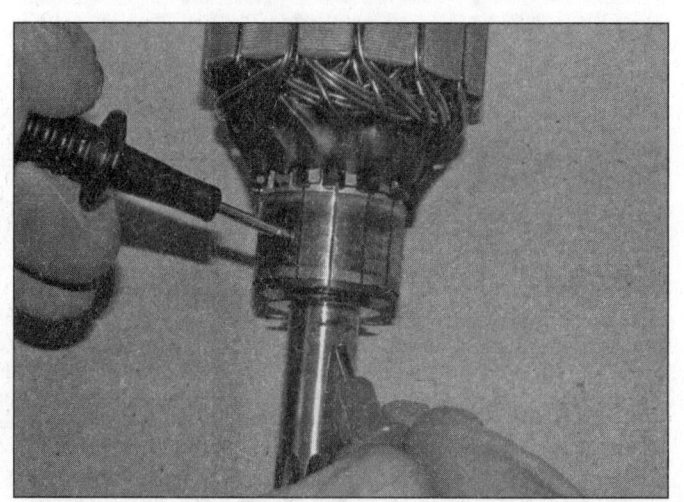

27.13b ...and no continuity between the bars and the shaft

27.15a Check the bearing and seal (arrowed)...

27.15b ...and the bush (arrowed)

Electrical system 8•25

27.21 Main housing sealing rings (arrowed)

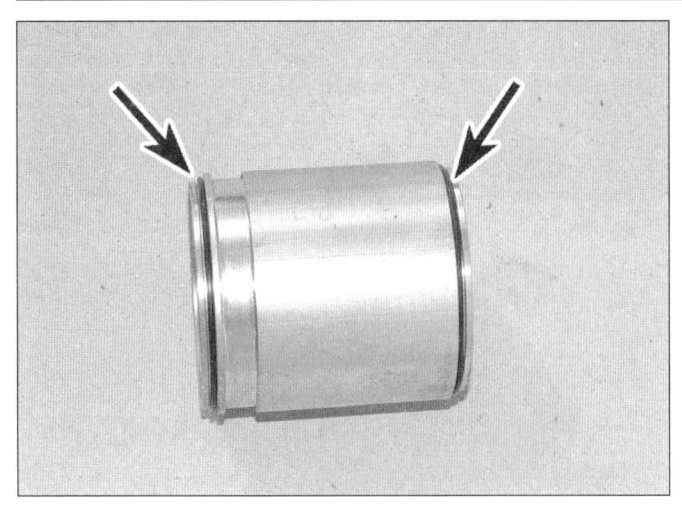

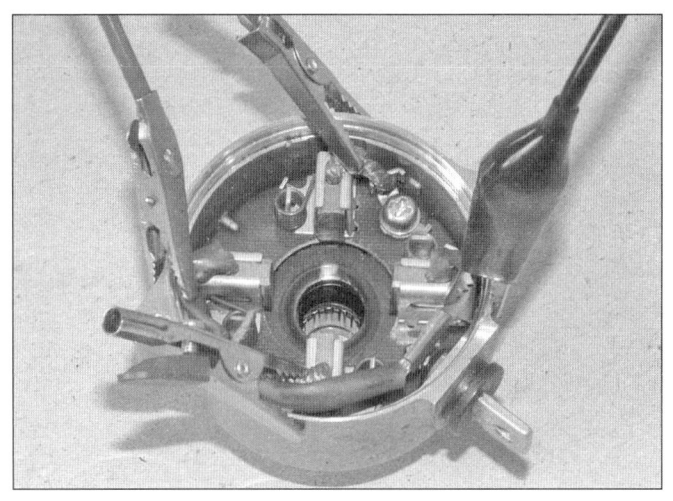

27.22a Retract and secure the brushes...

positioned according to the length of its wire, and solder the wire plate to the terminal as shown **(see illustrations 27.9 and 27.10)**.
19 Where removed fit the tabbed washer into the front cover. Fit the brushplate, aligning the cut-out in its outer rim with the tab on the cover. Fit the negative brushes and secure them with the screws **(see illustration 27.9)**. Make sure the brush springs are correctly in place. Locate the brushes in their housings.
20 To check for correct installation do the continuity checks described in Step 8.
21 If removed fit the sealing rings onto the main housing **(see illustration)**. Apply a smear of grease to the oil seal and bearing in the front cover **(see illustration 27.15a)**. Fit the washer onto the armature if removed **(see illustration 27.7b)**.
22 Retract each brush into its housing and secure it there using a crocodile clip as shown **(see illustration)**. Fit the armature into the front cover **(see illustration)**. Remove the clips and check that each brush lodges against the commutator, and the armature turns smoothly and freely.
23 The housing fits with its plain end towards the front cover. Hold the shaft and carefully allow the housing to be drawn on, making sure it is correctly aligned according to the marks made on disassembly **(see illustration 27.6)**.
24 Apply a smear of grease to the bush in the rear cover **(see illustration 27.15b)**. Fit the rear cover, aligning the marks **(see illustration 27.5b)**.
25 Check the marks are correctly aligned then fit the long bolts and tighten them **(see illustration 27.5a)**.
26 Install the starter motor (see Section 26).

28 Charging system testing

1 If the performance of the charging system is suspect, the system as a whole should be checked first, followed by testing of the individual components. **Note:** *Before beginning the checks, make sure the battery is fully charged and that all system connections are clean and tight.*
2 Checking the output of the charging system and the performance of the various components within the charging system requires the use of a multimeter (with voltage, current, resistance checking facilities).
3 When making the checks, follow the procedures carefully to prevent incorrect connections or short circuits resulting in irreparable damage to electrical system components.

Output test

4 Remove the battery access panel (see Chapter 7). Start the engine and warm it up.
5 To check the regulated (DC) voltage output, allow the engine to idle. Connect a multimeter set to the 0-20 volts DC scale across the terminals of the battery with the positive (+) meter probe to battery positive (+) terminal and the negative (-) meter probe to battery negative (-) terminal **(see illustration)**.

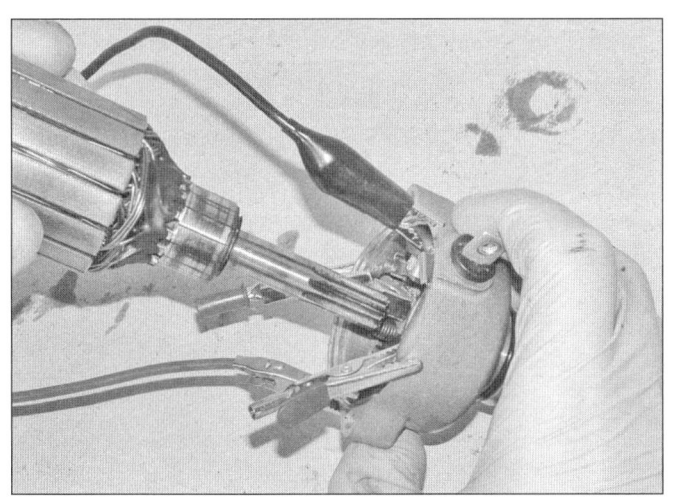

27.22b ...so the armature can be fitted

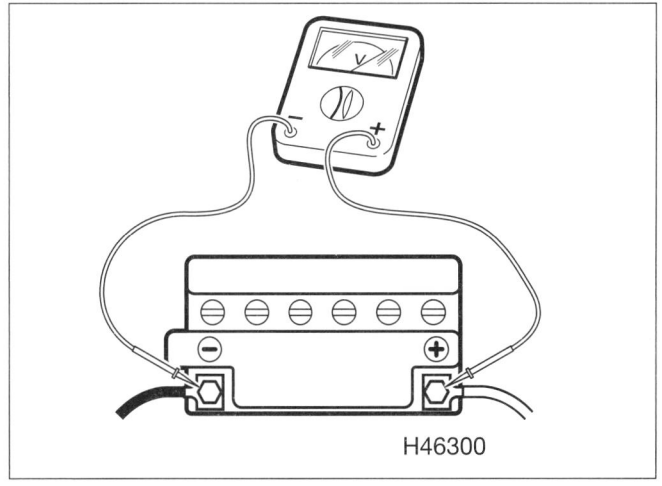

28.5 Checking the charging rate – connect the meter as shown

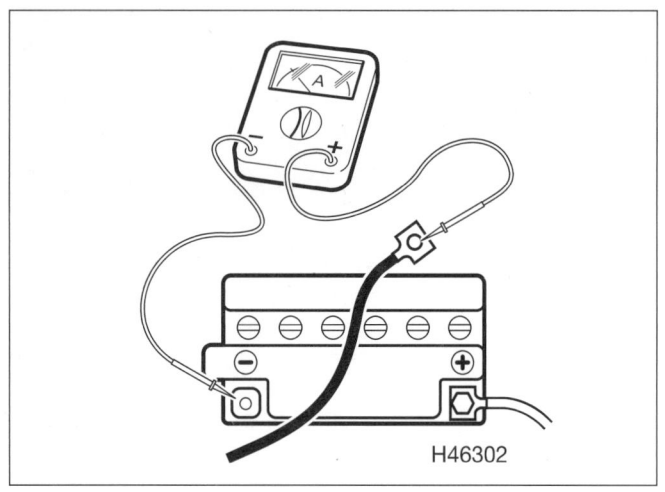

8•26 Electrical system

28.8 Checking the charging system leakage rate – connect the meter as shown

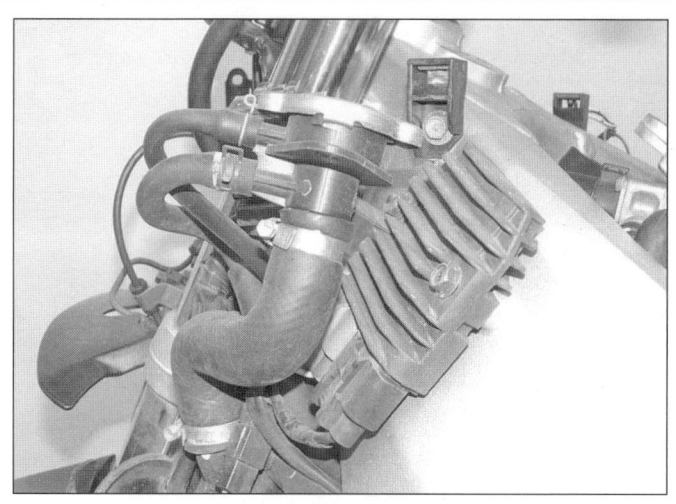

29.2a Regulator/rectifier – 2001 to 2005 models

6 Slowly increase the engine speed to 5000 rpm and note the reading obtained. Compare the result with the Specification at the beginning of this Chapter. If the regulated voltage output is outside the specification, check the alternator and the regulator/rectifier (see Sections 29 and 30).

HAYNES HiNT *Clues to a faulty regulator are constantly blowing bulbs, with brightness varying considerably with engine speed, and battery overheating.*

Leakage test

Caution: *Always connect an ammeter in series, never in parallel with the battery, otherwise it will be damaged. Do not turn the ignition ON or operate the starter motor when the ammeter is connected – a sudden surge in current will blow the meter's fuse.*

7 Remove the battery access panel (see Chapter 7). Disconnect the battery negative (-) lead (see Section 3).

8 Set the multimeter to the Amps function and connect its negative (-) probe to the battery negative (-) terminal, and positive (+) probe to the disconnected negative (-) lead **(see illustration)**. Always set the meter to a high amps range initially and then bring it down to the mA (milli Amps) range; if there is a high current flow in the circuit it may blow the meter's fuse.

9 Battery current leakage should not exceed the maximum limit (see Specifications). If a higher leakage rate is shown there is a short circuit in the wiring, although if an after-market immobiliser or alarm is fitted, its current draw should be taken into account. Disconnect the meter and reconnect the battery negative (-) lead.

10 If leakage is indicated, refer to Wiring Diagrams at the end of this Chapter to systematically disconnect individual electrical components and repeat the test until the source is identified.

29 Alternator stator

Check

1 On 2001 to 2005 models and 2013-on models remove the left-hand fairing side panel (see Chapter 7).

2 Disconnect the wiring connector with the three white wires from the regulator/rectifier **(see illustrations)**. Check the connector terminals for corrosion and security.

3 Using a multimeter set to the ohms x 1 (ohmmeter) scale measure the resistance between each of the white wire terminals in the connector, taking a total of three readings, then check for continuity between each terminal and ground (earth). If the stator coil windings are in good condition the three readings should be within the range shown in the Specifications at the start of this Chapter, and there should be no continuity (infinite resistance) between any of the terminals and ground (earth). If not,

29.2b Regulator/rectifier – 2006 to 2012 models

29.2c Regulator/rectifier – 2013-on models

Electrical system 8•27

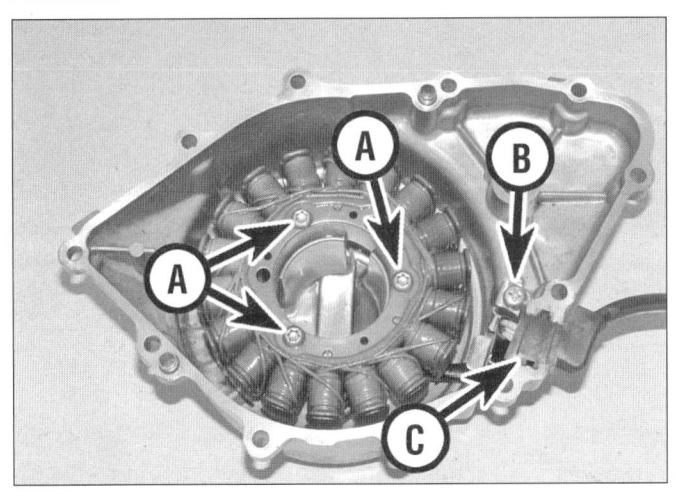

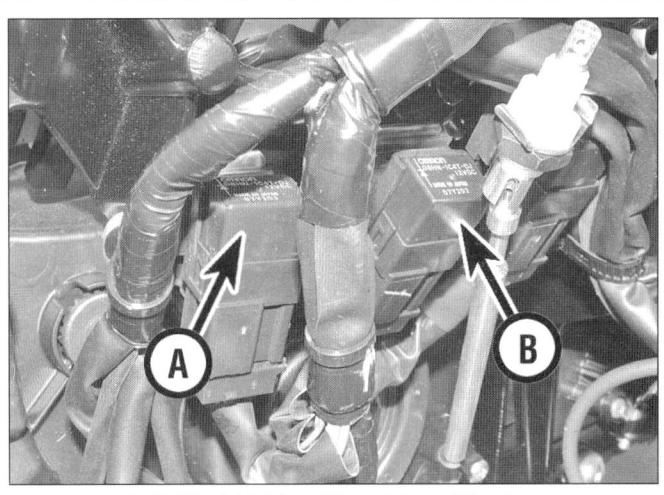

29.5 Stator screws (A), clamp screw (B), grommet (C)

31.2 Windshield up (A) and down (B) relays

the alternator stator coil assembly is at fault and should be replaced with a new one. **Note:** *Before condemning the stator coils, check the fault is not due to damaged wiring between the connector and the stator.*

Removal

Note: *The alternator rotor bolt has left-hand threads. This means it has to be slackened and tightened in the OPPOSITE direction to normal bolts. Turn the bolt clockwise to unscrew it, and anti-clockwise to tighten it.*

4 Refer to Section 13 in Chapter 2 and remove the alternator cover – the stator is mounted inside the cover.
5 Undo the stator screws, and the screw securing the wiring clamp, then remove the stator, noting how the rubber wiring grommet fits **(see illustration)**.

Installation

6 Clean all old sealant off the stator wiring grommet and its cut-out in the cover.
7 Clean the threads of the stator and wiring clamp screws then apply some fresh threadlock. Fit the stator into the cover, aligning the rubber wiring grommet with the groove **(see illustration 29.5)**. Fit the screws and tighten them to the torque setting specified at the beginning of the Chapter. Apply a suitable sealant to the wiring grommet, then press it into the cut-out in the cover. Secure the wiring with its clamp and tighten the screw.
8 Refer to Section 13 in Chapter 2 and install the alternator cover.

30 Regulator/rectifier

Check

1 On 2001 to 2005 models and 2013-on models remove the left-hand fairing side panel (see Chapter 7).
2 Disconnect the regulator/rectifier wiring connectors **(see illustration 29.2a, b or c)**.

Check the connectors for loose wires and terminals and corrosion.
3 Check the wiring and connectors between the battery, regulator/rectifier and alternator for shorts, breaks, and loose or corroded terminals (see the wiring diagrams at the end of this chapter).
4 If the wiring checks out, and the stator is good (see Section 29), the regulator/rectifier unit is probably faulty. Yamaha provide no test data for the unit itself. Take it to a Yamaha dealer for confirmation of its condition before replacing it with a new one.

> **HAYNES HiNT** *Clues to a faulty regulator are constantly blowing bulbs, with brightness varying considerably with engine speed, and battery overheating.*

Removal and installation

5 On 2001 to 2005 models and 2013-on models remove the left-hand fairing side panel (see Chapter 7).
6 Make sure the ignition is off. Disconnect the wiring connectors **(see illustration 29.2a or b)** – if you can't get them off on 2001 to 2005 models disconnect them after displacing the regulator/rectifier.
7 Unscrew the bolts or nuts, and remove the regulator/rectifier.
8 Installation is the reverse of removal.

31 Windshield motor

Check

1 If the motor does not work check the fuse (Section 5). Next remove the fairing and check the wiring and connectors for loose or broken terminals. If all is good so far check the switch (Section 19). If the windshield moves but does so roughly or noisily remove the motor (see below) and check for any dirt and debris

in the running tracks and gear, and make sure everything that moves is adequately lubricated.
2 On 2013-on models two relays control the movement, one for up, one for down, and they are mounted on the back of the fairing bracket on the left-hand side **(see illustration)**. If one is suspected of being faulty swop it with the other one and see if the fault is transferred. If required test each relay as follows **(see illustration 6.5)**: set a multimeter to test continuity and connect it across the terminals 3 and 4 on the relay – there should be continuity. Now connect across terminals 3 and 5 – there should be no continuity. Using a fully-charged 12 volt battery and two insulated jumper wires, connect the positive (+) terminal of the battery to terminal 1 on the relay, and the negative (–) terminal to terminal 2. Now there should be no continuity across 3 and 4, and there should be continuity across 3 and 5. If so, the relay is good. If not, replace the relay with a new one.

Removal and installation

3 Remove the fairing (see Chapter 7). On 2001 to 2012 models remove the mirrors, and the windshield and its (inner) bracket (see Chapter 7).
4 On 2001 to 2005 models undo the screw and remove the centre panel from the fairing **(see illustration)**. Disconnect the headlight wiring connectors and remove the sidelight

31.4a Remove the centre panel

8•28 Electrical system

31.4b Disconnect the headlights and remove the sidelights

31.4c Undo the screws (arrowed)...

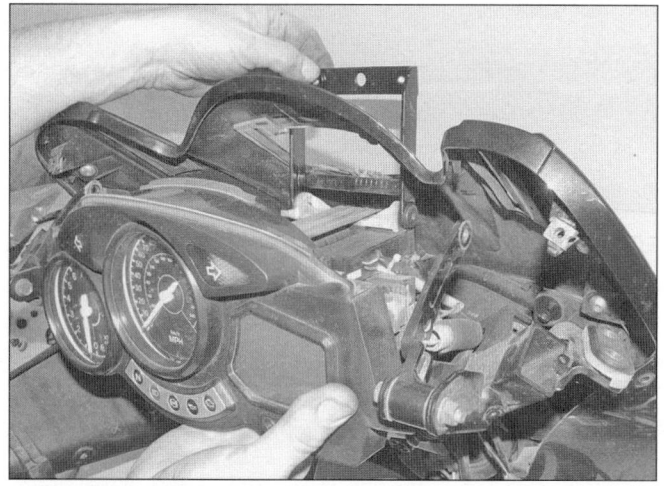

31.4d ...and remove the windshield motor/instrument assembly

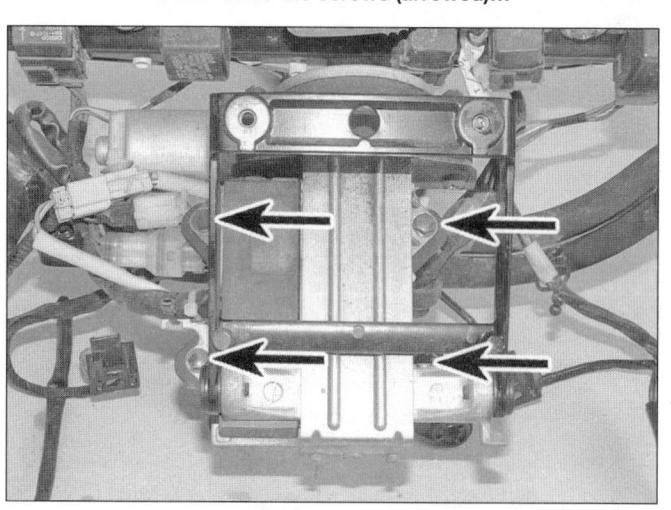

31.4e Windshield motor bolts (arrowed)

bulbholders **(see illustration)**. Unscrew the windshield motor/instrument assembly bracket screws and draw the assembly out of the fairing **(see illustrations)**. Retrieve the mirror pads. Disconnect the windshield motor wiring connectors, then unscrew the nuts, withdraw the bolts and remove the motor **(see illustration)**.

5 On 2006 to 2012 models disconnect the headlight wiring connectors and remove the sidelight bulbholders **(see illustration 31.4b)**. Undo the windshield motor/instrument assembly bracket screws and draw the assembly out of the fairing **(see illustrations)**. Retrieve the mirror pads. Disconnect the windshield motor wiring

31.5a Undo the screws (arrowed)...

31.5b ...and remove the windshield motor/instrument assembly

Electrical system 8•29

31.5c Windshield motor bolts (arrowed)

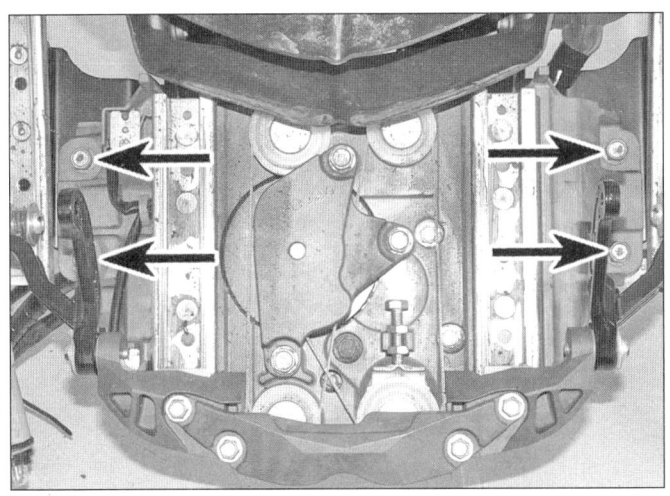

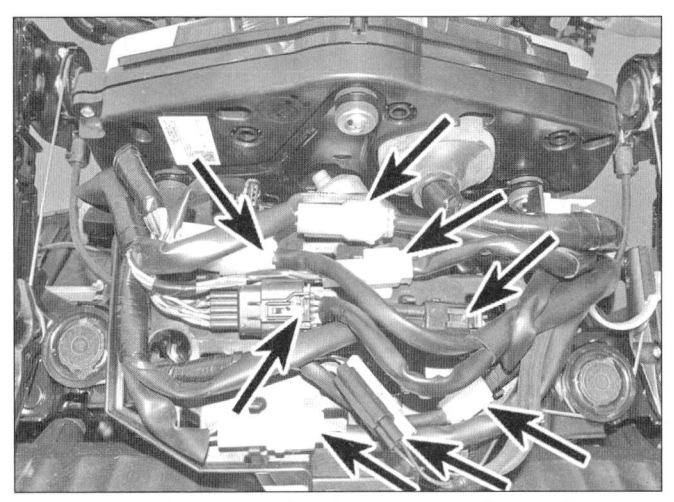

31.6a Disconnect the wire connectors (arrowed)

connectors. Unscrew the bolts and remove the motor **(see illustration)**.

6 On 2013-on models disconnect the wiring connectors which run across the front of the connector board **(see illustration)**. Remove the two bolts (retained by nuts on the back) and displace the connector board **(see illustration)**. Access is now available to the motor and cable mechanism **(see illustration)**. Note the spacers which are fitted with the connector board bolts **(see illustration)**.

7 Installation is the reverse of removal.

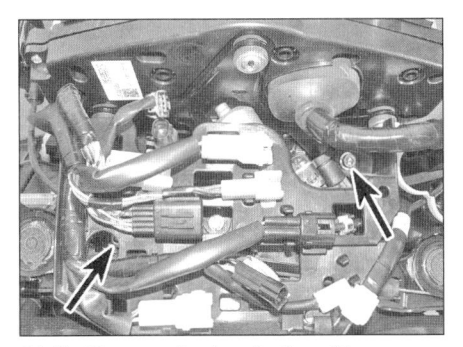

31.6b Remove the two bolts, with spacers and nuts, to free the connector board

31.6c The motor and cable/pulley mechanism

31.6d Spacers fit on the connector board mounting bolts

8•30 Wiring diagrams

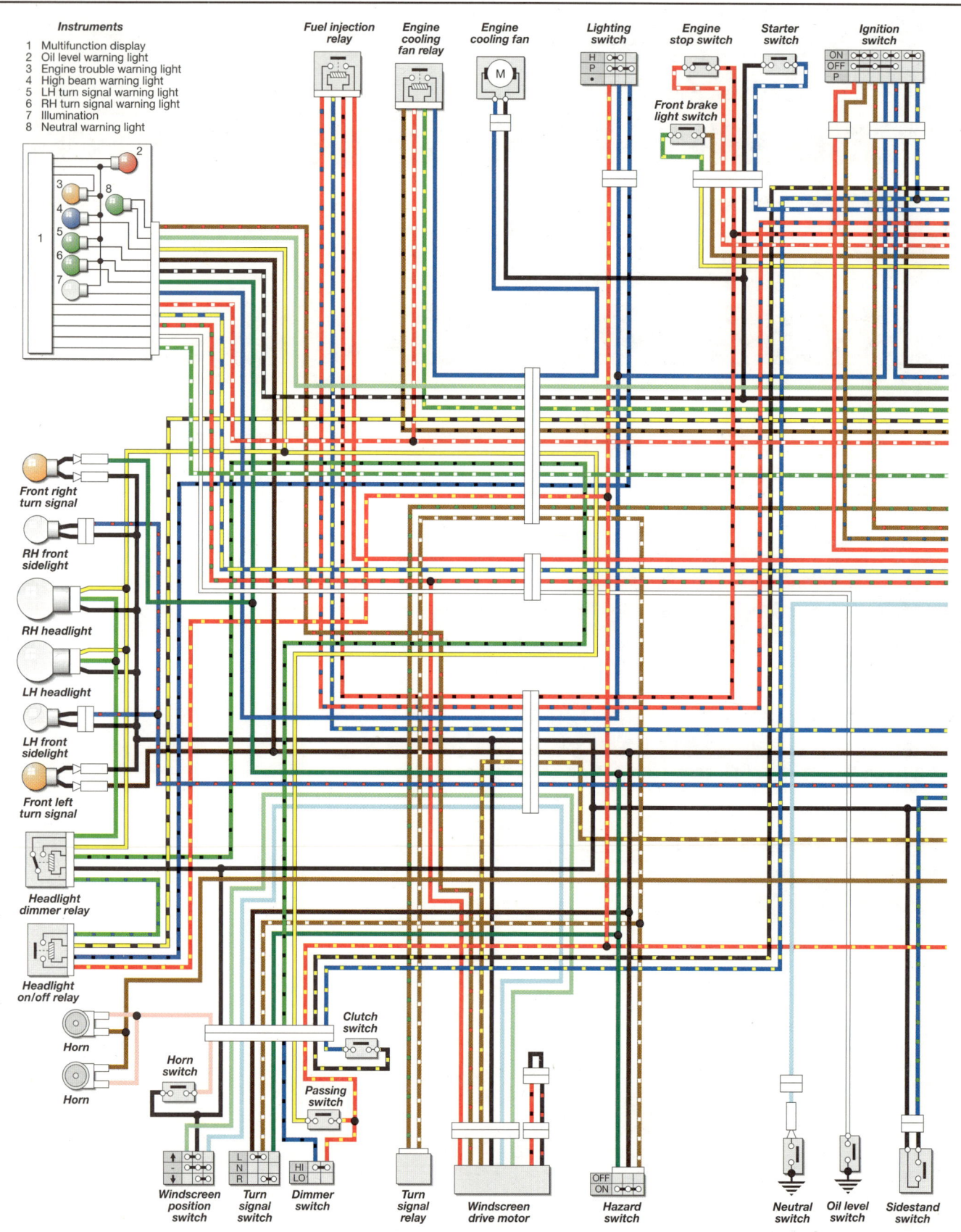

Instruments
1 Multifunction display
2 Oil level warning light
3 Engine trouble warning light
4 High beam warning light
5 LH turn signal warning light
6 RH turn signal warning light
7 Illumination
8 Neutral warning light

2001 and 2002 models

Wiring diagrams 8•31

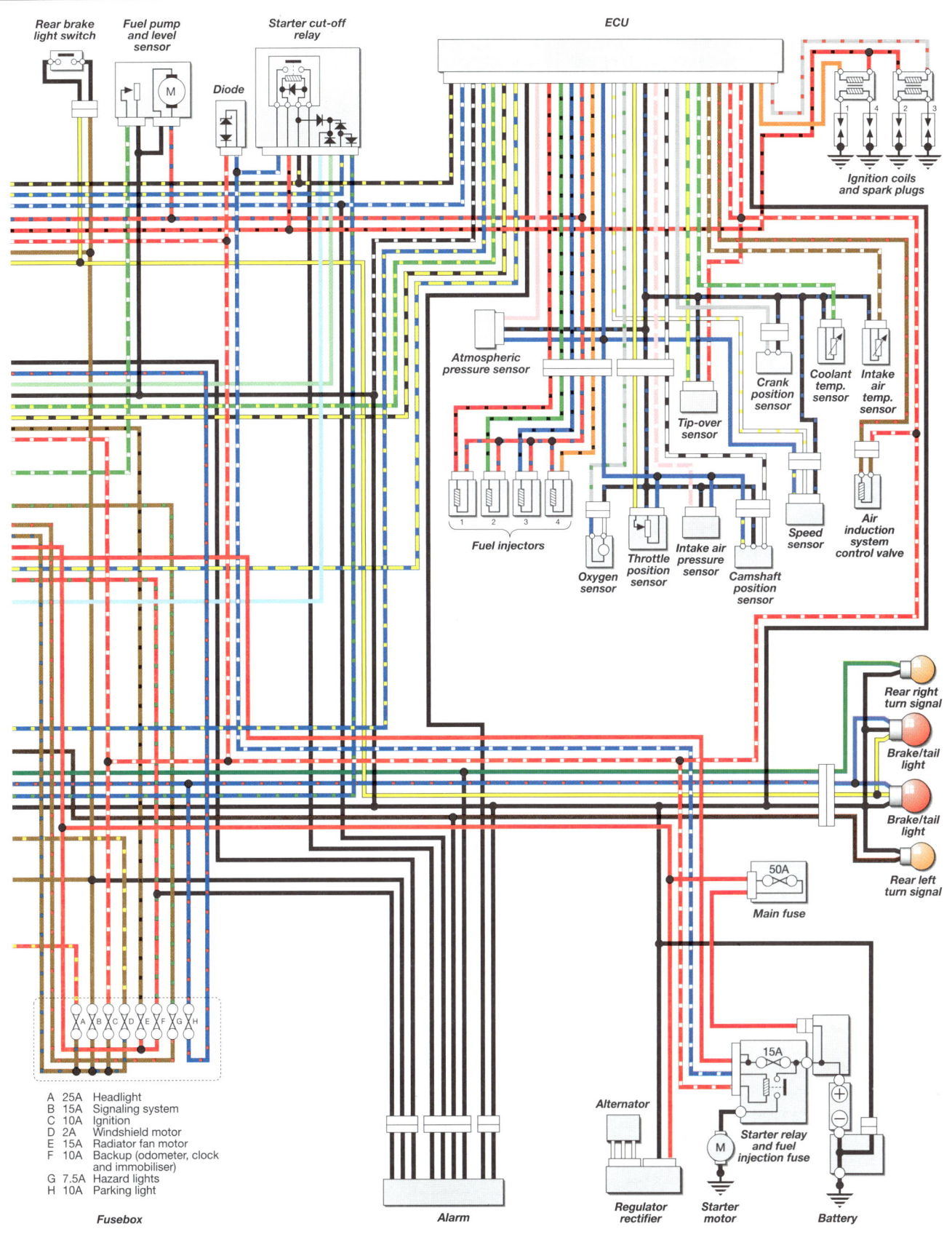

Rear brake light switch
Fuel pump and level sensor
Starter cut-off relay
Diode
ECU
Ignition coils and spark plugs
Atmospheric pressure sensor
Tip-over sensor
Crank position sensor
Coolant temp. sensor
Intake air temp. sensor
Fuel injectors
Oxygen sensor
Throttle position sensor
Intake air pressure sensor
Camshaft position sensor
Speed sensor
Air induction system control valve
Rear right turn signal
Brake/tail light
Brake/tail light
Rear left turn signal
Main fuse 50A
Alarm
Alternator
Regulator rectifier
Starter motor
Starter relay and fuel injection fuse 15A
Battery

Fusebox
A 25A Headlight
B 15A Signaling system
C 10A Ignition
D 2A   Windshield motor
E 15A Radiator fan motor
F 10A Backup (odometer, clock and immobiliser)
G 7.5A Hazard lights
H 10A Parking light

H47561

2001 and 2002 models

8•32 Wiring diagrams

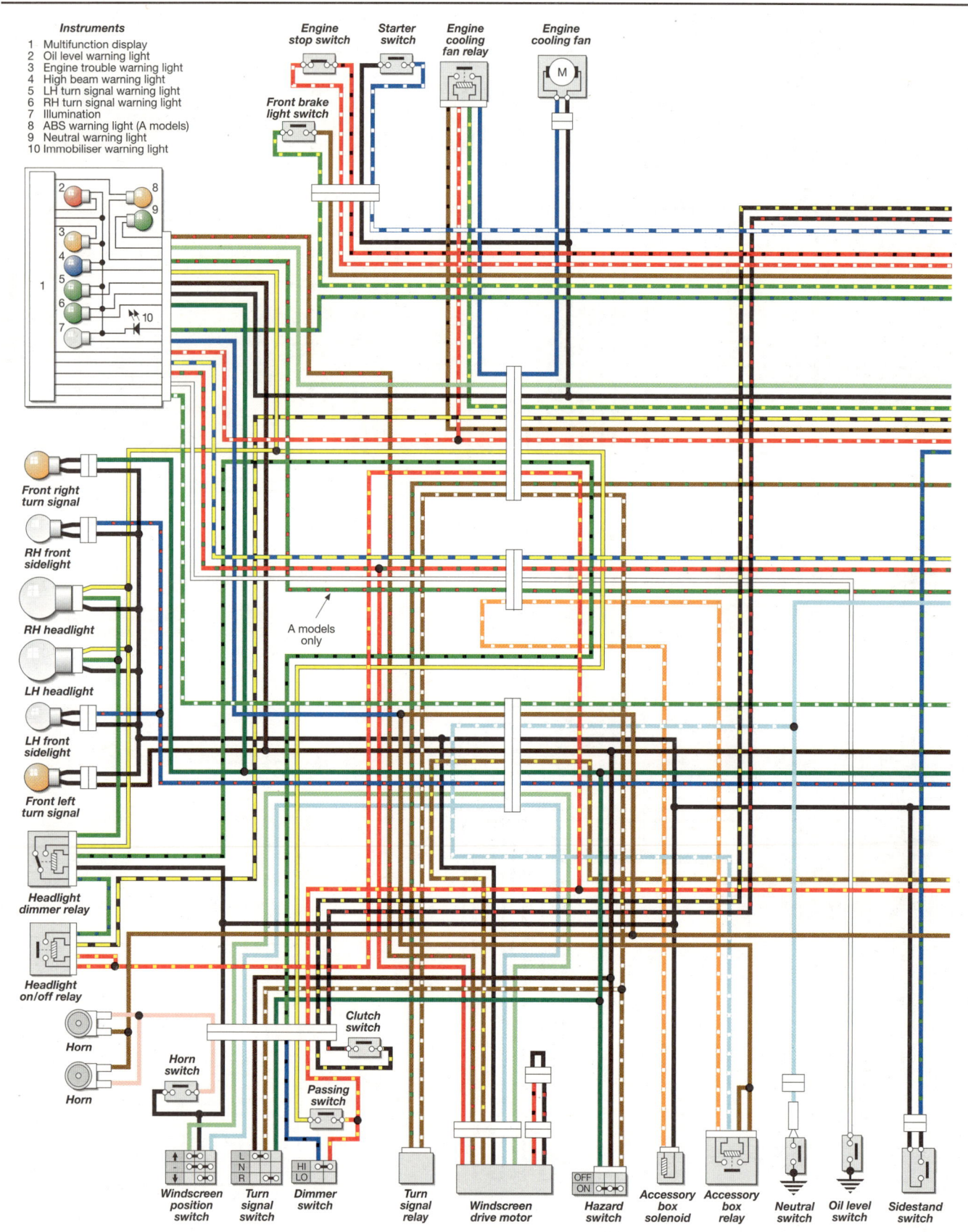

Instruments
1. Multifunction display
2. Oil level warning light
3. Engine trouble warning light
4. High beam warning light
5. LH turn signal warning light
6. RH turn signal warning light
7. Illumination
8. ABS warning light (A models)
9. Neutral warning light
10. Immobiliser warning light

2003 to 2005 models

H47562

Wiring diagrams 8•33

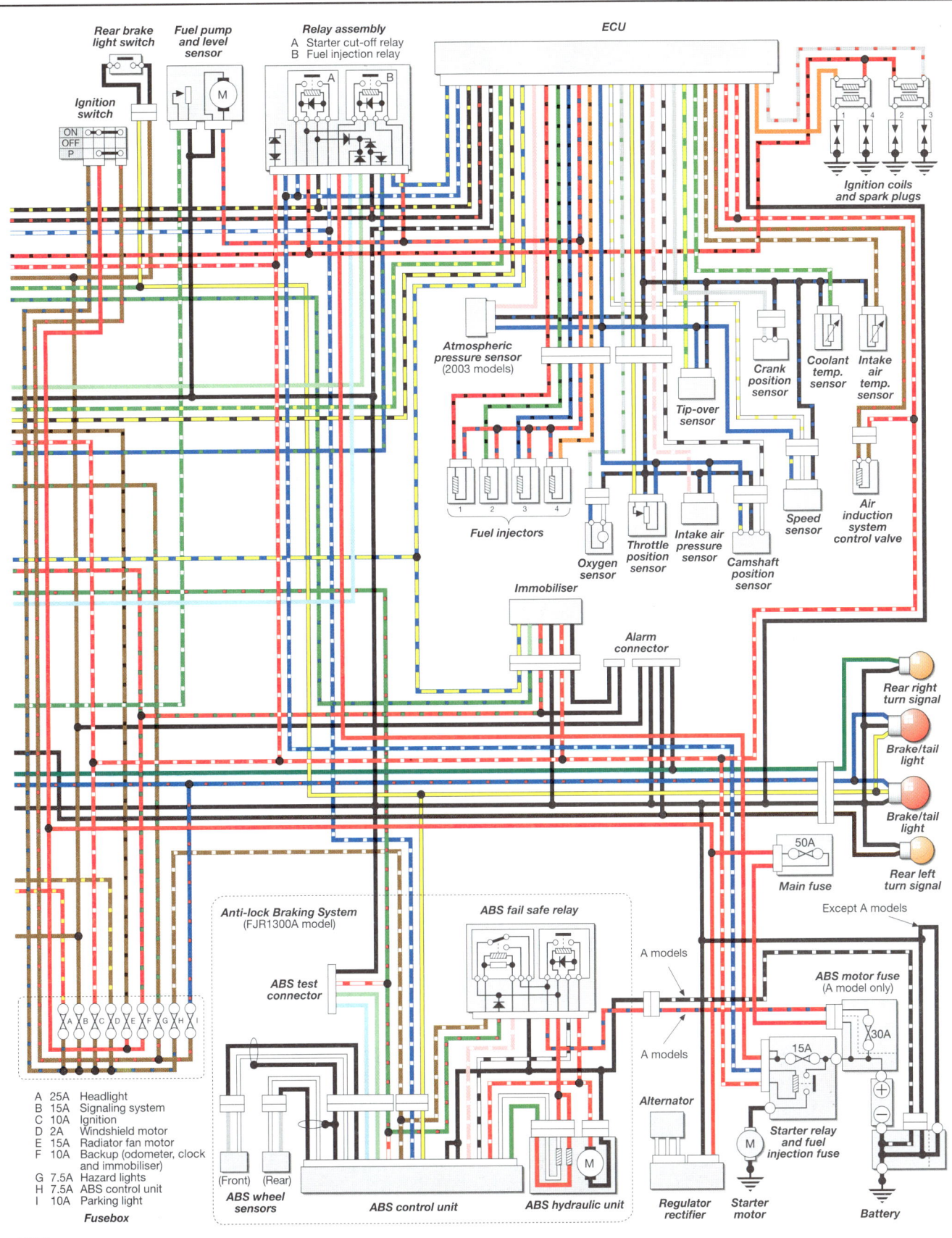

2003 to 2005 models

8•34 Wiring diagrams

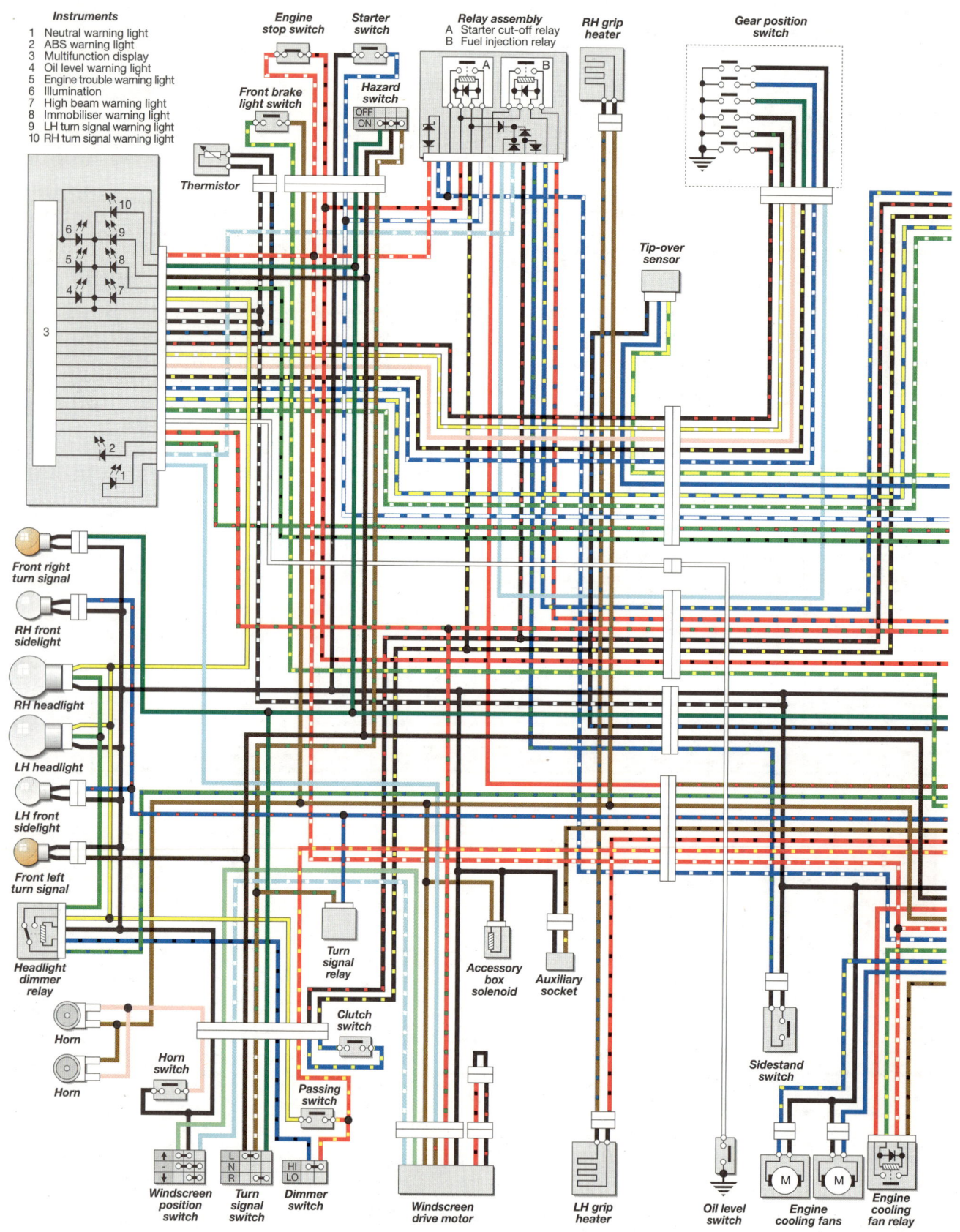

FJR1300A 2006 and 2007 models

Wiring diagrams 8•35

FJR1300A 2006 and 2007 models

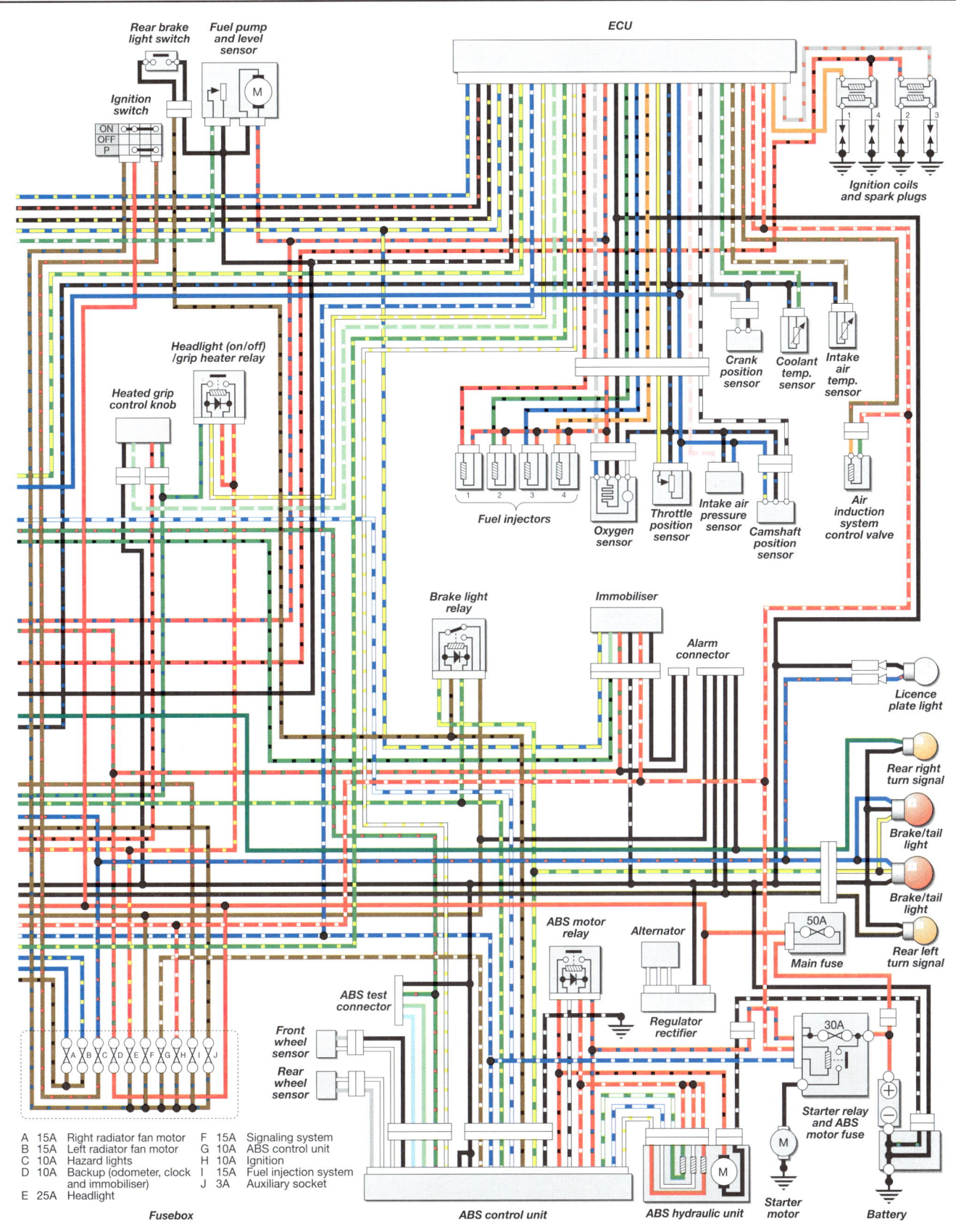

Fusebox:
- A 15A Right radiator fan motor
- B 15A Left radiator fan motor
- C 10A Hazard lights
- D 10A Backup (odometer, clock and immobiliser)
- E 25A Headlight
- F 15A Signaling system
- G 10A ABS control unit
- H 10A Ignition
- I 15A Fuel injection system
- J 3A Auxiliary socket

H47565

8•36 Wiring diagrams

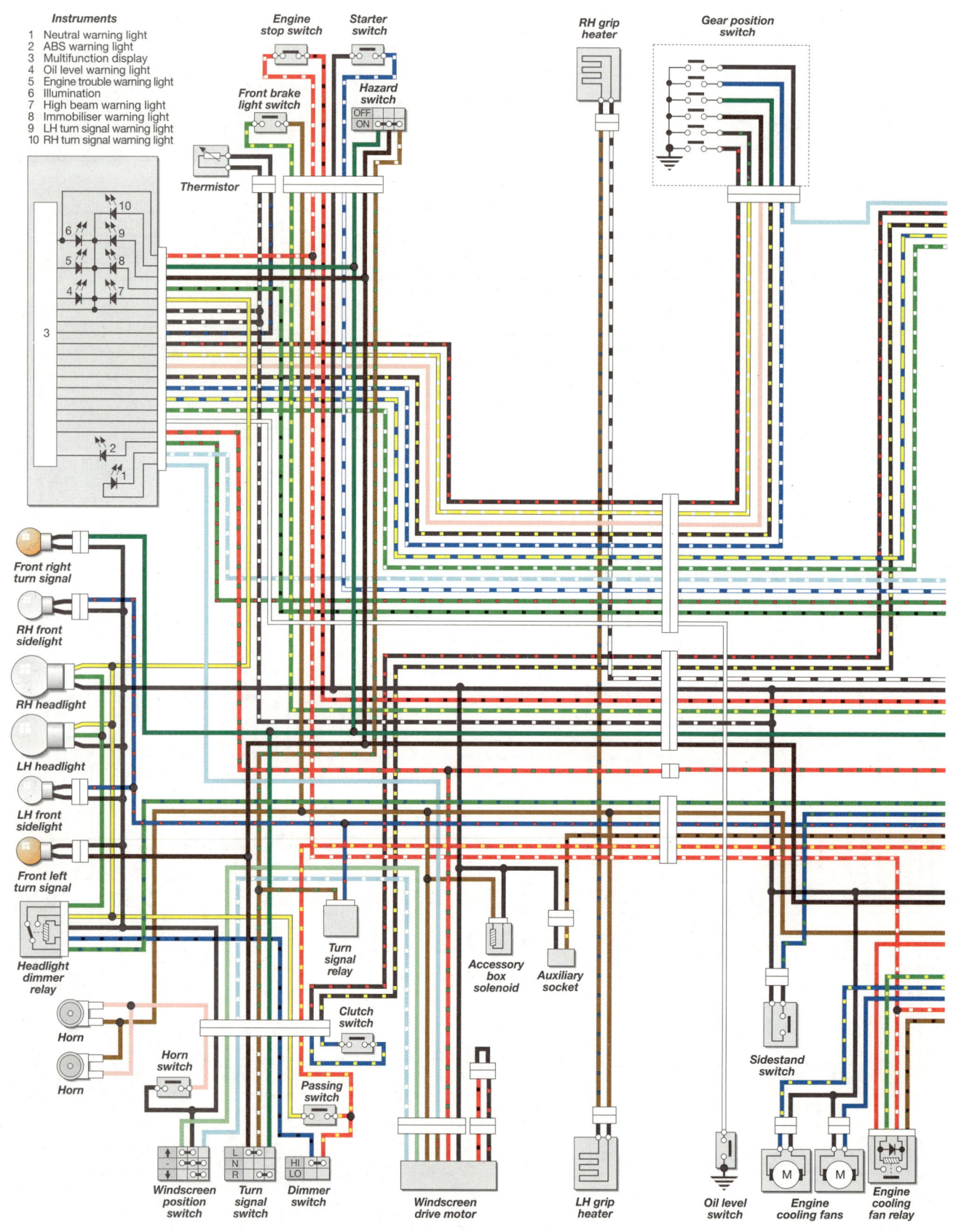

Instruments
1. Neutral warning light
2. ABS warning light
3. Multifunction display
4. Oil level warning light
5. Engine trouble warning light
6. Illumination
7. High beam warning light
8. Immobiliser warning light
9. LH turn signal warning light
10. RH turn signal warning light

FJR1300A 2008 to 2012 models

Wiring diagrams 8•37

FJR1300A 2008 to 2012 models

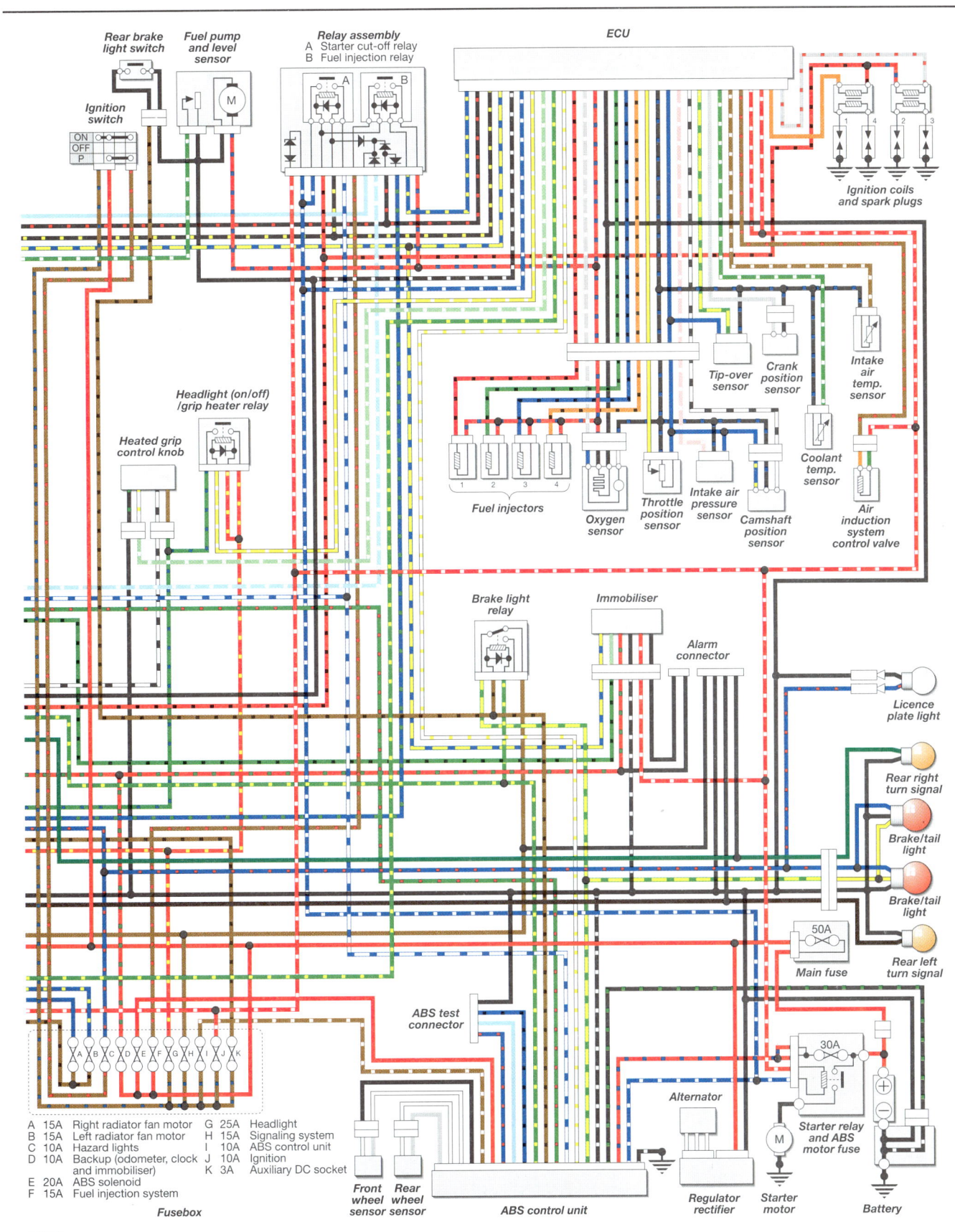

8•38 Wiring diagrams

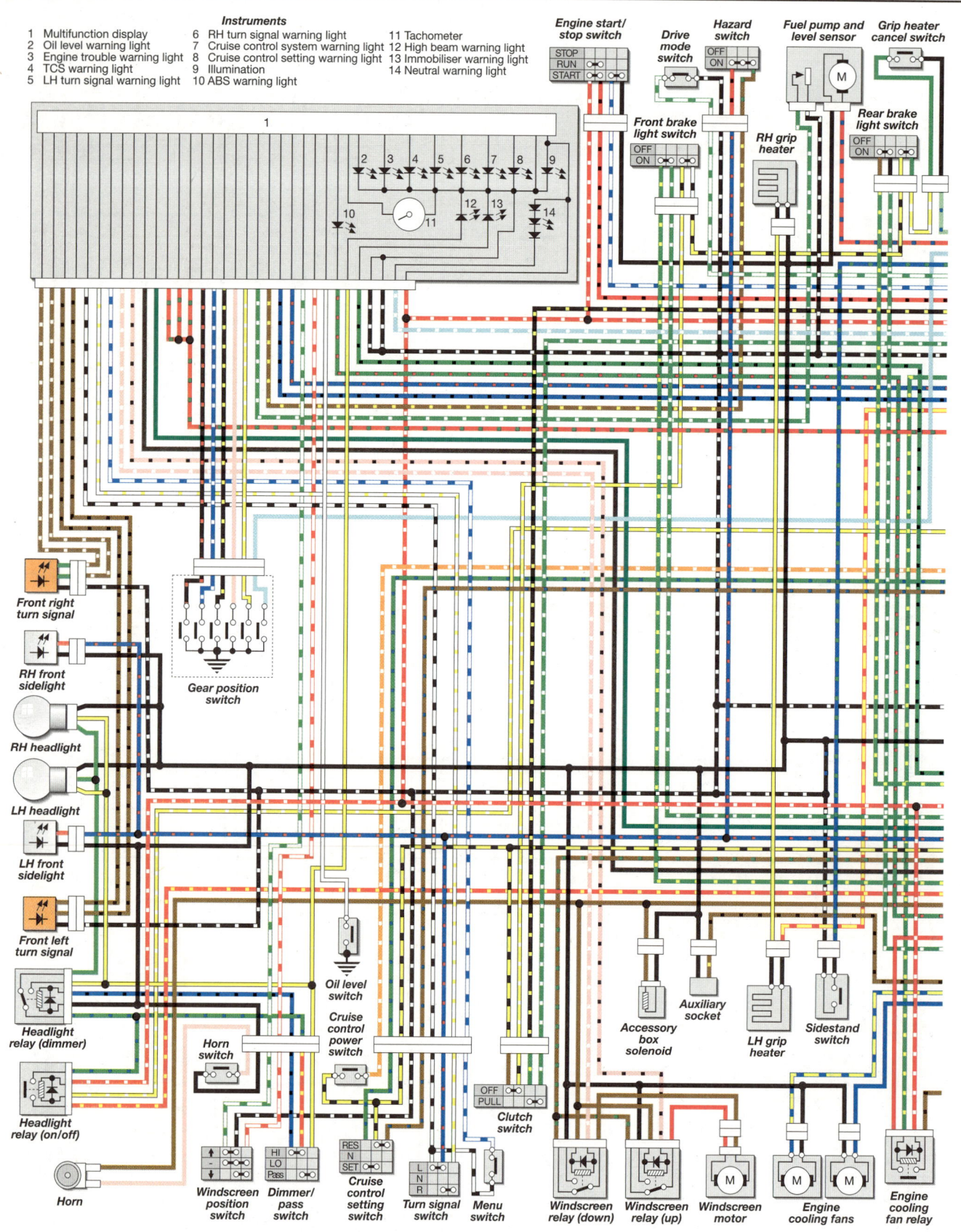

Instruments
1 Multifunction display
2 Oil level warning light
3 Engine trouble warning light
4 TCS warning light
5 LH turn signal warning light
6 RH turn signal warning light
7 Cruise control system warning light
8 Cruise control setting warning light
9 Illumination
10 ABS warning light
11 Tachometer
12 High beam warning light
13 Immobiliser warning light
14 Neutral warning light

FJR1300A 2013-on models

Wiring diagrams 8•39

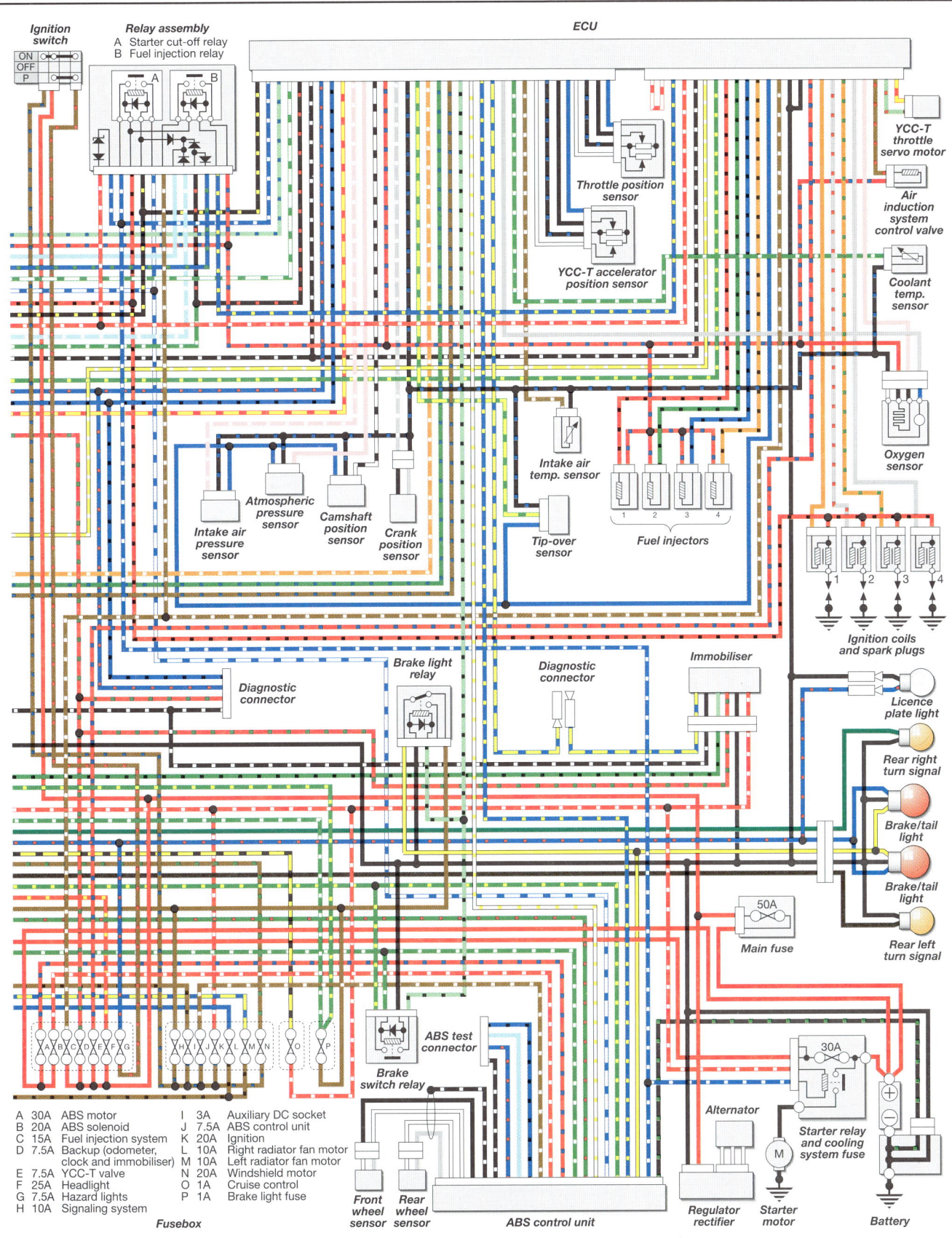

Ignition switch
ON / OFF / P

Relay assembly
A Starter cut-off relay
B Fuel injection relay

ECU

- Throttle position sensor
- YCC-T accelerator position sensor
- YCC-T throttle servo motor
- Air induction system control valve
- Coolant temp. sensor
- Oxygen sensor
- Intake air temp. sensor
- Fuel injectors 1 2 3 4
- Tip-over sensor
- Crank position sensor
- Camshaft position sensor
- Atmospheric pressure sensor
- Intake air pressure sensor
- Ignition coils and spark plugs 1 2 3 4
- Diagnostic connector
- Brake light relay
- Diagnostic connector
- Immobiliser
- Licence plate light
- Rear right turn signal
- Brake/tail light
- Brake/tail light
- Rear left turn signal
- Main fuse 50A
- ABS test connector
- Brake switch relay
- Front wheel sensor
- Rear wheel sensor
- ABS control unit
- Alternator
- Regulator rectifier
- Starter motor
- Starter relay and cooling system fuse 30A
- Battery

Fusebox
A B C D E F G H I J K L M N O P

A 30A ABS motor	I 3A Auxiliary DC socket	
B 20A ABS solenoid	J 7.5A ABS control unit	
C 15A Fuel injection system	K 20A Ignition	
D 7.5A Backup (odometer, clock and immobiliser)	L 10A Right radiator fan motor	
	M 10A Left radiator fan motor	
E 7.5A YCC-T valve	N 20A Windshield motor	
F 25A Headlight	O 1A Cruise control	
G 7.5A Hazard lights	P 1A Brake light fuse	
H 10A Signaling system		

H47569

FJR1300A 2013-on models

8•40 Wiring diagrams

FJR1300AS 2006 and 2007 models

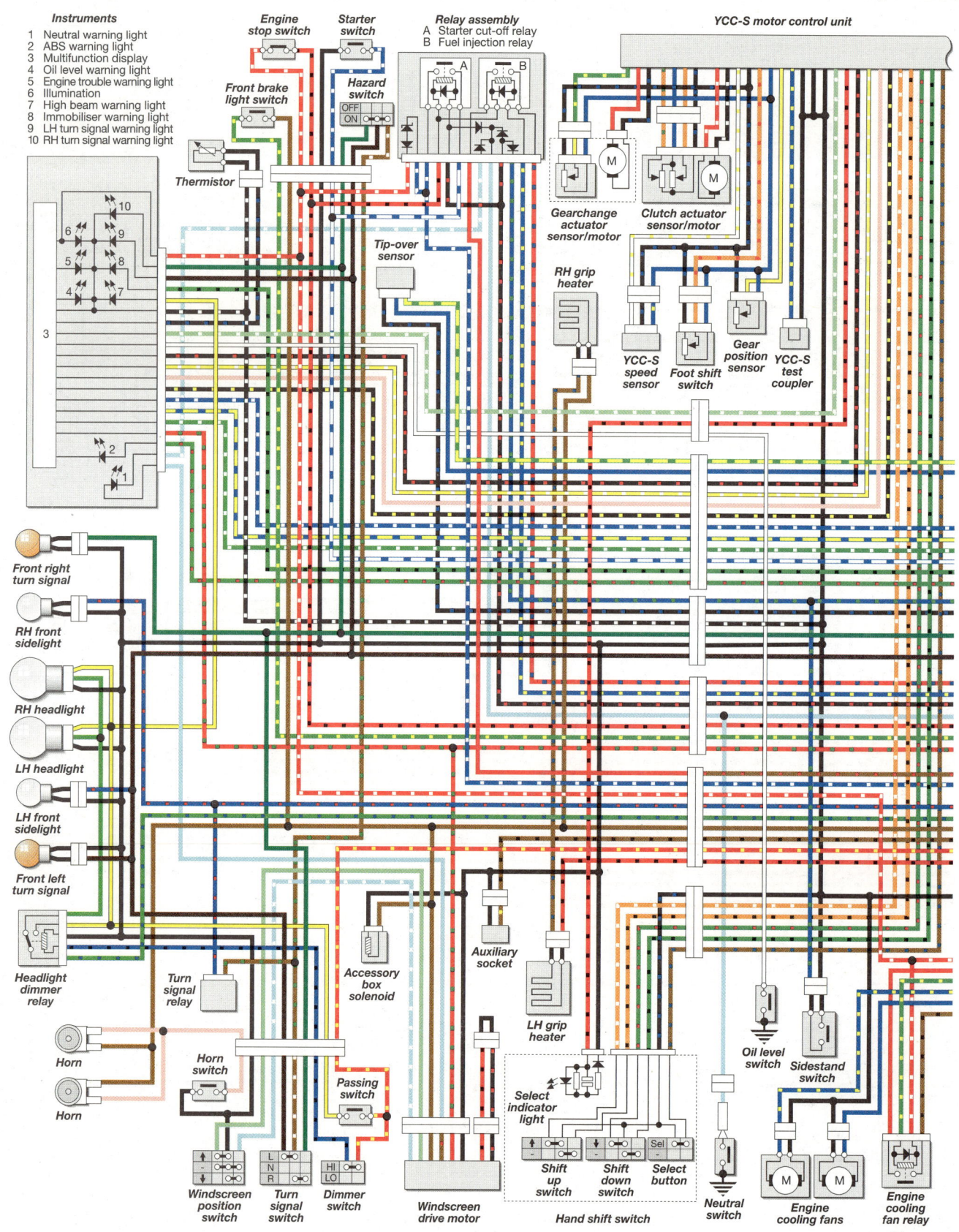

Wiring diagrams 8•41

FJR1300AS 2006 and 2007 models

Fusebox
- A 15A Right radiator fan motor
- B 15A Left radiator fan motor
- C 10A Hazard lights
- D 10A Backup (odometer, clock and immobiliser)
- E 15A Fuel injection system
- F 25A Headlight
- G 15A Signaling system
- H 10A ABS control unit
- I 10A Ignition
- J 3A   Auxiliary DC socket
- K 30A YCC-S motor

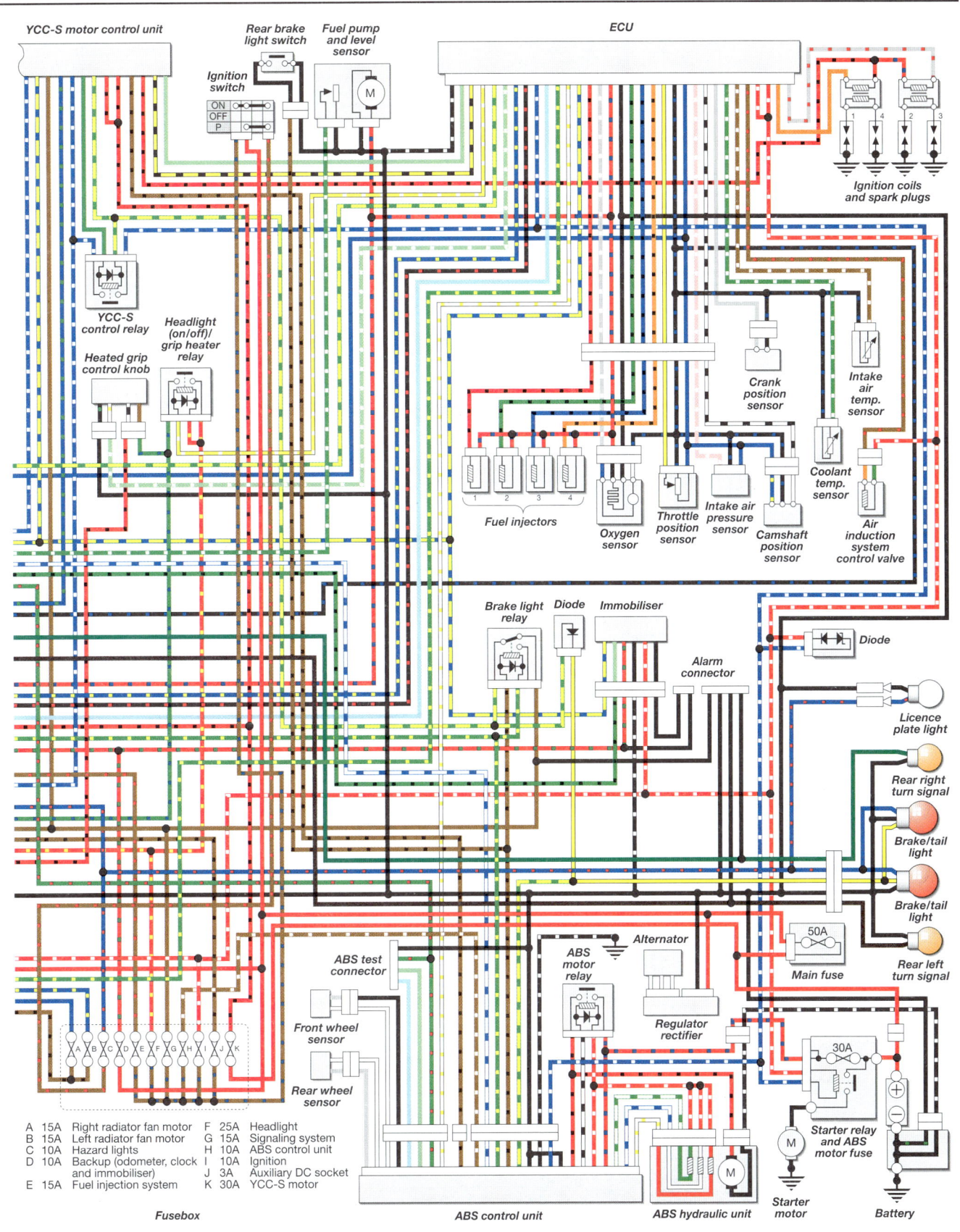

H47571

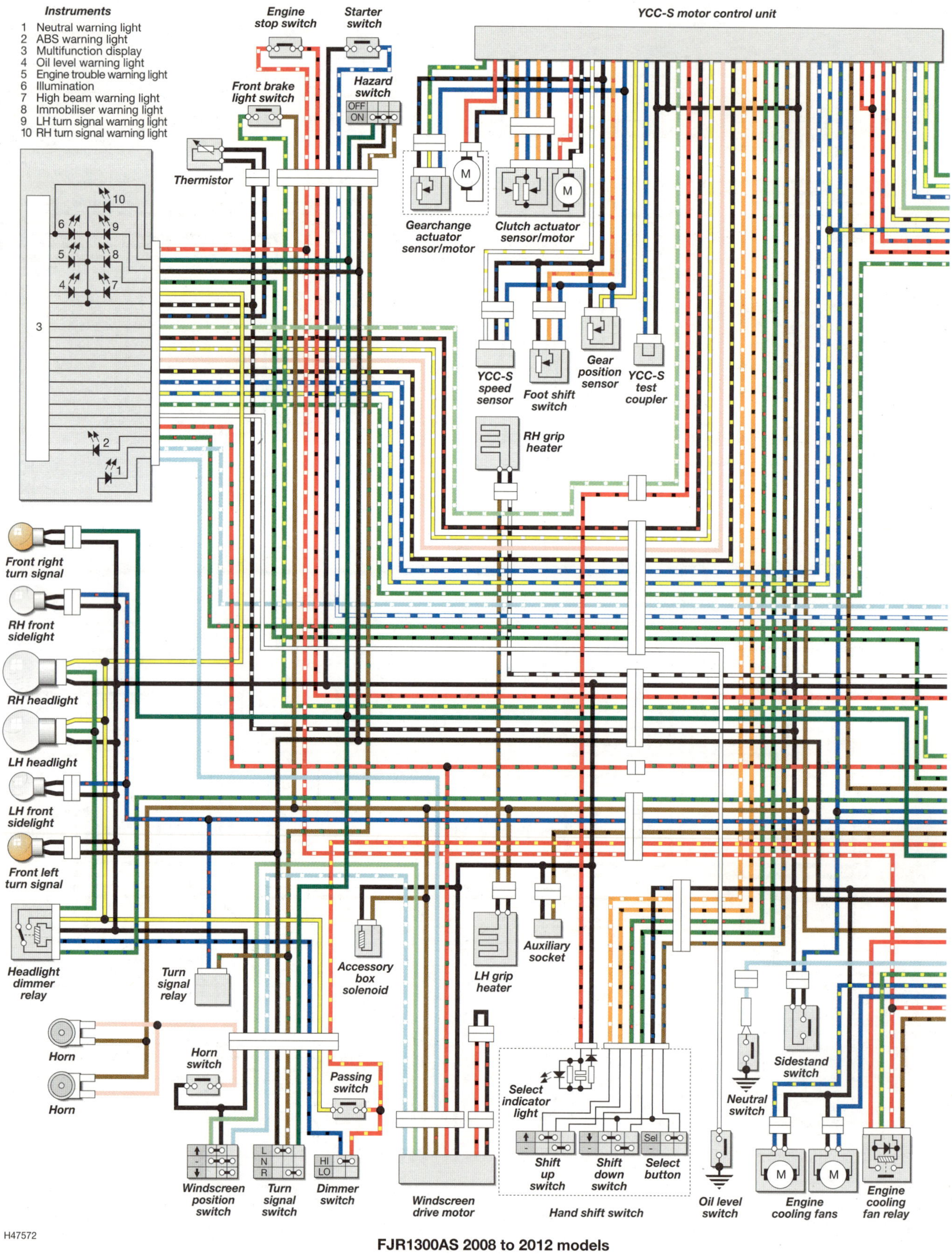

FJR1300AS 2008 to 2012 models

Wiring diagrams 8•43

FJR1300AS 2008 to 2012 models

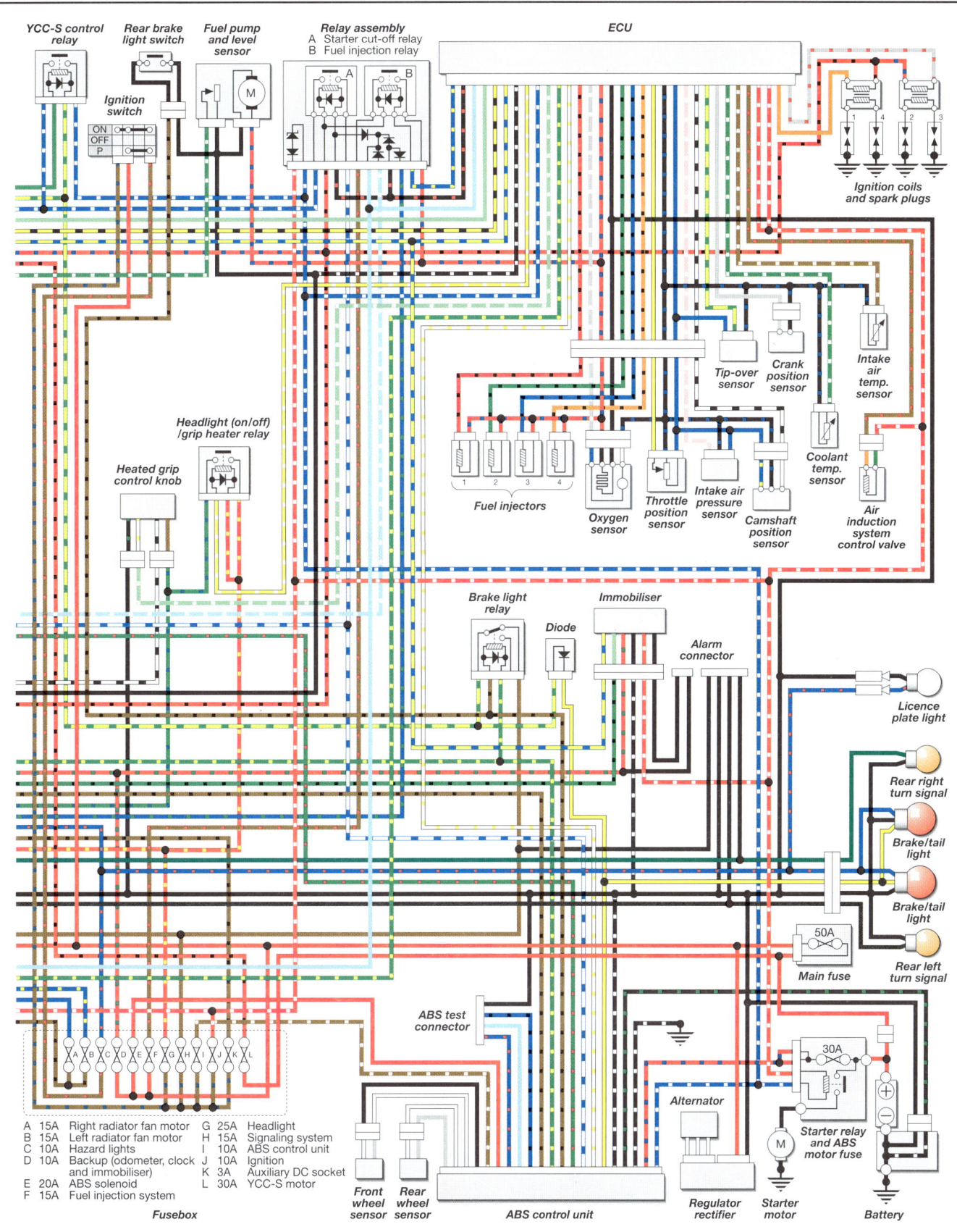

Fusebox:
- A 15A Right radiator fan motor
- B 15A Left radiator fan motor
- C 10A Hazard lights
- D 10A Backup (odometer, clock and immobiliser)
- E 20A ABS solenoid
- F 15A Fuel injection system
- G 25A Headlight
- H 15A Signaling system
- I 10A ABS control unit
- J 10A Ignition
- K 3A   Auxiliary DC socket
- L 30A YCC-S motor

H47573

Notes

Reference REF•1

Reference

Tools and Workshop Tips — REF•2
- Building up a tool kit and equipping your workshop
- Using tools
- Understanding bearing, seal, fastener and chain sizes and markings
- Repair techniques

Security — REF•20
- Locks and chains
- U-locks
- Disc locks
- Alarms and immobilisers
- Security marking systems
- Tips on how to prevent bike theft

Lubricants and fluids — REF•23
- Engine oils
- Transmission (gear) oils
- Coolant/anti-freeze
- Fork oils and suspension fluids
- Brake/clutch fluids
- Spray lubes, degreasers and solvents

Conversion Factors — REF•26
- Formulae for conversion of the metric (SI) units used throughout the manual into Imperial measures

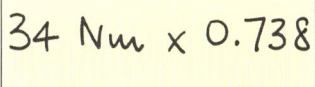

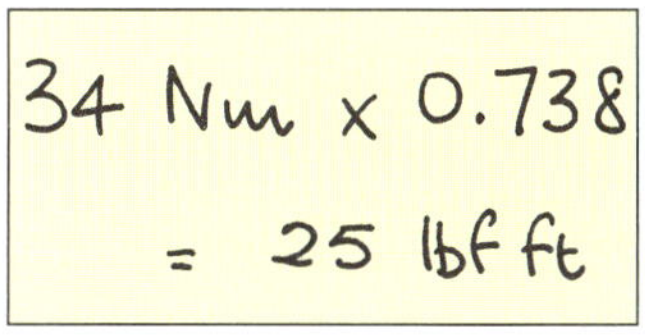

34 Nm x 0.738 = 25 lbf ft

MOT Test Checks — REF•27
- A guide to the UK MOT test
- Which items are tested
- How to prepare your motorcycle for the test and perform a pre-test check

Storage — REF•32
- How to prepare your motorcycle for going into storage and protect essential systems
- How to get the motorcycle back on the road

Fault Finding — REF•35
- Common faults and their likely causes
- Links to main chapters for testing and repair procedures

Technical Terms Explained — REF•44
- Component names, technical terms and common abbreviations explained

Index — REF•48

REF•2 Tools and Workshop Tips

Buying tools

A toolkit is a fundamental requirement for servicing and repairing a motorcycle. Although there will be an initial expense in building up enough tools for servicing, this will soon be offset by the savings made by doing the job yourself. As experience and confidence grow, additional tools can be added to enable the repair and overhaul of the motorcycle. Many of the specialist tools are expensive and not often used so it may be preferable to hire them, or for a group of friends or motorcycle club to join in the purchase.

As a rule, it is better to buy more expensive, good quality tools. Cheaper tools are likely to wear out faster and need to be renewed more often, nullifying the original saving.

> **Warning: To avoid the risk of a poor quality tool breaking in use, causing injury or damage to the component being worked on, always aim to purchase tools which meet the relevant national safety standards.**

The following lists of tools do not represent the manufacturer's service tools, but serve as a guide to help the owner decide which tools are needed for this level of work. In addition, items such as an electric drill, hacksaw, files, soldering iron and a workbench equipped with a vice, may be needed. Although not classed as tools, a selection of bolts, screws, nuts, washers and pieces of tubing always come in useful.

For more information about tools, refer to the Haynes *Motorcycle Workshop Practice Techbook* (Bk. No. 3470).

Manufacturer's service tools

Inevitably certain tasks require the use of a service tool. Where possible an alternative tool or method of approach is recommended, but sometimes there is no option if personal injury or damage to the component is to be avoided. Where required, service tools are referred to in the relevant procedure.

Service tools can usually only be purchased from a motorcycle dealer and are identified by a part number. Some of the commonly-used tools, such as rotor pullers, are available in aftermarket form from mail-order motorcycle tool and accessory suppliers.

Maintenance and minor repair tools

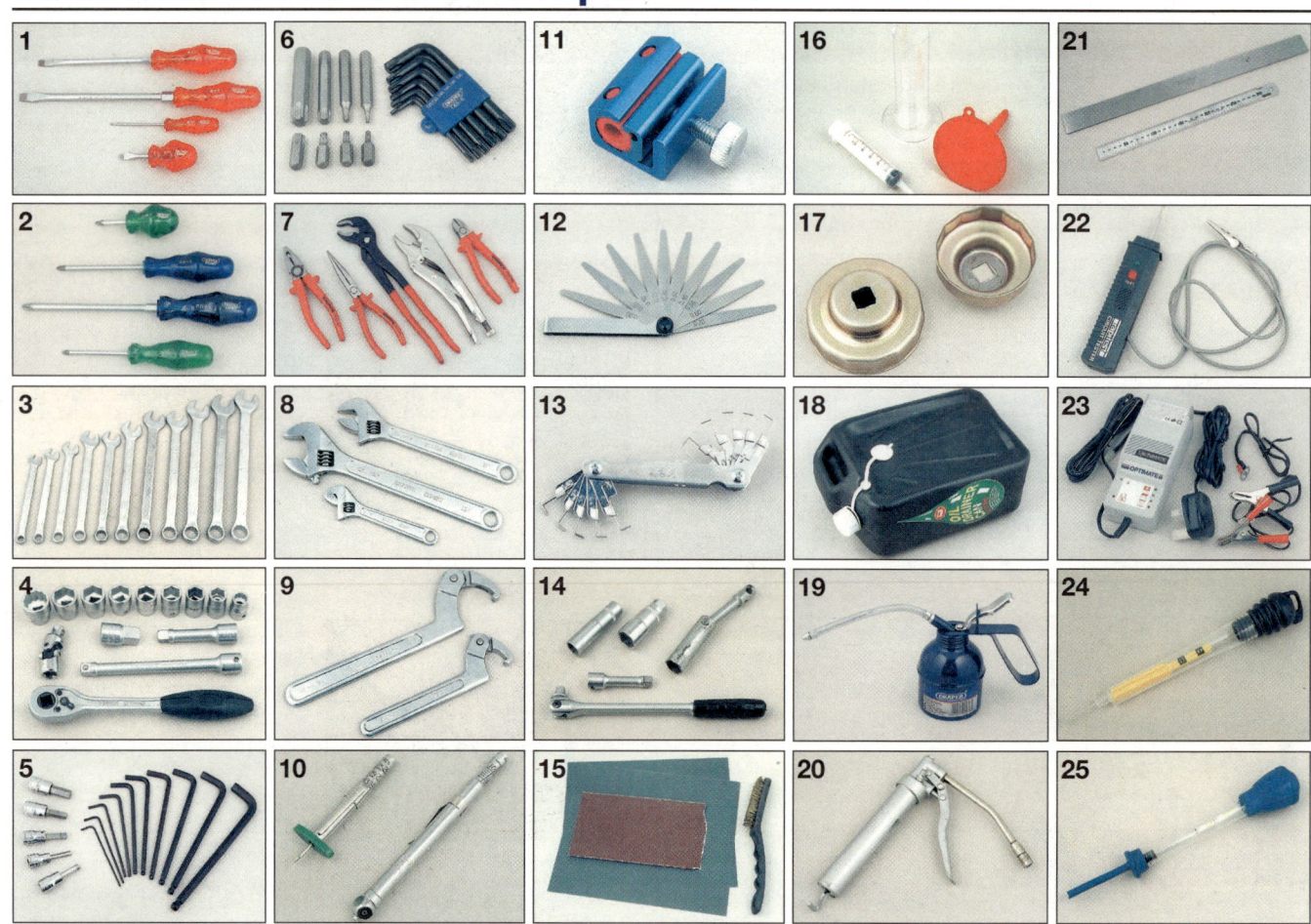

1 Set of flat-bladed screwdrivers
2 Set of Phillips head screwdrivers
3 Combination open-end and ring spanners
4 Socket set (3/8 inch or 1/2 inch drive)
5 Set of Allen keys or bits
6 Set of Torx keys or bits
7 Pliers, cutters and self-locking grips (Mole grips)
8 Adjustable spanners
9 C-spanners
10 Tread depth gauge and tyre pressure gauge
11 Cable oiler clamp
12 Feeler gauges
13 Spark plug gap measuring tool
14 Spark plug spanner or deep plug sockets
15 Wire brush and emery paper
16 Calibrated syringe, measuring vessel and funnel
17 Oil filter adapters
18 Oil drainer can or tray
19 Pump type oil can
20 Grease gun
21 Straight-edge and steel rule
22 Continuity tester
23 Battery charger
24 Hydrometer (for battery specific gravity check)
25 Anti-freeze tester (for liquid-cooled engines)

Tools and Workshop Tips REF•3

Repair and overhaul tools

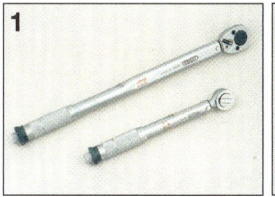

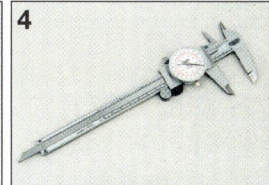

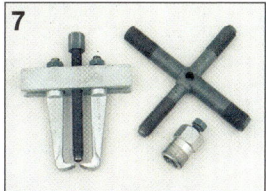

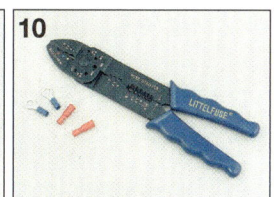

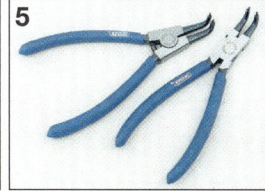

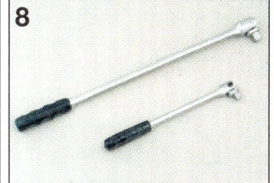

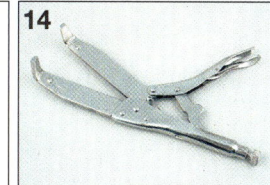

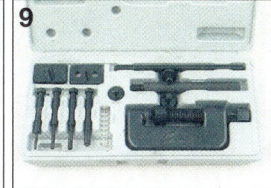

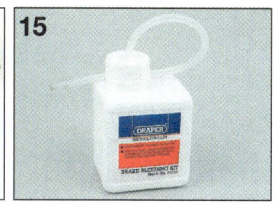

1 Torque wrench (small and mid-ranges)
2 Conventional, plastic or soft-faced hammers
3 Impact driver set
4 Vernier gauge
5 Circlip pliers (internal and external, or combination)
6 Set of cold chisels and punches
7 Selection of pullers
8 Breaker bars
9 Chain breaking/riveting tool set
10 Wire stripper and crimper tool
11 Multimeter (measures amps, volts and ohms)
12 Stroboscope (for dynamic timing checks)
13 Hose clamp (wingnut type shown)
14 Clutch holding tool
15 One-man brake/clutch bleeder kit

Specialist tools

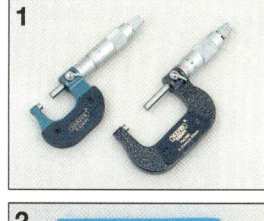

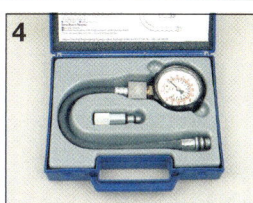

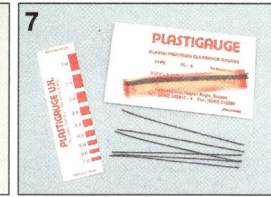

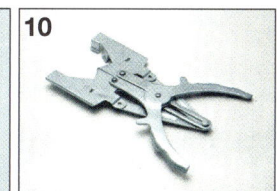

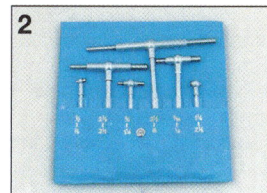

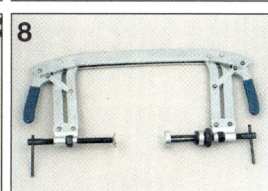

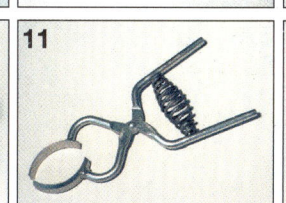

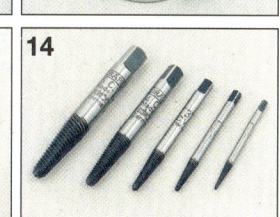

1 Micrometers (external type)
2 Telescoping gauges
3 Dial gauge
4 Cylinder compression gauge
5 Vacuum gauges (left) or manometer (right)
6 Oil pressure gauge
7 Plastigauge kit
8 Valve spring compressor (4-stroke engines)
9 Piston pin drawbolt tool
10 Piston ring removal and installation tool
11 Piston ring clamp
12 Cylinder bore hone (stone type shown)
13 Stud extractor
14 Screw extractor set
15 Bearing driver set

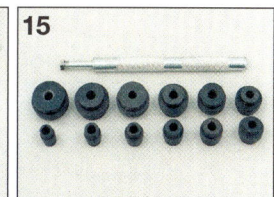

REF•4 Tools and Workshop Tips

1 Workshop equipment and facilities

The workbench

● Work is made much easier by raising the bike up on a ramp - components are much more accessible if raised to waist level. The hydraulic or pneumatic types seen in the dealer's workshop are a sound investment if you undertake a lot of repairs or overhauls **(see illustration 1.1)**.

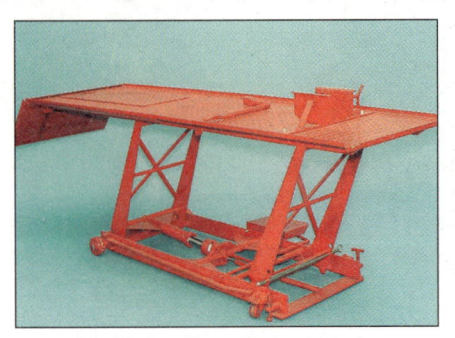

1.1 Hydraulic motorcycle ramp

● If raised off ground level, the bike must be supported on the ramp to avoid it falling. Most ramps incorporate a front wheel locating clamp which can be adjusted to suit different diameter wheels. When tightening the clamp, take care not to mark the wheel rim or damage the tyre - use wood blocks on each side to prevent this.
● Secure the bike to the ramp using tie-downs **(see illustration 1.2)**. If the bike has only a sidestand, and hence leans at a dangerous angle when raised, support the bike on an auxiliary stand.

1.2 Tie-downs are used around the passenger footrests to secure the bike

● Auxiliary (paddock) stands are widely available from mail order companies or motorcycle dealers and attach either to the wheel axle or swingarm pivot **(see illustration 1.3)**. If the motorcycle has a centrestand, you can support it under the crankcase to prevent it toppling whilst either wheel is removed **(see illustration 1.4)**.

1.3 This auxiliary stand attaches to the swingarm pivot

1.4 Always use a block of wood between the engine and jack head when supporting the engine in this way

Fumes and fire

● Refer to the Safety first! page at the beginning of the manual for full details. Make sure your workshop is equipped with a fire extinguisher suitable for fuel-related fires (Class B fire - flammable liquids) - it is not sufficient to have a water-filled extinguisher.
● Always ensure adequate ventilation is available. Unless an exhaust gas extraction system is available for use, ensure that the engine is run outside of the workshop.
● If working on the fuel system, make sure the workshop is ventilated to avoid a build-up of fumes. This applies equally to fume build-up when charging a battery. Do not smoke or allow anyone else to smoke in the workshop.

Fluids

● If you need to drain fuel from the tank, store it in an approved container marked as suitable for the storage of petrol (gasoline) **(see illustration 1.5)**. Do not store fuel in glass jars or bottles.

1.5 Use an approved can only for storing petrol (gasoline)

● Use proprietary engine degreasers or solvents which have a high flash-point, such as paraffin (kerosene), for cleaning off oil, grease and dirt - never use petrol (gasoline) for cleaning. Wear rubber gloves when handling solvent and engine degreaser. The fumes from certain solvents can be dangerous - always work in a well-ventilated area.

Dust, eye and hand protection

● Protect your lungs from inhalation of dust particles by wearing a filtering mask over the nose and mouth. Many frictional materials still contain asbestos which is dangerous to your health. Protect your eyes from spouts of liquid and sprung components by wearing a pair of protective goggles **(see illustration 1.6)**.

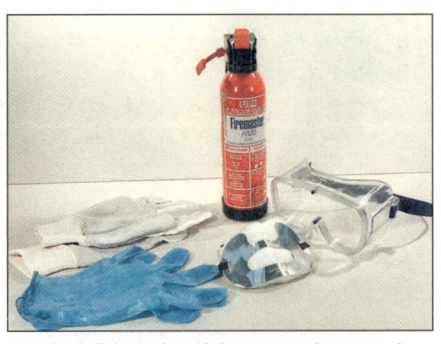

1.6 A fire extinguisher, goggles, mask and protective gloves should be at hand in the workshop

● Protect your hands from contact with solvents, fuel and oils by wearing rubber gloves. Alternatively apply a barrier cream to your hands before starting work. If handling hot components or fluids, wear suitable gloves to protect your hands from scalding and burns.

What to do with old fluids

● Old cleaning solvent, fuel, coolant and oils should not be poured down domestic drains or onto the ground. Package the fluid up in old oil containers, label it accordingly, and take it to a garage or disposal facility. Contact your local authority for location of such sites or ring the oil care hotline.

Note: It is antisocial and illegal to dump oil down the drain. To find the location of your local oil recycling bank in the UK, call 08708 506 506 or visit www.oilbankline.org.uk

In the USA, note that any oil supplier must accept used oil for recycling.

2 Fasteners - screws, bolts and nuts

Fastener types and applications

Bolts and screws

- Fastener head types are either of hexagonal, Torx or splined design, with internal and external versions of each type **(see illustrations 2.1 and 2.2)**; splined head fasteners are not in common use on motorcycles. The conventional slotted or Phillips head design is used for certain screws. Bolt or screw length is always measured from the underside of the head to the end of the item **(see illustration 2.11)**.

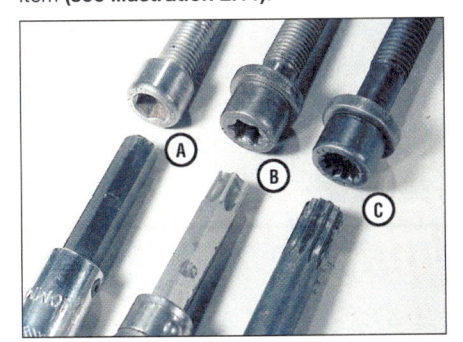

2.1 Internal hexagon/Allen (A), Torx (B) and splined (C) fasteners, with corresponding bits

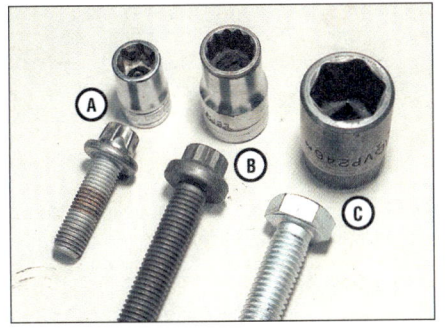

2.2 External Torx (A), splined (B) and hexagon (C) fasteners, with corresponding sockets

- Certain fasteners on the motorcycle have a tensile marking on their heads, the higher the marking the stronger the fastener. High tensile fasteners generally carry a 10 or higher marking. Never replace a high tensile fastener with one of a lower tensile strength.

Washers (see illustration 2.3)

- Plain washers are used between a fastener head and a component to prevent damage to the component or to spread the load when torque is applied. Plain washers can also be used as spacers or shims in certain assemblies. Copper or aluminium plain washers are often used as sealing washers on drain plugs.

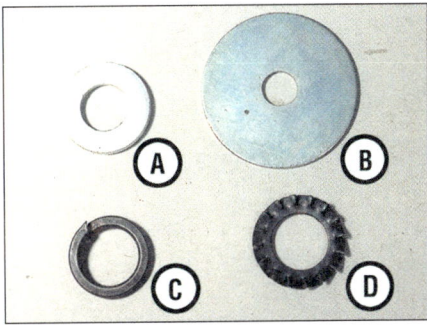

2.3 Plain washer (A), penny washer (B), spring washer (C) and serrated washer (D)

- The split-ring spring washer works by applying axial tension between the fastener head and component. If flattened, it is fatigued and must be renewed. If a plain (flat) washer is used on the fastener, position the spring washer between the fastener and the plain washer.
- Serrated star type washers dig into the fastener and component faces, preventing loosening. They are often used on electrical earth (ground) connections to the frame.
- Cone type washers (sometimes called Belleville) are conical and when tightened apply axial tension between the fastener head and component. They must be installed with the dished side against the component and often carry an OUTSIDE marking on their outer face. If flattened, they are fatigued and must be renewed.
- Tab washers are used to lock plain nuts or bolts on a shaft. A portion of the tab washer is bent up hard against one flat of the nut or bolt to prevent it loosening. Due to the tab washer being deformed in use, a new tab washer should be used every time it is disturbed.
- Wave washers are used to take up endfloat on a shaft. They provide light springing and prevent excessive side-to-side play of a component. Can be found on rocker arm shafts.

Nuts and split pins

- Conventional plain nuts are usually six-sided **(see illustration 2.4)**. They are sized by thread diameter and pitch. High tensile nuts carry a number on one end to denote their tensile strength.

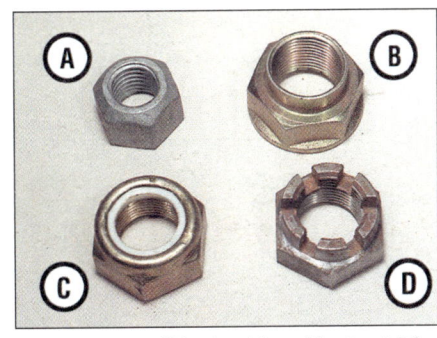

2.4 Plain nut (A), shouldered locknut (B), nylon insert nut (C) and castellated nut (D)

- Self-locking nuts either have a nylon insert, or two spring metal tabs, or a shoulder which is staked into a groove in the shaft - their advantage over conventional plain nuts is a resistance to loosening due to vibration. The nylon insert type can be used a number of times, but must be renewed when the friction of the nylon insert is reduced, ie when the nut spins freely on the shaft. The spring tab type can be reused unless the tabs are damaged. The shouldered type must be renewed every time it is disturbed.
- Split pins (cotter pins) are used to lock a castellated nut to a shaft or to prevent slackening of a plain nut. Common applications are wheel axles and brake torque arms. Because the split pin arms are deformed to lock around the nut a new split pin must always be used on installation - always fit the correct size split pin which will fit snugly in the shaft hole. Make sure the split pin arms are correctly located around the nut **(see illustrations 2.5 and 2.6)**.

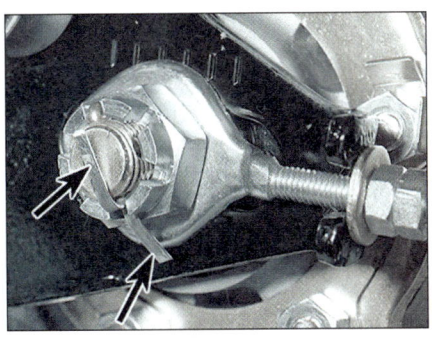

2.5 Bend split pin (cotter pin) arms as shown (arrows) to secure a castellated nut

2.6 Bend split pin (cotter pin) arms as shown to secure a plain nut

Caution: If the castellated nut slots do not align with the shaft hole after tightening to the torque setting, tighten the nut until the next slot aligns with the hole - never slacken the nut to align its slot.

- R-pins (shaped like the letter R), or slip pins as they are sometimes called, are sprung and can be reused if they are otherwise in good condition. Always install R-pins with their closed end facing forwards **(see illustration 2.7)**.

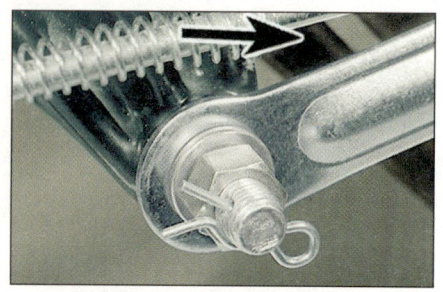

REF•6 Tools and Workshop Tips

2.7 Correct fitting of R-pin. Arrow indicates forward direction

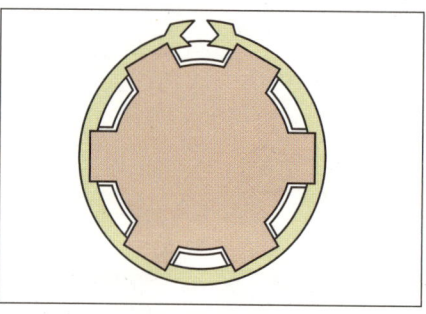

2.10 Align circlip opening with shaft channel

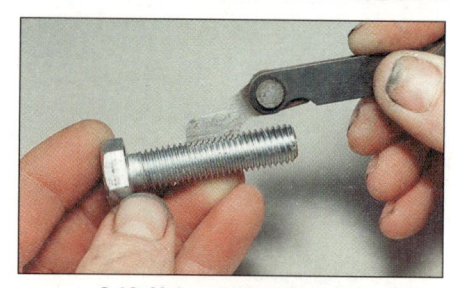

2.12 Using a thread gauge to measure pitch

AF size	Thread diameter x pitch (mm)
8 mm	M5 x 0.8
8 mm	M6 x 1.0
10 mm	M6 x 1.0
12 mm	M8 x 1.25
14 mm	M10 x 1.25
17 mm	M12 x 1.25

Circlips (see illustration 2.8)

● Circlips (sometimes called snap-rings) are used to retain components on a shaft or in a housing and have corresponding external or internal ears to permit removal. Parallel-sided (machined) circlips can be installed either way round in their groove, whereas stamped circlips (which have a chamfered edge on one face) must be installed with the chamfer facing away from the direction of thrust load **(see illustration 2.9)**.

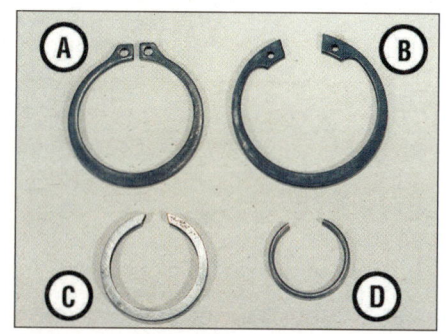

2.8 External stamped circlip (A), internal stamped circlip (B), machined circlip (C) and wire circlip (D)

● Always use circlip pliers to remove and install circlips; expand or compress them just enough to remove them. After installation, rotate the circlip in its groove to ensure it is securely seated. If installing a circlip on a splined shaft, always align its opening with a shaft channel to ensure the circlip ends are well supported and unlikely to catch **(see illustration 2.10)**.

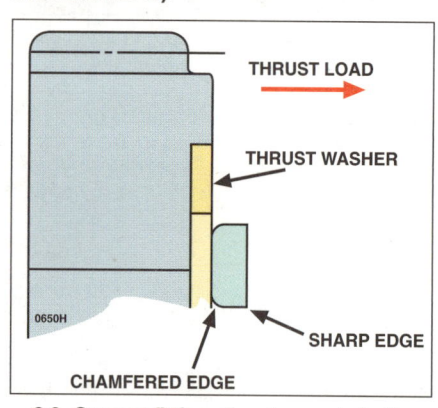

● Circlips can wear due to the thrust of components and become loose in their grooves, with the subsequent danger of becoming dislodged in operation. For this reason, renewal is advised every time a circlip is disturbed.

● Wire circlips are commonly used as piston pin retaining clips. If a removal tang is provided, long-nosed pliers can be used to dislodge them, otherwise careful use of a small flat-bladed screwdriver is necessary. Wire circlips should be renewed every time they are disturbed.

Thread diameter and pitch

● Diameter of a male thread (screw, bolt or stud) is the outside diameter of the threaded portion **(see illustration 2.11)**. Most motorcycle manufacturers use the ISO (International Standards Organisation) metric system expressed in millimetres, eg M6 refers to a 6 mm diameter thread. Sizing is the same for nuts, except that the thread diameter is measured across the valleys of the nut.

● Pitch is the distance between the peaks of the thread **(see illustration 2.11)**. It is expressed in millimetres, thus a common bolt size may be expressed as 6.0 x 1.0 mm (6 mm thread diameter and 1 mm pitch). Generally pitch increases in proportion to thread diameter, although there are always exceptions.

● Thread diameter and pitch are related for conventional fastener applications and the accompanying table can be used as a guide. Additionally, the AF (Across Flats), spanner or socket size dimension of the bolt or nut **(see illustration 2.11)** is linked to thread and pitch specification. Thread pitch can be measured with a thread gauge **(see illustration 2.12)**.

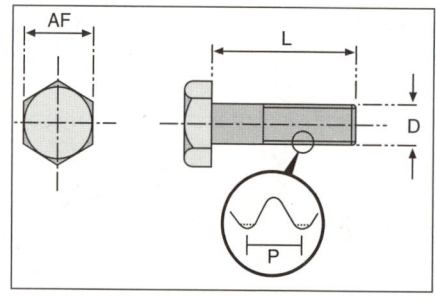

● The threads of most fasteners are of the right-hand type, ie they are turned clockwise to tighten and anti-clockwise to loosen. The reverse situation applies to left-hand thread fasteners, which are turned anti-clockwise to tighten and clockwise to loosen. Left-hand threads are used where rotation of a component might loosen a conventional right-hand thread fastener.

Seized fasteners

● Corrosion of external fasteners due to water or reaction between two dissimilar metals can occur over a period of time. It will build up sooner in wet conditions or in countries where salt is used on the roads during the winter. If a fastener is severely corroded it is likely that normal methods of removal will fail and result in its head being ruined. When you attempt removal, the fastener thread should be heard to crack free and unscrew easily - if it doesn't, stop there before damaging something.

● A smart tap on the head of the fastener will often succeed in breaking free corrosion which has occurred in the threads **(see illustration 2.13)**.

● An aerosol penetrating fluid (such as WD-40) applied the night beforehand may work its way down into the thread and ease removal. Depending on the location, you may be able to make up a Plasticine well around the fastener head and fill it with penetrating fluid.

2.9 Correct fitting of a stamped circlip
(THRUST LOAD, THRUST WASHER, SHARP EDGE, CHAMFERED EDGE)

2.11 Fastener length (L), thread diameter (D), thread pitch (P) and head size (AF)

2.13 A sharp tap on the head of a fastener will often break free a corroded thread

Tools and Workshop Tips REF•7

● If you are working on an engine internal component, corrosion will most likely not be a problem due to the well lubricated environment. However, components can be very tight and an impact driver is a useful tool in freeing them **(see illustration 2.14)**.

2.14 Using an impact driver to free a fastener

● Where corrosion has occurred between dissimilar metals (eg steel and aluminium alloy), the application of heat to the fastener head will create a disproportionate expansion rate between the two metals and break the seizure caused by the corrosion. Whether heat can be applied depends on the location of the fastener - any surrounding components likely to be damaged must first be removed **(see illustration 2.15)**. Heat can be applied using a paint stripper heat gun or clothes iron, or by immersing the component in boiling water - wear protective gloves to prevent scalding or burns to the hands.

2.15 Using heat to free a seized fastener

● As a last resort, it is possible to use a hammer and cold chisel to work the fastener head unscrewed **(see illustration 2.16)**. This will damage the fastener, but more importantly extreme care must be taken not to damage the surrounding component.

Caution: Remember that the component being secured is generally of more value than the bolt, nut or screw - when the fastener is freed, do not unscrew it with force, instead work the fastener back and forth when resistance is felt to prevent thread damage.

2.16 Using a hammer and chisel to free a seized fastener

Broken fasteners and damaged heads

● If the shank of a broken bolt or screw is accessible you can grip it with self-locking grips. The knurled wheel type stud extractor tool or self-gripping stud puller tool is particularly useful for removing the long studs which screw into the cylinder mouth surface of the crankcase or bolts and screws from which the head has broken off **(see illustration 2.17)**. Studs can also be removed by locking two nuts together on the threaded end of the stud and using a spanner on the lower nut **(see illustration 2.18)**.

2.17 Using a stud extractor tool to remove a broken crankcase stud

2.18 Two nuts can be locked together to unscrew a stud from a component

● A bolt or screw which has broken off below or level with the casing must be extracted using a screw extractor set. Centre punch the fastener to centralise the drill bit, then drill a hole in the fastener **(see illustration 2.19)**. Select a drill bit which is approximately half to three-quarters the diameter of the fastener

2.19 When using a screw extractor, first drill a hole in the fastener . . .

and drill to a depth which will accommodate the extractor. Use the largest size extractor possible, but avoid leaving too small a wall thickness otherwise the extractor will merely force the fastener walls outwards wedging it in the casing thread.

● If a spiral type extractor is used, thread it anti-clockwise into the fastener. As it is screwed in, it will grip the fastener and unscrew it from the casing **(see illustration 2.20)**.

2.20 . . . then thread the extractor anti-clockwise into the fastener

● If a taper type extractor is used, tap it into the fastener so that it is firmly wedged in place. Unscrew the extractor (anti-clockwise) to draw the fastener out.

⚠ *Warning: Stud extractors are very hard and may break off in the fastener if care is not taken - ask an engineer about spark erosion if this happens.*

● Alternatively, the broken bolt/screw can be drilled out and the hole retapped for an oversize bolt/screw or a diamond-section thread insert. It is essential that the drilling is carried out squarely and to the correct depth, otherwise the casing may be ruined - if in doubt, entrust the work to an engineer.

● Bolts and nuts with rounded corners cause the correct size spanner or socket to slip when force is applied. Of the types of spanner/socket available always use a six-point type rather than an eight or twelve-point type - better grip

REF•8 Tools and Workshop Tips

2.21 Comparison of surface drive ring spanner (left) with 12-point type (right)

is obtained. Surface drive spanners grip the middle of the hex flats, rather than the corners, and are thus good in cases of damaged heads **(see illustration 2.21)**.

● Slotted-head or Phillips-head screws are often damaged by the use of the wrong size screwdriver. Allen-head and Torx-head screws are much less likely to sustain damage. If enough of the screw head is exposed you can use a hacksaw to cut a slot in its head and then use a conventional flat-bladed screwdriver to remove it. Alternatively use a hammer and cold chisel to tap the head of the fastener around to slacken it. Always replace damaged fasteners with new ones, preferably Torx or Allen-head type.

> **HAYNES HiNT**
>
> *A dab of valve grinding compound between the screw head and screwdriver tip will often give a good grip.*

Thread repair

● Threads (particularly those in aluminium alloy components) can be damaged by overtightening, being assembled with dirt in the threads, or from a component working loose and vibrating. Eventually the thread will fail completely, and it will be impossible to tighten the fastener.

● If a thread is damaged or clogged with old locking compound it can be renovated with a thread repair tool (thread chaser) **(see illustrations 2.22 and 2.23)**; special thread

2.22 A thread repair tool being used to correct an internal thread

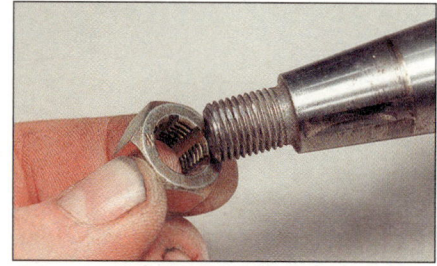

2.23 A thread repair tool being used to correct an external thread

chasers are available for spark plug hole threads. The tool will not cut a new thread, but clean and true the original thread. Make sure that you use the correct diameter and pitch tool. Similarly, external threads can be cleaned up with a die or a thread restorer file **(see illustration 2.24)**.

2.24 Using a thread restorer file

● It is possible to drill out the old thread and retap the component to the next thread size. This will work where there is enough surrounding material and a new bolt or screw can be obtained. Sometimes, however, this is not possible - such as where the bolt/screw passes through another component which must also be suitably modified, also in cases where a spark plug or oil drain plug cannot be obtained in a larger diameter thread size.

● The diamond-section thread insert (often known by its popular trade name of Heli-Coil) is a simple and effective method of renewing the thread and retaining the original size. A kit can be purchased which contains the tap, insert and installing tool **(see illustration 2.25)**. Drill out the damaged thread with the size drill specified **(see illustration 2.26)**. Carefully retap the thread **(see illustration 2.27)**. Install the

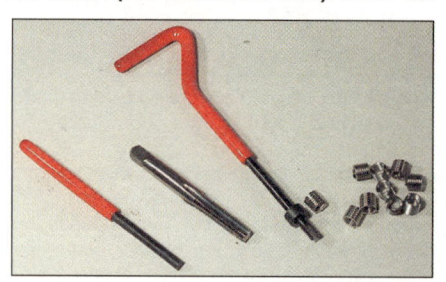

2.25 Obtain a thread insert kit to suit the thread diameter and pitch required

2.26 To install a thread insert, first drill out the original thread . . .

2.27 . . . tap a new thread . . .

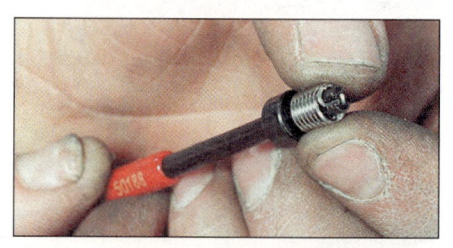

2.28 . . . fit insert on the installing tool . . .

2.29 . . . and thread into the component . . .

2.30 . . . break off the tang when complete

insert on the installing tool and thread it slowly into place using a light downward pressure **(see illustrations 2.28 and 2.29)**. When positioned between a 1/4 and 1/2 turn below the surface withdraw the installing tool and use the break-off tool to press down on the tang, breaking it off **(see illustration 2.30)**.

● There are epoxy thread repair kits on the market which can rebuild stripped internal threads, although this repair should not be used on high load-bearing components.

Tools and Workshop Tips REF•9

Thread locking and sealing compounds

● Locking compounds are used in locations where the fastener is prone to loosening due to vibration or on important safety-related items which might cause loss of control of the motorcycle if they fail. It is also used where important fasteners cannot be secured by other means such as lockwashers or split pins.

● Before applying locking compound, make sure that the threads (internal and external) are clean and dry with all old compound removed. Select a compound to suit the component being secured - a non-permanent general locking and sealing type is suitable for most applications, but a high strength type is needed for permanent fixing of studs in castings. Apply a drop or two of the compound to the first few threads of the fastener, then thread it into place and tighten to the specified torque. Do not apply excessive thread locking compound otherwise the thread may be damaged on subsequent removal.

● Certain fasteners are impregnated with a dry film type coating of locking compound on their threads. Always renew this type of fastener if disturbed.

● Anti-seize compounds, such as copper-based greases, can be applied to protect threads from seizure due to extreme heat and corrosion. A common instance is spark plug threads and exhaust system fasteners.

3 Measuring tools and gauges

Feeler gauges

● Feeler gauges (or blades) are used for measuring small gaps and clearances **(see illustration 3.1)**. They can also be used to measure endfloat (sideplay) of a component on a shaft where access is not possible with a dial gauge.

● Feeler gauge sets should be treated with care and not bent or damaged. They are etched with their size on one face. Keep them clean and very lightly oiled to prevent corrosion build-up.

3.1 Feeler gauges are used for measuring small gaps and clearances - thickness is marked on one face of gauge

● When measuring a clearance, select a gauge which is a light sliding fit between the two components. You may need to use two gauges together to measure the clearance accurately.

Micrometers

● A micrometer is a precision tool capable of measuring to 0.01 or 0.001 of a millimetre. It should always be stored in its case and not in the general toolbox. It must be kept clean and never dropped, otherwise its frame or measuring anvils could be distorted resulting in inaccurate readings.

● External micrometers are used for measuring outside diameters of components and have many more applications than internal micrometers. Micrometers are available in different size ranges, eg 0 to 25 mm, 25 to 50 mm, and upwards in 25 mm steps; some large micrometers have interchangeable anvils to allow a range of measurements to be taken. Generally the largest precision measurement you are likely to take on a motorcycle is the piston diameter.

● Internal micrometers (or bore micrometers) are used for measuring inside diameters, such as valve guides and cylinder bores. Telescoping gauges and small hole gauges are used in conjunction with an external micrometer, whereas the more expensive internal micrometers have their own measuring device.

External micrometer

Note: *The conventional analogue type instrument is described. Although much easier to read, digital micrometers are considerably more expensive.*

● Always check the calibration of the micrometer before use. With the anvils closed (0 to 25 mm type) or set over a test gauge (for the larger types) the scale should read zero **(see illustration 3.2)**; make sure that the anvils (and test piece) are clean first. Any discrepancy can be adjusted by referring to the instructions supplied with the tool. Remember that the micrometer is a precision measuring tool - don't force the anvils closed, use the ratchet (4) on the end of the micrometer to close it. In this way, a measured force is always applied.

● To use, first make sure that the item being measured is clean. Place the anvil of the micrometer (1) against the item and use the thimble (2) to bring the spindle (3) lightly into contact with the other side of the item **(see illustration 3.3)**. Don't tighten the thimble down because this will damage the micrometer - instead use the ratchet (4) on the end of the micrometer. The ratchet mechanism applies a measured force preventing damage to the instrument.

● The micrometer is read by referring to the linear scale on the sleeve and the annular scale on the thimble. Read off the sleeve first to obtain the base measurement, then add the fine measurement from the thimble to obtain the overall reading. The linear scale on the sleeve represents the measuring range of the micrometer (eg 0 to 25 mm). The annular scale

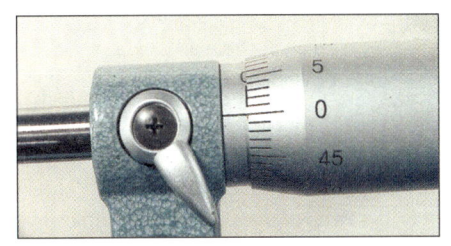

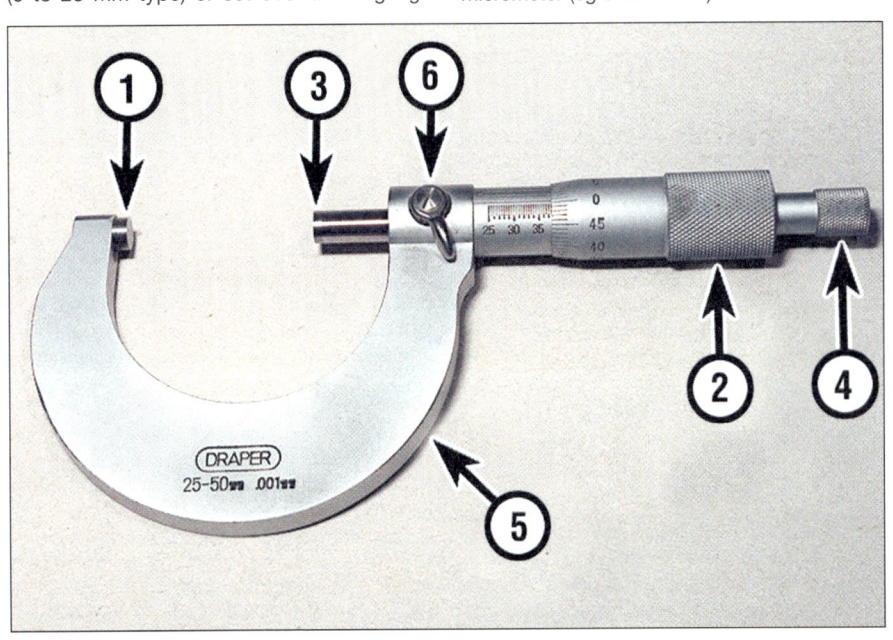

3.2 Check micrometer calibration before use

3.3 Micrometer component parts

1 Anvil
2 Thimble
3 Spindle
4 Ratchet
5 Frame
6 Locking lever

Tools and Workshop Tips

on the thimble will be in graduations of 0.01 mm (or as marked on the frame) - one full revolution of the thimble will move 0.5 mm on the linear scale. Take the reading where the datum line on the sleeve intersects the thimble's scale. Always position the eye directly above the scale otherwise an inaccurate reading will result.

In the example shown the item measures 2.95 mm **(see illustration 3.4)**:

Linear scale	2.00 mm
Linear scale	0.50 mm
Annular scale	0.45 mm
Total figure	2.95 mm

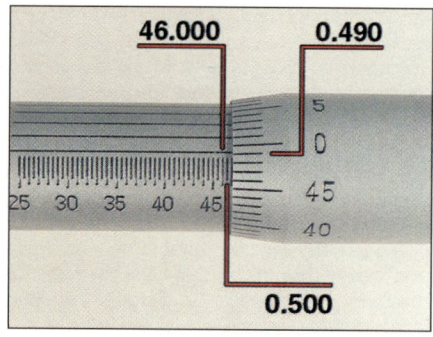

3.5 Micrometer reading of 46.99 mm on linear and annular scales . . .

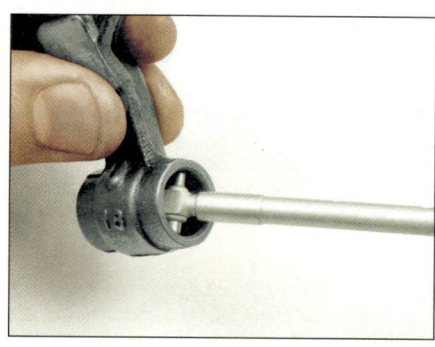

3.7 Expand the telescoping gauge in the bore, lock its position . . .

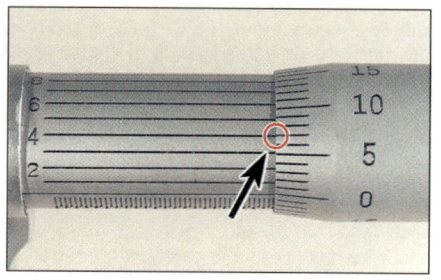

3.6 . . . and 0.004 mm on vernier scale

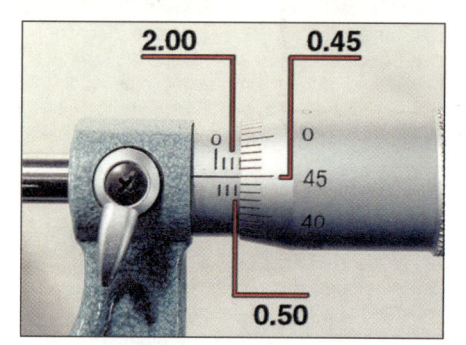

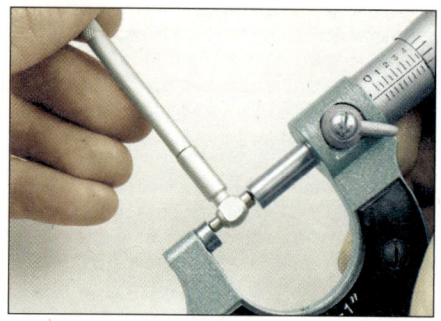

3.4 Micrometer reading of 2.95 mm

3.8 . . . then measure the gauge with a micrometer

Most micrometers have a locking lever (6) on the frame to hold the setting in place, allowing the item to be removed from the micrometer.
● Some micrometers have a vernier scale on their sleeve, providing an even finer measurement to be taken, in 0.001 increments of a millimetre. Take the sleeve and thimble measurement as described above, then check which graduation on the vernier scale aligns with that of the annular scale on the thimble **Note:** *The eye must be perpendicular to the scale when taking the vernier reading - if necessary rotate the body of the micrometer to ensure this.* Multiply the vernier scale figure by 0.001 and add it to the base and fine measurement figures.

In the example shown the item measures 46.994 mm **(see illustrations 3.5 and 3.6)**:

Linear scale (base)	46.000 mm
Linear scale (base)	00.500 mm
Annular scale (fine)	00.490 mm
Vernier scale	00.004 mm
Total figure	46.994 mm

Internal micrometer

● Internal micrometers are available for measuring bore diameters, but are expensive and unlikely to be available for home use. It is suggested that a set of telescoping gauges and small hole gauges, both of which must be used with an external micrometer, will suffice for taking internal measurements on a motorcycle.
● Telescoping gauges can be used to measure internal diameters of components. Select a gauge with the correct size range, make sure its ends are clean and insert it into the bore. Expand the gauge, then lock its position and withdraw it from the bore **(see illustration 3.7)**. Measure across the gauge ends with a micrometer **(see illustration 3.8)**.
● Very small diameter bores (such as valve guides) are measured with a small hole gauge. Once adjusted to a slip-fit inside the component, its position is locked and the gauge withdrawn for measurement with a micrometer **(see illustrations 3.9 and 3.10)**.

Vernier caliper

Note: *The conventional linear and dial gauge type instruments are described. Digital types are easier to read, but are far more expensive.*
● The vernier caliper does not provide the precision of a micrometer, but is versatile in being able to measure internal and external diameters. Some types also incorporate a depth gauge. It is ideal for measuring clutch plate friction material and spring free lengths.
● To use the conventional linear scale vernier, slacken off the vernier clamp screws (1) and set its jaws over (2), or inside (3), the item to be measured **(see illustration 3.11)**. Slide the jaw into contact, using the thumbwheel (4) for fine movement of the sliding scale (5) then tighten the clamp screws (1). Read off the main scale (6) where the zero on the sliding scale (5) intersects it, taking the whole number to the left of the zero; this provides the base measurement. View along the sliding scale and select the division which

3.9 Expand the small hole gauge in the bore, lock its position . . .

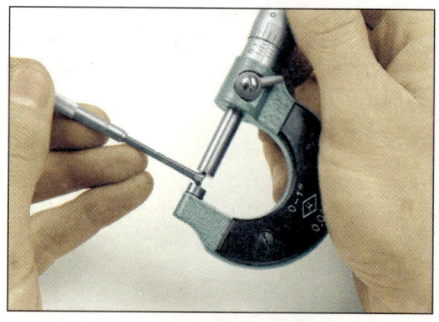

3.10 . . . then measure the gauge with a micrometer

lines up exactly with any of the divisions on the main scale, noting that the divisions usually represents 0.02 of a millimetre. Add this fine measurement to the base measurement to obtain the total reading.

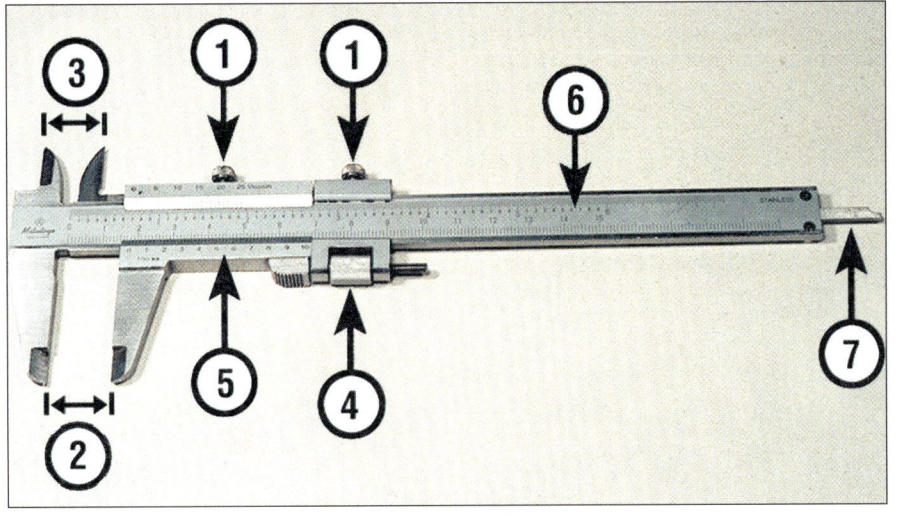

Tools and Workshop Tips REF•11

3.11 Vernier component parts (linear gauge)

1 Clamp screws
2 External jaws
3 Internal jaws
4 Thumbwheel
5 Sliding scale
6 Main scale
7 Depth gauge

In the example shown the item measures 55.92 mm **(see illustration 3.12)**:

Base measurement	55.00 mm
Fine measurement	00.92 mm
Total figure	55.92 mm

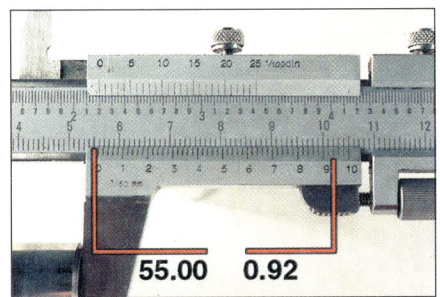

● Some vernier calipers are equipped with a dial gauge for fine measurement. Before use, check that the jaws are clean, then close them fully and check that the dial gauge reads zero. If necessary adjust the gauge ring accordingly. Slacken the vernier clamp screw (1) and set its jaws over (2), or inside (3), the item to be measured **(see illustration 3.13)**. Slide the jaws into contact, using the thumbwheel (4) for fine movement. Read off the main scale (5) where the edge of the sliding scale (6) intersects it, taking the whole number to the left of the zero; this provides the base measurement. Read off the needle position on the dial gauge (7) scale to provide the fine measurement; each division represents 0.05 of a millimetre. Add this fine measurement to the base measurement to obtain the total reading.

In the example shown the item measures 55.95 mm **(see illustration 3.14)**:

Base measurement	55.00 mm
Fine measurement	00.95 mm
Total figure	55.95 mm

3.12 Vernier gauge reading of 55.92 mm

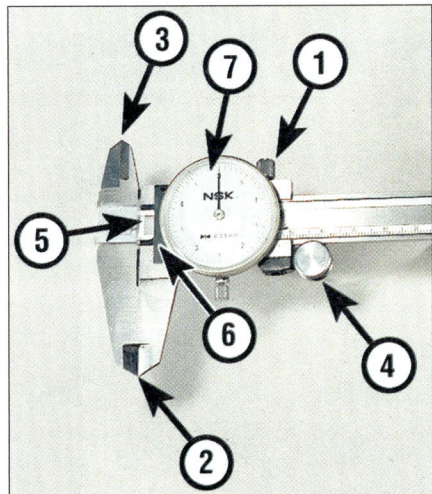

3.13 Vernier component parts (dial gauge)

1 Clamp screw
2 External jaws
3 Internal jaws
4 Thumbwheel
5 Main scale
6 Sliding scale
7 Dial gauge

3.14 Vernier gauge reading of 55.95 mm

Plastigauge

● Plastigauge is a plastic material which can be compressed between two surfaces to measure the oil clearance between them. The width of the compressed Plastigauge is measured against a calibrated scale to determine the clearance.

● Common uses of Plastigauge are for measuring the clearance between crankshaft journal and main bearing inserts, between crankshaft journal and big-end bearing inserts, and between camshaft and bearing surfaces. The following example describes big-end oil clearance measurement.

● Handle the Plastigauge material carefully to prevent distortion. Using a sharp knife, cut a length which corresponds with the width of the bearing being measured and place it carefully across the journal so that it is parallel with the shaft **(see illustration 3.15)**. Carefully install both bearing shells and the connecting rod. Without rotating the rod on the journal tighten its bolts or nuts (as applicable) to the specified torque. The connecting rod and bearings are then disassembled and the crushed Plastigauge examined.

3.15 Plastigauge placed across shaft journal

● Using the scale provided in the Plastigauge kit, measure the width of the material to determine the oil clearance **(see illustration 3.16)**. Always remove all traces of Plastigauge after use using your fingernails.

Caution: Arriving at the correct clearance demands that the assembly is torqued correctly, according to the settings and sequence (where applicable) provided by the motorcycle manufacturer.

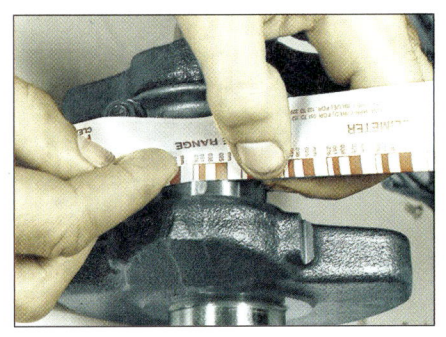

3.16 Measuring the width of the crushed Plastigauge

REF•12 Tools and Workshop Tips

Dial gauge or DTI (Dial Test Indicator)

● A dial gauge can be used to accurately measure small amounts of movement. Typical uses are measuring shaft runout or shaft endfloat (sideplay) and setting piston position for ignition timing on two-strokes. A dial gauge set usually comes with a range of different probes and adapters and mounting equipment.

● The gauge needle must point to zero when at rest. Rotate the ring around its periphery to zero the gauge.

● Check that the gauge is capable of reading the extent of movement in the work. Most gauges have a small dial set in the face which records whole millimetres of movement as well as the fine scale around the face periphery which is calibrated in 0.01 mm divisions. Read off the small dial first to obtain the base measurement, then add the measurement from the fine scale to obtain the total reading.

In the example shown the gauge reads 1.48 mm **(see illustration 3.17)**:

Base measurement	1.00 mm
Fine measurement	0.48 mm
Total figure	1.48 mm

3.17 Dial gauge reading of 1.48 mm

● If measuring shaft runout, the shaft must be supported in vee-blocks and the gauge mounted on a stand perpendicular to the shaft. Rest the tip of the gauge against the centre of the shaft and rotate the shaft slowly whilst watching the gauge reading **(see illustration 3.18)**. Take several measurements along the length of the shaft and record the maximum gauge reading as the amount of runout in the shaft. **Note:** *The reading obtained will be total runout at that point - some manufacturers specify that the runout figure is halved to compare with their specified runout limit.*

● Endfloat (sideplay) measurement requires that the gauge is mounted securely to the surrounding component with its probe touching the end of the shaft. Using hand pressure, push and pull on the shaft noting the maximum endfloat recorded on the gauge **(see illustration 3.19)**.

3.18 Using a dial gauge to measure shaft runout

3.19 Using a dial gauge to measure shaft endfloat

● A dial gauge with suitable adapters can be used to determine piston position BTDC on two-stroke engines for the purposes of ignition timing. The gauge, adapter and suitable length probe are installed in the place of the spark plug and the gauge zeroed at TDC. If the piston position is specified as 1.14 mm BTDC, rotate the engine back to 2.00 mm BTDC, then slowly forwards to 1.14 mm BTDC.

Cylinder compression gauges

● A compression gauge is used for measuring cylinder compression. Either the rubber-cone type or the threaded adapter type can be used. The latter is preferred to ensure a perfect seal against the cylinder head. A 0 to 300 psi (0 to 20 Bar) type gauge (for petrol/gasoline engines) will be suitable for motorcycles.

● The spark plug is removed and the gauge either held hard against the cylinder head (cone type) or the gauge adapter screwed into the cylinder head (threaded type) **(see illustration 3.20)**. Cylinder compression is measured with the engine turning over, but not running. The gauge will hold the reading until manually released.

3.20 Using a rubber-cone type cylinder compression gauge

Oil pressure gauge

● An oil pressure gauge is used for measuring engine oil pressure. Most gauges come with a set of adapters to fit the thread of the take-off point **(see illustration 3.21)**. If the take-off point specified by the motorcycle manufacturer is an external oil pipe union, make sure that the specified replacement union is used to prevent oil starvation.

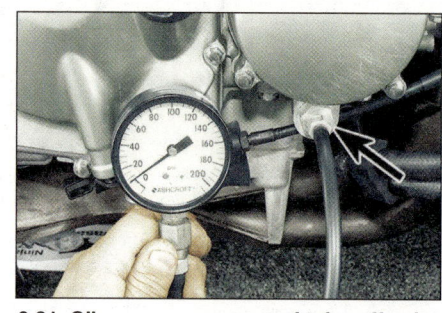

3.21 Oil pressure gauge and take-off point adapter (arrow)

● Oil pressure is measured with the engine running (at a specific rpm) and often the manufacturer will specify pressure limits for a cold and hot engine.

Straight-edge and surface plate

● If checking the gasket face of a component for warpage, place a steel rule or precision straight-edge across the gasket face and measure any gap between the straight-edge and component with feeler gauges **(see illustration 3.22)**. Check diagonally across the component and between mounting holes **(see illustration 3.23)**.

3.22 Use a straight-edge and feeler gauges to check for warpage

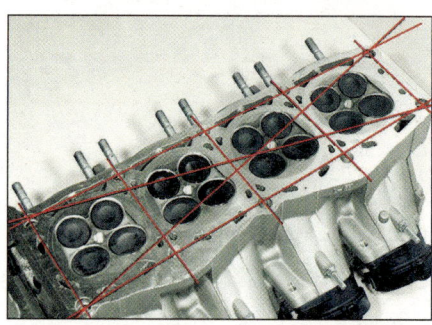

3.23 Check for warpage in these directions

Tools and Workshop Tips REF•13

● Checking individual components for warpage, such as clutch plain (metal) plates, requires a perfectly flat plate or piece or plate glass and feeler gauges.

4 Torque and leverage

What is torque?

● Torque describes the twisting force about a shaft. The amount of torque applied is determined by the distance from the centre of the shaft to the end of the lever and the amount of force being applied to the end of the lever; distance multiplied by force equals torque.

● The manufacturer applies a measured torque to a bolt or nut to ensure that it will not slacken in use and to hold two components securely together without movement in the joint. The actual torque setting depends on the thread size, bolt or nut material and the composition of the components being held.

● Too little torque may cause the fastener to loosen due to vibration, whereas too much torque will distort the joint faces of the component or cause the fastener to shear off. Always stick to the specified torque setting.

Using a torque wrench

● Check the calibration of the torque wrench and make sure it has a suitable range for the job. Torque wrenches are available in Nm (Newton-metres), kgf m (kilograms-force metre), lbf ft (pounds-feet), lbf in (inch-pounds). Do not confuse lbf ft with lbf in.

● Adjust the tool to the desired torque on the scale **(see illustration 4.1)**. If your torque wrench is not calibrated in the units specified, carefully convert the figure (see Conversion Factors). A manufacturer sometimes gives a torque setting as a range (8 to 10 Nm) rather than a single figure - in this case set the tool midway between the two settings. The same torque may be expressed as 9 Nm ± 1 Nm. Some torque wrenches have a method of locking the setting so that it isn't inadvertently altered during use.

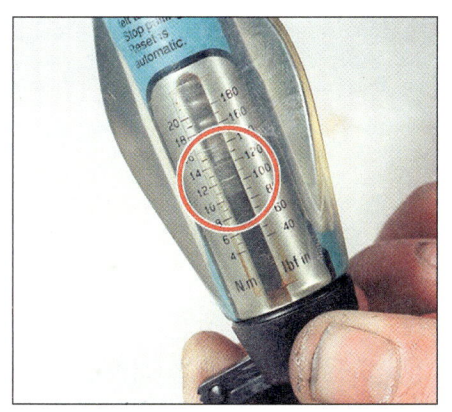

● Install the bolts/nuts in their correct location and secure them lightly. Their threads must be clean and free of any old locking compound. Unless specified the threads and flange should be dry - oiled threads are necessary in certain circumstances and the manufacturer will take this into account in the specified torque figure. Similarly, the manufacturer may also specify the application of thread-locking compound.

● Tighten the fasteners in the specified sequence until the torque wrench clicks, indicating that the torque setting has been reached. Apply the torque again to double-check the setting. Where different thread diameter fasteners secure the component, as a rule tighten the larger diameter ones first.

● When the torque wrench has been finished with, release the lock (where applicable) and fully back off its setting to zero - do not leave the torque wrench tensioned. Also, do not use a torque wrench for slackening a fastener.

Angle-tightening

● Manufacturers often specify a figure in degrees for final tightening of a fastener. This usually follows tightening to a specific torque setting.

● A degree disc can be set and attached to the socket **(see illustration 4.2)** or a protractor can be used to mark the angle of movement on the bolt/nut head and the surrounding casting **(see illustration 4.3)**.

4.2 Angle tightening can be accomplished with a torque-angle gauge . . .

4.3 . . . or by marking the angle on the surrounding component

4.1 Set the torque wrench index mark to the setting required, in this case 12 Nm

Loosening sequences

● Where more than one bolt/nut secures a component, loosen each fastener evenly a little at a time. In this way, not all the stress of the joint is held by one fastener and the components are not likely to distort.

● If a tightening sequence is provided, work in the REVERSE of this, but if not, work from the outside in, in a criss-cross sequence **(see illustration 4.4)**.

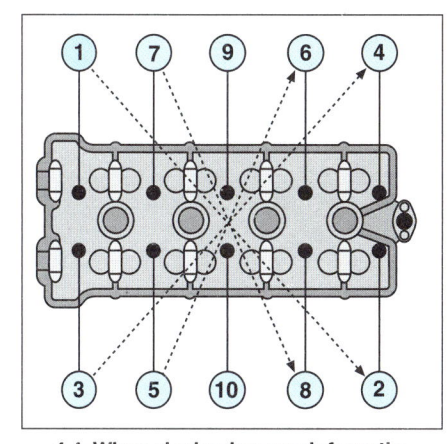

4.4 When slackening, work from the outside inwards

Tightening sequences

● If a component is held by more than one fastener it is important that the retaining bolts/nuts are tightened evenly to prevent uneven stress build-up and distortion of sealing faces. This is especially important on high-compression joints such as the cylinder head.

● A sequence is usually provided by the manufacturer, either in a diagram or actually marked in the casting. If not, always start in the centre and work outwards in a criss-cross pattern **(see illustration 4.5)**. Start off by securing all bolts/nuts finger-tight, then set the torque wrench and tighten each fastener by a small amount in sequence until the final torque is reached. By following this practice,

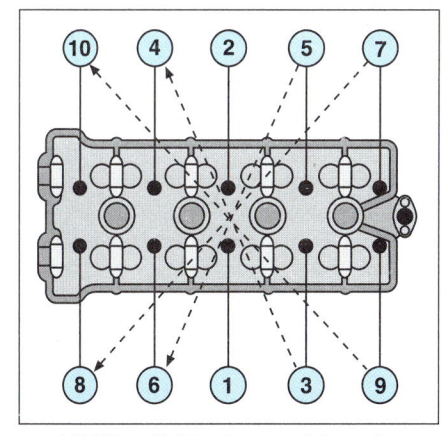

4.5 When tightening, work from the inside outwards

REF•14 Tools and Workshop Tips

the joint will be held evenly and will not be distorted. Important joints, such as the cylinder head and big-end fasteners often have two- or three-stage torque settings.

Applying leverage

● Use tools at the correct angle. Position a socket wrench or spanner on the bolt/nut so that you pull it towards you when loosening. If this can't be done, push the spanner without curling your fingers around it **(see illustration 4.6)** - the spanner may slip or the fastener loosen suddenly, resulting in your fingers being crushed against a component.

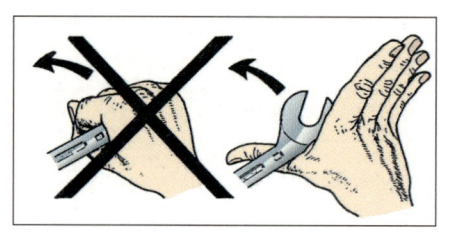

4.6 If you can't pull on the spanner to loosen a fastener, push with your hand open

● Additional leverage is gained by extending the length of the lever. The best way to do this is to use a breaker bar instead of the regular length tool, or to slip a length of tubing over the end of the spanner or socket wrench.
● If additional leverage will not work, the fastener head is either damaged or firmly corroded in place (see Fasteners).

5 Bearings

Bearing removal and installation
Drivers and sockets

● Before removing a bearing, always inspect the casing to see which way it must be driven out - some casings will have retaining plates or a cast step. Also check for any identifying markings on the bearing and if installed to a certain depth, measure this at this stage. Some roller bearings are sealed on one side - take note of the original fitted position.
● Bearings can be driven out of a casing using a bearing driver tool (with the correct size head) or a socket of the correct diameter. Select the driver head or socket so that it contacts the outer race of the bearing, not the balls/rollers or inner race. Always support the casing around the bearing housing with wood blocks, otherwise there is a risk of fracture. The bearing is driven out with a few blows on the driver or socket from a heavy mallet. Unless access is severely restricted (as with wheel bearings), a pin-punch is not recommended unless it is moved around the bearing to keep it square in its housing.

● The same equipment can be used to install bearings. Make sure the bearing housing is supported on wood blocks and line up the bearing in its housing. Fit the bearing as noted on removal - generally they are installed with their marked side facing outwards. Tap the bearing squarely into its housing using a driver or socket which bears only on the bearing's outer race - contact with the bearing balls/rollers or inner race will destroy it **(see illustrations 5.1 and 5.2)**.
● Check that the bearing inner race and balls/rollers rotate freely.

5.1 Using a bearing driver against the bearing's outer race

5.2 Using a large socket against the bearing's outer race

Pullers and slide-hammers

● Where a bearing is pressed on a shaft a puller will be required to extract it **(see illustration 5.3)**. Make sure that the puller clamp or legs fit securely behind the bearing and are unlikely to slip out. If pulling a bearing off a gear shaft for example, you may have to locate the puller behind a gear pinion if there is no access to the race and draw the gear pinion off the shaft as well **(see illustration 5.4)**.

Caution: Ensure that the puller's centre bolt locates securely against the end of the shaft and will not slip when pressure is applied. Also ensure that puller does not damage the shaft end.

5.4 Where no access is available to the rear of the bearing, it is sometimes possible to draw off the adjacent component

● Operate the puller so that its centre bolt exerts pressure on the shaft end and draws the bearing off the shaft.
● When installing the bearing on the shaft, tap only on the bearing's inner race - contact with the balls/rollers or outer race with destroy the bearing. Use a socket or length of tubing as a drift which fits over the shaft end **(see illustration 5.5)**.

5.5 When installing a bearing on a shaft use a piece of tubing which bears only on the bearing's inner race

● Where a bearing locates in a blind hole in a casing, it cannot be driven or pulled out as described above. A slide-hammer with knife-edged bearing puller attachment will be required. The puller attachment passes through the bearing and when tightened expands to fit firmly behind the bearing **(see illustration 5.6)**. By operating the slide-hammer part of the tool the bearing is jarred out of its housing **(see illustration 5.7)**.
● It is possible, if the bearing is of reasonable weight, for it to drop out of its housing if the casing is heated as described opposite.

5.3 This bearing puller clamps behind the bearing and pressure is applied to the shaft end to draw the bearing off

Tools and Workshop Tips REF•15

5.6 Expand the bearing puller so that it locks behind the bearing . . .

5.7 . . . attach the slide hammer to the bearing puller

If this method is attempted, first prepare a work surface which will enable the casing to be tapped face down to help dislodge the bearing - a wood surface is ideal since it will not damage the casing's gasket surface. Wearing protective gloves, tap the heated casing several times against the work surface to dislodge the bearing under its own weight **(see illustration 5.8)**.

5.8 Tapping a casing face down on wood blocks can often dislodge a bearing

● Bearings can be installed in blind holes using the driver or socket method described above.

Drawbolts

● Where a bearing or bush is set in the eye of a component, such as a suspension linkage arm or connecting rod small-end, removal by drift may damage the component. Furthermore, a rubber bushing in a shock absorber eye cannot successfully be driven out of position. If access is available to a engineering press, the task is straightforward. If not, a drawbolt can be fabricated to extract the bearing or bush.

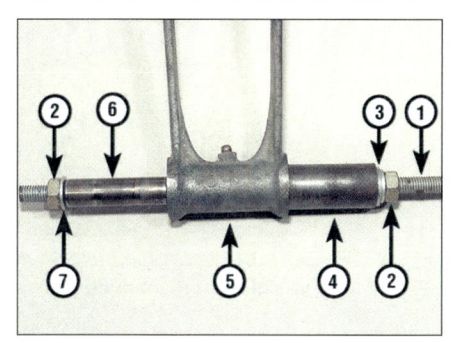

5.9 Drawbolt component parts assembled on a suspension arm

1 Bolt or length of threaded bar
2 Nuts
3 Washer (external diameter greater than tubing internal diameter)
4 Tubing (internal diameter sufficient to accommodate bearing)
5 Suspension arm with bearing
6 Tubing (external diameter slightly smaller than bearing)
7 Washer (external diameter slightly smaller than bearing)

5.10 Drawing the bearing out of the suspension arm

● To extract the bearing/bush you will need a long bolt with nut (or piece of threaded bar with two nuts), a piece of tubing which has an internal diameter larger than the bearing/bush, another piece of tubing which has an external diameter slightly smaller than the bearing/bush, and a selection of washers **(see illustrations 5.9 and 5.10)**. Note that the pieces of tubing must be of the same length, or longer, than the bearing/bush.

● The same kit (without the pieces of tubing) can be used to draw the new bearing/bush back into place **(see illustration 5.11)**.

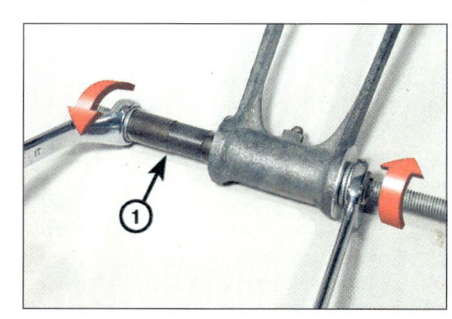

5.11 Installing a new bearing (1) in the suspension arm

Temperature change

● If the bearing's outer race is a tight fit in the casing, the aluminium casing can be heated to release its grip on the bearing. Aluminium will expand at a greater rate than the steel bearing outer race. There are several ways to do this, but avoid any localised extreme heat (such as a blow torch) - aluminium alloy has a low melting point.

● Approved methods of heating a casing are using a domestic oven (heated to 100°C) or immersing the casing in boiling water **(see illustration 5.12)**. Low temperature range localised heat sources such as a paint stripper heat gun or clothes iron can also be used **(see illustration 5.13)**. Alternatively, soak a rag in boiling water, wring it out and wrap it around the bearing housing.

> ⚠ **Warning: All of these methods require care in use to prevent scalding and burns to the hands. Wear protective gloves when handling hot components.**

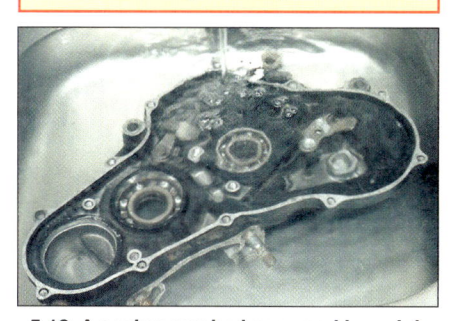

5.12 A casing can be immersed in a sink of boiling water to aid bearing removal

5.13 Using a localised heat source to aid bearing removal

● If heating the whole casing note that plastic components, such as the neutral switch, may suffer - remove them beforehand.

● After heating, remove the bearing as described above. You may find that the expansion is sufficient for the bearing to fall out of the casing under its own weight or with a light tap on the driver or socket.

● If necessary, the casing can be heated to aid bearing installation, and this is sometimes the recommended procedure if the motorcycle manufacturer has designed the housing and bearing fit with this intention.

Tools and Workshop Tips

- Installation of bearings can be eased by placing them in a freezer the night before installation. The steel bearing will contract slightly, allowing easy insertion in its housing. This is often useful when installing steering head outer races in the frame.

Bearing types and markings

- Plain shell bearings, ball bearings, needle roller bearings and tapered roller bearings will all be found on motorcycles **(see illustrations 5.14 and 5.15)**. The ball and roller types are usually caged between an inner and outer race, but uncaged variations may be found.

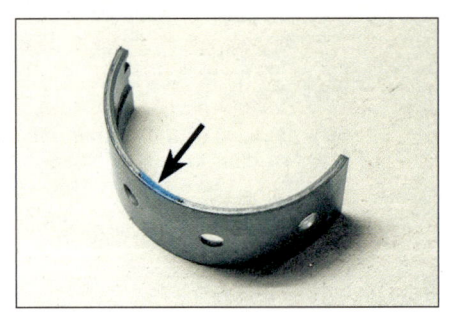

5.14 Shell bearings are either plain or grooved. They are usually identified by colour code (arrow)

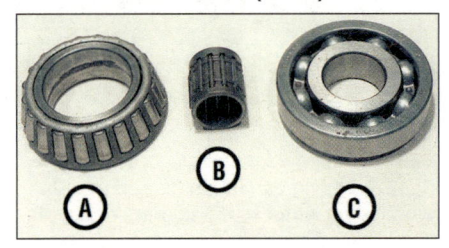

5.15 Tapered roller bearing (A), needle roller bearing (B) and ball journal bearing (C)

- Shell bearings (often called inserts) are usually found at the crankshaft main and connecting rod big-end where they are good at coping with high loads. They are made of a phosphor-bronze material and are impregnated with self-lubricating properties.
- Ball bearings and needle roller bearings consist of a steel inner and outer race with the balls or rollers between the races. They require constant lubrication by oil or grease and are good at coping with axial loads. Taper roller bearings consist of rollers set in a tapered cage set on the inner race; the outer race is separate. They are good at coping with axial loads and prevent movement along the shaft - a typical application is in the steering head.
- Bearing manufacturers produce bearings to ISO size standards and stamp one face of the bearing to indicate its internal and external diameter, load capacity and type **(see illustration 5.16)**.
- Metal bushes are usually of phosphor-bronze material. Rubber bushes are used in suspension mounting eyes. Fibre bushes have also been used in suspension pivots.

5.16 Typical bearing marking

Bearing fault finding

- If a bearing outer race has spun in its housing, the housing material will be damaged. You can use a bearing locking compound to bond the outer race in place if damage is not too severe.
- Shell bearings will fail due to damage of their working surface, as a result of lack of lubrication, corrosion or abrasive particles in the oil **(see illustration 5.17)**. Small particles of dirt in the oil may embed in the bearing material whereas larger particles will score the bearing and shaft journal. If a number of short journeys are made, insufficient heat will be generated to drive off condensation which has built up on the bearings.

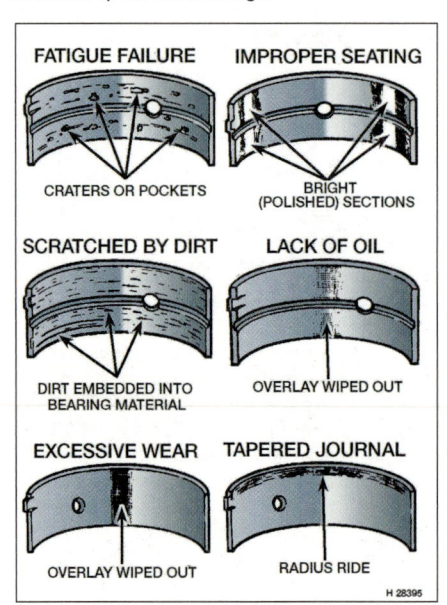

5.17 Typical bearing failures

- Ball and roller bearings will fail due to lack of lubrication or damage to the balls or rollers. Tapered-roller bearings can be damaged by overloading them. Unless the bearing is sealed on both sides, wash it in paraffin (kerosene) to remove all old grease then allow it to dry. Make a visual inspection looking to dented balls or rollers, damaged cages and worn or pitted races **(see illustration 5.18)**.
- A ball bearing can be checked for wear by listening to it when spun. Apply a film of light oil to the bearing and hold it close to the ear - hold the outer race with one hand and spin the inner race with the other hand **(see illustration 5.19)**. The bearing should be almost silent when spun; if it grates or rattles it is worn.

5.18 Example of ball journal bearing with damaged balls and cages

5.19 Hold outer race and listen to inner race when spun

6 Oil seals

Oil seal removal and installation

- Oil seals should be renewed every time a component is dismantled. This is because the seal lips will become set to the sealing surface and will not necessarily reseal.
- Oil seals can be prised out of position using a large flat-bladed screwdriver **(see illustration 6.1)**. In the case of crankcase seals, check first that the seal is not lipped on the inside, preventing its removal with the crankcases joined.

6.1 Prise out oil seals with a large flat-bladed screwdriver

- New seals are usually installed with their marked face (containing the seal reference code) outwards and the spring side towards the fluid being retained. In certain cases, such as a two-stroke engine crankshaft seal, a double lipped seal may be used due to there being fluid or gas on each side of the joint.

Tools and Workshop Tips REF•17

- Use a bearing driver or socket which bears only on the outer hard edge of the seal to install it in the casing - tapping on the inner edge will damage the sealing lip.

Oil seal types and markings

- Oil seals are usually of the single-lipped type. Double-lipped seals are found where a liquid or gas is on both sides of the joint.
- Oil seals can harden and lose their sealing ability if the motorcycle has been in storage for a long period - renewal is the only solution.
- Oil seal manufacturers also conform to the ISO markings for seal size - these are moulded into the outer face of the seal **(see illustration 6.2)**.

6.2 These oil seal markings indicate inside diameter, outside diameter and seal thickness

7 Gaskets and sealants

Types of gasket and sealant

- Gaskets are used to seal the mating surfaces between components and keep lubricants, fluids, vacuum or pressure contained within the assembly. Aluminium gaskets are sometimes found at the cylinder joints, but most gaskets are paper-based. If the mating surfaces of the components being joined are undamaged the gasket can be installed dry, although a dab of sealant or grease will be useful to hold it in place during assembly.
- RTV (Room Temperature Vulcanising) silicone rubber sealants cure when exposed to moisture in the atmosphere. These sealants are good at filling pits or irregular gasket faces, but will tend to be forced out of the joint under very high torque. They can be used to replace a paper gasket, but first make sure that the width of the paper gasket is not essential to the shimming of internal components. RTV sealants should not be used on components containing petrol (gasoline).
- Non-hardening, semi-hardening and hard setting liquid gasket compounds can be used with a gasket or between a metal-to-metal joint. Select the sealant to suit the application: universal non-hardening sealant can be used on virtually all joints; semi-hardening on joint faces which are rough or damaged; hard setting sealant on joints which require a permanent bond and are subjected to high temperature and pressure. **Note:** *Check first if the paper gasket has a bead of sealant impregnated in its surface before applying additional sealant.*
- When choosing a sealant, make sure it is suitable for the application, particularly if being applied in a high-temperature area or in the vicinity of fuel. Certain manufacturers produce sealants in either clear, silver or black colours to match the finish of the engine. This has a particular application on motorcycles where much of the engine is exposed.
- Do not over-apply sealant. That which is squeezed out on the outside of the joint can be wiped off, whereas an excess of sealant on the inside can break off and clog oilways.

Breaking a sealed joint

- Age, heat, pressure and the use of hard setting sealant can cause two components to stick together so tightly that they are difficult to separate using finger pressure alone. Do not resort to using levers unless there is a pry point provided for this purpose **(see illustration 7.1)** or else the gasket surfaces will be damaged.
- Use a soft-faced hammer **(see illustration 7.2)** or a wood block and conventional hammer to strike the component near the mating surface. Avoid hammering against cast extremities since they may break off. If this method fails, try using a wood wedge between the two components.

Caution: If the joint will not separate, double-check that you have removed all the fasteners.

7.1 If a pry point is provided, apply gently pressure with a flat-bladed screwdriver

7.2 Tap around the joint with a soft-faced mallet if necessary - don't strike cooling fins

Removal of old gasket and sealant

- Paper gaskets will most likely come away complete, leaving only a few traces stuck on the sealing faces of the components. It is imperative that all traces are removed to ensure correct sealing of the new gasket.
- Very carefully scrape all traces of gasket away making sure that the sealing surfaces are not gouged or scored by the scraper **(see illustrations 7.3, 7.4 and 7.5)**. Stubborn deposits can be removed by spraying with an aerosol gasket remover. Final preparation of

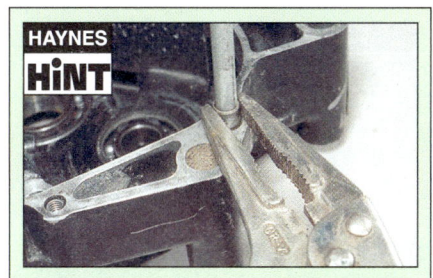

HAYNES HiNT

Most components have one or two hollow locating dowels between the two gasket faces. If a dowel cannot be removed, do not resort to gripping it with pliers - it will almost certainly be distorted. Install a close-fitting socket or Phillips screwdriver into the dowel and then grip the outer edge of the dowel to free it.

7.3 Paper gaskets can be scraped off with a gasket scraper tool . . .

7.4 . . . a knife blade . . .

7.5 . . . or a household scraper

REF•18 Tools and Workshop Tips

7.6 Fine abrasive paper is wrapped around a flat file to clean up the gasket face

7.7 A kitchen scourer can be used on stubborn deposits

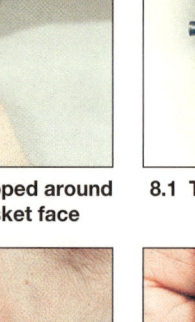

8.1 Tighten the chain breaker to push the pin out of the link . . .

8.2 . . . withdraw the pin, remove the tool . . .

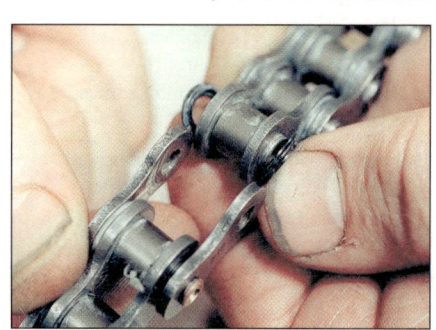

8.3 . . . and separate the chain link

8.4 Insert the new soft link, with O-rings, through the chain ends . . .

8.5 . . . install the O-rings over the pin ends . . .

8.6 . . . followed by the sideplate

8.7 Push the sideplate into position using a clamp

the gasket surface can be made with very fine abrasive paper or a plastic kitchen scourer **(see illustrations 7.6 and 7.7)**.
● Old sealant can be scraped or peeled off components, depending on the type originally used. Note that gasket removal compounds are available to avoid scraping the components clean; make sure the gasket remover suits the type of sealant used.

8 Chains

Breaking and joining final drive chains

● Drive chains for all but small bikes are continuous and do not have a clip-type connecting link. The chain must be broken using a chain breaker tool and the new chain securely riveted together using a new soft rivet-type link. Never use a clip-type connecting link instead of a rivet-type link, except in an emergency. Various chain breaking and riveting tools are available, either as separate tools or combined as illustrated in the accompanying photographs - read the instructions supplied with the tool carefully.

⚠ **Warning: The need to rivet the new link pins correctly cannot be overstressed - loss of control of the motorcycle is very likely to result if the chain breaks in use.**

● Rotate the chain and look for the soft link. The soft link pins look like they have been deeply centre-punched instead of peened over like all the other pins **(see illustration 8.9)** and its sideplate may be a different colour. Position the soft link midway between the sprockets and assemble the chain breaker tool over one of the soft link pins **(see illustration 8.1)**. Operate the tool to push the pin out through the chain **(see illustration 8.2)**. On an O-ring chain, remove the O-rings **(see illustration 8.3)**. Carry out the same procedure on the other soft link pin.

Caution: Certain soft link pins (particularly on the larger chains) may require their ends to be filed or ground off before they can be pressed out using the tool.

● Check that you have the correct size and strength (standard or heavy duty) new soft link - do not reuse the old link. Look for the size marking on the chain sideplates **(see illustration 8.10)**.
● Position the chain ends so that they are engaged over the rear sprocket. On an O-ring chain, install a new O-ring over each pin of the link and insert the link through the two chain ends **(see illustration 8.4)**. Install a new O-ring over the end of each pin, followed by the sideplate (with the chain manufacturer's marking facing outwards) **(see illustrations 8.5 and 8.6)**. On an unsealed chain, insert the link through the two chain ends, then install the sideplate with the chain manufacturer's marking facing outwards.
● Note that it may not be possible to install the sideplate using finger pressure alone. If using a joining tool, assemble it so that the plates of the tool clamp the link and press the sideplate over the pins **(see illustration 8.7)**. Otherwise, use two small sockets placed over

Tools and Workshop Tips REF•19

8.8 Assemble the chain riveting tool over one pin at a time and tighten it fully

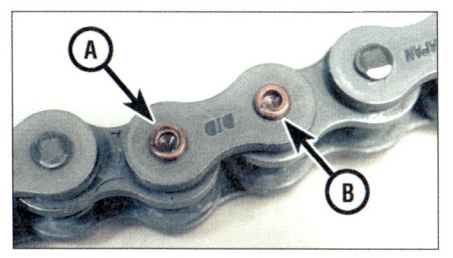

8.9 Pin end correctly riveted (A), pin end unriveted (B)

the rivet ends and two pieces of the wood between a G-clamp. Operate the clamp to press the sideplate over the pins.

● Assemble the joining tool over one pin (following the maker's instructions) and tighten the tool down to spread the pin end securely **(see illustrations 8.8 and 8.9)**. Do the same on the other pin.

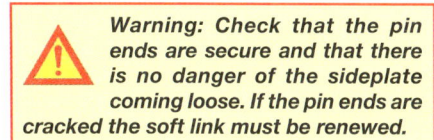

> ⚠ **Warning: Check that the pin ends are secure and that there is no danger of the sideplate coming loose. If the pin ends are cracked the soft link must be renewed.**

Final drive chain sizing

● Chains are sized using a three digit number, followed by a suffix to denote the chain type **(see illustration 8.10)**. Chain type is either standard or heavy duty (thicker sideplates), and also unsealed or O-ring/X-ring type.

● The first digit of the number relates to the pitch of the chain, ie the distance from the centre of one pin to the centre of the next pin **(see illustration 8.11)**. Pitch is expressed in eighths of an inch, as follows:

8.10 Typical chain size and type marking

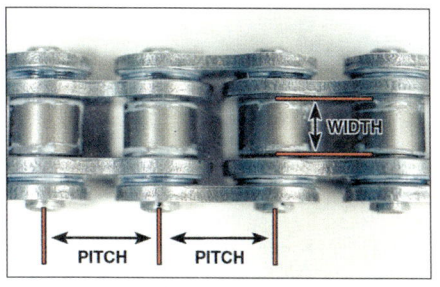

8.11 Chain dimensions

| Sizes commencing with a 4 (eg 428) have a pitch of 1/2 inch (12.7 mm) |
| Sizes commencing with a 5 (eg 520) have a pitch of 5/8 inch (15.9 mm) |
| Sizes commencing with a 6 (eg 630) have a pitch of 3/4 inch (19.1 mm) |

● The second and third digits of the chain size relate to the width of the rollers, again in imperial units, eg the 525 shown has 5/16 inch (7.94 mm) rollers **(see illustration 8.11)**.

9 Hoses

Clamping to prevent flow

● Small-bore flexible hoses can be clamped to prevent fluid flow whilst a component is worked on. Whichever method is used, ensure that the hose material is not permanently distorted or damaged by the clamp.
a) A brake hose clamp available from auto accessory shops **(see illustration 9.1)**.
b) A wingnut type hose clamp **(see illustration 9.2)**.
c) Two sockets placed each side of the hose and held with straight-jawed self-locking grips **(see illustration 9.3)**.
d) Thick card each side of the hose held between straight-jawed self-locking grips **(see illustration 9.4)**.

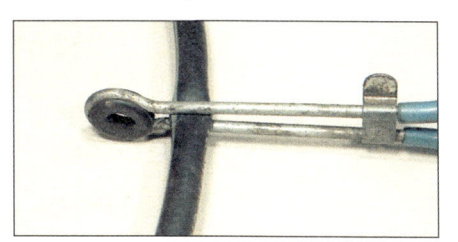

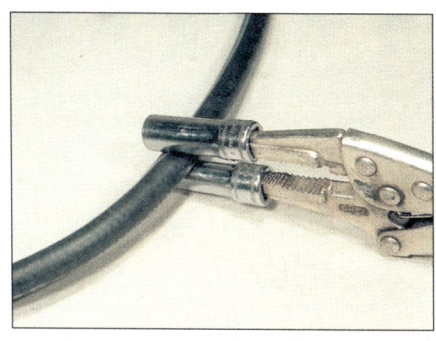

9.1 Hoses can be clamped with an automotive brake hose clamp . . .

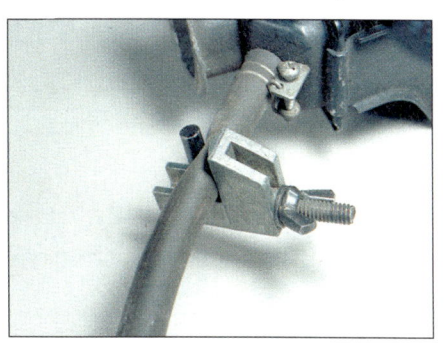

9.2 . . . a wingnut type hose clamp . . .

9.3 . . . two sockets and a pair of self-locking grips . . .

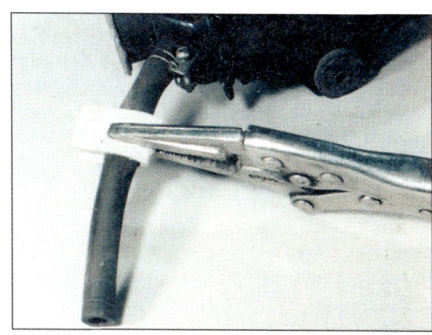

9.4 . . . or thick card and self-locking grips

Freeing and fitting hoses

● Always make sure the hose clamp is moved well clear of the hose end. Grip the hose with your hand and rotate it whilst pulling it off the union. If the hose has hardened due to age and will not move, slit it with a sharp knife and peel its ends off the union **(see illustration 9.5)**.

● Resist the temptation to use grease or soap on the unions to aid installation; although it helps the hose slip over the union it will equally aid the escape of fluid from the joint. It is preferable to soften the hose ends in hot water and wet the inside surface of the hose with water or a fluid which will evaporate.

9.5 Cutting a coolant hose free with a sharp knife

Security

Introduction

In less time than it takes to read this introduction, a thief could steal your motorcycle. Returning only to find your bike has gone is one of the worst feelings in the world. Even if the motorcycle is insured against theft, once you've got over the initial shock, you will have the inconvenience of dealing with the police and your insurance company.

The motorcycle is an easy target for the professional thief and the joyrider alike and the official figures on motorcycle theft make for depressing reading; on average a motor-cycle is stolen every 16 minutes in the UK!

Motorcycle thefts fall into two categories, those stolen 'to order' and those taken by opportunists. The thief stealing to order will be on the look out for a specific make and model and will go to extraordinary lengths to obtain that motorcycle. The opportunist thief on the other hand will look for easy targets which can be stolen with the minimum of effort and risk.

Whilst it is never going to be possible to make your machine 100% secure, it is estimated that around half of all stolen motorcycles are taken by opportunist thieves. Remember that the opportunist thief is always on the look out for the easy option: if there are two similar motorcycles parked side-by-side, they will target the one with the lowest level of security. By taking a few precautions, you can reduce the chances of your motorcycle being stolen.

Security equipment

There are many specialised motorcycle security devices available and the following text summarises their applications and their good and bad points.

Once you have decided on the type of security equipment which best suits your needs, we recommended that you read one of the many equipment tests regularly carried out by the motorcycle press. These tests compare the products from all the major manufacturers and give impartial ratings on their effectiveness, value-for-money and ease of use.

No one item of security equipment can provide complete protection. It is highly recommended that two or more of the items described below are combined to increase the security of your motorcycle (a lock and chain plus an alarm system is just about ideal). The more security measures fitted to the bike, the less likely it is to be stolen.

Lock and chain

Pros: Very flexible to use; can be used to secure the motorcycle to almost any immovable object. On some locks and chains, the lock can be used on its own as a disc lock (see below).

Cons: Can be very heavy and awkward to carry on the motorcycle, although some types will be supplied with a carry bag which can be strapped to the pillion seat.

- Heavy-duty chains and locks are an excellent security measure **(see illustration 1).** Whenever the motorcycle is parked, use the lock and chain to secure the machine to a solid, immovable object such as a post or railings. This will prevent the machine from being ridden away or being lifted into the back of a van.

- When fitting the chain, always ensure the chain is routed around the motorcycle frame or swingarm **(see illustrations 2 and 3).** Never merely pass the chain around one of the wheel rims; a thief may unbolt the wheel and lift the rest of the machine into a van, leaving you with just the wheel! Try to avoid having excess chain free, thus making it difficult to use cutting tools, and keep the chain and lock off the ground to prevent thieves attacking it with a cold chisel. Position the lock so that its lock barrel is facing downwards; this will make it harder for the thief to attack the lock mechanism.

1 Ensure the lock and chain you buy is of good quality and long enough to shackle your bike to a solid object

2 Pass the chain through the bike's frame, rather than just through a wheel . . .

3 . . . and loop it around a solid object

Security REF•21

U-locks

Pros: *Highly effective deterrent which can be used to secure the bike to a post or railings. Most U-locks come with a carrier which allows the lock to be easily carried on the bike.*

Cons: *Not as flexible to use as a lock and chain.*

- These are solid locks which are similar in use to a lock and chain. U-locks are lighter than a lock and chain but not so flexible to use. The length and shape of the lock shackle limit the objects to which the bike can be secured **(see illustration 4)**.

Disc locks

Pros: *Small, light and very easy to carry; most can be stored underneath the seat.*

Cons: *Does not prevent the motorcycle being lifted into a van. Can be very embarrassing if you forget to remove the lock before attempting to ride off!*

- Disc locks are designed to be attached to the front brake disc. The lock passes through one of the holes in the disc and prevents the wheel rotating by jamming against the fork/brake caliper **(see illustration 5)**. Some are equipped with an alarm siren which sounds if the disc lock is moved; this not only acts as a theft deterrent but also as a handy reminder if you try to move the bike with the lock still fitted.

- Combining the disc lock with a length of cable which can be looped around a post or railings provides an additional measure of security **(see illustration 6)**.

Alarms and immobilisers

Pros: *Once installed it is completely hassle-free to use. If the system is 'Thatcham' or 'Sold Secure-approved', insurance companies may give you a discount.*

Cons: *Can be expensive to buy and complex to install. No system will prevent the motorcycle from being lifted into a van and taken away.*

- Electronic alarms and immobilisers are available to suit a variety of budgets. There are three different types of system available: pure alarms, pure immobilisers, and the more expensive systems which are combined alarm/immobilisers **(see illustration 7)**.
- An alarm system is designed to emit an audible warning if the motorcycle is being tampered with.
- An immobiliser prevents the motorcycle being started and ridden away by disabling its electrical systems.
- When purchasing an alarm/immobiliser system, check the cost of installing the system unless you are able to do it yourself. If the motorcycle is not used regularly, another consideration is the current drain of the system. All alarm/immobiliser systems are powered by the motorcycle's battery; purchasing a system with a very low current drain could prevent the battery losing its charge whilst the motorcycle is not being used.

U-locks can be used to secure the bike to a solid object – ensure you purchase one which is long enough

A typical disc lock attached through one of the holes in the disc

A disc lock combined with a security cable provides additional protection

A typical alarm/immobiliser system

REF•22 Security

Indelible markings can be applied to most areas of the bike – always apply the manufacturer's sticker to warn off thieves

Chemically-etched code numbers can be applied to main body panels . . .

. . . again, always ensure that the kit manufacturer's sticker is applied in a prominent position

Security marking kits

Pros: Very cheap and effective deterrent. Many insurance companies will give you a discount on your insurance premium if a recognised security marking kit is used on your motorcycle.

Cons: Does not prevent the motorcycle being stolen by joyriders.

- There are many different types of security marking kits available. The idea is to mark as many parts of the motorcycle as possible with a unique security number **(see illustrations 8, 9 and 10)**. A form will be included with the kit to register your personal details and those of the motorcycle with the kit manufacturer. This register is made available to the police to help them trace the rightful owner of any motorcycle or components which they recover should all other forms of identification have been removed. Always apply the warning stickers provided with the kit to deter thieves.

Ground anchors, wheel clamps and security posts

Pros: An excellent form of security which will deter all but the most determined of thieves.

Cons: Awkward to install and can be expensive.

- Whilst the motorcycle is at home, it is a good idea to attach it securely to the floor or a solid wall, even if it is kept in a securely locked garage. Various types of ground anchors, security posts and wheel clamps are available for this purpose **(see illustration 11)**. These security devices are either bolted to a solid concrete or brick structure or can be cemented into the ground.

Permanent ground anchors provide an excellent level of security when the bike is at home

Security at home

A high percentage of motorcycle thefts are from the owner's home. Here are some things to consider whenever your motorcycle is at home:

- Where possible, always keep the motorcycle in a securely locked garage. Never rely solely on the standard lock on the garage door, these are usual hopelessly inadequate. Fit an additional locking mechanism to the door and consider having the garage alarmed. A security light, activated by a movement sensor, is also a good investment.
- Always secure the motorcycle to the ground or a wall, even if it is inside a securely locked garage.
- Do not regularly leave the motorcycle outside your home, try to keep it out of sight wherever possible. If a garage is not available, fit a motorcycle cover over the bike to disguise its true identity.
- It is not uncommon for thieves to follow a motorcyclist home to find out where the bike is kept. They will then return at a later date. Be aware of this whenever you are returning home on your motorcycle. If you suspect you are being followed, do not return home, instead ride to a garage or shop and stop as a precaution.
- When selling a motorcycle, do not provide your home address or the location where the bike is normally kept. Arrange to meet the buyer at a location away from your home. Thieves have been known to pose as potential buyers to find out where motorcycles are kept and then return later to steal them.

Security away from the home

As well as fitting security equipment to your motorcycle here are a few general rules to follow whenever you park your motorcycle.
- Park in a busy, public place.
- Use car parks which incorporate security features, such as CCTV.
- At night, park in a well-lit area, preferably directly underneath a street light.
- Engage the steering lock.
- Secure the motorcycle to a solid, immovable object such as a post or railings with an additional lock. If this is not possible, secure the bike to a friend's motorcycle. Some public parking places provide security loops for motorcycles.
- Never leave your helmet or luggage attached to the motorcycle. Take them with you at all times.

Lubricants and fluids

A wide range of lubricants, fluids and cleaning agents is available for motor-cycles. This is a guide as to what is available, its applications and properties.

Four-stroke engine oil

● Engine oil is without doubt the most important component of any four-stroke engine. Modern motorcycle engines place a lot of demands on their oil and choosing the right type is essential. Using an unsuitable oil will lead to an increased rate of engine wear and could result in serious engine damage. Before purchasing oil, always check the recommended oil specification given by the manufacturer. The manufacturer will state a recommended 'type or classification' and also a specific 'viscosity' range for engine oil.

● The oil 'type or classification' is identified by its API (American Petroleum Institute) rating. The API rating will be in the form of two letters, e.g. SG. The S identifies the oil as being suitable for use in a petrol (gasoline) engine (S stands for spark ignition) and the second letter, ranging from A to J, identifies the oil's performance rating. The later this letter, the higher the specification of the oil; for example API SG oil exceeds the requirements of API SF oil. **Note:** *On some oils there may also be a second rating consisting of another two letters, the first letter being C, e.g. API SF/CD. This rating indicates the oil is also suitable for use in a diesel engines (the C stands for compression ignition) and is thus of no relevance for motorcycle use.*

● The 'viscosity' of the oil is identified by its SAE (Society of Automotive Engineers) rating. All modern engines require multigrade oils and the SAE rating will consist of two numbers, the first followed by a W, e.g. 10W/40. The first number indicates the viscosity rating of the oil at low temperatures (W stands for winter – tested at –20°C) and the second number represents the viscosity of the oil at high temperatures (tested at 100°C). The lower the number, the thinner the oil. For example an oil with an SAE 10W/40 rating will give better cold starting and running than an SAE 15W/40 oil.

● As well as ensuring the 'type' and 'viscosity' of the oil match the recommendations, another consideration to make when buying engine oil is whether to purchase a standard mineral-based oil, a semi-synthetic oil (also known as a synthetic blend or synthetic-based oil) or a fully-synthetic oil. Although all oils will have a similar rating and viscosity, their cost will vary considerably; mineral-based oils are the cheapest, the fully-synthetic oils the most expensive with the semi-synthetic oils falling somewhere in-between. This decision is very much up to the owner, but it should be noted that modern synthetic oils have far better lubricating and cleaning qualities than traditional mineral-based oils and tend to retain these properties for far longer. Bearing in mind the operating conditions inside a modern, high-revving motorcycle engine it is highly recommended that a fully synthetic oil is used. The extra expense at each service could save you money in the long term by preventing premature engine wear.

● As a final note always ensure that the oil is specifically designed for use in motorcycle engines. Engine oils designed primarily for use in car engines sometimes contain additives or friction modifiers which could cause clutch slip on a motorcycle fitted with a wet-clutch.

Two-stroke engine oil

● Modern two-stroke engines, with their high power outputs, place high demands on their oil. If engine seizure is to be avoided it is essential that a high-quality oil is used. Two-stroke oils differ hugely from four-stroke oils. The oil lubricates only the crankshaft and piston(s) (the transmission has its own lubricating oil) and is used on a total-loss basis where it is burnt completely during the combustion process.

● The Japanese have recently introduced a classification system for two-stroke oils, the JASO rating. This rating is in the form of two letters, either FA, FB or FC – FA is the lowest classification and FC the highest. Ensure the oil being used meets or exceeds the recommended rating specified by the manufacturer.

● As well as ensuring the oil rating matches the recommendation, another consideration to make when buying engine oil is whether to purchase a standard mineral-based oil, a semi-synthetic oil (also known as a synthetic blend or synthetic-based oil) or a fully-synthetic oil. The cost of each type of oil varies considerably; mineral-based oils are the cheapest, the fully-synthetic oils the most expensive with the semi-synthetic oils falling somewhere in-between. This decision is very much up to the owner, but it should be noted that modern synthetic oils have far better lubricating properties and burn cleaner than traditional mineral-based oils. It is therefore recommended that a fully synthetic oil is used. The extra expense could save you money in the long term by preventing premature engine wear, engine performance will be improved, carbon deposits and exhaust smoke will be reduced.

Lubricants and fluids

● Always ensure that the oil is specifically designed for use in an injector system. Many high quality two-stroke oils are designed for competition use and need to be pre-mixed with fuel. These oils are of a much higher viscosity and are not designed to flow through the injector pumps used on road-going two-stroke motorcycles.

Transmission (gear) oil

● On a two-stroke engine, the transmission and clutch are lubricated by their own separate oil bath which must be changed in accordance with the Maintenance Schedule.
● Although the engine and transmission units of most four-strokes use a common lubrication supply, there are some exceptions where the engine and gearbox have separate oil reservoirs and a dry clutch is used.
● Motorcycle manufacturers will either recommend a monograde transmission oil or a four-stroke multigrade engine oil to lubricate the transmission.
● Transmission oils, or gear oils as they are often called, are designed specifically for use in transmission systems. The viscosity of these oils is represented by an SAE number, but the scale of measurement applied is different to that used to grade engine oils. As a rough guide a SAE90 gear oil will be of the same viscosity as an SAE50 engine oil.

Shaft drive oil

● On models equipped with shaft final drive, the shaft drive gears are will have their own oil supply. The manufacturer will state a recommended 'type or classification' and also a specific 'viscosity' range in the same manner as for four-stroke engine oil.
● Gear oil classification is given by the number which follows the API GL (GL standing for gear lubricant) rating, the higher the number, the higher the specification of the oil, e.g. API GL5 oil is a higher specification than API GL4 oil. Ensure the oil meets or exceeds the classification specified and is of the correct viscosity. The viscosity of gear oils is also represented by an SAE number but the scale of measurement used is different to that used to grade engine oils. As a rough guide an SAE90 gear oil will be of the same viscosity as an SAE50 engine oil.
● If the use of an EP (Extreme Pressure) gear oil is specified, ensure the oil purchased is suitable.

Fork oil and suspension fluid

● Conventional telescopic front forks are hydraulic and require fork oil to work. To ensure the forks function correctly, the fork oil must be changed in accordance with the Maintenance Schedule.
● Fork oil is available in a variety of viscosities, identified by their SAE rating; fork oil ratings vary from light (SAE 5) to heavy (SAE 30). When purchasing fork oil, ensure the viscosity rating matches that specified by the manufacturer.
● Some lubricant manufacturers also produce a range of high-quality suspension fluids which are very similar to fork oil but are designed mainly for competition use. These fluids may have a different viscosity rating system which is not to be confused with the SAE rating of normal fork oil. Refer to the manufacturer's instructions if in any doubt.

Brake and clutch fluid

● All disc brake systems and some clutch systems are hydraulically operated. To ensure correct operation, the hydraulic fluid must be changed in accordance with the Maintenance Schedule.
● Brake and clutch fluid is classified by its DOT rating with most motorcycle manufacturers specifying DOT 3 or 4 fluid. Both fluid types are glycol-based and can be mixed together without adverse effect; DOT 4 fluid exceeds the requirements of DOT 3 fluid. Although it is safe to use DOT 4 fluid in a system designed for use with DOT 3 fluid, never use DOT 3 fluid in a system which specifies the use of DOT 4 as this will adversely affect the system's performance. The type required for the system will be marked on the fluid reservoir cap.
● Some manufacturers also produce a DOT 5 hydraulic fluid. DOT 5 hydraulic fluid is silicone-based and is not compatible with the glycol-based DOT 3 and 4 fluids. Never mix DOT 5 fluid with DOT 3 or 4 fluid as this will seriously affect the performance of the hydraulic system.

Coolant/antifreeze

● When purchasing coolant/antifreeze, always ensure it is suitable for use in an aluminium engine and contains corrosion inhibitors to prevent possible blockages of the internal coolant passages of the system. As a general rule, most coolants are designed to be used neat and should not be diluted whereas antifreeze can be mixed with distilled water to provide a coolant solution of the required strength. Refer to the manufacturer's instructions on the bottle.
● Ensure the coolant is changed in accordance with the Maintenance Schedule.

Chain lube

● Chain lube is an aerosol-type spray lubricant specifically designed for use on motorcycle final drive chains. Chain lube has two functions, to minimise friction between the final drive chain and sprockets and to prevent corrosion of the chain. Regular use of a good-quality chain lube will extend the life of the drive chain and sprockets and thus maximise the power being transmitted from the transmission to the rear wheel.
● When using chain lube, always allow some time for the solvents in the lube to evaporate before riding the motorcycle. This will minimise the amount of lube which will

Lubricants and fluids REF•25

'fling' off from the chain when the motorcycle is used. If the motorcycle is equipped with an 'O-ring' chain, ensure the chain lube is labelled as being suitable for use on 'O-ring' chains.

Degreasers and solvents

● There are many different types of solvents and degreasers available to remove the grime and grease which accumulate around the motorcycle during normal use. Degreasers and solvents are usually available as an aerosol-type spray or as a liquid which you apply with a brush. Always closely follow the manufacturer's instructions and wear eye protection during use. Be aware that many solvents are flammable and may give off noxious fumes; take adequate precautions when using them (see Safety First!).

● For general cleaning, use one of the many solvents or degreasers available from most motorcycle accessory shops. These solvents are usually applied then left for a certain time before being washed off with water.

Brake cleaner is a solvent specifically designed to remove all traces of oil, grease and dust from braking system components. Brake cleaner is designed to evaporate quickly and leaves behind no residue.

Carburettor cleaner is an aerosol-type solvent specifically designed to clear carburettor blockages and break down the hard deposits and gum often found inside carburettors during overhaul.

Contact cleaner is an aerosol-type solvent designed for cleaning electrical components. The cleaner will remove all traces of oil and dirt from components such as switch contacts or fouled spark plugs and then dry, leaving behind no residue.

Gasket remover is an aerosol-type solvent designed for removing stubborn gaskets from engine components during overhaul. Gasket remover will minimise the amount of scraping required to remove the gasket and therefore reduce the risk of damage to the mating surface.

Spray lubricants

● Aerosol-based spray lubricants are widely available and are excellent for lubricating lever pivots and exposed cables and switches. Try to use a lubricant which is of the dry-film type as the fluid evaporates, leaving behind a dry-film of lubricant. Lubricants which leave behind an oily residue will attract dust and dirt which will increase the rate of wear of the cable/lever.

● Most lubricants also act as a moisture dispersant and a penetrating fluid. This means they can also be used to 'dry out' electrical components such as wiring connectors or switches as well as helping to free seized fasteners.

Greases

● Grease is used to lubricate many of the pivot-points. A good-quality multi-purpose grease is suitable for most applications but some manufacturers will specify the use of specialist greases for use on components such as swingarm and suspension linkage bushes. These specialist greases can be purchased from most motorcycle (or car) accessory shops; commonly specified types include molybdenum disulphide grease, lithium-based grease, graphite-based grease, silicone-based grease and high-temperature copper-based grease.

Gasket sealing compounds

● Gasket sealing compounds can be used in conjunction with gaskets, to improve their sealing capabilities, or on their own to seal metal-to-metal joints. Depending on their type, sealing compounds either set hard or stay relatively soft and pliable.

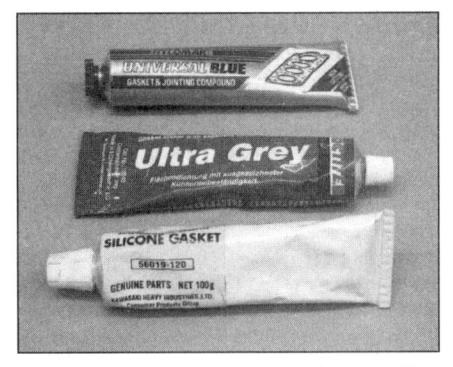

● When purchasing a gasket sealing compound, ensure that it is designed specifically for use on an internal combustion engine. General multi-purpose sealants available from DIY stores may appear visibly similar but they are not designed to withstand the extreme heat or contact with fuel and oil encountered when used on an engine (see 'Tools and Workshop Tips' for further information).

Thread locking compound

● Thread locking compounds are used to secure certain threaded fasteners in position to prevent them from loosening due to vibration. Thread locking compounds can be purchased from most motorcycle (and car) accessory shops. Ensure the threads of the both components are completely clean and dry before sparingly applying the locking compound (see 'Tools and Workshop Tips' for further information).

Fuel additives

● Fuel additives which protect and clean the fuel system components are widely available. These additives are designed to remove all traces of deposits that build up on the carburettors/injectors and prevent wear, helping the fuel system to operate more efficiently. If a fuel additive is being used, check that it is suitable for use with your motorcycle, especially if your motorcycle is equipped with a catalytic converter.

● Octane boosters are also available. These additives are designed to improve the performance of highly-tuned engines being run on normal pump-fuel and are of no real use on standard motorcycles.

REF•26 Conversion factors

Length (distance)
Inches (in)	x 25.4	= Millimetres (mm)	x 0.0394	= Inches (in)
Feet (ft)	x 0.305	= Metres (m)	x 3.281	= Feet (ft)
Miles	x 1.609	= Kilometres (km)	x 0.621	= Miles

Volume (capacity)
Cubic inches (cu in; in^3)	x 16.387	= Cubic centimetres (cc; cm^3)	x 0.061	= Cubic inches (cu in; in^3)
Imperial pints (Imp pt)	x 0.568	= Litres (l)	x 1.76	= Imperial pints (Imp pt)
Imperial quarts (Imp qt)	x 1.137	= Litres (l)	x 0.88	= Imperial quarts (Imp qt)
Imperial quarts (Imp qt)	x 1.201	= US quarts (US qt)	x 0.833	= Imperial quarts (Imp qt)
US quarts (US qt)	x 0.946	= Litres (l)	x 1.057	= US quarts (US qt)
Imperial gallons (Imp gal)	x 4.546	= Litres (l)	x 0.22	= Imperial gallons (Imp gal)
Imperial gallons (Imp gal)	x 1.201	= US gallons (US gal)	x 0.833	= Imperial gallons (Imp gal)
US gallons (US gal)	x 3.785	= Litres (l)	x 0.264	= US gallons (US gal)

Mass (weight)
Ounces (oz)	x 28.35	= Grams (g)	x 0.035	= Ounces (oz)
Pounds (lb)	x 0.454	= Kilograms (kg)	x 2.205	= Pounds (lb)

Force
Ounces-force (ozf; oz)	x 0.278	= Newtons (N)	x 3.6	= Ounces-force (ozf; oz)
Pounds-force (lbf; lb)	x 4.448	= Newtons (N)	x 0.225	= Pounds-force (lbf; lb)
Newtons (N)	x 0.1	= Kilograms-force (kgf; kg)	x 9.81	= Newtons (N)

Pressure
Pounds-force per square inch (psi; lbf/in^2; lb/in^2)	x 0.070	= Kilograms-force per square centimetre (kgf/cm^2; kg/cm^2)	x 14.223	= Pounds-force per square inch (psi; lbf/in^2; lb/in^2)
Pounds-force per square inch (psi; lbf/in^2; lb/in^2)	x 0.068	= Atmospheres (atm)	x 14.696	= Pounds-force per square inch (psi; lbf/in^2; lb/in^2)
Pounds-force per square inch (psi; lbf/in^2; lb/in^2)	x 0.069	= Bars	x 14.5	= Pounds-force per square inch (psi; lbf/in^2; lb/in^2)
Pounds-force per square inch (psi; lbf/in^2; lb/in^2)	x 6.895	= Kilopascals (kPa)	x 0.145	= Pounds-force per square inch (psi; lbf/in^2; lb/in^2)
Kilopascals (kPa)	x 0.01	= Kilograms-force per square centimetre (kgf/cm^2; kg/cm^2)	x 98.1	= Kilopascals (kPa)
Millibar (mbar)	x 100	= Pascals (Pa)	x 0.01	= Millibar (mbar)
Millibar (mbar)	x 0.0145	= Pounds-force per square inch (psi; lbf/in^2; lb/in^2)	x 68.947	= Millibar (mbar)
Millibar (mbar)	x 0.75	= Millimetres of mercury (mmHg)	x 1.333	= Millibar (mbar)
Millibar (mbar)	x 0.401	= Inches of water (inH$_2$O)	x 2.491	= Millibar (mbar)
Millimetres of mercury (mmHg)	x 0.535	= Inches of water (inH$_2$O)	x 1.868	= Millimetres of mercury (mmHg)
Inches of water (inH$_2$O)	x 0.036	= Pounds-force per square inch (psi; lbf/in^2; lb/in^2)	x 27.68	= Inches of water (inH$_2$O)

Torque (moment of force)
Pounds-force inches (lbf in; lb in)	x 1.152	= Kilograms-force centimetre (kgf cm; kg cm)	x 0.868	= Pounds-force inches (lbf in; lb in)
Pounds-force inches (lbf in; lb in)	x 0.113	= Newton metres (Nm)	x 8.85	= Pounds-force inches (lbf in; lb in)
Pounds-force inches (lbf in; lb in)	x 0.083	= Pounds-force feet (lbf ft; lb ft)	x 12	= Pounds-force inches (lbf in; lb in)
Pounds-force feet (lbf ft; lb ft)	x 0.138	= Kilograms-force metres (kgf m; kg m)	x 7.233	= Pounds-force feet (lbf ft; lb ft)
Pounds-force feet (lbf ft; lb ft)	x 1.356	= Newton metres (Nm)	x 0.738	= Pounds-force feet (lbf ft; lb ft)
Newton metres (Nm)	x 0.102	= Kilograms-force metres (kgf m; kg m)	x 9.804	= Newton metres (Nm)

Power
Horsepower (hp)	x 745.7	= Watts (W)	x 0.0013	= Horsepower (hp)

Velocity (speed)
Miles per hour (miles/hr; mph)	x 1.609	= Kilometres per hour (km/hr; kph)	x 0.621	= Miles per hour (miles/hr; mph)

Fuel consumption*
Miles per gallon, Imperial (mpg)	x 0.354	= Kilometres per litre (km/l)	x 2.825	= Miles per gallon, Imperial (mpg)
Miles per gallon, US (mpg)	x 0.425	= Kilometres per litre (km/l)	x 2.352	= Miles per gallon, US (mpg)

Temperature
Degrees Fahrenheit = (°C x 1.8) + 32   Degrees Celsius (Degrees Centigrade; °C) = (°F - 32) x 0.56

It is common practice to convert from miles per gallon (mpg) to litres/100 kilometres (l/100km), where mpg x l/100 km = 282

MOT Test Checks REF•27

About the MOT Test

In the UK, all vehicles more than three years old are subject to an annual test to ensure that they meet minimum safety requirements. A current test certificate must be issued before a machine can be used on public roads, and is required before a road fund licence can be issued. Riding without a current test certificate will also invalidate your insurance.

For most owners, the MOT test is an annual cause for anxiety, and this is largely due to owners not being sure what needs to be checked prior to submitting the motorcycle for testing. The simple answer is that a fully roadworthy motorcycle will have no difficulty in passing the test.

This is a guide to getting your motorcycle through the MOT test. Obviously it will not be possible to examine the motorcycle to the same standard as the professional MOT tester, particularly in view of the equipment required for some of the checks. However, working through the following procedures will enable you to identify any problem areas before submitting the motorcycle for the test.

It has only been possible to summarise the test requirements here, based on the regulations in force at the time of printing. Test standards are becoming increasingly stringent, although there are some exemptions for older vehicles. More information about the MOT test can be obtained from the TSO publications, *How Safe is your Motorcycle* and *The MOT Inspection Manual for Motorcycle Testing*.

Many of the checks require that one of the wheels is raised off the ground. If the motorcycle doesn't have a centre stand, note that an auxiliary stand will be required. Additionally, the help of an assistant may prove useful.

Certain exceptions apply to machines under 50 cc, machines without a lighting system, and Classic bikes - if in doubt about any of the requirements listed below seek confirmation from an MOT tester prior to submitting the motorcycle for the test.

Check that the frame number is clearly visible.

Electrical System

Lights, turn signals, horn and reflector

● With the ignition on, check the operation of the following electrical components. **Note:** *The electrical components on certain small-capacity machines are powered by the generator, requiring that the engine is run for this check.*

a) *Headlight and tail light. Check that both illuminate in the low and high beam switch positions.*
b) *Position lights. Check that the front position (or sidelight) and tail light illuminate in this switch position.*
c) *Turn signals. Check that all flash at the correct rate, and that the warning light(s) function correctly. Check that the turn signal switch works correctly.*
d) *Hazard warning system (where fitted). Check that all four turn signals flash in this switch position.*
e) *Brake stop light. Check that the light comes on when the front and rear brakes are independently applied. Models first used on or after 1st April 1986 must have a brake light switch on each brake.*
f) *Horn. Check that the sound is continuous and of reasonable volume.*

● Check that there is a red reflector on the rear of the machine, either mounted separately or as part of the tail light lens.
● Check the condition of the headlight, tail light and turn signal lenses.

Headlight beam height

● The MOT tester will perform a headlight beam height check using specialised beam setting equipment **(see illustration 1)**. This equipment will not be available to the home mechanic, but if you suspect that the headlight is incorrectly set or may have been maladjusted in the past, you can perform a rough test as follows.

● Position the bike in a straight line facing a brick wall. The bike must be off its stand, upright and with a rider seated. Measure the height from the ground to the centre of the headlight and mark a horizontal line on the wall at this height. Position the motorcycle 3.8 metres from the wall and draw a vertical line up the wall central to the centreline of the motorcycle. Switch to dipped beam and check that the beam pattern falls slightly lower than the horizontal line and to the left of the vertical line **(see illustration 2)**.

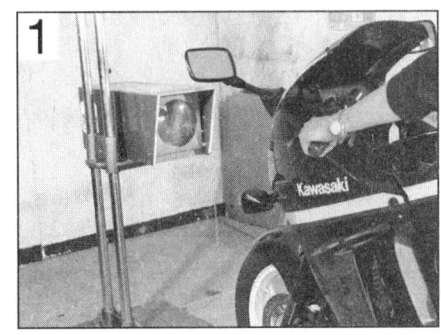

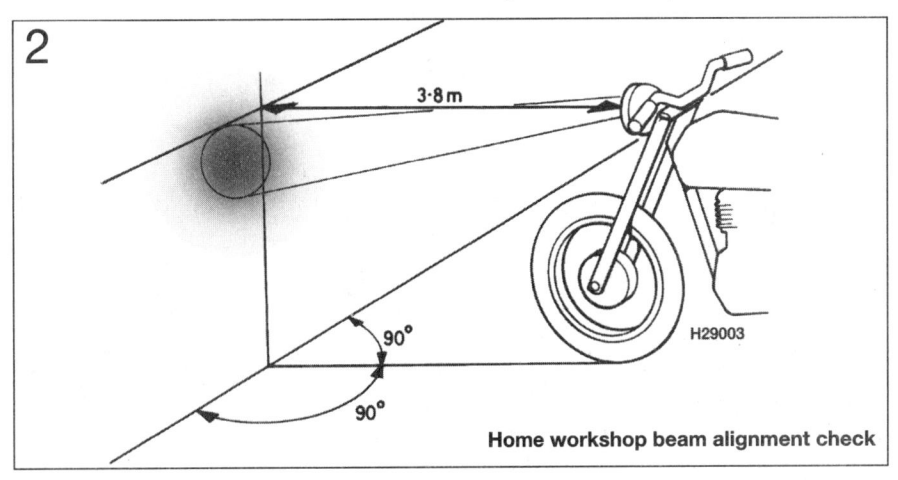

Headlight beam height checking equipment

Home workshop beam alignment check

MOT Test Checks

Exhaust System and Final Drive

Exhaust

- Check that the exhaust mountings are secure and that the system does not foul any of the rear suspension components.
- Start the motorcycle. When the revs are increased, check that the exhaust is neither holed nor leaking from any of its joints. On a linked system, check that the collector box is not leaking due to corrosion.
- Note that the exhaust decibel level ("loudness" of the exhaust) is assessed at the discretion of the tester. If the motorcycle was first used on or after 1st January 1985 the silencer must carry the BSAU 193 stamp, or a marking relating to its make and model, or be of OE (original equipment) manufacture. If the silencer is marked NOT FOR ROAD USE, RACING USE ONLY or similar, it will fail the MOT.

Final drive

- On chain or belt drive machines, check that the chain/belt is in good condition and does not have excessive slack. Also check that the sprocket is securely mounted on the rear wheel hub. Check that the chain/belt guard is in place.
- On shaft drive bikes, check for oil leaking from the drive unit and fouling the rear tyre.

Steering and Suspension

Steering

- With the front wheel raised off the ground, rotate the steering from lock to lock. The handlebar or switches must not contact the fuel tank or be close enough to trap the rider's hand. Problems can be caused by damaged lock stops on the lower yoke and frame, or by the fitting of non-standard handlebars.
- When performing the lock to lock check, also ensure that the steering moves freely without drag or notchiness. Steering movement can be impaired by poorly routed cables, or by overtight head bearings or worn bvearings. The tester will perform a check of the steering head bearing lower race by mounting the front wheel on a surface plate, then performing a lock to lock check with the weight of the machine on the lower bearing (see illustration 3).
- Grasp the fork sliders (lower legs) and attempt to push and pull on the forks

Front wheel mounted on a surface plate for steering head bearing lower race check

(see illustration 4). Any play in the steering head bearings will be felt. Note that in extreme cases, wear of the front fork bushes can be misinterpreted for head bearing play.
- Check that the handlebars are securely mounted.
- Check that the handlebar grip rubbers are secure. They should by bonded to the bar left end and to the throttle cable pulley on the right end.

Front suspension

- With the motorcycle off the stand, hold the front brake on and pump the front forks up and down (see illustration 5). Check that they are adequately damped.

Checking the steering head bearings for freeplay

Hold the front brake on and pump the front forks up and down to check operation

MOT Test Checks REF•29

Inspect the area around the fork dust seal for oil leakage (arrow)

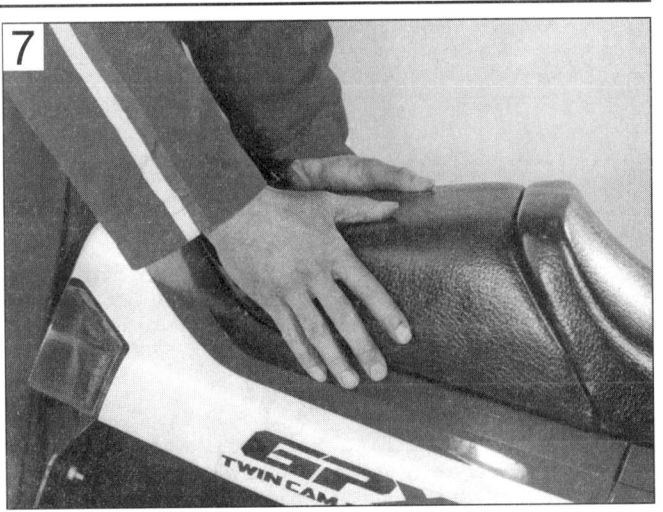

Bounce the rear of the motorcycle to check rear suspension operation

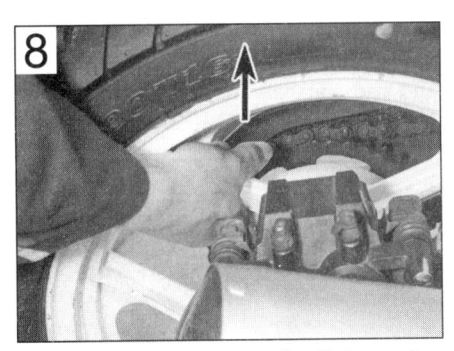

Checking for rear suspension linkage play

- Inspect the area above and around the front fork oil seals **(see illustration 6)**. There should be no sign of oil on the fork tube (stanchion) nor leaking down the slider (lower leg). On models so equipped, check that there is no oil leaking from the anti-dive units.
- On models with swingarm front suspension, check that there is no freeplay in the linkage when moved from side to side.

Rear suspension

- With the motorcycle off the stand and an assistant supporting the motorcycle by its handlebars, bounce the rear suspension **(see illustration 7)**. Check that the suspension components do not foul on any of the cycle parts and check that the shock absorber(s) provide adequate damping.
- Visually inspect the shock absorber(s) and check that there is no sign of oil leakage from its damper. This is somewhat restricted on certain single shock models due to the location of the shock absorber.
- With the rear wheel raised off the ground, grasp the wheel at the highest point and attempt to pull it up **(see illustration 8)**. Any play in the swingarm pivot or suspension linkage bearings will be felt as movement. **Note:** *Do not confuse play with actual suspension movement.* Failure to lubricate suspension linkage bearings can lead to bearing failure **(see illustration 9)**.
- With the rear wheel raised off the ground, grasp the swingarm ends and attempt to move the swingarm from side to side and forwards and backwards - any play indicates wear of the swingarm pivot bearings **(see illustration 10)**.

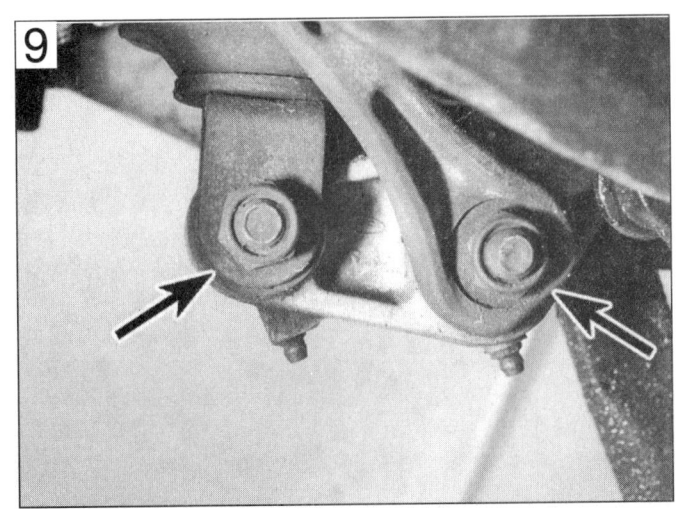

Worn suspension linkage pivots (arrows) are usually the cause of play in the rear suspension

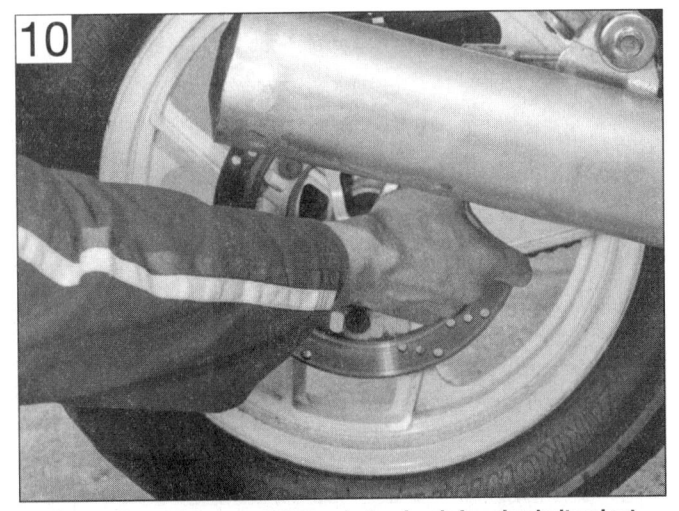

Grasp the swingarm at the ends to check for play in its pivot bearings

REF•30 MOT Test Checks

Brake pad wear can usually be viewed without removing the caliper. Most pads have wear indicator grooves (arrowed) and some also have indicator tangs or cut-outs.

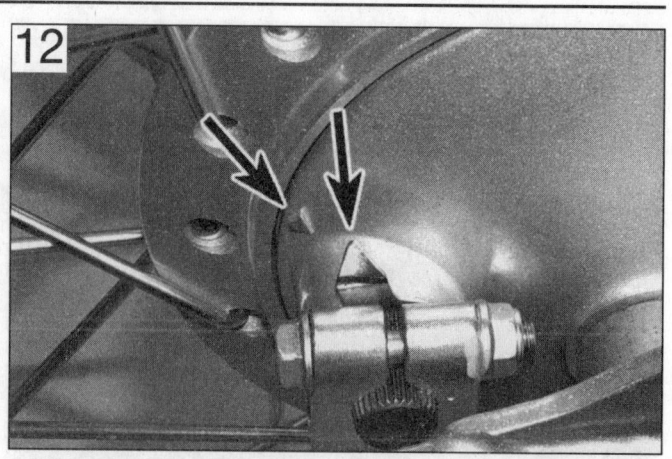

On drum brakes, check the angle of the operating lever with the brake fully applied. Most drum brakes have a wear indicator pointer or scale.

Brakes, Wheels and Tyres

Brakes

- With the wheel raised off the ground, apply the brake then free it off, and check that the wheel is about to revolve freely without brake drag.
- On disc brakes, examine the disc itself. Check that it is securely mounted and not cracked.
- On disc brakes, view the pad material through the caliper mouth and check that the pads are not worn down beyond the limit **(see illustration 11)**.
- On drum brakes, check that when the brake is applied the angle between the operating lever and cable or rod is not too great **(see illustration 12)**. Check also that the operating lever doesn't foul any other components.
- On disc brakes, examine the flexible hoses from top to bottom. Have an assistant hold the brake on so that the fluid in the hose is under pressure, and check that there is no sign of fluid leakage, bulges or cracking. If there are any metal brake pipes or unions, check that these are free from corrosion and damage. Where a brake-linked anti-dive system is fitted, check the hoses to the anti-dive in a similar manner.
- Check that the rear brake torque arm is secure and that its fasteners are secured by self-locking nuts or castellated nuts with split-pins or R-pins **(see illustration 13)**.
- On models with ABS, check that the self-check warning light in the instrument panel works.
- The MOT tester will perform a test of the motorcycle's braking efficiency based on a calculation of rider and motorcycle weight. Although this cannot be carried out at home, you can at least ensure that the braking systems are properly maintained. For hydraulic disc brakes, check the fluid level, lever/pedal feel (bleed of air if its spongy) and pad material. For drum brakes, check adjustment, cable or rod operation and shoe lining thickness.

Wheels and tyres

- Check the wheel condition. Cast wheels should be free from cracks and if of the built-up design, all fasteners should be secure. Spoked wheels should be checked for broken, corroded, loose or bent spokes.
- With the wheel raised off the ground, spin the wheel and visually check that the tyre and wheel run true. Check that the tyre does not foul the suspension or mudguards.
- With the wheel raised off the ground, grasp the wheel and attempt to move it about the axle (spindle) **(see illustration 14)**. Any play felt here indicates wheel bearing failure.

Brake torque arm must be properly secured at both ends

Check for wheel bearing play by trying to move the wheel about the axle (spindle)

MOT Test Checks REF•31

Checking the tyre tread depth

Tyre direction of rotation arrow can be found on tyre sidewall

Castellated type wheel axle (spindle) nut must be secured by a split pin or R-pin

Two straightedges are used to check wheel alignment

- Check the tyre tread depth, tread condition and sidewall condition (see illustration 15).
- Check the tyre type. Front and rear tyre types must be compatible and be suitable for road use. Tyres marked NOT FOR ROAD USE, COMPETITION USE ONLY or similar, will fail the MOT.
- If the tyre sidewall carries a direction of rotation arrow, this must be pointing in the direction of normal wheel rotation (see illustration 16).
- Check that the wheel axle (spindle) nuts (where applicable) are properly secured. A self-locking nut or castellated nut with a split-pin or R-pin can be used (see illustration 17).
- Wheel alignment is checked with the motorcycle off the stand and a rider seated. With the front wheel pointing straight ahead, two perfectly straight lengths of metal or wood and placed against the sidewalls of both tyres (see illustration 18). The gap each side of the front tyre must be equidistant on both sides. Incorrect wheel alignment may be due to a cocked rear wheel (often as the result of poor chain adjustment) or in extreme cases, a bent frame.

General checks and condition

- Check the security of all major fasteners, bodypanels, seat, fairings (where fitted) and mudguards.
- Check that the rider and pillion footrests, handlebar levers and brake pedal are securely mounted.
- Check for corrosion on the frame or any load-bearing components. If severe, this may affect the structure, particularly under stress.

Sidecars

A motorcycle fitted with a sidecar requires additional checks relating to the stability of the machine and security of attachment and swivel joints, plus specific wheel alignment (toe-in) requirements. Additionally, tyre and lighting requirements differ from conventional motorcycle use. Owners are advised to check MOT test requirements with an official test centre.

REF•32 Storage

Preparing for storage

Before you start

If repairs or an overhaul is needed, see that this is carried out now rather than left until you want to ride the bike again.

Give the bike a good wash and scrub all dirt from its underside. Make sure the bike dries completely before preparing for storage.

Engine

● Remove the spark plug(s) and lubricate the cylinder bores with approximately a teaspoon of motor oil using a spout-type oil can **(see illustration 1)**. Reinstall the spark plug(s). Crank the engine over a couple of times to coat the piston rings and bores with oil. If the bike has a kickstart, use this to turn the engine over. If not, flick the kill switch to the OFF position and crank the engine over on the starter **(see illustration 2)**. If the nature on the ignition system prevents the starter operating with the kill switch in the OFF position, remove the spark plugs and fit them back in their caps; ensure that the plugs are earthed (grounded) against the cylinder head when the starter is operated **(see illustration 3)**.

⚠️ **Warning: It is important that the plugs are earthed (grounded) away from the spark plug holes otherwise there is a risk of atomised fuel from the cylinders igniting.**

HAYNES HiNT *On a single cylinder four-stroke engine, you can seal the combustion chamber completely by positioning the piston at TDC on the compression stroke.*

● Drain the carburettor(s) otherwise there is a risk of jets becoming blocked by gum deposits from the fuel **(see illustration 4)**.

● If the bike is going into long-term storage, consider adding a fuel stabiliser to the fuel in the tank. If the tank is drained completely, corrosion of its internal surfaces may occur if left unprotected for a long period. The tank can be treated with a rust preventative especially for this purpose. Alternatively, remove the tank and pour half a litre of motor oil into it, install the filler cap and shake the tank to coat its internals with oil before draining off the excess. The same effect can also be achieved by spraying WD40 or a similar water-dispersant around the inside of the tank via its flexible nozzle.

● Make sure the cooling system contains the correct mix of antifreeze. Antifreeze also contains important corrosion inhibitors.

● The air intakes and exhaust can be sealed off by covering or plugging the openings. Ensure that you do not seal in any condensation; run the engine until it is hot,

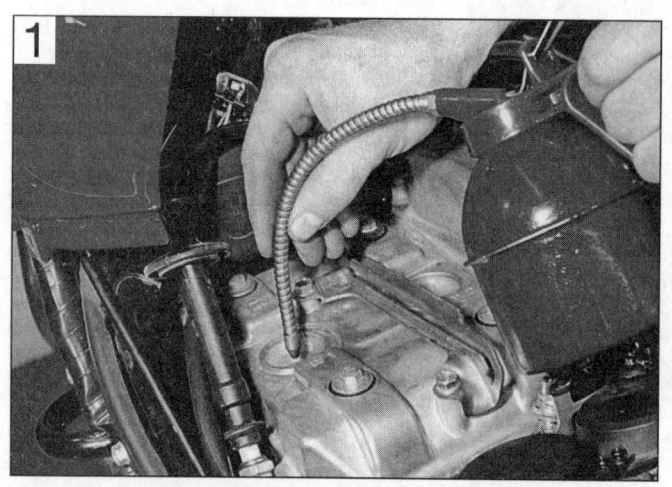

1 Squirt a drop of motor oil into each cylinder

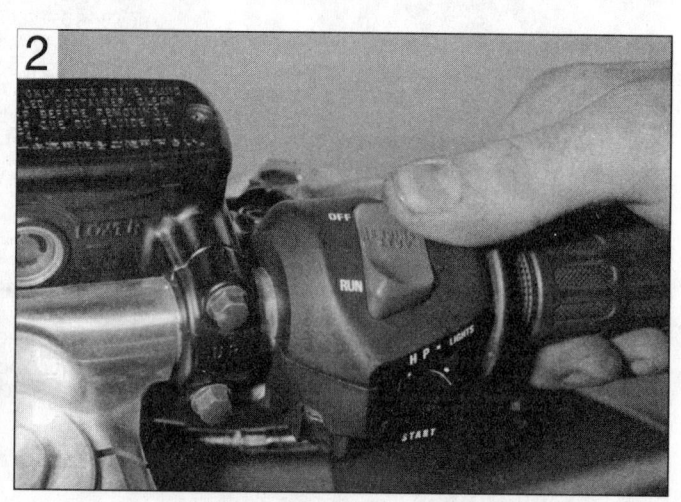

2 Flick the kill switch to OFF . . .

3 . . . and ensure that the metal bodies of the plugs (arrows) are earthed against the cylinder head

4 Connect a hose to the carburettor float chamber drain stub (arrow) and unscrew the drain screw

Storage   REF•33

Exhausts can be sealed off with a plastic bag

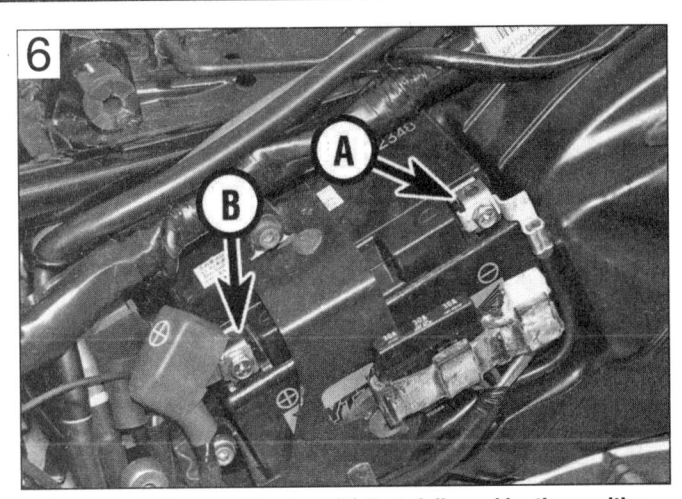

Disconnect the negative lead (A) first, followed by the positive lead (B)

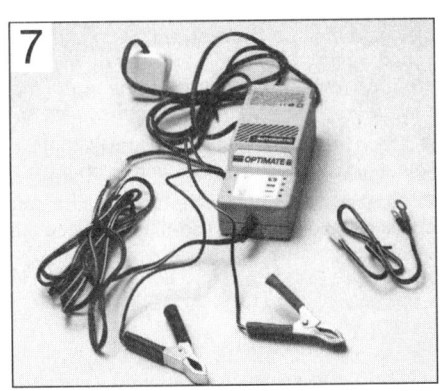

Use a suitable battery charger - this kit also assess battery condition

then switch off and allow to cool. Tape a piece of thick plastic over the silencer end(s) **(see illustration 5)**. Note that some advocate pouring a tablespoon of motor oil into the silencer(s) before sealing them off.

Battery

● Remove it from the bike - in extreme cases of cold the battery may freeze and crack its case **(see illustration 6)**.

● Check the electrolyte level and top up if necessary (conventional refillable batteries). Clean the terminals.
● Store the battery off the motorcycle and away from any sources of fire. Position a wooden block under the battery if it is to sit on the ground.
● Give the battery a trickle charge for a few hours every month **(see illustration 7)**.

Tyres

● Place the bike on its centrestand or an auxiliary stand which will support the motorcycle in an upright position. Position wood blocks under the tyres to keep them off the ground and to provide insulation from damp. If the bike is being put into long-term storage, ideally both tyres should be off the ground; not only will this protect the tyres, but will also ensure that no load is placed on the steering head or wheel bearings.
● Deflate each tyre by 5 to 10 psi, no more or the beads may unseat from the rim, making subsequent inflation difficult on tubeless tyres.

Pivots and controls

● Lubricate all lever, pedal, stand and footrest pivot points. If grease nipples are fitted to the rear suspension components, apply lubricant to the pivots.
● Lubricate all control cables.

Cycle components

● Apply a wax protectant to all painted and plastic components. Wipe off any excess, but don't polish to a shine. Where fitted, clean the screen with soap and water.
● Coat metal parts with Vaseline (petroleum jelly). When applying this to the fork tubes, do not compress the forks otherwise the seals will rot from contact with the Vaseline.
● Apply a vinyl cleaner to the seat.

Storage conditions

● Aim to store the bike in a shed or garage which does not leak and is free from damp.
● Drape an old blanket or bedspread over the bike to protect it from dust and direct contact with sunlight (which will fade paint). This also hides the bike from prying eyes. Beware of tight-fitting plastic covers which may allow condensation to form and settle on the bike.

Getting back on the road

Engine and transmission

● Change the oil and replace the oil filter. If this was done prior to storage, check that the oil hasn't emulsified - a thick whitish substance which occurs through condensation.
● Remove the spark plugs. Using a spout-type oil can, squirt a few drops of oil into the cylinder(s). This will provide initial lubrication as the piston rings and bores comes back into contact. Service the spark plugs, or fit new ones, and install them in the engine.

● Check that the clutch isn't stuck on. The plates can stick together if left standing for some time, preventing clutch operation. Engage a gear and try rocking the bike back and forth with the clutch lever held against the handlebar. If this doesn't work on cable-operated clutches, hold the clutch lever back against the handlebar with a strong elastic band or cable tie for a couple of hours **(see illustration 8)**.
● If the air intakes or silencer end(s) were blocked off, remove the bung or cover used.
● If the fuel tank was coated with a rust

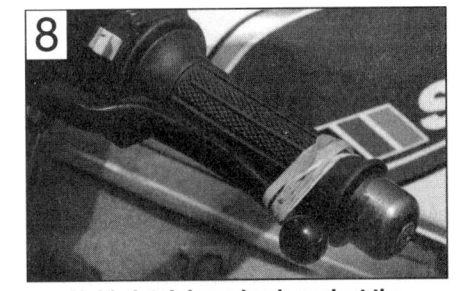

Hold clutch lever back against the handlebar with elastic bands or a cable tie

REF•34 Storage

preventative, oil or a stabiliser added to the fuel, drain and flush the tank and dispose of the fuel sensibly. If no action was taken with the fuel tank prior to storage, it is advised that the old fuel is disposed of since it will go off over a period of time. Refill the fuel tank with fresh fuel.

Frame and running gear

- Oil all pivot points and cables.
- Check the tyre pressures. They will definitely need inflating if pressures were reduced for storage.
- Lubricate the final drive chain (where applicable).
- Remove any protective coating applied to the fork tubes (stanchions) since this may well destroy the fork seals. If the fork tubes weren't protected and have picked up rust spots, remove them with very fine abrasive paper and refinish with metal polish.
- Check that both brakes operate correctly. Apply each brake hard and check that it's not possible to move the motorcycle forwards, then check that the brake frees off again once released. Brake caliper pistons can stick due to corrosion around the piston head, or on the sliding caliper types, due to corrosion of the slider pins. If the brake doesn't free after repeated operation, take the caliper off for examination. Similarly drum brakes can stick due to a seized operating cam, cable or rod linkage.
- If the motorcycle has been in long-term storage, renew the brake fluid and clutch fluid (where applicable).
- Depending on where the bike has been stored, the wiring, cables and hoses may have been nibbled by rodents. Make a visual check and investigate disturbed wiring loom tape.

Battery

- If the battery has been previously removal and given top up charges it can simply be reconnected. Remember to connect the positive cable first and the negative cable last.
- On conventional refillable batteries, if the battery has not received any attention, remove it from the motorcycle and check its electrolyte level. Top up if necessary then charge the battery. If the battery fails to hold a charge and a visual checks show heavy white sulphation of the plates, the battery is probably defective and must be renewed. This is particularly likely if the battery is old. Confirm battery condition with a specific gravity check.
- On sealed (MF) batteries, if the battery has not received any attention, remove it from the motorcycle and charge it according to the information on the battery case - if the battery fails to hold a charge it must be renewed.

Starting procedure

- If a kickstart is fitted, turn the engine over a couple of times with the ignition OFF to distribute oil around the engine. If no kickstart is fitted, flick the engine kill switch OFF and the ignition ON and crank the engine over a couple of times to work oil around the upper cylinder components. If the nature of the ignition system is such that the starter won't work with the kill switch OFF, remove the spark plugs, fit them back into their caps and earth (ground) their bodies on the cylinder head. Reinstall the spark plugs afterwards.
- Switch the kill switch to RUN, operate the choke and start the engine. If the engine won't start don't continue cranking the engine - not only will this flatten the battery, but the starter motor will overheat. Switch the ignition off and try again later. If the engine refuses to start, go through the fault finding procedures in this manual. **Note:** *If the bike has been in storage for a long time, old fuel or a carburettor blockage may be the problem. Gum deposits in carburettors can block jets - if a carburettor cleaner doesn't prove successful the carburettors must be dismantled for cleaning.*
- Once the engine has started, check that the lights, turn signals and horn work properly.
- Treat the bike gently for the first ride and check all fluid levels on completion. Settle the bike back into the maintenance schedule.

Fault Finding   REF•35

This Section provides an easy reference-guide to the more common faults that are likely to afflict your machine. Obviously, the opportunities are almost limitless for faults to occur as a result of obscure failures, and to try and cover all eventualities would require a book. Indeed, a number have been written on the subject.

Successful troubleshooting is not a mysterious 'black art' but the application of a bit of knowledge combined with a systematic and logical approach to the problem. Approach any troubleshooting by first accurately identifying the symptom and then checking through the list of possible causes, starting with the simplest or most obvious and progressing in stages to the most complex.

Take nothing for granted, but above all apply liberal quantities of common sense.

The main symptom of a fault is given in the text as a major heading below which are listed the various systems or areas which may contain the fault. Details of each possible cause for a fault and the remedial action to be taken are given, in brief, in the paragraphs below each heading. Further information should be sought in the relevant Chapter.

1 Engine doesn't start or is difficult to start
- [ ] Starter motor doesn't rotate
- [ ] Starter motor rotates but engine does not turn over
- [ ] Starter works but engine won't turn over (seized)
- [ ] No fuel flow
- [ ] Engine flooded
- [ ] No spark or weak spark
- [ ] Compression low
- [ ] Stalls after starting
- [ ] Rough idle

2 Poor running at low speed
- [ ] Spark weak
- [ ] Fuel/air mixture incorrect
- [ ] Compression low
- [ ] Poor acceleration

3 Poor running or no power at high speed
- [ ] Firing incorrect
- [ ] Fuel/air mixture incorrect
- [ ] Compression low
- [ ] Knocking or pinking
- [ ] Miscellaneous causes

4 Overheating
- [ ] Engine overheats
- [ ] Firing incorrect
- [ ] Fuel/air mixture incorrect
- [ ] Compression too high
- [ ] Engine load excessive
- [ ] Lubrication inadequate
- [ ] Miscellaneous causes

5 Clutch problems
- [ ] Clutch slipping
- [ ] Clutch not disengaging completely

6 Gearchanging problems
- [ ] Doesn't go into gear, or lever doesn't return
- [ ] Jumps out of gear
- [ ] Overselects

7 Abnormal engine noise
- [ ] Knocking or pinking
- [ ] Piston slap or rattling
- [ ] Valve noise
- [ ] Other noise

8 Abnormal driveline noise
- [ ] Clutch noise
- [ ] Transmission noise
- [ ] Final drive noise

9 Abnormal frame and suspension noise
- [ ] Front end noise
- [ ] Shock absorber noise
- [ ] Brake noise

10 Oil pressure low
- [ ] Engine lubrication system

11 Excessive exhaust smoke
- [ ] White smoke
- [ ] Black smoke
- [ ] Brown smoke

12 Poor handling or stability
- [ ] Handlebar hard to turn
- [ ] Handlebar shakes or vibrates excessively
- [ ] Handlebar pulls to one side
- [ ] Poor shock absorbing qualities

13 Braking problems
- [ ] Brakes are spongy, don't hold
- [ ] Brake lever or pedal pulsates
- [ ] Brakes drag

14 Electrical problems
- [ ] Battery dead or weak
- [ ] Battery overcharged

1 Engine doesn't start or is difficult to start

Starter motor doesn't rotate

- [ ] Engine kill switch OFF.
- [ ] Fuse blown. Check main fuse and FI fuse (Chapter 8).
- [ ] Battery voltage low. Check and recharge battery (Chapter 8).
- [ ] Starter motor defective. Make sure the wiring to the starter is secure. Make sure the starter relay clicks when the start button is pushed. If the relay clicks, then the fault is in the wiring or motor (Chapter 8).
- [ ] Starter switch not contacting. The contacts could be wet, corroded or dirty. Disassemble and clean the switch (Chapter 8).
- [ ] Wiring open or shorted. Check all wiring connections and harnesses to make sure that they are dry, tight and not corroded. Also check for broken or frayed wires that can cause a short to ground (earth) (see *Wiring diagrams*, Chapter 8).
- [ ] Ignition switch defective. Check the switch and replace with a new one if it is defective (Chapter 8).
- [ ] Engine kill switch defective. Check for wet, dirty or corroded contacts. Clean or replace the switch with a new one as necessary (Chapter 8).
- [ ] Faulty neutral switch, sidestand switch or clutch switch. Check the wiring to each switch and the switch itself (Chapter 8).
- [ ] Faulty starter circuit cut-off relay (Chapter 4).
- [ ] Fuel injection system shutdown due to system fault (Chapter 4).

Starter motor rotates but engine does not turn over

- [ ] Starter clutch defective. Inspect and repair or replace with a new one (Chapter 2).
- [ ] Damaged idler or starter gears. Inspect and replace the damaged parts (Chapter 2).

Starter works but engine won't turn over (seized)

- [ ] Seized engine caused by one or more internally damaged components. Failure due to wear, abuse or lack of lubrication. Damage can include seized valves, followers, camshafts, pistons, crankshaft, connecting rod bearings, or transmission gears or bearings. Refer to Chapter 2 for engine disassembly.

No fuel flow

- [ ] No fuel in tank.
- [ ] Fuel tank breather hose obstructed.
- [ ] Faulty fuel injection system relay. Check the relay (Chapter 4).
- [ ] Fuel pump faulty or blocked (Chapter 4).
- [ ] Fuel hose clogged. Remove the fuel hose and carefully blow through it.
- [ ] Fuel injector clogged. For all the injectors to be clogged, either a very bad batch of fuel with an unusual additive has been used, or some other foreign material has entered the tank. In some cases, if a machine has been unused for several months, the fuel turns to a varnish-like liquid which can cause an injector needle to stick to its seat. Drain the tank and fuel system (Chapter 4).

Engine flooded

- [ ] Injector needle valve worn or stuck open causing excess fuel to be admitted to the throttle body. In this case, the injectors should be renewed.
- [ ] Starting technique incorrect. Under normal circumstances (i.e. if all the components of the fuel injection system are good) the machine should start with the throttle closed.

No spark or weak spark

- [ ] Ignition switch OFF.
- [ ] Engine kill switch turned to the OFF position.
- [ ] Ignition or kill switch shorted. This is usually caused by water, corrosion, damage or excessive wear. The switches can be disassembled and cleaned with electrical contact cleaner. If cleaning does not help, replace the switches (Chapter 8).
- [ ] Battery voltage low. Check and recharge the battery as necessary (Chapter 8).
- [ ] Spark plug caps not making good contact. Make sure that the caps fit snugly over the plug ends.
- [ ] Spark plugs dirty, defective or worn out. Locate reason for fouled plugs using spark plug condition chart on the inside back cover and follow the plug maintenance procedures (Chapter 1).
- [ ] Incorrect spark plugs. Wrong type or heat range. Check and install correct plugs (Chapter 1).
- [ ] Ignition coil or spark plug cap defective. Test and replace if necessary (Chapter 4).
- [ ] Fuel injection system shutdown due to system fault (Chapter 4).
- [ ] Crankshaft position (CKP) sensor defective (Chapter 4).
- [ ] Faulty fuel injection relay or tip-over sensor (Chapter 4).
- [ ] Electronic control unit (ECU) defective (Chapter 4).
- [ ] Wiring shorted or broken between:
    - a) Ignition switch and engine kill switch (or blown fuse)
    - b) ECU and engine kill switch
    - c) ECU and ignition coils
    - d) ECU and CKP sensor
- [ ] Make sure that all wiring connections are clean, dry and tight. Look for chafed and broken wires (Chapters 4 and 8).

Compression low

- [ ] Spark plug loose. Remove the plugs and inspect their threads. Reinstall and tighten securely (Chapter 1).
- [ ] Cylinder head not sufficiently tightened down. If the cylinder head is suspected of being loose, then there's a chance that the gasket or head is damaged if the problem has persisted for any length of time. The head bolts should be tightened to the proper torque and in the correct sequence (Chapter 2).
- [ ] Improper valve clearance. This means that the valve is not closing completely and compression pressure is leaking past the valve. Check and adjust the valve clearances (Chapter 1).
- [ ] Cylinder and/or piston worn. Excessive wear will cause compression pressure to leak past the rings. This is usually accompanied by worn rings as well. A top-end overhaul is necessary (Chapter 2).
- [ ] Piston rings worn, weak, broken, or sticking. Broken or sticking piston rings usually indicate a lubrication or fuelling problem that causes excess carbon deposits to form on the pistons and rings. Top-end overhaul is necessary (Chapter 2).
- [ ] Piston ring-to-groove clearance excessive. This is caused by excessive wear of the piston ring lands. Piston renewal is necessary (Chapter 2).
- [ ] Cylinder head gasket damaged. If a head is allowed to become loose, or if excessive carbon build-up on the piston crown and combustion chamber causes extremely high compression, the head gasket may leak. Retorquing the head is not always sufficient to restore the seal, so a new gasket is necessary (Chapter 2).
- [ ] Cylinder head warped. This is caused by overheating or improperly tightened head bolts. Machine shop resurfacing or head renewal is necessary (Chapter 2).
- [ ] Valve spring broken or weak. Caused by component failure or wear; the springs must be renewed (Chapter 2).
- [ ] Valve not seating properly. This is caused by a bent valve (from over-revving or improper valve adjustment), burned valve or seat (improper fuelling) or an accumulation of carbon deposits on the seat. The valves must be cleaned and/or renewed and the seats serviced (Chapter 2).

Fault Finding REF•37

1 Engine doesn't start or is difficult to start (continued)

Stalls after starting
- ☐ Engine idle speed incorrect. Faulty idle speed control system (Chapter 4).
- ☐ Ignition malfunction (Chapter 4).
- ☐ Fuel injection system malfunction (Chapter 4).
- ☐ Fuel contaminated. The fuel can be contaminated with either dirt or water, or can change chemically if the machine has been unused for several months. Drain the tank and fuel system (Chapter 4).
- ☐ Intake air leak. Check for loose throttle body-to-intake duct connections or a loose or damaged AIS vacuum hose (Chapter 4).

Rough idle
- ☐ Idle speed incorrect (Chapter 4).
- ☐ Throttle bodies not synchronised (Chapter 1).
- ☐ Ignition fault (Chapter 4).
- ☐ Fuel injection system malfunction (Chapter 4).
- ☐ Fuel contaminated. The fuel can be contaminated with either dirt or water, or can change chemically if the machine has been unused for several months. Drain the tank and the fuel system (Chapter 4).
- ☐ Intake air leak. Check for loose throttle body-to-intake duct connections (Chapter 4).
- ☐ Air filter clogged. Clean the air filter element or replace it with a new one (Chapter 1).

2 Poor running at low speeds

Spark weak
- ☐ Battery voltage low. Check and recharge battery (Chapter 8).
- ☐ Spark plug caps not making good contact. Make sure that the caps fit snugly over the plug ends.
- ☐ Spark plugs dirty, defective or worn out. Locate reason for fouled plugs using spark plug condition chart on the inside back cover and follow the plug maintenance procedures (Chapter 1).
- ☐ Incorrect spark plugs. Wrong type or heat range. Check and install correct plugs (Chapter 1).
- ☐ Ignition coil or spark plug cap defective. Test and renew if necessary (Chapter 4).

Fuel/air mixture incorrect
- ☐ Fuel tank breather hose obstructed.
- ☐ Fuel pump faulty or blocked (Chapter 4).
- ☐ Fuel hose clogged. Remove the fuel hose and carefully blow through it.
- ☐ Fuel injector clogged. For all of the injectors to be clogged, either a very bad batch of fuel with an unusual additive has been used, or some other foreign material has entered the tank. In some cases, if a machine has been unused for several months, the fuel turns to a varnish-like liquid which can cause an injector needle to stick to its seat. Drain the tank and fuel system (Chapter 4).
- ☐ Intake air leak. Check for loose throttle body-to-intake duct connections, or loose or damaged vacuum hoses (Chapter 4).
- ☐ Air filter clogged. Clean the air filter element or replace it with a new one (Chapter 1).

Compression low
- ☐ Spark plug loose. Remove the plugs and inspect their threads. Reinstall and tighten securely (Chapter 1).
- ☐ Cylinder head not sufficiently tightened down. If the cylinder head is suspected of being loose, then there's a chance that the gasket or head is damaged if the problem has persisted for any length of time. The head bolts should be tightened to the proper torque and in the correct sequence (Chapter 2).
- ☐ Improper valve clearance. This means that the valve is not closing completely and compression pressure is leaking past the valve. Check and adjust the valve clearances (Chapter 1).
- ☐ Cylinder and/or piston worn. Excessive wear will cause compression pressure to leak past the rings. This is usually accompanied by worn rings as well. A top-end overhaul is necessary (Chapter 2).
- ☐ Piston rings worn, weak, broken, or sticking. Broken or sticking piston rings usually indicate a lubrication or fuelling problem that causes excess carbon deposits to form on the pistons and rings. Top-end overhaul is necessary (Chapter 2).
- ☐ Piston ring-to-groove clearance excessive. This is caused by excessive wear of the piston ring lands. Piston renewal is necessary (Chapter 2).
- ☐ Cylinder head gasket damaged. If the head is allowed to become loose, or if excessive carbon build-up on the piston crown and combustion chamber causes extremely high compression, the head gasket may leak. Retorquing the head is not always sufficient to restore the seal, so a new gasket is necessary (Chapter 2).
- ☐ Cylinder head warped. This is caused by overheating or improperly tightened head bolts. Machine shop resurfacing or head renewal is necessary (Chapter 2).
- ☐ Valve spring broken or weak. Caused by component failure or wear; the springs must be renewed (Chapter 2).
- ☐ Valve not seating properly. This is caused by a bent valve (from over-revving or improper valve adjustment), burned valve or seat (improper fuelling) or an accumulation of carbon deposits on the seat (from fuelling or lubrication problems). The valves must be cleaned and/or renewed and the seats serviced (Chapter 2).

Poor acceleration
- ☐ Timing not advancing. The crankshaft position sensor (CKP) or the electronic control unit (ECU) may be defective (Chapter 4). If so, they must be renewed.
- ☐ Engine oil viscosity too high. Using a heavier oil than that recommended in Chapter 1 can damage the oil pump or lubrication system and cause drag on the engine.
- ☐ Brakes dragging. Usually caused by debris which has entered the brake caliper piston seals, or from a warped disc or bent axle (Chapter 6).

3 Poor running or no power at high speed

Firing incorrect
- [ ] Spark plug caps not making good contact. Make sure that the caps fit snugly over the plug ends and that the wiring is secure.
- [ ] Spark plugs dirty, defective or worn out. Locate reason for fouled plugs using spark plug condition chart on the inside back cover and follow the plug maintenance procedures (Chapter 1).
- [ ] Incorrect spark plugs. Wrong type or heat range. Check and install correct plugs (Chapter 1).
- [ ] Ignition coil/spark plug cap defective. Test and renew if necessary (Chapter 4).
- [ ] Faulty ECU (electronic control unit) (Chapter 4).

Fuel/air mixture incorrect
- [ ] Fuel tank breather hose obstructed.
- [ ] Fuel pump faulty or blocked (Chapter 4).
- [ ] Fuel hose clogged. Remove the fuel hose and carefully blow through it.
- [ ] Fuel injector clogged. For all the injectors to be clogged, either a very bad batch of fuel with an unusual additive has been used, or some other foreign material has entered the tank. In some cases, if a machine has been unused for several months, the fuel turns to a varnish-like liquid which can cause an injector needle to stick to its seat. Drain the tank and fuel system (Chapter 4).
- [ ] Intake air leak. Check for loose throttle body-to-intake duct connections, or loose or damaged vacuum hoses (Chapter 4).
- [ ] Air filter clogged. Clean the air filter element or replace it with a new one (Chapter 1).

Compression low
- [ ] Spark plug loose. Remove the plugs and inspect their threads. Reinstall and tighten securely (Chapter 1).
- [ ] Cylinder head not sufficiently tightened down. If the cylinder head is suspected of being loose, then there's a chance that the gasket or head is damaged if the problem has persisted for any length of time. The head bolts should be tightened to the proper torque and in the correct sequence (Chapter 2).
- [ ] Improper valve clearance. This means that the valve is not closing completely and compression pressure is leaking past the valve. Check and adjust the valve clearances (Chapter 1).
- [ ] Cylinder and/or piston worn. Excessive wear will cause compression pressure to leak past the rings. This is usually accompanied by worn rings as well. A top-end overhaul is necessary (Chapter 2).
- [ ] Piston rings worn, weak, broken, or sticking. Broken or sticking piston rings usually indicate a lubrication or fuelling problem that causes excess carbon deposits to form on the pistons and rings. Top-end overhaul is necessary (Chapter 2).
- [ ] Piston ring-to-groove clearance excessive. This is caused by excessive wear of the piston ring lands. Piston renewal is necessary (Chapter 2).
- [ ] Cylinder head gasket damaged. If a head is allowed to become loose, or if excessive carbon build-up on the piston crown and combustion chamber causes extremely high compression, the head gasket may leak. Retorquing the head is not always sufficient to restore the seal, so a new gasket is necessary (Chapter 2).
- [ ] Cylinder head warped. This is caused by overheating or improperly tightened head bolts. Machine shop resurfacing or head renewal is necessary (Chapter 2).
- [ ] Valve spring broken or weak. Caused by component failure or wear; the springs must be replaced with new ones (Chapter 2).
- [ ] Valve not seating properly. This is caused by a bent valve (from over-revving or improper valve adjustment), burned valve or seat (improper fuelling) or an accumulation of carbon deposits on the seat (from fuelling or lubrication problems). The valves must be cleaned and/or renewed and the seats serviced (Chapter 2).

Knocking or pinking
- [ ] Carbon build-up in combustion chamber. Use of a fuel additive that will dissolve the adhesive bonding the carbon particles to the piston crown and chamber is the easiest way to remove the build-up. Otherwise, the cylinder head will have to be removed and decarbonised (Chapter 2).
- [ ] Incorrect or poor quality fuel. Old or improper grades of fuel can cause detonation. This causes the piston to rattle, thus the knocking or pinking sound. Drain old fuel and always use the recommended fuel grade.
- [ ] Spark plug heat range incorrect. Uncontrolled detonation indicates the plug heat range is too hot. The plug in effect becomes a glow plug, raising cylinder temperatures. Install the proper heat range plug (Chapter 1).
- [ ] Improper air/fuel mixture. This will cause the cylinders to run hot, which leads to detonation. A blockage in the fuel system or an air leak can cause this imbalance (Chapter 4).

Miscellaneous causes
- [ ] Throttle valve doesn't open fully. Adjust the throttle twistgrip freeplay (Chapter 1).
- [ ] Clutch slipping due loose or worn clutch components (Chapter 2).
- [ ] Timing not advancing. The crankshaft position sensor (CKP) or the electronic control unit (ECU) may be defective (Chapter 4). If so, they must be replaced with new ones.
- [ ] Engine oil viscosity too high. Using a heavier oil than the one recommended in Chapter 1 can damage the oil pump or lubrication system and cause drag on the engine.
- [ ] Brakes dragging. Usually caused by debris which has entered the brake caliper piston seals, or from a warped disc or bent axle (Chapter 6).

Fault Finding REF•39

4 Overheating

Engine overheats
- [ ] Coolant level low. Check the level and add coolant (see *Pre-ride checks*).
- [ ] Leak in cooling system. Check cooling system hoses and radiator for leaks and other damage. Repair or renew parts as necessary (Chapter 3).
- [ ] Faulty thermostat. Check and renew as described in Chapter 3.
- [ ] Faulty pressure cap. Remove the cap and have it pressure tested.
- [ ] Coolant passages clogged. Have the entire system drained and flushed, then refill with fresh coolant.
- [ ] Water pump defective. Remove the pump and check the components (Chapter 3).
- [ ] Clogged or damaged radiator fins (Chapter 3).
- [ ] Faulty cooling fan, relay or ECT sensor (Chapter 3).

Firing incorrect
- [ ] Wrongly connected ignition coil wiring or plug leads.
- [ ] Spark plugs dirty, defective or worn out. Locate reason for fouled plugs using spark plug condition chart on the inside back cover and follow the plug maintenance procedures (Chapter 1).
- [ ] Incorrect spark plugs. Wrong type or heat range. Check and install correct plugs (Chapter 1).
- [ ] Ignition coil or spark plug cap defective. Test and replace with a new one if necessary (Chapter 4).
- [ ] Faulty ECU (electronic control unit) or cylinder identification sensor (Chapter 4).

Fuel/air mixture incorrect
- [ ] Fuel tank breather hose obstructed.
- [ ] Fuel pump faulty or blocked (Chapter 4).
- [ ] Fuel hose clogged. Remove the fuel hose and carefully blow through it.
- [ ] Fuel injector clogged. For all the injectors to be clogged, either a very bad batch of fuel with an unusual additive has been used, or some other foreign material has entered the tank. In some cases, if a machine has been unused for several months, the fuel turns to a varnish-like liquid which can cause an injector needle to stick to its seat. Drain the tank and fuel system (Chapter 4).
- [ ] Intake air leak. Check for loose throttle body-to-intake duct connections, or loose or damaged vacuum hoses (Chapter 4).
- [ ] Air filter clogged. Clean the air filter element or replace it with a new one (Chapter 1).

Compression too high
- [ ] Carbon build-up in combustion chamber. Use of a fuel additive that will dissolve the adhesive bonding the carbon particles to the piston crown and chamber is the easiest way to remove the build-up. Otherwise, the cylinder head will have to be removed and decarbonised (Chapter 2).
- [ ] Improperly machined head surface or installation of incorrect gasket during engine assembly.

Engine load excessive
- [ ] Clutch slipping due to loose or worn clutch components (Chapter 2).
- [ ] Engine oil level too high. Too much oil will cause pressurisation of the crankcase and inefficient engine operation. Check Specifications and drain to proper level (Chapter 1 and *Pre-ride checks*).
- [ ] Engine oil viscosity too high. Using a heavier oil than the one recommended in Chapter 1 can damage the oil pump or lubrication system as well as cause drag on the engine.
- [ ] Brakes dragging. Usually caused by debris which has entered the brake caliper piston seals, or from a warped disc or bent axle (Chapter 6).

Lubrication inadequate
- [ ] Engine oil level too low. Friction caused by intermittent lack of lubrication or from oil that is overworked can cause overheating. The oil provides a definite cooling function in the engine. Check the oil level (see *Pre-ride checks*).
- [ ] Low engine oil pressure. Check the pressure (Chapter 2).
- [ ] Blocked oil filter or oil cooler (Chapters 1 and 2).
- [ ] Poor quality engine oil or incorrect viscosity or type. Oil is rated not only according to viscosity but also according to type. Some oils are not rated high enough for use in this engine. Check the Specifications section and change to the correct oil (Chapter 1).

Miscellaneous causes
- [ ] Modification to exhaust system. Most aftermarket exhaust systems cause the engine to run leaner, which make them run hotter. When installing an accessory exhaust system, always check with the manufacturer/supplier as to whether the ECM requires re-mapping.

5 Clutch problems

Clutch slipping
- [ ] Clutch plates worn or warped. Overhaul the clutch assembly (see Chapter 2).
- [ ] Clutch spring broken or weak. Old or heat-damaged (from slipping clutch) springs should be renewed (Chapter 2).
- [ ] Clutch centre or housing unevenly worn. This causes improper engagement of the plates. Replace the damaged or worn parts (see Chapter 2).
- [ ] Clutch release mechanism fault (see Chapter 2).
- [ ] Incorrect type of oil. Use of oils designed for car engines which include friction modifiers can cause clutch slip in a wet clutch application.

Clutch not disengaging completely
- [ ] Clutch fluid level low (see *Pre-ride checks*).
- [ ] Clutch release mechanism fault (see Chapter 2).
- [ ] Clutch plates warped or damaged. This will cause clutch drag, which in turn will cause the machine to creep. Overhaul the clutch assembly (see Chapter 2).
- [ ] Clutch springs fatigued or broken. Check and renew the springs (see Chapter 2).
- [ ] Engine oil deteriorated. Old, thin oil will not provide proper lubrication for the plates, causing the clutch to drag. Renew the oil and filter (see Chapter 1).
- [ ] Engine oil viscosity too high. Using a heavier oil than recommended in Chapter 1 can cause the plates to stick together. Change to the correct weight oil.
- [ ] Clutch housing bearing seized on the transmission input shaft. Lack of lubrication, severe wear or damage can cause the bearing to seize. Overhaul of the clutch, and perhaps transmission, may be necessary to repair the damage (see Chapter 2).
- [ ] Loose clutch centre nut. Causes housing and centre misalignment putting a drag on the engine. Engagement adjustment continually varies. Overhaul the clutch assembly (see Chapter 2).

REF•40 Fault Finding

6 Gearchanging problems

Doesn't go into gear or lever doesn't return
- [ ] Clutch not disengaging (above).
- [ ] Gearchange mechanism stopper arm spring weak or broken, or arm roller broken or worn. Replace the spring or arm with a new one (Chapter 2).
- [ ] Selector fork(s) bent, worn or seized. Overhaul the transmission (Chapter 2).
- [ ] Gear(s) stuck on shaft. Most often caused by a lack of lubrication or excessive wear in transmission bearings and bushes. Overhaul the transmission (Chapter 2).
- [ ] Selector drum binding. Caused by lubrication failure or excessive wear. Replace the drum and/or its bearing with a new one (Chapter 2).
- [ ] Gearchange mechanism return spring weak or broken (Chapter 2).
- [ ] Gearchange lever or linkage broken. Splines stripped out of arm or shaft, caused by a loose linkage arm pinch bolt or from dropping the machine (Chapter 2).

Jumps out of gear
- [ ] Selector fork(s) worn (Chapter 2).
- [ ] Selector fork groove(s) in selector drum worn (Chapter 2).
- [ ] Gear pinion dogs or dog slots worn or damaged. The gear pinions should be inspected and renewed. No attempt should be made to repair the worn parts.

Overselects
- [ ] Gearchange mechanism stopper arm spring weak or broken, or arm roller broken or worn. Renew the spring or arm (Chapter 2).
- [ ] Gearchange mechanism return spring weak or broken (Chapter 2).

YCC-S (Yamaha Chip Controlled Shift) system
- [ ] Fault code indicated or system malfunctions (Chapter 2).

7 Abnormal engine noise

Knocking or pinking
- [ ] Carbon build-up in combustion chamber. Use of a fuel additive that will dissolve the adhesive bonding the carbon particles to the piston crown and chamber is the easiest way to remove the build-up. Otherwise, the cylinder head will have to be removed and decarbonised (Chapter 2).
- [ ] Incorrect or poor quality fuel. Old or improper grades of fuel can cause detonation. This causes the pistons to rattle, thus the knocking or pinking sound. Drain old fuel and always use the recommended fuel grade.
- [ ] Spark plug heat range incorrect. Uncontrolled detonation indicates the plug heat range is too hot. The plug in effect becomes a glow plug, raising cylinder temperatures. Install the proper heat range plug (Chapter 1).
- [ ] Improper air/fuel mixture. This will cause the cylinders to run hot, which leads to detonation. A blockage in the fuel system or an air leak can cause this imbalance (Chapter 4).

Piston slap or rattling
- [ ] Cylinder-to-piston clearance excessive. Cylinder and/or piston worn, usually accompanied by worn rings as well. A top-end overhaul is necessary (Chapter 2).
- [ ] Piston ring(s) worn, broken or sticking. Overhaul the top-end (Chapter 2).
- [ ] Piston pin, piston pin bore or connecting rod small-end worn from high mileage or seized due to lack of lubrication (Chapter 2).
- [ ] Piston seizure damage. Usually from lack of lubrication or overheating. Replace the pistons and upper crankcase, as necessary (Chapter 2).
- [ ] Connecting rod big-end clearance excessive. Caused by excessive wear or lack of lubrication. Replace worn parts.
- [ ] Connecting rod bent. Caused by over-revving, trying to start a badly flooded engine or from ingesting a foreign object into the combustion chamber. Replace the damaged parts (Chapter 2).

Valve noise
- [ ] Incorrect valve clearances – check and adjust (Chapter 1).
- [ ] Valve spring broken or weak. Check and replace weak valve springs with new ones (Chapter 2).
- [ ] Camshaft or camshaft journals in the cylinder head worn or damaged. Lubrication failure at high rpm is usually the cause of damage due to insufficient oil or failure to change the oil at the recommended intervals. Since there are no replaceable bearings in the head, the head itself will have to be replaced with a new one (Chapter 2).

Other noise
- [ ] Cylinder head gasket leaking. Check around the joint for blowing with the engine running.
- [ ] Exhaust pipe leaking at cylinder head connection. Caused by incorrect fit of pipe(s), loose exhaust flange or damaged gasket. All exhaust system fasteners should be tightened evenly and carefully to avoid leaks (Chapter 4).
- [ ] Crankshaft runout excessive. Caused by a bent crankshaft (from over-revving) or damage from an upper cylinder component failure. Can also be attributed to dropping the machine on either of the crankshaft ends.
- [ ] Engine mounting bolts loose – ensure all the bolts are tightened to the specified torque settings (Chapter 2).
- [ ] Crankshaft bearings worn (Chapter 2).
- [ ] Cam chain rattle, due to worn chain or defective tensioner. Also worn chain tensioner/guide blades (Chapter 2).

Fault Finding REF•41

8 Abnormal driveline noise

Clutch noise
- [ ] Clutch housing/friction plate clearance excessive (Chapter 2).
- [ ] Wear between the clutch housing splines and input shaft splines (Chapter 2).
- [ ] Worn release bearing (Chapter 2).

Transmission noise
- [ ] Bearings worn. Also includes the possibility that the shafts are worn. Overhaul the transmission (Chapter 2).
- [ ] Gears worn or chipped (Chapter 2).
- [ ] Metal chips jammed in gear teeth. Probably pieces from a broken clutch, gear or selector mechanism that were picked up by the gears. This will cause early bearing failure (Chapter 2).
- [ ] Engine oil level too low. Causes a howl from transmission. Also affects engine power and clutch operation (see *Pre-ride checks*).

Final drive noise
- [ ] Final drive oil level low (Chapter 1).
- [ ] Rear wheel coupling worn or damaged (Chapter 6).
- [ ] Final drive gears worn or damaged (Chapter 6).
- [ ] Final drive bearings worn (Chapter 6).
- [ ] Driveshaft splines worn and slipping (Chapter 6).

9 Abnormal frame and suspension noise

Front end noise
- [ ] Low fluid level or improper viscosity oil in forks. This can sound like spurting and is usually accompanied by irregular fork action (Chapter 5).
- [ ] Spring weak or broken. Makes a clicking or scraping sound. Fork oil, when drained, will have a lot of metal particles in it (Chapter 5).
- [ ] Steering head bearings loose or damaged. Clicks when braking. Check and adjust or replace with new ones as necessary (Chapters 1 and 5).
- [ ] Fork yoke clamp bolts loose – ensure all the bolts are tightened to the specified torque (Chapter 6).
- [ ] Forks bent. Good possibility if machine has been dropped. Replace the inner and outer tubes with new ones as required (Chapter 5).
- [ ] Front axle or axle pinch bolts loose. Tighten them to the specified torque (Chapter 6).
- [ ] Loose or worn wheel bearings. Check and replace with new ones as needed (Chapters 1 and 6).

Rear end noise
- [ ] Shock absorber fluid level incorrect. Indicates a leak caused by defective seal. Shock will be covered with oil. Replace shock with a new one or seek advice on repair from a suspension specialist (Chapter 5).
- [ ] Defective shock absorber with internal damage. This is in the body of the shock and can't be remedied. The shock must be replaced with a new one or rebuilt (Chapter 5).
- [ ] Bent or damaged shock body. Replace the shock with a new one (Chapter 5).
- [ ] Loose or worn swingarm bearings. Check and replace with new ones as necessary (Chapter 5).
- [ ] Loose or worn suspension linkage bearings. Check and replace with new ones as necessary (Chapter 5).

Brake noise
- [ ] Squeal caused by pad shim not installed or positioned correctly (where fitted) (Chapter 6).
- [ ] Squeal caused by dust on brake pads. Usually found in combination with glazed pads. Clean using brake cleaning solvent (Chapter 6).
- [ ] Pads glazed. Caused by excessive heat from prolonged hard use or from contamination. DO NOT use sandpaper, emery cloth, carborundum cloth or any other abrasive to roughen the pad surfaces as abrasives will stay in the pad material and damage the disc. A very fine flat file can be used, but new pads is the best remedy (Chapter 6).
- [ ] Contamination of brake pads. Oil or brake fluid can cause the brake pads to chatter or squeal. Fit new pads. Identify the cause of the contamination, especially check the caliper piston seals for leaking fluid. Clean disc thoroughly with brake system cleaner (Chapter 6).
- [ ] Disc warped. Can cause a chattering, clicking or intermittent squeal. Usually accompanied by a pulsating lever and uneven braking. Replace the disc with new one (Chapter 6).
- [ ] Loose or worn wheel bearings. Check and replace with new ones as needed (Chapters 1 and 6).

10 Oil pressure low

Engine lubrication system
- [ ] Engine oil level low. Inspect for leak or other problem causing low oil level and add recommended oil (see *Pre-ride checks*).
- [ ] Engine oil pump defective, blocked oil strainer gauze or failed pressure relief valve. Carry out an oil pressure check (Chapter 2).
- [ ] Engine oil viscosity too low. Very old, thin oil or an improper weight of oil used in the engine. Change to correct oil (Chapter 1).
- [ ] Camshaft or crankshaft journals worn. Excessive wear causing drop in oil pressure. Abnormal wear could be caused by oil starvation at high rpm from low oil level or improper weight or type of oil (Chapter 1).

REF•42 Fault Finding

11 Excessive exhaust smoke

White smoke

- [ ] Piston rings worn or broken, causing oil from the crankcase to be pulled past the piston into the combustion chamber. Replace the rings with new ones (Chapter 2).
- [ ] Plating on cylinders worn or scored. Caused by overheating or oil starvation. Renew the crankcases and pistons (Chapter 2).
- [ ] Valve stem oil seal damaged or worn. Replace the oil seals with new ones (Chapter 2).
- [ ] Valve guide worn. Perform a complete valve job (Chapter 2).
- [ ] Engine oil level too high, which causes the oil to be forced past the rings. Drain oil to the proper level (see *Pre-ride checks*).
- [ ] Head gasket broken between oil return and cylinder. Causes oil to be pulled into the combustion chamber. Replace the head gasket with a new ones and check the head for warpage (Chapter 2).
- [ ] Abnormal crankcase pressurisation which forces oil past the rings, usually caused by a clogged breather.

Black smoke

- [ ] Air filter clogged. Clean the air filter element or replace it with a new one (Chapter 1).
- [ ] Fuel injection system malfunction (Chapter 4).

Brown smoke

- [ ] Air filter poorly sealed or not installed (Chapter 1).
- [ ] Fuel injection system malfunction (Chapter 4).

12 Poor handling or stability

Handlebar hard to turn

- [ ] Steering head bearing adjuster nut too tight. Check adjustment as described in Chapter 1.
- [ ] Bearings damaged. Roughness can be felt as the bars are turned from side-to-side. Replace the bearings with new ones (Chapter 5).
- [ ] Races dented or worn. Denting results from wear in only one position (e.g., straight ahead), from a collision or hitting a pothole or from dropping the machine. Replace the bearings with new ones (Chapter 5).
- [ ] Steering stem lubrication inadequate. Causes are grease getting hard from age or being washed out by high pressure car washes. Disassemble steering head and repack bearings (Chapter 5).
- [ ] Steering stem bent. Caused by a collision, hitting a pothole or by dropping the machine. Replace damaged part. Don't try to straighten the steering stem (Chapter 5).
- [ ] Front tyre air pressure too low (see *Pre-ride checks*).

Handlebar shakes or vibrates excessively

- [ ] Tyres worn or out of balance (Chapter 6).
- [ ] Swingarm bearings worn. Replace the bearings with new ones (Chapter 5).
- [ ] Wheel rim(s) warped or damaged. Inspect wheels for runout (Chapter 6).
- [ ] Wheel bearings worn. Worn front or rear wheel bearings can cause poor tracking. Worn front bearings will cause wobble (Chapters 1 and 6).
- [ ] Fork yoke clamp bolts or handlebar clamp bolts loose. Tighten them to the specified torque (Chapter 5).
- [ ] Engine mounting bolts loose. Will cause excessive vibration with increased engine rpm – ensure all the bolts are tightened to the specified torque settings (Chapter 2).

Machine pulls to one side

- [ ] Frame bent. Definitely suspect this if the machine has been dropped. May or may not be accompanied by cracking near the steering head, swingarm mountings or engine mountings. Replace the frame with a new one (Chapter 5).
- [ ] Wheels out of alignment. Caused by poor chain adjustment, improper location of axle spacers or from bent steering stem or frame (Chapters 1 and 5).
- [ ] Forks bent. Disassemble the forks and replace the damaged parts (Chapter 5).
- [ ] Swingarm bent or twisted. Replace the arm with a new one (Chapter 5).
- [ ] Fork oil level uneven. Check and add or drain as necessary (Chapter 5).

Poor shock absorbing qualities

- [ ] Too hard:
    - a) Suspension adjustment incorrect.
    - b) Fork oil level excessive (Chapter 5).
    - c) Fork oil viscosity too high. Use a lighter oil (see the Specifications in Chapter 5).
    - d) Fork tube bent. Causes a harsh, sticking feeling (Chapter 5).
    - e) Fork internal damage (Chapter 5).
    - f) Shock shaft or body bent or damaged (Chapter 5).
    - g) Shock internal damage.
    - h) Swingarm bearings or suspension linkage bearings seized (Chapter 5).
    - i) Tyre pressure too high (see *Pre-ride checks*).
- [ ] Too soft:
    - a) Suspension adjustment incorrect.
    - b) Fork oil level too low (Chapter 5).
    - c) Fork oil viscosity too light (Chapter 5).
    - d) Fork springs weak or broken (Chapter 5).
    - e) Fork or shock oil leaking (Chapter 5).
    - f) Shock internal damage (Chapter 5).

Fault Finding REF•43

13 Braking problems

Brakes are spongy, don't hold
- ☐ Low brake fluid level (see *Pre-ride checks*).
- ☐ Air in hydraulic system. Caused by inattention to master cylinder fluid level or by leakage. Locate problem and bleed brakes (Chapter 6).
- ☐ Pad or disc worn (Chapters 1 and 6).
- ☐ Contaminated pads. Caused by contamination with oil, grease, brake fluid, etc. Fit new pads. Identify the cause of the contamination, especially check the caliper piston seals for leaking fluid. Clean disc thoroughly with brake system cleaner (Chapter 6).
- ☐ Brake fluid deteriorated. Fluid is old or contaminated. Drain system, replenish with new fluid and bleed the system (Chapter 6).
- ☐ Master cylinder internal seals worn or damaged causing fluid to bypass (Chapter 6).
- ☐ Master cylinder bore scratched by foreign material or broken spring. Fit a new master cylinder (Chapter 6).
- ☐ Disc warped. Replace disc with new one (Chapter 6)
- ☐ ABS system faulty (where fitted, Chapter 6).

Brake lever or pedal pulsates
- ☐ Disc warped. Replace disc with new one (Chapter 6).
- ☐ Axle bent. Replace axle with new one (Chapter 6).
- ☐ Brake caliper bolts loose – tighten the bolts to the specified torque (Chapter 6).
- ☐ Wheel warped or otherwise damaged (Chapter 6).
- ☐ Wheel bearings damaged or worn (Chapters 1 and 6).
- ☐ ABS system faulty (where fitted, Chapter 6).

Brakes drag
- ☐ Master cylinder piston seized. Caused by wear or damage to piston or cylinder bore (Chapter 6).
- ☐ Lever balky or stuck. Check pivot and lubricate (Chapter 6).
- ☐ Brake caliper piston seized in bore. Caused by corrosion or ingestion of dirt past deteriorated seal (Chapter 6).
- ☐ Rear brake caliper slider pins sticking or corroded, prevent full movement of caliper (Chapter 6).
- ☐ Brake pad damaged. Pad material separated from backing plate. Usually caused by faulty manufacturing process or from contact with chemicals. Fit new pads (Chapter 6).
- ☐ Pads improperly installed (Chapter 6).
- ☐ Brake caliper incorrectly installed (Chapter 6).
- ☐ ABS system faulty (where fitted, Chapter 6).

14 Electrical problems

Battery dead or weak
- ☐ Battery faulty. Caused by sulphated plates which are shorted through sedimentation. Confirm with battery condition check (Chapter 8).
- ☐ Broken battery terminal making only occasional contact.
- ☐ Battery leads making poor contact (Chapter 8).
- ☐ Load excessive. Caused by addition of high wattage lights or other electrical accessories.
- ☐ Ignition switch defective. Switch either grounds (earths) internally or fails to shut off system. Renew the switch (Chapter 8).
- ☐ Regulator/rectifier defective (Chapter 8).
- ☐ Alternator stator coil open or shorted (Chapter 8).
- ☐ Charging system fault. Check for excessive current leakage (Chapter 8).
- ☐ Wiring faulty. Wiring grounded (earthed) or connections loose in ignition, charging or lighting circuits (Chapter 8).

Battery overcharged
- ☐ Regulator/rectifier defective. Overcharging is noticed when battery gets excessively warm (Chapter 8).
- ☐ Battery faulty. Confirm with battery condition check (Chapter 8).
- ☐ Battery amperage too low, wrong type or size of battery. Install manufacturer's specified amp-hour battery to handle charging load (Chapter 8).

REF•44 Technical Terms Explained

A

ABS (Anti-lock braking system) A system, usually electronically controlled, that senses incipient wheel lockup during braking and relieves hydraulic pressure at wheel which is about to skid.

Aftermarket Components suitable for the motorcycle, but not produced by the motorcycle manufacturer.

Allen key A hexagonal wrench which fits into a recessed hexagonal hole.

Alternating current (ac) Current produced by an alternator. Requires converting to direct current by a rectifier for charging purposes.

Alternator Converts mechanical energy from the engine into electrical energy to charge the battery and power the electrical system.

Ampere (amp) A unit of measurement for the flow of electrical current. Current = Volts ÷ Ohms.

Ampere-hour (Ah) Measure of battery capacity.

Angle-tightening A torque expressed in degrees. Often follows a conventional tightening torque for cylinder head or main bearing fasteners **(see illustration)**.

Angle-tightening con-rod bolts

Antifreeze A substance (usually ethylene glycol) mixed with water, and added to the cooling system, to prevent freezing of the coolant in winter. Antifreeze also contains chemicals to inhibit corrosion and the formation of rust and other deposits that would tend to clog the radiator and coolant passages and reduce cooling efficiency.

Anti-dive System attached to the fork lower leg (slider) to prevent fork dive when braking hard.

Anti-seize compound A coating that reduces the risk of seizing on fasteners that are subjected to high temperatures, such as exhaust clamp bolts and nuts.

API American Petroleum Institute. A quality standard for 4-stroke motor oils.

Asbestos A natural fibrous mineral with great heat resistance, commonly used in the composition of brake friction materials. Asbestos is a health hazard and the dust created by brake systems should never be inhaled or ingested.

ATF Automatic Transmission Fluid. Often used in front forks.

ATU Automatic Timing Unit. Mechanical device for advancing the ignition timing on early engines.

ATV All Terrain Vehicle. Often called a Quad.

Axial play Side-to-side movement.

Axle A shaft on which a wheel revolves. Also known as a spindle.

B

Backlash The amount of movement between meshed components when one component is held still. Usually applies to gear teeth.

Ball bearing A bearing consisting of a hardened inner and outer race with hardened steel balls between the two races.

Bearings Used between two working surfaces to prevent wear of the components and a build-up of heat. Four types of bearing are commonly used on motorcycles: plain shell bearings, ball bearings, tapered roller bearings and needle roller bearings.

Bevel gears Used to turn the drive through 90°. Typical applications are shaft final drive and camshaft drive **(see illustration)**.

Bevel gears are used to turn the drive through 90°

BHP Brake Horsepower. The British measurement for engine power output. Power output is now usually expressed in kilowatts (kW).

Bias-belted tyre Similar construction to radial tyre, but with outer belt running at an angle to the wheel rim.

Big-end bearing The bearing in the end of the connecting rod that's attached to the crankshaft.

Bleeding The process of removing air from an hydraulic system via a bleed nipple or bleed screw.

Bottom-end A description of an engine's crankcase components and all components contained there-in.

BTDC Before Top Dead Centre in terms of piston position. Ignition timing is often expressed in terms of degrees or millimetres BTDC.

Bush A cylindrical metal or rubber component used between two moving parts.

Burr Rough edge left on a component after machining or as a result of excessive wear.

C

Cam chain The chain which takes drive from the crankshaft to the camshaft(s).

Canister The main component in an evaporative emission control system (California market only); contains activated charcoal granules to trap vapours from the fuel system rather than allowing them to vent to the atmosphere.

Castellated Resembling the parapets along the top of a castle wall. For example, a castellated wheel axle or spindle nut.

Catalytic converter A device in the exhaust system of some machines which converts certain pollutants in the exhaust gases into less harmful substances.

Charging system Description of the components which charge the battery, ie the alternator, rectifer and regulator.

Circlip A ring-shaped clip used to prevent endwise movement of cylindrical parts and shafts. An internal circlip is installed in a groove in a housing; an external circlip fits into a groove on the outside of a cylindrical piece such as a shaft. Also known as a snap-ring.

Clearance The amount of space between two parts. For example, between a piston and a cylinder, between a bearing and a journal, etc.

Coil spring A spiral of elastic steel found in various sizes throughout a vehicle, for example as a springing medium in the suspension and in the valve train.

Compression Reduction in volume, and increase in pressure and temperature, of a gas, caused by squeezing it into a smaller space.

Compression damping Controls the speed the suspension compresses when hitting a bump.

Compression ratio The relationship between cylinder volume when the piston is at top dead centre and cylinder volume when the piston is at bottom dead centre.

Continuity The uninterrupted path in the flow of electricity. Little or no measurable resistance.

Continuity tester Self-powered bleeper or test light which indicates continuity.

Cp Candlepower. Bulb rating commonly found on US motorcycles.

Crossply tyre Tyre plies arranged in a criss-cross pattern. Usually four or six plies used, hence 4PR or 6PR in tyre size codes.

Cush drive Rubber damper segments fitted between the rear wheel and final drive sprocket to absorb transmission shocks **(see illustration)**.

Cush drive rubbers dampen out transmission shocks

D

Decarbonisation The process of removing carbon deposits - typically from the combustion chamber, valves and exhaust port/system.

Degree disc Calibrated disc for measuring piston position. Expressed in degrees.

Detonation Destructive and damaging explosion of fuel/air mixture in combustion chamber instead of controlled burning.

Dial gauge Clock-type gauge with adapters for measuring runout and piston position. Expressed in mm or inches.

Technical Terms Explained

Diaphragm The rubber membrane in a master cylinder or carburettor which seals the upper chamber.
Diaphragm spring A single sprung plate often used in clutches.
Direct current (dc) Current produced by a dc generator.
Diode An electrical valve which only allows current to flow in one direction. Commonly used in rectifiers and starter interlock systems.
Disc valve (or rotary valve) A induction system used on some two-stroke engines.
Double-overhead camshaft (DOHC) An engine that uses two overhead camshafts, one for the intake valves and one for the exhaust valves.
Drivebelt A toothed belt used to transmit drive to the rear wheel on some motorcycles. A drivebelt has also been used to drive the camshafts. Drivebelts are usually made of Kevlar.
Driveshaft Any shaft used to transmit motion. Commonly used when referring to the final driveshaft on shaft drive motorcycles.

E

Earth return The return path of an electrical circuit, utilising the motorcycle's frame.
ECU (Electronic Control Unit) A computer which controls (for instance) an ignition system, or an anti-lock braking system.
EGO Exhaust Gas Oxygen sensor. Sometimes called a Lambda sensor.
Electrolyte The fluid in a lead-acid battery.
EMS (Engine Management System) A computer controlled system which manages the fuel injection and the ignition systems in an integrated fashion.
Endfloat The amount of lengthways movement between two parts. As applied to a crankshaft, the distance that the crankshaft can move side-to-side in the crankcase.
Endless chain A chain having no joining link. Common use for cam chains and final drive chains.
EP (Extreme Pressure) Oil type used in locations where high loads are applied, such as between gear teeth.
Evaporative emission control system Describes a charcoal filled canister which stores fuel vapours from the tank rather than allowing them to vent to the atmosphere. Usually only fitted to California models and referred to as an EVAP system.
Expansion chamber Section of two-stroke engine exhaust system so designed to improve engine efficiency and boost power.

F

Feeler blade or gauge A thin strip or blade of hardened steel, ground to an exact thickness, used to check or measure clearances between parts.
Final drive Description of the drive from the transmission to the rear wheel. Usually by chain or shaft, but sometimes by belt.
Firing order The order in which the engine cylinders fire, or deliver their power strokes, beginning with the number one cylinder.
Flooding Term used to describe a high fuel level in the carburettor float chambers, leading to fuel overflow. Also refers to excess fuel in the combustion chamber due to incorrect starting technique.
Free length The no-load state of a component when measured. Clutch, valve and fork spring lengths are measured at rest, without any preload.
Freeplay The amount of travel before any action takes place. The looseness in a linkage, or an assembly of parts, between the initial application of force and actual movement. For example, the distance the rear brake pedal moves before the rear brake is actuated.
Fuel injection The fuel/air mixture is metered electronically and directed into the engine intake ports (indirect injection) or into the cylinders (direct injection). Sensors supply information on engine speed and conditions.
Fuel/air mixture The charge of fuel and air going into the engine. See Stoichiometric ratio.
Fuse An electrical device which protects a circuit against accidental overload. The typical fuse contains a soft piece of metal which is calibrated to melt at a predetermined current flow (expressed as amps) and break the circuit.

G

Gap The distance the spark must travel in jumping from the centre electrode to the side electrode in a spark plug. Also refers to the distance between the ignition rotor and the pickup coil in an electronic ignition system.
Gasket Any thin, soft material - usually cork, cardboard, asbestos or soft metal - installed between two metal surfaces to ensure a good seal. For instance, the cylinder head gasket seals the joint between the block and the cylinder head.
Gauge An instrument panel display used to monitor engine conditions. A gauge with a movable pointer on a dial or a fixed scale is an analogue gauge. A gauge with a numerical readout is called a digital gauge.
Gear ratios The drive ratio of a pair of gears in a gearbox, calculated on their number of teeth.
Glaze-busting see **Honing**
Grinding Process for renovating the valve face and valve seat contact area in the cylinder head.
Gudgeon pin The shaft which connects the connecting rod small-end with the piston. Often called a piston pin or wrist pin.

H

Helical gears Gear teeth are slightly curved and produce less gear noise that straight-cut gears. Often used for primary drives.
Helicoil A thread insert repair system. Commonly used as a repair for stripped spark plug threads **(see illustration)**.

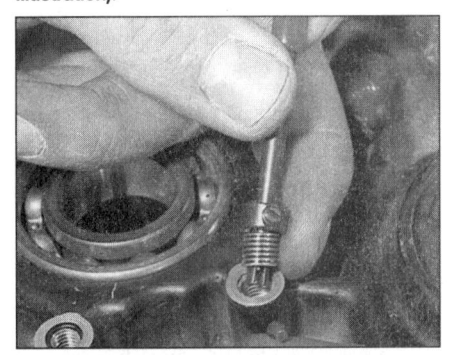

Installing a Helicoil thread insert

Honing A process used to break down the glaze on a cylinder bore (also called glaze-busting). Can also be carried out to roughen a rebored cylinder to aid ring bedding-in.
HT (High Tension) Description of the electrical circuit from the secondary winding of the ignition coil to the spark plug.
Hydraulic A liquid filled system used to transmit pressure from one component to another. Common uses on motorcycles are brakes and clutches.
Hydrometer An instrument for measuring the specific gravity of a lead-acid battery.
Hygroscopic Water absorbing. In motorcycle applications, braking efficiency will be reduced if DOT 3 or 4 hydraulic fluid absorbs water from the air - care must be taken to keep new brake fluid in tightly sealed containers.

I

lbf ft Pounds-force feet. An imperial unit of torque. Sometimes written as ft-lbs.
lbf in Pound-force inch. An imperial unit of torque, applied to components where a very low torque is required. Sometimes written as in-lbs.
IC Abbreviation for Integrated Circuit.
Ignition advance Means of increasing the timing of the spark at higher engine speeds. Done by mechanical means (ATU) on early engines or electronically by the ignition control unit on later engines.
Ignition timing The moment at which the spark plug fires, expressed in the number of crankshaft degrees before the piston reaches the top of its stroke, or in the number of millimetres before the piston reaches the top of its stroke.
Infinity (∞) Description of an open-circuit electrical state, where no continuity exists.
Inverted forks (upside down forks) The sliders or lower legs are held in the yokes and the fork tubes or stanchions are connected to the wheel axle (spindle). Less unsprung weight and stiffer construction than conventional forks.

J

JASO Quality standard for 2-stroke oils.
Joule The unit of electrical energy.
Journal The bearing surface of a shaft.

K

Kickstart Mechanical means of turning the engine over for starting purposes. Only usually fitted to mopeds, small capacity motorcycles and off-road motorcycles.
Kill switch Handebar-mounted switch for emergency ignition cut-out. Cuts the ignition circuit on all models, and additionally prevent starter motor operation on others.
km Symbol for kilometre.
kmh Abbreviation for kilometres per hour.

L

Lambda (λ) sensor A sensor fitted in the exhaust system to measure the exhaust gas oxygen content (excess air factor).

Technical Terms Explained

Lapping see Grinding.
LCD Abbreviation for Liquid Crystal Display.
LED Abbreviation for Light Emitting Diode.
Liner A steel cylinder liner inserted in a aluminium alloy cylinder block.
Locknut A nut used to lock an adjustment nut, or other threaded component, in place.
Lockstops The lugs on the lower triple clamp (yoke) which abut those on the frame, preventing handlebar-to-fuel tank contact.
Lockwasher A form of washer designed to prevent an attaching nut from working loose.
LT Low Tension Description of the electrical circuit from the power supply to the primary winding of the ignition coil.

M

Main bearings The bearings between the crankshaft and crankcase.
Maintenance-free (MF) battery A sealed battery which cannot be topped up.
Manometer Mercury-filled calibrated tubes used to measure intake tract vacuum. Used to synchronise carburettors on multi-cylinder engines.
Micrometer A precision measuring instrument that measures component outside diameters **(see illustration)**.

Tappet shims are measured with a micrometer

MON (Motor Octane Number) A measure of a fuel's resistance to knock.
Monograde oil An oil with a single viscosity, eg SAE80W.
Monoshock A single suspension unit linking the swingarm or suspension linkage to the frame.
mph Abbreviation for miles per hour.
Multigrade oil Having a wide viscosity range (eg 10W40). The W stands for Winter, thus the viscosity ranges from SAE10 when cold to SAE40 when hot.
Multimeter An electrical test instrument with the capability to measure voltage, current and resistance. Some meters also incorporate a continuity tester and buzzer.

N

Needle roller bearing Inner race of caged needle rollers and hardened outer race. Examples of uncaged needle rollers can be found on some engines. Commonly used in rear suspension applications and in two-stroke engines.
Nm Newton metres.
NOx Oxides of Nitrogen. A common toxic pollutant emitted by petrol engines at higher temperatures.

O

Octane The measure of a fuel's resistance to knock.
OE (Original Equipment) Relates to components fitted to a motorcycle as standard or replacement parts supplied by the motorcycle manufacturer.
Ohm The unit of electrical resistance. Ohms = Volts ÷ Current.
Ohmmeter An instrument for measuring electrical resistance.
Oil cooler System for diverting engine oil outside of the engine to a radiator for cooling purposes.
Oil injection A system of two-stroke engine lubrication where oil is pump-fed to the engine in accordance with throttle position.
Open-circuit An electrical condition where there is a break in the flow of electricity - no continuity (high resistance).
O-ring A type of sealing ring made of a special rubber-like material; in use, the O-ring is compressed into a groove to provide the sealing action.
Oversize (OS) Term used for piston and ring size options fitted to a rebored cylinder.
Overhead cam (sohc) engine An engine with single camshaft located on top of the cylinder head.
Overhead valve (ohv) engine An engine with the valves located in the cylinder head, but with the camshaft located in the engine block or crankcase.
Oxygen sensor A device installed in the exhaust system which senses the oxygen content in the exhaust and converts this information into an electric current. Also called a Lambda sensor.

P

Plastigauge A thin strip of plastic thread, available in different sizes, used for measuring clearances. For example, a strip of Plastigauge is laid across a bearing journal. The parts are assembled and dismantled; the width of the crushed strip indicates the clearance between journal and bearing.
Polarity Either negative or positive earth (ground), determined by which battery lead is connected to the frame (earth return). Modern motorcycles are usually negative earth.
Pre-ignition A situation where the fuel/air mixture ignites before the spark plug fires. Often due to a hot spot in the combustion chamber caused by carbon build-up. Engine has a tendency to 'run-on'.
Pre-load (suspension) The amount a spring is compressed when in the unloaded state. Preload can be applied by gas, spacer or mechanical adjuster.
Premix The method of engine lubrication on older two-stroke engines. Engine oil is mixed with the petrol in the fuel tank in a specific ratio. The fuel/oil mix is sometimes referred to as "petroil".
Primary drive Description of the drive from the crankshaft to the clutch. Usually by gear or chain.
PS Pfedestärke - a German interpretation of BHP.
PSI Pounds-force per square inch. Imperial measurement of tyre pressure and cylinder pressure measurement.
PTFE Polytetrafluroethylene. A low friction substance.
Pulse secondary air injection system A process of promoting the burning of excess fuel present in the exhaust gases by routing fresh air into the exhaust ports.

Q

Quartz halogen bulb Tungsten filament surrounded by a halogen gas. Typically used for the headlight **(see illustration)**.

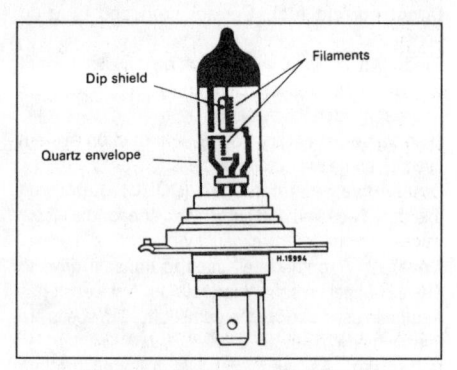

Quartz halogen headlight bulb construction

R

Rack-and-pinion A pinion gear on the end of a shaft that mates with a rack (think of a geared wheel opened up and laid flat). Sometimes used in clutch operating systems.
Radial play Up and down movement about a shaft.
Radial ply tyres Tyre plies run across the tyre (from bead to bead) and around the circumference of the tyre. Less resistant to tread distortion than other tyre types.
Radiator A liquid-to-air heat transfer device designed to reduce the temperature of the coolant in a liquid cooled engine.
Rake A feature of steering geometry - the angle of the steering head in relation to the vertical **(see illustration)**.

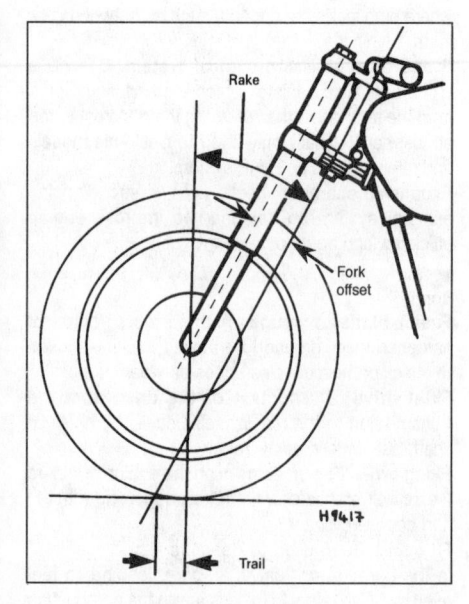

Steering geometry

Technical Terms Explained

Rebore Providing a new working surface to the cylinder bore by boring out the old surface. Necessitates the use of oversize piston and rings.
Rebound damping A means of controlling the oscillation of a suspension unit spring after it has been compressed. Resists the spring's natural tendency to bounce back after being compressed.
Rectifier Device for converting the ac output of an alternator into dc for battery charging.
Reed valve An induction system commonly used on two-stroke engines.
Regulator Device for maintaining the charging voltage from the generator or alternator within a specified range.
Relay A electrical device used to switch heavy current on and off by using a low current auxiliary circuit.
Resistance Measured in ohms. An electrical component's ability to pass electrical current.
RON (Research Octane Number) A measure of a fuel's resistance to knock.
rpm revolutions per minute.
Runout The amount of wobble (in-and-out movement) of a wheel or shaft as it's rotated. The amount a shaft rotates `out-of-true'. The out-of-round condition of a rotating part.

S

SAE (Society of Automotive Engineers) A standard for the viscosity of a fluid.
Sealant A liquid or paste used to prevent leakage at a joint. Sometimes used in conjunction with a gasket.
Service limit Term for the point where a component is no longer useable and must be renewed.
Shaft drive A method of transmitting drive from the transmission to the rear wheel.
Shell bearings Plain bearings consisting of two shell halves. Most often used as big-end and main bearings in a four-stroke engine. Often called bearing inserts.
Shim Thin spacer, commonly used to adjust the clearance or relative positions between two parts. For example, shims inserted into or under tappets or followers to control valve clearances. Clearance is adjusted by changing the thickness of the shim.
Short-circuit An electrical condition where current shorts to earth (ground) bypassing the circuit components.
Skimming Process to correct warpage or repair a damaged surface, eg on brake discs or drums.
Slide-hammer A special puller that screws into or hooks onto a component such as a shaft or bearing; a heavy sliding handle on the shaft bottoms against the end of the shaft to knock the component free.
Small-end bearing The bearing in the upper end of the connecting rod at its joint with the gudgeon pin.
Spalling Damage to camshaft lobes or bearing journals shown as pitting of the working surface.
Specific gravity (SG) The state of charge of the electrolyte in a lead-acid battery. A measure of the electrolyte's density compared with water.
Straight-cut gears Common type gear used on gearbox shafts and for oil pump and water pump drives.
Stanchion The inner sliding part of the front forks, held by the yokes. Often called a fork tube.

Stoichiometric ratio The optimum chemical air/fuel ratio for a petrol engine, said to be 14.7 parts of air to 1 part of fuel.
Sulphuric acid The liquid (electrolyte) used in a lead-acid battery. Poisonous and extremely corrosive.
Surface grinding (lapping) Process to correct a warped gasket face, commonly used on cylinder heads.

T

Tapered-roller bearing Tapered inner race of caged needle rollers and separate tapered outer race. Examples of taper roller bearings can be found on steering heads.
Tappet A cylindrical component which transmits motion from the cam to the valve stem, either directly or via a pushrod and rocker arm. Also called a cam follower.
TCS Traction Control System. An electronically-controlled system which senses wheel spin and reduces engine speed accordingly.
TDC Top Dead Centre denotes that the piston is at its highest point in the cylinder.
Thread-locking compound Solution applied to fastener threads to prevent slackening. Select type to suit application.
Thrust washer A washer positioned between two moving components on a shaft. For example, between gear pinions on gearshaft.
Timing chain See **Cam Chain**.
Timing light Stroboscopic lamp for carrying out ignition timing checks with the engine running.
Top-end A description of an engine's cylinder block, head and valve gear components.
Torque Turning or twisting force about a shaft.
Torque setting A prescribed tightness specified by the motorcycle manufacturer to ensure that the bolt or nut is secured correctly. Undertightening can result in the bolt or nut coming loose or a surface not being sealed. Overtightening can result in stripped threads, distortion or damage to the component being retained.
Torx key A six-point wrench.
Tracer A stripe of a second colour applied to a wire insulator to distinguish that wire from another one with the same colour insulator. For example, Br/W is often used to denote a brown insulator with a white tracer.
Trail A feature of steering geometry. Distance from the steering head axis to the tyre's central contact point.
Triple clamps The cast components which extend from the steering head and support the fork stanchions or tubes. Often called fork yokes.
Turbocharger A centrifugal device, driven by exhaust gases, that pressurises the intake air. Normally used to increase the power output from a given engine displacement.
TWI Abbreviation for Tyre Wear Indicator. Indicates the location of the tread depth indicator bars on tyres.

U

Universal joint or U-joint (UJ) A double-pivoted connection for transmitting power from a driving to a driven shaft through an angle. Typically found in shaft drive assemblies.
Unsprung weight Anything not supported by the bike's suspension (ie the wheel, tyres, brakes, final drive and bottom (moving) part of the suspension).

V

Vacuum gauges Clock-type gauges for measuring intake tract vacuum. Used for carburettor synchronisation on multi-cylinder engines.
Valve A device through which the flow of liquid, gas or vacuum may be stopped, started or regulated by a moveable part that opens, shuts or partially obstructs one or more ports or passageways. The intake and exhaust valves in the cylinder head are of the poppet type.
Valve clearance The clearance between the valve tip (the end of the valve stem) and the rocker arm or tappet/follower. The valve clearance is measured when the valve is closed. The correct clearance is important - if too small the valve won't close fully and will burn out, whereas if too large noisy operation will result.
Valve lift The amount a valve is lifted off its seat by the camshaft lobe.
Valve timing The exact setting for the opening and closing of the valves in relation to piston position.
Vernier caliper A precision measuring instrument that measures inside and outside dimensions. Not quite as accurate as a micrometer, but more convenient.

Wet liner arrangement

VIN Vehicle Identification Number. Term for the bike's engine and frame numbers.
Viscosity The thickness of a liquid or its resistance to flow.
Volt A unit for expressing electrical "pressure" in a circuit. Volts = current x ohms.

W

Water pump A mechanically-driven device for moving coolant around the engine.
Watt A unit for expressing electrical power. Watts = volts x current.
Wear limit see **Service limit**
Wet liner A liquid-cooled engine design where the pistons run in liners which are directly surrounded by coolant **(see illustration)**.
Wheelbase Distance from the centre of the front wheel to the centre of the rear wheel.
Wiring harness or loom Describes the electrical wires running the length of the motorcycle and enclosed in tape or plastic sheathing. Wiring coming off the main harness is usually referred to as a sub harness.
Woodruff key A key of semi-circular or square section used to locate a gear to a shaft. Often used to locate the alternator rotor on the crankshaft.
Wrist pin Another name for gudgeon or piston pin.

Index

Note: References throughout this index are in the form - "Chapter number" • "Page number"

A

ABS – 6•16, 6•17
Acknowledgements – 0•8
Air filter – 1•10
Air filter housing – 4•7
Air induction system – 1•14, 4•23
Alternator rotor – 2•25
Alternator stator – 8•1, 8•26
Atmospheric pressure sensor – 4•19

B

Balancer shafts – 2•63
Battery – 1•26, 8•1, 8•4, 8•5
Battery access panel
   2001 to 2005 models – 7•4
   2006 to 2012 models – 7•10
   2013-on models – 7•13
Bike spec – 0•17
Bodywork – 7•1 et seq
Brake
   ABS – 6•16
   bleeding – 6•12
   calipers – 1•10, 6•4, 6•10
   fluid – 1•2
   fluid change – 1•9, 6•15
   fluid level check – 0•12
   hoses – 1•9, 6•12
   master cylinders – 1•10, 6•6, 6•11
   pads – 1•8, 6•3, 6•8
   pedal – 5•3
   specifications – 6•1
   system check – 1•8
Brake light
   bulbs – 8•2, 8•11
   circuit test and relay – 8•8
Brake light switches – 1•8, 8•14
Bulbs – 8•2
   brake/tail lights – 8•11
   headlight – 8•9
   instrument – 8•16
   licence plate – 8•12
   sidelight – 8•10
   turn signal – 8•13

C

Cables (throttle) – 1•16, 1•26, 4•12
Caliper
   front – 6•4
   rear – 6•10
Cam chain and guides – 2•19

Cam chain tensioner – 2•14
Camshaft position sensor – 4•17
Camshafts – 2•2, 2•15
Catalytic converter – 4•23
Centrestand – 1•25, 5•4
Charging (battery) – 8•5
Charging system – 8•1, 8•25
Clutch – 2•29
   fluid – 1•2
   fluid level – 0•14
   lever – 5•6
   master cylinder – 2•35
   release cylinder – 2•37
   release mechanism – 2•35
   specifications – 2•2
   system check – 1•10
   YCC-S checks – 1•10
Clutch switch – 8•20
Cockpit trim panel
   2006 to 2012 models – 7•10
   2013-on models – 7•14
Colour code label – 0•9
Connecting rods – 2•4, 2•55, 2•60
Conversion factors – REF•26
Coolant – 1•2
   change – 1•21
   level check – 0•12
   reservoir – 3•9
Cooling system – 3•1 et seq
   checks – 1•20
   hoses, pipes and unions – 3•9
   fan and relay – 3•2
   radiator – 3•4
   specifications – 3•1
   temperature display and ECT sensor – 3•2
   thermostat – 3•4
   water pump – 3•6
Crankcase breather – 1•15
Crankcases – 2•51, 2•54
Crankshaft and bearings – 2•4, 2•56, 2•59
Crankshaft position sensor – 4•17
Cruise control – 4•15
Cylinder bores – 2•4, 2•55
Cylinder compression check – 2•6
Cylinder head – 2•2, 2•20, 2•21
Cylinder numbering – 1•1

D

Dimensions – 0•17
Diodes – 4•21
Discs
   front – 6•6
   rear – 6•10
Driveshaft – 6•28

E

ECU – 4•20
Electrical system – 8•1 et seq
   alternator stator – 8•26
   battery – 1•26, 8•4, 8•5
   brake/tail light – 8•11
   brake light switches – 8•14
   clutch switch – 8•20
   fuses – 8•6
   handlebar switches – 8•17
   headlight – 8•9, 8•10
   heated grips – 8•20
   horn – 8•20
   ignition switch – 8•17
   instruments – 8•14, 8•15
   licence plate light – 8•12
   lighting system – 8•7
   neutral/gear position switches – 8•18
   oil level sensor – 8•16
   regulator/rectifier – 8•27
   sidelight – 8•10
   sidestand switch – 8•19
   specifications – 8•1
   starter motor – 8•21, 8•22
   starter relay – 8•21
   tail light – 8•12
   turn signals – 8•12, 8•13
   windshield motor – 8•27
   wiring diagrams – 8•30 et seq
Engine – 2•1 et seq
   alternator rotor – 2•25
   balancer shafts – 2•63
   cam chain and guides – 2•19
   cam chain tensioner – 2•14
   camshafts – 2•15
   compression check – 2•6
   connecting rods – 2•55, 2•56, 2•60
   crankcases – 2•51, 2•54
   crankshaft – 2•56
   cylinder bores – 2•55
   cylinder head – 2•20, 2•21
   lubrication system – 2•3
   oil cooler – 2•13
   oil change and filter – 1•17
   oil level – 0•11
   oil pressure check – 2•6
   piston rings – 2•62
   pistons – 2•61
   removal from frame – 2•7
   running-in – 2•74
   specifications – 0•18, 1•1, 2•1
   starter clutch – 2•25
   timing rotor – 2•28
   valve clearances – 1•26
   valve cover – 2•13
   valves – 2•21

Index

Engine coolant temperature sensor – 3•1, 3•3
Engine management system – 4•1 et seq
  description – 4•16
  fault diagnosis and codes – 4•16
  sensors – 4•17
Engine number – 0•9
Exhaust system – 4•22

F

Fairing
  2001 to 2005 models – 7•5
  2006 to 2012 models – 7•12
  2013-on models – 7•16
Fairing pocket
  2003 to 2005 models – 7•4
  2006 to 2012 models – 7•10
  2013-on models – 7•14
Fairing side panels
  2001 to 2005 models – 7•3
  2006 to 2012 models – 7•8
  2013-on models – 7•14, 7•15
Fan – 3•2
Fault codes
  ABS – 6•16
  engine management – 4•16
  immobiliser – 4•29
  YCC-S – 2•43
Fault finding – REF•35 et seq
  electrical system – 8•3
  engine management – 4•16
  ignition system – 4•25
Fast idle system – 4•14
Filter
  air – 1•10
  fuel – 1•14
  oil – 1•17
Final drive
  checks – 0•11, 1•19
  drive coupling – 6•32
  drive coupling bearing – 6•27
  housing, driveshaft and UJ – 6•28
  middle gear shafts – 2•48
  oil level check and oil change – 1•2, 1•19
Footrests – 5•2
Frame – 5•2
Frame number – 0•9
Front brake
  calipers – 6•4
  discs – 6•1
  fluid level – 0•12
  lever – 5•6
  lever span adjuster – 1•9
  master cylinder – 6•6
  pads – 6•1, 6•3

Front forks
  adjustment – 5•21
  checks – 1•23
  oil – 5•1
  oil change – 1•24, 5•7
  overhaul – 5•9
  removal and installation – 5•7
  specifications – 5•1
Front mudguard – 7•12
Front wheel – 6•22
Front wheel bearings – 6•25
Front wheel sensor and rotor (ABS) – 6•17
Fuel injection system
  fault diagnosis and codes – 4•16
  rail and injectors – 4•13
  relay – 4•21
  sensors – 4•17
  specifications – 4•2
  throttle bodies – 1•15, 4•8
Fuel supply system
  checks – 1•13
  level sensor – 4•7
  pressure check – 4•7
  pump – 4•5
  specifications – 4•1
  tank – 4•1, 4•3
Fuses – 8•2, 8•6

G

Gear position sensor/switch – 8•19
  YCC-S – 2•44
Gearchange lever and linkage
  standard models – 5•3
  YCC-S models – 2•42
Gearchange mechanism – 2•4, 2•38, 2•41
Grab-rack
  2001 to 2005 models – 7•3
  2006 to 2013 models – 7•8

H

Handlebar switches – 8•17
Handlebars – 5•5
Hazard switch panel – 7•4
Headlight – 8•10
  aim – 8•11
  bulbs – 8•2, 8•9
  circuit test and relays – 8•7
Heated grip control panel – 7•10
Heated grips – 8•20
Horn – 8•20

I

Idle speed – 1•1, 1•16
Idle system – 4•14
Ignition coils – 4•2, 4•25
Ignition switch – 8•17
Ignition system check – 4•25
Ignition timing – 4•27
Immobiliser – 4•28
Injectors (fuel) – 4•13
Instrument surround panel
  2001 to 2005 models – 7•5
  2006 to 2012 models – 7•11
  2013-on models 7•13
Instruments – 8•14, 8•15
Intake air pressure sensor – 4•18
Intake air temperature sensor – 4•19

L

Leak-down test – 2•6
Legal checks – 0•11
Levers (handlebar) – 5•6
Licence plate light – 8•12
Lighting system – 8•7
Lubricants
  general information – REF•23
  recommended – 1•2
Lubrication
  cables – 1•26,
  pivot points – 1•26
  rear suspension bearings – 1•24
  steering head bearings – 1•25
Lubrication system (engine)
  oil change and filter – 1•17
  oil cooler – 2•13
  oil level check – 0•11
  oil level sensor – 8•15
  oil pressure check – 2•6
  oil pump – 2•47
  oil sump, strainer and pressure relief valve – 2•45
  specifications – 2•3

M

Main bearings – 2•55, 2•59
Maintenance schedule – 1•3, 1•4
Master cylinder
  clutch – 2•35
  front brake – 6•2, 6•6
  rear brake – 6•2, 6•11
Metering valve (ABS) – 6•19
Middle gear shafts – 2•48

Index

Mirrors
  2001 to 2005 models – 7•7
  2006 to 2012 models – 7•13
  2013-on models – 7•17
Model development – 0•16
Modulator (ABS) – 6•18
MOT Test Checks – REF•27

N

Neutral switch – 8•18

O

Oil (engine) – 0•11, 1•2, 1•17
Oil (final drive) – 1•2, 1•19
Oil (front forks) – 1•24, 5•1, 5•7
Oil cooler – 2•13
Oil level sensor – 8•15
Oil pressure check – 2•6
Oil pump – 2•47
Oil sump, strainer and pressure relief valve – 2•45
Oxygen sensor – 4•20

P

Pads (brake)
  front – 6•3
  rear – 6•8
Piston rings – 2•3, 2•62
Pistons – 2•3, 2•61
Pre-ride checks – 0•11 et seq
Pressure cap (cooling system) – 1•21, 3•1
Pressure check
  cylinder compression – 2•6
  fuel – 4•7
  oil – 2•6
  tyre – 0•15
Pressure relief valve – 2•45
Proportional control valve (ABS) – 6•19
Pump (fuel) – 4•5
Pump (oil) – 2•47
Pump (water) – 3•6

R

Radiator – 3•4
Rail (fuel) – 4•13
Rear brake
  caliper – 6•10
  disc – 6•10
  fluid level – 0•12
  master cylinder – 6•11
  pads – 6•1, 6•8
  pedal – 5•3
  pedal height adjustment – 1•9
Rear cover
  2001 to 2005 models – 7•3
  2006 to 2013 models – 7•8
Rear suspension
  bearing lubrication – 1•24
  checks – 1•23
  linkage – 5•18
  shock absorber – 5•17, 5•22
Rear wheel – 6•23
Rear wheel bearings – 6•26
Rear wheel drive coupling – 6•32
Rear wheel sensor and rotor – 6•18
Regulator/rectifier – 8•27
Relays
  ABS – 6•20
  brake light – 8•8
  brake switch – 8•9
  fan – 3•2
  fuel injection – 4•21
  headlight – 8•7
  starter – 8•21
  starter cut-off – 4•21
  windshield motor – 8•27
  YCC-S control – 2•44
Release cylinder (clutch) – 2•37
Routine maintenance and servicing – 1•1 et seq
Running-in – 2•74

S

Safety – 0•10, 0•11
Seats
  2001 to 2005 models – 7•2
  2006 to 2013 models – 7•7
Security – REF•20
Selector drum and forks – 2•74
Side covers
  2001 to 2005 models – 7•3
  2006 to 2013 models – 7•7
Sidelight bulbs – 8•10
Sidestand – 1•25, 5•3
Sidestand switch – 8•19
Silencers – 4•22
Spark plugs – 1•1, 1•11
Speed sensor – 2•44, 4•19
Starter clutch – 2•25
Starter cut-off relay – 4•21
Starter motor – 8•1, 8•21, 8•22
Starter relay – 8•21
Starter safety circuit – 1•26
Steering
  checks – 0•11, 1•24
  stem – 5•13
Steering head bearings – 1•24, 5•16
Storage advice – REF•32
Strainer (oil) – 2•45
Suspension
  adjustment – 5•21
  checks – 0•11, 1•22
  front forks – 5•7, 5•9
  rear linkage – 5•18
  rear shock – 5•17
Swingarm – 5•19

T

Tail light – 8•12
  bulbs – 8•11
Tank (fuel) – 4•1, 4•3
Temperature display – 3•3
Thermostat – 3•1, 3•4
Throttle bodies – 4•8
  synchronisation – 1•15
Throttle cables – 1•16, 1•26, 4•12
Throttle position sensor – 4•18
Throttle twistgrip – 1•17
Timing rotor – 2•28
Tip-over sensor – 4•20
Tools and Workshop Tips – REF•2 et seq
Torque settings – 1•2, 2•4, 3•1, 4•2, 5•2, 6•2, 8•3
Transmission
  selector drum and forks – 2•74
  shafts overhaul – 2•68
  shafts removal and installation – 2•66
  specifications – 2•4
Trim clips – 7•2
Turn signal – 8•13
  bulbs – 8•2, 8•13
  circuit check and relay – 8•12
Tyres – 6•28
  pressures and tread depth – 0•15
  sizes – 6•2
  valves – 1•22

U

Universal joint – 6•31

V

Valve clearances – 1•1, 1•26
Valve cover – 2•13
Valves – 2•2, 2•21
VIN – 0•9

W

Water pump – 3•6
Weights – 0•17
Wheels – 6•22, 6•23
  alignment – 6•21
  bearings – 1•22, 6•25
  checks – 1•22
  inspection and repair – 6•21
  specifications – 6•2
Windshield
  2001 to 2005 models – 7•5
  2006 to 2012 models – 7•11
  2013-on models – 7•16
Windshield motor and relays – 8•27
Wiring diagrams – 8•30 et seq

Y

YCC-S – 2•42
  checks – 1•10
  gearchange mechanism – 2•41
  release mechanism – 2•38
YCC-T – 4•15

Haynes Motorcycle Manuals – The Complete List

Title	Book No
APRILIA RS50 (99 - 06) & RS125 (93 - 06)	4298
Aprilia RSV1000 Mille (98 - 03)	♦ 4255
Aprilia SR50	4755
BMW 2-valve Twins (70 - 96)	♦ 0249
BMW F650	♦ 4761
BMW K100 & 75 2-valve Models (83 - 96)	♦ 1373
BMW R850, 1100 & 1150 4-valve Twins (93 - 04)	♦ 3466
BMW R1200 (04 - 06)	♦ 4598
BSA Bantam (48 - 71)	0117
BSA Unit Singles (58 - 72)	0127
BSA Pre-unit Singles (54 - 61)	0326
BSA A7 & A10 Twins (47 - 62)	0121
BSA A50 & A65 Twins (62 - 73)	0155
Chinese Scooters	4768
DUCATI 600, 620, 750 and 900 2-valve V-Twins (91 - 05)	♦ 3290
Ducati MK III & Desmo Singles (69 - 76)	◊ 0445
Ducati 748, 916 & 996 4-valve V-Twins (94 - 01)	♦ 3756
GILERA Runner, DNA, Ice & SKP/Stalker (97 - 07)	4163
HARLEY-DAVIDSON Sportsters (70 - 08)	♦ 2534
Harley-Davidson Shovelhead and Evolution Big Twins (70 - 99)	♦ 2536
Harley-Davidson Twin Cam 88 (99 - 03)	♦ 2478
HONDA NB, ND, NP & NS50 Melody (81 - 85)	◊ 0622
Honda NE/NB50 Vision & SA50 Vision Met-in (85 - 95)	◊ 1278
Honda MB, MBX, MT & MTX50 (80 - 93)	0731
Honda C50, C70 & C90 (67 - 03)	0324
Honda XR80/100R & CRF80/100F (85 - 04)	2218
Honda XL/XR 80, 100, 125, 185 & 200 2-valve Models (78 - 87)	0566
Honda H100 & H100S Singles (80 - 92)	◊ 0734
Honda CB/CD125T & CM125C Twins (77 - 88)	◊ 0571
Honda CG125 (76 - 07)	◊ 0433
Honda NS125 (86 - 93)	◊ 3056
Honda CBR125R (04 - 07)	4620
Honda MBX/MTX125 & MTX200 (83 - 93)	◊ 1132
Honda CD/CM185 200T & CM250C 2-valve Twins (77 - 85)	0572
Honda XL/XR 250 & 500 (78 - 84)	0567
Honda XR250L, XR250R & XR400R (86 - 03)	2219
Honda CB250 & CB400N Super Dreams (78 - 84)	◊ 0540
Honda CR Motocross Bikes (86 - 01)	2222
Honda CRF250 & CRF450 (02 - 06)	2630
Honda CBR400RR Fours (88 - 99)	◊ ♦ 3552
Honda VFR400 (NC30) & RVF400 (NC35) V-Fours (89 - 98)	◊ ♦ 3496
Honda CB500 (93 - 02) & CBF500 03 - 08	◊ 3753
Honda CB400 & CB550 Fours (73 - 77)	0262
Honda CX/GL500 & 650 V-Twins (78 - 86)	0442
Honda CBX550 Four (82 - 86)	◊ 0940
Honda XL600R & XR600R (83 - 08)	♦ 2183
Honda XL600/650V Transalp & XRV750 Africa Twin (87 to 07)	♦ 3919
Honda CBR600F1 & 1000F Fours (87 - 96)	♦ 1730
Honda CBR600F2 & F3 Fours (91 - 98)	♦ 2070
Honda CBR600F4 (99 - 06)	♦ 3911
Honda CB600F Hornet & CBF600 (98 - 06)	◊ ♦ 3915
Honda CBR600RR (03 - 06)	♦ 4590
Honda CB650 sohc Fours (78 - 84)	0665
Honda NTV600 Revere, NTV650 and NT650V Deauville (88 - 05)	◊ 3243
Honda Shadow VT600 & 750 (USA) (88 - 03)	2312
Honda CB750 sohc Four (69 - 79)	0131
Honda V45/65 Sabre & Magna (82 - 88)	0820
Honda VFR750 & 700 V-Fours (86 - 97)	♦ 2101
Honda VFR800 V-Fours (97 - 01)	♦ 3703
Honda VFR800 V-Tec V-Fours (02 - 05)	♦ 4196
Honda CB750 & CB900 dohc Fours (78 - 84)	0535
Honda VTR1000 (FireStorm, Super Hawk) & XL1000V (Varadero) (97 - 08)	♦ 3744
Honda CBR900RR FireBlade (92 - 99)	♦ 2161
Honda CBR900RR FireBlade (00 - 03)	♦ 4060
Honda CBR1000RR Fireblade (04 - 07)	♦ 4604
Honda CBR1100XX Super Blackbird (97 - 07)	♦ 3901
Honda ST1100 Pan European V-Fours (90 - 02)	♦ 3384
Honda Shadow VT1100 (USA) (85 - 98)	2313
Honda GL1000 Gold Wing (75 - 79)	0309

Title	Book No
Honda GL1100 Gold Wing (79 - 81)	0669
Honda Gold Wing 1200 (USA) (84 - 87)	2199
Honda Gold Wing 1500 (USA) (88 - 00)	2225
KAWASAKI AE/AR 50 & 80 (81 - 95)	1007
Kawasaki KC, KE & KH100 (75 - 99)	1371
Kawasaki KMX125 & 200 (86 - 02)	◊ 3046
Kawasaki 250, 350 & 400 Triples (72 - 79)	0134
Kawasaki 400 & 440 Twins (74 - 81)	0281
Kawasaki 400, 500 & 550 Fours (79 - 91)	0910
Kawasaki EN450 & 500 Twins (Ltd/Vulcan) (85 - 07)	2053
Kawasaki EX500 (GPZ500S) & ER500 (ER-5) (87 - 08)	♦ 2052
Kawasaki ZX600 (ZZ-R600 & Ninja ZX-6) (90 - 06)	♦ 2146
Kawasaki ZX-6R Ninja Fours (95 - 02)	♦ 3541
Kawasaki ZX-6R (03 - 06)	♦ 4742
Kawasaki ZX600 (GPZ600R, GPX600R, Ninja 600R & RX) & ZX750 (GPX750R, Ninja 750R)	♦ 1780
Kawasaki 650 Four (76 - 78)	0373
Kawasaki Vulcan 700/750 & 800 (85 - 04)	♦ 2457
Kawasaki 750 Air-cooled Fours (80 - 91)	0574
Kawasaki ZR550 & 750 Zephyr Fours (90 - 97)	♦ 3382
Kawasaki Z750 & Z1000 (03 - 08)	♦ 4762
Kawasaki ZX750 (Ninja ZX-7 & ZXR750) Fours (89 - 96)	♦ 2054
Kawasaki Ninja ZX-7R & ZX-9R (94 - 04)	♦ 3721
Kawasaki 900 & 1000 Fours (73 - 77)	0222
Kawasaki ZX900, 1000 & 1100 Liquid-cooled Fours (83 - 97)	♦ 1681
KTM EXC Enduro & SX Motocross (00 - 07)	♦ 4629
MOTO GUZZI 750, 850 & 1000 V-Twins (74 - 78)	0339
MZ ETZ Models (81 - 95)	◊ 1680
NORTON 500, 600, 650 & 750 Twins (57 - 70)	0187
Norton Commando (68 - 77)	0125
PEUGEOT Speedfight, Trekker & Vivacity Scooters (96 - 08)	◊ 3920
PIAGGIO (Vespa) Scooters (91 - 06)	◊ 3492
SUZUKI GT, ZR & TS50 (77 - 90)	◊ 0799
Suzuki TS50X (84 - 00)	◊ 1599
Suzuki 100, 125, 185 & 250 Air-cooled Trail bikes (79 - 89)	0797
Suzuki GP100 & 125 Singles (78 - 93)	◊ 0576
Suzuki GS, GN, GZ & DR125 Singles (82 - 05)	◊ 0888
Suzuki GSX-R600/750 (06 - 09)	♦ 4790
Suzuki GS & DR 250 Twins (78 - 85)	0120
Suzuki GT250X7, GT200X5 & SB200 Twins (78 - 83)	◊ 0469
Suzuki GS/GSX250, 400 & 450 Twins (79 - 85)	0736
Suzuki GS500 Twin (89 - 06)	♦ 3238
Suzuki GS550 (77 - 82) & GS750 Fours (76 - 79)	0363
Suzuki GS/GSX550 4-valve Fours (83 - 88)	1133
Suzuki SV650 & SV650S (99 - 08)	♦ 3912
Suzuki GSX-R600 & 750 (96 - 00)	♦ 3553
Suzuki GSX-R600 (01 - 03), GSX-R750 (00 - 03) & GSX-R1000 (01 - 02)	♦ 3986
Suzuki GSX-R600/750 (04 - 05) & GSX-R1000 (03 - 06)	♦ 4382
Suzuki GSF600, 650 & 1200 Bandit Fours (95 - 06)	♦ 3367
Suzuki Intruder, Marauder, Volusia & Boulevard (85 - 06)	♦ 2618
Suzuki GS850 Fours (78 - 88)	0536
Suzuki GS1000 Four (77 - 79)	0484
Suzuki GSX-R750, GSX-R1100 (85 - 92), GSX600F, GSX750F, GSX1100F (Katana) Fours	♦ 2055
Suzuki GSX600/750F & GSX750 (98 - 02)	♦ 3987
Suzuki GS/GSX1000, 1100 & 1150 4-valve Fours (79 - 88)	0737
Suzuki TL1000S/R & DL1000 V-Strom (97 - 04)	♦ 4083
Suzuki GSF650/1250 (05 - 09)	♦ 4798
Suzuki GSX1300R Hayabusa (99 - 04)	♦ 4184
Suzuki GSX1400 (02 - 07)	♦ 4758
TRIUMPH Tiger Cub & Terrier (52 - 68)	0414
Triumph 350 & 500 Unit Twins (58 - 73)	0137
Triumph Pre-Unit Twins (47 - 62)	0251
Triumph 650 & 750 2-valve Unit Twins (63 - 83)	0122
Triumph Trident & BSA Rocket 3 (69 - 75)	0136
Triumph Bonneville (01 - 07)	♦ 4364
Triumph Daytona, Speed Triple, Sprint & Tiger (97 - 05)	♦ 3755
Triumph Triples and Fours (carburettor engines) (91 - 04)	♦ 2162
VESPA P/PX125, 150 & 200 Scooters (78 - 06)	0707
Vespa Scooters (59 - 78)	0126
YAMAHA DT50 & 80 Trail Bikes (78 - 95)	◊ 0800
Yamaha T50 & 80 Townmate (83 - 95)	1247

Title	Book No
Yamaha YB100 Singles (73 - 91)	◊ 0474
Yamaha RS/RXS100 & 125 Singles (74 - 95)	0331
Yamaha RD & DT125LC (82 - 95)	◊ 0887
Yamaha TZR125 (87 - 93) & DT125R (88 - 07)	◊ 1655
Yamaha TY50, 80, 125 & 175 (74 - 84)	◊ 0464
Yamaha XT & SR125 (82 - 03)	◊ 1021
Yamaha YBR125	4797
Yamaha Trail Bikes (81 - 00)	2350
Yamaha 2-stroke Motocross Bikes 1986 - 2006	2662
Yamaha YZ & WR 4-stroke Motocross Bikes (98 - 08)	2689
Yamaha 250 & 350 Twins (70 - 79)	0040
Yamaha XS250, 360 & 400 sohc Twins (75 - 84)	0378
Yamaha RD250 & 350LC Twins (80 - 82)	0803
Yamaha RD350 YPVS Twins (83 - 95)	1158
Yamaha RD400 Twin (75 - 79)	0333
Yamaha XT, TT & SR500 Singles (75 - 83)	0342
Yamaha XZ550 Vision V-Twins (82 - 85)	0821
Yamaha FJ, FZ, XJ & YX600 Radian (84 - 92)	2100
Yamaha XJ600S (Diversion, Seca II) & XJ600N Fours (92 - 03)	♦ 2145
Yamaha YZF600R Thundercat & FZS600 Fazer (96 - 03)	♦ 3702
Yamaha FZ-6 Fazer (04 - 07)	♦ 4751
Yamaha YZF-R6 (99 - 02)	♦ 3900
Yamaha YZF-R6 (03 - 06)	♦ 4601
Yamaha 650 Twins (70 - 83)	0341
Yamaha XJ650 & 750 Fours (80 - 84)	0738
Yamaha XS750 & 850 Triples (76 - 85)	0340
Yamaha TDM850, TRX850 & XTZ750 (89 - 99)	◊ 3540
Yamaha YZF750R & YZF1000R Thunderace (93 - 00)	♦ 3720
Yamaha FZR600, 750 & 1000 Fours (87 - 96)	♦ 2056
Yamaha XV (Virago) V-Twins (81 - 03)	♦ 0802
Yamaha XVS650 & 1100 Drag Star/V-Star (97 - 05)	♦ 4195
Yamaha XJ900F Fours (83 - 94)	♦ 3239
Yamaha XJ900S Diversion (94 - 01)	♦ 3739
Yamaha YZF-R1 (98 - 03)	♦ 3754
Yamaha YZF-R1 (04 - 06)	♦ 4605
Yamaha FZS1000 Fazer (01 - 05)	♦ 4287
Yamaha FJ1100 & 1200 Fours (84 - 96)	♦ 2057
Yamaha XJR1200 & 1300 (95 - 06)	♦ 3981
Yamaha V-Max (85 - 03)	♦ 4072
ATVs	
Honda ATC70, 90, 110, 185 & 200 (71 - 85)	0565
Honda Rancher, Recon & TRX250EX ATVs	2553
Honda TRX300 Shaft Drive ATVs (88 - 00)	2125
Honda Foreman (95 - 07)	2465
Honda TRX300EX, TRX400EX & TRX450R/ER ATVs (93 - 06)	2318
Kawasaki Bayou 220/250/300 & Prairie 300 ATVs (86 - 03)	2351
Polaris ATVs (85 - 97)	2302
Polaris ATVs (98 - 06)	2508
Yamaha YFS200 Blaster ATV (88 - 06)	2317
Yamaha YFB250 Timberwolf ATVs (92 - 00)	2217
Yamaha YFM350 & YFM400 (ER and Big Bear) ATVs (87 - 03)	2126
Yamaha Banshee and Warrior ATVs (87 - 03)	2314
Yamaha Kodiak and Grizzly ATVs (93 - 05)	2567
ATV Basics	10450
TECHBOOK SERIES	
Twist and Go (automatic transmission) Scooters Service and Repair Manual	4082
Motorcycle Basics TechBook (2nd Edition)	3515
Motorcycle Electrical TechBook (3rd Edition)	3471
Motorcycle Fuel Systems TechBook	3514
Motorcycle Maintenance TechBook	4071
Motorcycle Modifying	4272
Motorcycle Workshop Practice TechBook (2nd Edition)	3470

◊ = not available in the USA   ♦ = Superbike

The manuals on this page are available through good motorcycle dealers and accessory shops.
In case of difficulty, contact: **Haynes Publishing**
(UK) +44 1963 442030   (USA) +1 805 498 6703
(SV) +46 18 124016
(Australia/New Zealand) +61 3 9763 8100

MCL24.08/09

Preserving Our Motoring Heritage

The Model J Duesenberg Derham Tourster. Only eight of these magnificent cars were ever built – this is the only example to be found outside the United States of America

Almost every car you've ever loved, loathed or desired is gathered under one roof at the Haynes Motor Museum. Over 300 immaculately presented cars and motorbikes represent every aspect of our motoring heritage, from elegant reminders of bygone days, such as the superb Model J Duesenberg to curiosities like the bug-eyed BMW Isetta. There are also many old friends and flames. Perhaps you remember the 1959 Ford Popular that you did your courting in? The magnificent 'Red Collection' is a spectacle of classic sports cars including AC, Alfa Romeo, Austin Healey, Ferrari, Lamborghini, Maserati, MG, Riley, Porsche and Triumph.

A Perfect Day Out

Each and every vehicle at the Haynes Motor Museum has played its part in the history and culture of Motoring. Today, they make a wonderful spectacle and a great day out for all the family. Bring the kids, bring Mum and Dad, but above all bring your camera to capture those golden memories for ever. You will also find an impressive array of motoring memorabilia, a comfortable 70 seat video cinema and one of the most extensive transport book shops in Britain. The Pit Stop Cafe serves everything from a cup of tea to wholesome, home-made meals or, if you prefer, you can enjoy the large picnic area nestled in the beautiful rural surroundings of Somerset.

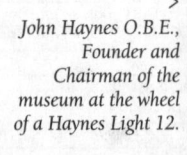

John Haynes O.B.E., Founder and Chairman of the museum at the wheel of a Haynes Light 12.

The 1936 490cc sohc-engined International Norton – well known for its racing success

The Museum is situated on the A359 Yeovil to Frome road at Sparkford, just off the A303 in Somerset. It is about 40 miles south of Bristol, and 25 minutes drive from the M5 intersection at Taunton.
Open 9.30am - 5.30pm (10.00am - 4.00pm Winter) 7 days a week, *except Christmas Day, Boxing Day and New Years Day*
Special rates available for schools, coach parties and outings Charitable Trust No. 292048